EYEWITNESS COMPANIONS

Art

ROBERT CUMMING

Text previously published in *Art: A Field Guide*

DK

LONDON, NEW YORK,
MUNICH, MELBOURNE, AND DELHI

Senior Art Editor	Juliette Norsworthy
Senior Editor	Ferdie McDonald
Design assistance	Peter Laws
Editorial assistance	David John, Rob Houston
Additional text contribution	Thomas Cussans
Picture Research	Sarah Smithies, Celia Dearing, Carlo Ortu
DTP	John Goldsmid
Production	Rita Sinha
Managing Editor	Debra Wolter
Managing Art Editor	Phil Ormerod
Executive Managing Editor	Liz Wheeler
Editorial Director	Andrew Heritage
Art Director	Bryn Walls
Publisher	Jonathan Metcalf

at Studio Cactus

Design	Laura Watson, Dawn Terrey, Sharon Rudd, Peter Radcliffe
Editorial	Aaron Brown, Jennifer Close, Lorna Hankin, Clare Wallis

First published in 2005 by
Dorling Kindersley Limited
80 Strand, London WC2R ORL
Penguin Group

First American Edition, 2005

Published in the United States by

DK Publishing, Inc.

375 Hudson Street, New York, New York 10014

04 05 06 08 09 10 9 8 7 6 5 4 3 2 1

Text © Robert Cumming 2005

ISBN 0 7566 1358 2

A CIP catalog record for this book is available from
the Library of Congress

Color reproduction GRB, Italy
Printed and bound in China by L Rex

Discover more at

www.dk.com

CONTENTS

INTRODUCTION
10

INTRODUCING
ART
14

WHAT IS ART?
16

MEDIA AND
MATERIALS
28

THE HISTORY
OF ART
44

EARLY ART
3000 BCE–1300 CE
46

GOTHIC AND EARLY
RENAISSANCE
c.1300–1500
72

HIGH RENAISSANCE
AND MANNERISM
c.1500–1700
128

THE BAROQUE ERA
c.1600–1700
162

FROM ROCOCO TO
NEOCLASSICISM
c.1700–1800
218

ROMANTIC AND
ACADEMIC ART
c.1800–1900
258

MODERNISM
c.1900–1970
340

CONTEMPORARY
ART
1970–
448

GLOSSARY
478

INDEX
501

THIS BOOK HAS EVOLVED OVER MANY YEARS OF LOOKING AT WORKS OF ART, OFTEN ON MY OWN, BUT PREFERABLY IN THE COMPANY OF OTHERS. THE EYE IS THE SOVEREIGN OF THE SENSES, AND TO SHARE LOOKING IS ONE OF LIFE'S GREAT PLEASURES—IT INCREASES WITH AGE AND IS NOT CONFINED TO WORKS OF ART.

My first job in the art world was at the Tate Gallery in London, as a new member of a small team whose task was to stand in front of the works on display and explain them to the public. I soon learned that four questions were asked over and over again:

1 What should I look for? What are the key features in a Picasso, a Rembrandt, a Raphael, a Turner?

2 What is going on? What is the story? Who is Hercules? What is the Nativity? Who is that girl with a broken wheel? Who is the man abducting the woman who looks like a tree? Does that big red square mean anything?

3 What is its value? Am I looking at $10? $10,000? $1 million? $10 million?

4 Is it any good? And, in front of a pile of bricks or an unmade bed, am I being taken for a ride?

I also found that most of my audience seemed to enjoy getting involved in an informed discussion or exchange of opinions about a particular work of art, or about specific issues (especially provocative or controversial ones) and about what *they* saw, thought, and felt.

In this book, I have tried to capture that kind of involvement and to address the four basic questions I have listed above. Also, I have been part of the art world long enough to know that when those of us who work in it are "off duty," looking at art purely for pleasure, uninhibited by the need to maintain professional credibility, we often voice different—and sometimes much more interesting—opinions than we do when "on duty."

POSTER FOR MIRÓ EXHIBITION

The present-day art world is a huge industry of museums, teaching institutions, commercial operations, and official bodies, all with reputations and postures to maintain. They are often desperate to convince us of the validity of their official messages.

I understand the pressures that impel all these official art institutions to maintain a party line, but in the face of all that vested self-interest there is a need for a no-nonsense alternative voice.

In the main section of the book, *The History of Art* (pages 44–477), you will

Hidden treasures, the Hermitage, St. Petersburg
This photograph, taken in 1994, gives some idea of the vast quantities of works of art that are not on display, but are held in museum archives around the world.

find painters and sculptors, from the early Renaissance onward, arranged as separate entries. In these I have indicated characteristics to serve as a guideline when looking at their works. My observations are entirely personal, but I have tried to pick out qualities that anyone with a pair of eyes can see, and have pleasure in searching for. Most of the entries were written, at least in note form, while looking at the works of art. In fact, nearly everything I have written in this book is what I would say if we were standing in front of a work of art. In such a situation it is, I think, better to say too little rather than too much, so as to allow those who are with me to make their own discoveries and connections.

I have included record prices paid for works by each artist because what people pay for works of art is fascinating, both in absolute terms and comparatively. Some works are worth every penny of the vast sums of money paid for them; some are ridiculously overpriced; and some wonderful works of art are almost given away because they are out of fashion or overlooked.

All prices are "hammer" prices, that is the value called out at auction when the item is "knocked down" to the bidder. The actual price paid by the successful bidder will be increased by the addition of a premium charged by the auction house (the amount varies between auction houses). Prices are given in US dollars, with no allowance for inflation. Where the sale was made in another currency, the price paid has been converted at the exchange rate at

the time. You will see that a record price is not given for all artists. Works by many of the old masters rarely come onto the market because most now are in public collections. I would like to thank Duncan Hislop of Art Sales Index Ltd., 54 Station Road, Egham, Surrey, TW20 9LF, UK

Viewing the *Mona Lisa* in her new setting
To allow more people to see the world's most famous painting, the Louvre created a special gallery costing over $6 million, which opened in April 2005.

(www.art-sales-index.com), for his generous help in providing the information on prices.

I hope this book will prove to be a friendly companion, an entertaining and practical aid for looking at art. If it fulfills its goals, it will provoke you, make you question your own opinions, cause you to stop, think, and, I hope, smile too. It should also encourage you to believe what you see, rather than what you are told and make you go back to a painting or sculpture and see aspects of it you had not perceived before. My first wish is to increase the pleasure you get when looking at a work of art.

ROBERT CUMMING
London, May 2005

Twenty Marilyns *Andy Warhol, 1962, silk screen, Private Collection.* Since the 1960s, prices for works of art have escalated and are now greater than at any other time in history.

INTRODUCING **ART**

WHAT IS ART?

Very few artists fit the stereotype of suffering for their art, starving in an unheated garret, producing one unrecognized masterpiece after another, and finally achieving recognition on their deathbed. The image of the artist as a lonely, neglected genius is attractive but misleading. The reality is much more prosaic.

Most artists are skilled in their trade, hard-working, professional, and aware of their business potential, often running busy, well-organized studios with assistants, not unlike a modern architectural practice. The artist whose talent goes unrecognized in his or her lifetime is rare. Much more common is the artist who attracts lavish praise and recognition in his or her lifetime only to sink into irrecoverable obscurity, a footnote in art history rather than a chapter.

THE ARTIST THROUGH HISTORY

This is not to say that the role of the artist does not change. It is possible to pinpoint three turning points when the role of the artist and his and her

Cold Dark Matter: An Exploded View Cornelia Parker, 1991, mixed media, London: Tate Modern. Cornelia Parker is one of the current stars specializing in installations for museum settings. In the art history of the future, will she merit a chapter or just a footnote?

relationship with the rest of society altered significantly. In Ancient, Classical, and Medieval times, artists were essentially skilled craftsmen working for an employer such as a monarch, the Church, or a corporate organization. Their activities were supported and regulated by a professional body or guild.

At the beginning of the 16th century, Leonardo da Vinci argued that the artist should be treated as the social and intellectual equal of aristocrats and scholars. The great artists of the High Renaissance shared this aspiration, and the majestic flowering of their art proves how successful they were in establishing this role. It suited both artist and patron and endured right up to the end of the 19th century. It allowed artists to play the fullest possible role in society, becoming the confidants of kings and popes, and sometimes even acting as diplomats and courtiers.

RADICAL CHANGE

The French Revolution of 1789 ushered in profound political and social changes. The privileged world of monarchy and aristocracy began to wane. With a new sense of individual liberty in the air, art attracted new personalities who previously would have ignored an artistic life. The Romantic spirit exploited this freedom to express individual emotions, and to create art about personal experiences. The Classical tradition, with its admiration for antiquity and disciplined professional training, continued to flourish alongside Romanticism, but it was in decline.

This spirit of independence led to a turning point in the second half of the 19th century, and to a new role for the artist. The change was most forcibly expounded by the radical French painter, Gustave Courbet, who argued that the true artist should be an outsider to the rest of society, free of all normal social conventions and at liberty to set his or her own rules. The idea was potent, particularly to the disaffected young, many of whom

Francis I Receives the Last Breaths of Leonardo da Vinci Ingres, 1818, oil on canvas, Paris: Musée du Petit-Palais. Ingres, a painter firmly in the Classical tradition of the Renaissance, presents the image of the artist as intellectual giant, the equal of kings.

wished to establish a new art that would address issues at the heart of industrial society and the new awareness of human relationships and emotions that were revealed, for example, by Freudian analysis. It was a necessary condition for the development of Modern Art, and led to a rare chapter in the history of art in which the prime motivation

Andy Warhol and friends
In the 1960s Warhol commented on his era through images of products such as Coca-Cola and iconic figures such as Marilyn Monroe. In the 1970s his art increasingly featured images of himself and his followers.

of the artist was not widespread recognition, professional advancement, riches, or social success, but a desire to reform society and human relationships and literally to change the way we see the world.

THE ARTIST TODAY

The most recent turning point occurred in the 1960s and the most articulate advocate for another role for the artist was Andy Warhol, who found the image of the artist as penniless reformer outdated and unattractive. He wanted artists to share in the material benefits of the postwar era and argued that they should have a role in society akin to that of Madison Avenue advertising executives or businessmen. If you look at the lifestyle and careers of most young artists born since the 1960s, you can see that they have, by and large, embraced Warhol's

Caricature of Gustave Courbet 1868. The French art establishment hated Courbet because of his radical political and aesthetic doctrines.

ideas with enthusiasm. The artist today is often a successful businessman or woman (in itself not that new a concept) selling to institutions or private clients such as large corporations or internet millionaires.

The most recent refinement is the artist's assumption of a managerial role—where the artist does not create a work of art in the traditional manner, but promotes an idea or concept, often in collaboration with others, and then manages it as a project or installation, delegating the physical manufacture or assembly of components to select subcontractors.

PATRONS AND PATRONAGE

A patron is someone who provides the necessary financial assistance for an artist to create a work from scratch.

In the early Renaissance, the patronage of one of the noble courts or the Church was the essential framework within which an artist was obliged to operate, and the influence of a creative and imaginative patron was immense. Any self-respecting monarch was now expected to be a patron of the arts, and this tradition continued even into the 20th century. Europe's rulers consciously used works of art to increase their prestige, credibility, and political power. The Church employed art in a similar way to spread the Christian message and to promote its influence. Without such patronage, the great artists of the Renaissance and the 17th century, such as Michelangelo and Rubens, could never have created their masterpieces.

COLLECTORS AND DEALERS

Collecting works of art without patronage is a different matter. It presupposes collecting the art of the past as well as that of living artists. If one had to

Cosimo I de' Medici Baccio Bandinelli, marble relief, Florence: Museo del Bargello. A reflection of Cosimo's self-image as a noble Roman in the mold of Caesar.

nominate a godfather figure it could be Cosimo I de' Medici (1519–74). Cosimo used art to consolidate commercial and political power, but he also collected for pleasure. Collecting is thus an aspect of that concept of individual personality which lies at the heart of much Western art and thought. Cosimo was also influenced by his love of antiquity. Seeking to emulate the ambitions of Classical Greece and Rome, he discovered how the Romans had been passionate collectors and bought and sold works of art at auction.

Private collectors, dealers, and auctioneers flourished in the new mercantile Dutch Republic in the 17th century. Much of the framework of today's art market was established then, but the golden age for the dealer was the 19th century and the early 20th century. Many of today's famous firms were founded then, and many great works of art, intended for a particular setting in a church or palace, were torn from their original context, sold by dealers to private clients, and have eventually come

DEALERS

In the late 19th century, as the artist found greater freedom to express a private vision, rather than one shared by, or demanded by, a patron, modern art dealers became a necessary intermediary between the artist and collector. Indeed, without the courage of a few adventurous dealers, such as Paul Durand-Ruel, Ambroise Vollard, and Daniel-Henry Kahnweiler, the Impressionists and great masters of Modernism would have found it impossible to survive economically, and would have lacked a valuable source of intellectual and moral encouragement.

Parisian art dealer Ambroise Vollard
Vollard (1866–1939) championed the great painters of the Post-Impressionist era, organizing the first one-man shows by Cézanne, Matisse, and Picasso.

to grace the National Galleries of the world. Other dealers effectively acted as patrons for young artists.

The art market used to be rather secretive. However, the rise of the international auction house since the 1960s and the buying and selling of works of art in full public view, has fueled popular interest in record-breaking prices. In relative and absolute terms, major works of art now command more money than ever before. This is partly because of their increasing scarcity in the market place, for once they enter a public collection, it is most improbable that they will come back on the market. And it is

also because rich people are prepared to go to almost any lengths to obtain the rarest of the rare.

FILLING SPACE

Very few works of art change the world or the way we see it. The reality is that most art does little more than fill a space. This is not a criticism, for

RECORD PRICES FOR ARTISTS' WORK

The figures given here are the prices paid at the time (in US dollars) with no account taken of subsequent inflation.

Garçon à la pipe	**$93m**, 2004	
Pablo Picasso		
Portrait of Dr. Gachet	**$75m**, 1990	
Vincent Van Gogh		
Au Moulin de la Galette	**$71m**, 2002	
Pierre-Auguste Renoir		
Massacre of the Innocents	**$68m**, 2002	
Sir Peter Paul Rubens		
Rideau, cruchon et compotier	**$55m**, 1999	
Paul Cézanne		
Portrait of Cosimo I de' Medici	**$32m**, 1989	
Jacopo Pontormo		
Madonna of the Pinks	**$39.4m**, 1999	
Raphael		
Interchange	**$18.8m**, 1989	
Willem de Kooning		
Record auction price for a living artist's work		

Fountain of Apollo Jean-Baptiste Tuby, 1670, gilded lead, Versailles. Louis XIV commissioned statuary glorifying himself as the "Sun King." Such patronage created an industry to supply art for his palaces.

Santa Trinità Altarpiece Fra Angelico, c. 1434, 69 ¼ x 72 ¾ in (176 x 185 cm), tempera and gold on panel, Florence: Museo di San Marco. Altarpieces of this high quality were rarities even in Renaissance Florence.

Dutch Republic had different spaces to fill. Wealthy merchants wanted to fill their townhouses with images of their newfound political freedom and prosperity—small-scale, meticulously crafted landscapes, portraits, domestic genre scenes, and still lives.

Eighteenth-century Britain created yet another new space, the country house. In addition to filling them with old art brought home from the Grand Tour, owners filled them with the art of their own day which seemed to them most relevant and desirable, namely landscapes and portraits.

it is possible to fill a space very well, enhancing life with beauty and style. Moreover, the works of art of a period—their subject, size, style, appearance—are influenced by the spaces they are expected to fill. The characteristic public spaces of the Renaissance were churches, and quantities of altarpieces were required to fill them. The finest of these now reside, paradoxically, in the secular public spaces of galleries, revered as icons of art history. But a visitor to Italy, making a tour of churches, will soon suspect that such life-changing icons are rare and that most Italian religious art does little more than fill spaces.

The monarchs of the 17th century quite literally created industries to produce works of art to fill their vast palaces. They required large sizes and complex mythological iconographies to proclaim their message of absolute temporal authority. By contrast, the newly established

GALLERIES AND ACADEMIES

The idea of a National Gallery—a public space containing works of art that somehow

Grand Gallery of the Louvre Hubert Robert, 1796, 44 ¼ x 56 ¼ in (112.5 x 143 cm), oil on canvas, Paris: Musée du Louvre. Robert was curator of the collection, which opened to the public in 1793.

define a nation's cultural identity—was a legacy of the Napoleonic era. But these spaces held only historic art, never the work of living artists. In the 19th century the major spaces for the display of contemporary art were controlled by the Academies. These powerful institutions trained young artists and put on regular displays prepared by their members. Although their intentions were worthy, the Academies became obsessed with rules and internal politics and this is reflected in the increasingly ostentatious, but vacuous works of art created to fill their spaces.

One of the unique characteristics of the art of the early Modern Movement is that it was not created to fill public spaces. Detested by the Academies, ignored by private collectors, and with no museum willing to house them, many of the avant-garde works of art produced by young artists, such as Picasso, never left the privacy of their studios. Their principal purpose was to change the way we see the world or to express a deep private personal sensibility. It was a rare and unusual interlude. Today, filling spaces has returned as a dominant influence in contemporary art.

The idea of a public place dedicated to a permanent display of work by living artists and of "Modern Art" in particular was pioneered by MOMA in New York in 1929. Not much imitated at first, in the last 50 years the idea has spread like wildfire. Museums dedicated to the display of Modern and contemporary

GREAT ART GALLERIES

Listed below are some of the world's largest and most famous public collections of art.

Galleria degli Uffizi *Florence, Italy* **1591**
The Medici art collection, viewable on request from 1591, bequeathed to the city of Florence in 1737

Musée du Louvre *Paris, France* **1793**
Originally the gallery of the royal palace; opened to the public by the revolutionary government

Museo del Prado, *Madrid, Spain* **1819**
The creation of King Ferdinand VII, encouraged by his wife, Maria Isabel de Braganza

National Gallery *London, England* **1824**
Moved in 1838 from its initial home in banker John Julius Angerstein's house to a specially built gallery

Gemäldegalerie *Berlin, Germany* **1830**
Originally the royal collection; finally reunited, after several name and location changes, in 1997

Hermitage Museum, *St. Petersburg, Russia* **1917**
Declared a state museum in 1917; began in 1764 as the private collection of Empress Catherine II

National Gallery of Art, *Washington, DC,* **1941**
Specially built gallery designed by John Russell Pope

Museo del Prado, Madrid
Spain's national gallery of fine art opened to the public in 1819, when Ferdinand VII transferred the royal collection to a fine Neo-Classical building in the center of Madrid.

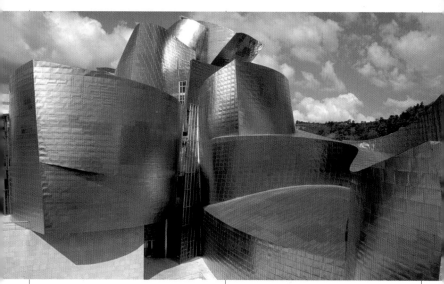

art are now to be found in every city
in the world. They have large spaces
to fill, and an enormous industry has
grown to supply them. Just as churches
required works that were identifiably
"religious" and "Christian," so these
spaces require works that are "modern"
and "contemporary," which is often
interpreted as shocking and provocative.
As the spaces become larger and more
architecturally spectacular, so, in order
not to be overwhelmed, do the works
of art. All of which begs the questions:

Guggenheim Museum, Bilbao
Since it opened in 1997, the spectacular museum of
Modern and contemporary art designed by Frank Gehry
has been the city of Bilbao's main tourist attraction.

Which came first? The altarpiece
or the church? The museum of
contemporary art or the installation?

ART HISTORY

There are many ways of looking at
and talking about art. When Queen
Victoria and Prince Albert wanted to
develop their appreciation of art, they

ART HISTORIANS, CRITICS, AND CONNOISSEURS

The natural habitat of the art historian
is the library and archive, the museum
and the lecture hall; that of the art critic
is the media, the studio and art school,
and the dinner table. The connoisseur
is likely to be found in the auction room,
the dealer's gallery, or in some long
neglected attic. The connoisseur combines
the best of the art historian and art critic
with something extra—a discrimination
and an instinctive eye for real quality plus
a knowledge that comes from years of
looking at works of art first hand.

Critic and connoisseur Bernard Berenson
An expert on Italian Renaissance art, whose opinions
are often still valid, American Berenson (1865–1959)
authenticated paintings for collectors and museums.

FAKES AND FORGERIES

There is a distinction between the two words, fake and forgery. A fake is a work of art made or altered so as to appear better, older, or other than what it is. A forgery is something made in fraudulent imitation of another thing. Throughout history people have produced what they claim to be lost paintings by Leonardo or Vermeer, for example, which they have created with great skill in their studios. Such works are not fakes but forgeries.

Christ in the House of Martha and Mary Jan Vermeer, c. 1654–56, 63 x 56 in (160 x 142 cm), oil on canvas, Edinburgh: National Gallery of Scotland (above).

The Dutch forger Han van Meegeren painted "Vermeers" that were authenticated by leading figures in the art world. He produced The Disciples at Emmaus (left) c. 1936–38.

followed the fashion of their day and took drawing and painting lessons. Today they would sign up for an art history course. Art history as an academic subject effectively began in Germany at the end of the 19th century. It has brought discipline, rigor, and objectivity to a notoriously fuzzy topic. It has rescued many reputations and even proved the existence of forgotten artists.

But art history also has a downside. Works of art are not just historical documents. Art has the ability to engage with individuals and create experiences that can range from tears to ecstasy. At its worst, art history can reduce even the greatest works of art to a tedious list of facts. There is a danger that one can become so obsessed by "history" that everything "old" comes to be blindly revered like the bones of long dead saints.

ART CRITICISM
Good art criticism respects facts and history but is principally concerned with value judgments. It questions and probes an artist's purpose, intentions, and technical ability, asking whether the final outcome delivers what the artist has set out to do. Equally, in a historic display of art, such as an exhibition, the critic should examine the validity of the curator's interpretation. For contemporary art the critic ought to cut through the lavish rhetoric, which is often heaped on it by curators and dealers, to determine the true merit of what is being promoted.

Many reputations and much money ride on the current boom in contemporary art and there is a dangerous temptation, fueled by the supremacy of art history, to treat every new manifestation and star name instantly as historically significant. This is disingenuous since, in any field of human endeavor, whether what happens today will have any significance in the longer term depends almost entirely on what happens tomorrow, and that is completely unpredictable and unknowable.

THE MASTERPIECE

Is the idea of a "masterpiece" valid today? The term implies excellence and the desirability of the pushing of individual technical skill, ideas, and innovation to their limits. Ultimately it suggests the identification of those few works that have the ability to inspire emotion and communicate meaning long after their creation. Many works of art speak powerfully to the generation for which they were created, but very few have the power to continue to speak meaningfully to subsequent generations.

The origin of the term "masterpiece" dates back to when artists were considered to be craftsmen. It was the piece the artist presented to the guild to prove his ability and gain the coveted rank of "master." When the guild system became obsolete and the role of the artist changed, the word lost this meaning and became attached to those outstanding works in which an artist is judged to display the full range of his or her powers. Yet the word is overused. History is littered with the names of artists who have been hailed as the "Michelangelo of our times," but now barely merit a mention. Equally, the geniuses, such as van Gogh, who were neglected in their lifetimes only for their masterpieces to be found after their deaths, are surprisingly few and far between. And there are those interesting second-rate artists who

David Michelangelo Buonarroti, 1501–04, height 161 in (410 cm), marble, Florence: Galleria dell'Accademia.

manage to produce just one or two outstanding works worthy of the description "masterpiece."

Taste and perception also change. Few would deny that for us, Botticelli's *Birth of Venus* is one of the early Renaissance masterpieces. Yet in his own lifetime, Botticelli's style was condemned as old-fashioned, and his name lapsed into obscurity until his works were rediscovered at the end of the 19th century.

HARMONY AND IDEAS

So what makes a masterpiece? Perhaps there are two things to look for. First, a complete unity between subject, style, and technique. Raphael's paintings of the Madonna and Child are a good example. Raphael's harmonious, graceful style and flawless technique perfectly complement the qualities he seeks to portray in his divine subject. Second, and equally familiar to Raphael, is the belief that art should express an idea greater than art itself. Without such a belief, and a commitment to communicate that idea to others, all art, however accomplished technically, is confined to decoration and illustration. Technical skill can fill and decorate spaces, but only an idea connects at a deeper level with the needs of others and can change the way we see things. Artists live and work in a world peopled by patrons, collectors, dealers, art institutions, and fellow artists. To stand out from the crowd requires courage and individuality. Only those endowed with a depth of vision beyond the ordinary, and who use art, not as an end in itself or as a means of personal and commercial gratification, but as a means of trying to tell a greater human or spiritual truth, are those who will succeed in creating masterpieces that can survive the judgment of the sternest critic of all—time.

The Madonna of the Pinks Raphael, 1507–08, 11¼ x 9 in (30 x 23 cm), oil on canvas, London: National Gallery. An example of Raphael's skill and engagement with beauty and faith, this painting was unrecognized from 1855–1991, but recently sold for $39 million.

For Raphael, beauty was an essential element in the search for ultimate truth—an inspired vision was more important than doctrine

The two figures together form a triangle filling most of the picture space. It suggests stability, permanence, dignity, and seriousness

This tiny painting was to be an object of intense and private contemplation for a young widow who was entering a nunnery to take up a life of Christian devotion

Raphael's complete mastery of the technique of oil painting with rich colors, subtle gradations, and fine detail such as fingernails, honors the spiritual profundity of his subject

The playful activity and darting eyes of the Christ-child contrast with the stillness and lowered eyes of the Virgin; his naked maleness contrasts with her modesty and sweet femininity

MEDIA AND MATERIALS

Artists have always enjoyed appropriating, devising, and combining new media in pursuit of visual expression, from the rudimentary materials of charcoal, chalk, wood, and stone, to paint in the form of pigments and binders, through to the contemporary technology of digital editing.

The first artists collected and manipulated simple, basic materials to achieve a likeness or design. As tools and technologies developed, artists progressed from carving bone, wood, and stone to manipulating and firing clay. Sculptors later appropriated the technology of the forge and foundry to make bronzes. Painters, meanwhile, explored the environment for suitable pigments: chalk, charcoal, the dye of berries, crustaceans, and minerals extracted from the ground. For these materials (pigments) to be formed into paint, they needed to be mixed with a medium to bind them as a liquid. Effective media were resins, gums— such as gum arabic, still used to bind watercolors today—and wax. A tempera paint made from egg was the dominant medium in the Middle Ages until the 15th century, when oil painting came to the fore. Oils and watercolors dominated until the advent of acrylic in the 1940s.

Artists have often combined media, for example, in the 20th-century practice of collage. Contemporary artists often juxtapose incongruous images and materials in installations and land art, as a means of challenging our conceptions of both the world around us and the aesthetics of art.

REPRODUCING ART

Printing allows multiple images to be generated, for example, by using woodcuts, engraved copper plates, and by plates etched with acids. The other major means of reproduction is photography. Most recently the advent of computer technology has allowed artists an unprecedented level of image manipulation and editing.

Oil paint was, and continues to be, widely used for many reasons: flexible, durable, easily manipulated, it offers rich colors and can carry the personal style of the individual artist's hand.

Drawing

Drawing is the most immediate form of artistic expression. Before the Renaissance it was rarely valued as an art form in itself, but was seen as the preparatory design for a work in another medium. Cennini (c. 1370–1440) gave it a certain status, calling it "the triumphal arch" to painting, but the first artists who really exploited drawing as an independent expressive medium were Leonardo da Vinci and Michelangelo.

CHARCOAL

Charcoal is one of the oldest drawing media and remains popular with artists to this day. It is made from twigs of willow and created by a slow burning process that reduces the wood to carbon. It is available in varying thicknesses, ranging from the very thick scene-painters' charcoal to medium and thin sticks used for more detailed drawings. It is commonly used for drawing under painting since it is easily overpainted without discoloring the overlaid paint. Charcoal drawings can be edited very easily by means of a brush, putty eraser, or even soft doughy bread.

ARTIST'S CHARCOAL

Study of a Man Shouting *Michelangelo, 16th century, charcoal on paper, Florence: Gallerie degli Uffizi.* Michelangelo drew in many differnt media: pen and ink, pen and wash, charcoal, and red and black chalks.

CHALKS AND PASTELS

White chalk was originally used to add highlights to other drawing media and was particularly effective on toned papers. Pigments such as iron oxide were added to chalk to make the red chalk characteristic of the drawings of Renaissance artists. Chalks are now produced in a full range of colors. Pastels, made of powdered pigments lightly bound in gum tragacanth, became popular with portrait artists in the 18th century. With soft pastels, the pigment is imparted to the paper by the slightest touch and can be blended in the manner of painting to create gradations of subtle, vibrant color. Hard pastels, bound in a higher concentration of gum, are more suitable for drawing.

Blue Dancers *Edgar Degas, c. 1899, pastel on paper, 25 1/2 x 25 1/2 in (65 x 65 cm), Moscow: Pushkin Museum.* Degas' practice was to develop the drawing in charcoal and then to apply layers of soft pastel to create a vibrant optical mixture of color. Other well-known exponents of pastels include Mary Cassat, Odilon Redon, Picasso, and R. B. Kitaj.

MODERN CHALKS

SOFT PASTELS

PEN AND INK

The pen evolved as an alternative to the brush as a means of controlled line drawing. The advantage of inks over dry drawing media was the precision and permanence of the line. Inks have been made from a diversity of sources, ranging from sooty carbon-based materials (bister) to dyes derived from berries, oak galls, insects, cuttlefish, and crustaceans. Water-soluble inks are more prone to fading than the more permanent waterproof inks such as Indian ink prepared with gum or shellac. The dip pen was the mainstay of graphic art for generations and evolved into the fountain pen, felt-tip pen, and technical drawing pen.

REED PEN

FOUNTAIN PEN

DIP PEN WITH ASSORTED NIBS

Lion Resting Rembrandt, ink on paper, Paris: Musée du Louvre. Pen and ink as a drawing medium requires a supremely confident approach since the permanence of the ink precludes casual editing.

MONET'S QUILL PEN

MODERN COLORED INKS

PENCIL

The "lead" in pencils is actually graphite (a form of carbon). In the 16th and 17th centuries the only source of solid graphite was Borrowdale in the English Lake District. In the late 18th century the French devised a method of combining crumbly, amorphous graphite with clay. This mixture, encased in wood, is the pencil we are familiar with today. The use of graphite pencils thus became widespread in the age of Ingres, Turner, and Constable. Many artists today prefer to work with either a solid graphite stick or leads of variable width and density of tone, held in pencil holders. The term "pencil" is used for many graphic media, including compressed charcoal, chalks, and wax, that can be encased in wood like a pencil. Some use water-soluble pigments that can be reworked with a wet brush.

Industrial buildings in a northern English town by an unknown artist, pencil on paper. Private collection.

MECHANICAL CLUTCH PENCIL   GRAPHITE STICKS   PENCIL

Painting

All paints require a binding medium that can hold pigments in suspension and permits successful application to prepared supports—walls, wood panels, vellum, paper, or stretched fabric (canvas). Early forms of paint consisted of pigment bound by a water-based glue called size, made from animal skins. Alternatives were gums and resins extracted from trees, the white and yolk of eggs, and beeswax. From the 15th to the 20th century the dominant medium was vegetable—usually linseed—oil.

ENCAUSTIC

Encaustic (wax) painting is a very durable medium that was one of the principal techniques of the ancient world, used by the Egyptians, Greeks, and Romans to paint images on panels and walls. The word "encaustic" comes from the Greek and means "burned in." Artists would apply the paint using brushes and spatulas to create the image, and on completion they would run lit torches across the surface of the mural to reheat the wax, causing the wax and pigment to be absorbed permanently into the lime surface of the wall. Wax can also be added to oil paint to aid the separation of clear areas of color, a process used most notably by van Gogh. This ancient medium was surprisingly revived in the latter half of the 20th century by Jasper Johns (pages 442–43), who used encaustic paint for a series of images of the American flag.

Encaustic portrait from Egyptian tomb
Some of the best ancient encaustic paintings to have survived are mummy-case portraits from the 2nd century CE.

BEESWAX

EGG TEMPERA

Medieval painters of illuminated manuscripts used beaten egg white in a form of paint called clarum or glair. Painters on panel, on the other hand, used egg yolk mixed with pigment and a little water—egg tempera. This was the principal painting medium before the advent of oil paint. Although tempera is quick-drying, building up the colors of a painting was a slow process. Panels were prepared with layers of gesso, a mixture of size and chalk to form a smooth surface. The paint was applied over a prepared drawing. Gradations of color had to be built up slowly, by means a series of carefully juxtaposed applications of paint.

EGG YOLK

Entombment of Christ *Russian icon, 15th century, 18 x 13 in (45 x 32 cm), tempera on panel.* Tempera was used for most medieval Byzantine and Russian icons.

EGG AND
WATER
EMULSION

TEMPERA
PIGMENTS

FRESCO

Fresco (the Italian word for "fresh") denotes the method of painting in which pigments, mixed solely with water, are painted directly onto a freshly laid lime-plaster ground. The liquid paint is absorbed into the plaster and as the plaster dries the pigments are bound within the fabric of the wall surface. Fresco was practiced by the Minoans, the ancient Greeks, and the Romans long before its use by Michelangelo (page 136) and other painters during the Renaissance.

VERMILION PIGMENT

The Creation of Adam (detail)
Michelangelo Buonarroti, 1508–12, fresco (prerestoration), Rome: Sistine Chapel, Vatican Museums.

OILS

Vegetable oil—principally walnut, poppy, and linseed—had been used as a medium for painting for some time before the Renaissance, but was more popular in northern Europe than in Italy. It was the skill of Flemish painters such as Jan Van Eyck (page 110) at the beginning of the 15th century that convinced the Venetians and subsequently other Italians and the rest Europe that oils were the best medium for easel painting, especially portraits. The advantages of oil paint are its strength and flexibility. The paint can be applied in many ways from thin glazes, diluted with turpentine, to thick impasto. It can be worked when wet for much longer than any other form of paint, allowing the artist to create subtle blending effects, or built up in layers according to the artist's favored technique. The masters of the 16th and 17th centuries, from Titian (pages 143–145) to Velasquez (pages 187–190), exploited the new medium to create astonishing new effects of color and light.

MODERN OIL PAINTS

FLAT SYNTHETIC

ROUND SYNTHETIC

FILBERT HOG

SHORT FLAT HOG

ROUND HOG

The Arnolfini Portrait with detail, Jan van Eyck (see page 109). Van Eyck's mastery of oils produced remarkably fine detail and subtle gradations of color in the dress and draperies where the sunlight from the window strikes them.

Oil painters employ a wide range of techniques. Here an artist exploits the texture of the canvas in a technique known as "scumbling."

Paint brushes are traditionally made from animal hair, stiff brushes from hog's bristles, finer ones from squirrel or sable hair. Both kinds are now produced using synthetic fibers.

WATERCOLOR AND GOUACHE

Both watercolor and gouache paints are bound in gum arabic, the difference being that watercolor is transparent, while gouache, through the addition of white chalk, is opaque. Watercolor uses the brightness of the paper or other support to generate a distinctive luminescence. Light passes through overlaid transparent washes and is reflected back from the support—for example, white paper. The opacity of gouache, also known as body color, makes it ideal for overpainting and its capacity for continuous tone makes it suitable for bold design and flat color work. Watercolor as a specialized medium was raised to new heights in 18th- and 19th-century Britain, most notably in the works of J. M. W. Turner (pages 281–83). More recent exponents of watercolor include Emil Nolde (page 362) and Paul Klee (page 387), who exploited the medium's luminosity and ethereal properties.

WATER
AND
SPONGE

ROUND SABLE BRUSH

SYNTHETIC FAN BLENDER

FINE ROUND SABLE BRUSH

FLAT SYNTHETIC BRUSH

Sunset over a Ruined Castle *J. M. W. Turner, 1868, watercolor and gouache on paper, London: Tate Collection.* Turner mixed gouache with a little yellow watercolor to highlight the clouds above the scene created by washes of color laid over the toned ground of the paper.

MASKING
FLUID

PAN COLORS

Watercolor can be applied in a series of overlaid washes or, as here, using a wet-into-wet technique in which the colors bleed and merge.

TUBE COLOR

GUM ARABIC

ACRYLICS

Acrylics were developed in the 1940s and adopted by many modern artists for their fast drying and permanence. Pioneers included Mexican muralists Orozco (page 402) and Siqueros (page 402). The advantage of acrylics is that they are water-soluble when wet, but dry quickly to a durable surface. They can be used in transparent applications like watercolors or in thick, impasto applications like oil paints.

PALETTE WITH ACRYLICS

PAINTING KNIFE

PALETTE KNIFE

Tree Harvey Daniels (contemporary artist), acrylic on paper, 36 1/4 x 19 1/4 in (92 x 49 cm), Private Collection. The inert properties of acrylics mean they are not susceptible to cracking or darkening in the manner of oil paints.

ACRYLIC BRUSH STROKE

COLLAGE

Collage is an assembly of assorted materials—printed matter, pieces of fabric, even solid objects—stuck onto a support to form a composition. Early exponents were Picasso (pages 396–97) and Braque (page 351), who in their Cubist works (page 350) frequently combined pieces of newspaper and other objects with paint. The German Artist Kurt Schwitters (page 368) did most to develop the use of collage, incorporating bus tickets and all manner of litter from the streets in his poetic compositions. Other notable exponents were the German artist Max Ernst (page 369) and the American Joseph Cornell (page 406), who extended the idea of collage to three dimensional box constructions. What was at first something of a novelty was soon accepted as a respectable form of artistic expression.

Sleep for Yvonne Rainer Robert Rauschenberg, 1965, 84 x 60 in (213.3 x 152.4 cm), collage, Private Collection.

Minotaur Pablo Picasso, 1933, collage with paper, foil, and leaves, New York: Museum of Modern Art. One of Picasso's own drawings of the minotaur is incorporated into a collage of assorted debris.

Printmaking

The oldest form of printmaking is "relief printing," in which the image is created by means of raised areas that receive the ink, as in a woodcut. In intaglio techniques, such as engraving and etching, the ink is held in lines inscribed or bitten into a plate. Other printing processes used by artists include the planographic (flat-surface) techniques of lithography and silkscreen.

WOODCUTS

In Europe the great age of woodcuts was the late 15th century, when printing spread across the continent from Germany. To make a woodcut, a V-shaped chisel is used to remove the negative areas of the design, the raised positive areas of the block are then inked over, a sheet of paper is laid onto the inked block, and pressure applied by using either a screw- or lever-operated press.

More sophisticated halftones are generated by engraving finer lines in the manner of hatching. The greatest master of the art was Albrecht Dürer (pages 126–127). The Japanese artists of the 18th and 19th centuries perfected the art of multicolored prints, overprinting several woodblocks in succession with the final block applying a black line drawing.

The Engraver published by Hartman Schopper, 16th century, engraving, Private Collection.

Woodblock of a hussar on horseback c. 1850 This simple design for the amusement of children shows the raised positive areas that receive the ink to make a print.

ENGRAVING

Engraving and etching are related intaglio techniques that produce a finer line than is possible in woodcuts. In the process of engraving a diamond-shaped tool called a burin is used to inscribe a precise line in either a tight-grained wood such as boxwood or a soft metal such as copper plate. Etching differs from engraving in that acid is used to "bite" a line. The copper plate is first coated in a thin layer of wax, called an etching ground, to resist the action of the acid. The wax is inscribed using a

ENGRAVED COPPER PLATE

point to draw the image and where the wax is displaced the acid bites a line. Areas of tone can be created using a process called aquatint. This involves dusting resin powder onto the plate and heating it to make the resin adhere. When the plate is etched, the acid bites around each grain of resin and when inked produces a subtle uniform tone.

Of What Ill Will He Die? plate 40 of "Los Caprichos," Francisco José de Goya y Lucientes, 1799, etching, burnished aquatint, drypoint, and burin, Private Collection. Goya combined a number of engraving techniques to produce his striking satirical prints.

19TH-CENTURY ENGRAVING TOOLS

LITHOGRAPHY

Lithography is a planographic (flat-surface) method of printing, which works on the principle of the mutual repulsion of oil and water. The process was invented in 1798 by Aloys Senefelder, a Bavarian playwright. A drawing design is applied to a prepared limestone or ground litho plate. The unique attribute of lithography is the directness with which either drawing or painterly technique can be applied using either a brush, pen, or crayon to apply a greasy ink. Lithography also facilitates the building of an image in multiples of overlaid colored printing. The plate is kept damp with a dilution of gum arabic and a mild etch to assist both the resistance to the ink in the undrawn areas and the takeup of the oil-based ink to the drawn areas of the lithograph.

A Stag at Sharkey's lithograph by George Miller (1917) from a painting by George Wesley Bellows, Houston: Museum of Fine Arts. Miller was the US's leading fine art lithographer.

A lithographic print is lifted from a litho stone. As in all printing processes where the image is lifted directly from the stone, block, plate, or screen the print is a mirror image of the original.

To produce a lithograph, a sheet of paper is placed over the plate and run through a litho press. This press is an antique dating back to the 1870s that is being used to make top-quality prints of classic movie posters.

SCREEN PRINTS

Silkscreen printing or serigraphy was developed out of stencil printing, primarily used for commercial textile printing. In the 1930s, particularly in the United States, it became popular as a means of creating commercial prints in vivid opaque color. As in the process of lithography, a design can be drawn or painted directly onto the screen in an oil-based medium and then the undrawn areas sealed using a glue or varnish. Oil-based ink is then squeegeed through the mesh of the silk screen onto paper. Stencils can be used to mask areas of the print. Alternative methods of transferring an image to silkscreen are the use of photo stencils. Andy Warhol (page 444) popularized the technique using a combination of photo-silkscreen and painting in his multiple portraits of 1960s celebrities.

686 Good Morning City Friedensreich Hundertwasser, 1969–70, 33 1/2 x 21 3/4 in (85 x 55.5 cm), silkscreen. Silkscreen works tend to feature clear shape and areas of flat color.

Silkscreen printing on material
Ink is forced through the fine mesh of the silk screen with a squeegee. The masked areas form a stencil preventing ink from passing though the screen.

Sculpture

The first and most ubiquitous form of artistic expression. The earliest sculptures appear to have been created by modifying found objects that suggested either animal or human forms. As tools and technologies developed, artists progressed from carving bone, wood, and stone to manipulating and firing clay, then to casting in bronze. While we are familiar with the bleached remnants of Greek and Roman sculpture, Classical statues were, in fact, rarely left uncolored, as artists applied pigments and precious stones to decorate or enhance the realism of their work.

BRONZE

Pouring molten bronze
The funnels are created by the lost-wax process along with the mold.

Rodin in his studio
Rodin (pages 318–319) had several hundred copies cast of his great works such as *The Kiss* and *The Thinker*.

Sculpting in bronze is a complex process that was developed independently by many cultures—in South America, China, Ancient Egypt, and in West Africa. Bronze casting involves the modeling of a form in clay, plaster, or wax. The earliest bronzes were solid and small, created by means of a sand casting. In the lost-wax process two molds are usually made. First a mold is made of the original sculpture—nowadays using latex and plaster. This is used to make the wax form. To this is attached a funnel shape and gates or ducts, also made of wax. The wax form is covered in heat-resistant plaster, and the whole is placed in an oven. During heating, the plaster hardens and the wax melts and runs out through the ducts. The plaster mold is now inverted and packed in sand and molten bronze is poured into the funnel. The mold is subsequently chiseled away and then the gates chiseled and chased from the surface of the bronze cast. When creating a large statue the mold of the original model has to be cut into two or more pieces to make a wax shell, from which a hollow bronze can be cast.

The wax form of a solid statuette with two runners is created in a mold in the first stage of the lost-wax process.

WOODCARVING

Carving in wood is common to all cultures worldwide. It flourished in medieval Europe, and the carvings of the Romanesque period are particularly expressive. In medieval and Baroque workshops the wood was frequently coated in plaster stucco and painted, a practice that goes back to Ancient Egypt. The carving of wood requires an awareness of the flow of the grain. This respect for the natural form of the wood was a notable feature of the work of the British sculptors Henry Moore (page 399) and Barbara Hepworth (page 400). The woodcarvings of Brancusi (page 356) are outstanding for their simplicity and elegance.

MALLET

DOGLEG
CHISEL

GOUGE

Woodcarving tools
Today there are of hundreds of differently shaped carving tools available, suitable for work on any scale.

Lamentation over the Dead Christ
(detail), woodcarving, German school, early 16th century, Venzone Cathedral, Italy. The work shows traces of the paint and gilding with which it was originally decorated.

SCULPTING IN STONE

Prehistoric man first produced small-scale portable figures such as the Willendorf Venus (page 48) before progressing to freestanding figures. The Greeks adapted the stance of the striding figure from the Egyptians to create the stylized but expressive *kouros* (page 53). They subsequently developed the art of stone-carving to achieve astonishing degrees of naturalism. This was achieved through techniques of carving, pinning, drilling, and polishing. The most prestigious stone for sculpture since Greek times has been marble, which is very hard and difficult to carve. Alabaster, which can give a similar effect, is much softer. Limestone, granite, and sandstone are also popular media. In imitation of the Greeks and Romans, the Italian Renaissance revived the practice of creating large, freestanding sculptures of idealized human forms. The great innovator of the High Renaissance period was Michelangelo (pages 136–137).

Sculptor in his studio
There are two methods of stone-carving: directly carving into the stone or using mechanical means such as calipers to scale up from a smaller model made of clay or plaster. According to Pliny, this process was in use in the 4th century BCE.

BLOCK OF
GRANITE

SCULPTOR'S
CHISELS

HAMMER

Modern sculpture

The roots of modern sculpture lie in the early years of the 20th century, when European artists fell under the influence of "primitive" African art. They were also starting to realize the expressive power of abstraction. Two pioneers of new sculptural forms were Picasso (pages 396–97) and the Paris-based Romanian Brancusi (page 356). In the course of the 20th century more and more materials were appropriated by sculptors, while "ready-made" and "found" objects were incorporated in sculpture or exhibited as works of art themselves.

MODERN SCULPTURAL MEDIA

Modern sculpture has exploited almost every conceivable material, construction process, and method of assembling objects. While many sculptors still find their inspiration in human and natural forms, others, from the Russian Constructivists onward, have moved toward pure abstract geometry. One of the most influential figures in this field was American sculptor David Smith (page 410). Whereas Smith welded and polished his stainless-steel structures himself, many modern sculptors simply make a design which is then realized by a team of assistants. Modern sculpture also delights in re-creating everyday objects on an unexpected scale or using

Contemporary sculptors and their assistants routinely make use of modern industrial manufacturing processes such as arc welding.

unexpected materials. Artists such as Eva Hesse (page 460) and Claes Oldenburg (page 439) produced sculpture using soft materials, such as foam rubber and latex, as in Oldenburg's *Giant Hamburger*.

Four Units Unequal *David Smith, 1960, height 77 1/2 in (196.8 cm), stainless steel, Private Collection.*

Studio of Alexander Calder
The monumental steel structures and playful mobiles of Alexander Calder (page 438) were produced by all manner of industrial processes. Prefabricated steel parts were assembled and painted in his busy studio.

INSTALLATION ART

Installation art effectively inverts the principles of sculpture. Whereas sculpture is designed to be viewed from the outside as a self-contained arrangement of forms, installations frequently envelop the viewer in the space of the work. The viewer enters a controlled environment which may utilize constructed, found, and ready-made forms as

The Forked Forest Path Olafur Eliasson, 1998, Eastbourne, UK: Towner Art Gallery. Eliasson's gallery installations usually evoke the natural world with lighting effects contributing sunlight, fog, or rainbows.

well as light or projected imagery and sound. Installation-based art is related to conceptual art in that it frequently challenges the viewer's habitual spatial and cultural expectations.

Installations can be playful, solemn, or alarming, ranging from meticulously detailed reconstructions of everyday reality to memorials to the dead. They played an important role in the Italian Arte Povera movement of the 1960s and 1970s (page 425). Significant recent practitioners have included German artists Joseph Beuys (page 453) and Rebecca Horn (page 466) and French artist Christian Boltanski (page 466).

Some/One Do-Ho Suh, 2002. The Korean artist installs his piece, made of thousands of nickel military dogtags at the Serpentine Gallery, London.

CONCEPTUAL ART

The credit—or the blame—for modern conceptual art is often laid at the door of Marcel Duchamp (page 367), whose Dadaist, anti-aesthetic view of art led him to exhibit "ready-made" or "found" objects, giving them absurd and provocative titles. Duchamp's mischief sanctioned a new role for the artist as a purveyor of concepts independent of any craft. Some artists have now taken conceptual art to the extreme of presenting text alone so that any visual component of the art is generated solely in the mind of the viewer.

Hat Rack and *Urinal* Marcel Duchamp, 1917, metal and ceramic, Private Collection. Two of Duchamp's most famous ready-mades, the hat rack and urinal were re-created more than once by the artist. The urinal gained huge notoriety when the first version was exhibited in New York in 1913, titled *Fountain* and signed R. Mutt.

Modern media

Much of today's art aims to subvert the audience's expectations about art and life, often in a spirit of parody or pastiche. In the pursuit of originality, contemporary artists have turned to almost every conceivable means of communicating with an audience, including photography, flashing neon signs, film, and video. The 1970s saw a vogue for live performance and in many cases the artist's life or activities may be presented as a work of art. Other artists choose to rearrange the landscape to draw attention to our relationship with the environment.

PHOTOGRAPHY

Photography evolved from the camera obscura, a device for projecting an image through a small hole, which allowed artists to make an accurate tracing of a scene. In 1839 the development of light-sensitive emulsions enabled the "camera" to be used for black-and-white photography. While painters

Rayograph Man Ray, 1923, 19 1/4 x 15 1/2 in (49 x 39.5 cm), photograph, Private Collection. Man Ray created his witty, negative Rayographs by placing a selection of objects on, or suspending them just above, light-sensitive photographic paper and then exposing the composition to light.

explored the new medium— often without acknowledging their debt to it—photography itself was accepted as a minor art form. In the 20th century it achieved higher status through photojournalism and the landscape photography of the likes of Edward Weston and Ansel Adams. Artists such as Man Ray (page 394), meanwhile, used photographic processes more experimentally. Successful contemporary artist include the German Andreas Gursky (page 473), who uses large format film, edits the photographs digitally, and produces huge prints. By contrast, American Nan Goldin (page 470) uses the camera in the spirit of intimate photojournalism.

Image manipulation
Computer technology has freed the photographer from the dark room and opened up new possibilities of creative image manipulation and editing.

VIDEO ART

Video art developed from the art films made using 16-mm and 8-mm formats, notably by Andy Warhol's Factory studio in the 1960s. The invention of video opened up new possibilities with instant playback and in-camera editing. Video also allows artists to explore and manipulate the element of

time in new ways. Artists can subvert the viewer's reading of time by cutting, montaging, slowing, and reversing sequences of images. Video is also used to document much performance-based work. A notable practitioner of video art in recent years has been the American Bill Viola (page 469), who produces video installations—some of them total environments that envelop the viewer in images and sound—as well as videotapes, sound environments, and electronic music performances.

The Crossing Bill Viola, 1996, video/sound installation, as installed at the Grand Central Market, Los Angeles in 1997. Two screens are mounted back to back. On the one seen here a deluge of water falls from above on the figure of a man until he is obliterated. Simultaneously the other screen shows the man being consumed by flames that rise from his feet.

PERFORMANCE ART

The roots of modern performance art lie in the theatrical events staged by the Dadaists and Surrealists in the 1920s. In the 1960s and 1970s it was often associated with political protest in the form of "happenings." Performance art takes many forms. In 1961 French artist Yves Klein (pages 420–21) presented three nude models covered in his trademark blue paint, who moved their bodies around to leave prints on white paper. Other artists present their own actions or lives as art, for example the German artist Joseph Beuys (page 453), who on a trip to New York in 1974, spent some days in a cage with a coyote. Performance art differs from theater in that it does not depend on narrative, but rather seeks to encourage the audience to question their assumptions about life, politics, and social and psychological relationships.

Nude Installation Spencer Tunick, 2003 Grand Central Terminus, New York. The artist directs his 450 models, who then arranged themselves into sculptural poses and formations. Nudity is a common feature of provocative performance art and happenings.

LAND ART

Andy Goldsworthy at work
British artist Andy Goldsworthy (page 474) subtly rearranges natural materials. His ephemeral creations, such as the 13 huge snowballs he placed in London in 2000, sometimes last for just a few days.

Man from the earliest times has interacted with the landscape to create forms that do not exist in nature, for example, the elegant geometry of the formal garden. However, during the 1960s a number of American artists, such as Robert Smithson (page 462), wanted to heighten awareness of our relationship with the natural world by intervening in the landscape by means of thought-provoking constructions. The most dramatic interventions have been the massive enterprises of Christo and Jeanne-Claude (page 460)—curtains reaching across vast stretches of landscape as impressively as the Great Wall of China and his urban projects of wrapping buildings. Photography plays a crucial role in the success of land art since photographs will often be the only lasting visual record of an artist's work, such as the lines created by Richard Long (page 468) in remote, inaccessible landscapes.

Surrounded Islands Christo and Jeanne-Claude, 1980–83, Miami, Florida: Biscayne Bay. Eleven islands were surrounded with 6 ½m sq ft (603,850 sq m) of pink woven polypropylene fabric.

THE HISTORY OF **ART**

EARLY ART
c. 3000 BCE – 1300 CE

Artists, like children, are great borrowers and imitators
and take delight in what they see in the world around
them. However, curiosity and a desire to create do not
in themselves produce works of art. So how do
we identify that moment when what we choose to
call "art" first appears as a significant activity?

The oldest known works of art
to have been discovered in
Europe are stone carvings,
dating from perhaps 32,000 years
ago. Found across Europe and Russia,
they are rare survivals. It is no accident
that carvings, inherently durable,
should be the oldest surviving
examples of human art. They are
inevitably few in number, their
survival almost entirely a matter of
chance. The clues they offer as to the
nature of the hunter-gatherer
societies that produced them are
tantalizing at best. But their claims to
be considered art are undoubted.
They satisfy the innate human need
for aesthetic appeal, whether by means
of craftsmanship, color, or form.

Mask from mummy-case of Tutankhamun, *c. 1340
BCE, gold, enamel and semiprecious stones, height 21¼in
(54 cm), Cairo: Egyptian Museum.* The artists of early
civilizations, such as Ancient Egypt, used the most
precious materials to produce highly stylized depictions
of rulers and their families.

As important, they almost uniformly
seem to have had a mystical,
probably religious purpose. They
make clear the enduring human
need to understand—perhaps to
appease—an uncertain and
frequently hostile world by means of
deliberately contrived objects.

STONE-AGE SCULPTURE
The best-known of these chance
survivals is a tiny limestone figure
of a woman. It was found in Austria
and dates from between 32,000 and
27,000 years ago. The Venus of
Willendorf, as this oddly misshapen
figure is known, was almost certainly
a fertility offering. At first sight, she
appears to be just a crude caricature
of the female form. Closer inspection
reveals a remarkably rhythmic
treatment allied to considerable
technical sophistication on the part of
her unknown creator. The taut curls
that hug her head are not just closely
observed but precisely rendered.

The Great Hall, Lascaux, *c. 15,000 BCE.* Like the other Stone Age cave paintings in Europe, those at Lascaux survived because, once abandoned, they were then completely forgotten until rediscovered by chance.

CAVE PAINTING

More spectacular by far are the cave paintings of southwest France and northern Spain. It is no surprise that when the first was discovered, in 1879, it was widely assumed to be a fake. Virtuosity on such an epic scale was hard to reconcile with current beliefs about Stone Age man. Between about 25,000 and 12,000 years ago, during the peak of the last Ice Age, an astonishingly vigorous tradition of cave painting developed in which acutely observed and brilliantly depicted animals—mammoths, bison, hyenas, and horses—were painted onto cave walls. A variety of materials, chiefly red ocher and charcoal, were used. These were applied by sticks, feathers, or moss, sometimes by hand. In almost every

Venus of Willendorf, c. 30,000 BCE, limestone, height 11.5 cm (4 ½ in), Vienna: Naturhistorisches Museum. The carving's swelling limbs and breasts invest it with a strong sexual quality.

TIMELINE: EARLY ART

35,000 BCE	25,000	10,000	5,000
	c. 25,000 Stylized female figurines made throughout Europe; first cave paintings (France and Spain)	**c. 10,000** Retreat of glaciers; larger mammals extinct	**c. 7000** Pigs domesticated (Anatolia); farming spreads to SE Europe	**c. 5000** Cereal farming villages in western Europe; copper first used (Mesopotamia)
c. 35,000 *Homo sapiens sapiens* in Europe; Neanderthals extinct	**c. 20,000** Peak of last Ice Age	**c. 9000** Earliest evidence of wheat cultivation (Syria)	**c. 5500** Bandkeramik pottery produced (C Europe); metallurgy discovered (SE Europe)	**c. 4500** Megalithic tombs built in western Europe

case the most spectacular images were created deep inside the caves. That their purpose was religious—part fearful, part celebratory—can scarcely be doubted. That they constitute everything that we understand today as art is no more in question. Curiously, there are almost no representations of humans: those that do appear, in contrast to the immediately recognizable animals, are schematic and crude, more like a child's attempt to draw a person.

CITIES AND CIVILIZATION

Perhaps 5,000 years ago, the world's first civilizations were forming in the Middle East. As settled agriculture began, reinforced by the domestication of goats and sheep, so surplus food production permitted the development of divisions of labor and the emergence of ruling classes, often priestly. At the same time, cities began to appear. These were organized societies, self-aware, technically sophisticated, and literate, that recognized how artistic images could be pressed into service on their behalf. Impelled by a need to justify themselves to their gods or to assert their dominance over their subjects, a series of rulers commissioned

images that would underline their status and their right to rule.

The earliest of these civilizations was Sumer, in modern-day Iraq. What has survived—fragments of pottery, a handful of battered marble figures—shows this to have been a society with a well-developed sense of the power of visual images. Yet more remarkable is a product of Sumer's successors, the Akkadians, who from

Akkadian Ruler, c. 2300 BCE, bronze, height 14 in (36 cm), Baghdad: Iraq Museum. This head, tentatively identified as Sargon I, would originally have had jewels placed in its eye-sockets.

about 2300 BCE united much of Mesopotamia in a single empire. The bronze head of an Akkadian ruler, cast between 2,300 and 2,200 BCE, is not just a technical triumph but also a defining image of a hierarchical ruler: remote and magnificent.

c. 3400 First evidence hieroglyphic writing systems (Sumer)	c. 3300 First walled towns in Egypt	c. 3100 Namer, first pharaoh, unifies Egypt	c. 2650 First Egyptian pyramid, the step pyramid of Zoser, built at Saqqara	c. 2100–2000 Stonehenge built
3,500				**2,000**
c. 3500 Emergence of Uruk, first city-state (Mesopotamia); stone circles (NW Europe)	c. 3200 Wheeled transportation (Sumer); development cuneiform script (Mesopotamia)	c. 2900 Early Dynastic period (Egypt)	c. 2540 Great Pyramid of Khufu	c. 2300 Expansion of Akkadian Empire under Sargon

ANCIENT EGYPT
C. 3000—300 BCE

Ancient Egyptian art precisely reflected the rigidly hierarchical society from which it developed. It placed a premium on lavish materials and epic scale and, above all, it echoed Ancient Egypt's obsession with death and the afterlife. Once established, its forms hardly changed for almost 3,000 years. Such tenacious conservatism is matched only by the similarly inward-looking civilization of China.

Palette of Narmer, c. 3000 BCE, schist carved in low relief, Cairo: Egyptian National Museum.

Writing in the 4th century BCE, Plato claimed there had been no change in Egyptian art for 10,000 years. If his chronology was faulty, he nonetheless touched on a central truth: that the art of Ancient Egypt has a near-unique continuity. The Palette of Narmer, which celebrates the first pharaoh, Narmer, who

KEY EVENTS

c. 3100 BCE	Early Dynastic period (to 2686 BCE): Egypt unified under Narmer; Memphis made capital; hieroglyphic writing developed
2686 BCE	Old Kingdom (to 2181 BCE)
c. 2540 BCE	Construction of the Great Pyramid of Khufu
2180 BCE	First Intermediate Period (to 2040 BCE): centralized rule dissolves
2040 BCE	Middle Kingdom (to 1730 BCE)
1730 BCE	Second Intermediate Period (to 1552 BCE): much of Egypt ruled by Hyksos, an Asiatic people
1552 BCE	New Kingdom (to 1069 BCE): Egyptian power at its height: new capital founded at Thebes
1166 BCE	Death of Ramses III, last great pharaoh
1069 BCE	Third Intermediate Period (to 664 BCE)
664 BCE	Late Period (to 30 BCE)
332 BCE	Egypt conquered by Alexander the Great

unified Egypt around 3100 BCE, already contains many of the essential elements of this fixed tradition. Perhaps the most striking is the pose in which Narmer is depicted. Head, arms, and legs are in profile, with legs characteristically splayed. Yet in an obvious anatomical distortion, his chest faces directly outward. Exactly the same pose can be found in works produced 2,500 years later. Although individual details are rendered with great precision, the overall effect is anything but naturalistic. Egyptian art was almost entirely symbolic, intended to convey precise meanings, in this case the triumph of Narmer over his enemies. The sizes of the figures denote status: the larger the figure, the greater its importance (nakedness also indicated inferiority). Though the figures stand on a common ground, there is no attempt to represent the space they occupy naturalistically.

Bird-scarab pectoral from Tutankhamun's tomb, c. 1352 BCE, gold, semiprecious stones, and glass paste), Cairo: Egyptian National Museum.

The deceased is ushered into the hall of judgment

HIERARCHY AND SYMBOLISM

Because its rulers were considered gods, their "eternal well-being" was dependent on preserving their mortal remains with as much splendor as possible. Hence the deliberate grandeur of the pyramids and, later, the vast tombs at Thebes. Complex and absolute rules governed how the pharaohs should be represented in art. The imperturbably blank features of the four giant seated statues of Ramses II guarding the entrance to his temple at Abu Simbel express this formal monumentality just as the gold head of Tutenkhamun underlines the premium placed on precious metals and craftsmanship.

There were exceptions. The less important the subject—slaves, dancing girls, or musicians, for example—the more naturalistically they could be depicted. Further, for a brief period in New Kingdom Egypt, above all during the reign of the Akenaten (1379–1362 BCE), who shocked the priesthood by banishing all gods other than Aten (the "disk of the Sun"), a slight relaxation of this otherwise absolute formality is evident. In the tomb of Akenaten's chief minister, Ramose, is a relief of the brother of Ramose and his wife carved not just with extraordinary delicacy and skill but also with a hint, if nothing more, of genuine humanity.

More typical of the Egyptian attitude to art are the many surviving examples of the parchment known as the *Book of the Dead*. This was a book of spells, placed in a tomb and intended to guide the dead through the afterworld. Not only are the figures—gods and humans—depicted following exact conventions, but the hieroglyphs inserted above and between them, themselves essentially pictorial, contain equally precise and detailed instructions.

Relief from tomb of Ramose, *c. 1350 BCE, limestone, Thebes*. Originally, when painted, its impact would have been still more remarkable.

Weighing of the Heart against the Feather of Truth, *c. 1250 BCE, painted papyrus, London: British Museum*. This scene is found in every *Book of the Dead*.

Pantheon of Egyptian gods headed by Horus

The god Thoth records the result of the weighing of the heart

The heart is weighed against a feather in the other scale

Anubis, the jackal-headed god supervises the weighing of the heart

The "Eater of the Dead", a monster that swallows the heart of the deceased if it proves too heavy

THE EARLY AEGEAN WORLD
c. 2000—500 BCE

Between about 2000 and 1150 BCE, two distinctive though related early Greek civilizations were established in the eastern Mediterranean: by the Minoans on the island of Crete and, perhaps 400 years later, by the more warlike Mycenaeans on the Greek mainland. The reasons for their later disappearance remain unclear, but by the beginning of the first millennium a new, fully Greek, culture was emerging.

Mycenaean death mask from royal tomb, *c. 1550 BCE, gold, Athens: National Archeological Museum.*

Both Minoan Crete and Mycenae were stratified, literate societies, presided over by elites. They appear to have enjoyed substantial agricultural surpluses and to have had extensive trading links. What was originally assumed to be the labyrinth at the palace of Knossos, the principal center of power in Crete (though nothing is known of its rulers), was in fact a huge storage area for wine, grain, and oil.

That Minoan Crete was a society with a taste for luxury and a highly developed visual sense is clear from the decoration of its palaces and villas. Frescoes of ships, landscapes, animals, and cavorting dolphins convey an expressive delight in the natural world. The best-known are those of youths and girls bull-leaping. Though this practice may have had a religious significance—bulls are a recurring theme in Minoan art—overridingly these images suggest an exuberant pleasure in physicality.

The palaces and villas of Minoan Crete were successively rebuilt, perhaps following natural disasters such as the volcanic eruption that wiped out the Minoan colony on the island of Thera in the mid-17th century BCE. But this apparently unwarlike world was also threatened from outside. Around 1450 BCE Minoan Crete fell victim to the Mycenaeans from mainland Greece.

MYCENAEAN CULTURE

The heavily fortified remains at Mycenae itself underline just how much this was a society presided over by an aggressive warrior elite. Yet, as the remarkable gold death mask of a Mycenaean ruler demonstrates, theirs was a world that was not just materially rich but also capable of great technical sophistication.

With the collapse of these first Aegean civilizations, probably in the face of invasions from the north, for over 400 years Greek culture effectively disappeared. Almost nothing is known of this "Dark Age." Yet, by about 800 BCE a new, very different Greek world was emerging. Though politically fragmented, it came to enjoy an exceptionally strong sense not just of its identity but also of its intellectual superiority.

In the visual arts, there were two key developments: a trend toward an idealized naturalism and the adoption of the male nude as its chief subject. It is a measure of the dominance of Greek cultural values that, to

Bull-leaping fresco, c. 1500 BCE, Athens: National Archeological Museum. One of the prize discoveries when the palace of Knossos (below) was excavated in the early 1900s.

KEY EVENTS

c. 2000 BCE	Minoan civilization established on Crete; palace of Knossos built
c. 1600 BCE	Linear B script comes into use on Crete
c. 1500 BCE	Mycenaeans become dominant power on Greek mainland
c. 1450 BCE	Collapse of Minoans; Mycenaeans take control of island
c. 1150 BCE	Collapse of Mycenaean Greece
c. 1000 BCE	Greek colonists migrate to Asia Minor and eastern Aegean
776 BCE	First pan-Hellenic athletics festival, Olympia
c. 750 BCE	First evidence of use of Greek alphabet; Homer's *Iliad* first written down
c. 700 BCE	Beginning of Archaic period; emergence of city-states

Western eyes at least, these have come to seem obviously desirable goals. In fact, they express values no culture outside the West has ever particularly esteemed. To most societies, for example, nakedness was a clear indication of servility.

The Greek obsession with the male nude began in the 7th century BCE. Over 100 life-size (or larger) statues known as *kouroi* (youths) have survived. Though formalized—all face rigidly forward, with hands clenched and one foot in front of the other (evidence of Egyptian influences)—they demonstrate a new interest in naturally rendered anatomical detail. By the 5th century BCE, they would give rise to a naturalism unprecedented in the history of art.

Kouros, c. 540 BCE, height 41 in (105 cm), marble, Paris: Musée du Louvre.

CLASSICAL GREECE
c. 500—300 BCE

Between the 5th century and 100 BCE, when it was absorbed by Rome, Greece evolved ideals in art, philosophy, mathematics, literature, and politics that would exercise an extraordinary hold on subsequent Western beliefs. That it did so in the face of external threats and internal turmoil makes this achievement all the more remarkable.

Red-figure vase, *(c. 450 BCE), height 18 7/8 in (48 cm), ceramic, Paris: Louvre Museum.* The vase shows a Hoplite returning from war.

Victory over the Persians in 490 BCE and again in 480 BCE left Athens clearly the strongest of the Greek city-states. Despite the debilitating and eventually disastrous Peloponnesian War against rivals Sparta between 431 and 404 BCE, culturally at least the city would retain its leading role even after the rise of Macedonia in the following century. Fifth-

Centaur Triumphing over a Lapith, 447–432 BCE, marble, London: British Museum. The relief (below) was part of the frieze on the south side of the Parthenon (left). It was removed by Lord Elgin in the early 1800s.

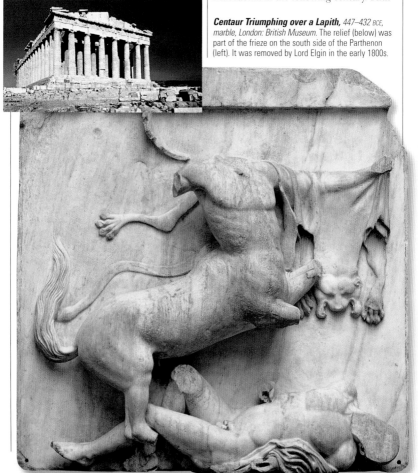

century BCE Athens saw an astonishingly fertile burst of artistic creation, establishing an artistic canon that would not only dominate the Roman world but, when rediscovered by Renaissance Europe, would also constitute an absolute artistic standard for a further 400 years.

Only a handful of fragments of Greek paintings have survived; many Greek sculptures are known only from Roman copies or written descriptions; and what architecture still exists is extensively ruined. But enough remains to make clear the extraordinary artistic impact of Classical Greece. The Parthenon, begun in 447 BCE, is the supreme example. Today, even stripped of its sculpture, its crumbling grandeur constitutes an emphatic statement of the lucid priorities that drove the Classical Greek world. Originally, brilliantly painted and embellished with statuary, its impact would have been more remarkable still.

GREEK SCULPTURE

The Parthenon's sculptures fall into three groups. On the triangular pediments at each end of the building were large-scale free-standing groups containing numerous figures showing the birth of Athena and her struggles with Poseidon for control of Attica; below these as well as along both sides were nearly 100 individual reliefs of struggling figures (men and centaurs; Greeks and Amazons; gods and giants); behind the outer colonnade and running round the entire building was a relief, 525 ft (160 m) long, depicting the Great Panathenaia, a religious festival held every four years in honor of Athena.

Even badly damaged, the Parthenon sculptures reveal the confidence and technical mastery of their creators. These are wholly convincing figures, dramatically grouped and heroically conceived. Other examples of Classical Greek sculpture are better preserved. The slightly more than life-size bronze *Boy from Antikythera* combines calm elegance with technical sophistication

Boy from Antikythera, c. 340 BCE, height 76 in (194 cm), bronze, Athens: National Archeological Museum.

in ways that were genuinely new, infusing the naturalistic with the ideal to produce a supremely self-confident image of a godlike youth. The sculpture manages the rare feat of being both supremely rational and yet at the same time extraordinarily sensual.

Descriptions of Greek painting suggest it, too, reached comparable levels of technical achievement. The Roman frescoes at Pompeii were almost certainly heavily influenced by Greek originals. Perspective, foreshortening, and the naturalistic representation of figures all seem to have been mastered in ways that would not reappear until Renaissance Italy. Greek vases reinforce the point. Though painted on curved and small-scale surfaces, their decoration contains complex and ambitious groups of figures in settings which have a real sense of space and depth.

KEY EVENTS

505 BCE	Democracy established in Athens
490 BCE	Greeks defeat Persians at Marathon
480 BCE	Greeks defeat Persians at Salamis and Plataea
478 BCE	Confederation of Delos founded; later transformed into Athenian Empire
461 BCE	Beginning of domination of Athenian political life by Pericles
447 BCE	Parthenon begun (completed 432)
431 BCE	Peloponnesian Wars between Athens and Sparta (to 404)
399 BCE	Athenian philosopher Socrates condemned to death for corrupting youth
385 BCE	Plato returns to Athens; opens Academy
384 BCE	Birth of Aristotle

HELLENISTIC GREEK ART c. 300—1 BCE

In 336 BCE, Alexander the Great began his blaze of conquest across the Middle East and Egypt. His empire fragmented after his death, but the cultural impact of Greece on these vast territories proved enduring. This process of "Hellenization" was further boosted by the Romans, who, by the 1st century BCE, had exported Greek artistic traditions across the whole Mediterranean.

Alexander and his successors implanted Greek cultural values across a vast swathe of the ancient world. Rather like the city-states of 5th-century Greece, these new Greek kingdoms were political rivals but shared a common cultural inheritance. A huge program of new city building was begun in Asia Minor, the Middle East, Mesopotamia, and North Africa. Alexandria, Antioch, and Pergamum for instance are all Hellenic cities. Greek prestige was enhanced, too, by learning. The library at Alexandria was the most famous in the ancient world. The influence of Aristotle, who died in 322 and had been Alexander's tutor,

The Battle of Issus (detail), 1st century BCE, mosaic, Naples: Museo Archeologico Nazionale. This mosaic from Pompeii is a Roman copy of a Greek original. The young Alexander (left) defeats Persian King Darius (center).

extended over the entire period and beyond. In the face of this huge expansion of the Greek world, the original city-states of Greece itself were overshadowed politically, but retained much of their cultural status.

Though Hellenistic art continues a clear line of development from the Classical period, with naturalism again the chief concern, there are important differences. The most obvious is that the restraint of Classical Greek art gives way to a sense of movement and drama. One reason may have been that increasing technical mastery led artists to set themselves harder problems to solve. But there is a

Dying Gaul, Roman copy of Greek original of c. 230 BCE, marble, Rome: Pinacoteca Capitolina. The original was created shortly after the kingdom of Pergamum defeated an army of invading Gauls in 230 BCE.

sense, too, that the Hellenistic world needed a more emphatic style of art to underline the fact of its conquests. Where on the Parthenon, for example, civic piety set the tone, on the Alexander Sarcophagus, a sumptuous marble tomb carved probably in 310 BCE for the ruler of Sidon, not only is there a sense that technical mastery is being celebrated for its own sake, a clear note of triumphalism creeps in. One side of the sarcophagus is a battle scene in which the figure of Alexander, clad in a lion-skin, is accorded the sort of heroic treatment previously reserved only for gods.

A NEW TREND IN SCULPTURE

The Altar of Zeus at Pergamum, perhaps the most famous work from the entire period, embodies another key characteristic: scale. The base of the platform on which the altar stands contains a frieze 7½ ft (2.3 m) high and fully 295 ft (90 m) long. On the upper level is a second frieze 5 ft (1.5 m) high and 240 ft (73 m) long. The vigor of the carvings, with their writhing, interlocking figures, is far removed from the placid assurance of the Classical period.

The expressiveness of heroic figures such as these found a different outlet in the almost equally well-known *Dying Gaul*. The stoic dignity with which he accepts

Altar of Zeus *(detail)*
c. 180 BCE, marble, Berlin: Pergamonmuseum. The sculpted frieze depicts the Gigantomachy, the battle between the Gods and the Giants.

his fate makes clear an interest in the individual that was reflected in the development of lifelike portraiture. This was partly prompted by the teachings of Aristotle. Whereas in Classical Greece individual worth was automatically equated with physical perfection, now personality was judged at least as important. The mid-3rd-century bronze statue of a philosopher, possibly Hermarchus, portrays an aging and crumpled figure. But his obvious nobility of spirit makes it clear that the sculpture is intended as a sympathetic portrayal, a point that is emphasized by his physical frailty and decrepitude.

OSTENTATION

The Hellenistic world also placed a premium on luxurious and elaborate surface decoration, an interest later fully shared by the luxury-loving Romans. The 4th-century Derveni krater is not just a technical tour de force but an object of conspicuous ostentation.

KEY EVENTS

336 BCE	Accession of Alexander the Great; begins conquest of Persia
332 BCE	Alexander conquers Egypt; lays foundations of Alexandria
323 BCE	Death of Alexander sparks breakup of his empire
322 BCE	Death of Aristotle
302 BCE	Final fragmentation of Alexander's empire
c. 230 BCE	Original bronze of *Dying Gaul* cast, Pergamum
c. 175 BCE	Altar of Zeus at Pergamum begun
168 BCE	Start of Roman expansion into eastern Mediterranean
146 BCE	Greece and North Africa fall under Roman rule
133 BCE	Pergamum bequeathed to Rome

Derveni krater, *late 4th-century BCE, height 34 in (86 cm), gilded bronze, Thessaloníki: Archeological Museum.* This enormous krater (vessel for mixing wine and water) was found at Derveni in northern Greece. The shoulders are decorated with statuettes, while the body has repoussé reliefs of Dionysus, Ariadne, and other mythological figures.

Laocoön

Hagesandrus, Polydorus, and Athenodorus   C. 42–20 BCE

Few Greek statues exercised a greater hold on the Renaissance imagination than the *Laocoön*. In part, this was due to the dramatic circumstances of its chance discovery in Rome in 1506, when Renaissance interest in Greek statuary was reaching a peak; in part, to the heroic nobility of its expressive, struggling figures.

The twist of the muscular torso adds dynamism and energy to the composition

The *Laocoön* is thought to have been carved in the second half of the 1st century BCE. This means it belongs to the very end of the Hellenistic period. Stylistically it derives from the Altar of Zeus at Pergamum of around 150 years before. It is an astonishingly accomplished work, acutely observed and highly finished. Overwhelmingly its impact stems from the sense of heightened and tragic emotion generated by its contorted, writhing figures. This kind of dramatic, large-scale treatment had a significant impact on Michelangelo and on later artists of the Roman Baroque. The statue illustrates an incident in Virgil's account of the Trojan Wars, the *Aeneid*. Laocoön was a Trojan priest punished by Poseidon, who sent two snakes to kill him and his sons, after he had urged the Trojans to reject the apparent Greek peace offering of a wooden horse. According to Pliny, the group was carved by three sculptors, Hagesandrus, Polydorus, and Athenodorus.

The flanking figures of the sons create a triangular composition, balancing and anchoring it

The figure of the son who is on the point of death is contrasted with the continuing, desperate struggles of the father and the other son.

TECHNIQUES

Despite its technical sophistication and complex interlocking figures, the work is only intended to be viewed from the front. It is essentially conceived in one plane, almost like a relief. It has been suggested that the figure of the elder son (right) may have been added later. He is physically separated from the other figures and also carved from a separate block. As with all Antique statues, it would originally have been painted.

Tortured expressions highlight the new interest accorded to the tragic dignity of suffering

The snakes bind the bodies of the father and his sons into a single composition, while their sinuous lines unify the group's rhythmic continuity.

Laocoön

Dimensions height, excluding base, 72 ½ in (184 cm)

Medium marble

Location Rome: Vatican Museums

Strong diagonals reinforce the sense of drama and movement

Draperies are contrasted with gleaming skin tones, increasing tactile values

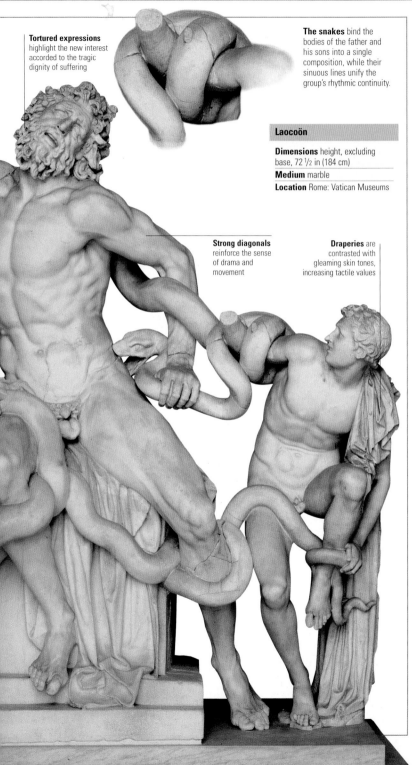

IMPERIAL ROME c. 27 BCE—C. 300 CE

Uniquely among the leading powers of the ancient world, Rome developed only a limited artistic language of its own. Roman architecture, like Roman engineering, was never less than bold, but Roman painting and sculpture were derived largely from Greek models. However potently Rome projected images of its political power, the visual means it used to do so were secondhand.

Roman art was largely imitative and utilitarian. Greece provided Rome with a huge range of models to adapt to its own ends. Yet rather than acting as a stimulus, the result was an apparently permanent Roman inferiority complex in the face of the Greek artistic achievement and the stifling of independent Roman schools of art. Hence the lifelessness traditionally and, on balance, rightly attributed to Roman art.

The 1st-century CE Medici Venus, for example, is just one of 33 surviving Roman copies of the Hellenistic original. Greek sculptures

Ara Pacis, *13–9 BCE, marble, Rome.* The frieze shows members of Augustus's family and state officials. The man in the detail (left) is Marcus Agrippa, the emperor's son-in-law .

weren't just copied by the Romans, they were actively recycled. Greek poses recast in Roman garb were pressed into service to reinforce Roman power. At its most extreme, this practice allowed a kind of off-the-rack shopping whereby heroic Greek figures, available in a variety of sizes, could be supplied headless, the buyer supplying his own, easily installed, portrait head.

This kind of pragmatism is illustrated by the celebrated late-2nd-century CE equestrian statue of Marcus Aurelius. Arm outstretched, head turned slightly to the side, his pose is just one of numerous Roman reworkings of the 5th-century BCE statue of Doryphorus, itself known only from Roman copies. What was originally an idealized image of male beauty has been slightly clumsily converted into a vehicle stressing Roman imperial might and the godlike person of the emperor.

Even the much earlier Ara Pacis Augustae (Altar of Augustan Peace), whilst seeking to stress the continuity between the rule of the Emperor Augustus and the earlier

KEY EVENTS

264 BCE	Rome completes conquest of Italy; first Punic War (to 241 BCE)
218 BCE	Second Punic War (to 201 BCE): Hannibal invades Italy
149 BCE	Third Punic War (to 146 BCE): Carthage destroyed by Roman army
46 BCE	Julius Caesar appointed dictator (assassinated 44 BCE)
27 BCE	Octavian becomes first Roman emperor (as Augustus); dies 14 CE
13–9 BCE	Ara Pacis Augustae created, Rome
79 CE	Pompeii and Herculaneum destroyed after eruption of Vesuvius
113 CE	Trajan's Column built, Rome
117 CE	Death of Emperor Trajan: Roman Empire at its greatest extent
161–180 CE	Equestrian statue of Marcus Aurelius cast, Rome

Roman republic, is obviously dependent on Greek models, above all in its use of a continuous large-scale frieze of figures. The virtues they seek to embody may be Roman; the manner in which they do so is unambiguously Greek.

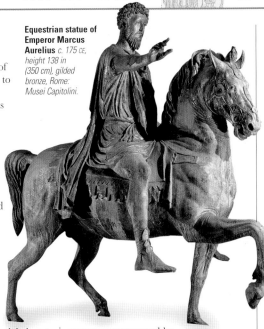

Equestrian statue of Emperor Marcus Aurelius *c. 175 CE, height 138 in (350 cm), gilded bronze, Rome: Musei Capitolini.*

ROMAN PAINTING

In imperial Rome the love of luxury, severely disapproved of by those seeking a return to the stern values of the republic, tended to equate opulence with quality. This was a world in which more almost always meant better.

Most of the surviving examples of Roman painting are from Pompeii (preserved thanks to the eruption that obliterated the city in 79 CE). These offer crucial clues to the earlier Greek painting on which they were modeled. In contrast to what is known of these Greek originals, the paintings at Pompeii seem to have been almost exclusively decorative murals for expensive villas. Landscapes and seascapes augmented by complex architectural settings using sophisticated illusionistic devices seem to have been the preferred subjects. As ever in the imperial Roman world, there was a premium on presentation over content. The surviving murals were clearly painted by journeymen, in most cases Greeks—superior interior decorators rather than artists as the Greeks would have understood the term.

Nile in Flood (detail) c. 80 BCE, mosaic, Palestrina: Museo Archeologico Prenestino. The Romans followed Greek models to produce magnificent floor mosaics.

LATE ROMAN & EARLY CHRISTIAN ART
c. 300—450 CE

As Rome's empire was eroded, Roman art increasingly departed from the naturalistic ideals it had inherited from the Greeks. In turn, these vigorous but less sophisticated artistic models were adapted by the early Christian Church in the search for a visual language appropriate to its theological needs.

Mummy-case portrait from Fayum, *encaustic on wood, London: British Museum.* A tradition of Roman-style portrait painting continued in Egypt through the 2nd and 3rd centuries CE.

The Arch of Constantine in Rome, built by the Emperor Constantine early in the 4th century, neatly encapsulates the move away from the rationalism of Greece. In addition to reliefs carved in the reign of Constantine himself, the arch incorporates a series of sculptured reliefs from earlier periods. The choice of these was deliberate: all come from the reigns of well-loved emperors with whom Constantine wished to identify, so as to legitimize his rule. The early reliefs are all carved in the fully naturalistic tradition inherited from Greece. The later reliefs, by contrast, contain figures that almost deliberately seem to caricature their more elegant predecessors: stumpy and badly proportioned, almost all shown in profile. In the same way, foreshortening and other devices to create a sense of space are totally ignored. The contrast is so great there is a sense that these reliefs are almost

flaunting their deliberate abandonment of the Greek visual tradition.

RADICAL CHANGE
Constantine's reign marked a crucial moment for Rome. His decision in 330 to move the capital of the empire from Rome to Constantinople (modern Istanbul) confirmed an existing shift of political and economic power to the east. His legitimization of Christianity in 313

KEY EVENTS

312 CE	Constantine confirmed as emperor
313	Edict of Milan: Constantine legitimizes Christianity in Roman Empire
325	Council of Nicaea called by Constantine to resolve theological differences within Church
329	St. Peter's basilica, Rome, completed
330	Constantine dedicates Constantinople as new capital of Roman Empire
391	Emperor Theodosius imposes Christianity on Roman Empire as sole religion
395	Death of Theodosius: Roman Empire definitively split into East and West
410	Visigoths under Alaric sack Rome
455	Vandals under Gaiseric sack Rome
476	Deposition of Romulus Augustulus, last Roman emperor in the west

constitute idolatry. No such strictures applied to the figure of Christ himself, it being a central tenet of Christianity that Christ had been made man. However, there was little agreement as to how he should be shown: young, old, stern, benign, even bearded or beardless. Although many scenes from the life of Christ were depicted quite early on, these never included the Crucifixion, a form of death reserved for the lowest class of criminal. Even the cross itself was only slowly adopted as a universal symbol. In the absence of surviving paintings, early Christian statuary and mosaics provide the only clues as to how these questions

Holy Women at the Tomb of Christ *c. 400, ivory, Milan: Castello Sforzesco.* Mary, the mother of Jesus, and Mary Magdalene worship the risen Christ, who is portrayed as a young, beardless man in Roman dress.

had consequences that were equally momentous. What had been a minor sect, frequently persecuted, now enjoyed the full weight of imperial patronage. Constantine's decision was overridingly political: he used the Church as a central point around which the empire could regroup, hence the urgency with which he set out to reconcile rival Christian sects. The challenge thereafter was to find visual means to express the Christian message. Inevitably, Roman, which is to say pagan, prototypes were used. The basic form of churches themselves came from secular Roman buildings known as basilicas, large oblong halls, often arcaded with aisles and an apse at the far end.

CHRISTIANITY AND ART

There was a long-running controversy as to whether God the Father could be represented or whether this would

Roundel from the Arch of Constantine
This medallion, which shows a sacrifice being made to Apollo, dates from the reign of Hadrian (117–138 CE). It was taken by Constantine from an earlier monument to decorate his triumphal arch in Rome, erected c. 315 CE.

were resolved. The sumptuous mid-4th-century sarcophagus of Junius Bassus, for example, has two tiers, each containing five scenes of sharply carved if crudely realized figures. In both a youthful Christ occupies the central scene. His pose in the upper tier, seated with arms outstretched in benediction, derives directly from an imperial Roman tradition.

A similar fusion of pagan forms and Christian subject matter is evident in an ivory of around 400 depicting the *Holy Women at the Tomb of Christ*. Again, if the figures are slightly awkwardly rendered, they clearly stem from the earlier Greek tradition.

BYZANTINE ART c. 500—1200 CE

Vastly richer than the beleaguered Western Empire and increasingly drawn toward the east, the Byzantine Empire evolved a new and elaborate visual language dominated by complex religious imagery. It marked an near absolute break with the Classical Greek inheritance that had driven earlier Roman art.

The most important subject of Byzantine art was Christianity. As the teachings of the Church were codified, precise rules came to govern how they could be depicted. Gestures and even colors came to acquire precise and unvariable meanings.

Among the earliest examples of Byzantine art are the glittering, near otherworldly mosaics in the Church of San Vitale in Ravenna in Italy. They are important not just as an emphatic assertion of the vigorous (if short-lived) Justinian reconquest—the attempt by the Eastern Emperor Justinian to recreate a unified Roman Empire in the face of the barbarian conquests in the west—but as a supreme example of the new sensibilities of the Byzantine world. The dominant image, over the altar, is of a luminous, seated Christ, flanked by angels and donors. But hardly less remarkable is that of Justinian and his

Madonna and Child, 12th century, mosaic in vault of apse (detail), Trieste: Cathedral of St. Just. The Byzantine tradition that Mary should be depicted wearing a blue robe was carried over into Western art.

retinue. This portrait of the splay-footed emperor, part gangster, part man of destiny, is one of the most compelling images in Western art. Justinian's Church of Hagia Sophia in Constantinople projects this mood of fierce piety even more strikingly. Even today, almost 600 years after the Ottoman conquest of Byzantium in 1453 when what was then still the largest church in Christendom became, as it remains, a mosque, its glinting mosaics and vast, shadowy recesses evoke an astonishing sense of the grandeur and mystery at the heart of imperial Byzantium.

The later formality of the Byzantine tradition

Byzantine capitals in Church of S. Vitale, Ravenna, 6th century. The interiors of Byzantine churches were richly decorated with mosaics, gilding, and reliefs, but not statues, which were not venerated as icons.

"the Mother of God," she became a central figure of Byzantine, and later of western, Christian art.

FAR-REACHING INFLUENCE

An image such as the 6th-century panel painting of the Virgin and Child from the Monastery of St. Catherine in the Sinai Peninsula, Egypt, highlights a further, central fact of Byzantine art: that religious "icons" (literally "images") were increasingly valued as aids to contemplation. Small and often portable, they would exercise a profound influence on the spreading world of "orthodox" Christianity ("orthodox" because sanctioned by the Byzantine Church). The conversions of Bulgaria in 864 and Kievan Russia in 988 to this distinctive brand of Christianity were crucial in expanding its reach and in implanting it in new lands.

belies just how inventive it originally was. The glowering mosaic figure of Christ Pantocrator, "Christ the ruler of all," staring down from the dome of the monastery church of Daphni in Greece, is an exceptionally potent image of an implacable God. It was in Byzantium, too, that the Virgin Mary was developed as one of the key icons of Christian art. In part this was a matter of doctrine. Yet once established in the 5th century that it was precisely her virginity that made her

KEY EVENTS

532	Hagia Sophia begun in Constantinople (consecrated 537)
533	Justinian launches reconquest of West Roman Empire
c. 547	Mosaics in San Vitale Ravenna
555	Byzantine conquest of Italy and southern Iberia complete
558	Dome of Hagia Sophia collapses (rebuilt by 563)
692	Trullan Council sanctions use of figures of Christ in art
726	Emperor Leo III bans worship of religious images, provoking "iconoclast" crisis
751	Ravenna, last Byzantine possession in Italy, falls to Lombards
843	Triumph of Orthodoxy: religious images officially promoted
864	Mission of Cyril and Methodius begins spread of orthodoxy in eastern Europe
1054	Final schism between Roman and Orthodox churches

Emperor Justinian I and his Retinue, c. 547 CE, mosaic, Ravenna: S. Vitale. Flanked by imperial officials, generals, and high-ranking members of the clergy, Justinian is portrayed as the political, military, and religious leader of the Byzantine Empire.

CELTIC, SAXON & VIKING ART c. 600—900

Northern Europe after the collapse of the Roman Empire has traditionally been seen as entering a "dark age," lost in impenetrable obscurity: marginal, shadowy, and violent. Yet drawing on earlier Celtic traditions and increasingly becoming part of the Christian world, it produced exceptionally vivid and sophisticated works of art.

The discovery at Sutton Hoo in 1939 of the burial goods of an early Anglo-Saxon king, generally agreed to be Raewald, ruler of East Anglia, transformed people's understanding of emerging Anglo-Saxon England. Raewald died around 625, not much more than 200 years after the Romans had abandoned Britain. Yet among the objects found in his grave were a Byzantine bowl and gold coins from Gaul, evidence of long-range trading contacts. At the same time, the treasure highlights a world poised between a pagan past and a Christian future. Already Christianity was penetrating Britain, from Ireland and from continental Europe. Once these rival traditions had been reconciled in 664 by the Synod of Whitby, Britain came firmly within the orbit of the Roman Church.

Belt buckle from Sutton Hoo, *early 7th century, gold, London: British Museum.* Inlaid with garnets and colored glass, the piece shows clear affinities with the intricately intertwined patterns of Celtic jewelry and illuminated manuscripts.

THE VIKINGS

By contrast, the Viking world as it emerged over the next 200 years was at first genuinely beyond Rome's reach. Nonetheless, drawing on the same Celtic roots that are obvious at Sutton Hoo, it, too, produced works of art of a remarkable and immediately recognizable potency. The 9th-century carved dragon ship's figurehead, found in a burial mound at Oseberg in Norway, is evidence of a warrior society capable of exceptional craftsmanship.

Viking ship's figurehead *c. 825, height 5 in (12.7 cm), wood, Oslo: Universetets Oldsaksamling.* This intricately carved dragon's head was among the grave goods found in a burial mound excavated in 1904.

KEY EVENTS

563	Irish monastery established at Iona
597	Mission of papal emissary St. Augustine to England
c. 650	Lindisfarne Gospels
664	Synod of Whitby: Roman Christianity adopted in England
731	Bede completes his Ecclesiastical History of England
c. 790	First Viking raids on western Europe
c. 800	*Book of Kells*

The Book of Kells c. 800

The monastery established in 563 on the remote island of Iona off the west coast of Scotland was one of a handful of isolated Dark Age Irish Christian communities that were responsible for an extraordinary outpouring of Celtic Christian art, above all a series of sumptuous illuminated manuscripts.

The Book of Kells, produced at Iona in about 800 and taken to Ireland for safekeeping when the Viking raids began, is the most famous product of the fusion of Celtic art and Christian subject matter. It is a book of verses, interspersed with extracts from the Gospels. The thousands of hours of patient labor lavished on it represented an act of worship just as much as the examination of it was intended to induce a mood of contemplation. Among its innovations was the use of richly decorated and elaborate capital letters at the start of each passage.

Interlaced patterns are a key characteristic of Celtic decorative art; they may have been influenced by Roman floor mosaics

Triskele—three legs radiating from a central point—are a recurring motif in Celtic art

The capitals—Chi and Rho—are first two letters of the Greek word for Christ and are one of the oldest Christian symbols

The complexity of the patterning is similar to contemporary Celtic jewelry

Naturalistic details—human heads, animals, and birds—are dotted among the swirling, swooping line work.

Book of Kells

Dimensions	13 x 10 in (33 x 25 cm)
Medium	ink on vellum
Location	Dublin: Trinity College Library

MEDIEVAL ART OF NORTHERN EUROPE
c. 800—1000

By the 8th century, the Frankish Empire had become the most successful of the new states formed after the collapse of Rome. It reached its largest extent under Charlemagne in the early 9th century when it covered France, Germany, the Low Countries, and most of Italy. Charlemagne also sparked a cultural revival that decisively influenced the development of later medieval art.

On Christmas day 800, Charlemagne, king of the Franks, was crowned emperor of a new Roman Empire by Pope Leo III in St. Peter's in Rome. It was a deliberate assertion of Rome reborn. As it turned out, Charlemagne's empire would prove vulnerable, its unity destroyed after his death in destructive dynastic quarrels. But his longer-term legacy proved remarkably enduring. In extending his rule deep into Germany, territories the Romans had been unable to subdue were brought within western Christendom. In the 10th century, Saxony, conquered and forcibly Christianized by Charlemagne after a

KEY EVENTS

771	Charlemagne sole ruler of Frankish Empire
772	Conquest of Saxony begun; complete 802
774	Lombardy brought within Charlemagne's empire
792	Imperial (Palatine) Chapel begun at Aachen; completed 805
800	Coronation of Charlemagne in Rome
814	Death of Charlemagne
843	Treaty of Verdun divides Carolingian Empire into three
845	Paris sacked by Vikings
875	Charles the Bald crowned first Holy Roman Emperor
910	Foundation of Benedictine abbey at Cluny, France
936	Accession of Otto I as Holy Roman Emperor

St. Mark from Carolingian Gospel Book *c. 800, purple vellum, Abbeville: Bibliothèque Municipale.* The strange-looking creature framed by the arch is the winged lion, symbol of St. Mark the Evangelist.

savage 30-year campaign, had become a major center of early medieval art and religious teaching. In effect, a nascent German state had been created. In the same way, the western half of the fractured empire would subsequently emerge as France. A shift of Europe's political and cultural center of gravity was taking place, away from the Mediterranean toward the north.

CULTURAL RENEWAL

Charlemagne's promotion of Latin not only helped preserve Roman texts that might otherwise have been lost, but it also established a common language among Europe's elites and strengthened the authority of the Roman Church.

Cross of Gero *c. 970, height 73 ⅝ in (187 cm), oak, Cologne Cathedral.* Unlike Byzantine art, western European religious art stresses the suffering of Christ.

An example of the artistic outpouring generated by the Carolingian *renovatio* (renewal) is a Gospel book produced at the city of Aachen, Charlemagne's capital, early in the 9th century. Its Classical origins are clear. The image of St. Mark, framed by a triumphal arch, is not just an obvious celebration of the evangelist, it is a clear attempt to imitate the richness of the late Roman world. In reality, however, it looks forward to the Middle Ages rather than back to Rome. There is no Roman precedent for the double-jointed twist of the evangelist's right wrist any more than there is for his oddly angled feet.

As important was the development of a narrative tradition in religious art that would endure throughout the Middle Ages. As early as the 6th century, Pope Gregory I had affirmed the didactic purpose of religious imagery: "What scripture is to the educated, images are to the ignorant." Under Charlemagne, narrative images of this kind became a fixed part of the western tradition. An early 9th-century ivory panel, subsequently used as the cover of devotional volume known as the *Pericopes* (meaning simply "extracts") of Henry II, set within an elaborately jeweled frame, contains three scenes, dominated by the Crucifixion, in an obvious narrative sequence. Similar painted scenes, only faded fragments of which survive, are known to have decorated Carolingian churches.

This depiction of the Crucifixion is an early example, its provenance hard to unravel, of what would become almost the single most important Christian image in medieval Europe: Christ not just on the cross but clearly human, suffering unbearable agonies. The so-called Cross of Gero, carved around 970 and now in Cologne Cathedral, encapsulates this new, tortured sensibility.

Book cover *8th century, silver gilt and ivory, Cividale del Friuli: Museo Archeologico.* The carving of the Crucifixion shows Longinus thrusting his spear into the dead Christ's side.

Otto II, Holy Roman Emperor *c. 985, illumination on vellum, Chantilly: Musée Condé.* Otto, the second Saxon Emperor, ruled 967–983. He married a Byzantine princess. The four women offering homage to the emperor represent the four parts of his empire.

ROMANESQUE & EARLY GOTHIC ART
c. 1000—1300

Despite external threats, whether Viking, Magyar, or Muslim, by about 1000 the Christian states of Europe had begun a slow process of recovery. At the heart of their regeneration was the Church, the only pan-European body in Christendom. Early medieval art, increasingly lavish, in architecture above all, was almost exclusively religious.

Rose window c. 1224, stained glass, south wall of Chartres Cathedral.

The foundation of a new monastery at Cluny in central France in 910 sparked a hugely important reform of the western Church. Under its second abbot, St. Odo, Cluny extended its control over a number of other monastic foundations. In the process, they were not merely reinvigorated themselves but the Church as a whole became much more expansive and assertive. One consequence was a program of new church building across much of western Europe.

ROMANESQUE ARCHITECTURE
Quite rapidly, a new architectural language, the Romanesque, came into being. As a reflection of the new power of the Church, these were buildings that were deliberately magnificent and, in many cases, much larger than anything yet seen in Europe. The cathedral of Santiago de Compostela, for example, built around 1120, possesses this austere gravity in abundance. There is a heaviness to its massive walls and

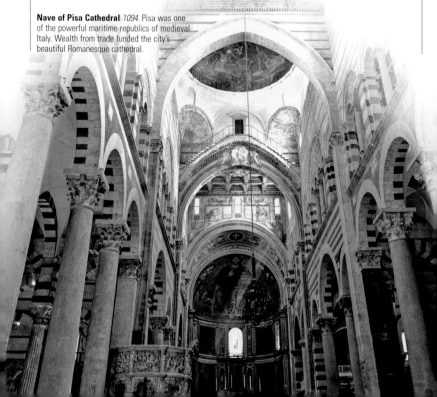

Nave of Pisa Cathedral 1094. Pisa was one of the powerful maritime republics of medieval Italy. Wealth from trade funded the city's beautiful Romanesque cathedral.

immense tunnel vaults that emphatically projects the new self-assurance of the Church. At much the same time, in France, a new manner of sculptural decoration was created. At Autun Cathedral, for example, the tympanum, the area immediately above the main entrance, is crowded with figures dominated by Christ in the center. The subject depicted, as it is on almost all later such carvings, is the Last Judgment, a reminder to worshippers entering the building of their mortality. The vigor and elegance of this teeming scene, filled with demons, angels, the damned, and the saved, the whole presided over by the serene figure of Christ, makes clear the revitalization of European sculpture, an art form almost abandoned after the fall of Rome. As with all medieval sculpture, originally it would have been painted.

THE GOTHIC

In 1144 Abbot Suger, abbot of the monastery of St. Denis just outside Paris, presided over the consecration of the rebuilt choir of the abbey church. That this is a radically different type of structure is obvious. Structurally, there is nothing new—its ribbed vaults and pointed arches had appeared in a number of earlier buildings—yet St. Denis has a unity, the whole lit by what Suger memorably called "the liquid light if heaven," that is quite different. Gothic art was more than just an extension of the Romanesque. It was different in every important sense, a visual language expressly designed to celebrate the central place of the Church in an increasingly confident European society. This was not a world looking back to Rome. Self-aware and increasingly self-assured, it sought to create its own towering monuments to God. The early Gothic cathedrals with their soaring verticals reaching up to pointed arches were triumphant assertions of a new sensibility that equated massive building projects with personal piety. It was a style that reached maturity at Chartres, begun in 1194, and

KEY EVENTS	
1031	Beginning of Christian reconquest of Spain
1065	Earliest known stained glass in Europe, at Augsburg cathedral, Germany
1066	Norman conquest of England
1077	Emperor Henry IV forced to seek absolution from Gregory VII, reinforcing papal authority
1085	Third abbey church at Cluny, the largest in the world, begun
1088	First university in Europe established, at Padua, Italy
1096	First Crusade (to 1099)
1098	Foundation of Cistercian order in France
1137	Rebuilding of St. Denis: first properly Gothic building
1147	Second Crusade (to 1148)
1154	Accession of Henry II unites much of France and England

Romanesque capital c. 1135. The pilgrimage church of Ste. Madeleine in Vézelay in the Burgundy region has many fine examples of Romanesque carving.

climaxed at Amiens, begun in 1220, and the Sainte-Chapelle in Paris (1243–48), where the floor-to-ceiling stained-glass windows are both a technical tour de force and an exultant celebration of a new monarchy certain of its own power.

The self-confidence of this world found other outlets. The mid-12th-century illustration of St. John from the Gospel of Liessies, for example, probably painted by an English illustrator in the Low Countries, projects a similar certainty of its own worth: stylized, lavish, and elegant. It is a compelling example of the self-belief that underpinned the art of medieval Europe.

Gothic carvings, Chartres Cathedral These Old Testament figures, flanking the central door of the the west facade, date from the late 12th century.

GOTHIC AND EARLY RENAISSANCE
c. 1300 – 1500

The word "Renaissance" (meaning "rebirth") was first used in the 15th century to describe a revival in Classical learning. At the same time, "Gothic" was used to describe a style of architecture regarded as barbaric, the creation of the Goths who had destroyed the glories of art and architecture in the Roman Empire.

It was only in the 19th century that "Renaissance" was used to explain the cultural flowering of the 14th and 15th centuries that launched the intellectual framework and artistic traditions of the modern world. Yet politically, socially, and economically, the soil from which the Renaissance grew could hardly have seemed more barren.

When in 1346, the Black Death, carried by ship-borne rats from Asia, began to wipe out one third of Europe's population, it seemed just the latest in a series of traumatic events. In the previous century, huge areas of eastern Europe had been seized by the Mongols. Between 1315 and 1319, there had been a run of catastrophic harvests. At the same time, the southeast of the continent was being menaced by the aggressively expanding Ottomans.

Europe looked ill equipped to deal with these threats. Technologically inferior and politically fragmented, it appeared destined to remain at the mercy of more powerful neighbors. In addition, it was wracked by periodic bouts of savage internal warfare. Edward III's attempted conquest of France in 1337 began over 100 years of brutal conflict between England and France. Meanwhile, the Catholic Church was divided by a period of schism.

RECOVERY THROUGH TRADE

Yet, in the face of these enormous handicaps, Europe staged a comeback. A sense of pan-European identity began to emerge, principally as the result of commerce. Throughout the Middle Ages, trade routes had been consolidated. By the end of the 14th

Camera degli Sposi *Andrea Mantegna, fresco, 1465–74, Mantua: Palazzo Ducale.* The virtuoso use of perspective, combined with Classical motifs, demonstrates the enthusiasm with which the Gonzaga family, the rulers of Mantua, embraced the new art and learning.

century, a network of sea and land routes linked much of the continent. Money and goods were exchanged, but so were ideas, and together these led to a general rise in prosperity. Venice and Genoa, city-states grown rich on trade with the Orient, led the way, but others were quick to imitate them. For example, the establishment of the Hanseatic League in 1360 created a series of northern European cities that could rival the traditionally dominant Mediterranean. Equally important was the establishment by Hans Fugger in Bavaria in 1380 of a banking network that in time would make the Fuggers the richest family in Europe.

The Triumph of Death *(detail) Pieter Brueghel the Elder, c. 1562, oil on panel, 46 x 63¾ in (117 x 162 cm) Madrid: Museo del Prado. The ravages of the Black Death were indiscriminate: the rich were as vulnerable as the poor.*

GOTHIC ART

"Gothic" describes principally a style of architecture common in Northern Europe between 1100 and 1500. It also includes the decorative art of the period, which was usually highly ornamental with realistic detail, but without any overall scheme of representation. In its later years Gothic art became increasingly decorative and elegant, with sophisticated patterns and rhythms, and when used by Italian painters is called "International Gothic."

Roettgen Pietà, *c.1300, limewood (originally painted), height 35 in (89 cm) Bonn: Rheinisches Landesmuseum.*

ITALY

Nevertheless, it was in Italy that the Renaissance achieved its fullest flowering. It was here that the physical remains of the ancient world—notably sculpture and architecture —were most numerous and so most easily studied. Also the newly rich city-states believed that they needed to embody the spirit of the Roman Empire itself. Florence, by the early 15th century the most powerful of these city-states, consciously chose to see itself as the direct heir of Rome. Financed by

TIMELINE: c. 1300—1500

c. 1300 Venetians improve Brenner Pass, facilitating trade with northern Europe

1337 Start of 100 Years' War between England and France

1380 Foundation of international banking system by Hans Fugger in Augsburg, Germany

1389 Battle of Kosovo: Ottomans gain control of Balkans

1300

1350

1304–12 Scrovegni Chapel, Padua, painted by Giotto

1346 First occurrence of Black Death; in three years reduces Europe's population by one third

1360 Hanseatic League founded

1378 The Great Schism: rival popes in Rome and Avignon (to 1417)

1387 Medici bank founded, Florence

its own indigenous banking dynasty, the Medici, Florentine artists not only proclaimed the superiority of Classical antiquity but asserted that it represented a golden age of creativity whose spirit needed to be revived in the present, and they condemned the recent past as a dark age. At the same time, European thought was becoming more questioning and freethinking. People began to look for rational explanations of the physical environment and human behavior, and were ready to reject the dogmatic propositions and blind faith that controlled the elaborately complex medieval world. Painters, sculptors, and architects were at the forefront in instigating these fundamental changes. When Brunelleschi demonstrated how perspective could be represented schematically on a flat surface, he was conscious that he was unifying science, philosophy and art, and was thus looking ahead to a world in which all three would be, and would look, permanently different.

POISED FOR EXPANSION
The most decisive contribution to this new spirit of inquiry was the invention of moveable type by Johannes Gutenberg in Germany

in the 1450s. This sparked an unprecedented revolution in the speed, ease, and cost of the spread of information and ideas. When Christopher Columbus crossed the Atlantic in 1492 he opened new horizons and at the same time confirmed that Europe had moved from the shadowy margins of the world to occupy center stage.

Dome of Florence Cathedral Completed by Filippo Brunelleschi in 1434, the dome of Florence Cathedral was an emphatic statement of civic pride in which science was used to produce architecture of outstanding beauty.

	1425 Masaccio's *Holy Trinity*, Santa Maria Novella, Florence	**1453** Constantinople falls to Ottomans; fall of Bordeaux to France ends 100 Years' War		**1492** Muslim Granada falls to Spain; Columbus's first Atlantic crossing
1421–44 Brunelleschi's Foundling Hospital, Florence, first properly classical building of the Renaissance			**1454** Gutenberg Bible, oldest known book printed with moveable type	
1400			**1450**	
1415 Burning of Jan Hus for heresy provokes religious wars in Bohemia	**1429** Joan of Arc sparks French revival in 100 Years' War	**1434** Dome of Florence cathedral completed	**1450** Alliance of Florence, Naples, and Milan dominates north and central Italy	**1469** Lorenzo de Medici (the Magnificent) assumes control of republic of Florence

Nicola and Giovanni **Pisano**

● 13TH–14TH CENTURIES ᴘᴜ ITALIAN

🏛 Pisa; Siena; Perugia; Pistoia; Padua
🎨 sculpture

Nicola (c. 1220–c. 1284) and Giovanni
(c. 1245–c. 1314/19) were father and
son. Nicola (also called Niccolò) founded
a workshop, at which Giovanni was a
pupil. Worked together, but each retained
a distinct individual style. Pioneers of the
Gothic style. Renowned for their religious
stonework, such as altars and pulpits.
The Fontana Maggiore in Perugia is the
most famous of their joint works. They
are credited with bringing a previously
unseen naturalism to stone sculpture.
KEY WORKS *Nativity* (pulpit), 1265–68 (Siena
Cathedral); *Madonna and Child*, c. 1305
(Padua: Cappella dei Scrovegni); *Madonna*,
c. 1315 (Prato Cathedral)

Bernardo **Daddi**

● c. 1290–c. 1349 ᴘᴜ ITALIAN

🏛 Florence 🎨 oils, fresco 🏛 London:
Courtauld Institute of Art 💲 $2,562,000
in 2004, *Coronation of the Virgin* (oils)

A younger contemporary of Giotto, who
was possibly Daddi's teacher. Blended
Giotto's tough realism with the sweetly
lyrical qualities of Sienese artists (such as
Ambrogio Lorenzetti). Look for smiling
Madonnas, cute children, flowers, and

Polyptych with the Crucifixion and Saints
Bernardo Daddi, c. 1348, approx. 61 x 85⅜ in
(155 x 217 cm), tempera and gold leaf on panel,
London: Courtauld Institute of Art.

draperies. Creator of popular, easy-to-
look-at, small-scale portable altarpieces.
Then, as now, art that is kind to the eye
and mind tends to have a wide following.
KEY WORKS *Arrival of St. Ursula at Cologne*, 1330
(Los Angeles: J. Paul Getty Museum); *The
Marriage of the Virgin*, c. 1330–40 (London:
National Gallery); *Martyrdoms of Sts. Lawrence
and Stephen*, c. 1330 (Florence: Santa Croce)

Jehan **Pucelle**

● c. 1300–c. 1350 ᴘᴜ FRENCH

🏛 France; Italy; Belgium 🎨 illumination

Pucelle was an eminent illuminator of
manuscripts and a master miniaturist;
recognized as such in his lifetime. Owned
an influential workshop in Paris at the
start of the 14th century. Traveled to Italy
and Belgium to learn new techniques.
A favorite of the French court, his works
were expensive and purchased by nobility
and royalty. Pucelle's works are renowned
for being more realistic in their depiction
of human features than those of the
traditional, "flat" icon painters.
KEY WORKS *Belleville Breviary*, 1323–26 (Paris:
Bibliothèque Nationale); *Hours of Jeanne
d'Evreux*, 1325–28 (New York: Metropolitan
Museum of Art)

Limbourg brothers

● ACTIVE 1390s – c. 1416 ◉ NETHERLANDISH

🏛 Paris; Italy   🎨 illumination   🏛 Chantilly (France): Musée Condé. New York: The Cloisters

Paul (or Pol), Herman, and Jean Limbourg were pioneering illuminators who trained as goldsmiths and then worked for the great French patron of the period, Jean, Duc de Berry, at a time of great political turmoil. They were born in the Netherlands, where their father was a wood carver. Through the influence of an uncle, who was a painter, they were sent to train in Paris. Paul was probably the head of the workshop, but it is not possible to distinguish his hand from those of his brothers.

   Their two great works are *Les Belles Heures* and *Les Très Riches Heures*. They used old forms (illustrated Books of Hours—personal prayer books) but with fresh and stunningly innovative illustrations—scenes of everyday life (courtiers and peasants), unusual biblical events, first-hand observation from life, and landscapes of real places (such as the Duc's châteaux). Their brilliant colors and meticulous technique marry perfectly with their subjects.

   Their best-known work is the "Months" from *Les Très Riches Heures* because they are most accessible to a secular society and look wonderful in reproduction. Note how they used contemporary advanced Italian ideas such as landscape background (one of the brothers went to Italy); and anticipated Netherlandish art—story-telling, fine detail, and observation. Their work and patronage reflect the notion that, for the wealthy, commissioning and collecting art is a celebration of God's glory and an act of true devotion.

KEY WORKS *The Nativity*, c. 1385–90 (Paris: Bibliothèque Nationale); *Les Très Riches Heures*, 1413–16 (Chantilly, France: Musée Condé); *The Anatomy of Man and Woman*; c. 1416 (Chantilly, France: Musée Condé)

Death, One of the Four Riders of the Apocalypse *Paul (or Pol) Limbourg, c. 1413–16, illumination on vellum, Chantilly (France): Musée Condé.* Note the fine detail—an obsession of the brothers.

ILLUMINATION   7th–15th centuries

"Illumination" is the term used to describe the hand-painting and handwriting of books decorated with motifs in rich colors. Characteristically, the initial letter of a page is much larger than the others and furnished with images and bold colors. The use of gold and vivid hues of red, blue, and green are employed. Other styles may include elaborate borders around the text or small pictorial scenes. The medium is often associated with religious books.

Illuminated "P" by Bartolomeo di Fruosino, 1421

Taddeo **Gaddi**

◯ c. 1300–c. 1366   🏳 ITALIAN

🏛 Florence   🎨 oils; fresco   🏛 Florence: Santa Croce (Baroncelli Chapel frescoes)
📊 $3,114,000 in 1991, *The Bromley Davenport Altarpiece—The Man of Sorrows, Sts. Peter, Francis, Paul, and Andrew* (oils)

He was Giotto's principal follower (and godson?). Gaddi popularized Giotto's tough realism by making it decorative, adding anecdotal details, and emphasizing the storytelling side of picture making.

KEY WORKS *Annunciation to the Shepherds*, c. 1328 (Florence: Santa Croce); *Madonna and Child Enthroned*, 1355 (Florence: Galleria degli Uffizi); *The Entombment of Christ*, c. 1360–66 (New Haven: Yale University Art Gallery)

Cimabue (Cenni di Peppi)

◯ c. 1240–1302   🏳 ITALIAN

🏛 Florence; Rome   🎨 oils; tempera; fresco; mosaic   🏛 Pisa: Cathedral (apse mosaic)

The most prominent artist working in Florence at the end of the 13th century, Cimabue was a contemporary of Dante. Traditionally said to be Giotto's teacher—i.e. it is claimed that he

Madonna and Child Enthroned with Eight Angels and Four Prophets (or Maestà)
Cimabue, c. 1280, 151½ x 87¾ in (385 x 223 cm), tempera on wood, Florence: Galleria degli Uffizi.

initiated the move from the static "old" and "unreal" Byzantine style to the "modern" and "realistic" style, with more credible 3-D space, human form, and emotion. So many works have been attributed to him that his name has almost come to represent a group of like-minded artists rather than an individual, though we know he existed.

KEY WORKS *Maestà*, 1280–85 (Florence: Galleria degli Uffizi); *Madonna and Child Enthroned with Two Angels and Sts. Francis and Dominic*, c. 1300 (Florence: Palazzo Pitti); *Christ Enthroned between the Virgin and St. John the Evangelist*, 1301–02 (Pisa Cathedral)

Duccio di Buoninsegna

◯ ACTIVE 1278–1319   🏳 ITALIAN

🏛 Siena; Florence; Paris   🎨 oils   📊 $1.77m in 1976, *The Crucifixion* (oils)

Key early Sienese painter, Duccio influenced all those that followed (just as Giotto influenced Florentine artists).

He tells a story with tenderness and humanity. He is not as innovative in style or technique as Giotto, who was his

Allegory of Good Government: Effects of Good Government in the City (detail) Ambrogio Lorenzetti, c. 1338–39, 116½ x 550⅜ in (296 x 1398 cm), fresco, Siena: Palazzo Pubblico.

contemporary, but he is a better narrator of events. Look at the way the people act and react together, and the way he uses the setting as part of the narrative. The perspective and scale may be haywire, but the buildings still look real and lived-in, and may be arranged so as to divide up the constituent parts of the story.

He paints no-nonsense (slightly sceptical?) faces with long, straight noses, small mouths, and almond-shaped eyes, which can be rather sly. His hand gestures help tell the story. He makes decorative use of color, notably blue, red, and pale green. Some of the oddities or quirkiness can be explained because his style is not actually of the Renaissance: it is essentially Byzantine and Gothic—that is, old-fashioned, but with a new twist, rather than completely new like Giotto's.

KEY WORKS *Maestà*, c. 1308 (Siena: Museo dell' Opera Metropolitana); *Nativity*, c. 1308–11 (Washington, DC: National Gallery of Art); *The Apostles Peter and Andrew*, c. 1308–11 (Siena: Museo dell'Opera Metropolitana); *The Holy Women at the Sepulchre*, c. 1308–11 (Washington, DC: National Gallery of Art)

Lorenzetti brothers

◗ ACTIVE c. 1319–1348　ⓙ ITALIAN

ⓟ Siena; Florence　🖌 fresco; oils
💰 $906,630 in 2001, *Crucifixion with Two Martyrs* (oils) by Pietro Lorenzetti

Siena's Pietro (1320–c. 1348) and Ambrogio (1319–c. 1348), followed in the steps of Duccio di Buoninsegna, but with more realism and expression. They had shadowy lives (there is a difficult chronology for extant work) and both died of plague. Ambrogio's work is warmer and less solemn than his brother's; his most important works are the frescoes of *Good* and *Bad Government* (Palazzo Pubblico, Siena)—the first Italian paintings where landscape is used as background.

KEY WORKS *The Charity of St. Nicholas of Bari*, Ambrogio Lorenzetti, 1335–40 (Paris: Musée du Louvre); *Scenes from the Life of Blessed Humility*, Pietro Lorenzetti, c. 1341 (Florence: Galleria degli Uffizi)

Giotto di Bondone

- c. 1267–1337   ITALIAN
- Florence; Padua; Naples; Assisi; Rome; Milan   fresco; oils   Padua: Cappella dei Scrovegni. Assisi: S. Francesco. Florence: S. Croce

The painter who brought a new level of realism to art, which would establish the framework for Western art until 20th-century Modernism changed the rules.

Despite humble beginnings as the son of a farmer, Giotto became an educated and cultivated man, who grew rich and important in Florentine society. An unsubstantiated story tells how he was discovered by chance by the great painter Cimabue who saw the boy Giotto sketching his father's sheep. Giotto then became Cimabue's apprentice. He lived through a period when Florence was becoming one of Europe's most important and influential cities.

WHAT TO LOOK FOR

Giotto's innovation was in the way he portrayed supposedly real-life events to appear as though enacted by lifelike people expressing believable emotions and occupying recognizable settings and spaces. He looked, painted what he saw, and then opened up a "window on the world." The impact, even now, is one of directness, simplicity, accessibility, and believability. In other words, his paintings are about *life*.

Look for his outstanding features: faces expressing genuine emotion; meaningful gestures; strong, self-explanatory storylines (like early silent movies, you only have to look to know exactly what is going on); the sense of space around and between the figures; how shape and movement of incidentals, such as trees and rocks, support the main action or emotion; large bones, well-built, solid figures. But notice also

> "When I see the Giotto frescoes at Padua, I do not trouble myself to recognize which scene of the life of Christ I have before me, but I immediately understand the sentiment which emerges from it. For it is the lines, the composition, the color."
>
> HENRI MATISSE

Campanile of the Duomo, Florence Giotto designed the Campanile in 1334, and construction was finished in 1359, 22 years after his death. Here it is viewed from the top of the Duomo.

Cappella dei Scrovegni, frescoes, Padua
Giotto di Bondone, c. 1305. The climax of the
chapel's glorious decoration is the large fresco
of the *Last Judgement* on the west wall.

where he finds problems that are difficult
for him to resolve; for example, he had
no knowledge of perspective or anatomy,
and a convincing sense of weightlessness
(e.g. flying angels) eluded him.

Giotto's key monument is the Scrovegni
(or Arena) Chapel in Padua (c. 1304–13),
which is decorated from floor to ceiling
with a complex arrangement of self-
contained scenes, most memorable for
their emotional and spiritual impact.

KEY WORKS *Stigmata of St. Francis*, c. 1295–1300
(Paris: Musée du Louvre); *The Lamentation
of Christ*, c. 1305 (Padua: Cappella dei
Scrovegni); *The Virgin and Child*, c. 1305–06
(Oxford: Ashmolean Museum); *Enthroned
Madonna with Saints and Angels*, c. 1305–10
(Florence: Galleria degli Uffizi)

The Ecstasy of St. Francis *Giotto di Bondone,
1297–99, 106⅛ x 90½ in (270 x 230 cm), fresco, Assisi:
S. Francesco.* One of the frescoes depicting "The Legend
of St. Francis," who had died less than 80 years earlier.

Simone Martini

◖ c. 1285–1344   ◪ ITALIAN

◩ Siena; Avignon   ◗ tempera; fresco; oils; illumination   ◪ $220,000 in 1991, *St. Peter* (oils)

One of the leading painters from Siena and a follower of Duccio. Although he experimented with new ideas (such as perspective), he was essentially a large-scale, decorative illustrator, not least of illuminated manuscripts.

Look for the qualities you might see in illuminated manuscripts (despite the difference in scale): glowing color; lively drawing; a precise, closely worked line; meticulous observation of detail; rhythmic, flowing, golden draperies. Simone's all-consuming emphasis was on decoration for sumptuous overall effect.

It is interesting to compare his work with that of his exact contemporary, Giotto, because, lovely as it is, it lacks everything that is in Giotto: Simone's figures are artificial, with convoluted poses and gestures; faces are stylized and without genuine emotion; the story-telling lacks deep meaning; everything is arranged decoratively, not to create ideas of space, form, and movement. Simone's work was a final chapter of the past; Giotto's was the future.

KEY WORKS *Maestà*, 1315 (Siena: Palazzo Pubblico); *Death of St. Martin*, c. 1326 (Assisi: Lower Church); *The Angel and the Annunciation*, 1333 (Florence: Galleria degli Uffizi); *Apotheosis of Virgil*, 1340–44 (Milan: Biblioteca Ambrosiana); *Christ Discovered in the Temple*, 1342 (Liverpool: Walker Art Gallery)

KEY WORKS *St. Mary Magdalene*, c. 1320 (Boston, MA: Museum of Fine Arts); *The Betrayal of Christ*, c. 1324–25 (London: National Gallery)

Lorenzo Monaco

◖ c. 1370–1425   ◪ ITALIAN

◩ Florence   ◗ oils; fresco; illumination   ◫ Florence: Galleria degli Uffizi; Galleria dell'Accademia   ◪ $1,665,517 in 2004, *Annunciation* (oils)

Lorenzo was born in Siena, but seems to have spent all his professional life in Florence. A highly gifted monk (*monaco* is Italian for "monk"). Creator of altarpieces and illuminated manuscripts (look for a love of detail; fine technique; luminous blues, reds, golds; rhythmical, decorative line). His poetic imagination strove to unite the natural with the supernatural, and decorative Gothic with Giotto's realism. Happiest when working on a small scale—predella panels and manuscripts.

KEY WORKS *The Nativity*, 1409 (New York: Metropolitan Museum of Art); *Madonna and Child*, 1413 (Washington, DC: National Gallery of Art); *The Adoration of the Magi*, c. 1422 (Florence: Galleria degli Uffizi)

Ugolino di Nerio

◖ ACTIVE 1317–27   ◪ ITALIAN

◩ Siena; Florence   ◗ oils   ◪ $200,200 in 1990, *Crucifixion* (oils)

He was Sienese, and also known as Ugolino da Siena. A close follower of Duccio, and with a similar style, but narrative is less well focused, colors are less clear, and the faces and gestures lack Duccio's precision.

Madonna Enthroned between Adoring Angels *Lorenzo Monaco, c. 1400, 12¾ x 8⅜ in (32.4 x 21.2 cm), panel, Cambridge: Fitzwilliam Museum.*

Gentile da Fabriano

🌐 1370–1427 🏛 ITALIAN

🏙 Fabriano; Florence; Venice   🎨 oils; fresco
📈 $497,624 in 1986, *The Annunciation* (oils)

He was an Italian painter, named after
his birthplace, Fabriano in the Marches.
One of the foremost artists of his day,
he was the most accomplished exponent
of the International Gothic style. Worked
all over Italy. Most of his work is either
lost or destroyed.

   His preference was to turn a work
of art into a highly luxurious object (a
characteristic of the International Gothic
style), rather than a window on the world
(Renaissance). His works could almost be
fabulous textiles woven with gold thread.

   As well as using traditional techniques
such as tooled gold, and with a liking for
patterned textiles and static figures, he
also experimented with light, space, and
narrative. He created delicate, unreal
figures with pink cheeks. Paid great
attention to natural detail—animals,
birds, plants—which he recorded with
delicacy and sympathy.

KEY WORKS *Virgin and Child Enthroned*, c. 1395
(Berlin: Staatliche Museum); *Coronation of
the Virgin*, 1420 (Los Angeles: J. Paul Getty
Museum); *Adoration of the Magi*, 1423 (Florence:
Galleria degli Uffizi); *The Nativity*, 1423
(Los Angeles: J. Paul Getty Museum)

**The Presentation in the Temple (from the
Altarpiece of the Adoration of the Magi)**
Gentile da Fabriano, 1423, 10½ x 30 in (26.5 x 66 cm),
oil on panel, Paris: Musée du Louvre.

Stefano di Giovanni
Sassetta

🌐 1392–1450 🏛 ITALIAN

🏙 Siena; Florence   🎨 oils

The best painter of early Renaissance
Siena. Combined the old decorative
style of the International Gothic with
the new ideas from Florence.

   Look for his charming, uninhibited
qualities—the kind that children show
when making a picture: a delight in
storytelling; lots of physical activity;
spaces and perspective that don't quite
work; sudden attention to unexplained
detail; unsophisticated, decorative colors.

   Note the bright little eyes with
prominent whites and, sometimes,
faces with wide-eyed expressions;
prissy, bow-shaped lips, and curious
harp-shaped ears; also observe stylized
crow's-feet on older male faces.

KEY WORKS *St. Margaret*, c. 1435 (Washington,
DC: National Gallery of Art); *San Sepolcro
Altarpiece*, 1437–44 (London: National Gallery);
The Madonna and Child Surrounded by Six Angels,
c. 1437–44 (Paris: Musée du Louvre); *The
Meeting of St. Anthony and St. Paul*, c. 1440
(Washington, DC: National Gallery of Art)

Pisanello (Antonio Pisano)
c. 1395–1455 ITALIAN

Verona; Rome oils; engravings; fresco
Verona: San Fermo; Santa Anastasia. London: National Gallery. Paris: Musée du Louvre (drawings)
$212,300 in 1990, *A Nobleman Attended by Knights and a Knight Fallen from his Charger in a Landscape* (works on paper)

He was very popular with princely courts as a painter, decorator, portraitist, and medallist, but few works now survive.

His work has qualities similar to those of illuminated manuscripts. It is good for an inconclusive art-historical debate: is he the late flowering of the International Gothic style or the pioneer of early Renaissance? (It is more profitable to forget the debate and just enjoy what you can, when you can.)

Notice his fascinating direct observation from life, and meticulous, fresh draftsmanship, especially of animals, birds, and costumes. He painted flat, decorative backgrounds like tapestries, using fresh colors. His portraits have distinctive profiles, which relate to his pioneering of the art of the portrait medal—a medium at which he excelled.

Portrait of Ginevra d'Este Antonio Pisano Pisanello, c. 1436–38, 17 x 11¾ in (43 x 30 cm), tempera on wood, Paris: Musée du Louvre. Notice how the leaves, flowers, and butterflies combine to create a rich tapestry effect.

The Last Judgment Stephan Lochner, 1440s, 48 x 67⅓ in (122 x 171 cm), oil on wood, Cologne: Wallraf-Richartz-Museum. Exquisite coloring and minute detail are characteristic of Lochner's work.

KEY WORKS *The Annunciation*, 1423–24 (Verona: San Fermo); *St. George and the Princess of Trebizond*, 1437–38 (Verona: Santa Anastasia)

Masolino da Panicale
c. 1383–1447 ITALIAN

Florence; Rome; Hungary oils; fresco Rome: San Clemente (fresco cycle). Como (Italy): Castiglione Olona
$270,000 in 1995, *Prophet or Evangelist* (oils)

Best remembered as collaborator of Masaccio, he was recognized as a painter of great distinction. He had a graceful figure style, learned by working with the sculptor Lorenzo Ghiberti, and made skilful use of perspective. He was an accomplished modeler of flesh and hair, and had an interest in everyday details.

KEY WORKS *Madonna of Humility*, c. 1415–20 (Florence: Galleria degli Uffizi); *St. John the Evangelist and St. Martin of Tours*, c. 1423 (Philadelphia: Museum of Art); *St. Liberius and St. Matthias*, c. 1428 (London: National Gallery)

Giovanni di Paolo
ACTIVE 1420–82 ITALIAN

Siena oils $800,000 in 2001, *Scenes from the Story of Esther* (oils)

"The El Greco of the Quattrocento." Sienese painter who adopted a deliberately old-fashioned style, in reply to the influential "modern" style of Duccio. Developed a charming, decorative, and convincing narrative style, in which the spaces, perspective, scale, emotions, and logic of the "real" world are deliberately ignored.

KEY WORKS *St. John the Baptist Retiring into the Wilderness*, c. 1453 (London: National Gallery); *The Feast of Herod*, c. 1453 (London: National Gallery); *The Nativity and the Adoration of the Magi*, c. 1455–59 (Paris: Musée du Louvre)

Stephan **Lochner**

c. 1400–51   GERMAN

Cologne   oils   Cologne

A shadowy early German painter about whom little is known and to whom few works are attributed for certain. The leading master of his time in Cologne, where he worked from 1442 until his death. Author of religious works of soft, rounded figures with slightly silly, chubby faces; glowing colors; rich, gold backgrounds; somewhat fussy, natural, and anecdotal detail.

KEY WORKS *The Virgin in the Rose Bush*, c. 1440 (Cologne: Wallraf-Richartz-Museum); *Annunciation*, c. 1440–45 (Cologne Cathedral); *Sts. Matthew, Catherine of Alexandria, and John the Evangelist*, c. 1445 (London: National Gallery)

The Moses Well *Claus Sluter, late 14th century, height of figures 70⅞ in (180 cm), stone, Dijon: Chartreuse de Champmol. Symbolic well surrounded by statues of Moses and other Old Testament prophets.*

Claus **Sluter**

c. 1350–c. 1405   DUTCH

Dijon; Brussels   sculpture

A sculptor and a founder of the Burgundian School. Hugely influential on the development of northern European sculpture. Born in Haarlem. Worked in Brussels, before moving to France. For 21 years, lived in Dijon as chief sculptor of Philip the Bold, Duke of Burgundy. His work is characterized by fine draperies, silken-looking hair, and realistic human figures.

Look for ordinary mortals introduced into religious works standing alongside divine figures.

KEY WORKS *Portal of the Chartreuse de Champmol*, 1385–93 (Dijon); *Arms of a Virgin or a Magdalene*, 14th century (Dijon: Musée Archéologique); *Fragment of Crucified Christ*, 14th century (Dijon: Musée Archéologique)

THE EARLY RENAISSANCE

Three major principles underlined the Renaissance (literally, rebirth) in early 15th-century Italy: a renewed, more systematic study of Classical Antiquity in the belief that it constituted an absolute standard of artistic worth; a faith in the nobility of man (Humanism); and the discovery and mastery of linear perspective. Together, they made up a revolution in Western art.

STYLE

From the start, Renaissance artists, especially those based in its birthplace, Florence, were conscious that their work represented a decisive break with the immediate past. The change came first—and most obviously—in sculpture. Ghiberti's panel for a new set of bronze doors for Florence Baptistry owes a direct and immediate debt to Roman models. Figures are modeled naturalistically; the sense of space is equally marked.

The Sacrifice of Isaac *Lorenzo Ghiberti, 1402, 21 x 17 in (53.3 x 43.4 cm), bronze, Florence: Museo Nazionale del Bargello.* The frame may be Gothic, but the key elements of the Renaissance are unmistakably present, e.g., the muscular Isaac derived from Classical originals.

SUBJECTS

Though religious subjects continued to predominate, there was an increasing interest in secular subjects. Gozzoli's mid-century *Procession of the Magi* artfully combined the two. His Magi are portraits of his patrons, the Medici, surrounded by numerous retainers, on a procession that is more regal than religious. If the shimmering, jewel-like picture surface looks back to the International Gothic, the figures and landscape are just as clearly products of the Renaissance.

The Procession of the Magi *(detail) Benozzo Gozzoli, 1459, fresco, Florence: Palazzo Medici-Riccardi.* The richly garbed figure on the white horse is Lorenzo de' Medici, commandingly certain of his worth in every sense.

KEY EVENTS

c. 1427	Masaccio completes frescoes in Brancacci Chapel, Santa Maria del Carmine, Florence, the first great Renaissance fresco cycle
1424	Ghiberti completes first set of Florence Baptistry bronze doors; more commissioned
1434–64	Florence ruled by Cosimo de' Medici
1445	Johannes Gutenberg's Bible, first printed book in Europe (Germany)
1452	Publication of Alberti's *De Re Aedificatoria*, first comprehensive treatise to set out principles of Classical architecture
1469–92	Lorenzo (the "Magnificent") de' Medici rules Florence

15th century

WHAT TO LOOK FOR

The two most obvious technical triumphs of Renaissance painting were the ability to portray convincingly naturalistic figures in equally convincingly realized illusionistic spaces. Piero della Francesca, author of three mathematical treatises, epitomized both developments. He constructed exceptionally elaborate perspective schemes while his figures have an overwhelming sense of assured monumentality. Yet however rational his paintings may be, ultimately what marks them is a distinctively haunting sense of serene detachment.

The architectural details—ceiling of the semi open-air structure and rich floor tiles—are painted exactly

The vanishing point is precisely calculated: exactly on the center line of the painting, dividing it in two, a quarter of the way up

The Flagellation of Christ *Piero della Francesca, c. 1470, 23 x 32 in (58.4 x 81.5 cm), oil and tempera, Urbino: Galleria Nazionale delle Marche.* A great and enigmatic masterpiece.

The flagellation is carried out with hardly any animation. On the left, the seated figure of Pontius Pilate gazes impassively at Christ's punishment

The significance of the three figures in the foreground has been endlessly questioned. Who are they, and why are they so detached from the flagellation?

The statue immediately above Christ's head provides clear evidence of Piero's interest in the Antique. Its precise meaning remains disputed but its soft modeling is ravishingly well done.

TECHNIQUES

Piero's palette, consistently cool and clear, is a key element in the curious air of mystery that pervades his work. Flesh tones (which use a base of green paint), no less than limpid skies, are realized with remarkable economy.

Lorenzo **Ghiberti**

◗ c. 1378–1455   Ⴖ ITALIAN

Ⴖ Florence; Siena   ⚑ sculpture; glass
🏛 $245,679 in 2000, *Madonna and Child* (sculpture)

He was a sculptor, goldsmith, designer,
and writer. Born and worked in Florence;
also worked in Siena. Renowned in his
lifetime as the best bronze-caster in
Florence. Famous for the bronze doors
of the Baptistry in Florence. Also
produced stained glass and sculptures.
Opened a large, influential workshop;
pupils included Donatello. Married
Marsilia c. 1415; two sons, Tommaso
and Vittorio, both worked in the studio.

Look for rich decoration and elegance
of sculpting. His relief work is defined by
clean lines and plenty of activity, with the
eye drawn by fluid drapery, movement in
the landscape, and ornate carving. Fusion
of classical artistic style with realism.
KEY WORKS *The Sacrifice of Isaac*, 1402
(Florence: Museo Nazionale del Bargello);
Joseph in Egypt (Porta del Paradiso), 1425–52
(Florence: Baptistry)

Masaccio (Tommaso Giovanni di Mone)

◗ 1401–28   Ⴖ ITALIAN

Ⴖ Florence   ⚑ fresco; tempera
🏛 Florence: Brancacci Chapel (fresco
cycle); Santa Maria Novella

The greatest of the early-Renaissance
Florentines, he revolutionized the art
of painting during his short lifetime
and was the bridge between Giotto and
Michelangelo. Masaccio means "Big ugly
Tom." He left very few known works.

His deeply moving pictures can plumb
the most basic and profound of human
emotions. He painted believable and
dignified human figures, expressing
qualities of feeling, emotion, and
intellectual curiosity that are as relevant
today as 500 years ago. His simple, well-
ordered compositions, in which the human
figure is the central feature, accord with
the Renaissance principle that human
beings are the measure of all things.

The individual expressions on the
faces show minds and emotions at
work—enquiring, doubting, suffering—
also expressed simultaneously through
gestures and hands (but why are the

The Trinity *Tommaso Masaccio, 1425, 263¾ x 124 in
(670 x 315 cm), fresco (post restoration), Florence: Santa
Maria Novella.* This piece was covered over in 1570 with
a panel painting by Vasari, and only rediscovered in 1861.

hands so small?). Creates believable
spaces, which human figures dominate
with authority. Uses light to model
draperies and figures (instead of outline,
so helping them to look real). Masaccio
was the first painter to understand and
use scientific perspective; the same is
true for foreshortening.
KEY WORKS *Crucifixion*, 1426 (Naples: Museo
di Capodimonte); *The Expulsion from Paradise*,
c. 1427 (Florence: Santa Maria del Carmine)

Fra Filippo **Lippi**

◗ c. 1406–69   Ⴖ ITALIAN

Ⴖ Tuscany   ⚑ fresco; tempera; oils   🏛 Spoleto:
Cathedral (frescoes); Prato: Cathedral (fresco
series)   🏛 $183,484 in 2002, *Madonna and Child
with St. Lucy, St. Lawrence, and St. Catherine* (oils)

An important early-Renaissance
Florentine whose work forms a bridge
between Masaccio and Botticelli.

His sincerely-felt religious works
expressed worship of God by sensitive
interpretation of the New Testament
and by mastery of all the chief technical
interests and developments of the period
(all of them, including the artist's skill,

being a gift from God): perspective; landscape; proportion; communication between human figures; finely painted decorative detail; carefully drawn drapery folds.

Look for the chubby figures with slightly glum youthful faces, and eyes that look as though they never blink. Note his love of rich detail—marble floors, gold grounds, decorated costumes.

KEY WORKS *Virgin and Child*, c. 1440–45 (Paris: Musée du Louvre); *The Annunciation*, c. 1448–50 (London: National Gallery); *Madonna and Child with Stories of the Life of St. Anne*, c. 1452 (Florence: Palazzo Pitti); *The Adoration with the Infant Baptist and St. Bernard*, c. 1459 (Berlin: Staatliche Museum)

Fra **Angelico**

● c. 1387–1455   ᴘᴊ ITALIAN

ᴘᴊ Florence; Fiesole; Orvieto; Perugia; Rome
⬥ fresco; tempera; oils   ⬥ Florence: Convent of San Marco (fresco series)   ⬥ $1,080,537 in 2003, *St. Peter and St. Thomas Aquinas by the Cross* (oils)

He was a Dominican friar whose work combines old-fashioned (Gothic) and progressive (Renaissance) ideas.

His paintings interpret the Christian message with directness, enthusiastically telling the story of God's goodness. They are delightfully happy, attractive, and holy, and have great innocent purity—as though he saw no evil in the world (perhaps he didn't.)

There is disarming and childlike innocence in the detail: youthful, happy faces with peaches and cream complexions and pink cheeks; everyone is busy doing something. Angelico takes evident pleasure in colors (especially pink and blue) and things that he has observed closely, such as flowers. He uses old-fashioned gold embellishments and modern perspective with equal enthusiasm; his soft draperies have highly detailed borders.

KEY WORKS *Noli me Tangere*, 1425–30 (Florence: Convent of San Marco); *The Annunciation*, 1435–45 (Madrid: Museo del Prado); *The Virgin and Child Enthroned with Angels and Saints*, c. 1438–40 (Florence: Convent of San Marco); *The Mocking of Christ*, c. 1439–43 (Florence: Convent of San Marco)

The Beheading of St. Cosmas and St. Damian
Fra Angelico, c 1438–40, 14½ x 18 in (37 x 46 cm), tempera on panel, Paris: Musée du Louvre. After previous failed attempts on their lives, the twin martyrs were finally killed.

David

Donatello c. 1435–53

This piece was created for the Medici, and was first mentioned in the report of the marriage of Lorenzo il Magnifico (1469). It stood in Florence's Palazzo Medici, paired with a statue of Judith and Holfernes. Both works told of the death of oppressors — a warning to enemies to keep away.

Donatello's *David* was a move away from traditional religious imagery. One of the first nude statues of the Renaissance; the homoeroticism is instantly apparent, as is the innovative twisting pose about the hips, known as "contrapposto." Although David stands with the head of Goliath at his feet, the figure does not seem capable of the great strength or violence needed to have killed the giant. Goliath's helmet displays Donatello's ability to sculpt in relief.

David's expression is strangely dreamy and contemplative

In his left hand, David holds the sling he used to bring down Goliath

Many Florentines were shocked by the statue's nudity

In his right hand is the sword that decapitates Goliath

He stands on a laurel wreath, symbol of victory and power

Donatello probably trained as a goldsmith. As a result, he was particularly skilled at working with bronze with fine detail and highly polished surfaces.

David	
Medium bronze	
Height 62¼ in (158 cm)	
Location Florence: Museo Nazionale del Bargello	

Donatello

● 1386–1466   ◢ ITALIAN

▣ Florence; Padua   ◨ sculpture
▤ Florence: Museo dell'Opera del Duomo;
Museo Nazionale del Bargello

Unquestionably the greatest sculptor of
the early Renaissance. Born in Florence,
traveled widely. Famous throughout Italy.

Essentially, he reinvented the art of
sculpture just as other contemporaries
were reinventing the art of painting.
His innovations and discoveries were
profoundly influential on Michelangelo.
He had complete mastery of sculpture
in bronze, stone, wood, and terracotta,
and nothing escaped his extraordinary
capabilities: relief sculpture, nudes,
equestrian statues, groups of figures
with single figures seated or standing.
Was able to bring sculpture to life by his
ability to tell a story, to combine realism
and powerful emotion, and give his figures
a sense of more than mere objects of
beauty for passive contemplation, but
creations filled with energy and thought,
ready to spring into action.

Physically strong and rough, prone
to anger, he was a popular member of
Florentine society and close to his patron,
Cosimo de Medici. Careless with money,
unmarried, and probably homosexual,
he was well known for choosing only
good-looking boys as studio apprentices.
KEY WORKS *St. Mark*, 1411 (Florence: Or San
Michele); *St. George*, c. 1415 (Florence: Museo
Nazionale del Bargello); *Zuccone*, c. 1436
(Florence: Museo dell'Opera del Duomo)

Luca della **Robbia**

● c. 1399–1482   ◢ ITALIAN

▣ Florence   ◨ sculpture; ceramics
▤ Florence: San Miniato al Monte
◪ $254,839 in 2002, *Madonna and
Child with Saints* (sculpture)

His full name was Luca di Simone
della Robbia; he came from a large
family of artists and artisans. Prolific
sculptor of the early Renaissance. A
warm personality who gave practical
help to struggling artisans. Trained
in textiles and as a goldsmith before
sculpture. Worked in stone and
terracotta. Follower of the humanistic
movement. Patronized by the Medici;
also patrons in Naples, Portugal,
and Spain. Achieved fame and wealth
through glazed terracotta artworks. Set
up successful studio in Florence; keeping
the formula of his tin glazes a secret.
Worked closely with his nephew Andrea
della Robbia (1435–1525).

Look for rich color and luminous tin
glazes, strict attention to detail, and an
awareness of the properties of draperies
and metalwork reflected in his sculpture.
His scenes are thick with symbolism and
the faces expressive.
KEY WORKS *The Resurrection*, c. 1442–45 (Florence:
Museo Nazionale del Bargello); *Roundels of the
Apostles*, c. 1444 (Florence: Pazzi Chapel)

Domenico **Veneziano**

● c. 1400–61   ◢ ITALIAN

▣ Perugia; Florence   ◨ tempera; fresco
▤ London: National Gallery. Florence:
Galleria degli Uffizi

He was an important and very influential
Venetian who worked in Florence. Almost
nothing is known about him now and
there are only a few known works
surviving. He was more interested in
constructing with light and color than
with modelled form and perspective.
KEY WORKS *St. John in the Desert*, c. 1445
(Washington, DC: National Gallery of Art);
The Martyrdom of St. Lucy, c. 1445–48 (Berlin:
Staatliche Museum)

Cantoria *(choir gallery, detail) Luca della Robbia,
c. 1432–38, 39⅜ x 37 in (100 x 94 cm), marble, Florence:
Museo dell'Opera del Duomo. The carvings illustrate the
150th Psalm and depict angels, boys, and girls in song.*

Paolo **Uccello**

● 1397–1475   ∎ ITALIAN

▣ Florence   ◐ tempera; oils; fresco
▦ Florence: Santa Maria Novella; Duomo
(frescoes); Galleria degli Uffizi

He was a Florentine painter, born
Paolo di Dono and nicknamed *Uccello*
("the bird"). His works are instantly
recognizable by the schematic use
of perspective and foreshortening.

His over-theoretical application of
the science of perspective tends to
swamp all other considerations, and
can make his work look rather wooden
and the figures toylike. But the sheer
enthusiasm and gusto with which he
used perspective stops his pictures from
becoming dry and boring. His wife,
however, complained that he loved
his perspectives more than her.

Does he use a single viewpoint for the
perspective, or are there several? Forget
perspective and foreshortening
for a moment, and enjoy his
strong sense of design and
attention to decorative detail.
Sadly, many of his works are
in very poor condition. They
are also often hung at the
wrong height in galleries so
that his carefully worked out
perspective effects are visually
ruined. (If necessary, sit or lie
on the floor and work out the
proper viewpoint.)

KEY WORKS *The Crucifixion*, mid-
1430s (New York: Metropolitan
Museum of Art); *Battle of San*

The Hunt in the Forest Paolo Uccello, c. 1465–70,
29½ x 70 in (75 x 178 cm), oil on canvas, Oxford:
Ashmolean Museum. One of Uccello's greatest works,
which demonstrates his fascination with perspective. The
leading stag (center) is the focus of the "vanishing point."

Romano, c. 1455 (Florence: Galleria degli
Uffizi); *St. George and the Dragon*, c. 1460
(London: National Gallery); *The Flood*,
1447–48 (Florence: Santa Maria Novella)

Benozzo di Lese **Gozzoli**

● c. 1421–97   ∎ ITALIAN

▣ Florence; Orvieto; Rome; Pisa   ◐ fresco;
tempera   ▦ Florence: Palazzo Medici-Riccardi
(fresco series); Galleria degli Uffizi   ⚡ $36,750
in 1993, *Study of Male Nude* (drawing)

Down-to-earth early-Renaissance
Florentine. A good craftsman who enjoyed
what he saw. Originally trained as a goldsmith, he worked in his early years with
Ghiberti on the doors of the Baptistry
in Florence.

Gozzoli was a painter of
high-quality altarpieces and
predella panels. He liked
crowded scenes, which
enabled him to show off
a combination of brilliant,
decorative qualities, and
carefully observed solid
figures, with no-nonsense
faces and expressions.

The Triumph of St. Thomas Aquinas
Benozzo di Lese Gozzoli, c. 1470–75,
90½ x 40¼ in (230 x 102 cm), tempera on
panel, Paris: Musée du Louvre. The saint
is enthroned between Aristotle and Plato.

Gozzoli's figures have good hands (with long fingers) and good feet, and are firmly placed on the ground. Note how well he arranges crowds, and has a propensity to paint the tops of heads, particularly if bald, or with a hat or helmet.

KEY WORKS *Procession of the Magi*, 1459–61 (Florence: Palazzo Medici-Riccardi); *The Dance of Salome*, 1461–62 (Washington, DC: National Gallery of Art); *Madonna and Child with Saints*, 1461–62 (London: National Gallery); *The Raising of Lazarus*, c. 1495 (Washington, DC: National Gallery of Art)

Andrea del **Verrocchio**

● c. 1435–88   ▯ ITALIAN

▯ Florence   ▯ sculpture; tempera; oils
▯ $30,910 in 1953, *Madonna and Child* (oils)

The son of a brickmaker, he trained with a goldsmith, whose name he took. Became a leading Florentine painter, goldsmith, and (principally) sculptor. Had a workshop where Leonardo da Vinci trained. Authentic paintings by him are very rare.

His altarpieces show an overall mood and style of refinement, grace, freshness, and delicate idealism. They have a dreamy, faraway atmosphere, which is reflected in the eyes and expressions on the faces. He portrayed two types of face or body: epicene youth and craggy, tough warrior. Also painted similarly fresh, delicate landscapes and skies that contrast with craggy outcrops and rocks. Look for clear, sharp outlines and bright colors.

Note his love of fine detail, showing in

Equestrian Monument to Bartolomeo Colleoni Andrea del Verrocchio, 1480s, height 395 cm (155½ in), bronze, Venice: Campo Santi Giovanni e Paolo. The work was a competitive challenge to Donatello.

expensive fabrics decorated with gold thread and jewelry. Notice the bow-shaped lips pressed together; the stylized curly, wiry hair; the refined hands touching each other or others; poses that imply movement through weight being placed on one foot or one leg. His figures seem modeled and conceived as sculpture.

KEY WORKS *Putto with Dolphins*, c. 1470 (Florence: Palazzo Vecchio); *Tobias and the Angel*, 1470–80 (London: National Gallery); *Beheading of John the Baptist*, 1477–80 (Florence: Museo dell'Opera del Duomo); *The Baptism of Christ*, c. 1478–80 (Florence: Galleria degli Uffizi)

Piero di Cosimo

c. 1462– c. 1521   ▯ ITALIAN

▯ Florence   ▯ oils   ▯ $150,000 in 2001, *Study of the Madonna. Kneeling Angel Writing with Forefinger and Two Shepherds* (works on paper)

He was an out-of-the-ordinary early-Renaissance Florentine who led a bohemian lifestyle and was fascinated by primitive, prehistoric life. He was a prime example of the artist as a craftsman.

He painted portraits, altarpieces, and mythologies. His love of animals and birds, his observations of nature, and his storytelling are especially endearing and memorable. His strange, mythological fantasy pictures are unique; they are entirely fanciful and can have disturbing suggestions of struggle and violence. Nobody knows what they mean or why they were painted, so we are free to interpret them as we like.

How do you interpret the strangely ambivalent role played by the animals in his pictures? Note the charming landscape details that look as though they have come out of a woven medieval tapestry. Many of his works were done as decorative panels for furniture (such as *cassoni*) or rooms, hence their elongated shape.

KEY WORKS *The Visitation with St. Nicholas and St. Anthony Abbot*, c. 1490 (Washington, DC: National Gallery of Art); *A Satyr Mourning over a Nymph*, c. 1495 (London: National Gallery); *Allegory*, c. 1500 (Washington, DC: National Gallery of Art)

Pollaiuolo brothers

◔ c. 1432–98   ⚑ ITALIAN

🅿 Florence   ◐ oils; sculpture; engravings

Antonio (c. 1432–98) was a shadowy
figure who, with his brother Piero
(c. 1441–96), ran one of the most
successful workshops in Florence.

They had a pioneering interest in
anatomy and landscape, choosing
subjects to display these interests and
skills to the full, notably anatomy—
the male, nude or seminaked, doing
something that shows straining muscles
and sinews. Shows front, side, and back
views in the manner of an anatomical
analysis (they are said to have dissected
corpses to study anatomy—a daring
and risky venture at the time).

They also painted detailed landscapes
and had an interest in spatial recession,
but their work jumps abruptly from
foreground to background. They never
worked out how to use the middleground.
KEY WORKS *Hercules and the Hydra*, c. 1470
(Florence: Galleria degli Uffizi); *Portrait
of a Woman*, c. 1470 (Milan: Museo Poldi
Pezzoli); *Apollo and Daphne*, c. 1470–80
(London: National Gallery)

Battle of the Ten Naked Men *Antonio Pollaiuolo,
c. 1465–70, 15⅛ x 23¼ in (38.3 x 59 cm), engraving,
Florence: Galleria degli Uffizi. This work shows the
artist's mastery of depicting the human body in motion.*

Cosimo **Rosselli**

◔ 1439–1507   ⚑ ITALIAN

🅿 Florence; Rome   ◐ tempera; oils; fresco
➋ $489,000 in 1998, *Crucifixion with Madonna,
John the Baptist, Mary Magdalen, Andrew and
Francis* (oils)

He was a well-known early-Renaissance
Florentine, but firmly in the second
division. He painted run-of-the-mill
religious works. His figures have stylized,
obsessively painted hair and a curiously
tired and drawn look around the eyes.
KEY WORKS *Virgin and Child with an Angel,*
c. 1470 (Boston, MA: Museum of Fine
Arts); *Portrait of a Man*, c. 1481–82 (New
York: Metropolitan Museum of Art)

Luca **Signorelli**

◔ c. 1441–1523   ⚑ ITALIAN

🅿 Arezzo; Florence; Orvieto; Perugia; Rome
◐ fresco; oils; tempera   🏛 Orvieto Cathedral
(fresco series)   ➋ $790,400 in 2002, *Study
for a Seated Prophet* (works on paper)

Signorelli was intense and gifted, but
outclassed by Raphael and Michelangelo.

His religious and secular subjects
were chosen to make the most of his
interest in dramatic (overdramatic?)
compositions. Observe the movement,
muscles, and gestures in his figures—

but sometimes there is too much of this and the paintings are overcrowded. Good draftsmanship.

He emphasized the sculptural quality of the figures to the point where they sometimes look as though they have been carved out of wood. (Michelangelo always showed flesh and blood.) He painted hands that look distorted by arthritis and mouths with set expressions.

KEY WORKS *The Holy Family*, 1486–90 (London: National Gallery); *The Circumcision*, c. 1491 (London: National Gallery); *St. Agostino Altarpiece*, 1498 (Berlin: Staatliche Museum)

Domenico **Ghirlandaio**
● 1449–94   ▶ ITALIAN

▣ Florence; Pisa; Rome   ◪ fresco; oils; tempera
▥ Florence: Santa Maria Novella; Santa Trinità. Rome: Sistine Chapel (all fresco series)
⬀ $318,000 in 1980, *San Pietro Martire* (oils)

Florentine painter who achieved success with a solid, old-fashioned yet realistic storytelling style. His most famous pupil was Michelangelo.

His frescoes were commissioned as decoration for important public buildings. Consequently many are still in situ. He used contemporary settings, dress, manners, faces, and portraits to illustrate religious subjects. Look for homely, domestic pictures, which could be illustrations to a story—a forerunner of the Dutch and 19th-century genre.

He painted serious, well-fed, middle-class people, like the patrons who commissioned these works. His figures have long hands, wrists, and legs. In tempera, he uses long, widely spaced strokes that follow the main curves and contours. Do not confuse with his brother David (1452–1525), who was left-handed and so used hatching that goes from top left to bottom right.

KEY WORKS *A Legend of Sts. Justus and Clement of Volterra*, c. 1479 (London: National Gallery); *Birth of John the Baptist*, 1479–85 (Florence:

The Visitation *Domenico Ghirlandaio, 1491, 67⅝ x 65 in (172 x 165 cm), tempera on panel, Paris: Musée du Louvre. Mary, pregnant with Jesus, visits her cousin Elizabeth (pregnant with St. John the Baptist).*

Santa Maria Novella); *Birth of the Virgin*, 1479–85 (Florence: Santa Maria Novella); *Portrait of an Old Man and a Boy*, c. 1485 (Paris: Musée du Louvre)

Filippino **Lippi**
● c. 1457–1504   ▶ ITALIAN

▣ Florence; Rome   ◪ fresco; oils; tempera
▥ Florence: Santa Maria Novella. Rome: Santa Maria sopra Minerva (both cities for fresco series)
⬀ $2m in 2005, *Penitent Mary Magdalen* (oils)

The son of Filippo Lippi. Successful, but stylistically outdated in his later years.

His religious subjects show all the standard technical qualities of early-Renaissance Florentine painting (see Filippo Lippi). He painted important fresco series and a few portraits.

Observe his sweet, young faces with soft eyes; good male bone structure; forward inclination of heads. Note his wonderful hands and fingers, which really do look as though they touch, feel, and grasp.

KEY WORKS *The Adoration of the Kings*, c. 1480 (London: National Gallery); *The Vision of St. Bernard*, c. 1486 (Florence: Badia Fiorentina)

> **"Ghirlandaio ... was created by Nature herself to become a painter."**
> GIORGIO VASARI

Alessandro **Botticelli**

◔ 1445–1510   ⚑ ITALIAN

🏛 Florence; Rome   🖌 tempera; fresco
🏛 Florence: Galleria degli Uffizi   💰 $1.2m
in 1982, *Portrait of Giovanni di Pierfrancesco de' Medici* (oils)

Known as Sandro, Alessandro di Mariano Filipepe Botticelli was a major Florentine artist, at a key moment, who emphasized ornament and sentiment rather than scientific observation and realism.

He painted deeply-felt religious pictures and pioneering large-scale mythologies. Note the way he portrays the human figure (on its own, in relationship to others, or in crowd scenes)—always with great dignity, strange and distant, with dreamlike unreality and distortions. One of the great draftsmen of all time. His later work is odd and retrogressive because he retreated into the past, unable to cope with Florence's turbulent descent into social and political turmoil.

His subjects have wonderful bone structure—especially in their cheeks and noses, long and refined hands, wrists, feet, and ankles—and beautifully manicured nails; they have fine and crisply drawn outlines like tense wires. Notice his fascination with pattern—in elaborate materials, hair, and crowds,

The Adoration of the Magi Alessandro Botticelli, 1481, 27½ x 41 in (70 x 104 cm), tempera and oil on panel, Washington, DC: National Gallery of Art. Botticelli may have painted this while in Rome working on the Sistine Chapel.

which he turns into designs of shape or color, or both. He found ideas like scientific perspective of no interest; instead, he cleverly combined old Gothic decorative styles with new, classical, and humanist ideals.

KEY WORKS *The Madonna of the Magnificat*, c. 1480–81 (Florence: Galleria degli Uffizi); *Virgin and Child with Eight Angels*, c. 1481–83 (Berlin: Staatliche Museum); *La Primavera* (see pages 98–99); *The Birth of Venus*, c. 1484 (Florence: Galleria degli Uffizi)

Lorenzo di **Credi**

◔ c. 1458–1537   ⚑ ITALIAN

🏛 Florence   🖌 oils; tempera   💰 $1.1m
in 1995, *St. Quirinus of Neuss* (oils)

A minor Florentine who had a similar style to the early works of fellow pupil, Leonardo da Vinci; they attended Verrocchio's workshop together. Lorenzo was a painter of altarpieces and portraits. Technically competent, but his style was lifeless and lacked individuality. Used an unpleasant, high-key palette with orange/reddish tone. Draperies and flesh both have the same squashy appearance; shows odd, upturned thumbs and toes.

The story goes that in 1497, influenced by the teachings of the fanatical friar Savonarola, Lorenzo destroyed many of his works featuring profane subjects.
KEY WORKS *The Annunciation*, c. 1480–85 (Florence: Galleria degli Uffizi); *Venus*, c. 1490 (Florence: Galleria degli Uffizi)

Pietro **Perugino**

◕ c. 1445–1523   ⚑ ITALIAN

🏛 Perugia   🎨 fresco; oils; tempera
💰 $5.58m in 1990, *Albizzi Pietà, Dead Christ with Virgin Mary and other Figures* (oils)

He was a hardworking, prolific, middle-ranking painter from Perugia, Umbria, hence his nickname: his real name was Pietro Vannucci. Trained in Florence. Raphael was trained in his workshop.

His religious pictures are painted in a soft, pretty, simplified, and sentimental (oversweet?) style, which tends to become routine—he reused figures from other compositions. His portraits can be very good, tough, and direct. His work declined in quality in later years.

Look for slender figures with gently tilting heads and the weight on one foot; oval-faced Madonnas; delicate fingers and a genteelly crooked little finger; lips pressed together, the bottom one fleshy; feathery trees and skies, milky on the horizon, graduating to deep blue at the zenith.
KEY WORKS *Crucifixion with the Virgin, St. John, St. Jerome, and Mary Magdalene*, c. 1485 (Washington, DC: National Gallery of Art); *Mary Magdalene*, 1490s (Florence: Palazzo Pitti)

Bernardino di Betto **Pinturicchio**

◕ c. 1454–1513   ⚑ ITALIAN

🏛 Perugia; Rome; Siena
🎨 fresco; tempera; oils
🏛 Rome: Vatican Museums. Siena: Piccolomini Library of the Cathedral   💰 $300,000 in 2001, *Madonna and Child* (oils)

The last serious artist from Perugia and Umbria. He was probably a pupil of Perugino. Highly skilled, prolific, ambitious, but not at forefront of new ideas. Ultimately second rank.

Pope Pius II Canonizes St. Catherine of Siena
Bernardino di Betto Pinturicchio, 1503–08, fresco, Siena: Cathedral. Note the brilliant colors, ornamental detail, and fanciful charm in this work.

He was a master of fresco painting and supremely skilled at fitting his decorative scheme to the space of the room. Hence he gives a particularly vivid sense of looking through the wall at a busy, bustling scene, full of incident. Enjoy his intense and childlike realism, attention to detail, and love of storytelling—and believe you have walked into the daily life of Umbria in the 15th or 16th century.

Notice his carefully planned and executed perspectives (geometric and aerial); his facility in recording almost microscopic details he has observed in nature. Uninhibited love of color. He painted lavish and brilliant decorative borders, which influenced Raphael.
KEY WORKS *St. Catherine of Alexandria with a Donor*, c. 1480–1500 (London: National Gallery); Borgia rooms frescoes, 1492–95 (Rome: Vatican); *Virgin and Child between St. Jerome and St. Gregory the Great*, c. 1502–08 (Paris: Musée du Louvre)

St. Sebastian *Pietro Perugino, c. 1495, 21 x 15in (53 x 39 cm), tempera and oil on panel, St. Petersburg: Hermitage Museum.* The artist's name is painted in gold lettering on the arrow embedded in the saint's neck.

La Primavera

Alessandro Botticelli c. 1482

La Primavera (Spring) shows the garden of Venus, the Goddess of
Love. From 1434 to 1737, Florence was controlled by the wealthy
Medici family, and the painting was probably commissioned by
Lorenzo di Pierfrancesco de' Medici (1463–1503) to hang in a
room adjoining the wedding chamber of his townhouse.

Sandro Botticelli was the principal
painter in Florence in the second half of
the 15th century. His refined, feminine
style found favor with the Florentine
intelligentsia in the troubled times in
which they lived. His masterpieces were
his large mythological paintings, which
promoted a particular type of divinely
inspired beauty, combined with complex
literary references.

Mercury, the messenger of the gods,
uses his caduceus—a wand entwined with
snakes—to hold back the clouds so that nothing
can blight the eternal spring of Venus's garden

Venus is shown wearing the
characteristic headdress of a Florentine
married woman—a reference to
the nuptial theme of the painting

La Primavera

Medium tempera on panel
Dimensions 80 x 123 in (203 x 314 cm)
Location Florence: Galleria degli Uffizi

Botticelli perfected a style in which crisp line was paramount. The intertwined hands, intricate drapery folds, and flowing hair of the Three Graces displays his skill to the full. Their pointed faces, long necks, sloping shoulders, curving bellies, and slender ankles embody the ideal of feminine beauty in Renaissance Florence.

Flora, the Goddess of Flowers, is the principal figure on the right-hand side of the painting. She tiptoes across the meadow of flowers, the embodiment of beauty, strewing blossoms around her

The blue, winged figure is one of Botticelli's most imaginative inventions. It is the ghostly Zephyrus, God of the West Wind and herald of Venus. He is pursuing his lover, Chloris.

Behind Flora, Botticelli shows her courtship with Zephyrus. When Zephyrus fell in love with Chloris, he pursued the startled nymph and took her as his bride, transforming her into the goddess Flora. Botticelli ingeniously, if somewhat artificially, shows how Flora emerged from the courtship

TECHNIQUES

Flora's gown is decorated with flowers that are slightly raised to imitate embroidery. Botticelli was fascinated by decoration and stylized pattern. Other examples are the "halo" of foliage that is silhouetted against the sky around Venus, and the carpet of flowers.

The Goddess Flora
has particular significance
for Florence (Firenze),
the City of Flowers

Piero della Francesca

● 1420–92 Ⓟ ITALIAN

Ⓟ Sansepolcro; Florence; Arezzo; Urbino
Ⓐ fresco; tempera; oils   🏛 Borgo Sansepolcro:
Museo Civico. Arezzo: San Francesco

One of the greatest masters of
the early Renaissance. Acted as
town councilor in his beloved native
Sansepolcro; currently very much in
fashion. Few works remain and many
are severely damaged.

His religious works and portraits
have special qualities of stillness and a
dignified serenity resulting from deep
Christian belief, and a humanist interest
in man's independence and observation
of the world. Had a passionate
fascination with mathematics and
perspective, which he used to construct
geometrically exact spaces and strictly
proportioned compositions. Loving,
instinctive feel for light and color.

His figures and faces are reserved,
aloof, and self-absorbed (a reflection
of Piero's own slow, hard-working,
intellectual character?). Was interested
in new ideas and experiments as a
means of reaching greater spiritual and
scientific truths. Look for his ability to
fill mathematical spaces with light; his
meticulous mastery of technique (fresco,
tempera, oil, and precise line). Nothing
was left to chance—he recorded
everything with total certainty and care.

KEY WORKS *Madonna della Misericordia*, c. 1445
(Borgo Sansepolcro: Museo Civico); *The
Story of the True Cross*, c. 1452–57 (Arezzo:
San Francesco); *The Baptism of Christ*, 1450s
(London: National Gallery); *The Flagellation
of Christ*, c. 1460s (Urbino: Galleria Nazionale
delle Marche)

Resurrection of Christ Piero della Francesca, c. 1463,
89 x 81 in (225 x 205 cm), fresco, Borgo Sansepolcro:
Museo Civico. The painting was commissioned for a
place in Italy called "Town of the Holy Sepulcher."

Matteo di Giovanni

1435–95   ITALIAN

Sansepolcro; Siena   tempera; oils   London: National Gallery $88,780 in 1990, *Madonna and Child with Holy Bishop, Young Martyr, and Two Angels* (oils)

One of the most prolific and popular painters of the Sienese School. In contrast to contemporary Florentines, he had a rather awkward and traditional style. His work shows the influence of modern ideas (perspective, foreshortening, movement, expression) uncomfortably combined with old-fashioned ones (gold grounds, figures placed one above the other, elaborate decoration). Look out for open mouths, flowing draperies; experiments with foreshortening.

KEY WORKS *Christ Crowned*, c. 1480–95 (London: National Gallery); *Saint Sebastian*, c. 1480–95 (London: National Gallery); *The Crucifixion*, c. 1490 (San Francisco: De Young Museum)

Madonna and Child with Sts. Catherine and Christopher Matteo di Giovanni, 1470, 23⅜ x 17⅜ in (62 x 44 cm), panel, Moscow: Pushkin Museum. The artist's style is elegant, decorative, and linear.

Toward the end of his life, he designed, built, and decorated an ornate burial chapel for himself and his wife Francesca inside Santa Maria della Scala, in Siena.

Look for Vecchietta's precise brushwork, densely populated scenes in his frescoes, an understanding of foreshortening, and forward-thinking lighting techniques. His figures are always realistically portrayed, with faces recreated without idealism; his works sometimes characterized by his self-portrait as one of the figures. His works also demonstrate his architectural training: look for intricately detailed buildings and architectural details in his paintings and sculptures.

KEY WORKS *Madonna and Child Enthroned with Saints*, 1457 (Florence: Galleria degli Uffizi); *Assumption of the Virgin*, c. 1461–62 (Pienza Cathedral); *St. Catherine*, c. 1461–62 (Siena: Palazzo Pubblico); *The Resurrection*, 1472 (New York: Frick Collection); *The Risen Christ*, 1476 (Siena: Santa Maria della Scala)

Vecchietta

1410–80   ITALIAN

Italy   tempera; fresco; illumination; sculpture   Siena: Palazzo Piccolomini $152,497 in 2000, *St. James* (polychrome wood)

He was an architect, painter, sculptor, goldsmith, and engineer. Also called by his birth-name, Lorenzo di Pietro (known by his nickname of "Vecchietta" from c. 1442 onward). Born and worked in Siena; influenced by Florentine art world. Far ahead of his peers in Siena in terms of understanding lighting and its painterly properties. Adept at working both in miniature and on a large scale. He also produced illuminated manuscripts, including the illuminations for Dante's *Divine Comedy*. In the 1430s, he was commissioned by Cardinal Branda Castiglione to paint a series of frescoes in Lombardy; he continued to paint frescoes for the rest of his career. In the 1450s, he met Donatello, who had a strong influence on his sculptural techniques.

Pope Pius II (1405–64) Crowned by Two Cardinals Vecchietta, 1458–64, tempera on panel, Siena: Palazzo Piccolomini. The use of foreshortening suggests the influence of Florentine art.

The Madonna of Humility adored by Leonello d'Este *Jacopo Bellini, 1407–50, 23⅝ x 15¾ in (60 x 40 cm), oil on panel, Paris: Musée du Louvre. The figure on the left is the donor who commissioned the painting.*

Jacopo **Bellini**

◗ c. 1400–70 ▣ ITALIAN

▣ Florence; Venice ▮ tempera; oils ▥ Paris: Musée du Louvre. London: British Museum (sketchbooks) ▨ $67,185 in 1998, *Santa Lucia* (oils)

He was Giovanni's father. Not much is known about him. Very little of his work survives other than sketchbooks. Progressive—was interested in latest artistic developments such as perspective, landscape, and architecture.
KEY WORKS *Madonna and Child*, 1448 (Milan: Pinacoteca di Brera); Sketchbooks, c. 1450 (London: British Museum/Paris: Musée du Louvre); *Madonna and Child Blessing*, 1455 (Venice: Gallerie dell'Accademia); *Saint Anthony Abbot and Saint Bernardino of Siena*, 1459–60 (Washington, DC: National Gallery of Art)

Gentile **Bellini**

◗ c. 1429–1507 ▣ ITALIAN

▣ Venice ▮ oils; tempera
▨ $696,000 in 2001, *Cardinal Bessarion attended by two brothers of the Scuola della Carità in Prayer with the Bessarion Reliquary* (oils)

He was Giovanni's brother. Much respected in his own lifetime. He was noted especially for panoramic views of his native Venice, peopled with crowds and processions; thus established a subject and tradition that reached its apogee in Canaletto. Many works have perished.
KEY WORKS *Portrait of Doge Giovanni Mocenigo*, c. 1480 (Venice: Museo Correr); *Sultan Mohammed II*, c. 1480 (London: National Gallery); *Miracle at Ponte di Lorenzo*, 1500 (Venice: Gallerie dell'Accademia)

Procession in St. Mark's Square *Gentile Bellini, 1496, 144½ x 293⅜ in (367 x 745 cm), oil on canvas, Venice: Gallerie dell'Accademia. One of a series of nine Venetian paintings showing the Miracles of the Cross.*

Giovanni **Bellini**

● c. 1430–1516 🇮🇹 ITALIAN

🇮🇹 Venice ◨ oils; tempera
🏛 Venice: Accademia and
various churches
💰 $1,237,500 in 1996, *Virgin
and Child with Male Donor,
Landscape Beyond* (oils)

One of the supreme
masters of the early
Renaissance and the
Father of Venetian
painting. The best
known of a distinguished
family of painters. Among the first to
exploit oil-painting technique in Venice.

Agony in the Garden *Giovanni Bellini, c. 1460,
32 x 50 in (81 x 127 cm), tempera on wood, London:
National Gallery.* The painting shows Bellini's sensitive
gift for understanding and representing light, as well as
a keen awareness of figures in space.

Known for his altarpieces, portraits,
and, above all, the depiction of light—
beautifully and carefully observed, lovingly
and accurately recorded, and always
warm. His work sings of the harmonious
relationship that should exist between
man, nature, and God. The profound
mood and spirituality of his religious
pictures results from his belief in God's
presence in light and nature.

His figures respond to light and often
turn their faces and bodies toward it, in
order to enjoy its physical and spiritual
benefits. Is he the first painter who really
looked at clouds and studied their structure
and formation? Notice his love of detail
in rocks, leaves, architecture, and rich
materials such as silks. Note
how his style becomes softer
as he gets older (a natural trait
in most humans?). No outlines,
just gradations of tone.

Bellini's influence on Venetian
painting was enormous. He was
appointed offical painter to the
republic in 1483, and almost all of
Venice's eminent painters during
the next generation are believed
to have trained in his workshop.

KEY WORKS *St. Francis in the Wilderness*,
c. 1480 (New York: Frick Collection);
Barbarigo Altarpiece, 1488, (Murano:
San Pietro Martire); *The Madonna
of the Meadow*, c. 1501 (London:
National Gallery); *The Doge Leonardo
Loredan*, 1501–04 (London: National
Gallery); *San Zaccaria Altarpiece*, 1505
(Venice: San Zaccaria)

> **"Giovanni Bellini
> is very old
> but still the
> best of all …"**
>
> ALBRECHT DÜRER, 1506

Antonello da Messina

◔ c. 1430–79   ▣ ITALIAN

▣ Messina; Naples; Milan; Venice   ◑ oils; tempera   ▣ London: National Gallery. Paris: Musée du Louvre   ⊠ $367,400 in 2003, *Madonna and Child with a Franciscan Monk. Ecce Homo in a trompe l'oeil* (oils)

He was from Messina, Sicily. Made a key visit to Venice in 1475–76. One of the pioneers of oil painting in Italy.

He combined Italian interests (sculptural modeling, rational space, and man-the-measure-of-all-things characterization) with northern European obsessions (minute detail and unadorned reality). He had a marvellous ability to observe and paint light, and created wonderful portraits and faces that seem to live and breathe, showing bones under the skin and an intelligence behind the eyes that looks and answers back. Sense that he shines both an intellectual and a physical spotlight on his subjects.

> **"Once this new secret that Antonello had brought from Flanders into the city of Milan had been understood, Antonello was admired and cherished by those magnificent noblemen for as long as he lived."**
>
> GIORGIO VASARI ON ANTONELLO DA MESSINA

He had a wonderful ability to recreate the appearance and feel of the skin—differentiating between lips, a stubbly or shaven chin, a hairless cheek—eyebrows, hair, the liquid surface of an eye (can only be done with oil paint and requires supreme technical mastery). Oil-paint equation: learns technique from northern artists in Naples and hands it on to clever Venetians, such as Bellini. It is very likely that he used a magnifying glass—and it is worth using one when looking at his paintings.

KEY WORKS *Christ Blessing*, 1465 (London: National Gallery); *Virgin Annunciate*, c. 1465 (Palermo: Galleria Nazionale); *Portrait of a Man*, c. 1475 (London: National Gallery); *St. Jerome in his Study*, c. 1475 (London: National Gallery)

Vivarini family

◔ ACTIVE 15TH CENTURY   ▣ ITALIAN

▣ Venice   ◑ oils; tempera ▣ London: National Gallery ⊠ $130,000 in 1990, *Head of St. Francis* (oils) by Antonio Vivarini

They were a Venetian family. Antonio (c. 1415–84) and his younger brother, Bartolomeo

Madonna and Child with Sts. Peter, Jerome, and Mary Magdalene with a Bishop *Alvise Vivarini, 1500, oil on panel, Amiens (France): Musée de Picardie.* Notice the way in which the baby Jesus is set in the absolute center of the painting, his pale skin drawing the eye toward him.

Monument to Doge Pietro Mocenigo Pietro Lombardo, 1476–81, Istrian stone and marble, Venice: SS. Giovanni e Paolo. As part of the tomb of Pietro Mocenigo, this intricate monument features 15 life-size marble figures.

(c. 1432–c. 1499) created old-fashioned, large polyptych altarpieces with stiff figures and elaborate carved frames. Antonio's son, Alvise (c. 1445–1505) did more modern work in the style of Bellini. Good example of craftsmen's business producing work to please conservative clientele.

KEY WORKS *The Madonna with the Blessed Child*, c. 1440 (Venice: Gallerie dell'Accademia); *Sts. Francis and Mark*, 1440–46 (London: National Gallery)

Lombardo family

● 15TH–16TH CENTURIES Ⓝ ITALIAN

Ⓟ Italy 🔨 sculpture 🏛 St. Petersburg: Hermitage Museum. New York: Metropolitan Museum of Art

Pietro Lombardo (c. 1435–1515), architect and sculptor, worked in several Italian cities before moving to Venice, c. 1467. He set up a workshop, employing large numbers of apprentices. His sculptor sons, Tullio (c. 1455–1532) and Antonio (c. 1458–1516), were among his pupils. Pietro was instrumental in bringing the Renaissance to Venice, reworking Florentine ideas about Classical antiquity into a Venetian ideal. His most famous work was rebuilding the Doge's palace (1498). By the 1480s, Tullio and Antonio were recognized as sculptors in their own right, often commissioned for tomb sculptures and religious pieces. Tullio collected Classical statues and is noted for poetic portraits like reliefs inspired by Roman grave portraits. Both of them worked for the courts of Northern Italy (see page 106). Pietro's grandsons continued as architects and sculptors well into the 16th century.

KEY WORKS *Adam*, Tullio Lombardo, c. 1493 (New York: Metropolitan Museum); *Monument to Andrea Vendramin*, Pietro & Tullio Lombardo, c. 1493 (Venice: SS. Giovanni e Paolo)

Carlo **Crivelli**
● ACTIVE 1457–93 Ⓝ ITALIAN

Ⓟ Venice; Marche Region (Italy); Croatia 🔨 tempera 🏛 London: National Gallery. Milan: Pinacoteca di Brera 💰 $840,000 in 1988, *Madonna and Child at a Marble Parapet* (oils)

He was an average Venetian artist with a self-conscious, old-fashioned style.

Crivelli's work shows an extraordinary and obsessive attention to detail, a system that virtually overwhelms everything else. His strange, hard, dry, linear style makes the figures look real but unreal (a bit like biological specimens); similarly with the architecture, his buildings look like painted stage sets rather than the real thing.

Note the lined faces with bags under the eyes and bulging veins on hands and feet. The real yet unreal-looking fruit and garlands, which have complicated symbolic meanings, resemble marzipan cake decorations.

KEY WORKS *Madonna and Child Enthroned with Donor*, c. 1470 (Washington, DC: National Gallery of Art); *St. Michael*, c. 1476 (London: National Gallery)

The Annunciation with St. Emidius Carlo Crivelli, 1486, 81½ x 57⅜ in (207 x 146.5 cm), tempera and oil on canvas, London: National Gallery. Painted for the Annunciation Church in Ascoli Piceno, Italy.

THE COURTS OF NORTHERN ITALY

During the Renaissance, being an artist could be a lucrative career. Most artists worked solely for commission and survived through patronage of the aristocratic courts. Italy was divided into city states or principalities and almost every city, large or small, had a system of artistic patronage. Among the most important of the large cities north of Florence were Mantua and Urbino.

In Mantua, the ruling family were called Gonzaga (prominent from the 14th to 17th centuries). Their court artists included Andrea

Mantegna and the Lombardi. Urbino came to artistic prominence in the 15th and 16th centuries, soon outshining the earlier established courts. With the naming of Federigo da Montefeltro (1422–82) as the 1st Duke of Urbino, the region became a center for artistic excellence. The Duke showed a partiality for Flemish art, but his most famous court painter was a fellow Italian, Piero della Francesca.

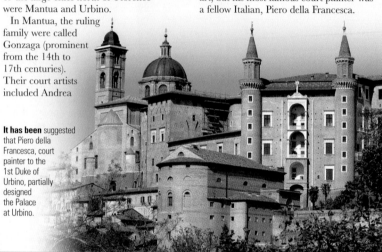

It has been suggested that Piero della Francesca, court painter to the 1st Duke of Urbino, partially designed the Palace at Urbino.

Ercole de' **Roberti**

⬤ c. 1450–96 |⛫| ITALIAN

|⛫| Ferrara; Bologna   🖌 tempera   🏛 Milan: Pinacoteca di Brera (for the *Madonna Enthroned with Saints* altarpiece, 1480)

His most famous post was as court painter to the d'Este family in Ferrara. Shadowy figure, with very few works firmly attributed to him.

Look for meticulous, fine detail and poetic sensibility; the careful placing of figures in space— well-proportioned with good movement. He was interested in perspective, architectural details, and the way buildings are constructed.

KEY WORKS *St. Jerome in the Wilderness*, c. 1470 (Los Angeles: J. Paul Getty Museum); *St. John the Baptist*, c. 1478–80

(Berlin: Dahlem Museum); *The Wife of Hasdrubal and Her Children*, c. 1480–90 (Washington, DC: National Gallery of Art)

Cima da Conegliano

⬤ c. 1459–c. 1517 |⛫| ITALIAN

|⛫| Venice   🖌 oils   🏛 London: National Gallery   💰 $84,948 in 1992, *Madonna and Child in Landscape* (oils)

He was a successful but minor Venetian, content just to follow others. "The poor man's Bellini"— similar use of light, but harder and less

Pietà Ercole de' Roberti, c. 1490–96, 13½ x 12⅜ in (34.4 x 31.3 cm), oil and tempera on panel, Liverpool: Walker Art Gallery. An altarpiece predella.

subtle. Works best on a small scale, when his crispness comes to the fore. Good light; satisfying blue mountains; intense faces; general air of busyness; slightly comical, frozen poses (as when a photographer says "hold it.")

KEY WORKS *Madonna with the Orange Tree*, 1487–88 (Venice: Gallerie dell'Accademia); *The Annunciation*, 1495 (St. Petersburg: Hermitage Museum); *Virgin and Child*, c. 1505 (London: National Gallery)

Andrea **Mantegna**

● 1431–1506 🇮🇹 ITALIAN

🏛 Padua; Mantua; Rome 🖌 engravings; oils; fresco; tempera 🏛 London: Hampton Court. Mantua: Ducal Palace 💲 $25.5m in 2003, *Descent into Limbo* (oils)

He was a precocious, highly individual master of the early Renaissance who worked for the dukes of Gonzaga at Mantua. An austere intellectual.

Mantegna's panel paintings are highly individual interpretations of standard Renaissance subjects such as altarpieces and portraits. He had a dry, scholarly style, which became obsessed with detail, especially when it came to the archaeology of classical antiquity and geology (but scholars do get obsessed by minutiae). His frescoes are wonderful large-scale schemes for churches and villas. Pioneering printmaker—with superb engraving technique, which suited his style perfectly.

Notice the extraordinary outcrops of rock and the way he could make everything (even human flesh) look like carved stone (late monochrome works consciously look like bas-relief sculpture). Stunning mastery of scientific perspective and foreshortening —seen at its most impressive (in situ) in his large, decorative schemes, which are more relaxed than the panel paintings.

KEY WORKS *St. James Led to His Execution*, c. 1455 (Padua: Ovetari Chapel, Church of the Eremitani); *St. Sebastian*, c. 1455–60 (Vienna: Kunsthistorisches Museum)

*The **Dead Christ*** Andrea Mantegna, 1480s, 26¾ x 31⅛ in (68 x 81 cm), oil on canvas, Milan: Pinacoteca di Brera. Mantegna's first teacher (Squarcione) criticized his work for "resembling ancient statues ... rather than living creatures." The just reply is that his figures resemble both.

THE NORTHERN RENAISSANCE

At the same time that the Renaissance was emerging in Italy, an equally significant artistic flowering was occurring in the Low Countries. Art in northern Europe was not "reborn" in the sense of rediscovering an Antique past. But it was crucially reinvigorated, above all by the development and almost immediate maturity of a new medium: oil painting.

STYLE

Oil painting was not the only important innovation introduced in the Low Countries. Of almost equal significance was easel painting. The notion, still prevalent today, of paintings as self-contained, independent of their settings, was being born. The combination was revolutionary. Unlike tempera and fresco, oil dries slowly, allowing precise reworkings; it can also be applied in tiny increments before drying to a hard, brilliant finish. Painted onto durable and largely nonabsorbent woods such as oak, the result is highly detailed and lustrously jewel-like. As early as the 1430s painters such as van Eyck had developed a form of linear perspective the equal of that devised in Italy, but arrived at pragmatically rather than theoretically. It was augmented by aerial perspective, the gradual softening of colors to suggest more distant objects.

Portrait of a Young Woman in a Pinned Hat Rogier van der Weyden, c. 1435, 18½ x 12⅜ in (47 x 32 cm), oil on oak, Berlin: Gemäldegalerie.

SUBJECTS

Religious subjects dominate the art of the period, but they are always given an earthly, hard-edged precision. There is no lack of opulence—in draperies, settings, or landscapes—but where the Italian Renaissance is characterized by unworldly idealism, northern European painting of the same date has an almost unnervingly clear-eyed and dispassionate directness.

St. Jerome in a Rocky Landscape Joachim Patenier, 1515–24, 14¼ x 13⅜ in (36 x 34 cm), oil on oak, London: National Gallery. Patenier, later widely imitated, was the first painter to make landscapes his principal subject.

KEY EVENTS

1432	Completion of van Eyck's monumental *Ghent Altarpiece*
1450	Presumed visit by Roger van der Weyden to Rome and Florence
1456	Van Eyck's spreading fame is confirmed by Neapolitan account of his achievements
1475	Hugo van der Goes's *Portinari Altarpiece* (see page 116) despatched to Florence

WHAT TO LOOK FOR

Figures seem always to have been painted from life. There is a growing stress on domestic detail. This may frequently be loaded with allegorical or other allusive meanings, but the sense that everyday objects—and by extension everyday life—are worthy of being precisely rendered for their own sake is central. In this work, van Eyck piles detail upon detail to create an entirely believable world.

The Arnolfini Portrait
Jan van Eyck, 1434, 32 x 23 in (82 x 60 cm), oil on oak, London: National Gallery. The work's exact subject, though it clearly concerns a wedding or betrothal, is unknown.

The Latin text reads: "Van Eyck was here." It may mean he was a witness or he was "here" in the sense of creating the painting. Either way, it underlines the new status claimed by artists

Both figures are very richly dressed, a statement of wealth and social status

The bride is in green, the color of fertility. Is she already pregnant or merely fashionably attired?

The convex mirror is a technical triumph. Window, bed, ceiling, and the two principals are shown from new angles, and two other figures are visible. The border shows 10 scenes from the life of Christ.

Neither figure wears shoes, an indication that they are on sacred ground

The dog may be a symbol of fidelity or lust. The bed is similarly suggestive

TECHNIQUES

Van Eyck's use of oil allowed him to achieve an extraordinary level of detail. Every object in the painting is depicted with the same concentrated clarity.

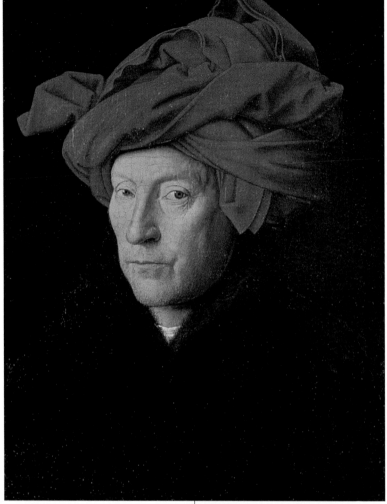

A Man in a Turban *Jan van Eyck, 1433, 10 x 7½ in (25.5 x 19 cm), oil on oak, London: National Gallery. The detailed depiction of the headdress and the way it sits on the head suggest that it may have been studied separately.*

Jan van **Eyck**

◯ c. 1390–1441   ⚐ NETHERLANDISH

🏛 The Hague; Lille; Bruges   🎨 oils   🏛 London: National Gallery. Ghent: St. Bavo's Cathedral. Paris: Musée du Louvre   📈 $1m in 1985, *The Three Maries at the Sepulcher* (oils)

He was an artist-cum-diplomat in service of Philip the Good, Duke of Burgundy. Obscure origins. Only known work is from 1430s onward. Key exponent of Netherlandish art and oil painting.

He was the first painter to portray the merchant class and bourgeoisie. His work reflects their priorities, such as having their portraits painted; taking themselves seriously (as donors of altarpieces, for example); art as the imitation of nature; art as evidence of painstaking work and of craftsmanship; prosperity and tidiness; wariness; restrained emotion. He had a brilliant oil-painting technique, which he was the first to perfect—luminous, glowing colors, and minute detail.

His three-quarter pose of face brought new realism to portraiture. He painted Madonnas that look like housewives, and saints that look like businessmen. Notice his precise delineation of all facial features, especially the eyes. He was fascinated with ears (they are miniature portraits) and by folds and creases in cloth. Also note the fall of light that unifies the objects and models them. Convincing but empirical perspective. Inscriptions on paintings and rich symbolism.

KEY WORKS *The Annunciation*, c. 1425–30 (Washington, DC: National Gallery of Art); *Ghent Altarpiece (The Adoration of the Lamb)*, 1432 (Ghent: St. Bavo's Cathedral); *The Arnolfini Marriage*, 1434 (London: National Gallery)

Robert **Campin**
(Master of Flemalle)
● c. 1378–1444   ◢ NETHERLANDISH

🏴 Tournai (Belgium)   ◼ oils
🏛 London: National Gallery

A shadowy figure whose identity is difficult to pin down. Attributions are rare and speculative. One of the founders of the Netherlandish School.

His devotional altarpieces and portraits are painted with the concentrated intensity that you get in a diminishing mirror (do visual intensity and detail equal spiritual intensity and commitment?). Virgin and Christ child are shown as down-to-earth people in everyday settings —not idealized, but presented in a way that creates a fascinating three-way tension between realism, symbolism, and distortion, which Campin is able to manipulate with the greatest subtlety.

Notice his acute powers of observation, especially in the way things (such as window shutters) are made, how light catches a corner, how drapery falls, or flames look. Uses light to isolate objects. The odd perspective is worked out experimentally, not scientifically. Use a magnifying glass to examine the extraordinarily fine detail; don't forget to look out of his windows at what is happening in the street. Objects and details usually contain or imply much complex symbolism.

KEY WORKS *Entombment*, c. 1420 (Private Collection); *A Woman*, c. 1430 (London: National Gallery); *The Virgin and Child before a Firescreen*, c. 1430 (London: National Gallery); *St. Barbara*, 1438 (Madrid: Museo del Prado)

Rogier van der **Weyden**
● c. 1399–1464   ◢ NETHERLANDISH

🏴 Tournai (Belgium); Brussels   ◼ oils
🏛 Madrid: Museo del Prado; Escorial. Berlin: Staatliche Museum   ⟱ $71,442 in 1938, *Dream of Pope Sergius* (oils)

The greatest and most influential northern painter of his day. Set the standard by which the rest are judged. Brussels-based. Worked for the dukes of Burgundy. Had a large workshop and was much imitated.

Look for the presence of Christ in contemporary life and powerful tension between reality and unreality. The meticulous detail of cloths, clothes, fingernails, and hair; faces drawn from life; anecdotal detail create an illusion of reality. But the stiff poses, cramped spaces, and static expressions are wholly unreal. Is it this tension that draws the eye so magnetically into the drama and the serious aspiration of the religious message (itself an interplay of the real and unreal)?

> **"Van Eyck's eye was at one and the same time a microscope and a telescope."**
> ERWIN PANOFSKY

Note also his superb portraits, each with minute, natural individuality—especially the fingernails, knuckles, red-rimmed eyes, and stitches on clothing. He was also fascinated by architectural and sculptural detail. See how he uses facial expression and poses that are appropriate to the emotion expressed, showing tear-streaked faces and an understanding of grief; observe how one figure echoes the poses and gestures of another, as if in emotional sympathy. He adopted a softer, more relaxed style after 1450 (Italian influence after visit to Rome).

KEY WORKS *St. Luke Drawing the Virgin*, 15th century (St. Petersburg: Hermitage Museum); *Descent from the Cross*, c. 1435 (Madrid: Museo del Prado); *Triptych: The Crucifixion*, c. 1440 (Vienna: Kunsthistorisches Museum); *Francesco d'Este*, c. 1455 (New York: Metropolitan Museum of Art); *Portrait of a Lady*, c. 1455 (Washington, DC: National Gallery of Art)

The Deposition

Rogier van der Weyden c. 1435–40

This altarpiece is a masterpiece of early
Netherlandish painting. The northern
European artists brought an intensity of
emotional expression and a minuteness
of realistic detail to their work, which
give it a quite different character and
appearance to that of their Italian
counterparts. This painting is the
central panel of a triptych.

The skull represents Adam, who is thus
symbolically present. Adam was cast out
of Paradise after eating the forbidden fruit.
Christ sacrificed himself on the cross to
redeem the world from Adam's original sin.

Many northern altarpieces at this
time were made with carved wooden
figures set in shallow boxlike spaces.
Van der Weyden seems to have accepted
this convention, but through the new
medium and technique of oil painting
he has brought the figures to life.

The artist heightens the sense of
tension by forcing the eye and mind to
reconcile conflicting qualities. Much of
the painting detail is intensely realistic,
such as the red-rimmed eyes and the
tears on the faces. This conflicts with
the highly unnatural composition in
which the almost life-size figures are
hunched and packed into a narrow
space beneath a tiny crucifix. The
shrinelike background shown in the
painting concentrates the viewer's
attention on the figures and avoids the
distractions of a true-to-life setting.

Set against a plain gold background,
The Deposition has an overriding sense
of dramatic power about it. Van der
Weyden was a master of depicting
human emotion, and his religious
painting reflects the strength of his
personal conviction. His work had a
profound effect on the course of art
throughout Europe.

**Mary, wife
of** the disciple
Cleopas—she was
supposedly present
at the Crucifixion

**St. John the
Evangelist** stoops
to comfort Mary,
Christ's Mother, who
swoons with grief

The Deposition

Medium oil on panel
Dimensions 86⅜ x 103¼ in (220 x 262 cm)
Location Madrid: Museo del Prado

TECHNIQUES

Notice the intriguing conflict
between the deep emotion
of the picture and the artist's
ability to look at an area such
as the cloak of Nicodemus
and record every detail with
dispassionate objectivity.

Joseph of Arimathea,
holding Christ's corpse,
was permitted to take
the body down from the
cross and lay it to rest

Van der Weyden was a celebrated
portrait painter. The expressions of grief
are highly individual. The face of St. John,
for example, is grave yet restrained as he
struggles to control his emotions.

Trickles of blood and
marbled flesh tones of
the dead Christ are
contrasted with the
white of the linen

A follower of Christ
holds a jar of ointment—
the attribute of St. Mary
Magdalene, who appears
inconsolably anguished

Dieric **Bouts**

⬬ c. 1415–78 🅟 NETHERLANDISH

🅟 Louvain (Belgium) 🅟 oils
📈 $3.74m in 1980, *The Resurrection* (oils)

Also known as Dirk Bouts. Possibly a pupil of Rogier van der Weyden. Very little is known about him and few attributable works exist. He created altarpieces, narrative scenes, and portraits. Solemn, restrained paintings with beautifully observed detail and painstaking craftsmanship. His static figures are exaggeratedly slender and graceful, and often set in landscapes of exquisite beauty. Lovely details of rocky backgrounds and shimmering light.

KEY WORKS *The Annunciation*, 1445 (Madrid: Museo del Prado); *Portrait of a Man*, 1462 (London: National Gallery); *Justice of the Emperor Otto*, 1470–75 (Bruges: Musées Royaux des Beaux-Arts)

Portrait of a Man Hans Memling, 1480s, 13 x 9¾ in (33 x 25 cm), oil on wood, Florence: Galleria degli Uffizi. Memling's gentle and occasionally sentimental style made him a popular acquisition for 19th-century collectors.

Hans **Memling**

⬬ c. 1430–94 🅟 FLEMISH

🅟 Bruges 🅟 oils 🏛 Bruges: Memling Museum 📈 $265,200 in 1992, *The Virgin and Child Enthroned with Two Angels* (oils)

Also known as Hans Memlinc. A prolific, Bruges-based successor to van der Weyden, from whom he borrowed a repertoire of motifs and compositions.

His large altarpieces are too rigid, with stiff figures like statues. He was better at small devotional pictures (full of life, with good space) and small portraits (he learned from manuscript illuminations). Liked soft textures (his drapery has soft, not crisp, folds); soft hair; soft landscapes and smooth, rounded, demure, idealized faces. Decorative, rather than intense, style.

Look out for his interesting skies of intense blue, melting to white on the horizon; clouds like chiffon veils; small, almost unnoticeable birds; pronounced eyelids. His motifs such as garlands of fruit and flowers held by putti are borrowed from the Italian Renaissance (from Mantegna?).

KEY WORKS *Portrait of a Man with an Arrow*, c. 1470–75 (Washington, DC: National Gallery of Art); *The Virgin and Child with an Angel*, c. 1470–80 (London: National Gallery); *Bathsheba*, c. 1482 (Stuttgart: Staatsgalerie)

Hell Dieric Bouts, 1450, 45¼ x 27⅜ in (115 x 69.5 cm), oil on wood, Lille: Musée des Beaux-Arts. This work was mistakenly believed to be part of a documented but destroyed triptych by Bouts of the Last Judgement. The panel is one of a pair displayed in the Musée des Beaux-Arts; the other depicts Paradise.

Petrus **Christus**

● ACTIVE 1444–72/3   Ⓕ FLEMISH

Ⓟ Bruges   🎨 oils   🏛 Bruges: Musées
Royaux des Beaux-Arts   💲 $182,400 in
1995, *The Virgin and Child* (oils)

He was a major painter from Bruges,
follower of van Eyck, and influenced
by van der Weyden. Underrated.

His intimate, small-scale
religious works and portraits
are organized and painted
with meticulous detail. Note
especially his interest in space
and light: liked deep space;
placed figures in the corners
of rooms to suggest both
space and intimacy. He was
the first northern painter to
understand and use Italian
single-point perspective.

Robes have elaborate, crisp
drapery, with folds arranged
decoratively, often flipped
back to show a lining or
undergarment in contrasting
color, sometimes brightly
outlined. Note how Christus
uses brownish rather than
pink flesh tones and favors red
and green color schemes. He
organized broad areas of tone and
filled in on top with meticulous detail,
which makes cleaning and restoration
especially risky.

KEY WORKS *The Man of Sorrows*, mid-15th
century (Birmingham, UK: Museums and
Art Gallery); *Edward Grimston*, 1446 (London:
National Gallery); *The Last Judgment*, 1452
(Berlin: Staatliche Museum); *Virgin and Child
with Sts. Jerome and Francis*, 1457 (Frankfurt:
Städelsches Kunstinstitut); *A Young Lady*,
c. 1470 (Berlin: Staatliche Museum)

Jan **Provost**

● c. 1465–1529   Ⓕ FLEMISH

Ⓟ Valenciennes (France); Antwerp; Bruges
🎨 oils   💲 $380,000 in 1990, *The Nativity* (oils)

He was a major original early-northern
Renaissance painter—pre-Italian
influences. Met Dürer in 1521; follower
of Massys. Painter of altarpieces, with
figures that are lifelike (for the time).
Look for his precise drawing (he trained
as a miniaturist); delicate modeling; good

color; long fingers bent at second joint;
tender faces with wide cheeks and
prominent lower lip; airy landscapes.

KEY WORKS *The Crucifixion*, c. 1495 (New York:
Metropolitan Museum of Art); *A Christian
Allegory*, c. 1500 (Paris: Musée du Louvre);
The Virgin in Glory, 1524 (St. Petersburg:
Hermitage Museum); *The Last Judgment*,
1525 (Bruges: Municipal Museums)

The Money Lender and his Wife *Quentin Massys,
1514, 29¼ x 26¼ in (74 x 68 cm), oil on panel, Paris:
Musée du Louvre.* The painting's attention to meticulous
detail forms a clear and satisfying artistic parallel with
the couple's evident obsession with material possessions.

Quentin **Massys**

● c. 1466–1530   Ⓕ FLEMISH

Ⓟ Antwerp; Italy   🎨 oils   🏛 London:
Courtauld Institute of Art   💲 $403,200
in 1988, *The Virgin at Prayer* (oils)

Also known as Quentin Metsys. Important
painter of unknown origins. Brought
Italian refinement to northern realist
tradition (visited Italy; admired Leonardo's
way with soft light and his interest in the
contrast between ugliness and beauty).
Best known for animated portraits of tax
collectors, bankers, merchants, and wives,
with understated satire (the influence of
Erasmus, whom he met?). Opulent details.

KEY WORKS *St. Anne*, 1507–09 (Bruges: Musées
Royaux des Beaux-Arts); *Portrait of a Canon*,
c. 1515 (Private Collection); *The Adoration of
the Magi*, 1526 (New York: Metropolitan
Museum of Art)

Hugo van der **Goes**

● ACTIVE 1467–82 🅽 NETHERLANDISH

🅿 Ghent; Brussels 🅾 oils 🏛 Florence: Galleria degli Uffizi (*Portinari Altarpiece*) 🔢 $84,000 in 1961, *Saint, probably St. Barbara Seated Holding a Book on her Knees* (works on paper)

He was an obscure genius about whom little is known (spent his last years in a monastery, going mad). Only work known for certain to be by him is the *Portinari Altarpiece* (c. 1475), which was commissioned for a chapel in Florence and introduced Italian artists to new ideas and techniques they had never seen before: oil paint, fine natural detail, and different symbolism.

The *Portinari Altarpiece* is of an unusually large scale for a Netherlandish painting (commissioned to be standard size of Italian triptych); there are Portinari men (members of a prosperous Florentine mercantile family) in the left panel, women in the right (each with patron saints); the composite central panel has Virgin and Child (naked child on floor is a northern idea), Joseph and shepherds (an Italian idea); the Magi are at the back of the right panel.

The kneeling man (right panel) is Tomasso Portinari (agent in Bruges for the Medici bank—he was reckless and the bank was closed). The kneeling woman (right panel) is his wife, Maria. The men look troubled; the women have fashionably high foreheads and pale faces. The very wobbly space and odd

The Adoration of the Shepherds *Hugo van der Goes, c. 1476, 100 x 120 in (254 x 305 cm), oil on panel, Florence: Galleria degli Uffizi. The center panel from the Portinari Altarpiece.*

changes of scale in the central panel perhaps suggest the artist was in difficulty with such a large-scale work? Much symbolism: scarlet lily as blood and passion of Christ; discarded shoe as holy ground; purple columbine as Virgin's sorrow, and so on.

KEY WORKS *Death of our Lady*, c. 1470 (Bruges: Municipal Museums); *The Fall of Man*, c. 1475 (Vienna: Kunsthistorisches Museum); *Portrait of a Man*, c. 1475 (New York: Metropolitan Museum of Art); *The Adoration of the Magi*, 1470s (Bath, UK: Victoria Art Gallery)

Jan **Gossaert**

● c. 1478–c.1532 🅽 FLEMISH

🅿 Netherlands; Rome 🅾 oils 🏛 London: National Gallery 🔢 $1.5m in 1998, *Madonna and Child Enthroned Accompanied by Six Musicmaking Angels* (oils)

Also called Jan Mabuse. He had a crucial role in the development of Netherlandish painting by introducing Italianate ideas (albeit a bit derivative). From Mauberge in Hainault, hence the name Mabuse.

His work is a fascinating (sometimes uncomfortable) synthesis of: 1) northern skills and vision—acute observation; fine oil technique; clear, precise drafts-manship à la Dürer; and 2) after visit to Rome in 1508–9, Italian aspirations—idealization of figures and faces; perspective; classical architecture and details; firm modeling, and subtle shading with light. Had a more conservative portrait style.

KEY WORKS *Neptune and Amphitrite*, 1516 (Berlin: Staatliche Museum); *Adam and Eve*, c. 1520 (London: National Gallery); *A Nobleman*, c. 1525–28 (Berlin: Staatliche Museum)

Joachim **Patenier**

● c. 1480–c. 1525 🅽 FLEMISH

🅿 Antwerp 🅾 oils 🏛 Madrid: Museo del Prado 🔢 $176,800 in 1968, *Wooded Landscape with Many Figures* (oils)

Also known as Joachim Patinir. The first painter to make landscape the principal theme. His works have a bird's-eye viewpoint, with improbably craggy inhabited mountains, blue distances with heavy clouds and cold seas, and

God the Father Blessing Gerrit David, 1506, 39¾ x 50⅜ in (101 x 128 cm), oil on panel, Paris: Musée du Louvre. Gerrit David's work was neglected for centuries, and "rediscovered" in the second half of the 19th century.

tiny-scale hermits, holy families, sometimes with Christ tucked in somewhere—fantasy at its most endearing. High-quality, detailed technique. There are few attributed works, but he had many imitators.

KEY WORKS *Rest on the Flight to Egypt*, c. 1515 (Minnesota: Minneapolis Institute of Arts); *The Baptism of Christ*, c. 1515 (Vienna: Kunsthistorisches Museum); *The Penitence of St. Jerome*, c. 1518 (New York: Metropolitan Museum of Art)

Joos van Cleve

◕ c. 1490–1540 🔲 NETHERLANDISH

🔲 Antwerp; France 🎨 oils 💰 $350,000 in 1993, *Christ on Cross with Mary, Mary Magdalen, and St. John the Evangelist* (oils)

He was a popular, Antwerp-based painter of devotional altarpieces and portraits. Combined tradition (finely detailed northern technique, overloaded symbolism, stiffly posed figures and draperies) with progressive ideas (landscapes and rocky formations, Italian-style modeling with light, extravagant costumes, detailed surfaces). Note cosy, homely details.

KEY WORKS *Joris Vezeleer*, c. 1518 (Washington, DC: National Gallery of Art); *The Last Judgment*, c. 1520–25 (Minnesota: Minneapolis Institute of Arts); *Virgin and Child with Angels*, c. 1520–25 (Liverpool: Walker Art Gallery); *The Annunciation*, c. 1525 (New York: Metropolitan Museum of Art)

Gerrit **David**

◕ 1484–1523 🔲 NETHERLANDISH

🔲 Bruges; Antwerp 🎨 oils 🏛 Bruges: Groeningemuseum 💰 $1,142,400 in 1988, *The Virgin feeding the Child from a Bowl of Soup* (oils)

Also known as Gerard David. Last great Netherlandish painter in tradition of van Eyck's and van der Weyden's meticulous realism. Worked in Bruges and Antwerp.

David was a painter of altarpieces and portraits. He loved exact details of objects and faces. Had a conscious awareness and acknowledgment of the Netherlandish tradition in which he was placed (and that was coming to an end). Fascinated with landscape and townscape, placing figures naturally and at ease within them—his landscapes are especially fine. Spaces are open and relaxed, not crowded, which gives a feeling of calm, poise, and harmony with nature and God.

Notice how the Italian influence on his work increases progressively and inexorably, but never takes over completely; moves from love of particular detail to more generalized storytelling. Note the individualism of each tree with detailed leaves. His characters have modest, solemn, but seemingly expressionless, faces. Splendid, subtle, rich colors, harmoniously woven together. His paintings remind us that fine craftsmanship and skill are God-given talents, and that he worshiped God by exercising his.

KEY WORKS *Christ Nailed to the Cross*, c. 1481 (London: National Gallery); *The Annunciation*, 1506 (New York: Metropolitan Museum of Art); *A Rest during the Flight to Egypt*, c. 1510 (Madrid: Museo del Prado)

Pietà with Two Donors *Fernando Gallego, c. 1470, 46½ x 48 in (118 x 122 cm), tempera on panel, Madrid: Museo del Prado.* Note the Northern influences: rigid poses, sorrowful expressions, and carefully depicted landscape.

Fernando **Gallego**

◔ c. 1440–c. 1507/10   **ℙ** SPANISH

ℙ Spain   **▮** oils; fresco   **▦** Paris: Musée du Louvre   **⚡** $221,200 in 1989, *Pentecost* (oils)

His birth and death dates are shrouded in mystery, surprisingly for an artist whose importance was recognized in his own lifetime. Credited as the "master" of Castilian painting and at the center of the Hispano–Flemish movement. Spent 14 years (1479–93) painting the ceiling in the Old Library at Salamanca University. Toward the end of his life, Gallego's palette changed from bright tones to muted shades, such as the use of a flat yellow instead of gold.

Look for paintings thick with symbols, figures with obviously Spanish features, and Gallego's use of realism, which is often uncomfortable. Strong use of gold and sumptuous draperies and jewelry. Markedly northern European in contrast to Italian paintings of the same era.

KEY WORKS *The Virgin, St. Andrew, and St. Christopher*, c. 1470 (Salamanca Cathedral, Spain); *San Idelfonso* (retable), c. 1475–80 (Zamora Cathedral, Spain); *Epiphany*, c. 1480–90 (Barcelona: Museu Nacional d'Art de Catalunya); *Pietà*, 1490 (Los Angeles: J. Paul Getty Museum); *Virgin and Child with Parrot*, 1468–1507 (Paris: Musée du Louvre)

> **"Art teaches us not only what to see, but what to be."**
>
> BERNARD BERENSON

Pedro **Berruguete**

◔ c. 1455–1504   **ℙ** SPANISH

ℙ Spain; Italy   **▮** oils; fresco   **▦** Madrid: Museo del Prado   **⚡** $240,000 in 1998, *The Adoration of the Magi* (oils)

He was court painter to King Ferdinand and Queen Isabella. Strongly influenced by Italian Renaissance and Flemish art. Works include the decoration of the palace at Urbino. His art greatly influenced the Castilian style, even after his death. Taught his son, Alonso (c. 1488–1561), to paint and sculpt. Alonso, whose style showed the influence of the early Italian Mannerists, became court painter to Charles V.

KEY WORKS *Virgin of the Milk (Virgen de la Leche)*, c. 1465 (Museo de Bellas Artes de Valencia); *St. Peter the Martyr*, c. 1494 (Madrid: Museo del Prado); *Death of St. Peter the Martyr*, late 15th century (Madrid: Museo del Prado); *St. Dominic Presiding over an Auto Da Fé*, late 15th century (Madrid: Museo del Prado)

Jean **Fouquet**

◔ c. 1415–c. 1481   **ℙ** FRANCE

ℙ France; Italy   **▮** oils; illumination; chalks   **▦** Chantilly (France): Musée Condé

Also spelled "Foucquet." He was master painter and illuminator allied to the royal court in Tours. One of the most important French painters of his time, although, sadly, little survives as testimony. Greatly influenced by Italian Renaissance. He was famed for bringing the Renaissance to France. Traveled to Italy c. 1446–48. Lived and worked in Tours for the rest of his life. Married and had at least two sons (birth dates unknown). Appointed *Peintre du Roi* in 1475, a post he held until death. Had a large workshop that produced important illuminated manuscripts. The style of his illuminations drew richly on his Italian experiences; the local surroundings of Tours were inspiration.

Jean **Bourdichon**

◔ 1457 – 1521   ◫ FRENCH

◫ France   ◪ illumination; sculpture; oils
▥ Paris: Bibliothèque Nationale. Los Angeles: J. Paul Getty Museum

A prolific illuminator, painter, gold- and silversmith, and designer. Born, lived, and worked in Tours; appears never to have traveled abroad. Seemingly a diplomatic and jovial man, he was a great favorite with a long line of French royalty, from Louis XI to Francis I. Appointed *Peintre du Roi* in 1481. His income from the royal court allowed him to become a wealthy landowner and ensured his family financial security. Had a workshop in the castle of Plessis-les-Tours and employed a large number of assistants. Little of his work is documented. Most renowned for illuminated manuscripts, of which his most famous work is the illuminated *Grandes Heures* for Queen Anne of Brittany.

Jean **Hey**

◔ 15TH – 16TH CENTURIES   ◫ UNKNOWN

◫ France; Netherlands   ◪ oils
▥ Paris: Musée du Louvre

Also known as Hay. A painter whose birth and death dates are a mystery, but his art is known around the last quarter of the 15th century, when he was living in France. His name suggests he or his parents originated from the Netherlands or Belgium; his art was greatly influenced by the Netherlandish style. In his lifetime he was respected and appears in the 1504 list of "Greatest Living Painters," compiled by Jean Lemaire de Belge. Another artist about whom very little is known today was nicknamed the "Master of Moulins;" some believe Hey and the Master were the same person, others are sceptical.

Anne of Brittany with St. Anne, St. Ursula, and St. Helen *Jean Bourdichon, c. 1503–08, illumination on vellum, Paris: Bibliothèque Nationale.* From the *Grandes Heures* of Anne of Brittany. Bourdichon's close-up technique placed large figures in the foreground.

Hieronymus Bosch

● c. 1450–1516   🏳 NETHERLANDISH

🏛 Hertogenbosch (Netherlands)
🎨 oils   🏛 Madrid: Museo
del Prado   💰 $62,300 in 1977,
*The Temptation of the Holy
Antonius* (oils)

*The Garden of Earthly Delights:
Hell* Hieronymus Bosch, c. 1510–15,
86⅓ x 37⅓ in (219 x 96 cm), oil on
panel, Madrid: Museo del Prado.
The right wing of a triptych, showing
scenes of anguish and humiliation
against a backdrop of mayhem.

Bosch is the last, and perhaps
the greatest, of the medieval
painters. Much admired
in his lifetime, especially
by ardent Catholics such
as Philip II of Spain,
who was an avid collector.

Best known for his complex,
moralizing works, of which
the central theme is the
sinful depravity of man,
human folly, deadly sin
(notably lust), the seductive
temptations of the flesh, and
the almost inevitable fate of eternal
damnation (salvation is possible but only
with the greatest difficulty). Like hellfire
sermons, they are a complete contrast to
the Renaissance view of man controlling
a rational world. Also produced more
conventional religious works.

Probably the greatest fantasy artist ever,
his works show bewildering detail and
unique imagery of part-animal, part-
human creatures; visions of depraved

activity and torture. Not
drug-induced but illustrations
of ideas and images in
wide circulation at the
time. Brilliant rapid
technique and luminous
color: flecked highlights
and chalk underdrawing.
Was influenced by ornate
manuscript illumination.
Acute, intricate intensity
reflects his belief that he
was depicting certainty
and reality, not fantasy.
Bosch had no real successor
until Bruegel (see page 157).

KEY WORKS *Death and the Miser*, c. 1485–90
(Washington, DC: National Gallery of Art);
The Ship of Fools, c. 1490–1500 (Paris: Musée
du Louvre); *Christ Mocked*, c. 1490–1500
(London: National Gallery); *The Path of
Life*, c. 1500–02 (Paris: Musée du Louvre)

Triptych of the Temptation of St. Anthony
Hieronymus Bosch, c. 1505, 52 x 47 in (132 x 120 cm),
oil on panel, Brussels: Musées Royaux. St. Anthony of
Egypt was tempted by demons and erotic visions.

Mathis **Grünewald**

● c. 1470–1528 ⚑ GERMAN

🏠 Mainz (Germany) 🎨 oils
🏛 Colmar (France): Unterlinden
Museum (*The Isenheim Altarpiece*)

Also known as Neithardt (after his
adopted son, Andreas) or Gothardt.
Obscure, austere, religious fanatic
who painted works of powerful,
spiritual intensity. Now regarded
as one of the all-time great painters,
but overlooked until the 20th century.
Successful both as an artist and
engineer. Worked for the Archbishop
of Mainz. Died of the plague.

His overwhelming masterpiece—
The Isenheim Altarpiece—is in Colmar,
near Strasbourg. His altarpieces
express his single-minded religious
fervor (he became a Lutheran) but
are full of visual contradictions and
anachronisms, especially imagery
lacking precedent or following. Little
interest in "realism" or "modern"
Renaissance ideas—his style has
more in common with the medieval
world and with 20th-century German
Expressionism (which he influenced).

Grünewald distorted scale to convey
emotion or significance. He used intense
colors, ranging from pitch black to
bright yellow, to express mood. His

distorted bodies and
anguished hands and
feet express inner
torment or suffering.
The settings range from
the bare and almost
abstract to the highly
detailed. The demons
come out of an imagined
medieval hell and are
mixed with faces or
details that have the
qualities of first-hand
observation of the
Italian Renaissance.

KEY WORKS *The Isenheim
Altarpiece* (see pages
122–123); *The Small
Crucifixion*, c. 1511–1520
(Washington, DC:
National Gallery of Art);
Saints Erasmus and Maurice,
c. 1520–24 (Munich:
Alte Pinakothek)

The Resurrection of Christ *Mathis Grünewald,
c. 1512–16, oil on panel, Colmar (France): Unterlinden
Museum.* From the right wing of the many-paneled
Isenheim Altarpiece, which was intended to give support
to patients in Isenheim's Anthonite monastery hospital.

Tilman **Riemenschneider**

● 1460–1531 ⚑ GERMAN

🏠 Germany 🎨 sculpture 💲 $420,000
in 1985, *Young Woman with Long Hair and
Wearing a Hat* (sculpture)

Major figure in German art history.
Renowned as the first sculptor in
limewood who produced altarpieces
finished in a monochrome brown
glaze rather than multicolored
polychrome. His works are mainly
religious: altarpieces, reliefs, busts, and
life-size statues, characterized by strong
Gothic symbolism and realistic carving.
Successful in his own time, became
very wealthy, owning land—including
vineyards. Married three times; had
five children. He lost his fortune in 1525
after backing the wrong side in a peasants'
revolt against the Prince Bishop.

KEY WORKS *St. Jerome and the Lion*, c. 1490 (Ohio:
Cleveland Museum of Art); *Seated Bishop*, 1495
(New York: Metropolitan Museum of Art);
Virgin of the Annunciation, end of 15th century
(Paris: Musée du Louvre); *Holy Blood Altarpiece*,
c. 1501 (Rothenburg: St. Jacob's Church)

Crucifixion (from *The Isenheim Altarpiece*)

Mathis Grünewald c. 1510–15

Grünewald's altarpiece was commissioned as the focus of the high altar of the chapel in the monastery of St. Anthony, at Isenheim near Strasbourg. Plague was the killer disease of the time and the monastery also contained a hospice where plague victims were cared for by the monks of the Anthonite Order.

The victims had no hope of recovery, and this image was intended to bring them comfort and to reinforce their faith—the message is that Christ, whose broken body is shown covered in sores like those caused by the plague, understands their condition and suffers with them and for them.

The figures on the left, Christ's Mother, Mary, and St. John the Evangelist—whom Christ asks to take care of his Mother—are nearly always present in Crucifixion scenes and display extreme mental anguish as they witness Christ's agony. The plague victims who knelt before this altar would have been able to associate with this vision of earthly and human suffering.

The wooden cross strains to bear the weight of Christ, adding to the emotional tension and anguish of the scene

In many Crucifixion scenes the crown of thorns is depicted almost as an ornament adorning the head of a serene, unblemished Christ figure. Here, it is unequivocally a cruel instrument of torture, which, along with his bleeding side and wrenched arms, intensifies the sense of Christ's suffering.

Crucifixion	
Medium	oil on panel
Dimensions	198 x 312 in (500 x 800 cm)
Location	Colmar (France): Unterlinden Museum

Christ's favorite disciple, St. John the Evangelist, comforts Mary, the Mother of Christ, who is dressed in symbolic white

Mary Magdelene is the fallen woman who anointed Christ's feet

TECHNIQUES

Grünewald's work is charged with emotional intensity heightened by his sublime skill with color. The illuminated saints at the base of the cross radiate their own mysterious light and the red of the two St. Johns' robes is almost incandescent.

Christ's hands express his intense physical and spiritual pain. Note the expressive hand gestures of all the other figures.

The size of the figures reflects their importance—Christ is the largest and Mary Magdelene is the smallest. This device was no longer employed by the majority of artists—one reason why this work is called the last great medieval altarpiece

The background of the painting is dark and threatening. Darkness has fallen onto the earth as described in the Gospels. Only those features that are essential to the spiritual message are included

The stoic figure of the Baptist dominates the right side of the painting. The Gospels tell us that John was beheaded by Herod long before the Crucifixion. His presence symbolizes the message of mankind's redemption. The words above his arm are "He must increase but I must diminish"

Christ's agony is depicted by his broken feet, his pierced skin, and his unbearably stretched arms

The lamb of God represents Christ's sacrifice in shedding his blood for the salvation of mankind

St. John the Baptist holds a book representing the scriptures, which refers to the sacrifice of Jesus

The St. Wolfgang Altarpiece Michael Pacher, 1471–81, wood with polychromy/oil on panel, St. Wolfgang Parish Church, Austria. Pacher's use of light and shade on the altarpiece create the impression of unlimited depth.

Veit **Stoss**

◕ c. 1445–1533　🅟 GERMAN

🅟 Nuremberg; Kraków　🅐 sculpture
🏛 Nuremberg: Bamberg Cathedral
🅩 $60,627 in 1992, *Madonna and Child* (oils)

Prominent German sculptor; also a painter and engraver. Renowned for his wood sculptures—with Riemenschneider, the greatest wood-carver of his age—executed in a unique, truly expressive style. Had a modest workshop in which he trained his apprentices—among them his sons—to a high standard. Produced only a handful of paintings and engravings, and none are as noteworthy as his sculpture. His rare paintings (only four are known) are characterized by a tame palette of muted colors. His most famous piece of stone sculpture is the altarpiece at Nuremberg's Bamberg Cathedral.
KEY WORKS *The Death of the Virgin*, 1477–89 (Kraków: Church of St. Mary); *Mourning Virgin*, c. 1500–10 (New York: Metropolitan Museum of Art); *Raphael and Tobias*, 1516 (Nuremberg: Germanisches Nationalmuseum); *The Annunciation*, 1518 (Nuremberg: Parish Church of St. Lorenz); *Crucifix*, 16th century (Nuremberg: Parish Church of St. Lorenz)

Michael **Pacher**

◕ ACTIVE 1462–98　🅟 UNKNOWN

🅟 Tyrol (Austria)　🅐 oils; sculpture
🏛 Würzburg: Mainfränkisches Museum
🅩 $289,793 in 2004, *Crucifixion* (sculpture)

Pacher was a panel-painter and wood-carver, although nothing is known of his training. He is believed to have been German, but it is conceivable that he was Austrian. The work he produced is strongly influenced by Italian art, suggesting he may have traveled to Italy. He is credited with melding Germanic and Italian techniques, and thus influencing the future of Northern European art. He died in Salzburg, but most of his career was spent in Bruneck (Brunico) in the South Tyrol.
KEY WORKS *St. Anne with the Virgin and Child*, 15th century (Barcelona: Museu Nacional d'Art de Catalunya); *The Annunciation*, 1465–70 (Munich: Alte Pinakothek); *The Virgin and Child Enthroned with Angels and Saints*, c. 1475 (London: National Gallery); *Altarpiece of the Four Latin Fathers*, c. 1483 (Munich: Alte Pinakothek)

Martin **Schongauer**

◕ c. 1430–91　🅟 GERMAN

🅟 Colmar (France)　🅐 tempera; oils; engravings　🅩 $146,138 in 1998, *Carrying the Cross* (works on paper)

Son of a goldsmith who settled in Colmar, Alsace. In his day, he was probably the most famous artist in Germany. Especially well known in his lifetime for his engravings, with precise lines and convincing volumes. Borrowed from Flemish techniques and ideas (especially from van der Weyden). Much influenced by Dürer. He concentrated on religious subjects and about 115 plates by him are known. His later work has a more delicate, soft touch—his gracefulness became the stuff of legend.
KEY WORKS *Madonna in the Rose Garden/Madonna of the Rose Bower*, 1473 (Colmar: St. Martin's); *The Large Carrying of the Cross*, c. 1474 (St. Petersburg: Hermitage Museum); *The Crucifixion with Soldiers Sharing Christ's Clothes*, c. 1480 (St. Petersburg: Hermitage Museum)

Hans **Baldung Grien**

◯ c. 1484–1545   ⚑ GERMAN

🏛 Strasbourg; Freiburg-im-Breisgau (Germany)
🎨 oils; woodcuts   🏛 Freiburg Cathedral
💰 $448,000 in 1978, *The Virgin as Queen of Heaven* (oils)

Painter and engraver from Strasbourg. May have trained with Dürer. Especially gifted at visionary themes, which incorporate the elemental and supernatural, and sometimes the gruesome and macabre. His early subjects tended to be religious; his later work is secular. Good draftsmanship; intense color. He also produced very high-quality woodcuts with strong *chiaroscuro*.

KEY WORKS *The Three Ages of Man and Death*, c. 1510 (Madrid: Museo del Prado); *Coronation of the Virgin*, c. 1512 (Freiburg Cathedral); *Girl and Death*, 1517 (Basel, Switzerland: Kunstmuseum); *The Bewitched Groom*, 1544 (Berlin: Staatliche Museum)

Lucas **Cranach** (the elder)

◯ 1472–1553   ⚑ GERMAN

🏛 Vienna; Wittenberg, Augsburg (Germany)
🎨 oils   🏛 Vienna: Kunsthistorisches Museum
💰 $7.92m in 1990, *Portraits of Kurfürst Herzog Johann von Sachsen and of his Son* (oils)

He was a leading figure of the German Renaissance. Worked for the Electors of Saxony in Wittenberg, although his style remained essentially provincial rather than international (Italian). Large, active studio. Staunch Protestant.

He painted impressive and solid court portraits, being especially good at old men's faces. Most notable for the strange, unique, and capricious pictures of female mythological subjects, which have a compelling power and character. These women are curiously reminiscent of the brittle, present-day high-fashion posed and posing models who strut along the catwalk. Both wear outrageous designer creations, and have hard little faces and faraway looks. He makes us adopt the role of voyeur.

Note the sloping shoulders; small, round breasts; feet turned out; long arms and legs; one leg twisted over another; prominent navels; crazy hats and clothes; rings on fingers; feathers; jeweled collars; rocky landscapes, and armor. Hard, glassy eyes, sometimes with strange highlights; manipulative hands; greedy, calculating facial expressions.

KEY WORKS *A Princess of Saxony*, c. 1517 (Washington, DC: National Gallery of Art); *Judith with the Head of Holofernes*, c. 1530 (Vienna: Kunsthistorisches Museum); *Cupid Complaining to Venus*, c. 1530s (London: National Gallery)

The Nymph of the Fountain *Lucas Cranach (the elder), 1534, 20⅛ x 30¼ in (51.3 x 76.8 cm), oil on panel, Liverpool: Walker Art Gallery. A teasing diaphanous wisp of silk simultaneously covers and reveals the nymph's loins.*

Albrecht **Dürer**

⬤ 1471–1528 🏳 GERMAN

🗺 Germany; Vienna   🎨 oils; woodcuts; engravings   🏛 Munich: Alte Pinakothek. London: British Museum (prints). Vienna: Albertina (watercolors)   💲 $1,203,200 in 1978, *The Isolated Rock of Doss Trento* (works on paper)

The greatest northern artist of the Renaissance. Born (four years before Michelangelo) in Nuremberg, he was prolific, tenacious, immensely ambitious, and very successful. He traveled widely in Europe and went on key visits to Italy in 1494 and 1505. Follower of Luther. Fused northern European and Italian styles and had a profound influence on art, both north and south of the Alps. Many thousands of his works survive to this day.

LIFE AND WORKS

His goldsmith father, who came from Hungary and trained in the Netherlands, taught Dürer the technique of engraving and an admiration for van Eyck and van der Weyden. He had rich, patrician patrons who encouraged him to travel,

> **"There lives no man upon the earth who can give a final judgment upon what the most beautiful shape of man might be; God only knows that."**
>
> ALBRECHT DÜRER

and he established his own busy workshop in Nuremberg. His marriage was unhappy and childless. His social pretensions, artistic ambitions, and his unusual degree of self-consciousness are revealed in his numerous self-portraits.

STYLE

Highly gifted but self-conscious as a painter, he was greater, more at ease, and more innovative as a printmaker:

Self-Portrait at the Age of Twenty-eight *1500, 26⅜ x 19⅜ in (67.1 x 48.7 cm), oil on panel, Munich: Alte Pinakothek.* Dürer portrays himself as an image reminiscent of Christ.

produced powerful woodcuts and pioneering engravings. Was a brilliant draftsman and painted exquisite watercolors. His portraits have strong lines; curious, lopsided faces with enlarged eyes that have liquid surfaces; beautiful, strong hands and feet. He was fascinated by landscape, plants, and animals, and anything unusual. Also look for objects as symbols.

WHAT TO LOOK FOR

Uniquely and subtly synthesized (often in the same work) characteristics of the old northern or medieval tradition and the new Italian and humanist discoveries. Look for northern features—apocalyptic imagery; emotional expression; complexity of design; crisp, angular line; minute observation of detail. Note also the Italian features—strong, dignified, composed, assured figures and faces; soft, rounded modeling; classical

A Young Hare *1502, 9¾ x 9 in (25 x 23 cm), watercolor on paper, Vienna: Graphische Sammlung Albertina.* Dürer's watercolors were created for his own pleasure.

Altarpiece of the Rose Garlands *1506,*
63⅜ x 76½ in (162 x 194.5 cm), oil on panel,
Prague: National Gallery. This painting was
Dürer's first attempt at a single-panel altar, though
its compositional structure is more like a triptych.

architecture; perspective and
foreshortening; New Testament
subjects; nudes.

KEY WORKS *The Four Horsemen of the Apocalypse,*
c. 1497–98 (Virginia: Museum of Fine
Arts); *Great Piece of Turf—Study of Weeds,*
1503 (Vienna: Graphische Sammlung
Albertina); *Virgin and Child Holding a Half-
Eaten Pear,* 1512 (Vienna: Kunsthistorisches
Museum); *Johannes Kleberger, aged 40,* 1526
(Vienna: Kunsthistorisches Museum)

Melancolia *1514, 9½ x 7½ in (24.2 x 19.1 cm),*
engraving, London: British Museum. The numbers in
the top right of the engraving form a "magic square,"
with the two middle cells of the bottom row giving
the date of the engraving: 1514.

HIGH RENAISSANCE AND MANNERISM
c. 1500 – 1600

The 16th century saw the establishment of an ideal that would be followed by all self-respecting European rulers until the 20th century, and accounts in no small measure for the great flowering of European art. It was twofold: be strong and fearless in battle, and a generous and knowledgeable patron and protector of the arts.

These principles were set out in one of the best-selling books of the 16th century, *Il Cortegiano* ("The Book of the Courtier") by Baldassare Castiglione, a diplomat from Urbino, Italy. Written in 1514 and first published in 1528, it summarized what had already been established as an ideal of behavior for monarchs, nobles, and ladies.

ESTABLISHED POWERS

By 1511, Europe had four major powers, each led by strong-willed men who did indeed fight hard and use art to display and reinforce their power and ambition. The fall of Constantinople in 1453 effectively left the Roman Church as the sole effective defender of Christendom. A succession of energetic popes made Rome an artistic showpiece that proclaimed this spiritual and political reality. Europe's most powerful temporal ruler was the Habsburg Holy Roman Emperor, Charles V, who controlled Spain, Austria, the Low Countries, and southern Italy. Francis I of France was determined that his country should compete with both these powers, while Henry VIII of England also wanted his nation, with its new ruling dynasty, to be a major player on the European stage.

At first there was a certain equilibrium between these rival power blocks, and their wish to outdo each other culturally, with virtually no limit on expense, was profoundly beneficial for the arts. Indeed, the achievements of the artists of the High Renaissance marked a high point that subsequent generations constantly revered and tried to emulate. But by the late 1520s warfare engulfed Europe, the Church began to fragment, and the

The Delphic Sibyl *(detail from Sistine Chapel ceiling) Michelangelo, 1508–12, fresco, Rome: Vatican Museums.* The Papacy cleverly combined Classical and Biblical authorities to assert its political and spiritual leadership.

Theatrum Orbis Terrarum: *Map of the World by Abraham Ortelius, 1574.* The pace of European exploration after the 1490s was exceptionally rapid. Even in the first decade of the 16th century, the African coastline was accurately known. By the second half of the century, the outline of the American continent was assuming recognizable shape.

intellectual certainties predicated on the perception of a universe in which the Earth was at the very center, and the Mediterranean at the center of the world, also fractured.

DISINTEGRATION

What had started as cultural rivalry degenerated into destructive warfare. In 1525, Francis I invaded Italy. In the course of the ensuing conflict, Charles V's army sacked Rome in 1527, burning and destroying what had become the finest city in the world. Meanwhile, the Catholic Church was severely weakened by the crisis sparked by Martin Luther in 1517. His supporters had intended to strengthen the Church by stamping out corruption. Instead, they created a permanent split between an emerging Protestant north and a Catholic south, and unleashed a campaign to destroy art treasures with

REFORMATION

Title Page, the Great Bible, *1539.* Printing was crucial in spreading the Reformation, as the Bible became available in vernacular languages, in this case English, instead of Latin.

When in 1517 Martin Luther nailed his *95 Theses* to a church door in Wittenberg, his goal was simply to protest against the corruption of the Church, especially in the sale of indulgences. But his further writings struck such a chord with antipapal feeling that the pope's authority was rejected across much of northern Europe. Many German princes, as well as the kings of Denmark and Sweden, were rapidly won over to the Lutheran doctrine, then Henry VIII of England— albeit for political rather than theological reasons—broke with Rome in 1534.

TIMELINE: 1500—1600

1500	1508–12 / 1509	1517 / 1519	1521 / 1522	1527	1534 / 1545	1543 / 1549

1500 Portuguese discovery of Brazil (Cabral)

1508–12 Michelangelo paints Sistine Chapel ceiling

1509 Spanish settlement of Central America begun; invention of the watch, Germany

1517 Martin Luther's *95 Theses* attacks abuses of Catholic Church

1519 Habsburg Charles V elected Holy Roman Emperor

1521 Cortés conquers Aztec Empire

1522 First circumnavigation of the globe completed (Magellan and del Cano)

1527 Sack of Rome

1534 Act of Supremacy: Henry VIII of England breaks with Rome

1545 Council of Trent called to counter threat of Protestantism

1543 *Of the Revolution of Celestial Bodies* published, Copernicus

1549 Direct Portuguese rule imposed on Brazil

1500

1520

1540

Catholic connections. This north-south divide gave a savage twist to the rivalries between the continent's leading powers. In 1565, a vicious, protracted conflict began in the Low Countries, where the Habsburgs were determined to crush an anti-Catholic revolt and reimpose their own rule.

With the Council of Trent, summoned in 1545, the Catholic Church committed itself to restoring its former supremacy, but in reality power was shifting away from Italy. By the mid-16th century, after an audacious act of conquest, Spain found itself in control of much of South America, and the staggering wealth gained as a result made it the richest country in Europe. By the end of the century, both England and France had established footholds in North America.

MANNERISM

The voyages of discovery showed that the world was much larger than had been imagined and full of curious new lands and creatures. In 1543, Copernicus published his proof that the Sun, not the Earth, was the center of our planetary system. Long-held scientific beliefs were being challenged as well as religious ones. Against this turbulent background, it is no surprise that the self-confidence of the art of the High Renaissance gave way to the uncertainties of Mannerism, whose principal characteristics were a deliberate flouting of rules and willful eccentricity and distortion.

Château de Chambord, Loire Valley Francis I's desire to emulate the cultural superiority of Italy found potent expression in the lavish châteaux of the Loire Valley. Chambord, begun in 1519, is the largest; 1,800 workmen were employed in its construction over 12 years.

1559 Treaty of Cateau-Cambrésis: France forced to concede Habsburg supremacy in Italy	**1570** Publication of Palladio's *Four Books of Architecture*, Italy	**1572** St. Bartholomew's Day Massacre: slaughter of French Protestants in Paris	**1588** Spanish Armada: attempted conquest of Protestant England by Spain

1560   **1580**   **1600**

1565 Dutch Revolt starts: extended attempt to gain independence from Spain; Philippines claimed by Spain	**1571** Battle of Lepanto: Ottoman navy defeated by united Christian fleet	**1598** Edict of Nantes ends 30-year religious war in France

Leonardo da Vinci

1452–1519   ITALIAN

Florence; Milan; France

oils; drawings; sculpture; fresco   Paris: Musée du Louvre (*Mona Lisa*). London: Royal Collection (drawings)

$10,360,001 in 2001, *Horse and Rider* (works on paper)

Unique, perhaps lonely, genius. The universal Renaissance man: scientist, inventor, philosopher, writer, designer, sculptor, architect, and painter. Had such a fertile mind that he rarely completed anything, and there are relatively few paintings by him. Changed the status of the artist from artisan to gentleman. Pivotal in the creation of the High Renaissance period of Florentine art.

LIFE AND WORKS

Leonardo was born in Vinci, near Florence, the illegitimate son of a notary at a time when illegitimacy was a serious stigma. This may have been a factor that led him to become detached from others.

Two Horsemen *after 1481, 5⅝ x 5 in (14.3 x 12.8 cm), metal point drawing, Cambridge: Fitzwilliam Museum. An example of Leonardo's lifelong fascination with animals.*

Leonardo trained with Verrochio but much of his life was spent working at the courts of foreign dukes and princes who, at times, were at war with Florence. The Medici ignored him entirely. After 1483, he worked for Ludovico Sforza, Duke of Milan, but returned to Florence following the French invasion of Milan in 1499. Between 1500 and 1516, he produced many of his most famous

> ## "The mind of the painter should be like a looking-glass that is filled with as many images as there are objects placed before him."
>
> LEONARDO DA VINCI

The Virgin of the Rocks *c. 1508, 74 x 47 in (189.5 x 120 cm), oil on panel, London: National Gallery.* Painted for the Milanese Foundation of San Francesco Grande. This is the second version created by da Vinci, showing the infant St. John the Baptist adoring the infant Christ accompanied by an angel.

paintings. He spent his last years in the service of Francis I of France and, according to legend, died in the king's arms near Amboise in the Loire Valley. Leonardo's most remarkable legacy is his notebooks filled with writings and sketches in which he explored his private thoughts about art and science, observations from nature, and diagrams for visionary scientific and mechanical projects.

STYLE

Leonardo had an insatiable curiosity to find out how everything operates. He then put this into practice (as witness his keenly observed anatomical drawings and his plans for flying machines, and so on). His paintings are multilayered, investigating these subjects; they also explore beauty, ugliness, spirituality, man's relationship with nature and God, and "the motions of the mind" (psychology). He was technically inventive, but careless.

WHAT TO LOOK FOR

Why is the *Mona Lisa* (see page 138) so important? It created a sensation (c. 1510) because it was lifelike in a way that had never been seen before. It comprises a brilliant bag of technical and perceptual innovation (the use of oil paint, a relaxed pose, soft and shadowy figure with no outlines, two landscapes) and demands that the viewer's imagination should supply the inner meaning and missing visual detail. It set a new standard—and it reaffirms that art you have to interact with creatively is always best.

KEY WORKS *Ginevra de'Benci,* c. 1474 (Washington, DC: National Gallery of Art); *Cecilia Gallarani/The Lady with an Ermine,* c. 1483 (Kraków: Czartoryski Museum); *Mona Lisa,* c. 1510 (Paris: Musée du Louvre)

The Last Supper *1495–97 (post-restoration), 181 x 346½ in (460 x 880 cm), mixed media fresco, Milan: Santa Maria delle Grazie.* More than a depiction of one event, the fresco refers to other episodes narrated in the Gospels.

Raphael (Raffaello Sanzio)

● 1483–1520   ⚑ ITALIAN

🏛 Tuscany; Umbria; Rome   🎨 oils; fresco
🏛 Rome: Vatican Stanze; Villa Farnese (fresco
series). London: Victoria & Albert Museum
(cartoons)   💰 $7.92m in 1996, *Study for
the Head of an Apostle* (drawing)

"Il Divino." A child prodigy who died
young, but one of the greatest masters
of the High Renaissance and therefore
of all time. Profoundly influential;
helped raise the social status of artists
from craftsmen to intellectuals.

He had complete mastery of all
Renaissance techniques, subjects, and
ideas, and used and developed them
with apparent ease: deep, emotional,
and intellectual expression; total
Christian belief; harmony; balance;
humanity; superb draftsmanship. In
short, he projected an ideal at almost
every level—which is why he was held
up as the model for all ambitious artists
until the overthrow of academic art by
the Modern Movement.

Notice how everything has a purpose,
especially how he uses contrast to

***Pope Leo X with Cardinals Giulio de' Medici
and Luigi de' Rossi*** *Raphael (Raffaello Sanzio),
1518–19, 60⅜ x 46⅛ in (154 x 119 cm), oil on wood,
Florence: Galleria degli Uffizi.*

heighten our perception and feeling (one
of the oldest and most successful devices):
stern men and sweet women;
stillness and movement;
contemplation and activity;
curved line and straight line;
tension and relaxation.
Observe too the continuity
in his works—how a gesture,
pose, or movement begun
in one part of the body, or in
one figure, is carried a stage
further in another.

KEY WORKS *The School of Athens*,
1510–11 (see page 139);
Madonna of the Chair, c. 1513
(Florence: Galleria degli
Uffizi); *Bindo Altoviti*, c. 1515
(Washington, DC: National
Gallery of Art); *Portrait of
Baldassare Castiglione*, pre-1516
(Paris: Musée du Louvre)

The Sistine Madonna
*Raphael (Raffaello Sanzio), 1513,
104⅓ x 77⅛ in (265 x 196 cm), oil on
canvas, Dresden: Gemäldegalerie. This
was Raphael's first major work on a
theme that was to become a central
feature of his art—the Madonna and
Child. He reworked the subject with
constant variation and invention.*

Sebastiano del Piombo

◔ c. 1485 – 1547 ▣ ITALIAN

🏛 Venice; Rome ◨ oils; fresco 🏛 Rome:
Villa Farnese (fresco series) 💰 $695,400
in 1987, *Portrait of Pope Clement VII* (oils)

Venetian expatriot and Titian's
contemporary, who settled in Rome
when Michelangelo and Raphael were
there. In 1531 obtained the sinecure
of keeper of the papal seal (made from
lead, or "piombo," hence his nickname).

He excelled at painting portraits—which
can be magnificent. Otherwise he flirted
with (relative) failure. He achieved a
certain marriage of muscularity and
poetry, which makes his figures look
like soulful athletes, but the compositions,
color, and figures became overblown
as he strove unsuccessfully to keep up
with his friend Michelangelo.

Look for rather fierce-looking, muscular
people, with good strong hands; dramatic
gestures, and plenty of foreshortening.
Interesting use of perspective. Rich color
and landscape backgrounds maintain his
links with Venice. Is it a misfortune to be
talented but not outstanding in an epoch
of giants? Do they cause you to live in
their shadow and diminish your talent?
Or do they inspire you to reach heights
you would otherwise not have achieved?
KEY WORKS *The Daughter of Herodias*, 1510
(London: National Gallery); *Fall of Icarus*,
c. 1511 (Rome: Villa Farnese); *Portrait
of a Woman*, 1512 (Florence: Galleria
degli Uffizi); *Flagellation*, 1516–21 (Rome:
S. Pietro in Montorio); *Raising of Lazarus*,
c. 1517–19 (London: National Gallery)

Fra Baccio della Porta
Bartolommeo

◔ c. 1474 – 1517 ▣ ITALIAN

🏛 Florence ◨ oils 🏛 Paris: Musée du Louvre
💰 $2.1m in 2001, *Nativity* (oils)

Major Florentine painter who influenced
the change in style between the early and
High Renaissance.

His large-scale, elaborate altarpieces of
throned Madonnas with the Christ child
show the main characteristics of the High
Renaissance style—monumental, solemn,
balanced, with dignified compositions
and figures. Bartolommeo replaced the
intensely observed detail of the early

Renaissance with generalizations
(notice it especially in faces and
drapery) and idealization.

Look for well-fed people with a
tendency to chubby cheeks, double
chins, and a self-satisfied look. Observe
landscapes that look prosperous and
well farmed. Warm color and light.
KEY WORKS *Portrait of Savonarola*, c. 1495
(Florence: Convent of San Marco);
Marriage of St. Catherine, 1511 (Paris:
Musée du Louvre); *Mother of Mercy*,
1515 (Lucca, Italy: Academy)

Andrea del Sarto

◔ 1486 – 1530 ▣ ITALIAN

🏛 Florence; Fontainebleau ◨ fresco; oils
💰 $1m in 2000, *Madonna and Child* (oils)

The last significant Florentine
High Renaissance painter. Influenced
in subjects, style, and technique by
Leonardo, Raphael, and Michelangelo.
Synthesized those influences to produce
handsome, monumental, religious
pictures and portraits, which are
harmonious in color, well balanced,
grand in conception and scale, but
lack real emotional depth and originality.
KEY WORKS *Punishment of the Gamblers*,
1510 (Florence: SS. Annunziata);
Madonna of the Harpies, 1517 (Florence:
Galleria degli Uffizi)

Lamentation over the Dead Christ *Andrea del Sarto,
1524, 93¾ x 78 in (238 x 198 cm), oil on wood panel,
Florence: Palazzo Pitti.* Forced to flee from the plague, del
Sarto painted this for the convent where he took refuge.

Michelangelo Buonarroti

◔ 1475–1564　📛 ITALIAN

🏛 Florence; Bologna; Rome　🗿 sculpture; fresco; tempera　🏛 Florence; Rome (especially Sistine Chapel)　💲 $11,174,001 in 2000, *The Risen Christ* (works on paper)

The outstanding genius (and infant prodigy), who cast his influence over all European art until Picasso broke the spell and changed the rules. Sculptor first, painter and architect second. Workaholic, melancholic, temperamental, lonely. Also argumentative and belligerent; he found relationships with others difficult.

He was born near Florence, the son of a minor official with noble lineage, and showed his talent at an early age. He had a profound belief in the human form (especially that of the male) as the ultimate expression of human sensibility and beauty. His early work shows the human being as the measure of all things: idealized, muscular, confident, quasi-divine. Gradually that image becomes more expressive, more human, less perfect, fallible, and flawed. Never a natural painter—he

The Last Judgment 1538–41, 576 x 528 in (1463 x 1341 cm), fresco, Vatican City: Sistine Chapel. In the center of the composition, Christ raises the good with his right hand and dismisses the damned with his left.

conceived the figure in sculptural terms and used light to model it, so it could be the design for shaping a block of marble.

In his paintings, he uses fiery reds, oranges, yellows against gray or blue; employs a wet-in-wet oil paint technique. Look for: tempera hatching, reminiscent of a sculptor exploring volume; brilliant draftsmanship exploring outline, contour, and volume; beautiful and expressive hands; twisting poses, full of latent energy; faces expressing the full range of human emotions. He was endlessly inventive—never repeats a pose (although he borrows some from famous Greek and Roman sculptures).

KEY WORKS *The Entombment*, c. 1500–01 (London: National Gallery); *David*, 1501–04 (Florence: Gallerie dell'Accademia); *Sistine Chapel ceiling frescoes*, 1508–12 (Rome: Vatican Museums)

Holy Family with St. John (Doni Tondo) 1504–05, diameter 47 in (120 cm), oil on panel, Florence: Galleria degli Uffizi.

Pietà

Michelangelo 1500

Michelangelo was only 25 when his *Pietà* was unveiled at St. Peter's Basilica in Rome. In this superb work, he removed the subject from its usual sphere. More than a lofty religious symbol, far removed from normal life, it has become a real moment in human existence: a sculpture that invites the viewer to share Mary's grief.

Pietà	
Medium marble	
Dimensions height 68½ in (174 cm); width at base 76¾ in (195 cm)	
Location Rome: St. Peter's Basilica	

Michelangelo took the study of anatomy very seriously. As an adolescent he befriended a priest who allowed him access to dead bodies lying in rest at the church before being buried. The dead Christ of the *Pietà* is a testimony to many hours spent studying genuine corpses, giving the work a realism most other sculptors were unable to attain. Michelangelo did not believe that his Christ should appear superhuman; he wrote that there was no need to conceal the human behind the divine. The work ensured his reputation as one of the Renaissance's finest artists.

Michelangelo's close study of anatomy is apparent in this mastery of the human form

The sorrowing face of the Madonna is an inspired union of classical idealism and Christian piety.

Christ's veins are distended, emphazing how recently the blood flowed in his body

Mary's outstretched hands show an acceptance of her fate

The *Pietà* was sculpted from one single block of marble, taken from the quarries at Carrara

THE HIGH RENAISSANCE

The years between about 1500 and the Sack of Rome in 1527 saw a prodigious outpouring in Italy in all the visual arts. In Rome, under the energetic patronage of an exceptionally able (and self-promoting) pope, Julius II, Raphael and Michelangelo simultaneously created works of startling novelty. In Venice, the celebrated Titian redefined the possibilities of painting.

STYLE

Idealization is the benchmark, but it manifests itself in different ways. For Raphael it meant heroic confidence, technical sophistication, and grace. Similar elegance allied to acute psychological insight and astonishingly close observation of the natural world are obvious in Leonardo. Both Michelangelo and Titian pioneered more personal if no less heroic styles, the former astoundingly audacious in his vision of the male form, the latter above all in his mastery of color.

The Emperor Charles V on Horseback in Mühlberg
Titian, 1548, 131 x 110 in (332 x 279 cm), oil on canvas, Madrid: Museo del Prado. Drama, idealization, and huge scale are unified by brilliant coloring and daring brushwork.

SUBJECTS

The visionary goal of High Renaissance art was a perfect union of the human and divine, Christian and pagan Antique, nature and imagination. Thus the male nude "made in God's image," the central motif of Michelangelo's painting and sculpture, heroic and often deliberately distorted, has an extraordinary power, which the Church used to convey a spiritual ideal. Yet though religious subjects generally remained pre-eminent, other subjects—whether Classical scenes, landscapes, or portraits—became increasingly important, significantly widening the repertoire of Western art. Titian's *poesie*, lyrical and dreamlike "visual poems", began to explore the relationship between the human figure and landscape.

Mona Lisa *Leonardo da Vinci, c. 1503–05, 30¼ x 21 in (77 x 53.5 cm), Paris: Musée du Louvre.* Praised by Giorgio Vasari because it "appeared to be living flesh rather than paint."

KEY EVENTS

1498	Milan—Leonardo completes his huge, psychologically penetrating *Last Supper*
1503	Michelangelo completes *David* in Florence, the largest statue carved since Antiquity
1506	Foundation stone of Bramante's new (and in the event never finished) St. Peter's laid by Julius II
1508–12	Michelangelo's almost single-handed epic labor on the ceiling of the Sistine Chapel, Rome
1528	Renaissance ideals defined by Castiglione in *The Book of the Courtier*

c. 1500–1527

WHAT TO LOOK FOR

The greatest triumph of the High Renaissance was the rebuilding of St. Peter's in Rome and its decoration through the leadership of Pope Julius II. As a complement to Michelangelo's religious theme in the Sistine Chapel, Raphael decorated the Pope's library with four subjects: Philosophy, Theology, Poetry, and Law. For his interpretation of Philosophy, Raphael drew exclusively on the inspiration and precedents of Greek and Roman Antiquity.

The architectural setting was based on designs by Bramante, the leading Classical architect in Rome

Plato and Aristotle, silhouetted against the sky, are awarded the dominant positions in the picture

The School of Athens
Raphael, 1509–11, base 304 in (772 cm), fresco, Vatican: Stanza della Segnatura

Euclid, giving a geometry lesson, was a portrait of Bramante

Pythagoras, the great Greek mathematician, demonstrates his propositions

Heraclitus was a portrait of Michelangelo, then working on his Sistine ceiling

Raphael included a self-portrait, an indication of the growing status accorded artists

TECHNIQUES

Each figure is a masterful, expressive portrait and each group a model of statuesque harmony and continuous, graceful movement. The color scheme, too, is serene and harmonious.

Raphael was renowned in his own day for his ability to include a huge variety of complex poses and realistic expressions in a single work. Many hundreds of preliminary drawings were made from life.

Giorgione

🌐 c. 1476–1510   🇮🇹 ITALIAN

🏛 Venice   🎨 oils   💰 $6,795 in 1957, *Caesar Enthroned Receives Head of Pompey* (oils)

Also known as Giorgio Barbarelli or Giorgio da Castelfranco, he was the young, short-lived genius of the Venetian School, who ranks in achievement, significance, and importance with the greatest of Renaissance painters. Few works are known to be his for certain.

His small-scale, mostly secular, pictures are consciously poetic, lyrical, and mysterious—carefully observed portraits of youthful and sensitive young men being beautiful. Dreamlike landscape settings. *The Sleeping Venus* and *The Tempest* opened the door for the development of the nude, landscape, and mythological painting on which so much of Western art has depended.

To own an authentic Giorgione has been one of the supreme ambitions of collectors since the Renaissance, so just think how many pictures have falsely or mistakenly had the label "Giorgione"

The Three Philosophers Giorgione, c. 1509, 47⅜ x 55½ in (121 x 141 cm), oil on canvas, Vienna: Kunsthistorisches Museum. Giorgione was patronized by collectors who enjoyed poetic ambiguity.

attached to them (and still do?). It is impossible to identify a recognizable technique (so few works known for certain, plus wicked restorations and overcleanings). Look for that indefinable, dreamy Giorgione mood, plus a passion for observing the real world.

KEY WORKS *Old Woman*, c. 1502–03 (Venice: Gallerie dell'Accademia); *The Tempest*, 1505–10 (Venice: Gallerie dell'Accademia); *The Sleeping Venus*, 1508–10 (Dresden: Gemäldegalerie)

Jacopo **Palma Vecchio**

🌐 1480–1528   🇮🇹 ITALIAN

🏛 Venice   🎨 oils   💰 $293,400 in 1991, *Sacra Conversazione—Madonna and Child with St. John the Baptist and St. Catherine* (oils, double-sided)

Short-lived (for an artist), well-regarded painter of the greatest period of Venetian art, of the same generation

Lady with a Lute Jacopo Palma Vecchio, c. 1520–25, 38¾ x 28 in (97 x 71 cm), Private Collection. Palma Vecchio's sensuous portraits of women were eagerly bought by wealthy Venetians, but few survive.

as Titian. His less good grandnephew was Palma Giovane (1544–1628).

His high-quality pictures are well executed and decorative, but have the misfortune to be emotionally empty (the fate of many artists who just fail to reach the first rank). Had great success with half-lengths of sumptuous blonds masquerading as goddesses and saints (high Venetian fashion of the day).

Look for skilful drawing, pleasingly soft and harmonious coloring, mastery of all the skills of perspective and the human figure, etc. But his most elaborate works, however, seem to be no more than an accumulation of small-scale visions and fine details, and lack the boldness and grandeur that they seem to be striving for.

KEY WORKS *Portrait of a Poet*, c. 1516 (London: National Gallery); *A Blonde Woman*, c. 1520 (London: National Gallery); *Venus and Cupid*, c. 1523–24 (Cambridge: Fitzwilliam Museum); *Judith*, 1525–28 (Florence: Galleria degli Uffizi)

Vittore **Carpaccio**

● ACTIVE 1490–1523   ⚑ ITALIAN

🇮🇹 Venice   🎨 tempera   🏛 Venice: Scuola di San Giorgio; Gallerie dell'Accademia (Scenes from *The Life of St. Ursula*)   💰 $360,000 in 1990, *Sacra Conversazione* (drawing)

Notable Venetian storyteller with an eye for homely, factual detail, crowds, and processions. Set his religious and mythological stories within images of his own familiar Venice and thus chronicled his own times. Carpaccio's faithful representation of the visible world is composed of many tiny parts. Not a pioneer, but a forerunner of later

Dream of St. Ursula (detail) Vittore Carpaccio, 1495, 9 x 9 in (23 x 23 cm), tempera on canvas, Venice: Galleria dell'Accademia. Carpaccio painted a series of works showing an unusually domesticated interpretation of the martyrdom of St. Ursula.

domestic genre painters and recorders of the Venetian scene, such as Canaletto.

KEY WORKS *The Dismissal of the English Ambassadors*, 1495 (Venice: Gallerie dell' Accademia); *The Flight into Egypt*, c. 1500 (Washington, DC: National Gallery of Art); *Young Knight in a Landscape*, 1510 (Madrid: Museo Thyssen-Bornemisza)

Dosso **Dossi**

● c. 1479–1542   ⚑ ITALIAN

🇮🇹 Venice; Mantua; Ferrara   🎨 oils   💰 $3.7m in 1989, *Allegory with Male and Female Figure* (oils)

Somewhat obscure Venetian painter in mold of Titian and Giorgione—moody, poetic, sensuous, using rich light and color. He painted myths, allegories, portraits, lush landscapes, and frothy trees. Had a liking for animals. Few works remain, most of which are badly damaged. It is fashionable to say he is wonderful—he ought to be, but he is somehow ungainly and gauche.

KEY WORKS *Sibyl*, c. 1516–20 (St. Petersburg: Hermitage Museum); *Melissa*, 1520s (Rome: Galleria Borghese); *Circe and her Lovers in a Landscape*, c. 1525 (Washington, DC: National Gallery of Art)

Lorenzo **Lotto**

c. 1480 – c. 1556   ITALIAN

Venice; Bergamo; Rome; Marche Region (Italy)   oils $404,800 in 1977, *Madonna and Child* (oils)

Minor and uneven Venetian with a difficult personality. Was much traveled. He died a forgotten man.

His portraits, altarpieces, and allegories have sumptuous colors and a rich, robust style, but are often uncomfortable compositions with overcramped spaces and inexplicable changes of scale. He never quite made all the parts work together. There are influences from many of his contemporaries, but too many borrowings that he never fully absorbs, so that his work can look like a mishmash of everyone else. At times it even comes close to caricature.

He was at his best in portrait painting, especially conjugal double portraits. He liked searching, soulful expressions and was obsessed by hand gestures and fingers. Works have uncertain anatomy, but good landscape details and bold modeling with light. Look for the stunning oriental carpets in his paintings of interiors. Was much admired by Bernard Berenson, who made a detailed study of his work.

KEY WORKS *The Annunciation*, 1520s (Recanati, Italy: Church of Sta Maria sopra Mercanti); *St. Catherine*, c. 1522 (Washington, DC: National Gallery of Art)

Paolo **Veronese**

c.1528 – 88   ITALIAN

Verona; Venice   oils   Venice: Gallerie dell'Accademia; Doge's Palace; churches. Vicenza: Villa Maser $2.7m in 1990, *Cupid Disarmed by Venus* (oils)

Also known as Paolo Caliari, he is one of the major Venetians and one of the greatest-ever creators of decorative schemes. So called because he came from Verona. He had a huge output.

See his work in situ – in one of his large-scale decorative schemes, such as a Venetian church or a nobleman's villa. Don't look for profound meaning or a deep experience; let your eye have a feast and enjoy the glorious visual and decorative qualities. Try to spot some of the illusionistic tricks and remember that these works were intended to go hand in hand with a particular building—with its space, architectural detail, and light.

Look for the posh people (his clients), surrounded by their servants, rich materials, and classy architecture. Look at the faces. Have they become bored by too much good living and leisure? These are the last days of the really good times for the Venetian Empire. Is that why the dogs and animals often seem more alive than the people? The Madonnas and deities he portrays are no more than Venetian nobility in fancy dress.

KEY WORKS *Allegory of Love, I (Unfaithfulness)*, c. 1570s (London: National Gallery); *The Finding of Moses*, c. 1570–75 (Washington, DC: National Gallery of Art)

Vincenzo **Catena**

c. 1480 – 1531   ITALIAN

Venice   oils $185,000 in 1995, *Madonna and Child with Two Angel Musicians and Landscape Beyond* (oils)

Reputable second-rank Venetian. Good middle-of-the-road painting—uninspired figures and composition, but well-observed light and attractive colors. Everything looks meticulously clean—because cleanliness is next to godliness?

KEY WORKS *Madonna and Child with the Infant St. John the Baptist*, c. 1506–1515 (London: National Gallery); *St. Jerome in his Study*, c. 1510 (London: National Gallery); *Christ Bearing the Cross*, c. 1520–1530 (Vienna: Liechtenstein Museum)

Marriage at Cana Paolo *Veronese, 1563, 262⅓ × 389¾ in (666 × 990 cm), oil on canvas, Paris: Musée du Louvre.* The scene is a fantasy interpretation of the occasion when Christ turned water into wine.

Venus and Adonis *Titian, 1553, 42 x 53½ in (107 x 136 cm), oil on canvas, Madrid: Museo del Prado. Titian's sensuous color tones accentuate the soft and shimmering beauty of the lovers' flesh.*

Titian

⬤ c. 1487 – 1576 🏳 ITALIAN

🏛 Venice; Rome 🎨 oils; fresco 🏛 Madrid: Museo del Prado. Vienna: Kunsthistorisches Museum. London: National Gallery

💲 $12,376,000 in 1991, *Venus and Adonis* (oils)

Named Tiziano Vecellio, but better known by the shortened version. He was the supreme master of the Venetian School and arguably the greatest painter of the High Renaissance and of all time. Probably a pupil of Giovanni Bellini. Also worked with Giorgione. One of the few painters whose reputation has never gone into eclipse or been overlooked.

He had a miraculous ability with rich color and luscious paint, and was constantly innovative, using new subjects or brilliant reinterpretations. Had a Shakespearean response to the human condition, showing us tragedy, comedy, realism, vulgarity, poetry, drama, ambition, frailty, spirituality—and always convincingly. He was a genius at creating a psychological relationship between figures so that the space between them crackles with unspoken messages.

Study the faces and the body language—portraits with a thrilling likeness (who was it I met or saw who was just like that?); also idealization and understanding of the hidden secrets of his subjects' characters. Was he too wise or discreet to tell quite all that he knew? Gods and saints seem to be as much human as divine (and therefore understandable and approachable). Titian never belittled anyone or anything. Superman is the measure of all things.

KEY WORKS *Christ Appearing to the Magdalen (Noli me Tangere)*, c. 1512 (London: National Gallery); *Portrait of Ranuccio Farnese*, 1542 (Washington, DC: National Gallery of Art); *Diana Surprised by Actaeon*, 1556–59 (Edinburgh: National Gallery of Scotland); *The Flaying of Marsyas*, c. 1570–75 (Kromeriz, Czech Republic: Château Archiépiscopal)

Bacchus and Ariadne

Titian c. 1522–23

Titian's crowning achievements are his mythological *poesie* (poems). This early work was one of a series commissioned by Alfonso d'Este, the duke of Ferrara, in northern Italy, to decorate an alabaster pleasure chamber at his country house.

Titian chooses to focus on the electrifying moment when Ariadne, daughter of King Minos of Crete, meets Bacchus, the god of wine, and they fall in love at first sight. He later married her, and she was eventually granted immortality.

There is an overriding sense of ordered chaos about the painting. Although the scene is crowded, Titian has worked out the composition with great care. Bacchus's right hand is at the center of the painting where the diagonals intersect. The revelers are all confined to the bottom right. Bacchus and Ariadne occupy the center and left. Bacchus's feet are still with his companions, but his head and heart have joined Ariadne.

The greatest painter of the Venetian school, Titian was based in Venice for his entire life, inspired by its magical union of light and water. He was one of the most successful painters in history, famous for his ability to inject his pictures with moments of crackling psychological energy of the kind that pervades this work. He was also the Renaissance master of color, and this painting's rich, glowing brilliance reflects its passionate subject.

After falling in love, Bacchus took Ariadne's crown and threw it into the sky where it became the constellation Corona Borealis.

Ariadne has been abandoned by her lover Theseus, whom she helped to escape from the Minotaur's labyrinth

Bacchus's chariot was traditionally pulled by leopards, signifying his triumphant return from his conquest of India. Titian uses artistic license by employing cheetahs for the task

TECHNIQUES

This close-up detail of Ariadne shows Titian relishing two of the special qualities of oil paint: translucent, lustrous color, and fine, precise detail.

Titian's name appears on an urn in Latin—"TICIANUS F[ecit]," or "Titian made this picture." He was one of the first artists to sign his work and was active in seeking to raise the social and intellectual status of painters.

The muscular figure shown wrestling with the snakes is based on a celebrated antique Roman statue of the Trojan priest Laocoön (who was killed by sea serpents), which was unearthed in 1506 (see pages 58–59). The statue's rediscovery caused a sensation, and many artists, including Raphael, incorporated cross-references to it in their work.

A maenad crashes cymbals together in a riotous procession

The longing glance that this maenad exchanges with the satyr contrasts with the intense expressions of the main characters

This drunken satyr, crowned and girdled with vine leaves, waves the leg of a calf above his head

Bacchus and Ariadne

Medium oil on canvas
Dimensions 69 x 75 in
(175 x 190 cm)
Location London: National Gallery

MANNERISM   c. 1520–1600

Mannerism is the name given to the predominant artistic style of the period bridging the High Renaissance and the Baroque. The term comes from the Italian *maniere*, meaning "manner" or "style." The cradle of Mannerism was Rome, where the style was developed by artists influenced by the late works of Raphael and Michelangelo. The movement was finished throughout Europe by c. 1700.

SUBJECTS AND STYLE

Mannerism was a reaction to social, political, and religious upheaval. The art of the period became violent, excitable, unnerving, often with a nightmarish, conflicting style; a huge step away from the harmony of High Renaissance. Key figures include Rosso Fiorentino, Jacopo Pontormo, Tintoretto, El Greco, Agnolo Bronzino, and Girolamo Parmigianino.

After the violent Sack of Rome in 1527, Mannerism spread throughout Italy, as terrified artists fled from the city. The style's subjects include religious

Self-Portrait in a Convex Mirror
Girolamo Parmigianino, c. 1523–24, diameter 9⅝ in (24.4 cm), oil on wood, Vienna: Kunsthistorisches Museum

scenes viewed from an unusual aspect; portraits whose sitters wear unexpected expressions; and mythological or allegorical scenes, often characterized by a sinister form of symbolism.

WHAT TO LOOK FOR

Look for distorted or elongated figures, artificial poses, complicated or obscure subject matter, tense symbolism, deliberate distortion of space, vivid color, unreal textures, deliberate lack of harmony and proportion, voyeuristic sexual scenes. Faces are rich with expression. Figures look deliberately tense or as though suspended halfway through an action. In sculpture, look for sense of movement, realism, exaggerated postures, strongly muscled anatomy. In architecture, look for anticlassicism and distortion of the viewer's expectations.

KEY EVENTS

1520	Death of Raphael. His later works were considered the beginning of Mannerism
1527	Sack of Rome. Spreads Mannerism across Italy and into France
c. 1528	Jacopo Pontormo finishes his *Deposition*, a Florentine altarpiece in the Mannerist style
1534–40	Girolamo Parmigianino paints *The Madonna of the Long Neck* (see page 150)
1541	Birth of El Greco

Cosimo de' Medici (Il Vecchio) *Jacopo Pontormo, 1518, 33¾ x 25⅜ in (86 x 65 cm), tempera on wood, Florence: Galleria degli Uffizi. A posthumous portrait of Cosimo il Vecchio (1389–1464), founder of the Medici dynasty.*

Giulio **Romano**

◯ c. 1496–1546 ▶ ITALIAN

🏛 Rome; Mantua 🖌 chalks; fresco; oils

Also known as Giulio Pippi. Architect
and painter; a major exponent of
Mannerism. Studied under and worked
with Raphael; strongly influenced
by his later style, and also by the work
of Michelangelo. After Raphael's
death, Giulio finished several of his
commissions. Also a pornographer—
designed a series of celebrated and
notorious pornographic engravings.
Threatened with prison in Rome,
Giulio moved to Mantua under
protection of the Gonzaga family;
most famous architectural work
is Mantua's Palazzo del Tè.

In paintings, look for a similar style
to Raphael, but exaggerated; also
look for realism, muscular anatomy,
and a strong sexual overtone. In
architecture, look for deliberate
"mistakes:" missing expected features,
such as central motifs; optical illusions,
for instance, columns that are sturdy
but look ready to tumble; or stonework
left rough, instead of being smoothly
carved and finished.

KEY WORKS *Crowning of the Virgin (Madonna
of Monteluce)*, c. 1505–25 (Rome: Vatican
Museums); *Mary Magdalene Borne by Angels*,
c. 1520 (London: National Gallery); *The
Holy Family*, c. 1520–23 (Los Angeles:
J. Paul Getty Museum); *The Fall of the
Giants*, 1532–34 (Mantua: Palazzo de Tè)

Madonna and Child Giulio Romano, c. 1530–40, 33⅓ x
30⅓ in (105 x 77 cm), oil on wood, Florence: Galleria degli
Uffizi. The Christ child reaches for grapes—a symbolic
reference to the Eucharist, the central Christian sacrament.

Giorgio **Vasari**

◯ 1511–74 ▶ ITALIAN

🏛 Florence 🖌 fresco; oils

He was a Mannerist
painter, architect, writer,
art historian, and
collector. A popular,
entertaining man—and
an inveterate gossip—
whose patrons were
said to have enjoyed
his storytelling ability
as much as his art. Most
famous for his volumes
of biography, *Lives of the
Artists* (1550; reprinted
and extended in 1568),

which was dedicated to Cosimo de'
Medici. Despite inconsistencies, errors,
and an overwhelming bias in favor of
Michelangelo, it remains an important
source for students of Renaissance art.

Vasari's writings have now outshone
his other works, but in his time he was a
highly successful painter, often decorating
the houses of the aristocratic. Also a
respected architect—most famous for
designing the Uffizi art gallery in Florence.

KEY WORKS *Paul III Directing the Continuence
of St. Peter's*, 1544 (Rome: Palazzo della
Cancelleria); Uffizi offices
(finished by others),
1560–80 (Florence);
The Prophet Elisha, c. 1566
(Florence: Galleria degli
Uffizi); *The Attack on the
Porta Camolia at Siena*, 1570
(Florence: Museo Ragazzi)

The Annunciation Giorgio
Vasari, c. 1564–67, 85 x 65⅓ in
(216 x 166cm), oil on panel, Paris:
Musée du Louvre. This intimate
scene formed the center panel of
a triptych for the dominican church
of Santa Maria Novella at Arezzo.

Jacopo **Pontormo**

◔ 1494–1557 ⚑ ITALIAN

🏛 Tuscany 🎨 oils; fresco 🏛 Florence: Galleria degli Uffizi and churches. Paris: Musée du Louvre (for drawings) 💰 $32m in 1989, *Portrait of Duke Cosimo I de' Medici* (oils)

He was also known as Jacopo Carucci. A Florentine, from Pontormo. Nervous, hysterical, solitary, melancholy, slow, capricious, and hypochondriacal, he was also a talented painter (good enough, anyway, to have studied with Leonardo). Taught Bronzino.

He painted altarpieces, religious and secular decorative schemes for churches and villas, and portraits. Took Michelangelo's and Dürer's classicism and energy and contorted them into beguiling works with irrational compositions—figures in complicated but frozen poses—and bright, high-key colors (acid greens, clear blues, and pale pinks). He was consciously radical and experimental—in line with his temperament and the political and social moods of his time. Brilliant drawings. Very good portraits—with

> ## "Sometimes when he went to work, he would fall into such deep thought that he came away at the end of the day without having done anything but think."
>
> GIORGIO VASARI ON JACOPO PONTORMO

elongated and arrogant poses, and sharp observation of character. Pontormo was one of the originators of the wayward style now known as Mannerism. (Like most good artists he did not care what style he painted in—he just got on with it.) Out of fashion in the 18th and 19th centuries, but has returned to favor in the 20th and 21st. (The word "Mannerism" was not invented or defined until the 20th century.)

KEY WORKS *The Visitation*, 1514–16 (Florence: SS. Annunziata); *Deposition*, c. 1528 (Florence: Santa Felicità, Cappella Capponi); *Portrait of Duke Cosimo I de' Medici*, c. 1537 (Malibu:

An Allegory with Venus and Cupid Agnolo Bronzino, c. 1540–50, 57⅔ x 45 in (146.5 x 116.8 cm), oil on panel, London: National Gallery. Designed for King Francis I of France, the meaning of Bronzino's allegory is unclear.

J. Paul Getty Museum); *Portrait of Maria Salviati*, c. 1537 (Florence: Galleria degli Uffizi); *Monsignor della Casa*, c. 1541–44 (Washington, DC: National Gallery of Art)

Agnolo **Bronzino**

◔ 1503–72 ⚑ ITALIAN

🏛 Tuscany 🎨 oils 🏛 Florence: Galleria degli Uffizi; Palazzo Vecchio 💰 $410,750 in 1996, *The Meeting of Joseph and Jacob in Egypt* (drawing)

He was best known for his aloof and icy portraits. Court painter to the Grand Duke of Tuscany. Humble background.

Painted portraits of brittle artificiality—he lived in an age when artifice and striking poses reigned supreme. He sums it up with rare beauty: note the body language of the poses and faces, which communicate such arrogance, contempt, or insolence; and the equally arrogant ease of his technique, with its superb facility, deliberately complex and artificial compositions, and intense, insolent colors.

Look for flesh that seems to be made of porcelain (as smooth as the people he portrays). Notice the elongated faces and bodies, and eyes that can often seem vacant, like those of a child's doll. Look also for more rarely seen allegories and religious works with intricate designs, involving many figures whose poses are deliberately stolen from Michelangelo.

KEY WORKS *A Lady with a Dog*, c. 1529–30 (Frankfurt: Städelsches Kunstinstitut); *The Panciatichi Holy Family*, 1540 (Florence: Galleria degli Uffizi)

Benvenuto **Cellini**

● 1500–71 🅿 ITALIAN

🅿 Italy; France   🖌 sculpture; engraving
🏛 Florence: Museo Nazionale del Bargello

A sculptor and engraver, and pupil of Michelangelo. Unpleasant, arrogant, sadistic, and violent. Exiled from Florence for dueling. Committed more than one murder. Rumored to have crucified a man and watched him die in order to sculpt a realistic Christ on the cross. Many influential patrons, including Francis I and Cosimo de' Medici. Bisexual—imprisoned twice for sodomy, but also fathered four children. Wrote an entertaining autobiography. Many of his famous works are monumental, but these lack the precision and excellence of his smaller pieces, such as Francis I's golden saltcellar.

KEY WORKS *Saltcellar, called the "Saliera,"* 1540–43 (Vienna: Kunsthistorisches Museum); *Nymph of Fontainebleau*, 1542–43 (Paris: Musée du Louvre)

Giambologna

● 1529–1608 🅿 FLEMISH

🅿 Belgium; Italy   🖌 sculpture
🏛 London: Victoria & Albert Museum

Also called Giovanni da Bologna or Jean de Boulogne. Mannerist sculptor; capable of producing both miniatures and monu-mental statues with equal ability. Patronized by the Medici.

Famous for the Fountain of Neptune in Bologna and the equestrian statue of Cosimo de' Medici in Florence. His works were hugely influential on the future of sculpture. Studied in Antwerp before arriving in Italy c. 1550 to study. Lived in Rome before settling in Florence.

KEY WORKS *Samson Slaying a Philistine*, c. 1561–62 (London: Victoria & Albert Museum); *The Fountain of Neptune*, 1563–66 (Bologna: Piazza del Nettuno); *Florence Triumphant over Pisa*, c. 1575 (Florence: Museo Nazionale del Bargello); *Hercules and the Centaur*, 1594–1600 (Florence: Loggia dei Lanzi)

Giovanni Battista **Moroni**

● c. 1525–78 🅿 ITALIAN

🅿 Albino; Bergamo   🖌 oils   🏛 London: National Gallery   💰 $1,101,440 in 1995, *Portrait of Prospero Alessandri* (oils)

Son of an architect. Artist from Bergamo who is best remembered as an accomplished painter of low-key, realist portraits, with good precise detail, in which the sitters are allowed to speak for themselves without too much manipulation by the artist. Had a wide range of sitters, including middle and lower classes. Possessed a strong preference for painting figures silhouetted against a plain background.

KEY WORKS *Portrait of a Gentleman*, c. 1555–60 (London: National Gallery); *Portrait of a Lady*, c. 1555–60 (London: National Gallery); *Portrait of a Man*, mid-1560s (St. Petersburg: Hermitage Museum); *Portrait of a Bearded Man in Black*, 1576 (Boston: Isabella Stewart Gardner Museum)

The Rape of the Sabines
Giambologna, c. 1583, height 163 in (414 cm), bronze, Florence: Galleria dell' Accademia. A brilliant resolution of the problem of uniting several figures in a single sculpture.

The Madonna of the Long Neck Girolamo Francesco Maria Mazzola Parmigianino,1534–40, 84⅗ x 52 in, (215 x 132 cm), oil on canvas, Florence: Galleria degli Uffizi. This work is a union of artificial elegance and spirituality.

Girolamo Francesco Maria Mazzola **Parmigianino**

🌐 1503–40　🇮🇹 ITALIAN

🏛 Parma; Rome; Bologna　🎨 fresco; oils; engravings; drawings　🏛 London: British Museum (drawings)　💰 $1,272,000 in 1995, *Madonna and Child* (oils)

He was short-lived, precocious, much admired ("Raphael reborn") and very influential. From Parma, in northern Italy—like his contemporary, Correggio.

Look for beautifully executed, refined, elegant, contrived, and precious works. He was especially great as a portraitist, projecting a cool, reserved, and enigmatic image. His religious and mythological paintings are a paradoxical combination of real and unreal. His art starts with acute observations from life, which he

then transforms into fantasies— like a musical composer making variations on a theme. He also produced small-scale panel paintings, large frescoes, and brilliant, prolific drawings.

Notice the recurrent bizarre, elongated human figures, their impossibly long necks, and knowing looks (especially in his late work, which was considered very beautiful at the time). Look for the distorted and convoluted perspectives and variety of scales (his style was the epitome of Mannerism). Had a sophisticated line in erotica. His drawings are full of energy, movement, and light; he loved drawing as an activity for its own sake, as well as a tool.

KEY WORKS *Self-Portrait in a Convex Mirror*, c. 1523 (Vienna: Kunsthistorisches Museum); *Vision of St. Jerome*, 1527 (London: National Gallery)

Antonio **Correggio**

🌐 c. 1494–1534　🇮🇹 ITALIAN

🏛 Parma　🎨 oils; drawings　🏛 Parma (churches, public buildings). London: British Museum (drawings)　💰 $322,000 in 1987, *Christ in Glory Flanked by Putti on Clouds* (works on paper)

Once hugely revered and popular (especially in 17th and 18th centuries), and consequently very influential. Now no longer well known: his virtues are completely out of fashion. Most important works are in Parma, northern Italy.

His works are full of genuine charm, intimacy, and tender emotion, and occasional sentimentality. Chose subjects from mythology and the Bible, and had a lyrical and sensitive style; everything (though immensely accomplished and not unambitious) is gentle—light, color, foreshortening. Compositions are complex but satisfying, with easy-to-read subjects displaying pleasing anatomy and relationships, youthful faces, and sweet smiles. Invented the idea of light radiating from the Christ child.

The in-situ decorations in Parma are forerunners of the over-the-top illusionistic decorations in Baroque Rome 100 years later (the link from one to the other was Lanfranco). See how he turns the ceiling into an illusionistic sky and then makes exciting things happen in it (Mantegna did this first and Correggio followed him). The charming, sentimental side derives from Leonardo and influenced French Rococo. Liked wistful faces and idealized profiles. Many fine drawings.

KEY WORKS *The Mystic Marriage of St. Catherine,* c. 1510–15 (Paris: Musée du Louvre); *Judith,* 1512–14 (Strasbourg: Musée des Beaux-Arts); *Venus, Satyr, and Cupid,* 1524–25 (Paris: Musée du Louvre); *Venus with Mercury and Cupid,* c. 1525 (London: National Gallery)

Paris **Bordone**

◔ 1500–71 🇮🇹 ITALIAN

🇮🇹 Italy; France; Germany　🎨 oils　🏛 Venice: Gallerie dell' Accademia

Venetian painter of portraits, religious works, landscapes, and mythological genre scenes. Strongly influenced by Giorgione and his teacher, Titian (despite disliking the latter intensely). Worked for King Francis I of France; important member of the first Fontainebleau School. His works, although facially realistic and finely detailed, demonstrate a problem with anatomy and perspective.

KEY WORKS *Rest on the Flight into Egypt,* 1520–30 (London: Courtauld Institute); *The Presentation of the Ring of St. Mark to the Doge,* c. 1535 (Venice: Galleria dell' Accademia)

Jacopo **Bassano**

◔ c. 1517–92 🇮🇹 ITALIAN

🇮🇹 Bassano; Venice　🎨 oils　🏛 Bassano: Museo Civico　💰 $2,020,144 in 1994, *Two Dogs Resting beside a Treetrunk* (oils)

Best-known member of the prominent Venetian da Ponte family, who lived at Bassano (where grappa is made).

He was a painter of standard religious subjects, chosen for their power and drama. Note how he interpreted them to make the best of his interest in stocky peasants, animals, stormy mountain landscapes, and spectacular lighting.

Note how Bassano packs great drama into small spaces—which is why everyone seems to be in such a hurry, and either

moving into the picture space or trying to get out of it. Beautifully painted hands and arms; striking light; marvelous, urgent handling of paint, which reflects the drama of the scene as though Bassano were part of it.

KEY WORKS *The Good Samaritan,* c. 1550–70 (London: National Gallery); *Sheep and Lamb,* c. 1560 (Rome: Galleria Borghese)

Federico **Barocci**

◔ 1526–1612 🇮🇹 ITALIAN

🇮🇹 Urbino (Italy); Rome　🎨 oils; fresco; chalks　🏛 Urbino　💰 $2,576,000 in 1987, *Madonna del Popolo* (works on paper)

Barocci was an Urbino-based painter of sentimental religious pictures, who suffered from terrible poor health (at times, evident in his work). Sugar-plum colors and soft forms (he was one of the first artists to use chalks), sweetly-faced Madonnas, and well-handled crowds. His work lacks bite, like cheap, sweet wine—all fruit and sugar, without acidity.

KEY WORKS *Rest on the Flight to Egypt,* 1570–73 (Vatican: Pinacoteca); *Madonna del Popolo,* 1576–79 (Florence: Galleria degli Uffizi)

The Circumcision of Christ *Federico Barocci, 1590, 140 x 98⅞ in (356 x 251 cm), oil on canvas, Paris: Musée du Louvre. The significance of the circumcision is that it is the first occasion on which Christ shed his blood.*

Jacopo Robusti **Tintoretto**

● 1518–94 📷 ITALIAN

📷 Venice 🎨 oils; drawings 🏛 Venice: Scuola di San Rocco; Ducal Palace; Accademia
💰 $825,000 in 1994, *The Raising of Lazarus* (oils)

Susanna Bathing *Jacopo Robusti Tintoretto, 1555–56, 57⅓ x 76⅓ in (146.5 x 193.6 cm), oil on canvas, Vienna: Kunsthistorisches Museum.* A popular subject as it provides an excuse for female nudity.

His father was a dyer (*tintore*)—hence his nickname, Tintoretto. Very little is known about his life. Although unpopular and unscrupulous, he was one of the major Venetian painters in the generation following Titian; he is said to have trained briefly with the greatest painter of the Venetian School. Very prolific, he was a formidable draftsman, too.

In his monumental and vast religious works and mythologies, everything was treated with the drama, verve, panache, scale—and sometimes the absurdity—of grand opera. Tintoretto used a model stage and wax figures to design his extraordinary and inventive compositions. His late religious work tended to be gloomy. His thick, hasty brushwork and exciting lighting show his passionate involvement in his creations. He painted portraits of notable Venetians but his busy studio produced many dull efforts.

When you find an extraordinary or off-center composition, try standing or kneeling to one side so that you view the work from an oblique angle: he designed many works to be seen in this way, especially if they were big works for the small or narrow spaces of Venetian churches, where the congregation would be both kneeling and looking up or forward to works hung on the side wall. Poor anatomy in some portraits—hands that don't belong to the body.

KEY WORKS *Summer*, c. 1555 (Washington, DC: National Gallery of Art); *The Woman who Discovers the Bosom*, c. 1570 (Madrid: Museo del Prado); *Christ at the Sea of Galilee*, c. 1575–80 (Washington, DC: National Gallery of Art)

St. George and the Dragon
Jacopo Robusti Tintoretto, c. 1570, 62⅓ x 39⅓ in (158 x 100 cm), oil on canvas, London: National Gallery. Such a small scale is unusual.

Rosso **Fiorentino**
● c. 1494/5–1540 ◪ ITALIAN

▣ Italy; France ◪ oils; fresco;
tempera; stucco ▥ Fontainebleau

Real name, Giovanni Battista di Jacopo.
Unconventional, eccentric painter.
Highly talented early Mannerist and
pupil of Andrea del Sarto. Member of
first Fontainebleau School. Born and
worked in Florence, before moving to
Venice, Rome, and France. Works include
large number of religious scenes (famous
for his *Musical Angel*, now in the Uffizi)
as well as excellent portraits. Also worked
in stucco, decorating the palace in
Fontainebleau with painting and stucco
decorations. Official painter of Francis I
in 1532–1537; died in Paris. Credited
with taking Italian Mannerism to France.

Look for lots of movement, bold colors,
prominent muscles, faces filled with
expression, and dreamlike sequences
that have a strange realism to them.

KEY WORKS *Portrait of a Young Man Holding
a Letter*, 1518 (London: National Gallery);
Musical Angel, c. 1520 (Florence: Galleria
degli Uffizi); *The Virgin and Child with Angels*,
c. 1522 (St. Petersburg: Hermitage Museum)

Francesco **Primaticcio**
● c. 1504–70 ◪ ITALIAN

▣ Italy; France ◪ oils; fresco; stucco
▥ Château de Fontainebleau ⚡ $424,600
in 1990, *Ulysses Shooting through the Rings*
(works on paper)

Painter, born and trained in Bologna.
Worked with Giulio Romano in Mantua.
In 1532, he moved to France under
patronage of Francis I. Became assistant to
Rosso Fiorentino and appointed official art
buyer to the king. Settled in Fontainebleau
(and died in France), but returned to
Italy regularly on art-buying trips. After
death of Fiorentino, Primaticcio took
over as leader of Fontainebleau School.
After death of Francis I, worked for
Henry II as Surveyor of Works.

Look for paintings and stucco, in
high relief, characterized by sensuality,
overcrowded scenes, tiny heads, and
elongated, elegant limbs. Influenced
by Mannerism, Michelangelo, Cellini,
and Correggio; look for anatomical
correctness, but over-muscled figures.

KEY WORKS *The Rape of Helen*, 1530–39 (County
Durham, UK: Bowes Museum); *Study of God*,
1555 (Los Angeles: J. Paul Getty Museum)

FONTAINEBLEAU
c. 1530–1560 & c. 1589–1610

The royal palace at Fontainebleau,
near Paris, fostered two brilliant schools
of decoration and architecture. The
first—and most influential—was
established by King Francis I in the
1530s. Francis (1514–47) employed a
variety of artists and artisans: painters,
poets, designers, sculptors, writers,
printmakers, architects, stucco workers,
gold- and silversmiths, and textile
workers. Most of the early workers,
such as Fiorentino and Primaticcio,
came from Italy, thereby spreading
Italianate art to northern Europe.

The second Fontainebleau School was
established by Henry IV in 1589, after
a period of great social and political
unrest in France. Principal painters
included Toussaint Dubreuil, Martin
Fréminet, and Ambroise Dubois.

***Former apartments of Anne de Pisseleu,
Duchesse d'Étampes*** Francesco Primaticcio,
1533–44, Château de Fontainebleau. The
influence of the Mannerist style seen here
spread quickly throughout northern Europe.

François **Clouet**

◉ c. 1510/16–72   ⚑ FRENCH

🇫🇷 France   🎨 oils; drawings
🏛 Chantilly (France): Musée Condé

Portrait painter, miniaturist, and draftsman; from family of painters. Often confused with his father, Jean Clouet, who trained him; both were favorites of Francis I and both nicknamed "Janet" or "Jehannet." Ran large, successful studio. Appointed court painter to Francis I in 1541 and remained so for Henry II, Francis II, and Charles IX; retired in 1570. Strongly influenced by the Italianate paintings of first Fontainebleau School. Painted portraits of the nobility as well as allegorical landscapes. Famous portrait of Francis I —lavish with gold—has been attributed to both François and Jean Clouet.

Look for meticulous detail, rich decoration, attention to contemporary fashions, natural-looking facial features, and realistic expression.

KEY WORKS *François I, King of France*, c. 1540 (Florence: Galleria degli Uffizi); *Pierre Quthe*, 1562 (Paris: Musée du Louvre); *Lady in her Bath*, c. 1570 (Washington, DC: National Gallery of Art)

Charles IX *François Clouet, 1550–74, 9⅞ x 8¼ in (25 x 21 cm), oil on wood, Vienna: Kunsthistorisches Museum.* At the time of painting, the young French king was only aged 11, but had already been reigning for a year. Clouet's portrait invests the young face with firmness and maturity, while retaining the bloom of youth.

Niccolò dell'**Abbate**

◉ c. 1512–71   ⚑ ITALIAN

🇮🇹 Modena; Bologna; France   🎨 oils; stucco
🏛 Bologna: Palazzo Pozzi   💲 $134,400 in 1998, *Portrait of a Young Man Wearing a Plumed Hat* (oils)

Italian-born decorator of palaces and portrait painter. He trained in his birthplace, Modena, and later developed a mature style in Bologna. He had a refined, elaborate, mannered, and artificial style playing with fantasy landscapes and themes of love. Settled in France in 1552 to work for the royal court. He was a key link figure between Correggio and Parmigianino (who influenced Niccolò with his elegant figure style), and the French classical landscape painters, such as Claude and Poussin (whom Niccolò influenced). He also painted portraits in both Italy and France.

KEY WORKS *Landscape with the Death of Eurydice*, c. 1552 (London: National Gallery); *The Continence of Scipio*, c. 1555 (Paris: Musée du Louvre)

Toussaint **Dubreuil**

◉ 1561–1602   ⚑ FRENCH

🇫🇷 France   🎨 fresco; oils

Dubreuil was a painter and draftsman who had a strong association with the second Fontainebleau School. He was apprenticed to Médéric Fréminet, father of Martin Fréminet. Appointed Premier Painter to Henry IV. Worked for the king in Fontainebleau and Paris; unknown to have left France. Little of his work survives, but his reputation as a talented painter remains intact.

Dubreuil designed large-scale tapestries and painted murals and frescoes, mainly of mythological and classical subjects. He is best known for the frescoes to be found in the Tuileries Palace, Paris. In his lifetime, he was famed for painting murals in the Louvre—all destroyed by fire in 1661. Credited with forging the link between Mannerism and Classicism.

KEY WORKS *Angélique and Médor*, 16th century (Paris: Musée du Louvre); *Dicé gives a Banquet for Francus*, c. 1594–1602 (Paris: Musée du Louvre); *Hyante and Climène at their Toilette*, c. 1594–1602 (Paris: Musée du Louvre); *Hyante and Climène offering a Sacrifice to Venus*, c. 1594–1602 (Paris: Musée du Louvre)

El Greco

🌊 1541–1614 🏛 GREEK/SPANISH

🗺 Crete; Italy; Toledo (Spain)
🎨 oils; sculpture 🏛 Madrid:
Museo del Prado. Toledo: Cathedral;
Museo del Greco 💰 $5,285,000
in 2000, *Christ on the Cross* (oils)

The Resurrection El Greco, 1584–94,
108¼ x 50 in (275 x 127 cm), oil on
canvas, Madrid: Museo del Prado. This
painting is a good example of the
visionary style that so displeased the
Spanish monarch Philip II, causing El
Greco to lose all of his royal patronage.

Real name Domenikos
Theotocopoulos. He was
born in Crete. Trained in
Venice but worked in Spain,
hence the name El Greco
(the Greek). At once intense,
arrogant, intellectual, and
spiritual. A one-off, with
a bewilderingly wide range
of sources. Favored by
Philip II of Spain until he
fell out of favor in 1582.

Art historians can have a good time
trying to piece together the sources:
directly applied color (Titian); writhing
figures (Michelangelo and Parmigianino),
fragmented spaces and jewel-like acid
colors (Byzantine mosaics and icons).
But to touch the real El Greco,
you have to forget this, and enter
the spiritual world of visionary
Christianity. Only then will
you appreciate his genius
and the significance of his
superb technical skills.

The elongated figures,
hands, feet, and faces
are not intended to
describe; rather to
reveal the inner
spirit. The soaring
compositions are
about the ascent
from the material
to the divine. The
strange colors are
a reflection and

revelation of spiritual light.
He believed that other-
worldly appearances were a
better aid to devotion than
naturalism. El Greco excelled
as a portraitist, painting
mainly ecclesiastics or
gentlemen; his works reveal
the essence and idea of a
person rather than a strict
likeness. Look for the thrilling
draftsmanship and the tense probing
line that outlines his forms.

KEY WORKS *St. Joseph and the Christ Child*,
1597–99 (Toledo: Museo de Santa Cruz);
*Madonna and Child with St. Martina and
St. Agnes*, 1597–99 (Washington, DC:
National Gallery of Art); *Laocoön*, c. 1610
(Washington, DC: National Gallery of Art)

*The Burial of Count
Orgaz, from a Legend
of 1323* El Greco, 1586–88,
192 x 141¾ in (488 x 360 cm),
oil on canvas, Toledo: Church
of Santo Tomé. The faces
of the mourners for the
saintly Count are clearly
portraits of contemporary
gentlemen of Toledo. The
boy, who is standing in the
bottom left-hand corner, may
be El Greco's eldest son.

Maerten van **Heemskerck**

● 1498–1574　🇳🇱 DUTCH

🎨 Haarlem; Italy　🖌 oils; engravings
🏛 Cambridge: Fitzwilliam Museum
💰 $652,219 in 1987, *Half-length
Portrait of a Woman* (oils)

Leading Haarlem painter of his day.
His works were portraits, altarpieces,
and mythologies. Van Heemskerck
was totally transformed by a visit to
Rome, 1532–36. Look for classical
profiles; Michelangelesque, muscular
figures; emotional (unrealistic) faces,
gestures, and colors (hot reds, strong
pinks, turquoise blue). Adopted Italian
idealization rather than northern realism.

KEY WORKS *The Crucifixion*, c. 1530 (Detroit
Institute of Arts); *Portrait of a Lady with a
Spindle and Distaff*, c. 1531 (Madrid: Museo
Thyssen-Bornemisza)

Pieter **Aertsen**

● c. 1508–75　🇳🇱 DUTCH

🎨 Antwerp　🖌 oils　💰 $317,042 in 1998,
Parable of Royal Wedding (oils)

Painter of altarpieces and large-scale
peasant subjects. Monumental genre
and still-life scenes (such as a butcher's
shop) that have a religious subject hiding
in the background. Good at modeling
with light in the Italian manner. Likes
movement. A Bruegel without the humor
and moral observation; a Rubens without
the panache and power.

KEY WORKS *Market Scene*, c. 1550 (Munich: Alte
Pinakothek); *Butcher's Stall with the Flight into
Egypt*, 1551 (University of Uppsala, Sweden);
Cook in front of the Stove, 1559 (Bruges: Musées
Royaux des Beaux-Arts)

Family Group *Maerten van Heemskerck, 1530,
45½ x 55 in (118 x 140 cm), oil on wood, Kassel
(Germany): Staatliche Museen. This portrait is in a
vigorous and relatively sober style and dates to before
Heemskerck's visit to Rome. He spent most of his life
in Haarlem and became Dean of the Painters' Guild.*

> ## "There are countries where they paint worse than in Flanders, but Flemish painting attempts to do so many things well that it does none well."
>
> MICHELANGELO

Marten de **Vos**

● c. 1531–1603　🇧🇪 FLEMISH

🎨 Antwerp; Italy　🖌 oils　🏛 Bruges: Musées
Royaux des Beaux-Arts　💰 $210,000 in 2002,
*St. John the Baptist and St. John Evangelist.
St. Lawrence and St. Catherine* (oils, a pair)

Leading painter in Antwerp. He
combined Flemish realism and detail
with Italianate subjects, grandeur, and
idealization (visited Rome, Florence,
and Venice 1552–58). Painted altarpieces
(vertical, with elegant, elongated figures);
portraits (worldly Flemish burghers
and plain backgrounds); and
mythologies (large in scale,
ambitious, and decorative).

KEY WORKS *St. Paul Stung by a Viper on the
Island of Malta*, c. 1566 (Paris: Musée
du Louvre); *Antoine Anselme and his
Family*, 1577 (Bruges: Musées Royaux
des Beaux-Arts); *Abduction of Europa*,
c. 1590 (Bilbao: Museo de Bellas Artes)

The Adoration of the Shepherds
*Pieter Aertsen (studio of), 16th century,
33¼ x 44¾ in (84.5 x 113.7 cm), oil on panel,
Private Collection. Many Aertsen altarpieces
were destroyed in the Reformation riots.*

Pieter **Bruegel** (the elder)

● c. 1525–69 🎨 FLEMISH

📍 Antwerp; France; Italy; Brussels 🎨 oils; drawings 🏛 Vienna: Kunsthistorisches Museum 💰 $4.56m in 2002, *Drunkard Pushed into the Pigsty* (oils)

Nicknamed "Peasant" Bruegel because of the subject matter of his paintings, not his character. Leading Flemish artist of his day whose subjects reflected contemporary religious and social issues. Paved the way for Dutch masters of the 17th century. Spelled his name Brueghel until 1559, then dropped the "h."

Brilliant works and accurately observed commentaries on the appearance and behavior of the ordinary people of his day—like a first-rate stage play or TV soap opera. They are powerful because, as well as enjoying the existence and minutiae of his day and age, we can recognize ourselves—especially when he illustrates human follies, greed, and misdemeanors. Like all great artists, Bruegel speaks simultaneously about the personal and the universal.

Bruegel's bird's-eye views place us outside his world (we look down, god-like, distanced, and superior); then by

Hunters in the Snow—February Pieter Bruegel (the elder), 1565, 46 x 63¾ in (117 x 162 cm), oil on canvas Vienna: Kunsthistorisches Museum. This famous series of depictions was commissioned by Niclaes Jonghelinck.

the fineness and charm of detail he draws us into it—we are simultaneously in his world and apart from it. Clear outlines and detail lead the eye through each picture. Early work (from Antwerp) is busy and anecdotal; later work (from Brussels) is simpler and more consciously and artistically composed and organized. Saw the Alps in 1552–53 on his way to Italy.
KEY WORKS *Netherlandish Proverbs*, 1559 (Berlin: Staatliche Museum); *The Gloomy Day*, 1565 (Vienna: Kunsthistorisches Museum); *The Wedding Feast*, c. 1567–68 (Madrid: Museo del Prado)

The Tower of Babel (detail) Pieter Bruegel (the elder), 1563, 45 x 61 in (114 x 155 cm), oil on panel, Vienna: Kunsthistorisches Museum. An attempt to build a tower so tall it would reach up to Heaven.

Albrecht **Altdorfer**

● c. 1480–1538 **GERMAN**

Austria; Regensburg (Germany) oils; engravings Munich: Alte Pinakothek

$7,021 in 1998, *Jahel and Sisera* (woodcut)

Mainly a painter of altarpieces. Their most notable features are strange, visionary landscapes with eerie light effects, and in which wild nature is in control, with man taking second place. Small output. Gave up painting to go into local government.

KEY WORKS *Christ Taking Leave of his Mother,* c. 1520 (London: National Gallery); *St. Florian Altar,* c. 1520 (Linz, Austria: Monastery of St. Florian; Florence: Galleria degli Uffizi)

Bartholomeus **Spranger**

● 1546–1611 **FLEMISH**

Belgium; Italy; France; Austria; Czech Republic fresco; oils; drawings

Painter, draftsman, and etcher; exponent of late Mannerist style. Key figure of Northern European Mannerism. Born in Antwerp, worked in France, then moved on to Rome, where he studied under Taddeo Zuccaro. He was appointed court painter to the Pope in 1570. In Vienna, he worked for Emperor Maximilian II. Then he moved on to Prague, where he stayed for the rest of his life. Became court painter to Emperor Rudolf II in 1581. His works were mainly of mythological or allegorical subjects. Very popular in northern Europe and hugely influential on Haarlem school.

Works are typical of the late Mannerist period. Look for a glut of nudes, improbable poses, a sensual style, luminosity of skin tone, and exaggerated features. His paintings are also filled with rich colors, finely executed small details, such as jewels, fruit, and flowers, and detailed decorations, such as on background furniture.

KEY WORKS *Christ, the Saviour of the World,* 16th century (Montauban, France: Musée Ingres); *Diana and Actaeon,* c. 1590–95 (New York: Metropolitan Museum of Art); *The Adoration of the Kings,* c. 1595 (London: National Gallery); *Venus and Adonis,* c. 1597 (Vienna: Kunsthistorisches Museum); *Allegory of Justice and of Prudence,* c. 1599 (Paris: Musée du Louvre)

Beheading of Saint Catherine Albrecht Altdorfer, *c. 1505–10, 22 x 14⅛ in (56 x 36 cm), oil on panel, Vienna: Kunsthistorisches Museum.* Altdorfer appealed to German humanists wanting to revive native German traditions.

Adam **Elsheimer**

● 1578–1610 **GERMAN**

Venice; Rome oils; engravings; drawings Munich: Alte Pinakothek $450,000 in 1990, *St. Jerome in the Wilderness* (oils)

Popular, early practitioner of small-scale, ideal landscapes. Spent his working life in Italy. Very influential on artists such as Rubens, Rembrandt, and Claude. Lazy — should have painted more pictures.

Full of the kind of remarkable precision and detail that you see when looking down the wrong end of a telescope. All his works are painted on copper plates, which allows such fine detail (he must have had brushes with only one bristle).

Often used several sources of light in one picture, such as sunset and moon, daylight and torchlight. Painted charming trees, which look like parsley.

KEY WORKS *Saint Christopher,* 1598–99 (St. Petersburg: Hermitage Museum); *The Baptism of Christ,* c. 1599 (London: National Gallery); *St. Paul on Malta,* 1600 (London: National Gallery); *Nymph Fleeing Satyrs,* c. 1605 (Berlin: Staatliche Museum); *The Flight into Egypt,* 1609 (Munich: Alte Pinakothek)

Giuseppe **Arcimboldo**

● 1527–93 🎏 ITALIAN

🏙 Milan; Vienna; Prague   🎨 oils
🏛 Stockholm: Nationalmuseum   💰 $1.3m
in 2000, *Reversible Anthropomorphic Portrait of a Man Composed of Fruit* (oils)

Best known for fantastical faces and bodies made up of vegetables, trees, fruits, fish, and the like—he had the type of artistic curiosity produced in times of cultural and political upheaval (as much in the late 20th century as in the late

16th century). Worked mostly in Prague for Rudolf II, who was addicted to alchemy and astrology. Arcimboldo returned to Milan in 1587.

KEY WORKS *Fire*, 1566 (Vienna: Kunsthistorisches Museum); *The Librarian*, 1566 (Balsta, Sweden: Skoklosters Slott); *Spring, Summer, Autumn,* and *Winter* (series of four), 1573 (Paris: Musée du Louvre)

Water Giuseppe Arcimboldo, 1566, 26⅛ x 20 in (66.5 x 50.5 cm), oil on canvas, Vienna: Kunsthistorisches Museum. The Four Elements—Earth, Air, Water, and Fire—were popular subjects for series paintings.

Lady with a Squirrel and a Starling
*Hans Holbein (the younger), c. 1526–28,
22 x 15⅓ in (56 x 39 cm), oil on panel,
London: National Gallery.* The animals in
the painting may allude to the the family
coat of arms of the sitter, Anne Lovell.

system. Also produced more
informal and flattering (but
never too relaxed) soft-focus
images of high society that
surrounded the court.

Note the way he draws and
models with light (as does a
photographer); the remarkable
sharp focus detail (stubble on
a chin, fur); intense lighting;
wonderful feel for structure of
a face and personality inside
it. Portraits before mid-1530s
are full of objects (sometimes
symbolic); later they are
flattened designs on a dark
background (like postage stamp
images?). The famous album
of 80 drawings at Windsor
contains the lovely, soft-focus,
informal portraits.

KEY WORKS *Portrait of a Woman*,
c. 1532–35 (Detroit Institute
of Arts); *The Ambassadors*, 1533
(London: National Gallery);
Christina of Denmark, c. 1538 (London: National
Gallery); *Edward VI as a Child*, c. 1538
(Washington, DC: National Gallery of Art)

Hans **Holbein** (the younger)

● c. 1497/8 – 1543   🏴 GERMAN/SWISS

🇩🇪 Germany; Switzerland; France; England
🎨 oils; drawings   🏛 Windsor Castle (England):
Royal Collection   💰 $1,957,500 in 1984,
Portrait of a Scholar (watercolors)

Painter and designer, chiefly celebrated
as one of the greatest of all portraitists.
Holbein was forced to leave Switzerland
because of the Reformation. He came
to England and established himself
successfully as the propaganda portrait
painter of the era of Henry VIII. He
died of the plague, and very little is
known about his life.

He was famous above all for his portraits
(many of his early religious works were
destroyed during the Reformation). There
are interesting parallels with official court
photographs of the mid-20th century, such
as the work of Cecil Beaton: masterly,
memorable, posed, officially commissioned
images—in sharp focus—of the monarch
and ruling officials, which are self-chosen
icons of the political and constitutional

Portrait of a Youth in a Broad-brimmed Hat *Hans
Holbein (the younger), c. 1524–26, 9⅓ x 8 in (24.5 x 20.2 cm)
chalk on paper, Derbyshire (UK): Chatsworth House.* The
artist learned his three-color pastel technique in France.

Hans **Eworth**

◕ c. 1520–c. 1574 Ⓝ FLEMISH

Ⓝ Netherlands; England 🎨 oils 🏛 London:
Courtauld Institute 💰 $91,800 in 1984, *Portrait
of Margaret Clifford* (oils)

Antwerp-born. Arrived in England in
1549. Difficult to identify. Look for very
pale faces with tight, hard eyes; carefully
observed and outlined figures, encased
in lavish costumes and jewelry.

***Queen Mary I** Hans Eworth, 1554, London: Society
of Antiquaries. Painted shortly after her marriage to
Philip II of Spain, Mary wears his gift of the famous
Peregrina pearl.*

KEY WORKS *Sir John Luttrell*, 1550 (Private
Collection); *Portrait of Elizabeth Roydon, Lady
Golding*, 1563 (London: Tate Collection); *Portrait
of a Lady*, c. 1565–68 (London: Tate Collection)

Nicholas **Hilliard**

◕ 1547–1619 Ⓝ BRITISH

Ⓝ England; France 🎨 watercolors
🏛 London: Victoria & Albert Museum
💰 $292,000 in 2002, *Portrait of
a Lady Wearing a Black Dress
and Hat* (miniature)

The son of an Exeter
goldsmith, he trained as a
jeweler. Principal portrait
painter during the reign of
Elizabeth I. Hilliard was especially

> **"A vacant mind invites
> dangerous inmates, as a
> deserted mansion tempts
> wandering outcasts to enter
> and take up their abode in
> its desolate apartments."**
>
> NICHOLAS HILLIARD

known for miniatures, which he produced
in quantity to pay the bills for a large
family. His reputation extended to
France, which he visited c. 1577–78.
  Look for innovative oval format,
symbolism, French elegance, fine outline.
Life-size portraits of Elizabeth I exist.
KEY WORKS *Queen Elizabeth I*, c. 1575 (London:
National Portrait Gallery); *Robert Dudley, Earl
of Leicester*, 1576 (London: National Portrait
Gallery); *Young Man Among Roses*, c. 1590
(London: Victoria & Albert Museum)

Isaac **Oliver**

◕ c. 1565–1617 Ⓝ BRITISH

Ⓝ England; Venice 🎨 watercolors; drawings
🏛 London: Victoria & Albert Museum 💰 $60,000
in 1996, *Young Gentleman in Black Silk Doublet,
Black Earring* (watercolor miniature)

Son of a Huguenot goldsmith who settled
in England in 1568. Painter of miniatures
(portraits, and mythological and religious
images). Was a pupil of Hilliard, but
adopted a different style, with strong
shadows. His life revolved around the
courts of Elizabeth I and James I. A
visit to Venice in 1590s led to
softer style and richer colors.
KEY WORKS *Charity*, c. 1596–1617
(London: Tate Collection);
*Lodovick Stuart, 1st Duke of
Richmond, and 2nd Duke
of Lennox*, c. 1605
(London: National
Portrait Gallery)

***Portrait of Robert
Devereux, Earl of
Essex** Isaac Oliver,
c. 1590s, miniature,
watercolor on vellum,
Beauchamp Collection, UK.
Devereux (1566–1601) was
a favorite of Queen Elizabeth I.*

THE BAROQUE ERA
c. 1600 – 1700

"Baroque" was first used disparagingly to describe something artificially extravagant and complex. Only relatively recently has it been used to denote the art and architecture of the 17th century—an era that saw the creation of some of the most grandiose and spectacular buildings, paintings, and sculpture in the history of art.

The spectacular art and architecture of the period was reminiscent of grand opera, an art form that developed in 17th-century Italy. Artists too assumed a grandeur not known before, sometimes adding to their role of creative practitioner that of impresario, art dealer, courtier, and diplomat.

IDEOLOGICAL DIVISION

The reasons for this extravagance lay in societies pulled apart by deep ideological and religious divisions. On one side were those fiercely committed to the absolute authority of the Catholic Church and the "Divine Right of Kings" with their requirements of unquestioning obedience. On the other were those

Fountain of the Four Rivers Gianlorenzo Bernini, 1651, marble and travertine, Piazza Navona, Rome. The magnificence of Bernini's sculptural projects was inspired by a belief that, through art, he was expressing the absolute authority of God and the Catholic Church.

committed to Protestant reform and a belief in self-determination, personally and nationally. The former used art without restraint to overwhelm and impress, creating such wonders as the Baroque churches and fountains of Rome and the palace of Versailles outside Paris. The latter disapproved of all worldly show, destroying religious art, whitewashing the interiors of churches and dispersing royal and noble collections.

The consequences of this ideological struggle are most clearly seen in three places. In England, Charles I's unyielding insistence on his divine right to rule led to his execution in 1649, the dispersal of his art treasures, and the institution of a Puritan Commonwealth that rejected any form of aesthetic experience. In the Netherlands, the Habsburgs attempted to stem the tide of Protestant revolt, finally conceding and then formally recognizing a compromise that split the

Low Countries in two: a Protestant north (the Netherlands) and a Catholic south (Flanders). The new republic of the Netherlands, mercantile and bourgeois, was able to strengthen and

The Hanging, after engraving by Jacques Callot (1592–1635), oil on canvas, Clermont-Ferrand: Musée Bargoin. Callot's series of engravings "The Miseries of War" illustrated many of the horrors of the Thirty Years' War.

expand its trading empire, especially in the East Indies. This new wealth funded a magnificent flowering of art. What the Dutch wanted were landscapes, seascapes, still lifes, and genre scenes of everyday life to hang on the walls of their townhouses, and

which they could buy and sell like other commercial goods.

RISE OF FRANCE

In central Europe the Austrian Habsburgs faced another Protestant revolt, this time in Bohemia. By 1618, this had given rise to general warfare, with other powers sucked in according to their religious affiliations: the Baltic powers, Denmark, and Sweden, on the Protestant side against the Habsburgs and their Catholic allies. Religion was the starting point but by the 1630s the war had become a trial of strength between France and the Habsburgs. The Thirty Years' War, as it was afterward known, was the most brutal yet fought in Europe, carving a swathe of destruction across Germany and leaving perhaps one million dead. In some areas, 40 percent of the population was killed. It ended in 1648, with France emerging as the most powerful state in Europe. This new dominance was brilliantly exploited by Louis XIV, whose direct personal

Chapelle Royale, Versailles Louis XIV's chapel was begun by royal architect Jules Hardouin-Mansart in 1689. During services the upper balcony was reserved for the royal family, while the nobles stood below.

TIMELINE: 14TH—15TH CENTURY

1609 Invention of telescope (Netherlands); Dutch Revolt ended by treaty between Spain and Netherlands
1618 Start of 30 Years' War
1630 Foundation of English Massachusetts Bay colony
1648 Treaty of Westphalia ends 30 Years' War

1600   **1620**   **1640**

1621 Hostilities renewed between Spain and Netherlands
1633 Galileo condemned for heresy by the Inquisition
1636 French intervene in 30 Years' War
1649 Execution of Charles I in England

SCIENCE IN THE 17TH CENTURY

In the course of the 17th century, European monarchs, as well as being generous patrons of the arts, also became patrons of the sciences, in particular astronomy and physics. State backing was given to science in England in 1662 when the Royal Society was established. A French equivalent, the Académie Royale des Sciences, followed in 1666. The century was characterized by an accelerating scientific revolution. The telescope, the microscope, the slide rule, the thermometer, and the barometer were all invented before 1650. As early as 1609, the Italian scientist Galileo Galilei used a telescope to discover four moons of Jupiter. He made other important observations that confirmed the Copernican theory of the solar system. By the end of the century, Sir Isaac Newton in England had laid the theoretical foundations of the new science of physics.

Isaac Newton's telescope
As well as discovering the laws of motion and gravity, Newton wrote a comprehensive treatise on optics.

Visit of Louis XIV to the Académie Royale des Sciences in 1667
By the mid-17th century, it was clear that scientific advances would play a key role in the development of states. Official patronage duly followed.

reign lasted 54 years. He asserted his authority by controlling his court from his own vast creation, the largest palace in Europe, Versailles. His brand of absolutist rule—centralizing and martial, visually spectacular and rigidly ceremonial—created a style of kingship that was increasingly imitated at other European courts, notably by Peter the Great in Russia.

A NEW STYLE OF MONARCHY

In the end the extravagance of Baroque art and architecture and the beliefs that it sought to promote were unsustainable. The future would lie not with unquestioning faith and obedience but with self-reliance. By then end of the century Spain was in decline politically and economically, central Europe was exhausted and devastated, and the Papacy forced to accept that it would have to live with rival Christian churches. France continued to prosper, but the soon-to-reemerge power was England, which was evolving a new form of constitutional monarchy and which was destined to supersede the Netherlands as the world's leading trading nation.

1659 Treaty of Pyrenees confirms French dominance in western Europe	**1667** Completion of Bernini's Piazza, St. Peter's, Rome	**1683** Ottoman threat contained after siege of Vienna	**1688** The Glorious Revolution in England: overthrow of James II

1660	**1680**	**1700**

1660 Restoration of monarchy in England	**1662** Royal Society established in England	**1678** Louis XIV initiates major building works at Versailles	**1685** Edict of Nantes revoked: French Protestants face renewed persecution	**1689** Accession of Peter the Great, Russia	**1699** Habsburgs recover Hungary from Ottomans

1694 Bank of England founded

Guido **Reni**

- 1575–1642   ITALIAN
- Bologna; Rome   oils; fresco
- Bologna: Pinacoteca $2.44m in 1985, *David with the Head of Goliath* (oils)

One of the principal Bolognese masters. Greatly inspired by Raphael, he was much admired in the 17th and 18th centuries, and much despised in the 20th.

THE SCHOOL OF BOLOGNA   c. 1550–1650

Bologna never achieved the artistic pre-eminence of Florence, Venice, or Rome, but nonetheless this ancient university town made a significant contribution to the arts of Italy and Europe. Situated midway between Florence and Venice, the School of Bologna drew inspiration from both, creating its own distinctive style. In particular, Bolognese artists tried to synthesize Florentine classicism with Venetian theatricality, seen most successfully in the works of Carracci, Domenichino, Guercino, and Reni. The Bolognese School style was much imitated in the 18th century, but has been despised for most of the 20th.

Atalanta and Hippomenes Guido Reni, c.1612, 206 x 297 cm (81 x 117 in), oil on canvas, Madrid: Museo del Prado. Atalanta the virgin huntress would challenge her suitors to a race in which losing was punishable by death. Hippomenes distracted her by dropping three golden apples given to him by Venus and thus overtook her.

Reni's style was much influenced by his visits to Rome, the first of which came soon after 1660. His images of intense and idealized (unreal and artificial) emotional experiences are usually religious. His mythological works do not have the same levels of intensity, but are highly polished pieces. He himself was very beautiful but remained celibate—two qualities that are reflected in his paintings, which convey a remote and unapproachable beauty. Are they too self-consciously slick, posed, and theatrical for popular 20th-century taste?

Look for eyeballs rolling up to heaven (as a means of signaling intensity of feeling), and surprisingly subtle and sensitive paint handling.

KEY WORKS *Deianeira Abducted by the Centaur Nessus*, 1621 (Paris: Musée du Louvre); *Susannah and the Elders*, c. 1620 (London: National Gallery); *Lady with a Lapis Lazuli Bowl*, c. 1630s (Birmingham: Museums and Art Gallery); *St. Mary Magdalene*, c. 1634–42 (London: National Gallery)

Annibale **Carracci**

● 1560–1609 📖 ITALIAN

📖 Bologna; Rome 🎨 fresco; oils
🏛 Rome: Farnese Gallery. Windsor Castle
(England): Royal Collection (for drawings)
💰 $2m in 1994, *Boy Drinking* (oils)

Born in Bologna, lived in Rome from
1595. Most talented member of a brilliant
trio (with brother Agostino and cousin
Ludovico). Revived Italian art from
doldrums that followed Michelangelo.
Victim of change of fashion from
around 1850.

The arguments for his greatness are
that he is as good as Raphael (brilliant
draftsmanship, observation of nude,
harmonious compositions); as good as
Michelangelo (anatomical knowledge,
heroic idealization—his frescoes in
the Farnese Palace are on a par with
Michelangelo's in the Sistine Chapel);
and as good as Titian (richness of color).
He was original: he invented caricature
and his early genre scenes and ideal
landscapes are full of fresh observation.
Influenced Rubens and Poussin.

The Holy Women at Christ's Tomb Annibale
Carracci, c. 1597–98, 47½ x 57½ in (121 x 145.5 cm),
oil on canvas, St. Petersburg: Hermitage Museum.
All the figures are from studies of live models.

The arguments against his greatness
are that he was too eclectic—merely a
plagiarist with no originality, the whole
less than the individual parts. Look who
his followers were—the awful Bolognese
School. But, look for a large number of

Fishing Annibale Carracci, 1585–88, 53½ x 99½ in
(136 x 253 cm), oil on canvas, Paris: Musée du Louvre.
He created the ideal landscape, in which a noble classical
vision of nature becomes the setting for a narrative.

wonderful drawings, full of humor and
personal touches. He had a strong belief
in drawing and observing from life as
an answer to sterile academicism—to
the point of establishing a school to teach
it—a belief shared in a different way by
Impressionists, especially Cézanne. He
gave up painting almost entirely in 1606.
KEY WORKS *The Butcher's Shop*, 1580s (Oxford:
Christ Church Picture Gallery); *Domine Quo
Vadis?*, 1601–02 (London: National Gallery)

The Last Sacrament of St. Jerome Domenichino, 1614, oil on canvas, Rome: Vatican Museums. St. Jerome was one of the four fathers of the Christian Church. The Host is the symbolic center of the scene.

Domenichino
◉ 1581–1641　🏳 ITALIAN

🏛 Bologna; Rome; Naples　🎨 fresco; oils; drawings　🏛 Windsor Castle (England)
💰 $3m in 2000, *Rebuke of Adam and Eve* (oils)

Bologna-born, worked in Rome and Naples. Small in stature (Domenichino means "little Dominic"). Look for idealization that is influenced by Raphael and antiquity (unlike his contemporary Caravaggio). Harmonious classical landscapes with mythological themes. Figures with expressive gestures that symbolize emotion but do not embody expression. He was a fine draftsman (Windsor Castle's Royal Library has a superb collection of his drawings) and an excellent portraitist.

KEY WORKS *Monsignor Agucchi*, c. 1610 (York: City Art Gallery); *Landscape with Tobias Laying Hold of the Fish*, c. 1617–18 (London: National Gallery); *St. Cecilia with an Angel Holding Music*, 1620 (Paris: Musée du Louvre)

Giovanni **Lanfranco**
◉ 1582–1647　🏳 ITALIAN

🏛 Parma; Rome; Naples　🎨 fresco; oils
🏛 Rome: Churches of S. Andrea della Valle and S. Carlo ai Catinari. Naples: Chapel of S. Gennaro (Duomo); Church of S. Martino
💰 $822,331 in 2003, *Crucifixion* (oils)

Key figure who established the enthusiasm for large-scale illusionistic decoration of churches and palaces in Rome and Naples. He painted crowds of figures on clouds floating on ceilings, with extreme foreshortening and brilliant light. Huge scale, excessive, inspiring—his work needs to be seen in situ.

KEY WORKS *Elijah Receiving Bread from the Widow of Zarephath*, c. 1621–24 (Los Angeles: J. Paul Getty Museum); *Moses and the Messengers from Canaan*, 1621–24 (Los Angeles: J. Paul Getty Museum); *Assumption of the Virgin*, 1625–27 (Rome: S. Andrea della Valle); *Ecstacy of St. Margaret of Cortona*, c. 1630s (Florence: Palazzo Pitti)

Christ and the Woman of Samaria Giovanni Lanfranco, 1625–28, 29½ x 33⅛ in (75 x 86 cm), oil on canvas, Oxford: Ashmolean Museum. A decorative interpretation of Christ's meeting with a prostitute.

Orazio **Gentileschi**

● 1563–1639   📫 ITALIAN

📫 Italy; Paris; England   🎨 oils
💰 $6,992,000 in 1995, *The Finding of Moses* (oils)

Greatly esteemed Tuscan. Born in Pisa, but settled in Rome in 1576. Much influenced by Caravaggio, but without his wild energy and imagination; he domesticated Caravaggio's excesses. Look for large-scale, decorative works, simplified subjects and compositions, cool colors, sharp-edged draperies, and unconvincing realism. In 1626, he became court painter to Charles I of England, a safe choice artistically.

KEY WORKS *The Lute Player*, c. 1610 (Washington, DC: National Gallery of Art); *Annunciation*, c. 1621–23 (Turin: Galleria Sabauda); *Lot and his Daughters*, 1622 (J. Paul Getty Museum, Los Angeles); *Cupid and Psyche*, 1610s (St. Petersburg: Hermitage Museum)

Rest on the Flight into Egypt *Orazio Gentileschi, c. 1615–20, 69 x 85⅞ in (175.6 x 218 cm), oil on canvas, Birmingham (UK): Museums and Art Gallery.* The use of harmonious blues and yellows is typical of Gentileschi.

Alessandro **Algardi**

● 1598–1654   📫 ITALIAN

📫 Rome; Bologna   🗿 sculpture   💰 $37,500 in 2005, *Hercules Mounting the Pyre* (works on paper)

Best sculptor in Baroque Rome after Bernini. They were great rivals and Algardi's studio seized control when Bernini was briefly out of favor with Pope Innocent X's court for shoddy work on St. Peter's. More obsessed than Bernini with classical ideal and the philosophy of the "Antique," so his work is more solid, permanent, and psychologically real than transitory fluidity of Bernini. Figures heavily classical in stance, robust, muscular, powerful. Pieces often symbolically crafted with attention to classical geometry and line. Preferred nobleness of cool white marble to Bernini's subtle color-play. He preserves the differences between painting and sculpture. His marble reliefs became prototype for supplanting painted altarpieces with sculptured ones. His intense classicism influenced French Baroque development and he became a great friend of Poussin.

KEY WORKS *Portrait of Gaspare Mola*, late 1630s (St. Petersburg: Hermitage Museum); *Tomb of Leo XI*, 1634–44 (Rome: St. Peter's); *Decapitation of St. Paul*, 1641–47 (Bologna: S. Paolo); *Pope Liberius Baptizing the Neophytes*, 1645–48 (Paris: Musée du Louvre)

Caravaggio

● 1571–1610 🇮🇹 ITALIAN

🏛 Rome; Malta; Sicily 🎨 oils 💲 $312,000 in 1971, *Martha Reproving Mary for her Vanity* (oils)

His full name was Michelangelo Merisi da Caravaggio. The only major artist with a serious criminal record (hooliganism and murder). Died of malarial fever at the age of 38. Contemporary of Shakespeare (1564–1616). Immensely influential.

LIFE AND WORKS

From his native Bologna he moved to Rome in 1592 where two distinct phases in his career occurred: an early period (1592–99) where he learned from the examples of the High Renaissance and the Antique; and a mature period (1599–1606) where he rejected decorum and turned to an exhilarating realism, displaying a complete disregard for proprieties and accepted rules. Nonetheless, he was well-received in Papal circles and executed many important Church commissions. He lived in a state of hyperexcitement, both in life and in his art. In 1606, at the height of his success, his tempestuous character led him into a murderous brawl over a wager on a tennis match. He was forced to flee to Malta, where, after another fight, he moved on to Sicily. Wounded in Palermo, he died near Naples while waiting for a Papal pardon. It arrived three days after his death. His many followers took up his mantle, ensuring his contribution to the future development of art, notably in Naples, Spain, and the Netherlands, and echoes of his influence are to be found in the works of artists as diverse as La Tour, Rembrandt, and Velasquez.

STYLE

He is known for sensational subjects, in which severed heads and martyrdom are shown in gory detail, and young men display charms that suggest decadence and corruption (his tastes were heterosexual, and his girlfriend a prostitute). His biblical subjects show immense moments of dramatic revelation, and his use of peasants and street urchins as models for Christ and the saints caused deep offense to many. His technique is equally

Judith and Holofernes *1599, 57 x 76¾ in (145 x 195 cm), oil on canvas, Rome: Palazzo Barberini.* Caravaggio's interpretation emphasizes real life drama and shock rather than the symbolism of virtue defeating sin.

The Supper at Emmaus *1601, 55½ x 77¼ in (141 x 196.2 cm), oil and tempera on canvas, London: National Gallery.* Caravaggio painted a second, more subdued version of this work five years later.

sensational and theatrical, with tense compositions, masterly foreshortening, and dramatic lighting with vivid contrasts of light and shade (*chiaroscuro*). His later work, after 1606, was hastily executed and is more contemplative and less forceful.

WHAT TO LOOK FOR

His early works tend to be quite small, with half-length figures, and still-life compositions. Later, his figures gained plasticity, and shadows became richer and deeper. Still-life details can contain symbolic meaning e.g. fruit that is full of wormholes. Also look closely at the modeling of flesh to observe the range of subtle rainbow colors used.

KEY WORKS *Calling of St. Matthew,* 1599–1600 (Rome: S. Luigi dei Francesi); *The Conversion of St. Paul,* 1601 (Rome: S. Maria del Popolo); *The Incredulity of St. Thomas,* 1601–02 (Florence: Galleria degli Uffizi)

The Sick Bacchus *1591, 26⅓ x 20⅞ in (67 x 53 cm), oil on canvas, Rome: Galleria Borghese.* Most of the early erotic works were commissioned by high-ranking Church dignitaries.

Bartolommeo **Manfredi**

◗ 1582–c. 1622   🏳 ITALIAN

🏛 Rome   🎨 oils   🏛 Florence: Galleria degli Uffizi. Art Institute of Chicago   💰 $65,854 in 1989, *Still Life with Grapes, Pomegranates, and Figs* (oils)

Little-known artist who was a successful imitator and follower of Caravaggio. Painted decadent everyday scenes as well as mythological and religious subjects. Preferred allegorical themes of conflict and discord. Style more rough and ready than his celebrated master but copies Caravaggio's theatrical lighting effects and also foreshortens the action so viewer feels an accomplice to the scene. Along with fellow Caravaggisti like Valentin, with whom Manfredi was often confused, he influenced northern artists who stayed in Rome, e.g. Honthorst and Terbrugghen.

KEY WORKS *Cupid Chastized*, 1610 (Art Institute of Chicago); *Allegory of the Four Seasons*, c. 1610 (Ohio: Dayton Art Institute); *Cain Murdering Abel*, c. 1610 (Vienna: Kunsthistorisches Museum); *The Fortune Teller*, c. 1610–15 (Detroit Institute of Arts); *The Triumph of David*, c. 1615 (Paris: Musée du Louvre)

Guercino

◗ 1591–1666   🏳 ITALIAN

🏛 Bologna; Rome   🎨 oils; fresco   🏛 Windsor (England): Royal Collection (for drawings)   💰 $1,672,000 in 2002, *Toilet of Venus* (oils)

Full name Giovanni Francesco Barbieri Guercino. Came from Bologna, was self-taught and successful in his day. Now regarded as one of the most important 17th-century Italian artists, but was neglected until recently. At his best in his early work, which is lively, natural, and has exciting light and strong color; also produced wonderful drawings. The Bolognese Pope summoned him to Rome in 1621; thereafter he lost his spontaneity and became boringly classical. "Guercino" means "crosseyed."

KEY WORKS *The Dead Christ Mourned by Two Angels*, c. 1617–18 (London: National Gallery); *The Woman Taken in Adultery*, c. 1621

(London: Dulwich Picture Gallery); *The Liberation of St. Peter by an Angel*, c. 1622–23 (Madrid: Museo del Prado)

Artemisia **Gentileschi**

◗ c. 1597–c. 1652   🏳 ITALIAN

🏛 Rome; Florence; Naples; England   🎨 oils   💰 $619,400 in 1998, *Portrait of a Woman Playing the Lute* (oils)

Daughter of Orazio Gentileschi, she was a better painter. Her tendency toward bloodthirsty themes was probably related to her own dramatic life, including being raped at 19 and tortured during the subsequent court case to see if she was truthful. Chose dramatic subjects, often erotic, bloody, and with a woman as victim or gaining revenge. Stylistically close to Caravaggio—made powerful use of foreshortening and *chiaroscuro*. She was the first female member of the Florentine Academy.

KEY WORKS *Judith Slaying Holofernes*, c. 1620 (Florence: Galleria degli Uffizi); *Self-Portrait as the Allegory of Painting*, 1630s (Royal Collection)

Judith and her Maidservant *Artemisia Gentileschi, 1612–1613, 44⅞ x 36⅞ in (114 x 93.5 cm), oil on canvas, Florence: Palazzo Pitti.* These depictions of Old Testament heroines such as Judith appealed greatly to private collectors throughout Europe.

Gianlorenzo **Bernini**

◐ 1598–1680   ⚑ ITALIAN

⚑ Naples; Rome   ◑ sculpture; oils   ⚹ $206,700
in 1981, *David with the Head of Goliath* (oils)

A devoted Roman Catholic for whom
art was the emotional inspiration and
glorification of godliness and purity.
Although gifted as a painter, he despised
the medium, regarding sculpture as the
"Truth." Bernini set sculpture free from
its previous occupation with earthly
gravity and intellectual emotion,
allowing it to discover a freedom,
which permitted it to move,
soar, and have a visionary
and theatrical quality, which
it had never had before.

A child prodigy, he had a sparkling
personality, brilliant wit, and wrote
comedies—qualities that shine
through his work in sculpture. He
was a virtuoso technically, able
to carve marble so as to make
it appear to move and come
to life or have the delicacy of
the finest lace. He epitomizes
the Baroque style with its
love of grandeur, theatricality,
movement, and passionate
emotion, and his
finest works are
to be found in
Rome where he
was the favorite artist
of the Catholic Church.

At his best, he blends sculpture,
architecture, and painting into an
extravagant theatrical ensemble,
nowhere more so than in his
fountains, where the play of
water and refractions of light
over his sculptured forms of
larger-than-life human figures
and animals creates a vision
that is literally out of this world.

KEY WORKS *The Rape of Proserpine*, 1621–22
(Rome: Galleria Borghese); *David*, 1623
(Rome: Galleria Borghese);
Constanza Buonarelli, 1635
(Florence: Museo
Nazionale del
Bargello); *Cornaro
Chapel* (see pages
174–175); *The Blessed
Lodovica Albertoni*, 1671–74
(Rome: S. Francesco a Ripa)

Apollo and Daphne
*Gianlorenzo Bernini, 1622–25,
height 95⅔ in (243 cm), marble,
Rome: Galleria Borghese.*
Bernini's unprecedented
life-size masterpiece depicts
the chaste nymph, Daphne,
turning into a laurel tree, while
Apollo, the Sun god,
pursues her in vain.

Cornaro Chapel

Gianlorenzo Bernini 1645–52

The centerpiece of the lavishly decorated but intimate and candlelit Baroque Church of Santa Maria della Vittoria in Rome is the Cornaro Chapel. It contains one of Bernini's most ambitious works, created to resemble a miniature theater.

Commissioned by Cardinal Federigo Cornaro, the chapel is a stunning amalgam of painting, sculpture, and architecture. Theatrically lit by a hidden window behind the altar, the divine light of God pours down on swooning Teresa at the very climax of her spiritual ecstasy. It is as though she is on a visionary cloud. The central figure group is of marble and gilded wood, and gilt bronze rays symbolically represent the power of divine light. High above are vaulted painted heavens, while below, the Cornaro family, in privileged front-row loggia boxes, are observers of this spectacle. Bernini stuck faithfully to St. Teresa's spiritual account of an angel piercing her heart with an arrow of divine love —her mystical union with Christ.

The angel looks adoringly at St. Teresa, ready to plunge his arrow into her heart for a second time

TECHNIQUES

No sculptor before Bernini used light to accomplish an illusion of life in 3-D sculpture. Unlike diffused light of the Renaissance, this directed light accentuates the poised moment of action. Warming reds and yellows in the lower human zone balance the religious purity of the white marble group.

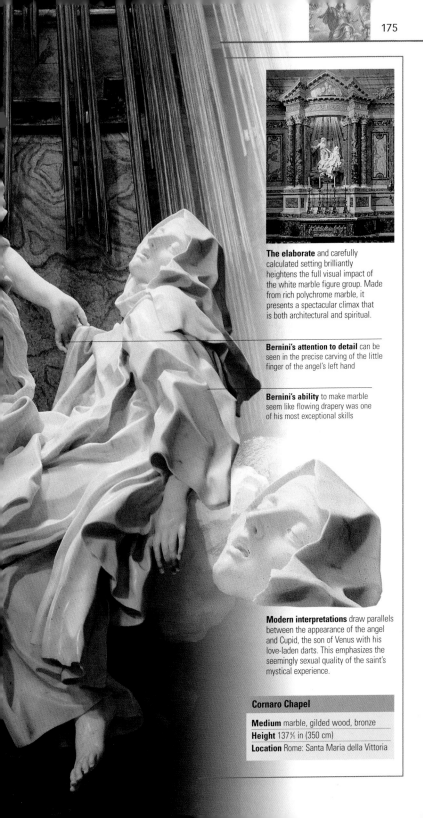

The elaborate and carefully calculated setting brilliantly heightens the full visual impact of the white marble figure group. Made from rich polychrome marble, it presents a spectacular climax that is both architectural and spiritual.

Bernini's attention to detail can be seen in the precise carving of the little finger of the angel's left hand

Bernini's ability to make marble seem like flowing drapery was one of his most exceptional skills

Modern interpretations draw parallels between the appearance of the angel and Cupid, the son of Venus with his love-laden darts. This emphasizes the seemingly sexual quality of the saint's mystical experience.

Cornaro Chapel

Medium marble, gilded wood, bronze
Height 137⅚ in (350 cm)
Location Rome: Santa Maria della Vittoria

Salvator **Rosa**

◗ c. 1615–73 ⚑ ITALIAN

🏛 Naples; Rome; Florence 🎨 oils; engravings
💰 $696,000 in 1992, *Portrait of Artist Wearing Doublet, Cap, Torn Glove, and Sword* (oils)

One of the first wild men of art—quarrelsome, anti-authority, self-promoting, lover of the macabre. Poet, actor, musician, satirist. Now best remembered for large, dark, stormy, fantastic mountainous landscapes and unpleasant witchcraft scenes (both much collected in the 18th and early 19th centuries). He was said to have fought by day and painted by night.

KEY WORKS *The Return of Astraea*, 1640–45 (Vienna: Kunsthistorisches Museum);

Self-Portrait Salvator Rosa, c. 1641, 45¾ x 37 in (116.3 x 94 cm), oil on canvas, London: National Gallery. The Latin inscription below Rosa's hand means "Be quiet, unless your speech be better than silence." He painted a companion portrait of his mistress Lucrezia whom he portrayed as one of the Muses of Poetry.

Human Fragility, c. 1656 (Cambridge: Fitzwilliam Museum); *The Spirit of Samuel Called up before Saul by the Witch of Endor*, 1668 (Paris: Musée du Louvre)

The Martyrdom of St. Paul, c. 1656-59 (Houston: Museum of Fine Arts); *Clorinda Rescuing Sofronia and Olindo*, c. 1660 (Los Angeles: J. Paul Getty Museum)

Pietro da **Cortona**

● 1596-1669   🏳 ITALIAN

🏛 Rome; Florence   🎨 fresco; oils; stucco
🏛 Rome: Palazzo Barberini; Santa Bibiana
📈 $391,200 in 1991, *Wooded River Landscape with Cascades and Men Dragging Net* (drawing)

Virtuoso architect, decorator, and painter, much sought after by Catholic grandees in Italy and France. Known as key creator of Roman High Baroque and for large-scale, extreme, illusionistic paintings where ceilings open up into a bold, dramatic, rich theater of space, color, human activity, architecture, learned allusion, and spiritual uplift.

KEY WORKS *Allegory of Divine Providence and Barberini Power*, 1633-39 (Rome: Palazzo Barberini); *Glorification of the Reign of Urban VIII*, 1633-39 (Rome: Palazzo Barberini); *Allegories of Virtue and Planets*, 1640-47 (Florence: Palazzo Pitti)

Mattia **Preti**

● c. 1613-99   🏳 ITALIAN

🏛 Rome; Naples; Malta   🎨 fresco; oils
📈 $1,185,000 in 1989, *The Liberation of St. Peter* (oils)

Accomplished painter of large-scale decoration that successfully combines the realism of Caravaggio and the theatricality of grand Venetian painting (it sounds unlikely, but he showed it could be done and thereby had much influence on the development of exuberant Baroque decorations).

KEY WORKS *Concert*, c. 1630 (St. Petersburg: Hermitage Museum); *The Marriage at Cana*, c. 1655-60 (London: National Gallery);

Luca **Giordano**

● c. 1634-1705   🏳 ITALIAN

🏛 Naples; Florence; Venice; Madrid
🎨 oils; drawings; fresco   📈 $453,600 in 1997, *The Raising of Lazarus* (oils)

The most important Italian decorative artist of the late 17th century. Prolific and energetic, created very theatrical, large-scale work; successful decorator of palaces (especially ceilings). Loved

The Crucifixion of St. Peter Luca Giordano, c. 1660, 77⅛ x 101⅝ in (196 x 258 cm), oil on canvas, Venice: Gallerie dell'Accademia. A dramatic representation of St. Peter, the leader of the 12 disciples of Christ, who was crucified upside down by Nero in 64 CE.

mythological subjects, which enabled him to emphasize dramatic action, bold compositions, contrasts of light and dark, silhouettes, violence and lust, and subjects that polarize good and evil. Giordano's last work was the Treasury Chapel ceiling of S. Martino, Naples. Nicknamed "Luca Fa Presto" (Luke works quickly).

KEY WORKS *The Fall of the Rebel Angels*, 1666 (Vienna: Kunsthistorisches Museum); *Allegory*, 1670 (Los Angeles: J. Paul Getty Museum); *Death of Seneca* c.1684 (Paris: Musée du Louvre)

> ## "Rosa is a great favorite with novel writers, particularly the ladies."
>
> JOHN CONSTABLE

THE BAROQUE

The dominant style of the 17th century, used by the Catholic Church to proclaim its continuing power—hence the best examples are to be found in Italy, Spain, France, Austria, Southern Germany, and Central Europe. Also loved by Absolute Monarchs who wanted to emphasize their worldly authority and the riches of their possessions and lifestyle.

STYLE

Fontana del Moro Gianlorenzo Bernini, 1653, stone, Rome: Piazza Navona. Originally designed in 1576 by Giacomo della Porta, the *Fontana del Moro* was then altered by Bernini in 1653. He designed the central statue of a muscular Moor holding a dolphin. The tritons blowing shells, from which water exits, are 19th-century additions.

"The style of absolutism" was used by the Catholic Church as a means of harnessing the magnificence of art to influence the largest possible audience. Exploiting the ideas of Classicism and religious doctrine, work was to be visually stunning and emotionally engaging to reflect the new Counter-Reformation confidence of the Church. The subsequent boldness of the artists' styles translates as huge freestanding sculptures, exaggerated decorations, intensely lit, emotional oil paintings with grand operatic-style themes, and a new architecture, planned around a series of geometrically controlled spaces to create an animated grandeur. Its hallmarks are illusion, movement, drama, rich color, and pomposity.

SUBJECTS

Religious subjects were paramount, especially the lives of saints and martyrs. These included recent saints such as St. Ignatius Loyola, founder of the Jesuits, and the Spanish mystic St. Teresa of Ávila (both canonized in 1622). Mythological characters, such as the chaste nymph Daphne or Proserpine, raped by Pluto, were used to illustrate religious ideals of purity. Statues of allegorical figures— Peace, Faith, Modesty, Chastity—were also common. Portraits tended to be bombastic and self-consciously dramatic. However, the everyday also found a place with scenes that included taverns, card players, and water sellers.

KEY EVENTS

1595	Annibale Carracci summoned from Bologna to decorate Farnese Palace, Rome
1601	Caravaggio paints the first of two versions of *The Supper at Emmaus*
1629	Bernini appointed architect of St. Peter's and of the Palazzo Barberini
1634	Charles I's Banqueting House, London: ceiling by Rubens completed
1663	Bernini's colonnaded piazza in front of St. Peter's
1669	Louis XIV orders massive reconstruction program at Versailles

WHAT TO LOOK FOR

The best example of secular Baroque decoration is Carracci's rarely seen frescoes for the vault of the sculpture gallery of the Farnese Palace in Rome. To complement the outstanding Farnese collection of Antique sculpture, Carracci created on the vaulted ceiling a picture gallery of mythological scenes illustrating stories from Ovid's *Metamorphoses*. The resulting effect is one of the triumphs of the Baroque ambition to marry architecture, painting, and sculpture.

All the figures are based on studies of live models

Landscape shows Mount Ida, where Anchises traditionally met the beautiful Venus

Venus disguised herself as a mortal and seduced Anchises. Their child was Aeneas, the founder of Rome

Venus and Anchises Annibale Carracci, 1597–1604. Part of Carracci's frescoed cycle depicting *The Loves of the Gods*. Anchises captures the heart of goddess Venus.

Anchises was a Trojan shepherd. He is shown in the act of removing Venus's sandal

Venus wore jewels and sweet-smelling perfume. The couch belonged to Anchises

Cupid, the son of Venus, is nearly always shown as a pretty, curly-haired boy who is present whenever love is in the air.

The central panel depicts the triumph of Bacchus and Ariadne, for which the artist made a detailed study of Classical reliefs. So disappointed was Carracci by the small fee he received for the work that he took to drink, and died aged only 49.

Nicolas **Poussin**

◗ c. 1593–1665　♙ FRENCH

🏛 Paris; Rome　🎨 oils　🏛 Paris: Musée
du Louvre. London: National Gallery. Madrid:
Museo del Prado　💰 $6.1m in 1999, *The
Agony in the Garden* (oils)

Founder of French classical painting.
Immensely influential on French artists
up to (and including) Cézanne, presenting
the standard to be lived up to.

LIFE AND WORKS

Son of a French farmer, became inspired
when an artist arrived to decorate his
village church. Struggled in early years
through poverty and ignorance until,
during a trip to Paris, engravings of
Raphael's works exposed him to Italian
High Renaissance, so set off for Rome.
Except for two years as court painter to
Louis XIII (1640–42), he worked in the
epicenter of Baroque Italy, though more
at home with his classical style. Did not
survive to see his style glorified by the
French Academy in the late 17th century.

STYLE

His paintings, usually biblical or from
Greco-Roman antiquity, are severe,
intense, and intellectual in subject matter,

> ## "Painting is the lover of beauty and the queen of the arts."
>
> NICOLAS POUSSIN

Portrait of the Artist
*1650, 38 x 29 in
(97 x 73 cm), oil on
canvas, Paris: Musée
du Louvre.* A grave
Poussin makes no
concession to vanity
in his portraiture.

style, and references: complex allegorical
subjects with a moral theme; constant
references to classical antiquity; a hidden
geometrical framework of verticals,
horizontals, and diagonals into which
the figures are placed and by which
they are tied together.

WHAT TO LOOK FOR

Note how the figure groups are
positioned flat on the surface of
the picture, like a carved bas relief
(another classical reference).

The figures, although notionally in
motion, have the stationary quality of

Arcadian Shepherds *c. 1648–50, 33½ x 47½ in
(58 x 121 cm), oil on canvas, Paris: Musée du Louvre.*
The shepherds examine an inscription whose meaning
is "Even in Arcadia, I [Death] am ever present."

statues. Poussin liked well-sculpted nudes, especially muscular backs, arms, and legs, and drapery that could have been carved out of marble. The interweaving arrangement of arms and legs are like an intellectual puzzle (which belong to whom?). The dark-reddish quality of many works is because he painted on a red ground, which is now showing through the oil paint that has gone transparent with time.

KEY WORKS *Cephalus and Aurora*, c. 1630 (London: National Gallery); *Landscape with the Ashes of Phocion*, c. 1648 (Liverpool: Walker Art Gallery); *The Holy Family*, 1648 (Washington, DC: National Gallery of Art)

The Rape of the Sabines *c. 1637–38, 62½ x 81 in (159 cm x 206 cm), oil on canvas, Paris: Musée du Louvre.* Worried about the declining birth rate, Romulus, Rome's founder, arranged a feast that resulted in young Romans marrying Sabine maidens.

Moïse **Valentin**

◒ c. 1593–1665   ⊠ FRENCH

⊞ Rome   🖌 oils   🏛 Paris: Musée du Louvre

Son of an Italian. From Boulogne in
France, he settled in Rome. His life
is obscure, but most of his known
work dates after 1620. One of the
Caravaggisti, loved the plebeian side
of art, continuing the master's style.
Probably met his friend Poussin in Rome
but was more emotional, dramatic.
Preferred seedy, bawdy scenes.
KEY WORKS *Christ and the Adulteress*, 1620s (Los
Angeles: J. Paul Getty Museum); *The Expulsion
of the Money-Changers from the Temple*, c. 1620–25
(St Petersburg: Hermitage Museum)

Claude **Lorrain**

◒ c. 1600–82   ⊠ FRENCH

⊞ Rome; Naples; Lorraine (France)
🖌 oils   🏛 London: National Gallery; British
Museum (drawings). Paris: Musée du Louvre
💲 $1.86m in 1999, *Evening Landscape with
Mercury and Battus* (oils)

Also called Le Lorrain or Claude Gellée.
Originator of the pastoral or picturesque
landscape. Immensely influential and
popular, especially in the 18th and early
19th centuries. Worked in and around
Rome. Claude's landscapes and seascapes
are enjoyable on two levels: as exquisite
depictions in their own right and as a
poetic setting for the staging of

Landscape with the Marriage of Isaac and Rebekah *Claude Lorrain, 1648, 58 x 77 in (149 x 197 cm), oil on canvas, London: National Gallery.* The Old Testament story lends artistic respectability to this pastoral landscape.

KEY WORKS *The Judgment of Paris*, 1645–46 (Washington, DC: National Gallery of Art); *Landscape with Hagar and the Angel*, 1646 (London: National Gallery); *Landscape with Ascanius Shooting the Stag of Silva*, 1682 (Oxford: Ashmolean Museum)

Phillippe de **Champaigne**

⬤ c. 1602–74 🇫🇷 FRENCH

🏛 Brussels; Paris 🖌 oils 💰 $423,077 in 2003, *Annunciation to Maria* (oils)

Born in Brussels; arrived in Paris in 1621. Brilliant, successful painter of portraits and religious pictures at the court of Louis XIII (favored by Cardinal Richelieu). Champaigne had a unique, memorable style, which combines over-the-top Baroque grandeur with severe, crisp, detailed, colorful, authoritarian austerity—you believe it should not be possible, but he showed that it could be done.

KEY WORKS *Triple Portrait of Cardinal Richelieu*, 1642 (London: National Gallery); *Moses with the Ten Commandments*, 1648 (St. Petersburg: Hermitage Museum); *Ex Voto*, 1662 (Paris: Musée du Louvre)

Gaspard **Dughet**

⬤ c. 1615–75 🇫🇷 FRENCH

🏛 Rome 🖌 oils; drawings; engravings 💰 $108,000 in 1994, *Italianate Wooded River Landscape with Fishermen on Boat* (oils)

He was the brother-in-law of Poussin. Very popular in the 18th century, but few works can be confidently attributed to him. Produced decorative landscapes in which he sometimes tries almost too hard to combine the heroic qualities of Poussin with the pastoral features of Claude. Ought to be very good, but frequently disappoints.

KEY WORKS *Landscape with Herdsman*, c. 1635 (London: National Gallery); *A Landscape with Mary Magdalene Worshipping the Cross*, c. 1660 (Madrid: Museo del Prado); *Classical Landscape with Figures*, c. 1672–75 (Birmingham, UK: Museums and Art Gallery)

mythological or religious scenes. Notice how he moves your eye from side to side across the picture in measured steps via well-placed figures, buildings, or paths (*coulisse*), and at the same time takes you from warm foreground to cool, minutely detailed distance (aerial perspective).

Magical painter of light—the first artist to paint the sun itself. Uses a formula of well-proven, balanced compositions and colors to produce a serene, luminous, calm, and harmonious atmosphere—although somewhere in the airless heat there is usually a refreshing breeze: a rustle in the tree tops, an unfurling flag, the sails of a boat in the far distance, or birds gliding on a current of air.

St. Joseph the Carpenter Georges da La Tour, c. 1640, 51⅛ x 39¾ in (130 x 100 cm), oil on canvas, Paris: Musée du Louvre. These humble settings for religious scenes were inspired by a Franciscan-led religious revival.

Georges de **La Tour**

◗ c. 1593–1652　◖ FRENCH

◖ Lorraine (France)　◖ oils　◖ $3,094,000 in 1991, *Blind Hurdy-Gurdy Player in Profile* (oils)

Shadowy figure with few attributed works, many in poor condition. In fashion with art historians, who are in the process of reconstructing his oeuvre. Major master or overrated enigma?

His work has two points of focus: peasant scenes (pre-1630s); nocturnes with spectacular handling of candlelight (post-1630s). Also painted cardsharpers and fortune-tellers. Beware of copies and imitations passing as the real thing.

Note how he paints peasants and saints with unnerving realism: wispy, greasy hair; lined brows and convincing old, dry skin; distinctive horny finger nails and peasant hands; sinister, cunning, piggy eyes. Used strong and beautiful *chiaroscuro* and lighting, and flat, non-existent backgrounds. Unconvincing when painting young flesh—the faces are wooden and masklike. Master at

creating virtuoso candlelight effects (such as the way it makes a hand look translucent).

KEY WORKS *Job and his Wife*, 1632–35 (Epinal, France: Musée Départemental des Vosges); *The Repentant Magdalen*, c. 1635 (Washington, DC: National Gallery of Art); *St. Jerome*, c. 1639 (Musée de Grenoble)

Le Nain brothers

◗ c. 1588–1677　◖ FRENCH

◖ Laon (France); Paris　◖ oils
◖ Paris: Musée du Louvre
◖ $194,922 in 1990, *Three Musicians Playing the Lute* (oils) by Mathieu Le Nain

Antoine (c. 1588–1648), Louis (c. 1593–1648), and Mathieu (c. 1607–77). Painters of large-scale mythologies, allegories, and altarpieces, but best known for smaller-scale portrayals of peasant groups sitting in an interior, doing nothing much, with dignity. Note the style; sensitivity when handling light and color; pleasing and detached powers of observation. Difficult to assign works as all signed their work by surname only. They were admired by Cézanne.

KEY WORKS *A Landscape with Peasants*, Louis Le Nain, c. 1640 (Washington, DC: National Gallery of Art); *Four Figures at a Table*, Le Nain brothers, c. 1643 (London: National Gallery)

François **Girardon**

◗ 1628–1715　◖ FRENCH

◖ Paris, Rome　◖ sculpture　◖ Paris: Palace of Versailles; Musée du Louvre. Los Angeles: J. Paul Getty Museum　◖ $2,302,362 in 1987, *The Rape of Proserpine* (sculpture)

Studied antiquities in Rome. Returned to dominate Sun King Louis XIV's sculptural projects, including decoration of Louvre, with distinct classical style. Unified muscular bodies. Lyrical with careful contrast of gesture and pose. Preferred Poussin's painting as chief influence rather than his sculptor counterparts. On death owned 800 sculptures, second biggest collection after King's.

KEY WORKS *Apollo Tended by the Nymphs*, c. 1666 (Château de Versailles); *Monument to Cardinal Richelieu*, 1675–77 (Paris: Sorbonne Church)

José **Ribera**

🔵 1591–1652 🏳 SPANISH

📍 Naples   🎨 oils; engravings; drawings
🏛 Naples: Museo di Capodimonte. Madrid:
Museo del Prado   💰 $4.5m in 1990,
Martyrdom of St. Bartholomew (oils)

Spanish-born, in 1616 Ribera settled
in Spanish-owned Naples where he
was known as "Lo Spagnoletto."
Naples was one of the main centers
of the Caravaggesque style at this time.
He was the major Neapolitan painter
of the 17th century. Particularly good
at martyrdom, shown through powerful
images of resigned suffering. Sometimes
the subject matter is repelling, but the
technique is exquisite and this results in
an almost unbearable "can't look but must
look" tension. He makes brilliant use of
chiaroscuro and tenebrism (light coming
from a single source above), and was an
early exponent of realism—his saints and
philosophers are real people from the
streets of Naples. Observe his marvelous
painting of textures and surfaces.

He paints old men's faces wonderfully,
with convincing, leathery flesh faces,
necks, and hands. Notice how the brushstrokes follow the contours of the flesh,
across a brow, down an arm. He couldn't
do convincing women's or boy's flesh and
faces, though. Is his brighter, Venetian-
style palette that he adopted from the
1630s a step forward or a step
backward? Be aware that many
pictures have darkened with time.

KEY WORKS *Martyrdom of St.
Bartholomew*, c. 1630 (Madrid:
Museo del Prado); *Apollo Flaying
Marsyas*, 1637 (Bruges: Musées
Royaux des Beaux-Arts); *Isaac
Blessing Jacob*, 1637 (Madrid:
Museo del Prado)

The Club Foot *José Ribera, 1642, 64⅛ x 36⅛ in (164 x 92 cm), oil
on canvas, Paris: Musée du Louvre.* In his late work, Ribera softens
his dramatic lighting, adopting a looser style with gentler modeling
and airy harmonious tones.

Francisco de **Zurbarán**

🔵 1598–1664 🏳 SPANISH

📍 Seville; Madrid   🎨 oils
🏛 Naples: Museo di Capodimonte.
Madrid: Museo del Prado
💰 $1.9m in 1998, *St. Dorothea* (oils)

"The major painter between
Velasquez and Murillo" (read
this as code for good, not great).
His principal patrons were
Spanish religious orders. His
most characteristic works are of
saints and monks in prayer or
meditation. Like Caravaggio, his
work has a hard-edged realism,
employs strong *chiaroscuro* effects,
and demonstrates a smooth
technique and care for precise
detail. It has dramatic visual
impact, but generally lacks
convincing emotion. Died out of
fashion and in financial difficulty.

KEY WORKS *Beato Serapio*, 1628
(Hartford, Connecticut: Wadsworth
Atheneum); *St. Margaret*, 1630–34
(London: National Gallery)

Juan de **Arellano**

◕ c. 1614–76   ◪ SPANISH

◪ Spain   ◧ oils   ◪ $1m in 1993, *Still Life of Mixed Flowers* (oils)

Pre-eminent Spanish flower painter of the 17th century. Detailed, skilful works, often executed and designed as pairs. Shows bouquets in baskets, on rough stone plinths, or in vases of crystal or metal, with a careful balancing of red, white, blue, and yellow. His later work is more loosely painted, with full-blown flowers and curling leaves.

KEY WORKS *Garland of Flowers with Landscape*, 1652 (Madrid: Museo del Prado); *Irises, Peonies, Convolvuli, and other Flowers in an Urn on a Pedestal*, 1671 (London: Christie's Images)

Still Life of Flowers in a Basket *Juan de Arellano, c. 1671, 33 x 41½ in (84 x 105.5 cm), oil on canvas, Bilbao: Museo de Bellas Artes.* Spain has a long tradition of still-life painting, influenced by Netherlandish art.

Bartolomé **Murillo**

◕ 1617–82   ◪ SPANISH

◪ Seville   ◧ oils   ◪ Seville: San Francisco; S. Maria la Blanca. London: Dulwich Picture Gallery (for genre)   ◪ $4,246,000 in 1990, *St. Joseph and Christ Child* (oils)

Regarded until about 1900 greater than Velasquez and as good as Raphael. Now the poor man's Velasquez. Born and bred in Seville. Pious family. Produced acres of soft-focus sentimental religious pictures for the home market. Fewer, better, genre scenes (good line in ragamuffins), done for the export market. Good portraits.

A Murillo revival campaign is currently under way. It is easy to extol his confident, masterly way with color, paint handling

light, and strong composition. The genre scenes are appealing as subjects; they influenced Reynolds and Gainsborough. Uphill struggle to find virtue in the overly sweet and sometimes sickly religious pictures—maybe being widowed at 45 made him excessively misty-eyed about young mothers and children.

KEY WORKS *The Young Beggar*, c. 1645 (Paris: Musée du Louvre); *The Virgin of the Rosary*, c. 1649 (Madrid: Museo del Prado)

Claudio **Coello**

◕ 1642–93   ◪ SPANISH

◪ Italy, Madrid   ◧ oils   ◪ Madrid: Museo del Prado. St. Petersburg: Hermitage Museum   ◪ $4.8m in 2000, *Portrait of Fernando Valenzuela* (oils)

Deeply influenced by Rubens, van Dyck, and Titian whose works were in Spanish Royal collection and studied for seven years in Italy. Painter to Charles II in 1683. Often complex and complicated works, fussy with exaggerated detail. Pre-empting Rococo. Employed loose brushstrokes, brilliant palette, and moody lighting. Masterpieces are his Titian-style portraits, particularly of Charles II, capturing degeneracy of last Hapsburg ruler of Spain.

KEY WORKS *Self-Portrait*, 1680s (St. Petersburg: Hermitage Museum); *The Repentant Mary Magdalene*, 1680s (St. Petersburg: Hermitage Museum)

Juan de **Valdés Leal**

◕ 1662–90   ◪ SPANISH

◪ Seville; Cordoba   ◧ oils; engravings   ◪ $1,261,000 in 2004, *Sacrifice of Isaac* (oils)

Spanish painter and engraver. Founded the Seville Academy of Painting with Murillo. Religious painter with fixation on the macabre. Vibrant coloring and dramatic lighting, vivid movements, volatile, verging on the operatic. Loved swirling forms, draperies, grand gestures. Anticipates the decorative exuberance of the 18th-century Rococo style.

KEY WORKS *The Assumption of the Virgin*, 1658–60 (Washington, DC: National Gallery of Art); *The Immaculate Conception of the Virgin, with Two Donors*, c. 1661 (London: National Gallery)

Velasquez
1599–1660 SPANISH

Seville; Madrid; Italy   oils
Madrid: Museo del Prado.
London: National Gallery
$8.1m in 1999, *St. Rufina* (oils)

Diego Rodríguez de Silva y Velazquez was the great Spanish painter of the 17th century whose life and work were inextricably linked with the court of King Philip IV. He wasn't a prolific artist but was precocious; while still in his teens he painted pictures that display powerful presence and total technical mastery. He was very influential on late-19th-century French avant-garde painting.

Observe the extraordinary and unique interweaving of grandeur, realism, and intimacy, which ought to self-cancel, but result in some of the finest official portraits ever painted. Notice the grand poses, characters, and costumes; eagle-eyed observation (he never flatters or idealizes); and a feeling of sensual intimacy through the use of seductive colors and paint handling. His religious

Waterseller of Seville *Velasquez, c. 1620, 42 x 31⅛ in (106.7 x 81 cm), oil on canvas, London: Wellington Museum.* Gifted to the Duke of Wellington by the king of Spain for his victory over Napoleon's army.

and mythological paintings sometimes fail to convince because he was simply too realistic in his work.

He had a great sensitivity to light, which is recorded with pinpoint accuracy in his early work and evoked by loose, flowing paint in later work. See how he makes ambiguous and mysterious use of space, which has the effect of drawing the viewer into the picture and therefore closer to the figures. Is better with static, solitary poses than with movement or people supposedly communicating with each other. Sensational color harmonies (especially pink and silver) in his late work.

KEY WORKS *The Forge of Vulcan*, 1630 (Madrid: Museo del Prado); *The Surrender of Breda*, 1634–35 (Madrid: Museo del Prado); *Las Meniñas*, (see pages 188–189); *Francisco Lezcano*, 1636–38 (Madrid: Museo del Prado)

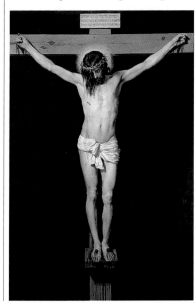

Christ on the Cross *Velasquez, c. 1631–32, 96 x 66½ in (248 x 169 cm), oil on canvas, Madrid: Museo del Prado.* An early work showing the continuing influence of Spanish polychrome sculpture.

Las Meniñas

Diego Velasquez 1656

As an ambitious courtier, Velasquez needed to be an expert in observation and manipulation. In this remarkable and influential group portrait of the Infanta Margarita and her maids of honor (*las meniñas*), he displays all his cunning as an artist and politician.

Velasquez plays an elaborate and artificial game with our perception, and the relationships in the portrait. He portrays himself on the left, painting on a large canvas, but why is he there and what is on the canvas? It cannot be that he is painting a portrait of the Infanta, since he stands behind her. The answer is in the mirror at the end of the room. It reflects the King and Queen, who must therefore be posing for Velasquez. The little Infanta has come into the room to look at them. By working this way, Velasquez has reversed all the rules and expectations of portraiture.

Velasquez achieved a very special sharpness of characterization in his portraiture. We can still see the childlike vulnerability in the Infanta Margarita's features despite her knowingness.

TECHNIQUES

Velasquez developed a technique whereby the details of a painting come into focus only at a certain distance. The lace cuffs worn by the maid of honor are nothing more than loose brushstrokes that suggest rather than describe.

The maid of honor on the left proffers a red terracotta jug on a gold plate to the Infanta, which probably would have contained cold perfumed water

Velasquez wears a royal decoration, the cross of the Order of Santiago (St. James), which was not given to him until three years after the date of the picture. The image of the cross on the artist's chest was added to the painting two or three years later, at the behest of the connoisseur king, who did much to promote painting to the status of the liberal arts.

Dwarves and clowns provided entertainment at Court, and often feature in the paintings by Velasquez. Another court favorite, Mari-Bárbola, stands behind the dog. Her grim features and dark dress serve to accentuate the Infanta's delicate beauty

The Court Jester Nicolasito playfully treads on the huge, sleepy mastiff. Such a detail helps to develop a feeling of spontaneity in this painting

The Infanta Margarita, the future Empress, is the central figure in the painting. She was just five years old when *Las Meniñas* was painted

A second maid of honor awaits the child's orders. Behind her a nun and a priest converse in the shadows. Their presence is a reminder of the power of the Church

Las Meniñas

Medium oil on canvas
Dimensions 125 x 108½ in (318 x 276 cm)
Location Madrid: Museo del Prado

Frans **Snyders**

● 1579–1657 ℙ FLEMISH

ℙ Antwerp; Italy ▮ oils ▥ Antwerp: Rockox
House. Madrid: Museo del Prado ▨ $1.4m in
1996, *Woman Selling Vegetables and Fruit* (oils)

The undisputed master of the Baroque
still life. Became as rich and successful
as his clients and so was able to consume
and enjoy the produce he painted. Prolific
and much imitated—there are many
wrong attributions. Son of an innkeeper.

Look for market scenes; pantries; large-
scale still lifes that literally groan and
overflow with fruit, vegetables, and fish,
flesh and fowl, both alive and dead. Look
also for the odd symbol of successful
bourgeois capitalism, such as rare
imported Wan Li Chinese porcelain.
After 1610, he painted hunting scenes,

Pantry Scene with a Page *Frans Snyders, c. 1615–20,
49⅛ x 78 in (125 cm x 198 cm), canvas, London: Wallace
Collection.* Snyder's paintings are often allegories
representing the five senses or the four physical elements.

but his best and most freely painted work
came after 1630—geometrically structured
compositions, which contain fluidity,
rhythm, balance, harmony, rich color.

He was much influenced by his visit to
Rome in 1608. Collaborated with other
artists (for example, he sometimes added
the still life or animal component of the
image/narrative to Rubens's work).
There is possible symbolism in the details
(grapes as Eucharist, for instance); plus
moralizing messages, proverbs, or animal
fables. If you visit the market area of
Brussels today, you will see shops and
restaurants with just such lavish displays
of produce—he painted embroidered
reality, not far-fetched fantasy.

KEY WORKS *Still Life with Dead Game, Fruits,
and Vegetables in a Market*, 1614 (Art Institute

of Chicago); *Hungry Cat with Still Life*,
c. 1615–20 (Berlin: Staatliche Museum);
Wild Boar Hunt, 1649 (Florence: Galleria degli
Uffizi)

Jacob **Jordaens**

● 1593–1678 ℙ FLEMISH

ℙ Antwerp ▮ oils; watercolors; gouache
▥ The Hague: Huis ten Bosch ▨ $2.8m in
2001, *Portrait of Rogier le Witer. Portrait of his Wife
Catharine* (oils, a pair)

Leading painter in Amsterdam after
the death of Rubens, whose style he
emulated (was an assistant for Rubens).
By comparison, his work seems hectic
and badly organized, without any clear
visual and emotional focus. Best when not
being too ambitious (for instance,
in genre scenes). Produced good
portraits. Large output from
commissions, but quantity took
precedence over quality. He also
etched and made designs for
tapestries. The work of the last two
decades of his life is more subdued.

KEY WORKS *The Artist and his
Family in a Garden*, c. 1621 (Madrid:
Museo del Prado); *The Four
Evangelists*, c. 1625 (Paris: Musée
du Louvre); *The Lamentation*,
c. 1650 (Hamburg: Kunsthalle)

Roelandt **Savery**

● 1576–1639 ℙ FLEMISH

ℙ Amsterdam; Prague; Vienna; Utrecht ▮ oils;
watercolours ▥ London: National Gallery
▨ $2.24m in 2001, *Still Life of Iris, Tulip, Rose,
and other Flowers Flanked by Lizard* (oils)

Prolific, successful, much traveled
(France, Prague, Vienna, the Alps).
He finally settled in Utrecht. Painted
landscapes—the wooded and mountainous
scenes are notable for their brilliant
cool blues. Also flowers and mythologies.
Best known for his painting of animals,
which he studied from life (including
the dodo in Rudolph II's menagerie).
Good landscape etchings.

KEY WORKS *Flowers in a Niche*, 1603 (Utrecht:
Centraal Museum); *Bouquet of Flowers
(the Liechtenstein Bouquet)*, 1612 (Vienna:
Liechtenstein Museum); *Landscape with
Birds*, 1622 (Prague: National Gallery)

Sir Peter Paul **Rubens**

◔ 1577–1640   ⴖ FLEMISH

ⵍ Antwerp; Rome; Paris   ◖ oils; drawings;
chalks   ⋔ Munich: Alte Pinakothek. Antwerp
⚡ $68.4m in 2002, *Massacre of the Innocents* (oils)

Extraordinary, widely traveled, gifted
man of many talents: painter, diplomat,
businessman, scholar. The greatest and
most influential figure in Baroque art
in northern Europe. Had a huge output
and a busy studio with many assistants,
including van Dyck. He was *the*
illustrator of the Catholic faith and
divine right of kings.

   His large-scale set-piece works, such as
altarpieces and ceiling decorations, must
be seen in situ in order to experience
their full impact and glory. However,
do not overlook his many sketches and
drawings, which are miracles of life
and vigor, and the genesis of the major
works. Rubens's work is always larger
than life, so enjoy the energy and
enthusiasm he brought to everything he
saw and did. Was never hesitant, never
introspective. A wonderful storyteller.

   There are three possible themes to
explore in Rubens's work: 1) Movement—
inventive compositions with energetic
diagonals and viewpoints; color contrasts
and harmonies that activate the eye;
figures at full stretch both physically and
emotionally. 2) Muscles—gods built like
Superman, muscular Christianity in
which well-developed martyrs suffer and
die with enthusiasm. 3) Mammaries—he
never missed a chance to reveal a choice
breast and cleavage. Note also the rosy,

Hélène Fourment in a Fur Wrap *Sir Peter Paul
Rubens, 1636–38, 69⅛ x 24⅜ in (176 x 63 cm), wood,
Vienna: Kunsthistorisches Museum. Rubens's second
wife (who was aged 16 when they married in 1630)
was the ideal female model for his art.*

blushing cheeks, and the businesslike
eye contact in the portraits.

   In his later years, Rubens developed
a new interest in landscape painting.
KEY WORKS *Samson and Delilah* (see pages
192–193); *The Life of Maria de Medici* series,
c. 1621–25 (Paris: Musée du Louvre); *The
Garden of Love*, 1632–34 (Madrid: Museo
del Prado); *The Judgment of Paris*, 1635–38
(London: National Gallery)

Battle of the Amazons and Greeks *(detail)
Sir Peter Paul Rubens, c. 1617, 47⅜ x 65½ in
(121 x 166 cm) oil on panel, Munich: Alte
Pinakothek. Rubens was in Italy from 1600–08
and this work shows the lasting influence of his
study of Greco-Roman and Italian Renaissance art.*

Samson and Delilah

Sir Peter Paul Rubens c. 1609

Rubens was only 31 years old when he painted this magnificent work, which resonates with the enthusiastic and energetic talent that brought him honors and riches. The picture tells the Old Testament story (Judges 16) of the downfall of Samson, the super-human Israelite warrior who was the scourge of the Philistines.

Samson's ruin was caused by his lust for the Philistine Delilah, who beguiled him into revealing the secret source of his strength—his uncut hair. The artist depicts the tense moment when the first lock is cut and the soldiers prepare to gouge out the Israelite's eyes. When his hair grew back, Samson used his returned strength to destroy the Philistines' temple, sacrificing his own life while taking his revenge.

The picture was painted for a close friend and patron, Nicolaas Rockox, who was a rich and influential alderman. It was designed to hang high on the wall above the mantelpiece of the Great Saloon of his Antwerp townhouse.

Cheeks flushed with pleasure, Delilah reclines languidly. The tilt of her head echoes the statue of Venus above

The intricate and intertwined hands holding the scissors are a brilliant visual metaphor for the deceitful and elaborate plot to cause Samson's downfall. The barber performs his task with deep concentration.

Each of the main characters has specific hand gestures that reveal their mental and physical state

The sweep of Samson's back leads the eye up to the climax of faces of the leading characters

TECHNIQUES

Note Rubens's expert use of light on Delilah and her flowing clothing. An intense, almost-white beam shoots from behind over her shoulder, emphasizing her pale, flawless skin and the shimmering glossiness of the rich, red gown that she wears.

Rubens's *chiaroscuro* treatment of light was strongly influenced by Caravaggio (see pages 170–171)

The faces of the Philistines are illuminated from below by a flaming torch. Entering stealthily through the doorway, they are carrying the sharpened stakes that they will use to put out Samson's eyes.

The dominant color in the lower left of the painting is a rich and vibrant red, set off against warm browns and gold, and Rubens's marvelously translucent flesh tones.

Samson and Delilah

Medium oil on wood

Dimensions 73 x 80½ in (185 x 205 cm)

Location London: National Gallery

Samson's enormous, muscular frame was inspired by the work of Michelangelo (see page 136)

The picture is strewn with rich materials and colors— silks, satins, and embroidery in vibrant reds and golds

Sir Anthony **van Dyck**

🌐 1599–1641   🏳 FLEMISH

🗺 Antwerp; Italy; England   🎨 oils; drawings
🏛 London: National Gallery. Edinburgh: National
Gallery of Scotland   🔀 $1.24m in 1989, *Portrait
of Mary, Princess Royal* (oils)

Antwerp-born infant prodigy from a
family of silk merchants. Best remembered
for his portraits, especially those of the

ill-fated Court of King Charles I
of England (who was beheaded
in 1649). He died relatively young.

As well as portraits, look for religious
and mythological subjects (the stock in

King Charles I of England out Hunting Sir Anthony
van Dyck, c. 1635, 104½ x 81½ in (226 x 207 cm), oil on
canvas, Paris: Musée du Louvre. Van Dyck painted 38
portraits of Charles I, of which this is the finest. The king
awarded him a knighthood in recognition of his talents.

trade of all artists of the time). Also painted rare landscape watercolors. His brilliant but restrained technique reflected the elegance, fineness, and impeccable taste and breeding assumed by his sitters—those subtly elongated fingers, bodies, noses, and poses, and the rich but unflashy silks and satins. Even his martyrs suffer with perfect manners.

Notice that air of aristocratic privilege (still around today). Van Dyck set the ultimate role model, much copied in (notably British) portraiture and life: the aloofness, disdain, and reserve adopted by people wishing to appear consciously set apart. These faces never smile; they know their duty and they will fight to retain their privileges to the end (the Divine Right to Rule). He painted wonderfully sensitive images of children. Realistic details, especially hair.

KEY WORKS *Portrait of Charles V on Horseback*, 1620 (Florence: Galleria degli Uffizi); *Geronima Brignole Sale and her Daughter Amelia*, c. 1621–25 (Genoa: Palazzo Rosso); *James Stewart, Duke of Richmond with Lennox*, 1635–36 (Private Collection); *A Lady as Erminia, Attended by Cupid*, c. 1638 (Oxfordshire: Bleinheim Palace)

A Village Festival in Honor of St. Hubert and St. Anthony Pieter Brueghel (the Younger), 1632, 46½ x 63⅓ in (118.1 x 158.4 cm), oil on panel, Cambridge: Fitzwilliam Museum.

David **Teniers** (the younger)
◉ 1610–90 🏳 FLEMISH

🏳 Antwerp; Rome; Brussels 🖌 oils
🏛 London: Courtauld Institute; Wallace Collection
💰 $4,185,000 in 1999, *Archduke Leopold Wilhelm and the Artist, Archducal Gallery* (oils)

Teniers is best remembered for his lively small-scale paintings of peasant and guardroom scenes (and depicting them misbehaving, as in *Boors Carousing*). After 1651, also known for his detailed views of the painting galleries of Archduke Leopold Wilhelm (Regent of the Netherlands). Later work is weak.

KEY WORKS *The Kitchen*, 1646 (St. Petersburg: Hermitage Museum); *An Old Peasant Caresses a Kitchen Maid in the Stable*, c. 1650 (London: National Gallery); *Peasants Making Music*, c. 1650 (Vienna: Liechtenstein Museum)

Pieter **Brueghel** (the younger)
◉ 1564–1638 🏳 FLEMISH

🏳 Antwerp 🖌 oils; tempera 💰 $4.9m
in 2001, *Village Kermesse* (oils)

He was the elder son of "Peasant" Bruegel. Made copies and imitations of his father's work. Later did fashionable hellfire scenes, which gave him the nickname "Hell" Brueghel (he also retained the "h" in his name).

KEY WORKS *Fight between Carnival and Lent*, c. 1595 (Bruges: Musées Royaux des Beaux-Arts); *The Adoration of the Magi*, c. 1595–1600 (St. Petersburg: Hermitage Museum)

Jan **Brueghel**
◉ 1568–1625 🏳 FLEMISH

🏳 Antwerp; Italy 🖌 oils 🏛 Munich: Alte Pinakothek 💰 $1.85m in 1990, *Wooded Landscape with Covered Wagons and Cattle on Road* (oils)

He was the second son of "Peasant" Breugel, nicknamed "Velvet" Breughel (also retaining the "h" in his name). Produced flower paintings, landscapes, and allegories with rich, velvety textures; very finely painted. He is known to have sometimes worked with Rubens.

KEY WORKS *The Battle of Issus*, 1602 (Paris: Musée du Louvre); *Forest's Edge (Flight into Egypt)*, 1610 (St. Petersburg: Hermitage Museum); *The Earthly Paradise*, 1610 (Madrid: Museo del Prado)

DUTCH REALISM

Seventeeth-century Holland consciously developed a new type of art. Small-scale, well made, and often full of symbolism and anecdotes, its principal subjects were secular and focused on the present day—landscapes, still lifes, and genre scenes that recorded their daily activities. They also had a liking for portraits but these too tended to be small-scale and distinctly bourgeois in character.

STYLE

The content of Dutch Realism reflected everyday domestic tastes: sensitive and unpretentious scenes, usually painted with a close attention to detail. This new style of art was made to decorate and please, but it was also created for financial gain. Investing in works of art was a major activity, and trading in works of art was commonplace at all levels of society.

River Landscape with Peasants Ferrying Cattle *Salomon van Ruysdael, 1633, oil on panel, Private Collection.* These early works are similar in style to Van Goyen.

SUBJECTS

National pride was the main subject. For example, landscapes, although rarely accurate descriptions of exact places, celebrate the particular qualities of the Dutch countryside: flat, neatly cultivated lands with gray skies, heavy with rain. Canals and shipping feature large, including naval battles and storms at sea, both of which threatened their prosperity. Being a nation of market gardeners, they painted superb flower pieces. Still lifes are

The Flea-Catcher (Boy with his Dog) *Gerard Terborch, c. 1655, 13½ x 10⅔ in (34.4 x 27.1 cm), oil on canvas, Munich: Alte Pinakothek.*

KEY EVENTS

1602	Dutch East India Company founded
1610	Utrecht School established. Group including Terbrugghen also returns from Rome excited by realism
1616	Frans Hals, *alla prima* pioneer, painting directly onto canvas, wins fame with Dutch "Civic Guards" group portrait
1648	Holland becomes an independent republic
1650	Founding of the Delft School with Vermeer as leading exponent
1659	Major late Rembrandt self-portrait. First artist to practice self-portraiture as speciality

full of rich and exotic goods, with glass often in evidence, as it was one of their luxury industries. Domestic scenes are full of themes of love, sexual morality, cleanliness, and household economy and order.

1600s

WHAT TO LOOK FOR

Nothing in Dutch art is ever quite what it seems, not even in a still life. The exotic objects, snuffed-out candles, and empty jugs are symbolic of the essential emptiness of earthly possessions, and often there is a skull or other symbol of death—a *momento mori*—a reminder that even for the richest citizen, there is no escape from the inevitability of death. What is ostensibly an object for visual enjoyment is, in fact, a sober Calvinist discussion.

The Vanities of Human Life
Harmen Steenwyck, c. 1645, 15½ x 20 in (39 x 51 cm), oil on oak, London: National Gallery. A visual sermon based on the Book of Ecclesiastes.

The shaft of light highlights the central object—the human skull, a principal reminder of mortality; light is a Christian symbol of the eternal

A ghostly Roman emperor's face is just visible on the urn, a reminder of the earthly powers and glory death takes away

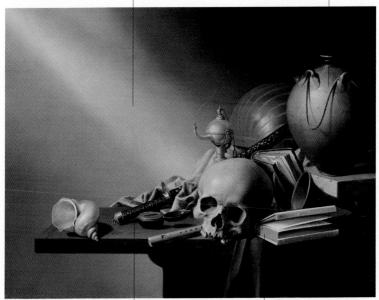

TECHNIQUES

Dutch painters were the first to establish a tradition of still-life painting; Steenwyck's subject gives him ample scope to show off his technical mastery, attention to detail, and evocation of reflected light on surfaces.

The Japanese sword is a symbol of worldly power, indicating that even the might of arms cannot defeat death

The vanity of knowledge is represented by a book, symbol of the human quest for the acquisition of knowledge and learning

The shell is a symbol of worldly wealth—it would also have been a rare and prized possession in the 17th century. But riches too are a vanity: "As he came forth of his mother's womb, naked shall he return to go … and shall take nothing of his labor" (Eccl. 5:15).

Frans **Hals**

● c. 1581–1666   ◪ DUTCH

◪ Haarlem   ◪ oils   ◫ Haarlem: Halsmuseum. Amsterdam: Rijksmuseum   ◪ $11,625,001 in 1999, *Tieleman Roosterman in Black Doublet, White Ruff* (oils)

Stay-at-home self-portraitist who never moved from Haarlem in the Netherlands. One of the first masters of the Dutch School (preceded Rembrandt). Although successful, he was constantly in debt (because he had eight children?).

Painter of portraits and group portraits (especially of the "Civic Guards," all-male social clubs) and of members of the newly established Dutch republic, who usually look pink-cheeked, well fed, well dressed, happy, and prosperous. Also painted single genre figures of children and peasantry. Was very influential in the late 19th century

***The Laughing Cavalier** Frans Hals, 1624, 32⅔ x 26⅛ in (83 x 67 cm), oil on canvas, London: Wallace Collection. The picture is inscribed "AETA.SVAE 26/A° 1624" (his age, 26, the year 1624), but the identity of the sitter remains unknown.*

when his style, having been totally out of fashion, became much admired by young artists such as Manet.

His exciting, lively, but simple poses are full of animation. He had a unique (for the time) sketchy painting technique, straight onto the canvas, with broad

brushstrokes and bright colors, adding to the sense of vivacity; yet he still captured the appearance and feel of different textures: plump flesh, pink cheeks, the shimmer of silk and satin, the intricacy of lace and embroidery. Masterly command of beautifully observed, well-formed, expressive eyes.

KEY WORKS *Young Man with a Skull*, 1626–28 (London: National Gallery); *Mad Babs*, c. 1629–30 (Berlin: Staatliche Museum); *Portrait of Willem Coymans*, 1645 (Washington, DC: National Gallery of Art); *Portrait of a Man*, early 1650s (New York: Metropolitan Museum of Art)

Daniel **Mytens**

● c. 1590–c. 1647   ◪ DUTCH/BRITISH

◪ The Hague; England   ◪ oils   ◫ London: National Portrait Gallery   ◪ $91,000 in 1988, *Portrait of Young Boy in Maroon Dress and White Ruff with Spaniel* (oils)

The major portrait painter in England before van Dyck. Dutch-born and trained. Arrived in London around 1618 and worked for Charles I. Painted elegant, rather stiff, formally posed portraits (but with insight into personality), which introduced a hitherto unknown level of realism to English art. His best works are his later full-length portraits, which are powerful, assured, and fluent.

KEY WORKS *Henry Wriothesley, 3rd Earl of Southampton*, c. 1618 (London: National Portrait Gallery); *King James I of England and VI of Scotland*, 1621 (London: National Portrait Gallery); *Endymion Porter*, 1627 (London: National Portrait Gallery)

Pieter **Lastman**

● 1583–1633   ◪ DUTCH

◪ Amsterdam; Italy   ◪ oils   ◫ Budapest: Museum of Fine Arts   ◪ $230,000 in 1985, *Hagar and the Angel* (oils)

Chiefly remembered as Rembrandt's most influential teacher. Painted lush, narrative pictures, full of gesture, and facial expression (see Rembrandt), but spoiled by over-fussy, anecdotal detail.

KEY WORKS *Abraham on the Way to Canaan*, 1614 (St. Petersburg: Hermitage Museum); *Juno Discovering Jupiter with Io*, 1618 (London: National Gallery)

The Expulsion of Hagar Pieter Lastman, 1612, oil on panel, Hamburg: Kunsthalle. The drama of the moment when Abraham banished Ishmael (his first son) and Hagar (his mother) is accompanied by an extensive landscape of equally dark mood.

Hendrick **Terbrugghen**

◔ 1588 – 1629 🄽 DUTCH

🄿 Utrecht; Rome 🄾 oils 🄼 Amsterdam: Rijksmuseum 💲 $1,460,000 in 1985, *Lute Player Carousing with a Young Woman* (oils)

The most important painter of the Utrecht School, who was deeply influenced by Caravaggio's subjects and style (he spent ten years in Italy). On his return to the Netherlands, he became with Honthorst the leader of the Caravaggism associated with the Utrecht School. His early work has hard, raking light, which throws detail into sharp relief. His later work is softer and quieter, sometimes to the point of stillness and silence. Was fascinated by reflected light. The rediscovery of his sensitive and poetic paintings has been part of the general reappraisal of Caravaggesque art in the 20th century.
KEY WORKS *Flute Players*, 1621 (Kassel, Germany: Staatliche Kunstsammlungen); *St. Sebastian Tended by Irene and her Maid*, 1625 (Oberlin, Ohio: Allen Memorial Art Museum); *The Annunciation*, 1629 (Amsterdam: Stedelijk Museum)

Jan Davidsz de **Heem**

◔ 1606 – 84 🄽 DUTCH

🄿 Utrecht; Antwerp 🄾 oils 🄼 Dresden: Gemäldegalerie 💲 $6m in 1988, *Banquet Still Life* (oils)

Utrecht-born, he lived and worked in Antwerp from 1636. Was famous and successful with his still-life paintings of flowers and groaning, exquisitely laid tables. Had many pupils and imitators.
KEY WORKS *Still Life with Books*, 1628 (The Hague: Mauritshuis Museum); *Fruit and Rich Tableware on a Table*, 1640 (Paris: Musée du Louvre); *A Table of Desserts*, 1640 (Paris: Musée du Louvre)

Still Life of Fruit and Flowers (detail) Jan Davidsz de Heem, c. 1640s, oil on canvas, Burnley, Lancashire: Towneley Hall Art Gallery. His style became more exotic and opulent after moving to Antwerp.

Rembrandt

◔ 1606–69 ⚑ DUTCH

🏴 Netherlands 🎨 oils; etchings; drawings
🏛 Amsterdam: Rijskmuseum. The Hague: The
Mauritshuis Museum 💲 $26,460,000 in 2000,
*Portrait of a Lady aged 62, Perhaps Aeltje Pietersdr,
Uylenburgh, Wife of Johannes Cornelisz* (oils)

His full name was Rembrandt
Harmensz van Rijn. Generally
considered to be the greatest,
but most elusive, Dutch
master. He created prolific,
stunning masterpieces,
treasured in galleries
worldwide. However, the
Rembrandt Commission
currently argues over how
many works he painted,
which is ultimately a
flawed enterprise: you
cannot resolve disputed
attributions by majority vote in
committee. Also one of the great
printmakers, developing the exciting,
new, free-flowing techniques of etching
into copper rather than the heavier,
surface-scratching of engraving.

LIFE

Born in Leiden. Son of a miller but,
reflecting Dutch social engineering
of the period, his modest parents
recognized the importance of education,
so he was sent to Leiden University.
Unlike the Utrecht School founders
and Rubens, he never visited
Italy to drink at the fountains of
Baroque but had access to High
Renaissance works and was taught
by Dutch "Caravaggio in a tea
cup" artist, Pieter Lastman,
who had worked in Italy.

*Studies of Old Men's
Heads and Three Women
with Children* (detail)
Rembrandt, c. 1635, ink on paper,
Birmingham (UK): The Barber
Institute of Fine Arts. From a group of
rapid sketches using thin pen strokes.

His personal life was increasingly touched with tragedy. At first money rolled in, thanks to marrying a successful art dealer's cousin, which resulted in wealthy portrait commissions and quickly won renown. He inherited his wife's fortune on her early death but later his popularity declined, resulting in debt, bankruptcy, and loss of his grand house and massive personal art collection. His beloved son, Titus, and housekeeper common-law wife saved him from ruin but when they died (Titus at the age of 27), he was left lonely and poor in his old age, dying 11 months later in Amsterdam.

SUBJECTS AND STYLE

His subjects were biblical history (his preference), portraits, and landscapes. He had a unique ability to find all humanity beautiful, in a way that can evoke deep, heart-rending emotions. He never flinched, even in front of the toughest subjects (the Crucifixion, or his own face). In fact, he is seen as art's first major self-portraitist as a recognized specialty. His direct honesty and intense personal scrutiny over the years reveals an aging face of a true human being, not beautiful but with penetrating realism. And this is the secret to his other works. Faces and gestures are the key—he was fascinated by the way faces reveal inner states of mind, and how hand and body language convey emotion. He was also interested in showing emotional crises and moral dilemmas—you sense that he has experienced the intense feelings he portrays.

WHAT TO LOOK FOR

Observe his emotional manipulation of light and shade—light being warming, purifying, revealing, spiritual; shadow being the domain of the unexplained, the threatening, the evil. He was enthralled by

Self-Portrait at the Age of 63 Rembrandt, 1669, 33⅞ x 27¾ in (86 x 70.5 cm), oil on canvas, London: National Gallery. This is one of the last of over 75 self-portraits—paintings, drawings, and prints.

the activity of painting; early work is detailed, later work is looser in style. His palette is distinctive: rich, warm, earthy, and comforting. He was intrigued by human skin, especially the fleshy areas around the eye and nose in old faces (no other artist has ever painted them with such care and so convincingly).

KEY WORKS *Saskia as Flora*, 1635 (London: National Gallery); *The Blinding of Samson*, 1636 (Frankfurt: Städelsches Kunstinstitut); *Joseph Accused by Potiphar's Wife*, 1655 (Washington, DC: National Gallery of Art); *Vase with Flowers*, c. 1670 (The Hague: Mauritshuis Museum)

Jacob Blessing the Children of Joseph Rembrandt, 1656, 69 x 82⅛ in (175.5 x 210.5 cm), oil on canvas, Kassel (Germany): Gemäldegalerie. One of Rembrandt's greatest achievements as a history painter.

The Three Crosses Rembrandt, 1653, 15 x 17¼ in (38.1 x 43.8 cm), etching, Cambridge: Fitzwilliam Museum. One of Rembrandt's best etchings: a complex, crowded work, with a stunning exploitation of light and shade.

Gerritt **Dou**

◯ 1613–75   ⚑ DUTCH

⬚ Leyden (Netherlands)   ⬤ oils   🏛 Paris:
Musée du Louvre. Budapest: Museum of Fine Arts
⚡ $2,030,864 in 2001, *The Dentist* (oils)

Also known as Gerard
Dou. Remembered as
Rembrandt's first pupil
(age 15). Small-scale
works with fine detail,
high, glassy finish, brilliant
colors, focused light and
shade (he trained initially
as an engraver and glass
painter). A conjurer's
world, dedicated to
self-conscious illusion,
obsession with surface
show, skilful special effects,
and hidden symbolism.

KEY WORKS *Astronomer by
Candlelight*, 1655 (Los
Angeles: J. Paul Getty
Museum); *Woman at a Window*, 1663
(St. Petersburg: Hermitage Museum);
The Hermit, 1670 (Washington, DC:
National Gallery of Art)

The Village Grocer *Gerrit Dou,
1647, 15 x 11⅜ in (38.5 x 29 cm), oil
on panel, Paris: Musée du Louvre.
Dou often used this composition
of figures engaged at a window.*

Govaert **Flinck**

◯ 1615–60   ⚑ DUTCH

⬚ Amsterdam   ⬤ oils   🏛 Amsterdam:
Rijksmuseum. Los Angeles: J. Paul Getty Museum
⚡ $325,000 in 1996, *Young Man Holding
Ottoman Short Sword* (oils)

A pupil of Rembrandt in
the 1630s and strongly
influenced by him in style
and subject matter, but his
works are generally lighter,
more elegant, and less
serious or gloomy. Flinck
was prolific and much
esteemed in his own day.
Recent revival of interest
due to reattributions by the
Rembrandt Commission
so that several so-called
Rembrandts are now
said to be by Flinck.

KEY WORKS *Countryside with
Bridge and Ruins*, 1637 (Paris:
Musée du Louvre); *Young Shepherdess with
Flowers*, c. 1637–40 (Paris: Musée du Louvre);
*Angels Announcing the Birth of Christ to the
Shepherds*, 1639 (Paris: Musée du Louvre)

Ferdinand **Bol**

◯ 1616–80   ⚑ DUTCH

⬚ Amsterdam   ⬤ oils
🏛 Amsterdam: Rijksmuseum.
Munich: Alte Pinakothek
⚡ $200,000 in 1998, *Portrait
of Young Woman Holding
Leather Fan* (oils)

Bol was a pupil of
Rembrandt. Working
very much in the master's
style, to whom his
works have often been
attributed (Rembrandt
being more prestigious
and much more
valuable). Liked the
formula of sitters posing
by an open window.

***Portrait of a Husband
and Wife*** *Ferdinand Bol,
1654, 67½ x 58¼ in (171 x 148 cm),
oil on canvas, Paris: Musée du
Louvre. In 1669, Bol married a rich
widow and, as a consequence, he
seems to have given up painting.*

Did allegories and history paintings for public buildings. Possessed a dark early style that becomes lighter after c. 1640.
KEY WORKS *Jacob's Dream*, 1642 (Dresden: Gemäldegalerie); *David's Dying Charge to Solomon*, 1643 (Dublin: National Gallery of Ireland)

Carel **Fabritius**
◐ 1622–54 ▣ DUTCH

▣ Amsterdam; Delft 🎨 oils 🏛 London: National Gallery. Amsterdam: Rijksmuseum
💰 $771,428 in 1985, *Mercury and Argos* (oils)

Had a tragically short life, and less than ten authenticated works are known, but they show great variety. Immensely talented—Rembrandt's best pupil, and a highly original and distinctive painter. Painted portraits, still lifes, genre, perspectives. Died in a gunpowder explosion in Delft, near his studio, which destroyed most of his work.

Used thick impastoed paint next to thin glazes (like Rembrandt). Preferred cool colors to Rembrandt's dark reds and browns. Sometimes silhouetted a dark figure against a light background (Rembrandt preferred vice versa).

An Eavesdropper with a Woman Scolding
Nicolaes Maes, 1655, 18¼ x 28⅗ in (46.3 x 72.2 cm), oil on panel, London: Harold Samuel Collection. Maes succeeded best when combining humor and complicity.

KEY WORKS *The Beheading of John the Baptist*, c. 1640 (Amsterdam: Rijksmuseum); *The Goldfinch*, 1654 (The Hague: Mauritshuis Museum)

Nicolaes **Maes**
◐ 1632–93 ▣ DUTCH

▣ Dordrecht (Netherlands); Antwerp 🎨 oils 🏛 Dordrecht: City Museum. Budapest: Museum of Fine Arts 💰 $708,400 in 1994, *Old Woman Making Lace in Kitchen* (oils)

Best known for his early genre paintings which often show kitchen life below stairs, or old women asleep (very popular at the time). Later in life went in for small, elegant, French-style portraits. Used strong *chiaroscuro* (he was a pupil of Rembrandt) and soft focus. Liked painting kitchen utensils. Good, but not great.
KEY WORKS *The Mocking of Christ*, c. 1650s (St. Petersburg: Hermitage Museum); *A Young Woman Sewing*, 1655 (London: Harold Samuel Collection)

> "The Dutch had no imagination, but they had extraordinary taste and an infallible feeling for composition."
> VINCENT VAN GOGH

Gerrit **van Honthorst**

⊖ 1590–1656　🇳 DUTCH

🅿 Italy; Utrecht; London　🎨 oils; fresco
🏛 London: National Gallery　💲 $434,000
in 1999, *Portrait of Laughing Violinist* (oils)

Only member of the Utrecht School
to establish an international reputation.
Studied in Rome 1610–12. Much
favored by royal and aristocratic patrons
for his history paintings and allegorical
decorations. Best remembered now for

Supper with the Minstrel and his Lute *Gerrit van
Honthorst, c. 1619, 56⅔ x 83½ in (144 x 212 cm), oil on
canvas, Private Collection. This use of artificial light
and silhouettes greatly influenced the young Rembrandt.*

striking treatment of illumination by
artificial light—especially good when he
hides light source and plays with silhouette.
KEY WORKS *Christ Before the High Priest*, c. 1671
(London: National Gallery); *Christ in the
Garden of Gethsemane (The Agony in the Garden)*,
c. 1671 (St. Petersburg: Hermitage Museum);
Christ Crowned with Thorns, 1620 (Los Angeles:
J. Paul Getty Museum)

Esaias **van de Velde**

⊖ c. 1591–1630　🇳 DUTCH

🅿 Haarlem; The Hague　🎨 oils　🏛 Amsterdam:
Rijksmuseum　💲 $450,000 in 1990, *Rocky Land-
scape with Travelers and Horsemen on Path* (oils)

One of the founder members of the
realist school of Dutch landscapes. His
soft, monochromatic scenes (often in

winter) are characterized by a feeling
of natural, unstagey open space and
atmosphere. He showed good detail,
especially in the anecdotal figures
going about their daily business. Also
a prolific etcher and draftsman.
KEY WORKS *Winter Games on the Town Moat*,
c. 1618 (Munich: Alte Pinakothek);
A Winter Landscape, 1623 (London:
National Gallery); *Villagers Skating on
a Frozen Pond*, 1625 (Washington, DC:
National Gallery of Art)

Willem **van de Velde**
(the elder)

⊖ 1611–93　🇳 DUTCH

🅿 Leyden (Netherlands); London　🎨 oils;
pen and ink　🏛 Amsterdam: Rijksmuseum
💲 $975,000 in 1998, *Dutch Harbor in a Calm
with Small Vessels Inshore* (works on paper)

Talented maritime painter, but eclipsed
in popular esteem by his oil-painter
son. His principal achievements are
drawings of ships and small craft and
pen paintings in ink on white canvas or
oak panel. The paintings have meticulous,
accurate detail. He spent much time at
sea with the Dutch fleet. Emigrated with
family to England (c. 1672) to escape
political confusion in Holland.
KEY WORKS *Figures on Board Small Merchant
Vessels*, 1650 (Los Angeles: J. Paul Getty
Museum); *Dutch Ships Near the Coast*,
1650s (Washington, DC: National
Gallery of Art); *The Battle of Terheide*,
1657 (Amsterdam: Rijksmuseum)

Sea Battle of the Anglo-Dutch Wars *Willem van de Velde (the younger), c. 1700, oil on canvas, New Haven: Yale Center for British Art. Both the elder and younger van de Veldes were official naval war artists to the English crown. The Anglo-Dutch wars (1652–84) were about control of trade routes.*

Willem **van de Velde** (the younger)

◯ 1633–1707   🏴 DUTCH

🏛 Leyden (Netherlands); London   🎨 oils
🏛 Amsterdam: Rijksmuseum. Los Angeles: J. Paul Getty Museum   📈 $2,349,000 in 1999, *The Morning Gun, Small English Man-o-War Firing a Salute* (oils)

Precocious son of hard-working maritime-painter father. His early work concentrates on accurately drawn and carefully placed fishing vessels on tranquil seas. After 1670, he produced portraits of particular ships, naval battles, and storms at sea. His later work (after 1693) was more freely painted. Worked extensively from his father's drawings.

KEY WORKS *Ships in a Calm Sea*, 1653 (St. Petersburg: Hermitage Museum); *Dutch Vessels at Low Tide*, 1661 (London: National Gallery); *Ships off the Coast*, 1672 (Vienna: Liechtenstein Museum)

Jan **van Goyen**

◯ 1596–1656   🏴 DUTCH

🏛 Leyden (Netherlands); Haarlem; The Hague   🎨 oils   🏛 St. Petersburg: Hermitage Museum. Paris: Musée du Louvre   📈 $1,874,500 in 1998, *Village on the Banks of River with Ferryboat and Peasants* (oils)

One of the most important Dutch landscape painters. Prolific and much imitated. Had many pupils. Repeated same motifs frequently—Dordrecht, sand dunes, ships, and Nijmegen River. Painted in subdued browns and grays, enlivened by a flash of red or blue. His paintings have attractive light, space, air, and cloud movement. Uses high viewpoint and low horizon. Likes gnarled oaks.

KEY WORKS *Skaters in Front of a Medieval Castle*, 1637 (Paris: Musée du Louvre); *A Windmill by a River*, 1642 (London: National Gallery); *Fort on a River*, 1644 (Boston: Museum of Fine Arts)

Pieter Jansz **Saenredam**

◯ 1597–1665   🏴 DUTCH

🏛 Haarlem   🎨 oils; chalks; watercolors
🏛 Amsterdam: Rijksmuseum. London: National Gallery   📈 $1.65m in 2004, *Haarlem, Interior of the Nieuwe Kerk* (oils)

Supremely gifted painter of architecture—both specific buildings in Dutch towns and interiors of identifiable churches (the once decorated Gothic buildings that were whitewashed to satisfy the Protestant belief in plainness). Made meticulous preliminary drawings and measurements. The light-filled church interiors are a metaphor for universal laws of mathematics and optics.

KEY WORKS *Interior of the Marienkirche in Utrecht*, 1638 (Hamburg: Kunsthalle); *Interior of St. James's Church in Utrecht*, 1642 (Munich: Alte Pinakothek)

River Landscape with Ferries Docked Before a Tower *Jan van Goyen, 1640s, 25¼ x 37 in (64.1 x 94 cm), oil on panel, Private Collection. The castle is real, the setting imaginary.*

Adriaen **van Ostade**

⚰ 1610–84 🏴 DUTCH

🏛 Haarlem 🎨 oils; drawings; watercolors
🏛 St. Petersburg: Hermitage Museum.
Amsterdam: Rijksmuseum 💰 $5,432,000
in 2004, *Peasants Carousing and Dancing
Outside Inn* (oils)

Haarlem-born specialist in good-natured,
uncritical, lowlife scenes of peasants
having a good time in their hovels or
taverns. Rich, earthy colors suit the
mood. Both the peasants' behavior and
Ostade's technique improve as his work
develops (perhaps marrying a well-to-do
woman toned down his style and subjects).

Adriaen's brother and pupil, Isaak
(1621–49), chose similar peasant subjects
in his early work. Later on he developed a
line in silvery-gray landscapes, with good
atmosphere and busy human activity.

The Piper *Adriaen van Ostade, c. 1650s, oil on canvas,
London: British Museum. Ostade was a prolific painter
(over 800 are known) and a skilled watercolorist and
etcher. All his works found a ready market.*

KEY WORKS *Rustic Concert*, 1638 (Madrid:
Museo del Prado); *A Peasant Courting an Elderly
Woman*, 1653 (London: National Gallery);
An Alchemist, 1661 (London: National Gallery).

Salomon **van Ruysdael**

⚰ c. 1600–70 🏴 DUTCH

🏛 Haarlem 🎨 oils 🏛 Amsterdam:
Rijksmuseum 💰 $3,465,000 in 1997,
Extensive River Landscape (oils)

Prolific and well-known painter of
landscapes and riverscapes. Uncle
of the better known Jacob van Ruisdael.

He painted scenes that sum up a
preconceived idea of Holland (water, flat

on a river bank; rowing boats with fishermen; sailing boats with flags; cows; buildings on horizon (town, windmill, church); cloudy skies; evening light on horizon; reflections in water. He painted with broad, sweeping brushstrokes, using thin paint on a light ground; the grain of the panel often shows through.

KEY WORKS *Sailboats on the Wijkermeer*, c. 1648 (Berlin: Staatliche Museum); *Landscape with Medieval Castle*, 1652 (Vienna: Liechtenstein Museum); *Dutch Landscape with Highwayman*, 1656 (Berlin: Staatliche Museum)

Aert **van der Neer**
◔ 1603–77 ◨ DUTCH

◫ Amsterdam ◧ oils ◫ St. Petersburg: Hermitage Museum ◪ $3,528,000 in 1997, *Winter Landscape with Figures on Path and Ice* (oils)

Specialist in night scenes (gloomily imaginative, with ghostly full moon or lit by burning candles) and winter landscapes (atmospheric, with pale, cold colors and lots of skaters). Oddly unsuccessful as a painter. Also failed as an innkeeper and went bankrupt.

KEY WORKS *Sports on a Frozen River*, c. 1600 (New York: Metropolitan Museum of Art); *River View by Moonlight*, c. 1645 (Amsterdam: Rijksmuseum)

Philips **Koninck**
◔ 1619–88 ◨ DUTCH

◫ Rotterdam; Amsterdam ◧ oils ◫ London: National Gallery ◪ $1,404,000 in 1992, *Panoramic River Landscape* (oils)

Pupil of Rembrandt who learned from the master's landscape etchings and went on to produce a formula for large-scale, panoramic landscapes of Holland: high viewpoint; horizon across middle; scudding clouds; small figures to increase sense of vast space; alternating bands of light and dark to give receding space. Good, but not great.

KEY WORKS *Wide River Landscape*, 1648 (New York: Metropolitan Museum of Art); *An Extensive Landscape*, 1666 (Edinburgh: National Gallery of Scotland)

lands, big skies)—applying a standard formula that was very popular with Dutch collectors. There are also a few late still lifes with hunting themes.

The riverscape formula that he employed inventively juggles the following elements: compositions that always have a diagonal axis; mature trees

Panoramic Landscape *Philips Koninck, 1665, 54½ x 65½ in (138.4 x 166.4 cm), oil on canvas, London: Harold Samuel Collection. The equal division of open sky and landscape is typical of this artist.*

Philips **Wouvermans**
🔹 1619–68 📛 DUTCH

📛 Haarlem 🎨 oils 🏛 Dresden: Royal College.
London: National Gallery. Paris: Musée du Louvre
📈 $1.57m in 2001, *Landscape with Stag Hunt in
Full Cry, Fording a Stream* (oils)

Small-scale landscapes of horsemen, battle
or hunting scenes (note trademark white
horse). Unpretentious decorative art at its
best. Popular. Simple compositions—clear,
white sky; harmonious, hilly landscape;
foreground figures; elegant coloring.
KEY WORKS *Horses Being Watered*, 1656–60 (St.
Petersburg: Hermitage Museum); *Landscape with
Bathers*, 1660 (Vienna: Liechtenstein Museum)

Paulus **Potter**
🔹 1625–54 📛 DUTCH

📛 Amsterdam 🎨 oils 🏛 St. Petersburg:
Hermitage Museum 📈 $1,519,000 in 1996,
Two Cows and a Bull in a Meadow (oils)

Best painter of cows (also horses, sheep,
goats). Noted for a few life-sized animal
pictures, but more at ease on a small scale.
Good at weather, atmospheres, observation
of light. Also vanitas-type still lifes.
KEY WORKS *Cattle and Sheep in a Stormy Landscape*,
1647 (London: National Gallery); *The Wolf-
Hound*, c. 1650 (Las Vegas: Guggenheim
Hermitage Museum)

Hendrick **Avercamp**
🔹 1585–1634 📛 DUTCH

📛 Amsterdam 🎨 oils; watercolors
🏛 Windsor Castle (England): Royal Collection
📈 $7.75m in 2004, *Winter Scene* (oils)

Mute painter from Kampen in the
Netherlands. Specialized in atmospheric
winter scenes, usually in a landscape with
bare trees, a pink castle, and a happy
throng on the ice and snow. Uses high
horizons and warm-colored buildings
that intensify the coldness of sky and
snow; the thin painting of his figures
gives them vitality and movement.
KEY WORKS *Winter Scene at Yselmuiden*, c. 1613
(Geneva: Musée d'Art et d'Histoire); *Fishermen
by Moonlight*, c. 1625 (Amsterdam: Rijksmuseum)

Jacob van **Ruisdael**
🔹 1628–82 📛 DUTCH

📛 Haarlem; Amsterdam 🎨 oils 🏛 Amsterdam:
Rijksmuseum. London: National Gallery
📈 $4,268,000 *Two Undershot Watermills
with Men Opening Sluice* (oils)

Jacob van Ruisdael was the principal
Dutch landscape painter of the second
half of the 17th century. His earliest
known works date from 1746. He was
prolific and about 700 known paintings
are happily attributed to him.

Winter Scene with Skaters near a Castle
*Hendrik Avercamp, c. 1608–09, diameter 16⅛ in(41 cm),
oil on panel, London: National Gallery.* These winter
scenes were painted in the studio, from sketches for
sale in the local art market.

Melancholic, he was nephew to the
landscape painter Salomon van Ruysdael
(c. 1600–70; the different spelling occurs
regularly in their signatures) and had
a second career as a surgeon. His work
has a certain amount of stock imagery
although he can be quite inventive
within the formula: mountains, waterfalls,
beaches and dunes, seascapes, and
winter scenes. Essentially, his paintings
are descriptive (no hidden symbolism)
with a yearning for grandeur. Before
1650, he worked on panel but
subsequently painted on canvas.

He favors skies with rain clouds and
flying birds (not convincing—it looks like
a stage backdrop). He is more naturalistic
than his predecessors and it is possible to
identify species of trees in his paintings
(note how he likes rotten trees and broken
branches). He is also attracted to massive
forms and often uses a low viewpoint to
silhouette features against the sky. His
work is painted on dark priming and,
as a result, has dark tones.

KEY WORKS *Panoramic View of Haarlem*,
c. 1660s (London: Harold Samuel
Collection); *The Jewish Cemetery*, c. 1660
(Dresden: Gemäldegalerie); *Forest Scene*,
c. 1660–65 (Washington, DC: National
Gallery of Art); *Oaks by a Lake with Watermills*,
c. 1665–69 (Berlin: Staatliche Museum)

The Young Bull *Paulus Potter, 1647, 93 x 133½ in
(236 x 339 cm), oil on canvas, The Hague: Mauritshuis
Museum.* This is Potter's most monumental work. His
father owned a factory for stamping and gilding leather.

Aelbert **Cuyp**

◯ 1620–91   ⚑ DUTCH

🏠 Dordrecht   🎨 oils, watercolors
🏛 London: National Gallery; Dulwich
Picture Gallery   💰 $5,852,000 in 1994,
Orpheus Charming the Animals (oils)

Son of a painter, Cuyp married
a wealthy widow in 1658 and
neglected his art for local politics.

He produced some of the most
beautiful landscapes and riverscapes
ever painted. Using Italianate, golden
light (which he took entirely from Italian
paintings) he transformed his native
Holland (especially Dordrecht) into a
fantasy dream world, which epitomizes
the start or end of a perfect day. The
patrician classes who commissioned
and collected his work appreciated the
qualities of order, stillness, security,
clarity, everything and everyone in their
appointed place, harmony with nature,
a sense of proprietorship and timelessness.

The light floods in from the left, casting
long, soft shadows (surprising how few
definite shadows there are). Note how
the golden light catches just the edges of
plants, clouds, or animals, with highlights
laid on in thick, impastoed paint. He
uses a warm palette of earthy golds and
browns contrasted with cool, silvery skies
and foliage. Nice ambiguities and easily
overlooked details, such as birds in flight;
Is it morning or evening? He was much
loved and collected in England.

KEY WORKS *The Sea by Moonlight*, c. 1648
(St. Petersburg: Hermitage Museum);
Sunset after Rain, 1648–52 (Cambridge:
Fitzwilliam Museum); *A Distant View of
Dordrecht with a Milkmaid and Four Cows*,
c. 1650 (London: National Gallery)

A Herdsman with Five Cows by a River *Aelbert
Cuyp, c. 1650, 17¾ x 29 in (45 x 74 cm), oil on wood,
London: National Gallery.* Works like these were produced
on commission for wealthy members of Dordrecht society.

Gerard **Terborch**

🔵 1617–81 📗 DUTCH

🏛 Amsterdam; Haarlem; England; Italy; Spain; Germany 🎨 oils 🏛 St. Petersburg: Hermitage Museum. London: National Gallery 💰 $4.2m in 1997, *Music Lesson* (oils)

Precocious and successful, Terborch (or Ter Borch) was one of the finest and most inventive masters of the Dutch School. His small-scale, very beautiful, restrained, and gentle genre scenes show self-absorbed moments of a mundane world being raised to immortality by art. One senses from the acuity of his observation and the minute care with which he applies the paint that he viewed this world, its people, its foibles, its ordinariness, and its objects (not forgetting the dogs) with the greatest of affection and pleasure.

Look for harmonies of brown, gold, and yellow, and silver and gray-blue, exquisitely balanced against dark backgrounds; his love of detail; the rendering of fabrics and the way clothes are made; his ability to draw us quietly into his intimate world and leave a lingering question over the secrets or affections that are being shared; his love of a lady's neck and the light reflecting off a surface. See how he uses gentle symbolism but without overt moralizing.

KEY WORKS *The Swearing of the Oath of Ratification of the Treaty of Münster*, 1648 (London: National Gallery); *The Message*, c. 1658 (Lyon: Musée des Beaux-Arts); *A Lady at her Toilet*, c. 1668 (Detroit Institute of Arts)

cloud—satisfying contrasts of warm and cool, hard and soft. A typical composition is of buildings closing in on one side with an open area leading out of the picture on the other—another good use of contrast.

KEY WORKS *A View in Cologne*, c. 1660–65 (London: National Gallery); *The Inn of the Black Pig at Maarsseveen*, c. 1668 (Los Angeles: J. Paul Getty Museum)

Jan **van der Heyden**

🔵 1637–1712 📗 DUTCH

🏛 Amsterdam 🎨 oils 🏛 London: National Gallery. Paris: Musée de Louvre 💰 $1,008,000 in 1997, *Düsseldorf, View of the Jesuit Church of St. Andreas* (oils)

A prosperous inventor and designer of fire engines and lighting, painting was a secondary activity for van der Heyden, who is best known for still lifes and meticulous, small-scale topographical and *capriccio* (see page 234) views of towns in the Netherlands and Rhineland.

Famous for dexterous painting of walls and masonry, he sets warm, sharp, detailed bricks against blue skies and fluffy white

Meyndert **Hobbema**

🔵 1638–1709 📗 DUTCH

🏛 Amsterdam 🎨 oils 🏛 London: National Gallery 💰 $8.26m in 2001, *Wooded Landscape with Travellers on a Path through a Hamlet* (oils)

Last of the major Dutch landscape artists of the 17th-century golden age, he gave up professional painting when he married in 1668 and became a wine gauger instead. His range is generally limited to repetitive scenes of finely painted dark landscapes with watermills and cottages round a pool, overgrown trees, and occasional figures.

KEY WORKS *A Stream by a Wood*, c. 1663 (London: National Gallery); *A Watermill*, c. 1665–68 (Amsterdam: Rijksmuseum)

The Christening Feast (detail)
Jan Steen, 1664, 34½ x 42 in
(87.8 x 107 cm), oil on canvas, London:
Wallace Collection. The complex
symbolism indicates that the "father"
holding the baby is a cuckold.

Pieter de **Hooch**

◐ 1629–83 ⚑ DUTCH

🏛 Delft; Amsterdam   🎨 oils
🏛 London: National Gallery
💰 $6.24m in 1992, *Courtyard
of House in Delft with Young
Woman and Two Men* (oils)

Pieter de Hooch is a
perennially popular Dutch
master and one of the best-
known and best-loved genre
painters. It is known that he
died insane but, otherwise,
little is known of his life.

His best and most widely
known work dates from
his years in Delft (1654–c.
1660/61), and generally
depicts sunny courtyards
and sunlit interiors,
celebrating well-behaved
middle-class life. Before
1655 he painted lowlife peasant and
soldier scenes. From Delft, he moved to
Amsterdam and, after 1665, portrayed
rich interiors with a bogus view of pseudo-
aristocratic life. His very late work (1670s)
is feeble but his best work bears a similarity
to that of Vermeer (see page 213), who
was his talented contemporary in Delft.

Observe the way he plays with, and
enjoys, space and light—he creates views
from one room or area to another and
uses the geometric patterns of the tiled
floors and courtyards to construct the
illusion of space, flooding them with
warm light and leaving the foreground
uncluttered. His compositions are
carefully designed with well-placed
verticals, horizontals, and diagonals,
and he uses carefully worked-out
geometric perspective, usually with a
single vanishing point. He also makes
discreet use of symbols and emblems.
KEY WORKS *The Pantry*, c. 1658 (Amsterdam:
Rijksmuseum); *Two Soldiers and a Woman
Drinking*, c. 1658–60 (Washington, DC:
National Gallery of Art); *A Dutch Courtyard*,
c. 1660 (Washington, DC: National
Gallery of Art)

Jan **Steen**

◐ c. 1626–79 ⚑ DUTCH

🏛 Netherlands   🎨 oils   🏛 London:
National Gallery   💰 $2.7m in 1989,
*Figures in an Interior with Man and Woman
Seated at Table Playing Cards* (oils)

Steen, one of the best and most important
Dutch genre painters, ran a tavern and
owned a brewery. His lively, crowded scenes
of taverns, feasts, and households with
stock characters and facial expressions
(rather like a TV soap opera—and maybe
his works fulfilled a similar need), were
prolific and popular. Watch out also for
portraits, mythological scenes, religious
works, and landscapes.

The lively and easy use of flowing, juicy
fresh colors (rose red, blue-green, pale
yellow) adds to the paintings' vitality and
reflects their character. Full of symbolism,
the genre scenes carry an unambiguous
(sometimes heavy-handed) message about
drunkenness, idleness, promiscuity, etc.
KEY WORKS *A Young Woman Playing a Harpsichord*,
c. 1659 (London: National Gallery); *Skittle
Players Outside an Inn*, c. 1660–63 (London:
National Gallery)

Jan **Both**

◔ c. 1618–52 🏴 DUTCH

🅿 Utrecht   🎨 oils   🏛 London: Wallace Collection
📈 $1.96m in 2000, *Italianate Evening with a
Muleteer and Goatherds on a Wooded Path* (oils)

Dutch landscape painter who studied
in Rome and introduced the Italianate
Arcadian landscape, *à la* Claude, to
Holland. More detailed and literal than
Claude (see page 182), he does not usually
make references to classical mythology.
KEY WORKS *Italian Landscape*, c. 1635–41
(Cambridge: Fitzwilliam Museum);
Bandits Leading Prisoners, c. 1646 (Boston:
Museum of Fine Arts)

Gabriel **Metsu**

◔ 1682–1749 🏴 DUTCH

🅿 Amsterdam   🎨 oils   🏛 Amsterdam:
Rijksmuseum   📈 $1,426,000 in 1999, *Officer
Paying Court to a Woman in Interior* (oils)

High-quality painter of intimate, small-
scale scenes of well-ordered, polite Dutch
households, whose carefully organized
compositions and meticulous technique
and palette reflect the lifestyle of the
Dutch bourgeoisie. Many of the objects
and still-life details are symbolic; if there
is lettering or a document, it is meant to
be read as part of the meaning of the
picture (a neat way of drawing you into
the intimacy and secrecy of the scene).

Note his liking for dark interiors—rooms
with windows closed or curtains drawn, or
a dark corner. His palette is warm and
personal, especially using reds and browns.
KEY WORKS *The Prodigal Son*, 1640s
(St. Petersburg: Hermitage Museum);
A Soldier Visiting a Young Lady, 1653
(Paris: Musée du Louvre); *A Dead Cock*,
c. 1655–59 (Madrid: Museo del Prado)

Jan **Weenix**

◔ 1640–1719 🏴 DUTCH

🅿 Amsterdam; Düsseldorf   🎨 oils
🏛 London: Wallace Collection   📈 $456,000
in 1995, *Dead Hare on Plinth by Urn, Fruit,
Birds, Boy Bearing Fruit* (oils)

Son of Jan Baptist Weenix (1621–63) who
called himself Giovanni Battista after his
trip to Italy 1642–1646. His son never
visited Italy but continued his father's

Still Life *Jan Weenix, c. 1690, 19½ x 15 in (49.5 x 38.1 cm),
oil on canvas, Leeds: City Art Gallery.* Weenix's early still
lifes caught the eye of the Elector Palatine, who employed
him in Düsseldorf from 1702–14.

popular Italianate seaports and courtyard
scenes. He also painted hunting trophies
and still lifes, and was skilled at textures,
such as silk, marble, silver, and glass.
KEY WORKS *The White Peacock*, 1692 (Vienna:
Liechtenstein Museum); *Falconer's Bag*, 1695
(New York: Metropolitan Museum of Art);
Portrait of Peter I, c. 1697 (St. Petersburg:
Hermitage Museum)

Jan **van Huysum**

◔ 1682–1749 🏴 DUTCH

🅿 Amsterdam   🎨 oils   🏛 Paris: Musée
du Louvre   📈 $3.2m in 1992, *Flowers in
a Terra-cotta Vase on a Marble Plinth* (oils)

One of the most prolific flower painters,
he gained an impressive international
reputation. Ornamental bouquets of
asymmetrical flower arrangements, not
necessarily of the same season. Smooth
enamel-like paint; cool tones; vivid blues
and greens. A few fruit pieces and landscapes. Whenever possible, he worked
directly from life rather than from studies.
KEY WORKS *Hollyhocks and Other Flowers in a
Vase*, c. 1702–20 (London: National Gallery);
Flowers and Fruit, 1723 (St. Petersburg:
Hermitage Museum); *Still Life with Flowers*,
1723 (Amsterdam: Rijksmuseum)

Jan **Vermeer**

- 1632–75 ♙ DUTCH

🏛 Delft 🖌 oils
🏛 Amsterdam: Rijksmuseum.
The Hague: Mauritshuis
Museum. Washington, DC:
National Gallery of Art
💰 $2.7m in 1990, *Cupid
Disarmed by Venus* (oils)

Now regarded as the
finest Dutch genre
painter. Unrecognized
in his own lifetime.
Forgotten until the end
of the 19th century.

Only 35 works known
for certain. With a few
memorable exceptions,
he constantly reworked
the same theme: the corner of a room,
but with a unique, exquisite, tantalizing
observation of the organization of space,
light, and enigmatic human relationships.

Look closely: nothing is quite in
focus—visually and emotionally he
selects that tantalizing fraction of a second
just before something that is anticipated
but not yet fully perceived or understood

Girl with a Pearl Earring *Jan
Vermeer, c. 1660–61, 18½ x 15¾ in
(46.5 x 40 cm), oil on canvas, The
Hague: Mauritshuis Museum.* In the
1880s this famous work was sold in
Holland for the equivalent of 50 cents.

becomes clear and
resolved, and in its
full realization, so
often disappointing.
By stopping short he
requires the individual
eye and imagination
to supply what it most
desires to see and feel.
This is perceptual and
poetic creativity, along
with manipulation of
breathtaking skill and
sensitivity. Makes the eye
linger over the seemingly
innocent but precisely
calculated interplay of
cool blues and sensuous
yellows and whites.

KEY WORKS *Kitchen Maid*,
1656–61 (Amsterdam: Rijksmuseum); *Woman
Holding a Balance*, c. 1664 (Washington. DC:
National Gallery of Art); *Lady Standing at the
Virginal*, c. 1670 (London: National Gallery)

View of Delft *Jan Vermeer, c. 1660–61, 39½ x 46 in
(100 x 117 cm), oil on canvas, The Hague: Mauritshuis
Museum.* It is likely that Vermeer used a camera obscura,
which projects a slightly fuzzy image. The work was much
admired by Marcel Proust.

The Artist's Studio

Vermeer c. 1665

This is one of Vermeer's later and most ambitious works, the fulfillment of many years of experience, meticulously developed craftsmanship, observation, study, and discussion. It operates on two levels: visually, it is a very subtle and intricate arrangement of space and light; intellectually and emotionally, it is a complex allegory about the art of painting.

Typical of Vermeer is the intimate glimpse of the relationship between two people, meticulous observation of light, and precise handling of color. Vermeer often used the placing of a chair in the foreground, the regular pattern of a slate and marble floor, and the interplay between two figures, like variations on a theme. The painting has also had an interesting history—in 1677 Vermeer's family petitioned the courts to prevent it from being auctioned to pay the artist's debts. It changed hands several times, and during World War II it was confiscated from its Austrian owners by Adolf Hitler, who hung it in his private rooms at Berchtesgaden.

The source of light is hidden behind a heavy curtain that is drawn aside to reveal the artist at work. Note how Vermeer turns highlights, especially on the curtain and the chairs, into delicate beads of light, not unlike pearls

The Muse of History carries a trumpet, which symbolizes the fame that can be achieved by an artist. Vermeer may be suggesting that an artist's fame need no longer rest with traditional history painting but can be achieved with new subjects, such as genre painting

The line of the tabletop draws the viewer's eye in to the painting toward a vanishing point positioned just below the bulbous finial of the map's roller bar

The model represents Clio, the Muse of History, whose attributes are the wreath of laurel and a book in which she records all heroic deeds. The nine Muses were the goddesses of inspiration in the arts and sciences. Vermeer confirms the status of painting as a liberal art.

The Artist's Studio

Medium oil on canvas
Dimensions 47 x 39½ in (120 x 100 cm)
Location Vienna: Kunsthistorisches Museum

The chandelier is decorated with the two-headed eagle of the Hapsburgs, the Spanish royal family. The lack of candles refers to their waning power. The Northern Dutch provinces gained full independence from Spain in 1648.

The roof beams create a strong horizontal pattern continued by the map's roller bars. The underlying structure of horizontals and verticals gives the picture its mood of stability and calm

The vertical crease marks the frontier between Protestant Holland and Catholic Flanders; the latter was still under the political control and cultural influence of Spain

The artist's easel points with new confidence toward the new republic of Holland

The painter is not dressed in the clothes of his own day, but wears a 15th-century costume. It would seem that Vermeer is connecting the art of his own era with the art of the time of the great masters van Eyck (see page 110) and van der Weyden (see page 111)

TECHNIQUES

Vermeer uses the tiles like stepping-stones to lead the eye into the composition. The line is reinforced by the angle of the tabletop.

William **Dobson**

- c. 1610–46 BRITISH

London oils London Galleries $161,920 in 1992, *Portrait of Sir Thomas Cricheley* (oils)

Brief career as a painter to the doomed court of Charles I at Oxford. Only 50 known paintings: nothing known pre-1642. Robust, direct style. Half-length portraits: red-faced, earthy, conservative male subjects with classical allusions and visual references, which emphasize the sitter's learning or bravery (or both).

KEY WORKS *The Executioner with the Baptist's Head*, c. 1630s (Liverpool: Walker Art Gallery); *Portrait of the Artist's Wife*, c. 1635–40 (London: Tate Collection)

Sir Peter **Lely**

- 1618–80 DUTCH/BRITISH

Haarlem; London oils London: National Maritime Museum, Greenwich; Hampton Court Palace $1,328,000 in 2003, *Chesterfield Portrait*, two boys, probably Philip Stanhope and brother Charles (oils)

German-born of Dutch parents, whose family name was van der Faes, Lely settled in England in the early 1640s. He was the principal portrait painter for Charles II, and especially notable for his

Anne Hyde, Duchess of York Sir Peter Lely, *c. 1660s, 71¾ x 56½ in (182.2 x 143 cm), Edinburgh: Scottish National Portrait Gallery.* The first wife of James II was reputedly more clever than beautiful.

fashionable, female portraits, which show richly dressed, slightly raffish-looking women with heavy eyes and long, mobile fingers. Studio assistants were responsible for much poor-quality work in his name.

A few very fine early works show his talent for landscape and observation of unimportant faces. When at his best, he had a wonderful feel for light.

KEY WORKS *Trial by Fire*, 1640s–50s (St. Petersburg: Hermitage Museum); *Two Ladies of the Lake Family*, c. 1660 (London: Tate Collection); *Barbara Villiers, Duchess of Cleveland*, c. 1665 (Private Collection)

John Michael **Wright**

- 1617–94 BRITISH

Edinburgh; Rome; Netherlands; London oils London: National Portrait Gallery. St. Petersburg: The Hermitage Museum $437,900 in 2000, *Portrait of Lord Mungo Murray in Highland Dress* (oils)

A talented Catholic portrait painter who spent the 1640s and 1650s in Rome and France, and learned the virtues of allegory and elegance. A direct contemporary of Lely, he established a successful practice during the reigns of Charles II and James II but his more direct and realistic style never quite suited fashionable taste. He died in poverty.

KEY WORKS *Elizabeth Claypole (née Cromwell)*, 1658 (London: National Portrait Gallery); *Thomas Hobbes*, c. 1669–70 (London: National Portrait Gallery)

Sir Godfrey **Kneller**

- 1646–1723 GERMAN/BRITISH

Amsterdam; Italy; England oils London: National Portrait Gallery $263,754 in 1997, *Portrait of King George I of England* (oils)

German-born, but had settled in England by the age of 30. Became principal state portrait painter from the reign of Charles II to George II. Established a successful formula (polite, masklike faces with repetitive mouths and eyes) that emphasized status rather than realism or personality. Many substandard works were produced by studio assistants.

KEY WORKS *Portrait of John Banckes*, 1676 (London: Tate Collection); *King Charles II*, 1685 (Liverpool: Walker Art Gallery)

Grinling **Gibbons**

⊖ 1648–1720 🏴 BRITISH/DUTCH

🏙 Rotterdam; London   🗿 sculpture
🏛 Surrey (England): Hampton Court.
Sussex (England) Petworth Park
💰 $140,000 in 1995, *Psalm 48, King
David Playing Harp, St. Cecilia an Organ*

England's most famous woodcarver
of all time. Born of English parents
in Rotterdam, he arrived in England
c. 1670/71. Very distinct personal
style—his sculptures seem organically
alive. His theme was often cascades: fruit,
leaves, flowers, birds, fish, which tumbled
down furniture, paneling, even chimneys
and walls. This famous cravat (right), *à
la* Venetian needlepoint, was so realistic
that an overseas visitor was convinced
it was the standard dress of an English
gent. Writer Sir Horace Walpole often
wore it as a joke. Royal patrons included
Charles II, William III, and George I,
as well as major stately homes where
his work is found today.

KEY WORKS Marble font, c. 1680s (London:
St. James's Church, Piccadilly); Ceiling,
c. 1680s (Suffolk: Petworth House)

> ## "There is nothing on
> ## earth so terrible
> ## as English music except
> ## English painting."
>
> HEINRICH HEINE

Woodcarving of a Cravat *Grinling Gibbons,
c. 1690, limewood, London: Victoria & Albert
Museum.* This intricately carved piece meticulously
imitates Venetian needlepoint lace, and once
belonged to 18th-century collector Sir Horace Walpole.

KEY WORKS *Thetis Accepting the Shield of
Achilles from Vulcan*, c. 1710 (London:
Tate Collection); *Time, Truth, and Justice,*
c. 1716 (Manchester: City Art Gallery)

Sir James **Thornhill**

⊖ 1675–1734 🏴 BRITISH

🏙 England   🗿 oils; fresco   🏛 London:
Greenwich, National Maritime Gallery
💰 $42,000 in 1999, *Capriccio with Saint
Paul before Agrippa* (oils)

Ambitious and successful. The only
English painter of fashionable, illusionistic
Baroque wall and ceiling paintings for
public buildings (including the Painted
Hall of Wren and Hawksmoor's naval
hospital in Greenwich, London) and
country houses. Retired from painting
in 1728 to become an MP and country
squire. Produced quality work, but it
lacks the necessary histrionic drama and
excess (the British always believed that
foreigners do that kind of thing better).

Michael **Dahl**

⊖ 1659–1743 🏴 SWEDISH/BRITISH

🏙 London   🗿 oils   🏛 London:
National Portrait Gallery; Tate Collection
💰 $88,920 in 1989, *View of Olyo
Farm, Valdres* (oils)

Born in Sweden, settled in London in
1689. Produced competent portraits
of aristocracy, royalty, and the literati.
Languorous, elegant style, but poor
characterization. Good on draperies;
used diffused, silvery tones and short
brushstrokes. Kneller's principal
competitor. Dahl was prolific and
successful. His earlier works are best.

KEY WORKS *Self-Portrait*, 1691 (London:
National Portrait Gallery); *Unknown
Woman, formerly known as Sarah Churchill,
Duchess of Marlborough*, 1695–1700
(London: National Portrait Gallery)

FROM ROCOCO TO NEO-CLASSICISM
c. 1700 – 1800

The 17th century had been a period of religious confrontation and warfare. By contrast, the 18th century, the Age of Reason, was a period of relative calm in which all the arts developed a refinement and elegance—often small in scale—suited to satisfying simple human needs and longings, rather than supporting ideologies.

At the heart of 18th-century thought and politics was the Enlightenment—a belief that human reason would resolve political and religious dilemmas, explain the workings of the world, the universe, and human nature, and create harmonious relationships in which superstition, tyranny, slavery, and oppression would be eliminated. This emphasis on "a pursuit of happiness" manifested itself in many ways: family life, children, and conjugal love became important; so did education, travel, industriousness, town planning, landscape gardening, parties, music, reading, discussion, food, comfort, and convenience. The Enlightenment also liked intellectual and emotional dualities, not as competing ideologies that would fight each other to the death, but to emphasize that choice was part and parcel of human fulfillment. Thus, the art, literature, and philosophy of the 18th century are full of references to the differences between sense and sensibility, frivolity and morality, reason and emotion, indulgence and sobriety, sensuality and self-denial. This duality is equally well represented in the two principal artistic styles of the century: the Rococo with its light-hearted subjects, delicate colors, and asymmetric curves emphasizing frivolity, and sensuality, and Neoclassicism with its serious historical subjects, straight lines, and precise outlines prioritizing morality and self-denial.

FRANCE AND ENGLAND
The principles of the Enlightenment were also reflected in the politics of the two major powers, France and England, but expressed in surprisingly

Interior of Abbey Church, Ottobeuren, Bavaria
In the 18th century Germany staged a cultural recovery. Spectacular church interiors were created from a blend of Baroque architecture and Rococo decoration.

Cry of Liberty and the Departure for the Frontier *Le Sueur brothers, 1792, print, Musée de la Ville de Paris.* The French Revolution brought 10 years of political chaos to France, during which the king and his family were executed and Europe was plunged into war.

different ways, and with very different outcomes. English ideas were filtered though a prism of robust middle-class pragmatism; French ideas through one of theory, philosophical speculation, and aristocratic otherworldliness.

Both nations benefited from scientific discoveries, population growth, and agricultural revolutions. Both also had substantial colonial territories—chiefly in India and North America—backed by powerful military and naval forces. However Anglo-French rivalry was more than just a question of power politics. As important, each stood for a fundamentally different approach to government. Catholic France remained committed to the absolutist model of kingship established by Louis XIV. Protestant England, more properly Britain after its formal

unification with Scotland in 1707, was rapidly evolving an early form of parliamentary rule. After 1763, with the end of the Seven Years' War, Britain's superiority was clear. France had been ejected from India and North America and British naval superiority, the linchpin of its maritime empire, was emphatically confirmed.

James Watt rotary steam engine
Britain's technological lead in the second half of the 18th century gave it a decisive advantage over its European trading rivals. Industrialization boosted productivity and lowered costs.

TIMELINE: 1700—1800

1700	**1720**	**1740**
1703 Foundation of St. Petersburg by Peter the Great	**1729** *Bach's St. Matthew Passion* first performed	**1751** Diderot begins publication of *L'Encyclopédie* (to 1780)
1714 Hanoverian succession in Britain		
1704 Grand Alliance forces under duke of Marlborough defeat French at Blenheim	**1735** War of the Polish Succession becomes Europe-wide conflict (to 1738)	**1740** Frederick II (the Great) of Prussia launches War of Austrian Succession (to 1748)
1715 France ruled by regency of Philippe II, duc d'Orléans, upon death of Louis XIV		

INDEPENDENCE AND REVOLUTION

British self-confidence received a stinging rebuff with the Declaration of Independence in 1776 by the American colonists. It was the clearest possible statement of the political and philosophical principles of the Enlightenment, modeled on the examples of both France and England, and it succeeded in creating what would eventually grow into a new world power. Britain recovered. Having lost her American colonies, she simply went on to build a second worldwide empire, an Anglo-Scottish enterprise that defined a British national identity, and added enormous riches to a land already grown fat on modern agriculture, and about to reap the economic benefits of an industrial revolution.

France, on the other hand, was a country that was kept unsteadily afloat by a volatile combination of aristocratic privilege, corruption, and debt, the whole centered on an inept monarchy. In the end, this fatally flawed structure fell apart in the turmoil of the French Revolution of 1789. The revolutionary rallying cry of "Liberty, Equality,

Fraternity" soon became hollow words, as the bloodshed and tyranny of the "Terror" and then the dictatorship of Napoleon usurped the Enlightenment principles that the Revolution had sought to establish.

Goethe in the Campagna *Johann Heinrich Wilhelm Tischbein, 1787, oil on canvas, 64 1/2 x 81 in (164 x 206 cm), Frankfurt: Städelsches Kunstinstitut.* Like many other 18th-century writers and artists, Goethe visited Italy to seek inspiration among the Classical ruins.

Elsewhere in Europe the Austrian Habsburgs (Empress Maria Theresa), Prussia (Frederick the Great), and Russia (Catherine the Great) were all growing in influence and power, even if they lacked the global reach of France and England. Poland was on the verge of extinction. Italy and Habsburg Spain were subsiding, the latter despite its still huge Latin American empire. Ottoman Turkey was also shrinking in terms of power and territory, reduced by the end of the century to little more than an impotent bystander.

1761 British destroy French power in India

1776 American colonies declare independence from Britain

1788 First British settlement in Australia

1793 Final partition of Poland

1799 Coup brings Napoleon to power in France

1760

1780

1800

1762 Accession of Catherine the Great of Russia

1763 Treaty of Paris confirms British supremacy in North America

1777 Watt develops first true steam engine (Britain)

1789 French Revolution

1784 *The Oath of the Horatii*, David (France)

1798 Napoleon invades Egypt

Jean-Antoine **Watteau**

● 1684–1721　**∾** FRENCH

🔲 Paris　⚫ oils; chalk　🏛 Paris: Musée du Louvre. London: Wallace Collection
↗ $3,234,000 in 2000, *Le Conteur, Artist from the Commedia dell'Arte in a Landscape* (oils)

The most important French painter of the first half of the 18th century. Created a fresh, new, unassuming style, which was badly needed at the time.

LIFE AND WORKS

Watteau came from a poor family and had indifferent health throughout his short life. From a Flemish town ceded to France from the Spanish Netherlands, he trained as a scene painter at the Paris Opéra from c. 1702–07. He then went to work for the curator of the Luxembourg Palace. There he had access to Rubens's *Marie de Medici* series, which was a major

> **"With a material art he has realized the miracle of representing a domain that it seemed only possible to evoke with music."**
>
> CAMILLE MAUCLAIR ON WATTEAU

influence, even though his own style was far more light and delicate.

He entered the French Academy in 1717 with *A Journey to Cythera* (right), which could not be fitted into any existing category and for which he received the new title of "peintre de fêtes galantes," a variant of the term "fête champêtre" or "outdoor feast," which had been applied to the 16th-century outdoor scenes of Giorgione (see page 140) and the Gardens of Love found in medieval manuscripts.

Two years later, in 1719, he went to London, possibly to consult a famous physician, but the grim English winter aggravated his condition and he died of TB in 1721. His last great work was a shop sign known as *L'Enseigne de Gersaint*, 1721 (Berlin: Staatliche Museum).

STYLE

He is famous for inventing the *fête galante* or "courtship party"—a sort of stage set and dream world of perfectly mannered human love and harmony with nature, grounded in an acute observation of reality. Never sentimental, there is a melancholy that is sometimes accredited to his poor health.

His forms are often half-suggested and require completion in the imagination (as in love, where a half-spoken sentence or a snatched glance can be made to mean everything). His statues seem about to become flesh and blood and join the human activity. The very titles of his works, *Conversation, Breakfast in the Open Air, Rural Pleasures*, become the spirit of the Rococo: daring, airy, carefree exuberance.

Pierrot: Gilles *1721, 72⅛ x 59 in (185 x 150 cm), oil on canvas, Paris: Musée du Louvre.* The character Pierrot: Gilles comes from the form of Italian improvised comedy known as *commedia dell'arte*. A laughing stock, this mournful clown is the rejected lover and pitiable fool.

Still Life *Jean Chardin, c. 1732, 6⅔ x 8¼ in (16.8 x 21 cm), oil on panel, Detroit Institute of Arts.* Although a member of the prestigious Royal Academy in Paris, Chardin was criticized for not attempting more ambitious subjects. The son of a master carpenter, and a man of simple tastes, he instead preferred to perfect what he knew he could do best.

Jean **Chardin**

● 1669–1779   🏳 FRENCH

🏛 Paris   🎨 oils   🏛 Paris: Musée du Louvre   📊 $2.3m in 1989, *Fish, Vegetables, Pots, and Cruets on a Table* (oils)

Diligent artist, widowed. Exemplified in paint the best qualities of the Age of Reason, producing exquisite small still lifes and genre scenes that demonstrate harmony of order, sober color, pleasure in simplicity and relationships.

Note his loving observation of light and handling of paint. Subjects and style reflect his modest, open personality with love of craftsmanship. The surfaces and textures of the still lifes are so believable that you want to touch them—you know exactly what everything is and where it is in space. The genre scenes crystallize moments of simple, restful intimacy, such as childish pleasures, Experience teaching Youth, the dignity of domestic labor, etc. Simple, easy-to-understand symbolism.

KEY WORKS *The House of Cards*, c. 1735 (Washington, DC: National Gallery of Art); *The Young Schoolmistress*, c. 1735–36 (London: National Gallery)

Nicolas **Lancret**

● 1690–1743   🏳 FRENCH

🏛 Paris   🎨 oils   🏛 Paris: Musée du Louvre. London: Wallace Collection   📊 $740,000 in 1997, *Huntsman and his Servant* (oils)

Lancret was a chief follower of Watteau's style, but his own style was more prosaic—he painted only the day-to-day

(albeit elegant) reality, whereas Watteau could transform reality and endow it with the magic of poetry and dreams. His works have a cruder color than Watteau's. Liked theater subjects. Popular with aristocratic collectors.

KEY WORKS *The Four Ages of Man: Maturity*, 1730–35 (London: National Gallery); *Dance before a Fountain*, c. 1730–35 (Los Angeles: J. Paul Getty Museum)

Jean-Baptiste **Pater**

● 1695–1736   🏳 FRENCH

🏛 Paris   🎨 oils   🏛 Paris: Musée du Louvre. St. Petersburg: Hermitage Museum   📊 $600,000 in 2003, *Bathers. The Swing* (oils; a pair)

Watteau's pupil. Had similar subjects and style, but his drawing and use of color lack confidence. His work doesn't have the depth of feeling and the richness of color that is the hallmark of Watteau.

KEY WORKS *Les Baigneuses* (*Women Bathing*), (St. Petersburg: Hermitage Museum); *The Dance*, (London: National Gallery); *Chinese Hunt*, 1736 (Paris: Musée du Louvre)

François **Boucher**

● 1703–70   🏳 FRENCH

🏛 Paris   🎨 oils   🏛 Paris: Musée du Louvre. London: Wallace Collection. Stockholm: National Museum   📊 $2,237,094 in 1988, *Les Amusements de la Campagne. La Musique Pastorale* (oils; a pair)

A key artist of the sumptuous, profligate, overindulgent *ancien régime* of Louis XV. A favorite of Madame de Pompadour. Epitomizes the full-blown Rococo style.

Creator of lavish images of, and for, a world of narcissistic, self-indulgent luxury, namely the French royal court of the mid-18th century (this does not stop them from being wonderful paintings). Most magnificent with his depictions of the classical gods, who (according to Boucher) enjoyed a similar lifestyle; also heavily sentimental pastoral and genre scenes. In addition, he designed for the royal tapestry works and porcelain factories and became King's Painter in 1765.

Notice the acres of soft, pink flesh set among frothy and false vegetation; lavish silks, satins, and lace in the portraits—all painted with great technical skill and caressing sensuality; a brilliant marriage between his patrons' needs (the subject matter) and style and technique—one of the hallmarks of great painting.

KEY WORKS *The Breakfast*, 1739 (Paris: Musée du Louvre); *Diana Bathing*, 1742 (Paris: Musée du Louvre); *Reclining Girl*, 1751 (Munich: Alte Pinakothek)

Jean-Baptiste **Greuze**

◔ 1725–1805   ⚑ FRENCH

🏛 Paris   🎨 oils   🏛 Paris: Musée du Louvre. Montpellier: Musée Fabre. London: Wallace Collection   💰 $900,000 in 1998, *Portrait of Benjamin Franklin* (oils)

Best known for his sentimental storytelling genre pictures and titillating images of young children that were part of his later work. Early on he had aspirations as a history painter. Played to a pre-French Revolution audience that turned luxury and idleness into an art form. Became very successful but fell into obscurity with the revolution and died in poverty. Had an unpleasant personality.

His overriding feature is excess of emotion—overexpressive faces and overdramatic gestures. You know what feeling he was trying to convey (or do you, in fact?) but, like bad acting, it can seem so false you may well be moved to laughter rather than tears.

Many weaknesses: false emotion, bad composition, poor drawing, unattractive color. In fairness, he did make some striking portraits, which are good and worth looking for.

KEY WORKS *Broken Eggs*, 1756 (New York: Metropolitan Museum of Art); *Boy with Lesson Book*, c. 1757 (Edinburgh: National Gallery of Scotland); *The Laundress*, 1761 (Los Angeles: J. Paul Getty Museum); *Spoilt Child*, 1765 (St. Petersburg: Hermitage Museum)

Le Geste Napolitain Jean-Baptiste Greuze, 1757, 28¼ x 37 in (73 x 94.3 cm), oil on canvas, Massachusetts: Worcester Art Museum. Greuze's anecdotal scenes were popular with a novel-reading public, and he played up to their enthusiasms by selling engravings of his works and elaborating their themes in notes in exhibition catalogs.

THE ROCOCO

By the early 18th century, the heroic certainties of the Baroque were giving way to the elegant intricacies of the Rococo (from the French "rocaille," meaning "shellwork," a recurring motif in Rococo interior decoration). A conspicuously courtly painting style, it appealed to sophisticated, aristocratic patrons. As a reflection of a supremely cultivated society, it was briefly supreme.

STYLE

Light colors and deft brushwork predominate, with a premium on highly finished, shimmering surfaces in which the depiction of gorgeous fabrics, melting skin tones, and luxuriant landscape backgrounds—often overgrown, never threatening—is relished for its own sake. In the hands of its most outstanding exponents—the French painters Boucher and Fragonard, the Italian Tiepolo—the result is a captivating, idealized world, elegant and seemingly effortless. Draperies flow, limbs intertwine, smiles entice and eyelids flutter. Allure is everything.

The Last Judgment (ceiling fresco) Johann Baptist Zimmermann, c. 1746–54, fresco and stucco, Wies (Germany): Wieskirche. German artists fused architecture and painting to create light-filled interiors that soar into visions of heaven.

SUBJECTS

"Education de l'Amour" (modeled by Etienne Falconet after Boucher), c. 1763, 12 in (30.5 cm), porcelain. The subject matter, self-evidently sexual, is as typical as the handling: eroticism meets highly finished treatment.

Sophisticated 18th-century society placed a premium on intimacy. It was a shift in taste precisely reflected by Rococo art, above all in France. In place of the large scale of the Baroque, whether antique or religious, Rococo painting concentrated on aristocratic dalliance, small scale and highly wrought. Antiquity became a matter of scantily clad shepherdesses, bosoms daintily exposed, ravished by muscular young giants. The Rococo rarely lent itself to religious subjects, but Tiepolo successfully linked the two.

KEY EVENTS

1702	Flemish-born Watteau arrives in Paris
1714	Death of Louis XIV
1717	Watteau paints his elegiac *A Journey to Cythera* (see page 223)
1750	Tiepolo spends three years at Würzburg. Completes the decorative cycle in 1752–53 with fresco of the continents, the world's largest painting, over the main staircase
1775	Boucher appointed director of the French Academy
1767	Fragonard paints his airy masterpiece, *The Swing* (see page 228)

WHAT TO LOOK FOR

Boucher epitomized the gorgeous colors, highly finished surfaces, and technical sophistication of the Rococo. It was an art that was self-consciously pleasing, reflecting the privileged aristocratic world that brought it into being. As early as the mid-18th century, the Rococo was being criticized for these apparent frivolities; by the French Revolution in 1789, what was left of Rococo sentiment had been obliterated. Yet at its best it encapsulated much more than aristocratic frippery.

Putti **underline** classical origins of this scene as well as its essential unreality

Soft background lighting focuses attention on the principal figures in this tableau

Precise painting of an apparently naturalistic setting highlights new interest in landscape

Bacchus and Erigone *François Boucher 1745, 39 x 53 in (99 x 134.5 cm), oil on canvas, London: Wallace Collection.* For Boucher, classical myths made most sense when transformed into scenes of ravished innocents. Seduction, here aided by the (fatal) promise of wine, is a recurring theme.

To seduce Erigone, Bacchus transformed himself into a bunch of grapes; Erigone swoons as her arm touches the fruit

TECHNIQUES

Darkened leaves are lit so that they appear iridescent at the edges from the light of the shaded sun. Similar light plays seductively on the girls' exposed breasts.

Flesh tones are precisely and lovingly rendered, exemplified in Erigone's delicate, elegant legs, sensually curved and exposed.

Jean-Honoré **Fragonard**

◯ 1732–1806　🏴 FRENCH

🏛 Paris; Rome; France　🎨 oils; chalks　🏛 Paris: Musée du Louvre. London: Wallace Collection
📈 $7,776,000 in 1999, *Le Verrou (The Bolt)* (oils)

Precocious, successful—much favored by the *ancien régime* for his easy-to-enjoy, virtuoso, and titillating private paintings. Rejected the trappings of official art. Died in poverty after the French Revolution.

The participants in his pictures of love and seduction may be in contemporary dress, from mythology, or have no clothes at all. He likes pink cheeks and heaving bosoms, sidelong glances, passionate embraces, and futile resistance. Even his drapery, landscape backgrounds, foliage, and clouds froth with equal erotic intensity.

His exciting, nervous, but confident style suits his subjects; his seductive pink-and-green palette and soft, dappled light prefigure Renoir. Paints hands with long, sensuous fingers. Note the lap dogs and fleshy statues ready to join the fun. Look for occasional early works in a "correct" official style—which he soon rejected.

The Swing (Les hasards heureux de l'escarpolette) *Jean-Honoré Fragonard, 1767, 32 x 25½ in (81 x 65 cm), oil on canvas, London: Wallace Collection. The trees were inspired by Tivoli Gardens.*

KEY WORKS *Bathers*, c. 1765 (Paris: Musée du Louvre); *Young Girl Reading*, 1776 (Washington, DC: National Gallery of Art); *The Stolen Kiss*, c. 1788 (St. Petersburg: Hermitage Museum)

Carle **van Loo**
● 1705–65   **FRENCH**

▣ Rome; Paris   ▣ oils   ▣ Paris: Musée du Louvre   ▤ $250,000 in 2000, *Venus Requesting Vulcan to Make Arms for Aeneas* (oils)

Also known as Charles-André van Loo. Most successful member of a family that dominated French painting in the mid-18th century, but is now, rightly, forgotten—his success due to quantity, not quality. Royal portraits, huge altarpieces, boudoir scenes. His nephew, Louis Michel (1707–71), is now rated as highly.

KEY WORKS *The Grand Turk giving a Concert to his Mistress*, 1727 (London: Wallace Collection); *Aeneas Carrying Anchises*, 1729 (Paris: Musée du Louvre)

Sebastiano **Ricci**
● 1659–1734   **ITALIAN**

▣ Venice; Vienna; England   ▣ oils   ▣ Windsor Castle (England): Royal Collection. Venice: Querini-Stampalia Galleria   ▤ $622,800 in 1991, *The Last Communion of St. Mary in Egypt* (oils)

Decorative painting at its best. Standard mythological and religious paintings. An engaging eyeful of easy compositions, fresh color, and attractive people. No pretentious intellectualizing or moralizing. Worked in the Venetian tradition.

KEY WORKS *The Rape of the Sabine Women*, c. 1700 (Vienna: Liechtenstein Museum); *Esther before Ahasuerus* c. 1730 (London: National Gallery)

Marco **Ricci**
● 1676–1729   **ITALIAN**

▣ Italy; England   ▣ oils; drawing   ▣ Windsor Castle (England): Royal Collection. Washington, DC: National Gallery of Art   ▤ $478,500 in 2001, *An Opera Rehearsal* (oils)

Nephew of Sebastiano. Worked in England 1708–16 and collaborated with his uncle on religious

Ships in a Gale *Marco Ricci, c. 1705–08, 36⅛ x 49 in (92 x 124.5 cm), oil on canvas, Indianapolis: Museum of Art. Ricci was widely traveled and was employed in London and Venice to create stage sets.*

and mythological pieces. Developed his own line of fresh, frothy, light-filled fantasy or semitopographical landscapes.

KEY WORKS *Fishing Boats*, 1715 (Los Angeles: J. Paul Getty Museum); *Landscape with Ruins*, 1725 (Los Angeles: J. Paul Getty Museum)

Rosalba Giovanna **Carriera**
● 1675–1758   **ITALIAN**

▣ Venice; Paris; Vienna   ▣ pastels   ▣ Dresden: Gemäldegalerie. London: Victoria & Albert Museum   ▤ $105,000 in 1998, *Female Personification of Summer* (works on paper)

Known for her highly successful portraits in pastels, which cleverly combine delicacy and graciousness with spontaneity, plus a judicious realism that neatly negotiates the fine divide between honesty and flattery. She was much sought after by the rich and fashion-conscious as she took her artistic skills around the capital cities of Europe. She inspired Maurice-Quentin de La Tour to use pastel.

KEY WORKS *Self-Portrait with a Portrait of her Sister*, 1709 (Florence: Galleria degli Uffizi); *Young Lady with a Parrot*, c. 1730 (Art Institute of Chicago)

Caterina Sagredo Barbarigo as "Bernice" *Rosalba Giovanna Carriera, c. 1741, 17½ x 12½ in (44.5 x 31.8 cm), pastel on paper mounted on canvas, Detroit Institute of Arts. One of the last works the artist produced; in 1745 she went blind.*

Giovanni Battista **Pittoni**

◉ 1687–1767   ⴷ ITALIAN

⬚ Venice   🎨 oils   🏛 Venice: Gallerie dell'
Accademia   💰 $443,005 in 1990, *Omphale* (oils)

Poor man's Tiepolo. Had a flashy, richly
colored, loosely painted style, which is
more a mishmash of earlier Venetian
artists and borrowings from Tiepolo
than truly original. His work—religious,
historical, and mythological subjects—
was much sought after in his lifetime,
both at home and abroad, demonstrating
that commercial and critical success is
sometimes (often?) achieved by showing
off, rather than through talent.

KEY WORKS *St. Prosdocimus Baptizing Daniel*,
1725 (York: City Art Gallery); *An Allegorical
Monument to Sir Isaac Newton*, 1727–29
(Cambridge: Fitzwilliam Museum)

The Delivery of the Keys to St. Peter *Giovanni
Battista Pittoni, c. 1710–67, 32⅓ x 16½ in (82 x 42 cm),
oil on canvas, Paris: Musée du Louvre.* Christ entrusts the
keys of heaven to the disciple Peter, watched by cherubs.

Giovanni Antonio **Pellegrini**

◉ 1675–1741   ⴷ ITALIAN

⬚ Venice; England; Paris   🎨 oils
🏛 Paris: Musée du Louvre   💰 $489,000
in 1998, *Venus, Cupid, and Faun* (oils)

Well-traveled (Germany, Vienna, Paris,
Netherlands, England) Venetian painter.
Bright, appealing, airy, illusionistic,
decorative compositions on a large scale
(very much the Venetian tradition, but
brought up to date), which were influential
in creating a fashion and demand for this
type of work, especially in England.

KEY WORKS *Rebecca at the Well*, 1708–13
(London: National Gallery); *The Marriage
of the Elector Palatine*, 1713–14 (London:
National Gallery); *Bacchus and Ariadne*,
c. 1720–21 (Paris: Musée du Louvre)

Giambattista **Tiepolo**

◉ 1696–1770   ⴷ ITALIAN

⬚ Italy; Würzburg (Germany); Madrid   🎨 oils;
frescoes   🏛 Würzburg: Residenz. Madrid: Royal
Palace   💰 $2,128,000 in 2002, *Lamentation* (oils)

Full name Giovanni Battista Tiepolo.
Last of the great Venetian decorators
in the Renaissance tradition. Easy-going,
happily married to Francesco Guardi's
sister, quick, and astonishingly gifted.
Was successful, sought after, and rich,
but his work is now out of fashion and
very underrated.

His great decorative schemes *in situ*
(Venice, the Veneto, Würzburg, Madrid)
are a truly miraculous combination of
fresco and architecture on a vast scale,
where walls and ceilings seemingly
disappear to reveal a celestial, luminous,
shimmering vision of happily radiant
gods, saints, and historical and allegorical
figures in an epic fantasy world. They
constitute one of the greatest artistic
experiences of all time.

Observe his brilliant storytelling and
perspectival illusion. He has a confident,
resolute technique and uses luminous
colors. Large-scale schemes were the
result of teamwork (the painting of
the architectural settings being especially
crucial). The preliminary sketches show
a deft, delicate technique with flickering
dark outlines, which weave under and
over color, giving life and crispness.
He loves rich textures, doe-eyed females,

Abraham and the Three Angels *Giambattista Tiepolo, c. 1720–70, oil on canvas, Venice: Scuola Grande di San Rocco. The Bible tells how the prophet Abraham offered a meal to three angels, representing the Trinity.*

muscular men, theatrical gestures—but always avoids cliché and frivolity.

KEY WORKS *Queen Zenobia Addressing her Soldiers* c. 1730 (Washington, DC: National Gallery of Art); *Apollo in his Sun Chariot* (see pages 232–233); *The Olympus*, c. 1750s (Madrid: Museo del Prado); *Allegory of the Marriage of Rezzonico to Savorgnan*, 1758 (Venice, Ca' Rezzonico: Museo del Settecento)

> "… the last, and most refined, stage of illusionistic ceiling decoration is represented by its greatest master, Giovanni Battista Tiepolo."
>
> H. W. JANSON

Giandomenico **Tiepolo**
◔ 1727–1804   ⚑ ITALIAN

📍 Venice   🎨 oils; frescoes   🏛 Vincenza: Villa Valmarana   💰 $874,500 in 1995, *The Tiepolo Family* (oils)

Son of Giambattista, with whom he worked on major projects and whose style he successfully imitated. He

flourished in his own right (but without his father's celestial inspiration and vision), preferring scenes of everyday life and witty anecdote. Skilled draftsman and printmaker.

KEY WORKS *The Marriage of Frederick Barbarossa*, c. 1752–53 (London: National Gallery); *The Building of the Trojan Horse*, c. 1760 (London: National Gallery); *Horseman with Punchinellos*, second half of 18th century (St. Petersburg: Hermitage Museum)

Pietro **Longhi**
◔ 1702–85   ⚑ ITALIAN

📍 Venice   🎨 oils; chalks   🏛 Venice: Querini-Stampalia Galleria   💰 $775,000 in 2005, *Ridotto in Venice* (oils)

Italian counterpart to Lancret and Hogarth (see pages 224 and 238) in that he successfully caught the 18th-century taste for small-scale scenes of everyday life—in his case, Venetian goings-on from aristocracy to lowlife. They still sparkle with spontaneity and sharp, dispassionate observation.

KEY WORKS *Theatrical Scene*, c. 1752 (St. Petersburg: Hermitage Museum); *The Display of the Elephant*, 1774 (Houston: Museum of Fine Arts)

Exhibition of a Rhinoceros at Venice *Pietro Longhi, 1751, 23⅝ x 18½ in (60 x 47 cm), oil on canvas, London: National Gallery. The rhino is exhibited for the amusement of revelers, one of whom brandishes its sawn-off horn.*

Apollo Bringing the Bride
Giambattista Tiepolo 1750–51

Tiepolo was the most celebrated fresco painter of the 18th century, famed for his seemingly ceaseless invention, astonishing fluency, and ability to tackle huge decorative schemes in record time. Among his most startling works are those at the Residenz, or palace, of the worldly Prince-Bishop of Würzburg.

The French court at Versailles was emulated by rulers in many parts of Europe. That at Würzburg in Bavaria was unusual only in attracting arguably the greatest Rococo architect, Balthasar Neumann, and its most accomplished frescoist, Tiepolo, as well. Together, they created an astonishingly sumptuous decorative program. The settings of Tiepolo's frescoes were always crucial. He may have relished his mastery of illusionistic techniques for its own sake. But as important, they allowed him to create works that extend the real space of these vast settings into his imaginary, painted world. Typically, he displays a bravura disregard for historical accuracy. Twelfth-century Germany—scene of the Burgundian princess Beatrice's arrival for her marriage to Emperor Frederick Barbarossa—is transmuted into a sky-borne 16th-century Venice.

With exceptional daring, large ares of cloud-flecked sky are left blank, increasing the sense of heroic expansiveness

Two other, no less magnificent, frescoes by Tiepolo complete the decorative cycle of the Imperial Hall

Though only a fragment of a building is shown, and from a steeply angled perspective, it implies a strongly imagined architectural setting

The merging of painting and setting makes the fresco seem as if it is an extension of the elaborate space

Beatrice is accompanied by the Sun God, Apollo, who escorts her in his chariot to her wedding. Appearing luminescent in her majestic matrimonial splendor, she is dressed as though in a painting by Veronese, the 16th-century Venetian painter, who exercised a profound influence on Tiepolo.

Apollo Bringing the Bride

Medium ceiling fresco
Dimensions 22⅔ x 46⅙ ft (6.97 x 14.07 m)
Location Würzburg Palace: Imperial Hall

> "He paints a picture in less time than it takes another to grind his colors."

COUNT CARL GUSTAV TESSIN

Pale, limpid colors add luminosity and underline the airy magnificence of the sky

Allegorical figures usher Apollo and Beatrice toward the princess's future husband

Tiepolo suspends reality to create a convincing parallel world

Clouds and figures spill over the frame of the fresco into the real space of the room

Tiepolo revels in his mastery of extreme foreshortening and the drama and excitement it projects. These magnificent horses testify to his virtuosity, apparently able to tackle any subject in the absolute certainty that it can be invested with his unique brand of epically elegant heroism.

Giovanni Paolo **Panini**

◔ c. 1691–1765   ᴾᵁ ITALIAN

🏛 Bologna; Rome   🎨 oils   💰 $3,843,000 in 2004, *Interior of St. Peter's, Rome* (oils)

Also known as Pannini. Highly successful view painter, contemporary of Canaletto, who anticipated Neoclassical taste. Born in Piacenza and trained in the school of stage designers in Bologna. Worked in Rome, and was much admired by the French. Had a good line in picturesque, ancient ruins, and views and events in modern Rome. His drawings were much sought after in his day.

KEY WORKS *Roman Ruins with Figures*, c. 1730 (London: National Gallery); *The Sermon of St. Paul Amid the Ruins*, 1744 (St. Petersburg: Hermitage Museum); *Roman Ruins with a Prophet*, 1751 (Vienna: Liechtenstein Museum)

Ruins with Figures *Giovanni Paolo Panini, 96¾ x 70⅛ in (38.1 x 27.9 cm), oil on canvas, Wilton (UK): Wilton House.* Panini trained in architectural drawing. He was married to a Frenchwoman.

THE GRAND TOUR   18th century

Once-in-a-lifetime tour around Europe to see the major sights and works of art, and to experience life and broaden horizons. It was very much the done thing in the early 18th and 19th centuries, especially for young English gentlemen, who would return home with quantities of works of art with which they filled their country homes. An elegant portrait painted in Rome by the Italian artist Batoni was the typical Grand Tour souvenir-cum-status symbol.

Giovanni Antonio **Canaletto**

◕ 1697–1768   ⚑ ITALIAN

🏙 Venice; London   🎨 oils; drawings; engravings
🏛 Royal Collection. London: National Gallery.
Dresden: Gemäldegalerie   💰 $16m in 1992,
*The Old Horse Guards, London, from St. James's
Park, with Figures Parading* (oils)

The most famous Venetian view painter
of the 18th century. Instantly recognizable.
He was much loved and collected by
English Grand Tourists, and also painted
views of England.

His early views of Venice (during
the 1720s and 1730s) are the best,
being surprisingly subtle and poetic
(later works tend to become mechanical
and dull). Stunning use of perspective and
composition (he may have used a camera
obscura). Views are not of reality, but
cunning fictions. One of the few painters
who has been able to capture not just
the light and feel of Venice, but also the
pageantry and history of a once-great
empire in its dying years.

See the way he enlivens perspective
with crisp, accurate, architectural details
and opens up a scene by using several
different viewpoints in one work. Shows
clever use of light and shade: judicious
balance of both with razor-sharp shadows
and an exciting, unexpected fall of light
on a wall. Delightful, original, anecdotal
(figure) details and firsthand observation;
sense of something (unseen) happening
around the corner. Also produced
exciting, fluent drawings and sketches.

KEY WORKS *The Stonemason's Yard*, 1726–30
(London: National Gallery); *Rome: The Arch
of Constantine*, 1742 (Windsor Castle, England:
Royal Collection); *London, St. Paul's Cathedral*,
1754 (New Haven: Yale Center for British
Art); *A View of the Ducal Palace in Venice*,
pre-1755 (Florence: Galleria degli Uffizi)

The Basin of San Marco on Ascension Day
*Giovanni Antonio Canaletto, c. 1740, 48 x 72 in (122 x
183 cm), oil on canvas, London: National Gallery.* Every year
on Ascension Day the Doge of Venice went to the Lido to
perform a ceremony whereby Venice was "married" to the
Adriatic Sea. The Doge's golden barge is moored ready.

236

Francesco **Guardi**

- 1712–93 ITALIAN

Venice   oils; drawings
$13,943,218 in 1989, *View of the
Giudecca and the Zattere, Venice* (oils)

Prolific Venetian view painter and
best-known member of a family of
painters, Guardi was widely collected
in the 18th century, but his paintings
sold for half the price of Canaletto's.

His charming Venetian scenes capture
the spirit of the city more by atmosphere
and mood than by topographical accuracy.
The cool, misty, relaxed, small-scale style
is in complete contrast to the intense, busy,
sharp, and bigger-scale style of Canaletto
(their works are usually hung together).

Note the inaccurate perspective and
seeming indifference when people or
buildings get out of scale; suppression of
detail; loose, flickering style of painting;
and hazy, cool colors and somber palette.
KEY WORKS *A Seaport and Classical Ruins in
Italy*, 1730s (Washington, DC: National
Gallery of Art); *St. Mark's Square*, c. 1760–65
(London: National Gallery); *Venice: The
Grand Canal with the Riva del Vin and Rialto
Bridge*, c. 1765 (London: Wallace Collection);
*View of the Venetian Lagoon with the Tower
of Malghera*, c. 1770s (London: National
Gallery); *An Architectural Caprice*, 1770s
(London: National Gallery)

View of Warsaw from the Royal Castle
*Bernardo Bellotto, 1772, oil on canvas, Warsaw:
National Museum.* Bellotto's views of Warsaw were
used in the reconstruction of the city after 1945.

Landscape with Ruins *Francesco Guardi, c. 1775,
28⅓ x 20½ in (72 x 52 cm), oil on canvas, London:
Victoria & Albert Museum.* Guardi liked capricci—fantasy
townscapes with real and imaginary buildings.

Bernardo **Bellotto**

- 1720–80 ITALIAN

Venice; Dresden; Warsaw   oils
Dresden: Gemäldegalerie. Warsaw:
National Museum $5,642,000 in
1991, *Fortress of Königstein* (oils)

A nephew of Canaletto, from whom
he learned his craft, Bellotto left Italy
in 1747 because of family problems,
never to return. His coloring is generally
more somber than his uncle's.

He painted views of northern European
towns, commissioned by the old-fashioned,
aristocratic patrons who ruled them and

An Italianate River Landscape *Francesco Zuccarelli, 41½ x 35⅓ in (105.3 x 89.8 cm), oil on canvas, London: Christie's Images. Zuccarelli's work was usually made to become part of a decorative room setting.*

who employed him on a salary as court painter (Dresden, Vienna, Warsaw).

His impressive, large-scale works are distinguishable from Canaletto's by their different subject matter and cooler, blue-green, silvery palette (he painted on darkly primed canvases). Less imaginative use of space (used only a standard single-viewpoint perspective), but a better response to trees and vegetation. His anecdotal detail is good , but the figure-painting is more crude than Canaletto's.

KEY WORKS *Dresden, the Frauenkirche and the Rampische Gasse*, 1749–53 (Dresden: Gemäldegalerie); *The Neustadter Market in Dresden*, 1750 (Dresden: Gemäldegalerie); *Architectural Capriccio*, c. 1765 (San Diego Museum of Art)

Francesco **Zuccarelli**

● 1702–88   ℙ ITALIAN

ℙ Rome; Venice; England   ◆ oils
🏛 Royal Collection. Glasgow Art Gallery
💲 $313,500 in 1997, *Wooded Landscape with Washerwomen by River* (oils)

A Florentine painter of Venetian-style high quality, Zuccarelli produced sugary, softly colored, easily painted pastoral landscapes and cityscapes. Was much admired by collectors of his day (especially the English, who favored his soft, Rococo style and made him a founding member of the Royal Academy). Once spoken

about in the same breath as Canaletto, he is now virtually forgotten.

KEY WORKS *Landscape with a Woman Leading a Cow*, 1740s (St. Petersburg: Hermitage Museum); *Landscape with the Education of Bacchus*, 1744 (Los Angeles: J. Paul Getty Museum); *Landscape with Shepherds*, 1750 (Los Angeles: J. Paul Getty Museum)

Pompeo Girolamo **Batoni**

● 1708–87   ℙ ITALIAN

ℙ Rome   ◆ oils   💲 $625,800 in 1993, *Portrait of Sir Charles Watson* (oils)

He was a highly successful portrait painter, especially of English visitors to Italy on the Grand Tour. Polished and finely painted work, careful attention to detail (lace, stitches in clothing), with beautiful results. Established a formula that favored stock poses with stylish clothes, ruins in the background, and dogs at the feet—or both. He knew exactly what his snobby clientele wanted and provided them with it.

KEY WORKS *Christ in Glory with Four Saints*, 1736–38 (Los Angeles: J. Paul Getty Museum); *Time Orders Old Age to Destroy Beauty*, 1746 (London: National Gallery)

William **Hogarth**

● 1697–1764　🅿 BRITISH

🅟 London　🛈 oils; engravings　🏛 London:
National Gallery; Tate Collection; Sir John Soane's
Museum　💰 $602,250 in 1991, *The Edwards
Hamilton family on Terrace in Kensington* (oils)

Hogarth is considered the "father of
English painting." He was a quirky,
argumentative antiforeigner, with a tough
childhood. Talented both as a painter and
printmaker, he laid the foundations that
led to Reynolds and the Royal Academy.

Hogarth is best known for his portraits
(individual and group) and modern, moral
subjects—slices of contemporary life,
which were often developed as a series
(for instance, *The Rake's Progress* and
Marriage à la Mode). In neither does
he idealize nor criticize; he shows people
and their behavior for what they are.

Brilliant as a storyteller. Also a very fine
handler of paint, producing confident
drawing and color-rich textures. Painted
attractive, open faces in portraits and was
especially good at representing children.

Marriage à la Mode: VI, The Lady's Death William
*Hogarth, c. 1743, 27½ x 35⅜ in (70 x 91 cm), oil on
canvas, London: National Gallery.* The final grimly comic
scene in a story of a disastrous fashionable marriage.

Self-Portrait *William Hogarth, engraving,
Private Collection.* Hogarth helped to establish
the first permanent public display of English art
at the Foundling Hospital in central London.

Showed engaging, anecdotal details and
"warts and all" realism, but we are left
to draw our own moral conclusions.
KEY WORKS *The Strode Family*, 1738 (London:
Tate Collection); *The Graham Children*, 1742
(London: National Gallery); *The Shrimp
Girl*, c. 1745 (London: National Gallery)

Arthur **Devis**

◔ 1711–87 🏳 BRITISH

🅿 London; Lancashire 🎨 oils 📈 $478,800 in 1989, *Portrait of Mr. and Mrs. Robert Dashwood of Stanford Hall, Nottinghamshire* (oils)

Small-scale family conversation pieces with doll-like figures (he used dolls as models), neatly dressed and arranged in their houses and parks. Successful with the newly emerging middle classes. Gives us a charming and authoritative insight into 18th-century society.

KEY WORKS *Jacob Bacon and His Family*, c. 1742–43 (New Haven: Yale Center for British Art); *Portrait of a Lady*, c. 1750–51 (London: Tate Collection)

Sir Joshua **Reynolds**

◔ 1723–92 🏳 BRITISH

🅿 London; Devon; Italy 🎨 oils 🏛 London: National Gallery; Tate Collection 📈 $13,348,000 in 2000, *Portrait of Omai, Standing in a Landscape, Wearing Robes and a Headdress* (oils)

Best known for his portraits. Raised the status of portraiture, the arts generally, and the social standing of artists in Britain. A discriminating collector of old-master prints and drawings. Well connected, and the first President of the Royal Academy.

His principal achievement is the brilliant way he used allusion and cross-references to enhance the dignity of his sitters and turn portraiture into a type of history painting, with lots of references to classical mythology, antique statues, and architecture. His sitters are often in the poses of well-known examples of Greek and Roman sculpture or the Madonna and Child. Was especially good with children, but terrible as a "history" painter.

He made inventive use of hands and gesture to bring life and character to his figures. In 1781 he went to Flanders and Holland, and afterward one can see the influence of Rubens and Rembrandt on his work. Had poor technique—his pictures are often in bad condition because of his use of inferior materials such as bitumen and carmine.

KEY WORKS *Self-Portrait Shading the Eyes*, 1747 (London: National Portrait Gallery); *Commodore Keppel*, 1753–54 (Greenwich, London: National Maritime Museum); *Lady Caroline Howard*, 1778 (Washington, DC: National Gallery of Art)

Allan **Ramsay**

◔ 1713–84 🏳 BRITISH

🅿 London; Italy 🎨 oils; drawings 📈 $760,000 in 1993, *Portrait of Sir Edward and Lady Turner seated holding Lace and Basket* (oils)

Interesting and successful Scottish portrait painter who worked mainly in London, from 1739. His early work is often very labored and derivative, and his official full-length portraits are rather wooden. His later work, from the 1760s onward, is better. At his best with small and intimate three-quarter-length portraits, especially of women; these have a lovely softness, charm, and delicacy.

The turn of the head on the body gives life to the figures, in spite of repetitive and unimaginative poses. His intensity of observation is worthy of the best still-life painters: note the detail on costumes; the careful painting of objects; the eyes, where even the color of the iris is noted exactly; the beautiful use of light.

KEY WORKS *Richard Mead*, 1740 (London: National Portrait Gallery); *Norman "The Red Man," 22nd Chief of Macleod*, c. 1747 (Isle of Skye, UK: Dunvegan Castle); *Miss Janet Shairp*, 1750 (Aberdeen: Art Gallery and Museums)

Master Thomas Lister (The Brown Boy) *Sir Joshua Reynolds, 1764, 91 x 55 in (231 x 139 cm), oil on canvas, Bradford (UK): Art Galleries and Museums.* The pose mimics an Antique statue of Mercury.

Mr. and Mrs. Andrews *Thomas Gainsborough, c. 1749, 28 x 47 in (71 x120 cm), oil on canvas, London: National Gallery.* The newly married couple sit in their estate, whose topography is precisely recorded.

Thomas **Gainsborough**

◉ 1727 – 88 ⚑ BRITISH

🎨 London; Ipswich; Bath 🖌 oils 🏛 London: National Gallery; Victoria & Albert Museum; Kenwood House 💰 $3,504,000 in 2002, *Portrait of Colonel John Bullock* (oils)

Best known for his portraits (which he could sell), his heart was more in landscapes (difficult to sell). Fashionable and successful. An amorous man.

Born in Sudbury, Suffolk, he went to London in 1740 and studied engraving before setting up as a portrait painter in 1752. Gainsborough's sensibility and instinct, and his imaginative, experimental craftsmanship were the antithesis to Reynolds's intellectualism and bad technique. His portraits after 1760 are of natural, untheatrical poses—gorgeous best clothes and hats, sympathetic observation and response to character in a face (especially that of a pretty woman). His landscapes are imaginary, lyrical, poetic—a conscious escape from a hard day's labor. Lovely, free chalk drawings. Also prints.

Wonderful paint handling, used very thinly, freely, and sketchily, enabling him to capture the shimmer of silks and satins, the rustle of breeze-touched foliage, the natural blush on a girl's cheek, or rouge on a matron's face. There are parallels with early Mozart (1756–91): interweaving of structure and texture; light-hearted seriousness; physical pleasure in being alive. His early works lack the easy relaxation of the later works; they are charming but the portrait figures look like dolls and the landscapes concentrate on detail rather than atmosphere.

No fan of literature, his only great interest outside of painting was music.

KEY WORKS *"The Blue Boy,"* c. 1770 (San Marino: Huntingdon Art Collections); *Portrait of Anne, Countess of Chesterfield*, c. 1777 (Los Angeles: J. Paul Getty Museum); *Mrs. Richard Brinsley Sheridan*, c. 1785 (Washington, DC: National Gallery of Art)

The Painter's Daughters Chasing a Butterfly *Thomas Gainsborough, c. 1759, 44⅔ x 41 in (113.5 x 105 cm), oil on canvas, London: National Gallery.* Observed with love; 7 and 11.

Gavin **Hamilton**

● 1723–98   **⚑** BRITISH

🏛 Rome   **🎨** oils   **💰** $35,000
in 1993, *Hygieia* (oils)

Scottish-born, resident in Rome;
archeologist, painter, picture dealer.
A pioneer of the international,
archeological, and severely intellectual
branch of Neoclassicism, but outpaced
by other, better, painters. Also painted
portraits and conversation pieces
endowed with an austere charm.

KEY WORKS *Dawkins and Wood Discovering
the Ruins of Palmyra*, 1758 (Edinburgh:
National Gallery of Scotland); *Achilles
Lamenting the Death of Patroclus*, 1763
(Edinburgh: National Gallery of Scotland);
*Agrippina Landing at Brundisium with the Ashes of
Germanicus*, 1765–72 (London: Tate Collection)

Johann **Zoffany**

● c. 1734–1810   **⚑** GERMAN/BRITISH

🏛 Rome; London; Florence; India   **🎨** oils
💰 $4,480,000 in 2001, *Dutton Family in the Drawing
Room of Sherborne Park, Gloucestershire* (oils)

Also known as John Zoffany. German-
born painter who established his career
in Rome and London from 1760. He
lived in India from 1783 to 1789, and
made a fortune painting native princes
and British colonialists. His delightful,
informal group portraits are his best

works—they capture the ease and
prosperous confidence of Georgian
upper-class society. Look for good
anecdotal details such as costumes, and
sporting, artistic, and literary activities.

KEY WORKS *The Academicians of the Royal
Academy*, 1772 (Royal Collection); *The
Tribuna of the Uffizi*, 1772–77 (Royal
Collection); *Charles Townley's Library at 7
Park Street, Westminster*, 1781–83 (Burnley,
UK: Towneley Hall Art Gallery)

James **Barry**

● 1741–1806   **⚑** BRITISH

🏛 London; Italy   **🎨** oils   **💰** $18,000
in 1990, *Venus Anadyomene* (oils)

Highly gifted Irish-born history painter
who became a professor at the Royal
Academy, only to be expelled in 1799
after a series of quarrels. Aimed for the
top: large-scale history painting on the
scale of Raphael's Vatican frescoes.
Was so paranoid and pretentious as a
person that he ruined his opportunities
and died lonely and unloved.

KEY WORKS *The Progress of Human Culture*,
1777–83 (London: Royal Society of
Arts); *Portrait of Samuel Johnson*, c. 1778–80
(London: National Portrait Gallery)

The Drummond Family Johann Zoffany, c. 1769,
oil on canvas, New Haven: Yale Center for British Art.
Zoffany's portraits were popular with George III and
Queen Charlotte, who became his patrons.

Angelica **Kauffmann**

◉ 1741–1807   🏴 SWISS

🏛 Rome; London   🎨 oils   🏦 Devon (UK): Saltram Park   💰 $747,000 *Portrait of Philip Tisdal with his Wife and Family* (oils)

Best known for work done during her stay in England (1765–80), when she was very successful with elegant, delicate portraits, history paintings, and decorations, in the style of Reynolds, for Adam houses. She was partial to sentimental figures with pink faces and cheeks.

KEY WORKS *Ariadne Abandoned by Theseus*, 1774 (Houston: Museum of Fine Arts); *Self-Portrait Hesitating Between the Arts of Music and Painting*, 1775 (Yorkshire, UK: Nostell Priory)

Richard **Cosway**

◉ 1742–1821   🏴 BRITISH

🏛 England   🎨 watercolors; oils   🏦 London: National Portrait Gallery   💰 $49,500 in 1998, *Group Portrait of the Children of Edmund Boyle, 7th Earl of Cork* (oils)

Best remembered as the most fashionable and outstanding miniaturist of the 18th century. Look for long, aquiline noses with very noticeable nostrils and shadows under the nose. A few unsuccessful large-scale oils. Married Maria Hadfield (1759–1838), a successful Irish/Italian painter, miniaturist, and illustrator. Friend of the Prince of Wales (later Prince Regent).

KEY WORKS *Self-Portrait*, c. 1770–75 (New York: Metropolitan Museum of Art); *Group of Connoisseurs*, 1771–75 (Burnley, UK:

Towneley Hall Art Gallery); *Portrait of Mrs. Marley*, c. 1780 (Washington, DC: Hillwood Museum and Gardens); *Unknown Lady of the Sotheby or Isted Families*, c. 1795 (Cambridge: Fitzwilliam Museum)

Sir Henry **Raeburn**

◉ 1756–1823   🏴 BRITISH

🏛 Edinburgh; London   🎨 oils
💰 $270,000 in 1995, *Portrait of Sir George Stewart Mackenzie, 7th Baronet* (oils)

Best-ever Scottish portrait painter. No-nonsense character, just as happy playing golf or speculating on property (went bankrupt). He was the first Scottish painter to be knighted.

Note the matinée-idol style of portraiture—heroic stances and soft focus with "alone but self-assured" poses, often against dramatic skies and landscape backgrounds. His work is at its best with handsome, strong-jawed male figures, looking vaguely disheveled and adopting the stern, faraway look. He was never at home with female sitters, who often look dull and plain, but was very good with children. Figures are bathed in light and animated by brilliant, inventive, theatrical play of light over face and costume.

Look for pink faces and rich colors. He has a strong, confident, broadly brushed technique using square brushes straight onto coarse canvas, without underdrawing—he paints directly from life, with carefully observed tones and shadows. His best works have no alterations or reworkings—he becomes messy and clumsy when he is forced to make changes. His no-nonsense, confident method is in harmony with the temperament he sees in (or imposed on?) his sitters. Note single dab of bright highlight on noses.

KEY WORKS *Miss Eleanor Urquhart*, c. 1793 (Washington, DC: National Gallery of Art); *William Glendonwyn*, c. 1795 (Cambridge: Fitzwilliam Museum); *Isabella McLeod, Mrs. James Gregory*, c. 1798 (Aberdeenshire: Fyvie Castle); *Mrs. Scott Moncrieff*, c. 1814 (Edinburgh: National Gallery of Scotland)

Portrait of Sir Walter Scott *Sir Henry Raeburn, c. 1810, 29¾ x 23⅛ in (75.5 x 59 cm), oil on canvas, Private Collection.* Scott's "Waverley" novels made him the most important and influential Scottish novelist.

THE ENGLISH LANDSCAPE TRADITION
18th century

From as early as 1750, a distinctive tradition of landscape painting was emerging in England, partly a reflection of 18th-century English landscape gardening, the subtle reordering of nature for aristocratic patrons in imitation of the classical landscapes of 17th-century painters like Claude Lorrain. In the hands of a series of exceptional painters, it developed into a rich celebration of a distinctively English approach to nature.

SUBJECTS AND STYLE

The White House, Chelsea *Thomas Girtin, 1800, watercolor on paper, Private Collection.* Turner greatly admired Girtin's brilliant watercolor technique and later said "Had Tom Girtin lived, I would have starved."

Landscapes were rarely regarded as an end in themselves. Rather, they were considered evidence of the divine harmony of nature, in particular of its domestication in an England that was increasingly prosperous and self-confident. At any rate, in the 18th century, the prevailing mood was accordingly almost always contemplative and calm. The intimate and the ordered were valued above the dramatic. It is then no surprise that the majority of these works were small in scale.

WHAT TO LOOK FOR

Precisely rendered and closely observed details contrast with flat, pale skies. Similarly, the impact of man, in buildings as much as in landscaped parklands, is seen as a complement to nature rather than an intrusion. This is a landscape that is fundamentally benign and tranquil, a reflection of the similarly well-ordered English society that produced it.

London from Greenwich Hill *John Robert Cozens c. 1791, watercolor and black ink, New Haven: Yale Center for British Art.* Cozens strongly influenced Girtin and Turner, who made copies of his works.

Richard **Wilson**

◉ c. 1713–82   🇬🇧 BRITISH

🔲 Wales; London; Italy   🎨 oils   🏛 Cardiff: National Museum of Wales. London: Tate Collection. Oxford: Ashmolean Museum   ➤ $286,900 in 1996, *Welsh Landscape with Cottages Near Lake* (oils)

The first major British landscape painter, he produced lovely, direct topographical views and sketches, which were influenced by Dutch masters. He is especially known for successful set-piece works that are a synthesis of idealized classical formulae and actual places. His work shows great sensitivity to light, notably during and after his visit to Italy 1750–57, but it can become overfamiliar and repetitious.

Snowdon *Richard Wilson, c. 1760s, oil on canvas, Nottingham: City Museums & Galleries.* Wilson was especially attracted to the Welsh countryside, which he transformed into visions of classical Arcadia.

KEY WORKS *Caernarvon Castle*, c. 1760 (Cardiff: National Museum of Wales); *The Valley of the Dee*, c. 1761 (London: National Gallery); *Lake Albano*, 1762 (Washington, DC: National Gallery of Art)

Alexander **Cozens**

◉ 1717–86   🇷🇺 RUSSIAN/BRITISH

🔲 Russia; Rome; England   🎨 drawings
➤ $631,800 in 1997, *After Rain* (oils)

English landscape draftsman. Born in Russia, but educated in Rome. Watercolor landscapes and etchings. Fascinated by systems, and famous for his method of using accidental blots on a piece of paper as a visual inspiration out of which an

idea, such as a landscape, might develop (still worth trying, as the Surrealists realized).

KEY WORKS *The Valley of the Rhone*, 1746 (London: Tate Collection); *A Blot: Landscape Composition*, 1770–80 (London: Tate Collection); *Mountain Landscape with a Hollow*, c. 1770 (Washington, DC: National Gallery of Art)

John Robert **Cozens**

◉ 1752–97   🇬🇧 BRITISH

🔲 Italy; Switzerland   🎨 watercolors; drawings   ➤ $444,000 *Cetera, Gulf of Salerno, Italy* (works on paper)

Alexander's melancholic son; also a landscape painter. Well traveled (Alps, Italy, Naples). Wonderful early watercolors, prefiguring those of Turner, in which he shows how a landscape can be a vehicle for emotion and mood when made with imagination and inventive techniques. Luminous skies full of atmosphere, space, and light. In 1793 he went insane.

KEY WORKS *Satan Summoning his Legions*, c. 1776 (London: Tate Collection); *Sepulchral Remains in the Campagna*, c. 1783 (Oxford: Ashmolean Museum); *Two Great Temples at Paestum*, c. 1783 (Oldham, UK: Lees Collection)

Thomas **Girtin**

◉ 1775–1802   🇬🇧 BRITISH

🔲 UK; Paris   🎨 watercolors; oils
➤ $468,000 in 1990, *Jedburgh Abbey from the South-East* (watercolors)

Potentially a rival to Turner, but died of consumption aged 27. Painted brilliant watercolors that pushed the interpretation of landscape and watercolor technique through to new frontiers. Had a wonderful sense of color and of the noble grandeur of nature.

KEY WORKS *Village Along a River Estuary in Devon*, 1797–98 (Washington, DC: National Gallery of Art); *Lindisfarne*, c. 1798 (Cambridge: Fitzwilliam Museum); *The White House at Chelsea*, 1800 (London: Tate Collection)

William **Marlow**

🌐 1740–1813   🏴 BRITISH

🏛 England; France; Italy   🎨 watercolors;
oils; drawings   🏛 London: Tate Collection
💰 $92,960 in 1989, *Distant View of Rome
with Vatican and Castel Sant'Angelo* (oils)

Successful, topographical painter in
watercolor and oils. Much traveled in
the UK, France, Italy. Produced successful
Grand Tour souvenir views, seascapes,
river scenes, and portraits of country
houses. Created satisfying, balanced
compositions and was able to capture
the cool light and well-ordered topography
of England, as well as the intense light
and rougher topography of Italy.

KEY WORKS *The Pont Royal, Paris* c. 1765–68
(Cambridge: Fitzwilliam Museum); *View of
the Tiber and the Ripetta with St. Peter's in the
Distance,* c. 1768 (Northamptonshire, UK:
Boughton House); *A Post-House near Florence,*
c. 1770 (London: Tate Collection)

Jacques Philippe de **Loutherbourg**

🌐 1740–1812   🏴 FRENCH/BRITISH

🏛 France; England   🎨 oils; drawings
💰 $264,793 *Scene de Patinage à Hyde Park* (oils)

Strasbourg painter and stage designer
who settled in England in 1771 and
produced stagey landscapes and
seascapes. Important as a link between
the old Arcadian classical landscape

The Pont du Gard, Nîmes *William Marlow, c. 1767,
15 x 22 in (38 x 56 cm), oil on canvas, London: Charles
Young Fine Paintings. Marlow traveled in France and
Italy in 1765–66, painting Grand Tour souvenir views.*

traditions and the new realism and
Romanticism of Turner and Constable.
He also painted battle scenes and
biblical subjects in an energetic style.
One of the first to celebrate the delights
of English native scenery.

KEY WORKS *Landscape with Cattle,* c. 1767 (London:
Dulwich Picture Gallery); *A Midsummer's
Afternoon with a Methodist Preacher,* 1777 (Ottawa:
National Gallery of Canada); *Travellers Attacked
by Banditti,* 1781 (London: Tate Collection);
The Falls of the Rhine at Schaffhausen, 1788
(London: Victoria & Albert Museum)

**Battle Between Richard I Lionheart (1157–99)
and Saladin (1137–93) in Palestine** *Jacques
Philippe de Loutherbourg, c. 1790, oil on canvas,
Leicester: New Walk Museum. The artist loved drama
and designed stage sets for Drury Lane Theatre, London.*

Joseph **Wright**

◔ 1734–97 ⚐ BRITISH

🏛 London; Derby; Italy 🎨 oils 🏛 London: National Gallery; Tate Collection. Derby (England): Museum and Art Gallery 💰 $1,625,000 in 1984, *Mr. and Mrs. Thomas Coltman about to Set Out on a Ride* (oils)

Known as the "Wright of Derby." Talented and versatile painter, but out of the mainstream. Developed new and original subjects: night scenes, scientific experiments, and early industrial forges. His paintings often have unusual light effects and offer fascinating insights into the Age of Reason and nascent Industrial Revolution. He painted goodish, occasionally great, portraits.

KEY WORKS *Two Boys Fighting over a Bladder*, c. 1767 (Private Collection); *An Experiment on a Bird in the Air Pump*, 1768 (London: National Gallery); *Mrs. John Ashton*, c. 1769 (Cambridge: Fitzwilliam Museum)

David **Allan**

◔ 1744–96 ⚐ BRITISH

🏛 Italy; London; Edinburgh 🎨 oils; drawings 💰 $109,120 in 1992, *Portrait of Three Boys Wearing Windsor Uniform* (oils)

The Scottish Hogarth, he was deeply influenced by a visit to Rome. Wanted to be remembered as a history painter (*de rigueur* at the time, but not his forte); was a successful portrait painter and established the tradition of Scottish genre paintings with anecdotal illustrations of Scottish life and history.

KEY WORKS *A Neapolitan Music Party*, c. 1775 (Private Collection); *The Connoisseurs*, 1783 (Edinburgh: National Gallery of Scotland); *John, the 4th Duke of Atholl and His Family*, c. 1773 (Private Collection)

George **Stubbs**

◔ 1724–1806 ⚐ BRITISH

🏛 Northern England; Rome; London 🎨 oils 💰 $4,611,000 in 1995, *Portrait of the Royal Tiger* (oils)

The greatest-ever painter of the horse, hunting, racing, and horsebreeding. Also painted scenes of rural life. Successful, with powerful patrons, but always a loner. His book, *Anatomy of the*

Horse (1766), is one of the most remarkable published works of art and science.

His deep, personal fascination with the anatomy and character of the horse touched something more widespread and profound: man's relationship with nature (wholly dependent on the horse until the invention of mechanical power)—plus the mid-18th-century belief in rational investigation as a means of understanding the natural world and comprehending the qualities of beauty. Produced wonderful, measured, modest pictures, which exemplify the saying "beauty is truth, truth beauty."

His paintings are models of rational beauty: subtle, careful, half-concealed geometry of horizontal and vertical structures around which play curving cadences (like Mozart); loving observation

> ### "Beauty is truth, truth beauty,
> ### That is all …
> ### ye need to know."
>
> JOHN KEATS

of space, anatomy, and the unspoken relationship between animal and man. Stunning draftsmanship. The exquisite, harmonious, gentle color has too often been tragically destroyed by insensitive cleaning and restoration.

KEY WORKS *Mares and Foals*, 1762 (London: Tate Collection); *Mares and Foals beneath Large Oak Trees*, c. 1764–68 (Private Collection); *Cheetah and Stag with Two Indians*, c. 1765 (Manchester: City Art Gallery)

A Horse Frightened by a Lion George Stubbs, 1770, 37 x 49 in (94 x 125 cm), oil on canvas, Liverpool: Walker Art Gallery. Stubbs's inspiration was not real life but an Antique sculpture he saw in Rome in 1754.

Thomas **Rowlandson**

⬤ 1756–1827 🏴 BRITISH

🔲 England; France; Germany; the Low Countries
🎨 drawings; prints ➡️ $91,800 *Place des Victoires, Paris* (works on paper)

Prolific draftsman and printmaker; chronicler of 18th-century life and morals. Had huge technical facility, eager enthusiasm for life, and a great eye for detail and character. Expressed all his observations with admirable economy of line. Walked the tightrope between observation and caricature with skill.
KEY WORKS *Box-Lobby Loungers*, 1785 (Los Angeles: J. Paul Getty Museum); *The Dinner*, 1787 (St. Petersburg: Hermitage Museum)

Jacques-Laurent **Agasse**

⬤ 1767–1849 🏴 SWISS

🔲 Switzerland; Paris; England 🎨 oils
🏛 Geneva: Musée d'Art et d'Histoire
➡️ $5.81m in 1988, *Two Leopards Playing in the Exeter Change Menagerie* (oils)

Swiss-born, Paris-trained (by J. L. David, and as a vet), worked in England. He was known for his faithfully observed, meticulously executed paintings

Miss Casenove on a Grey Hunter *Jacques-Laurent Agasse, c. 1800, 12 x 10 in (30.5 x 25.5 cm), oil on canvas, Private Collection. The artist was much influenced by Stubbs in subject matter and technique.*

A French Coffee House *Thomas Rowlandson, 1790s, 9 x 12⅛ in (23 x 33 cm), pen and ink with watercolor on paper, Cambridge: Fitzwilliam Museum. Revolutionary France was a popular target for British caricaturists.*

of animals and their owners or keepers. A truly great painter, but had a small output and died poor and unknown; animals were not considered a serious art subject (and still aren't, even today).
KEY WORKS *Sleeping Fox*, 1794 (Private Collection); *The Nubian Giraffe*, 1827 (Windsor Castle, England: Royal Collection)

The Nightmare *Henry Fuseli, 1781, 39¼ x 50 in (101 x 127 cm), oil on canvas, Michigan: Detroit Institute of Arts.* The woman represents Fuseli's lost love, Anna Landolt.

Henry **Fuseli**

● 1741–1825　**ᴾᴺ** SWISS/BRITISH

🏛 England; Italy　🎨 oils; drawings
💰 $1,162,000 in 1998, *Satan Starting from the Touch of Ithuriel's Lance* (oils)

Also known as Johann Heinrich Füssli. Swiss-born eccentric. Inspired by Michelangelo, Shakespeare, and Milton. Highly dramatic interpretations of literature in which facial expression and intense, overdeveloped body language is all. A defective technique has ruined many of his oil paintings.

Fuseli produced wonderful drawings; he also had a special line in female cruelty and bondaged males. Was obsessed with women's hair.

KEY WORKS *Lady Macbeth Sleepwalking,* c. 1784 (Paris: Musée du Louvre); *Oedipus Cursing His Son, Polynices,* 1786 (Washington, DC: National Gallery of Art)

William **Blake**

● 1757–1827　**ᴾᴺ** BRITISH

🏛 London; Sussex　🎨 engravings; watercolors; drawings　🏛 London: Tate Collection; British Museum　💰 $3.5m in 2004, *The Good and Evil Angels Struggling for Possession of a Child* (pen and watercolors)

Genuine visionary Romantic—truly inspired and driven by inner voices and sights, difficult to understand. Impoverished. Neglected in his lifetime.

He had an extraordinary originality in imagery, technique, and symbolism. An artist who created mostly small(ish) works on paper—watercolors and drawings—and a combination of these with print techniques (engraving). Blake's imagery and symbolism are highly personal but at heart is the wish to express his dislike of all forms of oppression. Championed creativity over reason; love over repression; individuality over state conformity. Believed in the liberating power of the human spirit.

Look for idealized human figures with spiritual expressions, and a fascination with fire and hair, which are similarly stylized. Uses biblical sources, especially from the Old Testament.

KEY WORKS *Frontispiece to Visions of the Daughters of Albion,* 1795 (London: Tate Collection); *Newton,* 1795 (London: Tate Collection); *Job and his Daughters,* 1799–1800 (Washington, DC: National Gallery of Art); *Ghost of a Flea,* 1819–20 (London: Tate Collection)

The Ancient of Days *William Blake, 1824, 9 x 6⅔ in (23 x 17 cm), etching with watercolor, pen, and ink on paper, Manchester: Whitworth Art Gallery.* Blake's God is an oppressive lawmaker imprisoning the imagination.

Giovanni Battista **Piranesi**

◉ 1720–78   ⼝ ITALIAN

🏛 Rome   ✎ engravings   💲 $310,000 in 1999, *Studies of Four Figures, Three Standing and One Seated Pointing to Left* (works on paper)

Architect, archeologist, and printmaker (etchings). Venetian-born. Settled in Rome in 1740, and made a reputation from popular prints of Ancient and modern Rome. Used inventive imagery, which moved from archeological exactitude to dramatic, overwhelming Romantic grandeur, made all the more powerful by a brilliant technique and a mastery of perspective, light, and shade. His most original works are images of fantastic prisons (1745–61), which are Surrealist before time. His etching work was continued by his son, Francesco.

KEY WORKS *Round Tower*, c. 1749 (St. Petersburg: Hermitage Museum); *The Gothic Arch*, c. 1749 (Washington, DC: National Gallery of Art); *The Well*, 1750–58 (Washington, DC: National Gallery of Art)

Carceri d'Invenzione (Prisons) Plate IV *Giovanni Battista Piranesi, 1760, 21½ x 16½ in (54.5 x 41.5 cm), etching, Hamburg: Kunsthalle.* Piranesi was also a successful restorer and dealer in Roman art and artifacts.

Anton Raphael **Mengs**

◉ 1728–79   ⼝ GERMAN

🏛 Dresden; Rome   ✎ oils; fresco   💲 $275,745 in 2003, *The Adoration of the Shepherds* (oils)

"The German Raphael," one of the founders of Neoclassicism and one of the foremost artists of his day. Worked in Germany, Italy, and Spain, and was a committed teacher, with an active studio. Wrote an influential theoretical treatise.

He is proof that having all the right credentials—being well taught, well thought of in official circles, and obeying all the currently correct aesthetic principles—does not lead to lasting fame. His religious paintings, mythologies, and portraits consciously aimed to contain the best of Raphael (expression), Correggio (grace), and Titian (color). In a way they do, but in spite of their competence they also end up looking lifeless and contrived.

Note his paint surface that looks like polished lacquer. His compositions and poses are so carefully calculated as to be merely stagey: notice how in the portraits the head often turns in one direction while the hands and body turn in the other. Painted flesh and faces that look impossibly and perfectly healthy. Rich textures and colors (especially a velvety royal blue, rich bottle-green, and dusky pinks). His portraits are now considered better than his history paintings.

KEY WORKS *Parnassus* (ceiling fresco), 1761 (Rome: Villa Albani); *Noli me Tangere*, 1771 (London: National Gallery); *The Immaculate Conception*, 1770–79 (Paris: Musée du Louvre)

Franz Xaver **Messerschmidt**

◉ 1736–1783   ⼝ AUSTRIAN

🏛 Munich; Graz; Vienna; Bratislava   🗿 sculpture   🏛 Vienna: Österreichische Galerie   💲 $4,300,000 in 2005, *Ill-humored Man* (sculpture)

Sculptor, trained by his uncles, whose Baroque busts won early approval with the Austrian Court. Later he became deeply influenced by famous Roman Republican heads after a visit to Rome and his style became more Neoclassical. Famous for his "Character Heads," a series of busts, many self-portraits, in which he explored facial distortions and grimaces after he started to suffer from delusions and paranoia. He thought the work would help heal and protect him from evil spirits.

KEY WORKS *Character Heads: The Gentle, Quiet Sleep; The Hanged; The Lecher; The Arched Evil*, 1770–83 (Vienna: Österreichische Galerie)

NEOCLASSICISM

Neoclassicism was a deliberate reaction against the decorative priorities of the Rococo. It was a self-conscious return to what were thought the absolute, severe standards of the ancient world. On the whole, it generated huge, dreary paintings of "improving" history subjects, but its most brilliant exponent, the painter David, radically fused contemporary political concerns with a new artistic language.

STYLE

The German theorist and art historian, Johann Winckelmann, decisively influenced Neoclassicism, persuasively advocating the "noble simplicity and calm grandeur" of ancient art, Greek especially. Typically, Neoclassical works became measured, grave, and self-consciously noble. Color schemes are often somber, though with brilliant highlights. Paint is applied with smoothly precise consistency. Light falls evenly, draperies are simple and chaste, poses invariably sternly heroic.

Paulina Bonaparte Borghese as Venus
Antonio Canova, 1808, marble, Rome: Galleria Borghese. Canova, who settled in Rome after 1779, was the most influential Neoclassical sculptor. To Greek purity he brought an exceptionally finished technique.

SUBJECTS

Overwhelmingly, subjects from Classical literature and history were favored. Religious subjects always coexisted uneasily with Neoclassicism, not surprisingly since the vast majority of Classical art was pagan. Greece and Republican (not Imperial) Rome furnished most subjects. Self-sacrifice and self-denying heroism were recurring themes, underlining the supposed moral worth and superiority, and thus truth, of ancient art.

KEY EVENTS

1738	Excavations begin at Herculaneum, and at Pompeii in 1748
1755	Publication of Winckelmann's *Thoughts on the Imitation of Greek Works of Art*
1775	Jacques-Louis David visits Rome, remaining there until 1780
1789	French Revolution begins. The Bastille, symbol of the *ancien régime*, is stormed
1806	Work begins on the Arc de Triomphe by sculptor Claude Michel Clodion
1815	Restoration of the French monarchy and final overthrow of Napoleon at Waterloo

Kedleston Hall, Derbyshire, *c. 1760,* interior of the marble hall designed by Robert Adam, showing alabaster columns and plasterwork by Joseph Rose. Following a visit to Rome in 1754, the Scot Robert Adam actively sought to emulate the grandeur of Ancient Roman, building in a series of opulent and imposing English houses, such as Kenwood House, Hampstead, and Bowood House, Wiltshire.

1770–1830

WHAT TO LOOK FOR

This landmark painting was the high point of Neoclassical painting, and is a deliberate celebration of the art, life, and stern moral values of Republican Rome. Authoritative, heroic, and impeccably composed, it is also a statement about moral and political ideals. Three brothers (the Horatii) swear allegiance to the Roman Republic, but are also bound by ties of love to an enemy family, the Curatii. They choose loyalty to the state over personal emotion.

The helmets, swords, and togas are copied from known Roman examples

The dominant color of the male grouping is a vivid red, the color of passion and revolution

Each of the three Doric arches frames a group of figures, suggesting both their isolation and their ties to each other

The Oath of the Horatii

Jacques-Louis David, 1784, oil 130 x 167 in (330 x 425 cm) on canvas, Paris: Musée du Louvre. The picture became a rallying cry for the French Revolution. Ironically, it had been commissioned by Louis XVI.

The shadow of death is cast by the men over the women and innocent children

TECHNIQUES

Despite its massive size, *The Oath of the Horatii* is painted with the fine and polished technique usually found in a small Dutch still life.

Sabina (right) is one of the Curatii, but married to one of the Horatii. Camilla (left), a Horatii, is betrothed to a Curatii. She will be killed by her brother for lamenting her lover's death.

Jean-Antoine **Houdon**

● 1741–1828   🏴 FRENCH

🏛 Paris; Rome; North America   🗿 sculpture
🏛 Paris: Musée du Louvre. London: Courtauld
Institute of Art   💰 $2.65m in 1996, *Bust of Benjamin Franklin* (marble)

One of the most important French
sculptors of the 18th century. Born and
died in France; studied in Rome after
receiving the *Prix de Rome* in 1761. Famed
in his lifetime throughout Europe and
America. Survived the French Revolution.
The majority of his works are portrait
busts. Famously commissioned to sculpt
George Washington, for which he
visited North America. Influenced
by the Baroque before becoming a
Neoclassicist; his works emulate the
busts of Ancient Greece and Rome.

KEY WORKS *St. Bruno* 1767, (Rome: S. Maria
degli Angeli); *Morpheus*, 1777 (Paris: Musée
du Louvre); *George Washington as the
Modern Cincinnatus*, 1788
(Richmond: Virginia
State Capitol); *Diana,
the Huntress*, 1790
(Paris: Musée
du Louvre)

Louis-François **Roubiliac**

● 1702–62   🏴 FRENCH

🏛 England; Germany; France   🗿 sculpture
🏛 Cambridge: Trinity College   💰 $1.53m in
1990, *Bust of Alexander Pope* (marble)

Born in France but worked mainly in
England, where he became the greatest
sculptor of his time. Made his name
sculpting statues of famous men and
ornate tombs. Pupil of the Baroque
sculptor Balthasar Permoserin in
Germany. His works are characterized
by a vitality seldom seen in those of his
contemporaries, as though his statues are
simply pausing in the middle of an action.

KEY WORKS *George Frederic Handel*, 1738
(London: Victoria & Albert Museum); *Sir Isaac
Newton*, 1755 (Cambridge: Trinity College)

Comte Joseph-Marie **Vien**

● 1716–1809   🏴 FRENCH

🏛 France; Rome   🎨 oils   🏛 Paris:
Musée du Louvre   💰 $450,544 in 2004,
Woman Leaving the Baths (oils)

One of a happy band of competent
artists who bridge the gap between styles
(Rococo and Neoclassicism, in his case)
without establishing a significant place in
either. Delicate, whimsical works, softly
Neoclassical in subject and setting, but
Rococo in mood and lack of seriousness.

KEY WORKS *Dedalus in the Labyrinth Attaching
the Wings to Icarus*, 1754 (Paris: Musée du
Louvre); *Love Fleeing Slavery*, 1789
(Toulouse: Musée des Augustins)

Jacques-Louis **David**

● 1748–1825   🏴 FRENCH

🏛 Paris; Rome; Brussels   🎨 oils; drawings;
chalks   🏛 Paris: Musée du Louvre
💰 $5,542,000 in 1997, *Portrait of Suzanne
le Peletier de Saint-Fargeau* (oils)

Passionate, volatile character—
an artistic Napoleon (dictatorial,
austere, inflexible). Deeply

François-Marie Arouet Voltaire
*Jean-Antoine Houdon, 1781, height 55½ in
(133.5 cm), marble, Paris: Bibliothèque
de la Comédie Française. This
likeness of the writer was
commissioned by Voltaire's
niece, Madame Denis.*

Napoleon Crossing the Alps on May 20th, 1800
*Jacques-Louis David, 1803, 105 x 87⅖ in (267 x 223 cm),
oil on canvas, Château de Versailles.* Four separate
versions exist, differing only in the coloring of the cape.

involved in the politics of French
Revolution and Napoleonic Empire. Died
in exile in Brussels. Founder of French
Neoclassical painting, but was an arts
administrator as well as a creative genius.

If you want authority in art—this is it.
He applies the precision of the painter of
miniatures on a massive scale. Stern moral
and artistic rules: behind the theater and
storytelling is the ideological commitment
to art as a public and political statement
in the service of the state. Body language
and facial expressions used as drama. No
place for ambiguity: what you see and
feel are as precise and as clear as can be.

Observe his attention to detail, especially
in hands, feet, tassles, armor, and stones.
His flesh is as smooth as porcelain, with
never a hair in sight. Portraits of victors of
the French Revolution have direct, busy-
body eyes. Even shadows and light seem
to have been disciplined and regimented.
Love of antiquity and archeological
accuracy (Roman noses everywhere). You
have to experience the sheer physical size
of the big set pieces firsthand.

KEY WORKS *The Oath of the Horatii*, 1784–85
(Paris: Musée du Louvre); *The Death of Socrates*,
1787 (New York: Metropolitan Museum of
Art); *Death of Marat*, 1793 (Bruges: Musées
Royaux des Beaux-Arts); *Madame Récamier*
c. 1800 (Paris: Musée du Louvre)

Antonio **Canova**

◔ 1757–1822   🏳 ITALIAN

🇮🇹 Italy; France; Austria   🗿 sculpture
🏛 Possagno (Italy): Museo Canova. Venice:
Museo Correr. St. Petersburg: Hermitage Museum
📈 $547,200 in 1995, *Bust of a Lady* (marble)

The leading Neoclassical sculptor,
certainly the most celebrated; enjoyed
huge fame across Europe and was
widely credited with reviving "lost art"
of sculpture and frequently compared
with best of the ancients. Combined
astonishingly accomplished technique—
best works are highly finished—with
rare talent for human figure, females
especially, in a variety of winningly
graceful poses. Many group
sculptures can only be

> "Canova … invented
> a new type
> of ideal
> beauty, closer
> to our taste
> than that of
> the Greeks."
>
> STENDHAL, 1824

appreciated in the round, i.e.,
from different viewpoints, so no
longer dependent on architectural
settings. Highly significant that
many later works were created
for museums rather than patrons,
underlining the changing status of the
artist. Born Treviso, moved to Venice,
where opened studio in 1774. Visited
Rome and Naples in 1780 as his interest
in Neoclassicism developed; settled
permanently in Rome in 1781. Enjoyed
early success with monuments to popes
Clement XIV (1782–87) and Clement
XIII (1787–92). In 1797, the French
invasion forced him into exile in Vienna,
but in 1802 he accepted commissions
from Napoleon after visiting Paris.
Canova's most famous work was of
Napoleon's sister, Pauline Borghese,

in 1808 (see page 250). After 1815, visited
Paris again overseeing return of looted
Italian art, with side trip to London.
In 1817, a grateful pope granted him
title of Marchese (marquis) of Ischia.
KEY WORKS *Daedalus and Icarus*, 1779 (Venice:
Museo Correr); *Theseus and the Minotaur*,
1781–83 (London: Victoria & Albert
Museum); *Theseus Slaying a Centaur*, 1780s
(Vienna: Kunsthistorisches
Museum); *The Penitent
Magdalene*, 1796 (Genoa:
Palazzo Bianca); *Pauline
Borghese as Venus*
(see page 250)

Cupid and Psyche Antonio Canova,
*1796–97, height 59 in (150 cm), marble,
Paris: Musée du Louvre.* Canova was
fascinated by hands and fingers.

The Storm Claude-Joseph Vernet, 1777, oil on canvas, Avignon: Musée Calvet. Vernet married an Englishwoman, and many of his clients were British Grand Tourists.

instead of employing live models. A museum was built in his honor in Copenhagen (1839–48).

KEY WORKS *The Triumph of Alexander the Great*, 1810s (Preston, UK: Harris Museum and Art Gallery); *Hebe*, 1806 (Copenhagen: Thorvaldsens Museum)

Elisabeth **Vigée-Lebrun**

● 1755–1842 ◢ FRENCH

🏛 France; Russia; England ◢ oils 🏛 Paris: Musée du Louvre ◢ $735,347 in 1984, *La Duchesse de Gramont-Caderousse en Vendangeuse* (oils)

Successful portraitist in last years of the *ancien régime*; member of the French Academy. Best at sentimental, lushly colored portraits of fashionable women (allegedly painted Marie Antoinette 25 times). Left France in 1789 to tour Europe. Wrote a good autobiography.

KEY WORKS *Hubert Robert, Artist*, 1788 (Paris: Musée du Louvre); *Madame Perregaux*, 1789 (London: Wallace Collection)

Claude-Joseph **Vernet**

● 1714–89 ◢ FRENCH

🏛 Rome; France ◢ oils 🏛 Paris: Musée de la Marine ◢ $3,507,000 in 2003, *Landscape at Sunset with Fisherman Returning. Shipwreck in Stormy Seas* (oils, a pair)

Established a successful formula for rather stagey, evocative views of Italianate landscapes, coastlines, and especially shipwrecks, much admired by 18th-century collectors. His major project (commissioned by Louis XV) was 16 views of major French seaports (1753–65).

KEY WORKS *View of Naples*, 1748 (Paris: Musée du Louvre); *The Town and Harbor of Toulon*, 1756 (Paris: Musée du Louvre); *Shipwreck*, 1759 (Bruges: Groeninge Museum)

Bertel **Thorvaldsen**

● c. 1770–1844 ◢ DANISH

🏛 Rome; Denmark ◢ sculpture; oils 🏛 Copenhagen: Thorvaldsens Museum. Stockholm: National Museum ◢ $331,250 in 2003, *Mythological Figures* (sculpture)

Thorvaldsen is Denmark's most important Neoclassicist. Ranked alongside Canova, although his works lack the Italian's sensitive surfaces. His career took off with the statue *Jason with the Golden Fleece*. Stationed mainly in Rome, he preferred to work from copies

Portrait of a Young Woman Elisabeth Vigée-Lebrun, c. 1797, 32⅛ x 27¾ in (82.2 x 70.5 cm), oil on canvas, Boston: Museum of Fine Arts. The artist organized famous parties at which guests wore Greek costumes.

Benjamin **West**

● 1738–1820 ⏺ AMERICAN

🏛 US; Italy; England   🎨 oils   🏛 London:
National Portrait Gallery. Washington, DC: National
Gallery of Art. Boston: Museum of Fine Arts.
New York: Metropolitan Museum of Art
💰 $2.6m in 1987, *Portrait of Sir Joseph Banks* (oils)

Pennsylvania-born and the first American
artist to achieve international recognition.
Trained and based in Europe after 1760,
he became the second President of the
Royal Academy, London (after Joshua
Reynolds), and was employed by George
III (who lost the American colonies). His
work is an acquired taste for modern eyes.

His art is secondhand—derived, if not
exactly copied, from others. He had the
enviable ability of anticipating the next
fashion and was thus always successful and
in the public eye. His early large works
often portray obscure literary subjects and
have a stiff, rather flat, wooden style that
caught the taste for the Neoclassical.

From 1770 onward, he cleverly adapted
Neoclassicism by delivering the same
heroic message using modern rather than
ancient history—this was popular with
the public and collectors, and shook up
less progressive artists. He later anticipated
Romanticism by introducing melodramatic
subjects of death and destruction with
powerful contrast of light and shade.
He was also a popular portraitist.

KEY WORKS *Venus Lamenting the Death of Adonis*,
late-18th century (Pittsburgh: Carnegie
Museum of Art); *Colonel Guy Johnson*, c. 1775
(Washington, DC: National Gallery of Art);
The Burghers of Calais, 1789 (Windsor Castle,
England: Royal Collection)

John Singleton **Copley**

● 1738–1815 ⏺ AMERICAN

🏛 US; Europe; England   🎨 oils   🏛 Washington,
DC: National Gallery of Art   💰 $260,000 in 2000,
Mrs. Elizabeth Coffin Amory (oils)

The greatest American painter of the
colonial period. Self-taught. Slow, earnest,
timid, indecisive as a person but assured,
talented, and pioneering as a painter. Son
of poor Irish immigrants, he married well
(the daughter of a rich Tory merchant).

Had two separate and successful careers and styles. Pre-1774, in Boston, established himself as the leading portrait painter. Decisive, high-quality, sober works, which show his own and his sitters' liking for empirical realism. Precise (overhard?) line, clear detail and enumeration of material objects, severe light and dark contrasts. In 1774 he left Boston, disliking politics, fearful that he would be dubbed a pacifist and Tory hanger-on.

Note how he adapted to the grand-manner style of portrait painting (more decorative, pompous, and frothy) after his visit to Italy. It did his portraiture no good, but he achieved great success in London with huge-scale modern-history paintings (heroic actual events presented as though they were moral tales from Ancient History). Late, melancholic decline as he went out of fashion and felt exiled (he never returned to the US).

KEY WORKS *Paul Revere*, c. 1768–70 (Boston: Museum of Fine Arts); *The Copley Family*, 1776–77 (Washington, DC: National Gallery of Art); *Watson and the Shark*, 1778 (Washington, DC: National Gallery of Art); *The Three Youngest Daughters of George III*, 1785 (Windsor Castle, England: Royal Collection)

Ralph **Earl**
● 1751–1801 ⬛ AMERICAN

🄿 US; England 🎨 oils
🏛 New York: Metropolitan Museum of Art 💰 $210,000 in 1996, *Portrait of John Phelps* (oils)

Prominent member of a family of craftsmen and artists; loyalist who left for England in 1778, returning in 1785. Notable for portraits of Connecticut patrons—typically, a plain likeness in their own familiar setting. His sketches of the sites of the battles of Lexington and Concord were turned into popular prints. Bigamist, carouser, failed businessman.

The Death of General Wolfe Benjamin West, c. 1771, 17 x 24 in (43.2 x 61 cm), oil on panel, Private Collection. An episode from the conquest of Quebec, 1759. Wolfe died at the moment of victory.

THE RISE OF AN AMERICAN SCHOOL   mid-18th century

From the mid-18th century, a number of painters appeared in Colonial America. This may have been a measure of growing American prosperity but the colony's cultural insecurity was underlined by the fact that they all trained in Europe, falling under the influence of Neoclassicism. The best known, Benjamin West, settled permanently in England. As late as 1784, when the State of Virginia commissioned a statue of George Washington, it turned to a Frenchman, Jean-Antoine Houdon. A distinctively American school did not emerge until the 19th century.

KEY WORKS *The Striker Sisters*, 1787 (Ohio: Butler Institute of American Art); *Dr. David Rogers*, 1788 (Washington, DC: National Gallery of Art); *Mrs. Noah Smith and her Children*, 1798 (New York: Metropolitan Museum of Art)

Gilbert **Stuart**
● 1755–1828 ⬛ AMERICAN

🄿 US; London; Dublin 🎨 oils 🏛 Boston: Museum of Fine Arts. Washington, DC: Museum of Fine Art. New York: Metropolitan Museum of Art 💰 $900,000 in 1986, *Portrait of John Jay* (oils)

Penniless, uneducated son of a Rhode Island tobacconist. Was a heavy drinker, often in debt, bad-tempered, and addicted to snuff. Was also a highly successful portrait painter and America's first virtuoso exponent of the grand manner.

He learned his trade in Edinburgh (1772) and London (1775) as an assistant to Benjamin West. Produced Romantic, dignified portrait images of independence and self-assurance, softly modeled and silhouetted against a plain background. Painted almost every contemporary of note, especially Washington. Of his 114 portraits of Washington, only three were made from life; the rest are replicas.

Characteristic features and touches are a pinkish-green palette; a white dot on the end of a shiny nose; light shining on a forehead; and rapid execution without preliminary drawing.

KEY WORKS *The Skater*, 1782 (Washington, DC: National Gallery of Art); *George Washington and Martha Washington*, 1796 (Boston: Museum of Fine Arts)

ROMANTIC AND ACADEMIC ART
c. 1800 – 1900

The art of the 19th century was complex and multifaceted. Radical new styles were invented that delighted some and caused deep offence to others. Old styles were revived or combined in unexpected ways. Some artists followed the market, motivated by money; others were prepared to starve for the purity of their art.

Romanticism was embraced by those who wanted to redefine the place of art and humankind in a rapidly changing world. Academicism was supported by those who resisted change and wanted art to maintain the cultural and social status quo. These attitudes to the art of the era reflect the complex politics of the 19th century.

THE NAPOLEONIC ERA
In Europe the decisive event of the early part of the century was the resurgence of France under the galvanizing influence of Napoleon. What had begun in 1789 as a struggle for liberty evolved into a war of conquest. In 1812, at the height of Napoleon's success, French rule extended across almost the whole of

western Europe. Only Britain, Portugal, and Scandinavia remained free of French control.

NATIONALISM AND REVOLUTION
Napoleon's defeat in 1815 restored Europe's pre-revolutionary status quo, but ideas of liberty, once planted, proved tenacious. Growing demands for self-rule by oppressed minorities saw Belgium, Greece, Serbia, and Romania emerge as independent nations by the end of the century. Popular nationalism also drove the unification of Italy (after 1859) and of Germany (after 1866).

There was fierce reaction against self-rule by conservative regimes, above all the multinational Austrian Empire. These conflicting ideologies clashed in 1848 when Poles, Czechs, and Hungarians rose against their Austrian rulers, engulfing central and eastern Europe in revolution. France, which had already seen the abdication of

The Turkish Bath (detail), Jean-Auguste-Dominique Ingres, 1863, oil on canvas, diameter 78 in (198 cm), Paris, Musée du Louvre. Ingres embodies 19th-century taste for Classical academic style combined with exotic Orientalism.

Napoleon Giving Orders before Austerlitz Antoine-Charles Horace Vernet, 1808, oil on canvas, 150 x 254 in (380 x 645 cm), Château de Versailles. The memory of Napoleon influenced French politics throughout the 19th century.

Germany's southern states committed themselves to the powerful new Prussian-dominated German Empire and, following the downfall of Napoleon III, France established the Third Republic.

one king in 1830, was also swept by popular uprisings, forcing a second king to abdicate and the inauguration of a new republic. In 1852, this was replaced by the Second Empire under Napoleon III, Napoleon's nephew.

The crushing defeat of France in the Franco-Prussian War of 1870–71 provided the final impetus for the unification of Germany. In its wake,

INDUSTRIALIZATION

Britain became increasingly aloof from European affairs, preoccupied with its vast empire and the consequences of industrialization. First Britain, and then Europe after 1850, were changing

PHOTOGRAPHY

Photography was first demonstrated to the wider world by Louis-Jacques-Mandé Daguerre in 1839. In its early years it was used principally for studio portraits, mimicking those painted for the wealthy at a fraction of the cost. Gradually, however, it replaced drawing as the most immediate method of making a record of visual

MUYBRIDGE PHOTOGRAPHS OF A JUMPING HORSE

appearance. In the 1870s, US-based English photographer Eadweard Muybridge, using a battery of cameras with fast shutter-speed, began to make studies of horses and humans in motion. This allowed people to see for the first time the action of a galloping horse.

EARLY DAGUERRE CAMERA FROM THE 1840S

TIMELINE: 1800—1900

1804 Napoleon declares himself emperor of France

1825 First passenger steam train (Britain)

1812 Napoleon defeated in Russia

1839 Photographs by Louis Daguerre exhibited in Paris

1837 Accession of Queen Victoria (Britain)

1848 Nationalist uprisings in central Europe repressed; last French king deposed

1800

1820

1840

1805 Spanish-French fleet defeated at Trafalgar

1815 Napoleon defeated at Waterloo; Congress of Vienna restores pre-revolutionary order

1830 Abdication of Charles X in France and accession of more liberal regime under Louis-Philippe

1838 Invention of first electric telegraph (Britain)

1852 Accession of Napoleon III

The Crystal Palace in Hyde Park, London
Built for the Great Exhibition of 1851, the iron-and-glass structure was 1,848 ft (563 m) long. Industrial processes and goods were displayed from all around the world.

rapidly from rural to urban societies amid great social upheaval. Britain had set the pace but France, and, significantly, Germany proved ever more effective rivals. Huge new industrial cities appeared, with railroads, steam ships, and the electric telegraph causing a revolution in communications. After the trauma of the Civil War of 1861–65, the United States established a new, confident identity and continued to expand westward, adding new states to the Union. It too became a major industrial power.

EUROPE AND THE WORLD

At the same time an important shift in attitude toward Europe's overseas colonies took place. Originally the goal had been trade rather than territory. After about 1870 empire in itself came to be seen as desirable. Europe's states engaged in a frenzied race to take over as much of the globe as they could.

The impact of these enormous changes was highly significant for continental European art especially in France, though less so for Britain and the United States. From 1870 onward the principles that had governed the western tradition for over 400 years began to dissolve. The Modern was being born.

1861 Unification of Italy; abolition of serfdom in Russia

1863 Paris Salon rejects Manet's *Déjeuner sur l'Herbe*; first Salon des Refusés held

1876 Bell patents telephone (Britain)

1885 Development of first automobile (Germany)

1860

1880

1900

1859 Publication of Origin of Species (Darwin)

1867 Dual monarchy of Austria-Hungary established

1870–71 Franco-Prussian War and unification of Germany

1884 Berlin Conference initiates "scramble" for Africa

1895 Invention of wireless telegraphy (Marconi)

Francisco **Goya**

● 1746–1828   ◪ SPANISH

◨ Spain; France   🎨 oils; engravings; drawings   🏛 Madrid: Museo del Prado. London: British Museum (prints)   💰 $7.02m in 1992, *Bullfight—Suerte de Varas* (oils)

A solitary and lonely figure, Goya became stone deaf aged 48. He produced a wide range of powerful work, and was one of the greatest portrait painters of all time. He influenced several French 19th-century painters, especially Manet (see page 307).

LIFE AND WORKS

Born in Saragossa. Full name Francisco di Goya y Lucientes. Went to Madrid in 1763. Visited Italy c. 1770–71, returned to work on the cathedral in Saragossa in 1772. In Madrid by 1775 and in 1776 began drawing tapestry cartoons for the Royal factory. Became principal court painter in 1799, which was also the year he completed his *Los Caprichos* series. Following the Napoleonic invasion of Spain in 1808, he worked for the French-held Spanish court until 1814. Painted *The Disasters of War* series 1810–14. Was then pardoned by reinstated Ferdinand VII. Retired to Bordeaux in 1824.

STYLE

An admirer of the French Enlightenment, his overriding interest was appearance and behavior. He understood youth and age, hope and despair, sweet innocence, and the worst aspects of man's inhumanity to man. His art is about Spain and its

The Clothed Maja c. 1800, 37⅓ x 78⅓ in (95 x 190 cm), oil on canvas, Madrid: Museo del Prado. Goya painted a nude and a clothed Maja, causing him to be denounced to the Inquisition for obscenity.

obsessions. He is hauntingly memorable because he is never judgmental (simply showing human behavior as it is), and because his work is always beautiful to look at, even when the subject matter is horrific.

His portraits are untraditional. With Goya one has the uneasy sensation that the relationship between viewer and sitter is reversed; they examine you and your views on human behavior as much as you scrutinize them.

WHAT TO LOOK FOR

Intensity and introspection; drama; untraditional, free, impressionistic paintwork; gray tones against color.
KEY WORKS *Therese Louise de Sureda,* c. 1803–04 (Madrid: Museo del Prado);

Here Neither, Plate 36, The Disasters of War
1810–14, published 1863, 6⅛ x 8⅛ in (15.8 x 20.8 cm), etching, Private Collection. Goya created a series of 82 prints showing the brutality of war.

The Duke of Wellington, 1812–14 (London: National Gallery); *The Third of May 1808,* 1814 (Washington, DC: National Gallery of Art)

Antoine-Jean **Gros**

◕ 1771–1835   🎨 FRENCH

🏛 France; Italy   🖌 oils   🏛 Paris: Musée du Louvre   💰 $695,652 in 1988, *Napoleon on the Battlefield at Eylau* (oils)

David's most famous pupil and the most successful painter of the early Napoleonic period. Despite Neoclassical background, he was a crucial precursor of Romanticism. Had David's ability to manage huge-scale compositions with many figures, yet drew his subject matter from modern life, not the Antique. Best known work is *Napoleon in the Plague House at Jaffa* (1804), which portrays Napoleon as a Christ-like figure surrounded by dying French troops. Loose, brilliant handling of paint, strong contrasts of light and shade, and interest in Eastern exoticism. Later works increasingly sterile. Eventually driven to suicide.

KEY WORKS *Sappho at Leucate*, 1801 (Bayeux: Musée Baron Gérard); *Napoleon on the Battlefield at Eylau*, 1808 (Paris: Musée du Louvre)

Portrait of Madame Bruyère *Antoine-Jean Gros, 1796, 31 x 25 in (79 x 65 cm), oil on canvas, Bristol: City Museum and Art Gallery.* Painted in Genoa, where the sitter's husband was president of the French Chamber of Commerce.

Anne-Louis **Girodet-Trioson**

◕ 1767–1824   🎨 FRENCH

🏛 France; Italy   🖌 oils; pen and ink 🏛 Paris: Musée du Louvre   💰 $328,572 in 1987, *La Révolte du Caire* (oils)

Also known as Anne-Louis Girodet de Roucy or Roussy. Male painter of aristocratic portraits, associated with the cort of Napoleon I. Renowned for refusing to paint faces he did not find psychologically interesting. A talented, capable, and in-demand painter who gave up art in his mid-40s after inheriting a large sum of money. Became a writer.

KEY WORKS *The Sleep of Endymion*, 1792 (Paris: Musée du Louvre); *Napoleon Bonaparte Receiving the Keys of Vienna at the Schloss Schönbrunn, 13th November 1805*, 1808 (Château de Versailles)

Jean-Auguste-Dominique **Ingres**

◕ 1780–1867   🎨 FRENCH

🏛 Paris; Rome; Florence   🖌 oils; drawings   🏛 Paris: Musée du Louvre. Montauban (France): Musée Ingres 💰 $2,132,492 in 1989, *Jupiter and Thetis* (oils)

One of the major heroes of French art and the master of high-flown academic illusionism. Great admirer of the Italian Renaissance and Raphael. Tortured, uptight personality.

His work conveys total certainty—his subjects were well established and officially approved: portraits, nudes, and mythologies, all painted with the high "finish" required by the Academy. He created the most manicured paintings in the history of art—everything carefully arranged (hair, hands, poses, clothes, settings, faces, smiles, attitudes, even light)—and some of the most exquisite drawings ever made, with a total mastery of line and precise observation.

Notice the way he (usually, but not always) manipulated this artificial idealism and fused realism with distortion, so that the end result is alive and thrilling, and never dead academicism: chubby hands with tapering fingers (can look like flippers), strange necks, and sloping shoulders. He had an interest in mirrors, painting figures that are reflected in mirrors; maybe his (and his society's) whole world was that glassy reality/ unreality of the looking glass?

KEY WORKS *La Grande Odalisque*, 1814 (Paris: Musée du Louvre); *The Apotheosis of Homer*, 1827 (Paris: Musée du Louvre); *Madame Moitessier*, 1856 (London: National Gallery)

The Valpinçon Bather *Jean-Auguste-Dominique Ingres, 1808, 57½ x 38½ in (146 x 98 cm), oil on canvas, Paris: Musée du Louvre.* To produce artistic harmony, the body is distorted; for example, the back is too long.

ROMANTICISM

As the rationalism promised by the Enlightenment dissolved in the bloodletting of the French Revolution, artists struggled to come to terms with a world that had plunged from apparent certainty into chaos. Perhaps predictably, the results were mixed. Heroic individualism defined Romanticism. It also marked a decisive break with the conformities of the past.

STYLE

It is no surprise that Romanticism resists neat categorization; a single definition is impossible. Self-expression in the modern sense—that the artist is not just

uniquely well equipped to see into the human soul but has a duty to do so— inevitably led to a huge variety of artistic styles. The desire to see everything as larger than life frequently expressed itself in bold color, vigorous brushwork, and themes of love, death, heroism, and the wonders of nature. It appealed particularly to northern European temperaments and flourished most creatively in Germany, Britain, and France.

Couvent du Bonhomme, Chamonix J. M. W. Turner, c. 1836–42, 9½ in x 12 in (24.2 x 30.2 cm), watercolors, Cambridge: Fitzwilliam Museum. The artist turned the calm certainties of later 18th-century English landscape painting upside-down. Colors exploded, brushwork knew no limits.

SUBJECTS

Heightened emotions dominated. Artists turned away from the logical and rational, allowing themselves freedom to express raw, usually suppressed feelings. Movement, color, and drama were actively championed, exoticism favored. This was a world of vast, elemental

forces, frequently destructive, almost always beyond the reach of man to control. Landscapes became larger, brooding, and more threatening. For the first time, the subconscious was recognized as a mainspring of human activity. In stark contrast to the optimism of the 18th century, humanity was seen as puny and subservient to nature.

KEY EVENTS

1789	French Revolution
1793	Execution of Louis XVI: apparent triumph of new liberal French political order is followed by the Terror
1798	Wordsworth and Coleridge publish *Lyrical Ballads*, key doctrine of Romantic feeling; Schlegel coins term "romantic poetry"
1799	Napoleonic coup: Bonaparte becomes First Consul (1804 Emperor)
1814	Constable's *Stour Valley and Dedham Church* appears same year as Goya's great antiwar polemic *The Third of May*

Monk by the Sea Caspar David Friedrich, 1809, 43⅓ x 67¾ in (110 x 172 cm), oil on canvas: Berlin Staatliche Museum. Friedrich excelled in images of an implacable nature under whose vast skies man inevitably shrank.

18th and 19th centuries

WHAT TO LOOK FOR

The Romantics believed in the freedom of the individual. They were not interested in compromise—better to be a heroic success or a total failure. Géricault's masterpiece encapsulates these virtues and takes art into the realm of political protest. It theatrically recreates a real-life incident when the captain of a shipwrecked French frigate saved himself and abandoned the passengers and crew. Here the survivors see the vessel that will save them. The story and the painting scandalized the French nation. Whereas David's art (page 252) encouraged service to the State, Géricault castigates the State for abandoning those who serve.

The tattered remains of a billowing sail contrast with the menace of an approaching wave

Emotions are deliberately played on. A distraught father grieves over his dead son

A silhouetted figure against a dramatic sky features in many of Géricault's works

TECHNIQUES

The dark, somber mood of the painting is not entirely deliberate. Géricault used bitumen, a tar-based pigment, to add luster to his color scheme. Once dry, it decays. The picture is not just fading, it is slowly disintegrating before our eyes.

The Raft of the Medusa *Théodore Géricault, 1819, 193 x 282 in (491 x 716 cm), oil on canvas, Paris: Musée du Louvre.* Géricault's huge painting was intended to be deliberately challenging—to a complacent state presided over by a newly restored monarchy as much as to a smug bourgeoisie.

The face of death. In pursuit of authenticity, Géricault visited the local hospital, *L'Hôpital Beaujon*, to make detailed studies of the sick and dying. He even took a severed head and an assortment of limbs from the morgue back to his studio in the *Faubourg du Roule*.

Eugène **Delacroix**

◉ 1798–1863   ℗ FRENCH

🏛 Paris; England; Morocco   🖌 oils;
drawings; pastels   🏛 Paris: Musée du
Louvre; Palais Bourbon; Palais Luxembourg;
Saint Sulpice; Musée Delacroix   💲 $7,765,500
in 1998, *Choc de Cavaliers Arabes* (oils)

Small in stature but big in spirit—
the fashionable, fiery hero of French
Romanticism. Allegedly the illegitimate
son of the aristocrat/diplomat, Talleyrand.
Was willing to shock with strong subject
matter and vigorous style, and often did.

He chose big, romantic subjects where
the linking theme is heightened emotion,
especially through sexuality, struggle, and
death. Inspired by literature (Dante, Byron),
current politics, historical events, wild
animals, North Africa (visited in 1832).
Before the 1830s he produced set-piece
works for the official Salon (now mostly
in the Louvre). Had complex working
methods, which produced much
preliminary work, often sketches: these are
what you will most often see outside Paris.

He uses color as the main means of
expression: color and the play of light
keep the eye moving, without a specific
point of focus or climax. Loves rich
material and texture, lush reds, and intense,
coppery greens. His later work exploited
color theory and used complementary

colors and the color wheel. After 1833
his major works are set-piece official
commissions (for the Bourbon Palace,
for instance), which can only be seen
in situ. His *Journal* is essential reading.

KEY WORKS *Orphan Girl at the Cemetery*, 1824
(Paris: Musée du Louvre); *The Death of
Sardanapalus*, 1827 (Paris: Musée du Louvre);
Odalisque, 1845–50 (Cambridge: Fitzwilliam
Museum); *The Barque of Dante*, 1882 (Paris:
Musée du Louvre)

Richard Parkes **Bonington**

◉ 1802–28   ℗ BRITISH

🏛 Paris; England; Venice   🖌 oils; watercolors
🏛 London: Wallace Collection   💲 $564,400
in 1987, *The Palazzi Manolesso-Ferro on the
Grand Canal, Venice* (oils)

The English Delacroix, with whom he
worked closely. Died of consumption, aged
26. Lovely, small-scale, fresh, luminous
oils and watercolors of picturesque places
(Normandy, Venice, Paris), and costume
history pieces, all done with consummate
skill and ease. Works to savor and enjoy.
A genius and a sad, early loss.

KEY WORKS *Venetian Campanili*, c. 1826 (Maidstone
Museum and Art Gallery); *The Corsa Saint
Anastasia, Verona, with the Palace of Prince*

Scenes from the Massacre of Chios *Eugène
Delacroix, 1824, 165 x 139½ in (419 x 354 cm), oil on
canvas, Paris: Musée du Louvre. Directly inspired by the
slaughter of the Greek population of Chios by the Turks.*

contemporary political subject in a manner truly comparable with the grandest history painting (see page 267). His talents extended further: he was also a producer of stunning, innovative lithographs.

Géricault's compositions are memorably simple: he often uses silhouette against a dramatic sky and lifts the eye up to a single point of climax near the top of the picture. He depicts soulful human beings and horses (the expression in the horse's eye is the same as in the human's)—note his trick of turning the human face one way and the horse the other. His strong sense of color and lively paint handling were sometimes ruined by the use of bitumen and poor-quality technique (was a lazy student, should have studied harder).

KEY WORKS *A Horse Frightened by Lightning*, 1813–14 (London: National Gallery); *Officer of the Hussars*, 1814 (Paris: Musée du Louvre); *The Raft of the Medusa*, 1819 (Paris: Musée du Louvre); *The Madwoman*, 1822–23 (Lyon: Musée des Beaux-Arts)

The Undercliff Richard Parkes Bonington, 1828, 5 x 8½ in (13 x 21.6 cm), watercolor on paper, Nottingham: City Museums and Galleries. Watercolor sketches were made on summer travels to be used in the studio in winter.

Maffet, 1826 (London: Victoria & Albert Museum); *Venice: the Piazza S. Marco*, c. 1828 (London: Wallace Collection)

Théodore **Géricault**

◉ 1791–1824   ⚑ FRENCH

🏛 Paris; Italy; England   🎨 oils; drawings
🏛 Paris: Musée du Louvre   💲 $5.21m in 1989, *Portrait de Laure Bro, née de Comères* (oils)

A true Romantic: he was unorthodox, passionate (about horses, women, and art), temperamental, depressive, virile, and inspiring. Had an early death (fell off a horse). Was wealthy and only painted when he felt like it. Was hugely influential on Delacroix.

Géricault had two main subjects: horses and moments of danger or uncertainty (and often combined both). His early work was much influenced by Rubens (rich color and movement) and Michelangelo (muscles and monumentality). Scandalized French art and the political establishment, and changed the rules of art with *The Raft of the Medusa*—the first rendering of a

Portrait of a Woman Addicted to Gambling
Théodore Géricault, c. 1822, 30⅓ x 25½ in (77 x 65 cm), oil on canvas, Paris: Musée du Louvre. A psychiatrist encouraged Géricault to paint portraits of the insane.

Liberty Leading the People

Eugène Delacroix 1830

Leader of the French Romantic Movement in painting, a close friend of Baudelaire and Victor Hugo, Delacroix's own life is like that of the hero of a romantic novel. With restless energy but frail health, he had many love affairs yet remained unmarried. He died alone, exhausted by his artistic labors.

This highly controversial painting commemorates the political uprising in Paris in July 1830, when Parisians took to the streets for three days in revolt against the greedy and tyrannical regime of the king, Charles X. Delacroix had high hopes for the critical reception of this work, but he was disappointed. The proletarian emphasis was considered so dangerous that the painting was removed from public view until 1855. Delacroix's use of color here is uncharacteristically subdued but serves to heighten the brilliance of the saturated tones of the flag.

All classes of society, except the dyed-in-the-wool monarchists, supported the revolution. Delacroix conveys this by displaying a variety of hats worn by the streetfighters—top hats, berets, and cloth caps are all represented.

TECHNIQUES

Delacroix often used short, broken brushwork, anticipating artists such as Monet (see page 310). He also investigated the juxtaposition of colors to increase their individual richness and vibrancy. His journals document his insights into color theory.

Delacroix shows dying and dead men, victims of the battle, their faces and bodies picked out by the dramatic halo of light shining behind Liberty. To the right lie two soldiers; many soldiers refused to fire on their fellow citizens—some even joined the rebel ranks

Liberty Leading the People

Medium oil on canvas
Size 129 x 169 in (330 x 425 cm)
Location Paris: Musée du Louvre

Emerging from the gunsmoke are the towers of Notre Dame. On one of the towers flies the tricolor. Delacroix was in Paris during the three-day revolution but did not play an active part.

The tricolor flag was a symbol of the 1789 Revolution and Delacroix knew it would bring to mind the glories of the early Napoleonic Empire

Liberty wears a Phrygian cap, a symbol of freedom during the French Revolution. Women played a leading role in the street fighting of the 1830 revolution

Delacroix balances realistic detail with a powerful abstracted composition—a pyramid rising up to the right hand of Liberty

The young patriot to the right of Liberty represents a popular hero named Arcole, who was killed in the fighting around the Hôtel de Ville. He also prefigures the popular character Gavroche in Victor Hugo's *Les Misérables*.

A mortally wounded citizen strains with his dying breath to take a last look at Liberty. His arched pose is a crucial element in the pyramidal composition. Significantly, the artist echoes the colors of the tricolor flag in the dying patriot's clothing

The artist's signature is written boldly in symbolic red with the date 1830. Shortly after this he visited Morocco, finding Arab civilization more exciting than the dead history of the ancient world

Caspar David **Friedrich**

◗ 1774–1840   ⚑ GERMAN

🎨 Copenhagen; Dresden   🖌 oils; drawings;
watercolors   🏛 St. Petersburg: Hermitage
Museum   💰 $3,213,000 in 1993, *Spaziergang
in der Abenddämmerung (A Walk at Dusk)* (oils)

Now the best-known German Romantic
landscape painter, but neglected in his
day. Friedrich came into his own later,
influencing late-19th-century Symbolists.

Born at Greifswald, near the Baltic
coast, but later settled permanently in
Dresden. Although a meticulous and
careful painter of small pictures, he
was full of big ideas. His Romantic
relationship with nature was intensely
spiritual and Christian, and loaded
with symbolism. His work is also full
of yearning: for the spiritual life beyond
the grave; for greatness; for intense
experience. Studied nature's details
closely, but all his landscapes are
imaginary or composite—painted out
of his head, not sitting in front of nature.

Look for his symbolism, for instance, oak
trees and Gothic churches as representing
Christianity; dead trees as death and
despair; ships as the transition from the
here and now to otherworldliness; figures

Winter Landscape *Caspar David Friedrich, c. 1811,
13 x 17¾ in (33 x 45 cm), oil on canvas, London:
National Gallery.* Shoots of grass push through the
snow to symbolize the hope of Resurrection.

looking out of windows or at the horizon
as yearning. Times of day and the seasons,
when one state is about to become
another. Sunrise turning to sunset, or
winter turning to spring as spiritual
transition and hope of resurrection.

KEY WORKS *The Cross in the Mountains,* 1808
(Berlin: Staatliche Museum); *Monk by the
Sea,* 1809 (Berlin: Staatliche Museum);
The Polar Sea, 1824 (Hamburg Kunsthalle)

The Stages of Life *Caspar David Friedrich, c. 1835, 28½ x
37 in (72.5 x 94 cm), oil on canvas, Leipzig: Museum der
Bildenden Künste.* The five ships correspond to the figures
on the shore, each at a different stage of life's journey.

Peter von **Cornelius**

1783–1867 GERMAN

Italy; England oils; fresco
Hamburg: Kunsthalle $8,852 in 1990, *Eros with the Eagle* (oils)

Responsible for bringing frescoes back into prominence in the 19th century. His early works are Neoclassical, but later works evince the influence of German Gothicism. Spent several years in Rome (from 1811), where he joined the Nazarenes (see box below). Commissioned by Louis I of Bavaria to paint the frescoes in Munich's Glyptothek (1819–30), the museum of ancient art designed by Leo von Klenze. Visited England in 1841 to advise on frescoes for the new Houses of Parliament. Also worked on frescoes for Frederick William IV of Prussia in Berlin but the project was canceled after the revolution in 1848. Cornelius was also an accomplished book illustrator, most notably of *Faust*.

KEY WORKS *The Vision of the Rabenstein*, 1811 (Frankfurt: Städelsches Kunstinstitut); *Joseph Interpreting Pharaoh's Dream*, 1816–17 (Berlin: Nationalgalerie); *The Recognition of Joseph by his Brothers*, 1816–17 (Berlin: Nationalgalerie)

Self-Portrait *Philipp Otto Runge, 1802, 14½ x 12⅓ in (37 x 31.5 cm), oil on canvas, Hamburg: Kunsthalle.* Runge hoped to create a new art that would fill the voids created by revolution and the collapse of the old certainties.

Philipp Otto **Runge**

1777–1810 GERMAN

Germany; Denmark watercolors; chalks; pen and ink Hamburg: Kunsthalle
$151,773 in 1995, *Study of Lily* (works on paper)

Born in Germany, where he spent most of his short life (died at 33). Studied at the Copenhagen Art Academy for two years. Also a musician and lyricist. He knew Freidrich (see opposite) and met Goethe. His art brought him little fame in his lifetime, but he was recognized posthumously for his sharp—often naïve—style and vivid use of color. Greatly interested in the properties of color, he wrote a hugely influential treatise about it, *Die Farbenkugel* (The Color Sphere), which has remained pivotal to the study and teachings of color.

Runge was interested in trying to express the harmony of the universe and painted pantheistic, mythical subjects as well as portraits. Look for intense (often symbolic) color, and the use of local German landscapes as background to religious and genre paintings.

KEY WORKS *The Lesson of the Nightingale*, 1804–05 (Hamburg Kunsthalle); *The Hülsenbeck Children*, 1805–06 (Hamburg: Kunsthalle); *The Child in the Meadow*, 1809 (Hamburg: Kunsthalle); *The Great Morning*, 1809–10 (Hamburg: Kunsthalle)

THE NAZARENES c. 1818–1840s

A group of Roman Catholic German and Austrian painters who were brought together in Vienna as the *Lukasbrüder* (Brotherhood of St. Luke) in 1809 by art students Friedrich Overbeck and Franz Pforr. They wished to revive German religious art in the manner of Perugino, Dürer, and the young Raphael. From 1810, they lived and worked in a monastery in Rome, where they welcomed others who shared their ideals of intensely spiritual subject matter and the religious properties of light. They were nicknamed the Nazarenes and they dressed like monks. They were a major influence throughout Europe, including the early Pre-Raphaelites.

John **Trumbull**

● 1756–1843 🏴 AMERICAN

🏛 US; London 🎨 oils 🏛 Washington, DC:
Capitol Collection. Yale: University Art Gallery

💰 $260,000 in 1986, *Portrait of John Adams* (oils)

Ambitious, pretentious, unfortunate
(blessed with an uncanny sense of bad
timing), and finally embittered. The
first college graduate (Harvard) in the
US to become a professional painter
(although his parents thought art to
be a frivolous and unworthy activity).

His main goal was to excel in history
painting, but this was going out of fashion.
He took as his subjects the recent history
of the triumphs of revolutionary American
colonies. Completed eight of a projected
series of 13 and was commissioned
by an unenthusiastic Congress to do
four for the rotunda of the Capitol
in Washington. Struggled to achieve
success—had to earn his way as a
portrait painter, which he disliked.

Look for stagey compositions, theatrical
lighting, and good, convincing faces done
from life. (In another age he would have
gone to Hollywood to make B-movies.)
Why the bad timing? He served with
Washington, but then went to London
and was arrested and very nearly
executed in reprisal for the hanging
of a British agent in America; he was
imprisoned instead. Went back to
the US, then returned to London in
1808—but any hope of success was
dashed by the War of 1812. His last work
was his autobiography, published in 1841.

KEY WORKS *Patrick Tracy*, c. 1784–86 (Washington,
DC: National Gallery of Art); *Signing the
Declaration of Independence, July 4th, 1776*,
1786–1820 (New Haven:
Yale University Art
Gallery); *The Sortie Made
by the Garrison of Gibraltar*,
1789 (New York:
Metropolitan Museum of
Art); *Mrs. William Pinkney
(Ann Maria Rodgers)*,
c. 1800 (San Francisco:
Fine Arts Museums)

*Portrait of Alexander
Hamilton* John Trumbull, c. 1806,
30¼ x 24¼ in (77 x 61 cm),
oil on canvas, Washington, DC:
White House. Hamilton founded
the First Bank of the United States.

Emmanuel Gottlieb **Leutze**

● 1816–68 🏴 AMERICAN/GERMAN

🏛 US; Düsseldorf 🎨 oils; drawings 🏛 New
York: Metropolitan Museum of Art. Washington,
DC: Smithsonian Institute 💰 $400,000 in 2004,
General Ulysses S. Grant in his Tent (oils)

German-born, Philadelphia-raised, he
returned to Düsseldorf in 1841 to study
history painting and stayed there (making
it a Mecca for US
artists). Was noted for
large, memorable, easy-
to-understand, patriotic
scenes of American
history. Would have
made a great movie
director. Was antislavery
and racism.

KEY WORKS *Columbus before
the Queen*, 1843 (New York:
Brooklyn Museum of
Art); *Westward the Course
of Empire Takes its Way*,
1861–62 (Washington,
DC: Capitol Collection)

Washington Crossing the Delaware River, 25th December 1776 *Emanuel Gottlieb Leutze, 1851 (copy of an original painted in 1848), 149 x 254¾ in (378.5 x 647 cm), oil on canvas, New York: Metropolitan Museum of Art. The original work was damaged by fire in 1850.*

"No subject can be proper
that is not generally
interesting. It ought to be
either some eminent
instance of heroick action
or heroick suffering."

SIR JOSHUA REYNOLDS

Edward **Hicks**

◉ 1780–1849 🇺 AMERICAN

🏴 Pennsylvania 🎨 oils 🏛 Washington, DC:
National Gallery of Art 💰 $900,000 in 1990,
Penn's Treaty with the Indians (oils)

Hicks had a Quaker upbringing in
Pennsylvania (and became a Quaker
minister in 1811). Initially, he learned
the trade of decorative coach painting.
An otherwise untrained artist with a
primitive style, he is best known for his
Peaceable Kingdom paintings illustrating

Isaiah 11:6–9 (words are sometimes
inscribed round the picture)—the belief
in a peaceful coexistence. Quakers
disapproved of art, but illustrating
Isaiah was acceptable.

He painted at least 60 different versions
of *Peaceable Kingdom* between 1816 and
1849. The animals' expressions change
from tense and fearful to sad and
resigned, reflecting the current political
divisions among the Quakers; in the
background William Penn concludes a
treaty with the Indians. Late in his life
Hicks also painted depictions of the
Declaration of Independence and
Washington crossing the Delaware River.
KEY WORKS *The Falls of Niagara, c.* 1825 (New
York: Metropolitan Museum of Art); *Noah's
Ark*, 1846 (Philadelphia: Museum of Art);
The Cornell Farm, 1848 (Washington, DC:
National Gallery of Art)

THE NORWICH SCHOOL
1803–1880s

An important English school of artists founded by John Crome that grew from the Norwich Society of Artists (founded 1803). The group produced landscapes, coasts, and marine scenes from around Norwich and Norfolk, and favored outdoor painting, as opposed to studio work. They used both oils—as favored by Crome—and watercolors—favored by John Sell Cotman, who took over as president after Crome's death. From 1805 until 1833, an annual exhibition was held in Norwich (the only exceptions being the years 1826 and 1827). This school was 19th-century England's only successful attempt at establishing a regional artistic scene, in emulation of the many Italian examples. It was a provincial school in every aspect as the artists were actively patronized by local wealthy families, who bought their works and hired them as drawing tutors. Artists of the Norwich School continued working through the 1880s.

The Marl Pit *John Sell Cotman, c. 1809–10, 11¾ x 10¼ in (30 x 26 cm), watercolor on paper, Norwich: Castle Museum & Art Gallery. Cotman's early watercolors are noted for their simplicity and translucency.*

View of Mousehold Heath, near Norwich *John Crome, c. 1812, 21½ x 32 in (54.5 x 81.2 cm), oil on canvas, London: Victoria & Albert Museum. "Old Crome" was self-taught and worked only part-time as a painter.*

John **Varley**
● 1778–1842 🏳 BRITISH

📖 London 🎨 watercolors 💲 $79,040 in 1996, *Views of Bamburgh Castle, Northumberland* (watercolors)

Sublime Romantic watercolor painter, whose landscapes are contemporaneous with Turner's and who similarly began the development from topographical drawings to fully developed watercolor painting. Was most influential as a teacher (of Linnel, Cox, Holman Hunt et al).

KEY WORKS *View of Bodenham and the Malvern Hills, Herefordshire,* 1801 (London: Tate Collection); *A Half-Timbered House,* c. 1820 (Boston: Museum of Fine Arts)

"No two days are alike, not even two hours; neither were there two leaves alike since the creation of the world."

JOHN CONSTABLE

John **Constable**

◔ 1776–1837   ⚐ BRITISH

🏛 Suffolk; Hampstead   🎨 oils   🏛 London:
National Gallery; Tate Collection; Victoria & Albert
Museum   💰 $19,306,000 in 1990, *The Lock* (oils)

One of the great landscape painters
who pioneered a new type of plein-air
painting based on the direct observation
of nature. He believed that nature,
with its dewy freshness, sunlight, trees,
shadows, streams, and so forth, was
full of moral and spiritual goodness.
He was a devoted family man.

   Limited subject matter: he only painted
the places he knew best. Seems to know
every square inch of ground and all the
local day-to-day activity. Note how the
light in the sky and the fall of light on
the landscape are directly connected
(not so in Dutch landscapes). The
sketches (not for public display) have
a direct spontaneity, absent from the
more labored, finished paintings
(especially the "six-footers") with which
he hoped to make his reputation.

   How does he get that sense of dewy
freshness? Look at the way he juxtaposes
different greens (full of subtle color
variation) and introduces small accents
of red (the complementary color) to
enliven them. Note, also, the layering
of clouds to create perspective recession;
the figures, sometimes almost hidden
in the landscape. Late work much more
emotional, darker, more thickly painted.

KEY WORKS *Dedham from Langham*, c. 1813
(London: Victoria & Albert Museum); *Weymouth
Bay*, 1816 (London: National Gallery); *Wivenhoe
Park, Essex*, 1816 (Washington, DC: National
Gallery of Art);
Hampstead Heath,
1821 (Manchester:
City Art Gallery);
The Hay Wain (see
pages 278–279)

**Flatford Old Mill
Cottage on the
Stour** *John Constable,
c. 1811, pen and wash,
London: Victoria &
Albert Museum.*
Constable combined a
detailed objective study
of nature with a deeply
personal vision of his
childhood scenery.

David **Cox**

◔ 1783–1859   ⚐ BRITISH

🏛 Birmingham; London; Hereford
🎨 watercolors; oils   🏛 Birmingham (UK):
City Art Gallery   💰 $158,760 in 1997,
Crossing Lancaster Sands (watercolors)

Well traveled (France, Flanders, Wales);
lived in Hereford, London, Birmingham.
Produced talented, small-scale, freely
executed oils and watercolors that capture
the spontaneity of rapidly shifting light and
breezes, experienced in the open air. One
of the few painters to make one feel wind
and rain (the French Impressionists rarely,
if ever, attempted it).

KEY WORKS *Moorland Road*, 1851 (London:
Tate Collection); *Rhyl Sands*, c. 1854
(London: Tate Collection)

James **Ward**

◔ 1769–1859   ⚐ BRITISH

🏛 England   🎨 oils; engravings   🏛 London:
Tate Collection   💰 $380,000 in 1996, *Adonis,
King George III's Favourite Charger* (oils)

Brother-in-law of George Morland.
Memorable mostly for large-scale
pictures of animals, and landscapes
bursting with Romantic drama and
emotion, notably the vast *Gordale Scar*
(Tate Collection) with bulging-eyed heroic
cattle, exaggerated cliffs, and stormy
skies. He was not appreciated in
his time—died in poverty—although
he was an inspiration to Géricault.

KEY WORKS *Bulls Fighting*, c. 1804 (London:
Victoria & Albert Museum); *Gordale Scar*,
1811–15 (London: Tate Collection)

The Hay Wain

John Constable 1821

"Constable's Country" is now a much visited beauty spot and this image adorns many tourist souvenirs. Constable put all his efforts into this picture, but when first exhibited, it failed to sell, and the artist was hurt by the constant rejection of his work.

To many people, Constable's picture represents a nostalgic image of the English countryside, with mankind working in perfect harmony with nature, a golden age before the industrial problems of modern times. It is perfectly legitimate to read the picture in this way, but Constable was in fact trying to create a new subject matter for painting, but few of his fellow artists or collectors could accept it as serious art. At the time it was painted, there was an economic depression in agriculture, with riots and farms burned down.

The carefully observed high, billowing clouds are a special feature of this part of eastern England, caused by water vapor drawn up from the nearby Stour Estuary

The cottage on the left is known, even today, as Willy Lot's cottage. He was a deaf and eccentric farmer who was born in the cottage and lived there for over 80 years; he would have been the inhabitant at the date of this picture

Constable was a slow worker, and behind this work lie many small sketches made in the open air of this actual place. The finished picture was made in his studio in London as stated in his signature, which is included along the bottom edge of the painting.

TECHNIQUES

If you look carefully, you can see that all areas of green are an interweaving of many different shades of green, and there are touches of red, such as in the figure of the man fishing. Red is the complementary color to green, and so intensifies its impact. Similarly, Constable infuses the water with brown and orange hues.

Outside Willy Lot's cottage a woman is either collecting water or washing clothes in the estuary. The detail shows Constable's traditional palette of earth colors, and his highlights of thick white paint.

Constable avoids treating clouds merely as a backdrop and makes them an integral part of the picture

The play of light and shadow over the land is consistent with the pattern of light and clouds in the sky

The water prevents the wheels from shrinking, which would cause the metal band around the rim to loosen

In the far distance it is possible to see the haymakers in the fields carrying their scythes, and loading hay onto a cart

The dog is an essential part of the composition, leading the eye toward the focus of interest, which is the hay cart. It was added quite late in the development of the picture.

The Hay Wain

Medium oil on canvas
Dimensions 51 x 73 in (130 x 185 cm)
Location London: National Gallery

Sir David **Wilkie**

◔ 1785–1841 ⚑ BRITISH

🏛 Edinburgh; London   🎨 oils   🏛 Edinburgh:
National Gallery of Scotland   💰 $544,000 in
2003, *Spanish Girl* (oils)

Scottish, direct, down-to-earth, and
ambitious. His individual style, which
embraced the narrative subjects of
everyday life and loaded them with
authentic detail, was very influential
throughout Europe. His manner
became more contrived and Romantic
after a visit to the Continent in 1825–28.
He was much admired by the Prince
Regent (George IV) who bought
Wilkie's paintings and ignored
Turner and Constable.

**The Chelsea Pensioners Reading the Waterloo
Dispatch** *Sir David Wilkie, 1822, 38¼ x 62¼ in (97 x
158 cm), oil on wood, London: Wellington Museum. The
painting was commissioned by the Duke of Wellington.*

KEY WORKS *The Letter of Introduction*, 1813
(Edinburgh: National Gallery of Scotland);
Self-Portrait, 1813 (Pau: Musée des Beaux-Arts)

John **Martin**

◔ 1789–1854 ⚑ BRITISH

🏛 England; France   🎨 oils; engravings
🏛 London: Tate Collection. Newcastle upon
Tyne: Laing Art Gallery   💰 $2,415,000
in 2003, *Pandemonium* (oils)

Famous in his own day (but then went
completely out of fashion). Overdramatic
detailed representations of apocalyptic
events from history—they anticipate the
Hollywood spectaculars of Cecil B. de
Mille. They win commendations for
special effects rather than content.

Martin's work combines impressive scale
and imagination with architectural detail
and tiny figures. Impressive mezzotints.

KEY WORKS *The Bard*, c. 1817 (New Haven:
Yale Center for British Art); *The Eve of the
Deluge*, 1840 (Windsor Castle, England:
Royal Collection); *Great Day of his Wrath*,
1851–53 (London: Tate Collection)

John **Linnell**

◔ 1792–1882 ⚑ BRITISH

🏛 England   🎨 watercolors; oils
💰 $241,500 in 2003, *Return of Ulysses* (oils)

Romantic landscape painter who was
successful commercially. He provided
artistic and financial support to Blake
and Palmer. Linnell
was an eccentric,
argumentative, radical
nonconformist, best
known for his rural
landscapes, often
showing laborers
at work or rest.
He believed that
landscape paintings
could carry a religious
message—hence their
intense visionary
quality and style.

KEY WORKS *Leading a
Barge*, c. 1806 (London:
Tate Collection); *Kensington Gravel Pits*, 1811–12
(London: Tate Collection); *Mid-day Rest*, 1816
(Manchester: City Art Gallery)

Samuel **Palmer**

◔ 1805–81 ⚑ BRITISH

🏛 London; Kent   🎨 watercolors; engravings
🏛 London: British Museum; Tate Collection. Oxford:
Ashmolean Museum   💰 $1.02m in 2000, *Oak Tree
and Beech, Lullingstone Park* (works on paper)

Child prodigy from Kent (the "Garden
of England"). Had a very intense pastoral
and Christian vision—nature as the
gateway to a revelation of paradise.
Made exquisite, magical, small drawings
in the 1820s, with microscopic details.
After his marriage in 1837, he turned
to a less intense, classical, pastoral vision.

KEY WORKS *Self-Portrait*, c. 1825 (Oxford:
Ashmolean Museum); *Early Morning*,
1825 (Oxford: Ashmolean Museum)

Crichton Castle (Mountainous Landscape with a Rainbow) J. M. W. Turner, c. 1818, 6 ¼ x 9 ½ in (17.1 x 24 cm), watercolor over graphite on wove paper, New Haven: Yale Center for British Art.

J. M. W. **Turner**

● 1775–1851   ⚑ BRITISH

London; France; Switzerland; Italy; Scotland
oils; watercolors; engravings   London:
Tate Collection; Clore Gallery $9,045,000
in 1984, *Seascape, Folkestone* (oils)

The champion of Romantic landscape and seascape. The greatest British painter yet (apologies, Constable).

Observe his ability to portray nature in all her moods, from the sweetest and most lyrical to the stormiest and most destructive. He had a deep, personal response to nature, using a wide-ranging source of inspiration (from Scotland to Italy). Applied a remarkable range of working methods, with fascinating technical and stylistic innovation,

especially in his watercolors and later work. Had a never-ending interest in light, and a deep reverence for the old masters, especially in his early work.

Look for the sun—where it is; what it is doing; its physical qualities as light, but also its symbolism (rising, setting, hiding, warming, frightening; of a bitter northern winter, of a balmy Mediterranean summer, and so on). His early "old master" style changes dramatically after his visit to Italy in 1819 (introducing a brighter palette, freer style and imagery). Note the detail in finished watercolors. Complex personal—sometimes secret—symbolism. He left sketchbooks that show his working process.

KEY WORKS *Mortlake Terrace*, c. 1826 (Washington, DC: National Gallery of Art); *Norham Castle, Sunrise*, c. 1835–40 (London: Tate Collection); *Snowstorm: Steam-Boat off a Harbour's Mouth*, 1842 (London: Tate Collection); *Approach to Venice*, c. 1843 (Washington, DC: National Gallery of Art)

Rain, Steam, and Speed—The Great Western Railway J. M. W. Turner, c. 1840, 35 ¾ x 48 in (90.8 x 121.9 cm), oil on canvas, London: National Gallery. Turner was inspired by his own journey on a steam train.

The Fighting Téméraire

J. M. W. Turner   1839

Turner lived in revolutionary times. At home, he witnessed the Industrial Revolution and the dawn of the steam age. Abroad, he observed the French Revolution and the rise and fall of the Napoleonic Empire. In this late work, he explores both these themes, along with his Romantic response to the beauty of nature.

On September 6th, 1838, Turner was a passenger on a steamboat from Margate with the sculptor W. F. Woodington when they witnessed the *Téméraire* being towed up the Thames from Sheerness to Rotherhithe to be broken up. Turner always carried a notebook in his pocket, and made sketches of this historic event, which he later transformed into this masterpiece. The famous ship had been part of Nelson's fleet, and her moment of glory had come in 1805 with distinguished service at the Battle of Trafalgar. Turner's art was at its best when it was inspired by a subject that resonated with history and with a sense of time, fate, and nature sweeping all before them.

In 1877, correspondents to *The Times* attacked Turner's lack of accuracy, such as incorrect rigging, the sun setting in the east, and the mast of the steamer incorrectly shown behind the smokestack.

The silver light of a crescent moon, reflected in the water, illuminates the ship and gives it a ghostlike quality

The *Téméraire* was a ship of the line with 98 guns. She took her name from a French ship captured at Lagos Bay in 1759

The Fighting Téméraire

Medium oil on canvas
Dimensions 35¾ x 48 in (90.7 x 121.6 cm)
Location London: National Gallery

Turner is reported to have seen the *Téméraire* on an evening with a blazing sunset. In his picture he exploits both the appearance and symbolism of the setting sun, heightening each by contrasting them with a delicate new moon, and by repeating the fiery glow of the sky in the burning gases streaming from the smokestack.

Turner was able to use the recently discovered synthetic pigments such as chrome yellow to bring a new brightness and intensity to his palette

The picture was exhibited at the Royal Academy in 1839. The catalog contained lines from Thomas Campbell's *Ye Mariners of England:* "The flag which braved the battle and the breeze, now no longer owns her."

Turner's treatment of light and handling of paint influenced the young Monet, who studied his works in London in 1870

Turner chose never to sell this picture. The National Gallery acquired it in 1856 as part of the Turner Bequest. The artist left a disputed will through which the nation received all his unsold works

The first paddle-wheel steamboat was launched in 1783; the first steam warship in 1815 – both in Turner's lifetime

Although Turner's late works often received harsh criticism, this composition was highly praised. *The Morning Chronicle* singled out the poignantly symbolic "gorgeous horizon"

TECHNIQUES

Turner combined his early training in watercolors with the scope for variation in texture of oils to form a style involving washes of great fluidity and impasto details to evoke different surfaces.

THE ACADEMIES   1562–late 19th century

Academies were the official institutions, funded by a princely
ruler or a State, that arranged and promoted exhibitions,
organized art education, and dictated rules and standards.
Enormously influential between the mid-17th
and late 19th centuries, the first academy
was founded in Florence in 1562.

THE FRENCH ACADEMY

The academy par excellence was the
French Royal Academy, founded in 1648
under Louis XIV and directed by LeBrun.
It had a monopoly of exhibitions and
hiring models for life classes, awarded
scholarships, and established branches
in provincial cities and in Rome. A
remarkable example of the imposition
of centralized bureaucracy on the arts,
its example was widely followed, e.g.
in Berlin in 1697, Vienna 1705,
St. Petersburg 1721, Stockholm 1735,
and Madrid 1752, as well as in many

principalities
and municipalities in
Germany, Switzerland,
Italy, and Holland. The
exception was London
where the Royal
Academy was, and
remains, private
and independent.

Gloria Victis Marius Jean Antonin
Mercie, 1874, height 55⅛ in (140 cm),
bronze, Paris: Musée de la Ville.
Archetypal academic sculpture.

THE 19TH CENTURY

Academies were at their most stultifying
and conservative in the mid- to late 19th
century, especially in France with its
annual salon that was much patronized
by Napoleon III and his Empress
Eugénie. In many ways, their most
important achievement was to provoke

young artists to react against them,
e.g. Courbet, Manet, and the various
Secession movements (see page 338).

*Empress Eugénie (1826–1920) Surrounded by
her Ladies-in-Waiting* Franz Xavier Winterhalter,
1855, 118¼ x 158¼ in (300 x 402 cm), oil on canvas,
Oise (France): Château de Compiègne.

Cleopatra Testing Poisons on those Condemned to Death
Alexandre Cabanel, 1887, oil on canvas, Private Collection.

Alexandre **Cabanel**

● 1823–89 ▣ FRENCH

▣ Paris ⬤ oils ▣ Paris: Musée d'Orsay
⚡ $400,000 in 1993, *Cleopatra Testing Poisons on those Condemned to Death* (oils)

One of the pillars of the establishment of late 19th-century Paris. Conventional, fashionable, much sought after. Painted nudes, allegories, portraits. Now seen in true light—academic painting at its worst and most flatulent. Weak technique; sickly, garish colors; banal subjects. A warning that much-praised contemporary art can be dire (then and now).

KEY WORKS *The Birth of Venus*, 1862 (Paris: Musée d'Orsay); *Death of Francesca da Rimini and Paolo Malatesta*, 1870 (Paris: Musée d'Orsay); *The Life of St. Louis*, 1870s (Paris: Pantheon)

William-Adolphe **Bouguereau**

● 1825–1905 ▣ FRENCH

▣ France; Rome ⬤ oils
⚡ $3.2m in 2000, *La charité* (oils)

Bouguereau was the archetypal conservative pillar of the French academic system in its final years, refusing to abandon the language and manners of a by-now debased Classical tradition.

He delighted his public with large-scale theme paintings and a dazzlingly accomplished technique. However, his work now looks curiously stilted and unconvincing—a dinosaur of art history. His lofty rhetorical subject matter (for example, nude Venuses) invites us to suspend disbelief in reality, but his style, which apes the reality of photography, contradicts or denies the

invitation. Art that aspires to be this great requires a convincing unity between subject and style.

Smooth, hairless, firm flesh and rosy nipples, which anticipate (inspire?) the airbrushed girlie pin-ups of World War II or *Playboy* magazine. His paintings of everyday peasant life are more convincing than his grander works because they do not aim so high (so cannot fall so low) and do not demand suspension of disbelief to the same degree. A recent revival of interest in his works has resulted in some massive prices at auction.

KEY WORKS *Young Girl Defending Herself Against Eros*, c. 1880 (Los Angeles: J. Paul Getty Museum); *A Little Shepherdess*, 1891 (London: Christie's Images); *Cupidon*, 1891 (London: Roy Miles Fine Painting)

The Birth of Venus *William-Adolphe Bouguereau, 1879, 118¼ x 85¾ in (300 x 218 cm), oil on canvas, Paris: Musée d'Orsay. Bouguereau's mythological paintings were avidly collected, and sold for huge prices.*

Franz Xavier **Winterhalter**

● 1805–73 🅟 GERMAN

🏛 Paris   🎨 oils   🏛 London: Wallace Collection
💰 $1.6m in 1997, *Jeune fille de l'Ariccia* (oils)

He was a smooth-mannered, highly
popular Munich-trained portrait painter,
notably of the European monarchy
(English, Belgian, and French) in their
19th-century golden age. He captured
their preferred self-image—royalty as
bourgeoisie. His work brilliantly combines
formality, intimacy, and anecdote. Was
a rapid worker, straight onto canvas,
with an effortless, impersonal style.
Winterhalter also made lithographs.

KEY WORKS *Princess Leonilla*, 1844 (Los Angeles:
J. Paul Getty Museum); *The First of May*, 1851
(Windsor Castle, England: Royal Collection);
Portrait of Princess Tatyana Alexandrovna Yusupova,
1858 (St. Petersburg: Hermitage Museum)

Hans **Makart**

● 1840–84 🅟 AUSTRIAN

🏛 Munich; Vienna   🎨 oils   🏛 Vienna:
Österreichische Galerie   💰 $223,200 in 2000,
Frauenporträt in ägyptischem Kostum (oils)

A highly successful Viennese painter,
Makart delighted his rich clientele by
plundering the art of the great masters
of the Venetian Renaissance and the
17th and 18th centuries to create
decorative allegories and historical
images that promised (but in the end,
failed to deliver) great talent and
emotional content. Despised by avant-
garde artists such as Schiele and Klimt.

KEY WORKS *The Dream after the Ball*, 1870s
(New York: Metropolitan Museum of Art);
The Triumph of Ariadne, 1870s (Vienna:

Österreichische Galerie); *Charlotte Wolter
as the Empress Messalina*, c. 1875 (Vienna:
Historisches Museum der Stadt)

Sir Thomas **Lawrence**

● 1769–1830 🅟 BRITISH

🏛 London; Europe   🎨 oils   🏛 Oxford:
Ashmolean Museum   💰 $1,092,000 in
1988, *Portrait of Prince Regent* (oils)

The precociously talented son of an
innkeeper, Lawrence went on to become
the leading portrait painter of the day.
Over-production led to uneven quality.

His paintings have style, elegance, and
haughty confidence. He was the chosen
portrait painter of the ruling class of
the richest and most powerful nation on
earth—they believed it and he confirmed
it. They were also hungry for aesthetic
experience; his portraits revealed this
side of their personalities and gave a
strong aesthetic thrill (they still do).

Observe the way he conveys the
above: inventive, dramatic, self-conscious
poses; flowing dresses, flowing hair; heads
confidently turned on overlong necks,
to show off; long arms; finely formed,
sloping shoulders; rich colors; luscious,
free-flowing paint applied with total
confidence and sensual pleasure; above
all, dark eyes, with crisp, white highlights
that are deep pools of romantic
experience and feeling.

KEY WORKS *Elizabeth Farren*, 1790 (New York:
Metropolitan Museum of Art); *Mrs. Isaac
Cuthbert*, c. 1817 (Paris: Musée du Louvre);

Derby Day William Powell Frith, 1856–58, 40 x 88 in
(101.6 x 223.5 cm), oil on canvas, London: Bonhams.
When first exhibited, crash barriers were erected
around the painting to hold back overexcited crowds.

Portrait of Arthur Wellesley (1769–1852), 1st Duke of Wellington *Sir Thomas Lawrence, 1814, oil on canvas, London: The Wellington Museum.* Lawrence painted portraits of all the European victors over Napoleon.

Samuel Woodburn, c. 1820 (Cambridge: Fitzwilliam Museum); *Sir John Julius Angerstein*, c. 1823–28 (London: National Gallery)

William Powell **Frith**

● 1819–1909 ⚑ BRITISH

🏴 England 🎨 oils 🏛 London: Tate Collection. Surrey: Royal Holloway and Bedford New College

🏆 $3,701,300 in 2003, *For Better, For Worse* (oils)

A popular painter, admired by Queen Victoria, famous for his detailed, panoramic chronicles of Victorian life (railway stations, races, the seaside). Refreshingly unpretentious, unambitious, and free from moral comment. Used photographs but was reluctant to admit it. Unwisely attempted to do history and moral paintings.

KEY WORKS *Othello and Desdemona*, 1840–56 (Cambridge: Fitzwilliam Museum); *Portrait of Charles Dickens*, c. 1850s (London: Victoria & Albert Museum); *The Railway Station*, 1862 (Surrey: Royal Holloway and Bedford New College)

Lord Frederic **Leighton**

● 1830–96 ⚑ BRITISH

🏴 Frankfurt; Rome; Paris; London 🎨 oils; sculpture 🏛 London: National Gallery; Tate Collection. Wirral (UK): Lady Lever Art Gallery

🏆 $1,812,000 in 2000, *The Bracelet* (oils)

The first British painter to be made a Lord. Was educated in Europe. Aimed to be, and was called, the Michelangelo of his day. Adept at art politics and diplomacy. Very successful. Counted Queen Victoria among his buyers.

His works are immaculate and faultless in every way: they display wonderful technique and draftsmanship; superb, sophisticated, and inventive handling of light, color, composition; correct academic subject matter (portraits, biblical and mythological themes). So why are his works so often cold, aloof, and soulless? Because overt support for the status quo always wins support from those with most to lose—but lasting fame requires real innovation.

Look for borrowings from (also homages to) Michelangelo and from other great Italian and French masters (Titian, Ingres). Also notice the places where he lets go and, instead of playing the pompous, godlike, so-called great artist, is himself: sketches from nature, occasional quirky oil painting, joy at painting white textures. It is then that the warmth and freshness that is absent from his "official" works begin to come across.

KEY WORKS *Cimabue's Madonna Carried in Procession through the Streets of Florence*, 1853–55 (London: National Gallery); *On the Nile*, 1868 (Cambridge: Fitzwilliam Museum); *Athlete Struggling with a Python*, 1874–77 (London: Tate Collection); *Study of a Nubian Young Man*, 1880s (London: Bonhams); *Study*, 1877 (Liverpool: Sudley House)

Garden of the Hesperides *Lord Frederic Leighton, c. 1892, oil on canvas, Wirral (UK): Lady Lever Art Gallery.* Bought by the soap manufacturer Lord Leverhulme, the epitome of the successful Victorian businessman.

Sir Edwin **Landseer**

● 1802–73 🏴 BRITISH

📱 London; Scotland   🎨 oils; sculpture; engravings
🏛 London: Tate Collection; Victoria & Albert
Museum   💰 $1,851,500 in 2003, *Scene in
Chillingham Park, Portrait of Lord Ossulston* (oils)

Hugely successful and much admired by
Queen Victoria, Landseer had a prolific
output of sentimental portraits and
animal and sporting pictures (particular
affinity with Highland cattle, stags, lions,
and polar bears). Was ideally in tune
with his times—his animals express
the key Victorian virtues: nobility,
courage, pride, success, conquest, male
dominance, and female subservience.

His small plein-air sketches, done
on the spot, are as good as anything
by Constable or French contemporaries.
KEY WORKS *The Old Shepherd's Mourner,* 1837
(London: Victoria & Albert Museum); *Dignity
and Impudence,* 1839 (London: Tate Collection)

Sir Lawrence **Alma-Tadema**

● 1836–1912   🏴 BRITISH

📱 Netherlands; London   🎨 oils
🏛 Los Angeles: J. Paul Getty Museum
💰 $2.5m in 1995, *The Finding of Moses* (oils)

He was Dutch-born, naturalized British.
Highly successful with the Victorian
business classes for whom he produced
fashionable, meticulously painted, erotic
but safe fantasy images of the leisured
classes of Greece and Rome—usually
the women in private with their clothes
off. Dedicated archaeologist. He used
photographs and his own site drawings.
KEY WORKS *Phidias and the Parthenon,* 1868
(Birmingham, UK: Museums and Art
Gallery); *The Sculptor's Model,* 1877
(Private Collection)

Sir Luke **Fildes**

● 1843–1927   🏴 BRITISH

📱 Liverpool; London; Venice   🎨 oils
💰 $462,500 in 1992, *The Village Wedding* (oils)

A very successful and popular pillar of
the establishment who freshened stale
Victorian academic tradition with a whiff
of acceptable new French ideas—loose
paint handling, modern subjects, and
an interest in light. Portraits, landscapes,
social themes. His *Doctor* was one of the
most internationally popular paintings
of the late 19th century.
KEY WORKS *Venetians,* 1885 (Manchester:
City Art Gallery); *Doctor,* 1891 (London:
Tate Collection); *A Devotee,* 1908
(Manchester: City Art Gallery)

The Tepidarium *Sir Lawrence Alma-Tadema, 1881,
9½ x 13 in (24 x 33 cm), oil on panel, Wirral, UK: Lady
Lever Art Gallery.* In the 1880s, Alma-Tadema's paintings
often fetched higher prices than quality old masters.

John Frederick **Lewis**

◔ 1805–76 ⚑ BRITISH

🏠 London; Cairo 🖌 watercolors; oils; engravings
📈 $1.26m in 1996, *Lilium Auratum* (watercolors)

Best-known member of a prolific artistic
dynasty, famous for his impressive scenes
of Egyptian markets, bazaars, and harems,
using intricate watercolor technique
(clever use of gouache) and obsessive detail.
Also produced less good oils. Early work
has sporting, wildlife, and topographical
subjects. Visited Spain and Morocco
(1832–34); lived in Egypt (1841–51).
KEY WORKS *A Syrian Sheik, Egypt*, 1856
(Cambridge: Fitzwilliam Museum); *The
Coffee Bearer*, 1857 (Manchester: City Art
Gallery); *The Door of a Café in Cairo*, 1865
(London: Royal Academy of Arts)

River Bank at Emilliekilde *Christen Købke, c. 1836,
7½ x 12¼ in (19 x 31 cm), oil on canvas, Paris: Musée du
Louvre.* Købke's famous lake scenes were painted in the
studio from numerous outdoor drawings and sketches.

Indoor Gossip, Cairo *John Frederick Lewis, 1873,
12 x 8 in (30.4 x 20.2 cm), oil on panel, Manchester:
Whitworth Art Gallery.* Lewis preferred the solitude
of Egypt's deserts to the bustling social life of Cairo.

Christen **Købke**

◔ 1810–48 ⚑ DANISH

🏠 Copenhagen 🖌 oils 🏛 Copenhagen:
Statens Museum for Kunst 📈 $322,712 in 2000,
View from a Window in Eckersberg's Studio (oils)

He was a short-lived (died of pneumonia),
gifted painter who caught the prevailing
Biedermeier middle-class taste for
reassuring portraits of themselves and
their dwelling places. The liveliest works
are his sketches from nature (from which
he made finished exhibition paintings).
Traveled in Italy in 1838–40. He was
rejected by the Academy.

The luminous calm hides a quiet
national pride and strong sense of moral
virtues. Both sentiments are essential
Biedermeier qualities and are revealed
in his attention to detail, emphasis on
cleanliness and orderliness (which is
probably unreal and overexaggerated),
and understated symbolic details.
KEY WORKS *Portrait of Frederik Sødring*, 1832
(Copenhagen: Hirschsprungske Samling);
A View of a Street in Copenhagen, 1836
(Copenhagen: Statens Museum for Kunst);
*The Northern Drawbridge to the Citadel in
Copenhagen*, 1837 (London: National Gallery);
A View of One of the Lakes in Copenhagen, 1838
(Copenhagen: Statens Museum for Kunst)

Richard **Dadd**

◔ 1817–86 ⚑ BRITISH

🏠 Bedlam, Broadmoor (UK) 🖌 oils
🏛 London: Tate Collection 📈 $2,775,000 in
1992, *Contradiction, Oberon, and Titania* (oils)

"Mad Dadd" murdered his father
in 1843 and was locked up, but his
doctors encouraged him to continue
with his painting. Has recently become
famous through his meticulous and
obsessively detailed paintings of fairy
subjects made in the 1850s.
KEY WORKS *The Flight out of Egypt*, 1849–50
(London: Tate Collection); *Mercy: David Spareth
Saul's Life*, 1854 (Los Angeles: J. Paul Getty
Museum); *The Fairy Feller's Master-Stroke*,
1855–64 (London: Tate Collection)

Thomas **Cole**

◑ 1801–48　⚐ AMERICAN

🏠 Pennsylvania; New York; Catskill Mountains; Europe　🖌 oils　🏛 New York: Munson-Williams-Proctor Art Institute　📈 $1.3m in 2003, *Catskill Mountain Houses* (oils)

Cole was British-born (Bolton, Lancashire), but his family emigrated to the United States in 1818. Major figure in American art—founder of the Hudson River School and the tradition of the grand landscape. Romantic, conservative, melancholic, often at odds with a world given to fast-changing materialism.

His early picturesque Hudson River landscapes (done in the 1820s) interpret the American rural scene through the European conventions of the picturesque and sublime. His later work gets larger in scale and overlaid with literary and moralizing ideas, which he also expresses in verse and diaries. Combines landscape with biblical and historical themes, which to modern eyes can go completely over the top in the manner of bad operas or Hollywood spectaculars.

The reason for the earlier works is a genuine response to the beauties of relatively virgin US nature unsullied by too much tourism, development, or artistic interpretation (unlike Europe). The reason for the later work is his fear of the clash between this nature and an aggressive material culture, which he feared would gobble it up. "The Course of Empire" and "The Voyage of Life" predict the rise and fall of American culture.

KEY WORKS *Distant View of Niagara Falls,* 1830 (Art Institute of Chicago); *The Course of Empire: The Savage State,* 1836 (New York Historical Society); *View on the Catskill—Early Autumn;* 1837 (New York: Metropolitan Museum of Art); *Schroon Mountain, Adirondacks,* 1838 (Ohio: Cleveland Museum of Art); *The Notch of the White Mountains,* 1839 (Washington, DC: National Gallery of Art)

Frederic Edwin **Church**

◑ 1826–1900　⚐ AMERICAN

🏠 US; Canada; South America　🖌 oils　🏛 New York: Metropolitan Museum of Art. Hudson (New York State): Olana State Historic Site　📈 $7.5m in 1989, *Home by the Lake, Scene in the Catskill Mountains* (oils)

The greatest American landscape painter. Combined detailed observation of nature with the heroic, sublime vision of Romantics such as Turner. God-fearing and patriotic (and it shows).

His large-scale, stunning vistas or panoramas of North and South America have natural phenomena (Niagara Falls), mountains, and dramatic light (blood-red sunsets) to the fore. Uses high viewpoints, which give a birdlike feeling of being free to go anywhere, and combines this with the quasi-scientific observation of microscopic details—indicating his deep spiritual belief in the morality of Nature and presence of God in the largest and the smallest feature.

Note the thrilling shafts of light falling on the landscape; exquisite painting of

---

THE HUDSON RIVER SCHOOL　　　1820s–1870s

Loosely organized group of American painters whose founding father, Thomas Cole, painted picturesque views of the beautiful Hudson River Valley in Upper New York State in the 1820s, thereby establishing a new tradition for landscape painting in the United States. Most of the artists associated with the school traveled widely throughout the US and worked in New York. They often painted the Hudson River landscape interspersed with other scenes taken from all over the country. The group's vigor waned after the Civil War (1861–65), but it was a great influence on the Luminist School that followed.

Scene from "The Last of the Mohicans"
Thomas Cole, 1827, oil on canvas, New York: Fenimore Art Museum. This is one of four works inspired by James Fenimore Cooper's novel.

Cotopaxi *Frederic Edwin Church, 1862, 48 x 85 in (122 x 216 cm), oil on canvas, Michigan: Detroit Institute of Arts.* Church made two visits to South America, following in the footsteps of German explorer Alexander von Humboldt. He sketched Ecuador's Cotopaxi volcano in 1857.

distant mountains and waterfalls; and sharp, bright colors (used new, heavy, metal pigments). At his peak in the 1860s, he had a long, slow decline (suffered from bad rheumatism in his hands).

KEY WORKS *South American Landscape,* c.1856 (New York: Berry-Hill Galleries); *Heart of the Andes,* 1859 (New York: Metropolitan Museum of Art); *Aurora Borealis,* 1865 (Washington, DC: National Gallery of Art); *Niagara Falls,* 1867 (Edinburgh: National Gallery of Scotland)

Martin Johnson **Heade**

● 1819–1904   ⚑ AMERICAN

🏛 US; Europe; South America   ◑ oils
🏛 New York: Brooklyn Museum of Art
➤ $1,750,000 in 1987, *Two Fighting Hummingbirds with Two Orchids* (oils)

Johnson Heade was an important Luminist and long-lived hack portraitist who "came good" after meeting Frederic Church in 1859. He is best known for his haunting landscapes of flat lands with low horizons. Author of simple, clear compositions—wide, open spaces where each element is placed with the utmost precision. Had a special ability to show that mysterious, ominous light that precedes a storm. Also remembered for

his travels to Brazil where he did notable paintings of hummingbirds and orchids.

KEY WORKS *Approaching Thunderstorm,* 1859 (New York: Metropolitan Museum of Art); *Seascape: Sunset,* 1861 (Detroit Institute of Arts); *Rio de Janeiro Bay,* 1864 (Washington, DC: National Gallery of Art)

Fitz Hugh **Lane**

● 1804–65   ⚑ AMERICAN

🏛 Boston; Maine; Gloucester (US)   ◑ oils
➤ $5m in 2004, *Manchester Harbour* (oils)

Leading member of the Luminist School. A master of the frozen moment when time apparently stops—creator of scenes of eerie unpopulated stillness with a golden light that suffuses all. Also finely detailed paintings of ships and coastlines. The visual equivalent of transcendentalism in literature—the search for the essence of a reality beyond mere appearance.

KEY WORKS *The Golden State Entering New York Harbour,* 1854 (New York: Metropolitan Museum of Art); *Off Mount Desert Island,* 1856 (New York: Brooklyn Museum of Art)

> **"The real voyage of discovery consists not in seeking new landscapes, but in having new eyes."**
>
> MARCEL PROUST

Albert **Bierstadt**

◉ 1830–1902   🇩🇪 GERMAN/AMERICAN

🏛 US   🎨 oils   🏛 New York: Metropolitan
Museum of Art. Boston: Museum of Fine Arts
💰 $6.4m in 2003, *Yosemite Valley* (oils)

Bierstadt was German-born, but raised
in Massachusetts. He painted large-scale
landscapes of the American West during
the era of early railroads, with low
viewpoints, convincing but fanciful
compositions, good anecdotal detail,
and crisp use of light and shade. Did for
the American West what Canaletto did
for Venice. Also worked in Switzerland
and Bermuda. Brilliant oil sketches.
KEY WORKS *Yosemite Valley*, c. 1863 (New York:
Berry-Hill Galleries); *A Storm in the Rocky
Mountains*, 1866 (New York: Brooklyn
Museum of Art); *Among the Sierra Nevada
Mountains, California*, 1868 (Washington,
DC: National Museum of American Art)

Thomas **Moran**

◉ 1837–1926   🇺🇸 AMERICAN

🏛 US; Europe; Mexico   🎨 oils   🏛 Bolton (UK):
Museums, Art Gallery, and Aquarium   💰 $4.4m
in 2004, *Mist in the Yellowstone* (oils)

He was a self-taught, Irish-English
émigré raised in Philadelphia. Made
his reputation after a pioneering visit to

The Grand Canyon of the Yellowstone *Thomas
Moran, 1872, 96½ x 168½ in (245.1 x 427.8 cm), oil on
canvas, New York: Smithsonian Institute. Inspired after
accompanying a government expedition to Yellowstone.*

Yellowstone (1871), depicting its natural
grandeur in the style of Turner's
Romanticism. His superb watercolors
are built up from pencil underdrawing
and were much influenced by Turner. He
also painted scenes of Venice (Turner
again), Long Island, and California.
KEY WORKS *Nearing Camp, Evening on the
Upper Colorado River*, 1882 (Bolton, UK:
Museums, Art Gallery, and Aquarium);
The Much Resounding Sea, 1884 (Washington,
DC: National Gallery of Art); *The River
Schuylkill*, 1890s (Private Collection)

George Caleb **Bingham**

◉ 1811–79   🇺🇸 AMERICAN

🏛 Missouri   🎨 oils   🏛 New York:
Metropolitan Museum of Art   💰 $980,000
in 1978, *Jolly Flatboatmen No.2* (oils)

Born in Virginia and brought up in
Missouri, he was the first significant
painter from the Midwest. Had a decade
of brilliant talent, 1845–55, painting
scenes of the American frontier, and
"jolly flatboatmen." Contrived simple
compositions bathed in golden light.
As formal as Poussin and as proudly
documentary of his new Republic as
any 17th-century Dutch master.
KEY WORKS *Ferrymen Playing Cards*, 1847
(Missouri: St. Louis Art Museum); *Country
Politician*, 1849 (San Francisco: Fine Arts
Museum); *Shooting for the Beef*, 1850 (New
York: Brooklyn Museum of Art); *The Squatters*,
1850 (Boston: Museum of Fine Arts)

The Blanket Signal *Frederic Remington, c. 1896, oil on canvas, Houston: Museum of Fine Arts.* One of the Native Americans employed by the United States Army as irregulars, a military trend Remington strongly supported in the 1890s.

> "Art is a she-devil of a mistress, and if at times in earlier days she would not even stoop to my way of thinking, I have persevered and will so continue."
>
> FREDERIC REMINGTON

Frederic **Remington**

◔ 1861–1909   🏳 AMERICAN

🎨 US; Europe; North Africa   🖌 oils; sculpture
🏛 New York State: Remington Art Memorial
📈 $4.7m in 1999, *Reconnaissance* (oils)

The most famous painter of the cowboy West. Also made sculptures. Was haunted by the notion that he was a mere illustrator (which in truth he was), rather than a "proper" artist—his late works experiment unsuccessfully with Impressionism and arty ideas. Was pro the US cavalry, unsympathetic to Indians. Bigoted. Friend of Theodore Roosevelt.

Remington was a great mythmaker who liked to promote the idea that he was a former cowboy, US cavalry officer, but in fact he was Yale-educated and lived mostly in New York. His images of the "good" whites protecting "their" territory against the savage "foreign" Indians were consciously adopted by Hollywood cowboy movie directors. Reproductions of his illustrations in *Harper's Weekly* and other popular publications made him a household name throughout the US. Remington also spent time as a journalist, covering the Indian Wars of 1890–01 and the Spanish-American War (in Cuba) of 1898. Keen writer; published eight books.

KEY WORKS *The Mexican Major*, 1889 (Art Institute of Chicago); *Aiding a Comrade*, c. 1890 (Houston: Museum of Fine Arts); *The Advance-Guard, or the Military Sacrifice*, 1890 (Art Institute of Chicago); *Coming Through the Rye*, 1902 (New York: Metropolitan Museum of Art)

Charles M. **Russell**

◔ 1864–1926   🏳 AMERICAN

🎨 Montana   🖌 watercolors; oils; sculpture
🏛 Montana: C. M. Russell Museum   📈 $2.1m in 2001, *Disputed Trail* (oils)

He was the premier painter of the American West—alongside Remington but very different: Russell was self-taught, had genuinely worked as a cowboy, was sympathetic to Indians, and had a sense of humor. Good at working in oils, but superb in watercolor. He didn't hit his stride until 1900, but then got better and better. Was also a producer of high-quality sculptures.

KEY WORKS *Indian Braves*, 1899 (New York: Metropolitan Museum of Art); *The Death Song of Lone Wolf*, 1902 (Minnesota: Minneapolis Institute of Arts); *Smoking Up*, 1904 (New York: Metropolitan Museum of Art); *The Wagons*, 1910 (New York: Kennedy Galleries)

Eight Bells *Winslow Homer, 1886, 25⅓ x 30⅓ in (64.5 x 77.2 cm), oil on canvas, Andover (US): Addison Gallery of American Art.* Homer lived for many years on the Atlantic seaboard in Maine.

Winslow **Homer**

● 1836–1910 ⚑ AMERICAN

🏛 US; Paris; England   🎨 watercolors; oils
🏛 New York: Metropolitan Museum of Art.
Boston: Museum of Fine Arts   💰 $4.4m in
1999, *Red Canoe* (drawing)

Homer was one of the great 19th-century painters. He was able to interpret nature in a way that convincingly reflected the American pioneering spirit. Well traveled in the US, England, and the Bahamas. He was self-taught.

Homer was a creator of highly satisfying, virile images: sea paintings of the Atlantic coast; images of down-to-earth, practical people, especially when coping with adversity; modern women; robust children. Made a pragmatic exploration of light and color, and produced strong, well-designed, and boldly painted pictures. Also painted exquisite, fresh, fluid watercolors. His work has a strong narrative content (it's no coincidence that he started out as a magazine illustrator), but he lifted his art beyond the ordinary by infusing it with a sincerely felt, underlying moral message, and a subtle ambiguity of meaning.

His no-nonsense practical painting is completely in tune with its subject matter, time, and place. Has an enviable ability to simplify and leave out unnecessary detail. Uses strong contrasts of light and shade with assurance. Note the solid, unhesitating draftsman and frequent use of a silhouetted figure, often in heroic attitude. He employs the imagery of children as a metaphor for the future of America. Note also the progression of his style and subjects as they grow larger, stronger, more confident, and freer with age and experience.

KEY WORKS *Snap the Whip*, 1872 (Ohio: Butler Institute of American Art); *Tending Sheep, Houghton Farm*; c. 1878 (Private Collection); *The Herring Net*, 1885 (Art Institute of Chicago); *The Turtle Pound*, 1898 (New York: Brooklyn Museum of Art); *The Sharpshooters*, c. 1900 (London: Christie's Images)

William Sidney **Mount**

◔ 1807–68 ⋈ AMERICAN

🏙 New York 🎨 oils; drawings 🏛 Detroit Institute of Arts 💰 $800,000 in 1983, *The Trap Sprung* (oils)

The premier genre painter of mid-19th-century America. Lived in Long Island and produced scenes of rural life that appealed to New York city-dwellers. His images of farm life, horse dealing, music-making, and his sensitive portrayals of African-American farmers appealed to a public hungry for expressions of national self-awareness and self-consciousness. Clear, precise draftsmanship and colors.

KEY WORKS *Bar-room Scene*, 1835 (Art Institute of Chicago); *The Raffle (Raffling for the Goose)*, 1837 (New York: Metropolitan Museum of Art)

Albert Pinkham **Ryder**

◔ 1847–1917 ⋈ AMERICAN

🏙 New York 🎨 oils 🏛 Ohio: Cleveland Museum of Art 💰 $180,000 in 2004, *Landscape* (oils)

He was an erratic bohemian character who painted brooding, romantic scenes such as *Jonah and the Whale*, *Siegfried and the Rhinemaidens*, and boats on stormy moonlit seas. Used jewel-like colors and thick, cumbersome paint, but bad technique and the use of bitumen mean that most of his paintings are damaged beyond repair. He was considered to represent the height of poetic sensibility and was somewhat of a guru figure for the likes of Hartley and Pollock.

KEY WORKS *Siegfried and the Rhinemaidens*, 1888–91 (Washington, DC: National Gallery of Art); *The Forest of Arden*, c. 1888–97 (New York: Metropolitan Museum of Art); *The Race Track (Death on a Pale Horse)*, c. 1896–1908 (Ohio: Cleveland Museum of Art)

Roadside Meeting Albert Pinkham Ryder, 1901, 15 x 12 in (38.1 x 30.5 cm), oil on canvas, Ohio: Butler Institute of American Art. Like many symbolist painters, Ryder was an admirer of the poet Edgar Allen Poe.

Thomas **Eakins**

◔ 1844–1916 ⋈ AMERICAN

🏙 Philadelphia; Paris 🎨 oils 🏛 Philadelphia: Museum of Art 💰 $4.8m in 2003, *Cowboys in the Badlands* (oils)

He was Philadelphia-born and bred. Studied in Paris and Spain; was a gifted teacher at the Pennsylvania Academy. Said by some to be the greatest of all American artists, but he was little honored in his lifetime. Pragmatic but difficult, unyielding personality. Eager boatman.

His frank, candid portraits are of people from a fairly narrow social circle. He had more interest in matters like status, achievement, and position in society than in personality—and responded best to achievers (he was one himself). His middle period (from 1869 onward) features matter-of-fact successful professionals; his later period was more dreamy. Had a deep interest in science, medicine, and how things work. Employed human anatomy, motion, and perspective to make his pictures work.

Look for imaginative poses and movement; workmanlike hands; rich, dark color harmonies; atmospheric 19th-century interiors. He uses extra objects or incidents to tell the story behind a portrait, and light to animate compositions. Likes color and emotion but is even more interested in shadows—notice how he uses them to create space. Has any other painter observed shadows so accurately?

KEY WORKS *The Biglin Brothers Racing*, 1872 (Washington, DC: National Gallery of Art); *The Gross Clinic*, 1875 (Philadelphia: Thomas Jefferson University); *William Rush carving his Allegorical Figure of the Schuylkill River*, 1877 (Philadelphia Museum of Art); *The Swimming Hole*, 1884–85 (Texas: Modern Art Museum of Fort Worth)

John **Ruskin**

◉ 1819–1900   🏴 BRITISH

🏛 UK; Europe   🎨 watercolors   🖼 Venice:
Scuola di S. Rocco   💰 $408,000 in 2003, *Bellinzona,
Switzerland, Looking North toward the St. Gotthard
Pass* (watercolors)

He was most important as a critic and
writer. As a painter had a central belief
in the supremacy of truth to nature
(not the same as a slavish imitation of
nature), but abandoned this belief after
1858. His intensely observed and detailed
watercolors reflect his passion and
knowledge of geology and architecture.
KEY WORKS *J. M. W. Turner, RA*, c. 1840
(London: Royal Academy of Arts); *View of
Bologna*, c. 1845–46 (London: Tate Collection)

Ford Madox **Brown**

◉ 1821–93   🏴 BRITISH

🏛 Antwerp; Paris; Rome; England   🎨 oils; watercolors; drawings   🖼 Manchester: City Art Gallery
💰 $334,800 in 2004, *The Last of England* (oils)

Trained in France and was a close
follower of the Pre-Raphaelites. Highly
detailed work—landscapes painted in the
open air and figurative works containing
social commentaries on contemporary
life, which reached out to intellectual
political activists. Too idiosyncratic
to be successful in his own day.
KEY WORKS *The Seeds and Fruits
of English Poetry,*

1845–51 (Oxford: Ashmolean Museum);
Chaucer at the Court of Edward III, 1851
(Sydney: Art Gallery of New South Wales)

Dante Gabriel **Rossetti**

◉ 1828–82   🏴 BRITISH

🏛 London   🎨 oils; watercolors; drawings
🖼 London: Tate Collection. Birmingham, UK:
City Art Gallery. Manchester: City Art Gallery
💰 $3,624,000 in 2000, *Pandora* (works on paper)

He was a painter, poet, and the leading
Pre-Raphaelite. Had a complicated love
life and died of alcohol and drug abuse.

   He is best known for images of erotic
femmes fatales painted from the 1860s
onward. Also went in for romantic
medieval themes. Early Pre-Raphaelite
work is rather awkward and stiff at times.
His *femmes fatales* are characterized by
luscious lips, sinuous hands, and thick,
glistening hair. Brilliant draftsman
but his painting technique is a bit suspect.
Look for works of much intensity (the
most desirable state of existence for
artistic folk at that time). Fine, detailed,
and heavily worked watercolors.
KEY WORKS *Girlhood of Mary Virgin*, 1849
(London: Tate Collection); *Mary Nazarene*,
1857 (London: Tate Collection)

Work Ford Madox Brown, 1852–65, 54 x 77⅔ in
*(137 x 197.3 cm), oil on canvas, Manchester: City
Art Gallery.* Brown's picture is intended to
encapsulate the appearances and
activities of the different
social classes.

PRE-RAPHAELITES   19th century

Artistic movement stemming from the Pre-Raphaelite Brotherhood (PRB), an ambitious and confident group of seven male artists, aged between 19 and 23. They decided art had "gone wrong" around the time of Raphael and sought to return to ideals shared by artists before Raphael's time. The brotherhood was established in 1848 and lasted until c. 1853. The movement was much more long-lived and wide-reaching.

SUBJECTS AND STYLE

Pre-Raphaelites drew their inspiration from literature, especially the Bible, Shakespeare, the Romantics, and contemporary poets, such as Browning and Tennyson. They were also inspired by medievalism, especially Malory's *Morte d'Arthur*. They developed their own paint colors and came up with a new technique of painting on a "wet white" background, so the colors shone with luminosity. Women feature heavily in their works, especially those of Dante Gabriel Rossetti and Edward Burne-Jones.

The Rescue Sir John Everett Millais, 1855, 8½ x 33 in (21.5 x 83.6 cm), oil on canvas, Melbourne: National Gallery of Victoria. Note his spectacular command of light, with faces lit up by the glow.

WHAT TO LOOK FOR

Vivid use of color—sometimes exquisite, at other times gaudy. Scenes of chivalry and deep emotion; sentimentalism; strong literary references, with the same scene often painted by several artists; rich and quite obvious symbolism. They often used one another as models, so look for recognizable portraits and self-portraits among genre paintings. In early paintings seek out the stylized "PRB" monogram somewhere in the scene.

Isabella and the Pot of Basil William Holman Hunt, 1867, 23 x 15 in (60.7 x 38.7 cm), oil on canvas, Wilmington: Delaware Art Museum. Based on Keats's poem; the model was Holman Hunt's pregnant wife.

KEY EVENTS

1848	The Pre-Raphaelite Brotherhood holds its first meeting at 7 Gower Street, London
1850	The meaning of "PRB" revealed by mistake to a journalist
1855	Pre-Raphaelite paintings are shown at the Paris Exhibition
1857	Rossetti meets William Morris and Burne-Jones, a new generation of Pre-Raphaelites

William Holman **Hunt**

● 1827–1910　📕 BRITISH

📕 England; Egypt; Palestine　🎨 oils; watercolors
🏛 London: Tate Collection　💰 $2.72m in 1994,
The Shadow of Death (oils)

Hunt was a founding member of the
Pre-Raphaelite Brotherhood and its
most consistent exponent. Religious,
obsessive, and stubborn, producing
work with insistent moralizing and
didactic themes. A true Victorian, who
verges on greatness but whose obsession
with detail and coloring can be intense
to the point of unpleasantness.

KEY WORKS *On English Coasts*, 1852 (London:
Tate Collection); *The Scapegoat*, 1854 (Wirral,
UK: Lady Lever Art Gallery)

Sir John Everett **Millais**

● 1829–96　📕 BRITISH

📕 London　🎨 oils; drawings　🏛 London:
Tate Collection. Birmingham (UK): City Art Gallery.
Liverpool: Walker Art Gallery. Manchester: City
Art Gallery　💰 $3.04m in 1999, *Sleeping* (oils)

He was an infant prodigy who became
extremely fashionable, rich, and famous.
Founding member of Pre-Raphaelite
Brotherhood and pillar of the Royal
Academy (became its president in 1896).

> **"Sometimes as I paint
> I may find my work
> becoming laborious
> But as soon as I detect
> any evidence of that
> labor I paint the
> whole thing out."**
>
> SIR JOHN EVERETT MILLAIS

His early work (up to the 1850s) was
genuinely Pre-Raphaelite, with a
meticulous, tight style; strict observation
of nature; choice of moral themes.
The later work is more freely painted,
with subjects overtly designed to catch
the fashion of the times and sell well—
sentimental scenes, historical romances,
portraits (he needed the money with eight
children and a lavish lifestyle to support).

His virtuoso craftsmanship and attention
to detail (natural and historical) makes it
all look so easy. Look out for delightful,
often humorous, sketches; note also the
commercial prints made from his paintings,
which sold as well as current-day rock
group recordings.

KEY WORKS *Ophelia*, 1851–52 (London:
Tate Collection); *The Blind Girl*, c. 1856
(Birmingham, UK: Museums and Art
Gallery); *The Ransom*, 1860–62 (Los
Angeles: J. Paul Getty Museum)

John **Brett**

● 1830–1902　📕 BRITISH

📕 England; Italy; Europe　🎨 oils
🏛 Liverpool: Walker Art Gallery
💰 $1,848,000 in 1989, *Val d'Aosta* (oils)

He was a devotee of Ruskin, emulator
of Holman Hunt, resulting in early,
intensely detailed, high-colored landscapes
that are a *tour de force* of precise observation
and technique. Painting trips to Italy
and the Alps (as approved by Ruskin).
Commercially more successful with later
works (especially panoramic views of the
ocean), but they are flabby by comparison
with his earlier works.

KEY WORKS *Glacier of Rosenlaui*, 1856
(London: Tate Collection); *Florence from
Bellosguardo*, 1863 (London: Tate Collection)

Sir Edward Coley **Burne-Jones**

● 1833–98　📕 BRITISH

📕 England　🎨 oils; watercolors
🏛 Birmingham: City Art Gallery　💰 $1.47m
in 2001, *Prince Entering the Briar Wood* (oils)

A quiet, retiring, otherworldly painter, with
a streak of calculating shrewdness. Famous
and successful after 1877. His paintings
reflect his character and one aspect of the
age he lived in. His early medieval and
mythological subjects are heavily laden
with mysticism and symbolism that look
back to a "golden" age, chosen to fulfill a
wish to escape from modern urban and
industrial reality; yet the large-scale, precise
style, fascination with materials and realistic
details are very worldly, showing a personal
(and typical Victorian) duality.

Highly developed sense of 2-D design
(due to his closeness to William Morris,
who encouraged him to become an artist

St. George and the Dragon *Sir Edward Coley Burne-Jones, 1868, gouache on paper, London: William Morris Gallery.* Burne-Jones worked closely with William Morris from 1855–59. This painting postdates his visit to Italy with Ruskin in 1862.

instead of following a career in the Church) and a technique that shows a love of meticulous craftsmanship (due to his closeness to Ruskin). Was also influenced by early Renaissance art (such as Botticelli). Produced very successful designs for tapestry and stained glass; and illustrations for texts of medieval and classical legends.

KEY WORKS *Music*, 1880s (New York: Roy Miles Fine Paintings); *King Cophetua and the Beggar Maid*, 1880 (London: Tate Collection)

George Frederick **Watts**

● 1817–1904 **BRITISH**

 England; Italy   oils; sculpture
 Guildford (UK): Watts Gallery
 $1,121,800 in 1986, *Hope* (oils)

He aimed to emulate the grandeur and achievements of Titian and Michelangelo; known in his day as "England's Michelangelo." Produced portraits, allegories, and landscapes that reflect the influence of his two exemplars but can now seem pompous and overambitious. His portraits are his best work.

KEY WORKS *Choosing*, 1864 (Private Collection); *Sir Galahad*, 1880s (Liverpool: Walker Art Gallery)

REALISM

The progressive movement in art and literature in the mid-19th century (especially in France). It began in earnest in 1855, with an exhibition of works by Gustave Courbet. Its centerpiece, *The Painter's Studio,* had been refused by the Universal Exhibition, so Courbet set up his own in a nearby tent. The artist produced a manifesto to go with his exhibition, which he entitled *Le Réalisme*.

STYLE

The Gleaners Jean-François Millet, 1857, 33 x 44 in (83 x 111 cm), oil on canvas, Paris: Musée d'Orsay. In 1857, Millet was described by one critic as "a great painter who walks in clogs the road of Michelangelo."

Realism was concerned with social realities, and wanted to show fact rather than ideals or aesthetics. It rejected Academic art as being too artificial, and Romanticism as being too concerned with the imagination. Realists wanted to cut through the cant of society—and not just in art; as such, the movement became a mechanism for social change, with a committed political agenda, being associated with new, democratic ways of thinking, with antiestablishment causes, and with championing individuals' rights. The movement was highly influential, spreading into Germany, Russia, the Netherlands, and the US. Realism also influenced literary giants such as Tolstoy, Balzac, Zola, Dickens, and Flaubert.

The losers include a Chinese, a Jew, an Irishwoman, a poacher, a war veteran, and a laborer

Wearing huntsman's dress is Napolean III, the effective dictator of the French Second Empire

SUBJECTS

Subject matter is diverse: portraits, landscapes, groups, genre scenes. Refusing to hark back to historic or pastoral idylls, Realism dealt with the harshness of life, such as human degradation and poverty, as well as with natural landscapes and human emotions. Whereas artists had traditionally romanticized the poor and their harsh existence, Realists wanted to depict the truth. Above all, Realists also painted what they saw in everyday life, rejoicing in the contrariness of the natural world. The movement had a strong following, with artists from other traditions often borrowing the ideas and language of Realism.

KEY EVENTS

1848	Revolution in France; rise to power of Napoleon III
1850	Courbet's *Stonebreakers*, remarkable for its social realism, shown at Salon
1855	Universal Exhibition. Courbet mounts rival show, including *The Painter's Studio*
1863	Manet's *Le déjeuner sur l'herbe* at Salon des Refusés
1867	Publication of Emile Zola's first major realist novel, *Thérèse Raquin*

c. 1855–1900

WHAT TO LOOK FOR

Courbet's masterpiece, although painted early in his career, is a manifesto of Realism in which he sets out his central beliefs and opinions. It shows his studio in Paris with three groups of figures. The artist is in the center. To his right are his friends—"those who thrive on life." To his left are those who "thrive on death," not just his enemies (notably the Head of State, Napoleon III), but also the evils he fought against, and those exploited and oppressed by them, represented as the poor, the destitute, and the losers in life.

The Painter's Studio Gustave Courbet, 1855, 142 x 235½ in (361 x 598 cm) oil on canvas, Paris: Musée d'Orsay. We know a great deal about this work because Courbet described it in detail while he worked on it.

A figure in the pose of the Crucifixion. This "lay figure" symbolizes academic art, which Courbet rejected

The plaster medallion of a woman's profile is one of very few props depicted in the studio

Light enters through a window on the right side—the side of life. A skylight also lit the studio

A large floppy hat with a feather, a cloak and dagger, and a guitar—the typical gear of the Romantic artist

On the easel is a large landscape, depicting the artist's homeland. The art establishment frowned upon such subject matter

This woman represents naked truth guiding Courbet's brush

On a table to the left of the artist is a skull, which is the archetypal symbol of death. The skull is resting on top of a newspaper. This is Courbet's unambivalent comment on the critics who were extremely powerful in shaping 19th-century artistic opinion.

TECHNIQUES

The boy makes a crude sketch, uninhibited by rules or overrefined techniques. Courbet wanted his art to have similar qualities.

Henri **Fantin-Latour**

◗ 1836–1904 ◳ FRENCH

🏛 France 🎨 oils; prints 🏛 Paris: Musée d'Orsay 💲 $3.2m in 2000, *Bouquet de fleurs* (oils)

He was a painter of allegories inspired by music (especially Wagner), still lifes, and stodgy, wooden portraits with sitters who look distinctly uncomfortable or bored. Flowers and fruit are highly worked and end up looking artificial. Benefited from close connections with his more gifted artistic contemporaries.
KEY WORKS *Flowers and Fruit*, 1865 (Paris: Musée d'Orsay); *Portrait of Edouard Manet*, 1867 (Art Institute of Chicago); *Still Life: Corner of a Table*, 1873 (Art Institute of Chicago)

Max **Liebermann**

◗ 1847–1935 ◳ GERMAN

🏛 Germany; France 🎨 oils; prints 🏛 London: Christie's Images 💲 $1.4m in 2003, *The Garden of the Artist in Wannsee* (oils)

A successful painter of middle-class daily life and places—updated replay of Dutch 17th-century and Biedermeier art. Produced freely painted, not very difficult paintings, which reassured his clients and appeal to modern-day nostalgia. Used the earth-color palette of the old masters, not

the modern rainbow palette of the French Impressionists.
KEY WORKS *An Old Woman with Cat*, 1878 (Los Angeles: J. Paul Getty Museum); *Memorial Service for Kaiser Friedrich at Kösen*, 1888–89 (London: National Gallery); *The Ropewalk in Edam*, 1904 (New York: Metropolitan Museum of Art)

James **Tissot**

◗ 1836–1902 ◳ FRENCH

🏛 France; London; Palestine 🎨 oils; prints; drawings 🏛 London: The Fine Art Society. Manchester: City Art Gallery 💲 $4.8m in 1994, *Le banc de jardin* (oils)

He was French-born, but lived in London between 1871 and 1882, where he became a highly successful, fashionable painter of small-scale polished depictions of society (especially slim-waisted women) at play. Had a brilliant technique, which compensated for lack of depth and insight. His late religious conversion following the death of his much-painted mistress led to Bible illustrations.

A Country Brasserie, Brannenburg, Bavaria Max Liebermann, 1894, 27½ x 39½ in (70 x 100 cm), oil on canvas, Paris: Musée d'Orsay. Liebermann was regarded as a cultural enemy by the Kaiser because he admired modern foreign art (like French Barbizon and Impressionism), and rejected German nationalist and academic traditions.

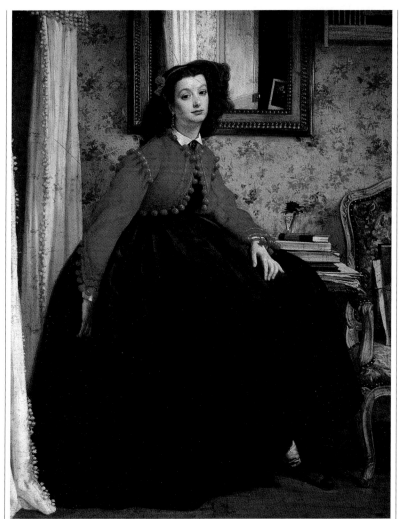

KEY WORKS *London Visitors*, c. 1874 (Ohio: Toledo Museum of Art); *Reading the News*, c. 1874 (London: Christie's Images); *Inner Voices (Christ Consoling the Wanderers)*, 1885 (St. Petersburg: Hermitage Museum)

Portrait of Mlle. L. L. *James Tissot, 1864, 48¾ x 39½ in (124 x 100 cm), oil on canvas, Paris: Musée d'Orsay.* Tissot's art was attacked by the critics Oscar Wilde, Henry James, and John Ruskin, for its appeal to the *nouveaux riches*.

Carl **Larsson**

● 1853–1919 ⚑ SWEDISH

🏠 Sweden 🖌 watercolors; oils; prints
🏛 Stockholm: Nationalmuseum 💰 $1,345,714
in 1989, *Near Kattegat* (watercolors)

A key Swedish artist whose idealized illustrations of his own country cottage (rustic furniture, scrubbed floors, wife's designer textiles, simplicity) were internationally influential and established the idea of the Scandinavian style. Earlier in his life he painted large-scale decorative, allegorical murals. Also portraits and self-portraits. Became manic-depressive after 1906.

KEY WORKS *Watering the Plants, Sitting Room—View Two*, 1899 (Private Collection); *The Midwinter Sacrifice*, 1914–15 (Stockholm: National Museum); *Indian Summer*, c. 1915 (Private Collection)

Woman with a Pearl *Jean-Baptiste-Camille Corot,
c. 1842, 27½ x 21½ in (70 x 55 cm), oil on canvas, Paris:
Musée du Louvre.* Corot has based the woman's pose—
hands crossed over one another, head turned toward
us—on Leonardo da Vinci's masterpiece the *Mona Lisa.*

Jean-Baptiste-Camille **Corot**

● 1796–1875　🅵 FRENCH

🅵 France; England; Switzerland; Italy　🅰 oils
🏛 Paris: Musée du Louvre　💰 $3.5m in 1984, *La
femme à la grande toque et à la mandoline* (oils)

A major landscape painter of the
19th century. A bridge between the
English landscape tradition and French
Impressionism. Kind, gentle, and
unusually unegocentric for an artist.

　His late, best-known paintings (post-
1860)—silvery green, soft focus, lyrical
landscapes—are based on remembered
emotions ("souvenirs") and sketches
from nature. But notice, too, the earlier,
artificial, more conventional (academic
and sometimes ludicrous) landscapes;
also enchanting figure paintings. Much
copied and faked—there are said to be
more "genuine" Corots in the US than
all the pictures he painted in his lifetime.

　Unquestionably at his best with his
small plein-air, on-the-spot sketches
(called *pochades*). Shows wonderful
observation of light and clouds in the
sky and empirical exploration of space;
note the way he tightens the soft focus
with sharp dark accents of paint.

KEY WORKS *The Forum Seen from the Farnese
Gardens*, 1826 (Paris: Musée du Louvre);
Ville d'Avray, c. 1867–70 (New York:
Brooklyn Museum of Art)

Théodore **Rousseau**

● 1812–67　🅵 FRENCH

🅵 France　🅰 oils　🏛 Chantilly (France):
Musée Condé　💰 $485,000 in 2004, *Soleil
couchant sur les sables du Jean-de-Paris* (oils)

An important pioneer of plein-air painting
and principal figure of the Barbizon
School (thereby linking Constable to
Monet). He allowed nature to speak
for itself, abolishing the convention
of inserting human figures in order to
animate or interpret the landscape.
Trod a difficult and not always successful
path between Romanticism and realism.

　He was excited by woods and trees,
and sought to convey both the spirit
(Romanticism) and appearance (realism)
of nature growing and vegetating.
Distinguish between the small-scale
sketches made on the spot and the
larger detailed works made in the studio.
Dramatic skies, such as one finds on
fall evenings. Some works have darkened
with time.

KEY WORKS *Sunset in the Auvergne*, 1830
(London: National Gallery); *Paysage
panoramique*, 1830–40 (Cambridge: Fitzwilliam
Museum); *Forest in Boisrémond; Cottage*, 1842
(Los Angeles: J. Paul Getty Museum)

Eugène **Boudin**

● 1824–98　🅵 FRENCH

🅵 Northern France　🅰 oils; watercolors
🏛 Le Havre: Musée des Beaux-Arts
💰 $1,467,000 in 2003, *Scène de plage* (oils)

Best known for charming small-scale
beach scenes of vacationers on the
Normandy coast (Trouville), dressed up
in their crinolines and bonnets on cloudy,
breezy days. Had a sketchy style and
was an exponent of plein-air spontaneity,
a forerunner of the Impressionists (very
influential on young Monet). Also painted
scenes of Venice, the Netherlands, and
France. If you can't sense the breeze,
it's probably not a Boudin.

KEY WORKS *Approaching Storm*, 1864 (Art Institute
of Chicago); *The Beach at Tourgeville-les-Sablons*,
1893 (London: National Gallery)

Jean-François **Millet**

● 1814–75 ⚑ FRENCH

🏛 Paris; England; Netherlands 🎨 oils; engravings
🏛 London: National Gallery. Paris: Musée d'Orsay
📈 $3.1m in 1996, *The Wool Carder* (oils)

The son of a Normandy farmer, who painted the final scenes of a rural world and lifestyle at the moment when it was beginning to disappear because of the industrialization of France.

His small-scale works describe a self-contained world of humble people working on and with the land. He portrays, depending on your point of view, either the dignity or the cruelty of manual peasant labor. Shows a magical stillness, silence, and peace that is not overloaded with drama or symbolism.

Notice the low viewpoint, so you feel you are standing on the same level as the people you see. Freshly observed light; sense of direct contact with the land, the light, and the atmosphere. Works directly onto the canvas—so you can often see pentimenti (alterations), the way he worked

The Angelus Jean-François Millet, 1857–59, 26 x 29 in (55.5 x 66 cm), oil on canvas, Paris: Musée d'Orsay.
This picture was a star exhibit at the Paris World Fair of 1867, and vast numbers of reproductions were sold.

PLEIN AIR PAINTING AND THE BARBIZON SCHOOL c. 1840–1870

A group of progressive, mid-19th century painters who worked in and around the French village of Barbizon near Paris, surrounded by the forest of Fontainebleau. The leader of the school was Theodore Rousseau, whose great innovation was to allow landscape and nature to speak for themselves without human intervention or presence. The group made landscape as important as portraiture and genre painting, and paved the way for Impressionism. The Barbizon painters promoted the concept of "plein air" painting, meaning paintings that were begun and completed in the open air instead of inside the studio, or studio paintings that consciously set out to capture on canvas the qualities and sensations of being outside in the open air.

the paint, and his carefully considered line. (It is as if his style and working methods were a sort of parallel with the way in which his peasants work the land.)
KEY WORKS *The Winnower*, 1847–48 (London: National Gallery); *The Sower*, 1850 (Boston: Museum of Fine Arts); *Peasant Girls with Brushwood*, 1852 (St. Petersburg: Hermitage Museum)

Gustave **Courbet**

◔ 1819–77 ⚑ FRENCH

🏠 France; Switzerland 🎨 oils 🏛 Paris: Musée d'Orsay. Montpellier: Musée Fabre 💰 $2.7m in 1998, *Portrait de Jo, la belle Irlandaise* (oils)

Courbet was the radical scourge of corrupt Second Empire France and the tedious old-fashioned traditions of the French Academy. The major exponent of 19th-century realism.

He chose large-scale subjects (such as life, death, destiny, the ocean, the forest) and often produced physically large paintings. Brilliant, gutsy technique with thick, physical paint. Portrayed toughness and realism—real people carrying out unglamorous, everyday activities. Had an intimate knowledge of all the activities, people, and places he painted and valued down-to-earth, provincial life more highly than fashionable Parisian glamour.

His work can range from the most brilliantly inspired and executed to sloppy, uninspired, and bad painting. Note the

> **"The sea's voice is tremendous, but not loud enough to drown the voice of Fame crying my name to the entire world."**
>
> GUSTAVE COURBET

very unusual rich green, especially in his landscapes—it is not artistic license: in his beloved homeland (Ornans, near Besançon) the copper in the soil turns the vegetation that color. The area is worth visiting for its stunning beauty, but also to see what it was that inspired him and how real his "realism" is. Note his prominent red signature—what a big ego!

KEY WORKS *The Painter's Studio*, (see page 301); *The Source of the Loue*, 1864 (Washington, DC: National Gallery of Art); *The Cliff at Etretat after the Storm*, 1869 (Paris: Musée d'Orsay); *The Sea*, 1872 (Caen: Musée des Beaux-Arts)

The Bar at the Folies-Bergère
Edouard Manet, 1881–82, 38 x 51 in (97 x 130 cm), oil on canvas, London: Courtauld Institute of Art. Upper-class dandies like Manet rubbed shoulders with workers and prostitutes at the Folies-Bergère. The bottles (from beer to champagne) symbolize this interaction.

Edouard **Manet**

● 1832–83 ◪ FRENCH

◳ France; Europe ◧ oils; prints; engravings ▥ Paris: Musée d'Orsay. London: Courtauld Institute of Art ◮ $24m in 1989, *La rue Mosnier aux drapeaux* (oils)

A hugely important, very influential, key figure in late 19th-century Paris. Spurned by official art circles, he was a father figure for the young avant-garde. Took Courbet's realism one step further.

His fascinatingly ambiguous subject matter and style portray modern (sometimes seamy) urban and suburban life and people, or parodies traditional themes dear to the heart of academic artists. At his best he does both at the same time. He was unique in that he had a brilliant, very visual and sketchy painting technique, involving the use of large areas of flat color. Has anyone ever used black so lusciously and with such visual impact?

His work is a paradoxical combination of intimacy and aloofness: one of Manet's personal characteristics was wanting to be accepted in official art circles but his whole approach to art and those in authority ensured that he wasn't. Thus, many paintings show one or more people in a scene of great intimacy or drama, but someone is often withdrawn or preoccupied and not immediately involved in what is going on.

KEY WORKS *Olympia* (see pages 308–309); *Still Life with Melon and Peaches*, c. 1866 (Washington, DC: National Gallery of Art); *The Fifer*, 1866 (Paris: Musée d'Orsay); *Gare Saint-Lazare*, 1873 (Washington, DC: National Gallery of Art); *Madame Manet on a Blue Sofa*, 1874, 1874 (Paris: Musée d'Orsay)

Honoré **Daumier**

● 1808–79 ◪ FRENCH

◳ France ◧ prints; drawings; oils; sculpture ▥ London: Courtauld Institute of Art ◮ $2,235,000 in 1993, *Le fardeau—la blanchisseuse* (oils)

Called the "greatest 19th-century caricaturist," but is much more because he reveals universal truths about the human condition. His subjects are French men and women living in a corrupt, greedy, bourgeois regime (French Second Empire), but the message is timeless.

His compelling images observe the absurdities and obsessions of husbands, wives, lawyers, politicians, artists, actors, etc. Had a prolific output: prints (he was a pioneer of lithography), especially, watercolors, sketches; some oil paintings after 1860 (he was never comfortable with the scale and technique—at his best with a smaller and more spontaneous scale and medium). Never judgmental or unkind, even though his work was censored. Went semiblind in 1870.

Notice his captivating facial expressions, body language, hands—all speaking volumes. His use of light, shade, and atmosphere is as good as Rembrandt's. Works have a probing, lively line. He produced miraculous, small clay-model caricatures of politicians. Ignored the rich and famous, and was never successful commercially. Makes the everyday sublime and moving.

KEY WORKS *The Laundress*, c. 1860 (Paris: Musée d'Orsay); *The Print Collector*, c. 1860 (Glasgow Museums); *Advice to a Young Artist*, after 1860 (Washington, DC: National Gallery of Art); *The Studio*, c. 1870 (Los Angeles: J. Paul Getty Museum)

The Third-Class Carriage *Honoré Daumier, 1864, 8 x 11¼ in (20.3 x 29.5 cm), watercolor, ink wash, and charcoal on paper, Baltimore: Walters Art Museum.* Railroads brought the rural poor to Paris seeking employment and a new life.

Olympia

Edouard Manet 1863

Edouard Manet never achieved his ambition: to be officially honored as the true modern successor of the old masters. Coming from a well-to-do Parisian family, he was born to such a role. Good-looking, charming, strong, worldly-wise, and very gifted, he was always at ease in society.

This picture was shown at the official Paris Salon of 1865. Manet was nervous about how it would be received, as his famous painting *Déjeuner sur l'Herbe* had already caused a scandal. *Olympia* caused a storm of outraged protest. It was seen not as a modern interpretation of a respected theme, but as a crude parody of a sacred artistic tradition going back to the greatest masters such as Titian and Goya (see pages 143 and 262–263). It was obvious to everyone that the reclining woman was not a goddess, but a prostitute.

The constant criticism and rejection of his work caused Manet to have a nervous breakdown in 1871. He considered *Olympia* to be his finest work, and he never sold it. When he died, it went to auction, but it did not find a buyer. In 1888, Sargent (see page 326) learned that Manet's widow was about to sell the painting to an American collector, and he warned Monet, who organized a public appeal to buy it for the Louvre.

Manet mostly used his family and friends to pose as models. Here he has employed a professional model, Victorine Meurent, aged 30. She became a painter herself, but ended life as an alcoholic

TECHNIQUES

The candid style shows Manet at his best. He uses a bold composition with strong outlines to the forms. There is virtually no shadow or modeling with soft light. There is no fine detail, but the color harmonies are very subtle. Some critics saw this style as merely incompetent when compared with that of Ingres (see page 264), and it was described as being crude.

Black is one of the most difficult of pigments for an artist to exploit as it can easily overwhelm and kill all other colors and qualities. Manet is the great master of black: he was able to use it to bring a rich tonality and elegance to his work. Manet, who dressed with great care, habitually wore the black frock coat and silk top hat that was fashionable in his day.

The servant brings in flowers—a gift from a previous admirer—but Olympia does not acknowledge her presence. She is ready for her next client: the spectator of the painting.

Manet was a master of still life, which he often painted for his own pleasure. The bouquet symbolically suggests the sweet pleasures offered by Olympia

The image of the reclining nude is one of the most revered in the old master tradition. Manet knew that his audience would understand his reference to Giorgione's *Sleeping Venus* (see page 140)

Manet's creation is not the goddess Venus, but a young woman in a recognizable role. Her slipper dangles impatiently on her foot. She is explicitly naked with pearls at her neck and ears, and an orchid in her hair.

Olympia

Medium oil on canvas

Dimensions 51 x 75 in (130 x 190 cm)

Location Paris: Musée d'Orsay

Claude **Monet**

● 1840–1926 ▶ FRENCH

🏠 France; London; Italy; Norway
🎨 oils 🏛 Paris: Musée
d'Orsay; Musée Marmottan.
Giverny (near Paris) for Monet's
house, studio, and garden
💰 $29,520,000 in 1998,
*Bassin aux nymphéas et
sentier au bord de l'eau* (oils)

Waterlily Pond *Claude Monet,
1899, 34¾ x 36⅓ in (88.3 x 93.1 cm),
oil on canvas, London: National
Gallery.* One of a series of 18
paintings depicting the Japanese
bridge in Monet's water garden.

The true leader of the
Impressionists—he was constantly
exploring "What do I see and
how do I record it in painting?"

Monet had a never-ending interest in
observing and painting that most elusive
quality, light—notably in the "Series"
paintings, where he painted the same
subject dozens of times, under different
light conditions (the Rouen Cathedral,
haystacks, scenes in London). Spent 40
years (the second half of his life) creating
his garden, at Giverny,
from scratch—a subject
that he could control in
every detail (except the
light). He would sit in the
middle of it and paint it.

Stand back and enjoy the imagery—
familiar and nostalgic for us now, but
challenging and modern in its day. Or
stand close up to his compositions and
enjoy the complexity, texture, and interweaving of paint and color. Note the thick,
crusty paint, which gets thicker as the light
gets more interesting—particularly when it
catches the edges of objects.

KEY WORKS *The Petit Bras of the Seine at Argenteuil*,
1872 (London: National Gallery); *Impression:
Sunrise* (see page 312); *The Haystacks, or The
End of Summer, at Giverny*, 1891 (Paris: Musée
d'Orsay); *The Houses of Parliament, London*,
1904 (Paris: Musée d'Orsay); *Waterlilies*,
1908 (London: Christie's Images)

The Japanese Bridge at Giverny *Claude Monet,
1918–24, 35 x 39⅓ in (89 x 100 cm), oil on canvas,
Paris: Musée Marmottan.* In old age Monet's eyesight
deteriorated because of cataracts and he depended
on instinct and memory to paint his later works.

Bather Arranging her Hair
Pierre-Auguste Renoir, 1893, 36½ x 29 in (92 x 74 cm), oil on canvas, Washington, DC: National Gallery of Art. Renoir was much influenced by Delacroix and Ingres. Socially conservative, he destroyed many works he deemed inadequate.

makes one think of soft feather cushions and Turkish Delight?

See how the sensuality of his technique marries with the subject matter: long, free brushstrokes of warm color, which caress the canvas. Note the blushes on the cheeks and the obsession with small, firm breasts. The early works have cooler colors, more black, and less mush.

KEY WORKS *The Gust of Wind*, c. 1872 (Cambridge: Fitzwilliam Museum); *The Parisienne*, 1874 (Cardiff: National Museum of Wales); *The Boating Party* (see page 313); *Girl Combing her Hair*, 1907–08 (Paris: Musée d'Orsay)

"There is something in painting which cannot be explained, and that something is essential. You come to nature with your theories, and nature knocks them all flat."

PIERRE-AUGUSTE RENOIR

Pierre-Auguste **Renoir**

● 1841–1919 🇫🇷 FRENCH

🇫🇷 France; Italy 🎨 oils 🏛 Philadelphia: Barnes Collection. Paris: Musée d'Orsay
💰 $71m in 1990, *Le Moulin de la Galette* (oils)

Renoir was one of the first Impressionists, but soon developed an individual and un-Impressionist style. Most remembered for his lyrical paintings of pink, buxom young girls. Very prolific.

He is the greatest ever master of dappled light, which pervades all his work, giving it a seductive, sensual, and soft-focus quality. The early works have bite and observation; the late works become rather repetitive at times. Did he never become bored by all that comfortable, pink, female flesh, which

Gustave **Caillebotte**

● 1848–94 🇫🇷 FRENCH

🇫🇷 France 🎨 oils 🏛 Paris: Musée d'Orsay
💰 $13m in 2000, *L'homme au balcon, boulevard Haussmann* (oils)

He was a second-rate painter who knew what talent was (one of the first collectors of great Impressionist paintings), and who occasionally showed some in his own work.

Typical Impressionist subject matter and technique (very similar to Monet and Manet). Scenes of everyday contemporary Paris, especially street scenes with exaggerated, plunging perspectives. Interesting work but essentially derivative, and hampered by being too anecdotal— it could often be one of those illustrations for a 19th-century novel that visualize a specific phrase or sentence in the text.

Recognizable pink-green-blue-purple palette—often too strident and overdoes the purple. Cropped compositions influenced by photography.

KEY WORKS *Rue de Paris, Wet Weather*, 1877 (Art Institute of Chicago); *View of Rooftops (Snow)*, 1878 (Paris: Musée d'Orsay); *At the Café, Rouen*, 1880 (Rouen: Musée des Beaux-Arts)

IMPRESSIONISM

Impressionism marked the birth of modern painting. It was never consciously revolutionary, its goal simply to depict the immediacy of the world with complete fidelity. Yet in seeing this as accidental, the product of transitory lighting conditions and chance moments, it prompted a strikingly different pictorial language that began the overthrow of the naturalistic tradition the Renaissance established.

STYLE

Impression: Sunrise *Claude Monet, 1872, 48 x 63 cm (19 x 24¾ in), oil on canvas, Paris: Musée Marmottan. By painting rapidly, Monet aimed to capture fleeting moments. Impermanence of light and atmosphere are his real focus.*

Delicate, mosaiclike brushstrokes in light, brilliant colors intended to capture an instant briefly glimpsed define Impressionism. The artists aimed at more than just spontaneity. By replacing tonal gradations—the gradual lightening or darkening of a color to suggest shadows and depth—with tiny dabs of pure color, the Impressionists pointed the way to a new way of seeing. Yet although almost every major avant garde French painter of the period was influenced by Impressionism, only Pissarro, Sisley, and Monet, the giant of the movement, remained consistently true to its goals.

SUBJECTS

The here and now dominated. Whether picnics, boating parties, still lifes, railroad stations, city views or sun-flooded landscapes vibrantly alive with color, the emphasis was consistently on the world immediately surrounding the painter.

The modern world became paramount. As important, the studio was abandoned for painting on the spot directly onto the canvas. Plein air (literally, "open air") painting (see page 305) not only demanded an immediacy on the part of the painter—the speed of work necessary was a key reason for the fragmented, shimmering visual language of Impressionism—it naturally placed a premium on landscapes and outdoor scenes. It amounted to a decisive rejection of the Academy's ponderous "official" history-painting.

KEY EVENTS

1869	Monet and Renoir establish key Impressionism characteristics, painting at Bougival on the Seine
1870	Monet and Pissarro in London, escaping Franco-Prussian war; joined by Sisley (1871)
1874	Critic derisively coins name "Impressionism" at first exhibition
1881	Renoir increasingly abandons Impressionism after visiting Rome
1886	Last Impressionist exhibition held
1890	Monet begins epic cycles, repainting same subjects in different conditions

Little Dancer, Aged 14 *Edgar Degas, 1880–81, height 38½ in (97.8 cm), polychrome bronze with muslin, satin ribbon and wood base, Private Collection. Impressionism exulted in the everyday. Degas excelled in exquisite, apparently random, slices of life.*

WHAT TO LOOK FOR

Impressionism was near universally derided as "unfinished." Critics complained that its subjects were trivial and its execution crude, an apparently deliberate flaunting of the accepted canons of Academic painting. Renoir's *Boating Party* encapsulates Impressionism's unshackled *joie de vivre*. It unapologetically celebrates the pleasures of youth and summer. Yet his most enduring achievement was to combine the visual imperatives of Impressionism, above all in his quivering, feathery brushwork, with the traditions of European figure painting. However, his seeming spontaneity was the product of painstaking labor.

M. Fournaise (in the straw hat) was the proprietor of the restaurant

Baron Raoul Barbier, a close friend of Renoir's, is chatting to the proprietor's daughter

Paul Lhote, wearing pince-nez glasses, flirts with the actress Jeanne Samary. He had a reputation as a ladies' man

The Boating Party Pierre-Auguste Renoir, 1881, 51 x 68 in (129.5 x 173 cm), oil on canvas, Washington, DC: Phillips Collection. Renoir artfully used Impressionistic techniques to create complex groups of rhythmically composed figures.

Deep in conversation, the man in the straw hat is Gustave Caillebotte, a talented artist (see page 311)

TECHNIQUES

Typically, Impressionists used canvases with white backgrounds. The result was an unprecedented luminosity that shone through their work, heightening colors, reinforcing deft brushwork.

Renoir was an accomplished still-life painter, and the debris of this meal is a sparkling achievement. The spontaneity is deceptive, since he constantly reworked the painting.

Berthe **Morisot**

◗ 1841–95 ⚑ FRENCH

📖 Paris 🎨 oils; watercolors 🏛 Paris: Musée Marmottan; Musée d'Orsay 💲 $4m in 2000, *Cache-cache* (oils)

She was a member of the Impressionists and effective hostess and go-between to the writers, poets, and painters in their circle. Attractive, free, delicate style derived from Manet (she married his brother, Eugène). Her works are, in effect, an autobiographical diary.
KEY WORKS *The Harbor at Lorient*, 1869 (Washington, DC: National Gallery of Art); *Portrait of the Artist's Mother and Sister*, 1869–70 (London: National Gallery)

Camille **Pissarro**

◗ 1830–1903 ⚑ FRENCH

📖 France; England 🎨 oils; watercolors; drawings 🏛 Paris: Musée d'Orsay. Oxford: Ashmolean Museum 💲 $8m in 2004, *Les quatre saisons* (oils)

He was a reclusive, curmudgeonly, and unsettled artist who, nonetheless, takes his place as one of the major Impressionists and Post-Impressionists. Always an anarchist and always poor.

Pissarro chose a wide range of subjects: landscapes (Seine valley), modern city-scapes (Paris, Rouen—note the factory chimneys), still lifes, portraits, peasant scenes (especially laundresses). Was most confident in later work, but never really settled into a style with which he was completely at ease or that was completely his own. He progressed from dark, early landscapes to Impressionism and to experiments with Divisionism, then back to Impressionism.

He often chose high viewpoints (such as cityscapes painted from windows). His developed palette is quite chalky and pale, with predominant greens and blues. Surfaces are thickly painted

The Bridge at Moret *Alfred Sisley, 1893, 29 x 36⅜ in (73.5 x 92.5 cm), oil on canvas, Paris: Musée d'Orsay.* Sisley had to earn a living as a painter when the family business collapsed in 1870.

(sometimes patchily) with a sketchy look, as if they could be worked further if he could decide what to do with them (a sign of his uncertainty?). Note the play of contrasts in content: rural against industrial; transient against permanent; natural against artificial; old against new; warm against cool.
KEY WORKS *View from Louveciennes*, 1869–70 (London: National Gallery); *Autumn*, 1870 (Los Angeles: J. Paul Getty Museum); *The Climbing Path, L'Hermitage Pontoise*, 1875 (New York: Brooklyn Museum of Art)

Alfred **Sisley**

◗ 1839–99 ⚑ BRITISH/FRENCH

📖 Paris; England 🎨 oils 🏛 London: Courtauld Institute of Art; Tate Collection 💲 $3.2m in 2000, *Un jardin à Louveciennes, chemin de l'Etarche* (oils)

"The forgotten Impressionist"—the most underrated of the group, then and now.

Look for places, structures, and connections. Like Constable, Sisley only painted places he knew well and he particularly responded to the Seine and Thames valleys. He also liked well-structured compositions (notice the verticals, horizontals, diagonals). Cleverly used structural details like roads and bridges to take the eye through the landscape and link all the parts together.

Note the interesting color combinations (especially pinks and greens, blues and purples) to produce the sensation of light.
KEY WORKS *Women Going to the Woods*, 1866 (Tokyo: Bridgestone Museum of Art); *Floods at Port Marly*, 1876 (Paris: Musée d'Orsay); *The Walk*, 1890 (Nice: Musée d'Art et d'Histoire)

Woman Drying Herself *Edgar Degas, c. 1888–92, 49 x 38¼ in (103.8 x 98.4 cm), pastel, London: National Gallery. Degas increasingly worked with soft waxy pastels as his eyesight deteriorated, depending on touch and feel.*

experimented in many media: pastel, prints, and sculpture. Also was interested in photography—he borrowed and used the cut-off effect brilliantly. Worked and reworked the same subject or theme to achieve ever greater understanding and perfection. Notice how often he used the receding diagonal as the main armature for his compositions. Had astonishing color sensitivity, even when he was old and nearly blind.

Edgar **Degas**

● 1834 – 1917   🇫🇷 FRENCH

🇫🇷 France; Italy   🎨 oils; pastels; prints; sculpture   🏛 Paris: Musée d'Orsay. New York: Metropolitan Museum of Art   💰 $25.28m in 1999, *Danseuse au repos* (pastels)

Degas was one of the greatest draftsmen of all time. Successfully bridged the gap between the old master tradition and modernity. Shy, haughty, conservative, and single.

Each picture shows a self-contained and self-absorbed world, whatever the topic. Even when the subjects of his portraits make eye contact, they give nothing away. Ballet and racing scenes are a means of exploring complex space and movement. His technique, his extraordinary capacity for drawing, and attention to detail are equally self-absorbed—one of those rare, perfect unions between subject matter and means of expression.

Degas was fascinated by meticulous but innovative craftsmanship, and

> ## "Anyone can have a talent at 25. The difficulty is to have talent at 50!"
> EDGAR DEGAS

KEY WORKS *Madame René de Gas*, 1872–73 (Washington, DC: National Gallery of Art); *The Millinery Shop*, 1884–90 (Art Institute of Chicago); *The Tub*, 1886 (Paris: Musée d'Orsay)

The Star, or Dancer on the Stage *Edgar Degas, c. 1876–77, 23¾ x 17½ in (60 x 44 cm), pastel on paper, Paris: Musée d'Orsay. His technique shows the same qualities of precision and balance as classical ballet.*

Childe **Hassam**

● 1859–1935   ⋈ AMERICAN

🏳 US; Paris   🎨 oils; prints   🏛 New York:
Metropolitan Museum of Art   ⚡ $7.2m in
1998, *Flags, Afternoon on the Avenue* (oils)

America's foremost Impressionist artist,
Hassam painted more than 4,000 works
(oil and watercolors). Best remembered
for his late (post-1917) "flag paintings,"
where brightly colored, richly painted
flags at wartime parades act as an
exciting visual motif and symbol of
patriotism. In his earlier work, the
emphasis was on *contre-jour*.

Next to the French, the Americans
were the best and largest group of
Impressionists, but they were late in
the day by 20 years—post-1890s, as
they did not often visit Paris until the
1880s. Before that, they had tended
to learn their art in Germany.
KEY WORKS *Grand Prix Day*, 1887 (Boston:
Museum of Fine Arts); *Evening in New York*,
c. 1890 (Boston: Museum of Fine Arts);
Manhattan's Misty Sunset, 1911 (Youngstown,
Ohio: Butler Institute of American Art);
Allies Day, May 1917 (Washington, DC:
National Gallery of Art); *Avenue of the
Allies, Great Britain, 1918* (New York:
Metropolitan Museum of Art)

Mary **Cassatt**

● 1844–1926   ⋈ AMERICAN

🏳 Paris   🎨 oils; prints   🏛 New York:
Metropolitan Museum of Art   ⚡ $3.7m
in 1996, *In the Box* (oils)

The daughter of a wealthy Pittsburgh
family, Cassatt settled in Paris. She
mixed with avant-garde and helped
American collectors spend their
loot (very Henry James). A friend
of Degas, she also helped the
Impressionists. Produced attractive
works with strong sense of design,
courageous color, and cropped
angled viewpoints that capture
personal, meaningful moments of the
well-to-do. Spottable influences from
Degas, Japanese prints, and Ingres.
KEY WORKS *Musical Party*, 1874 (Paris: Musée
du Petit Palais); *Mother about to Wash her
Sleepy Child*, 1880 (Los Angeles County
Museum of Art); *Girl Arranging her Hair*, 1886
(Washington, DC: National Gallery of Art);
The Bath, 1891 (Art Institute of Chicago)

William Merritt **Chase**

● 1849–1916   ⋈ AMERICAN

🏳 Munich; New York   🎨 oils   🏛 Houston:
Museum of Fine Arts   ⚡ $3.6m in 1993,
Peonies (work on paper)

Chase was a prolific and versatile artist
from a prosperous Indiana background.
Successful, gregarious, witty, flashy
dresser, cultivated in the European
manner (friend of Whistler). Developed
two distinct styles, both direct and
spontaneous: his early works are dark,
heavy, elegant portraits (style learned
in Munich); after 1890s they become
light-filled French-Impressionist-style
scenes of Long Island (Shinnecock).

Portrait of a Lady in Black *William Merritt
Chase, c. 1895, 72 x 36 in (182.9 x 91.4 cm), oil on
canvas, Detroit Institute of Arts. Chase is best
known for his spirited portraits and still lifes in oil.*

At the Piano Theodore Robinson, 1887, 16½ x 25¼ in (41.8 x 64.2 cm), oil on canvas, Washington, DC: Smithsonian Institute. Known only as Marie, the true identity of Robinson's mysterious model remains unknown, despite her appearance in numerous works.

KEY WORKS *At the Seaside*, c. 1892 (New York: Metropolitan Museum of Art); *Portrait of Moses Swaim*, 1867 (Indianapolis: Museum of Art); *The Brass Bowl*, 1899 (Indianapolis: Museum of Art)

Julian Alden **Weir**

◔ 1852–1919   ⚑ AMERICAN

⚑ Paris; US   ◑ oils; watercolors; drawings   ⏛ New York: Metropolitan Museum of Art   ⚡ $400,000 in 1987, *Nassau, Bahamas* (oils)

Weir was the most academically successful American Impressionist. He studied in Paris. Was conservative in technique and temperament. His early work was much influenced by Manet; later work is closer to Monet. Was most successful in his smaller works, particularly in watercolor and silverpoint. Became president of the National Academy of Design.

KEY WORKS *Union Square*, c. 1879 (New York: Brooklyn Museum of Art); *Willimantic Thread Factory*, 1893 (New York: Brooklyn Museum of Art); *The Red Bridge*, 1895 (New York: Metropolitan Museum of Art)

Theodore **Robinson**

◔ 1852–96   ⚑ AMERICAN

⚑ US; France   ◑ oils   ⏛ New York: Metropolitan Museum of Art   ⚡ $1.9m in 1994, *Boats at a Landing* (oils)

Robinson was the leading American Impressionist painter. He made several visits to France between 1876 and 1892, and was a close friend of Monet, whom he had met at Giverny in 1887. Painted landscapes and vignettes of village and farm life. He found East Coast American light too bright compared with the light in France, and had difficulty painting it. He died relatively young, his later years marred by poor health and poverty.

In the US, he was a pioneer, but his Impressionist style is cautious by French standards—compositions are rather static, and the brushstrokes too carefully considered. He sometimes worked from photographs, which he used by squaring up—traces of the grid can occasionally be seen on the canvas.

KEY WORKS *Self-Portrait*, c. 1884–87 (Washington, DC: National Gallery of Art); *Watching the Cows*, 1892 (Youngstown, Ohio: Butler Institute of American Art); *Miss Motes and her Dog Shep*, 1893 (London: Christie's Images); *Low Tide, Riverside Yacht Club*, 1894 (Washington, DC: National Gallery of Art)

Auguste **Rodin**

◗ 1840–1917　🇫🇷 FRENCH

🏴 France; Italy　◑ sculpture　🏛 Paris: Musée Rodin. San Francisco: Palace of the Legion of Honor　💰 $4.4m in 1999, *Eve* (sculpture)

The glorious, triumphant finale to the sculptural tradition that starts with Donatello. Rightly spoken of in the same breath as Michelangelo (although they were quite different: Michelangelo carved, Rodin molded). Shy, workaholic, impoverished beginnings, untidy, friend of poets, physically enormous. Became an international celebrity and was deeply attractive to smart women.

He carried out an extraordinary and enriching hide-and-seek exploration with the processes of his art, and the relationship between intellectual and artistic creativity. His famous set-piece projects (such as *The Gates of Hell*) evolved over many years. Also sculpted portraits, nudes, and small models, which show ideas in evolution. Observe the ways he uses the fluidity of clay and plaster (even when cast in bronze), to release his figures, human feelings, and the unknown forces in nature. Was fascinated with biological procreativity.

Note his stunningly beautiful recreation of (large) hands, embraces, kisses, and whole body poses as an expression of human libido and anima (he always worked from life, even when borrowing from antiquity or classics). Bases are important because he makes his figures grow out of them. Washes his figures in light (try to see them in natural light). He used studio assistants or commercial firms to make large-scale versions of his original models—what you see may never have been touched by Rodin (he wanted to disseminate his work widely).

Married his lifetime companion Rose Beuret in 1917 in Meudon, Paris, at the age of 77. Rose died two weeks later and Rodin nine months after. A cast of *The Thinker* overlooks his grave in Meudon.

KEY WORKS *The Thinker*, 1880–81 (Private Collection); *The Gates of Hell*, 1880–1917 (Paris: Musée d'Orsay); *Andromeda*, c. 1885 (Private Collection); *Sinner*, c. 1885 (St. Petersburg: Hermitage Museum)

The Burghers of Calais *Auguste Rodin, 1884–89, height 79½ in (201.7 cm), bronze, Washington, DC: Hirshhorn Museum.* One of a number of casts of Rodin's original plaster model. It was commissioned by the city of Calais to commemorate six 14th-century civic heroes.

The Kiss

Auguste Rodin 1901–04

One of the most powerful sculptures ever created, its influence reached far into the 20th century. It is a perfect example of Rodin's ability to express intense emotion through the physicality of sculpture and one of the great images of sexual love.

Originally part of Rodin's huge *The Gates of Hell*, the sculpture depicts the illicit lovers, Francesca da Rimini and Paolo Malatesta, whose story is told in poet Dante Alighieri's masterwork *The Divine Comedy* (1321). Francesca was stabbed to death by husband Giovanni as she exchanged her first kiss with his brother Paolo after falling madly in love with him. The statue eventually became an independent work because the blend of eroticism and pure happiness didn't fit *The Gates*'s damnation theme.

The man leans down, but depending on where you stand, either lover can look like the instigator

Rodin's profound knowledge of anatomy allowed him to incorporate subtle exaggerations and distortions in order to achieve his aim of rendering inner feeling through muscular movement

The Kiss exists in three different marble versions, none of which were carved by Rodin, accounting for the smooth, anonymous surface. This version was commissioned by a wealthy Bostonian collector living in England

The Kiss

Medium marble
Height 71 in (182 cm)
Location Paris: Musée Rodin.
London: Tate Collection (copy)

The figures appear to emerge preformed from the stone. Rodin believed man and woman were one entity united through erotic love

DIVISIONISM   1880s

Divisionism is the name for a way of painting, in which color effects are obtained optically rather than by mixing colors on the palette: i.e. small areas of pure color are put side-by-side on the canvas so that at a distance, the eye cannot differentiate between them but mixes them together and so experiences another color (optical mixing). More convincing as a theory than in practice. Seurat was its originator, but he died young, and so Signac became its chief promulgator. Pointillism is Divisionism as practiced by Seurat, using small dots of color.

Georges **Seurat**

⊖ 1859–91   ⚑ FRENCH

🏠 France   🎨 oils; drawings   🏛 New York: Metropolitan Museum of Art. Art Institute of Chicago   💰 $32m in 1999, *A Sunday Afternoon on the Island of La Grande Jatte* (oils)

Seurat, a shy, reclusive man who died suddenly from meningitis aged 31, having produced very great work. The originator of Pointillism and Divisionism.

His subjects are modern life and places. His work can seem austere and rigid because he painted according to worked-out theories, not what he saw or felt. He applied the latest ideas of color and optical mixing—painting separate dots of pure color on the canvas (Pointillism), which mix and vibrate in the eye and are intended to give the same sensation as light itself. Used a formula of lines to express emotion: upward diagonal = happiness; downward diagonal = sadness; horizontal = calmness.

Color theories don't work in practice because pigments lose their brightness and the mixing in the eye tends to end up as a gray mush. Why did he ignore the significance of vertical lines? He made wonderful drawings using soft black crayon on textured paper, and tiny, free, preliminary sketches for his big works. Used color borders that complement the areas of color in the picture. There is hidden symbolism and references to old masters in the set-piece figure paintings.

KEY WORKS *Model from the Back*, 1887 (Paris: Musée d'Orsay); *Port of Gravelines Channel*, 1890 (Indianapolis: Herron Art Institute); *The Circus*, 1891 (Paris: Musée d'Orsay)

Paul **Signac**

⊖ 1863–1935   ⚑ FRENCH

🏠 France   🎨 oils   🏛 St. Petersburg: Hermitage Museum   💰 $4m in 1998, *Concarneau, calme du matin* (oils)

Frenchman Signac was a patient follower and disciple of Seurat. Through his work and writings he was the chief promulgator of the theory and practice of Divisionism. He moved from observed outdoor scenes to studio-based subjects, and from small dots to larger brushstrokes. Good plein-air watercolors. His own work was overly theoretical and tidy, but despite this, he influenced others (Matisse, for instance). He was a dogmatic man.

A keen yachtsman, Signac spent a lot of time on the Mediterranean and Atlantic coasts; harbor scenes became his favorite subjects.

KEY WORKS *Gas Tanks at Clichy*, 1886 (Melbourne: National Gallery of Victoria); *Lighthouse at Groix*, 1925 (New York: Metropolitan Museum of Art); *Port of Concarneau*, 1925 (Tokyo: Bridgestone Museum of Art)

A Sunday Afternoon on the Island of La Grande Jatte *Georges Seurat, 1884–86, 81⅝ x 121¼ in (207.5 x 308 cm), oil on canvas, Art Institute of Chicago.* Seurat labored extensively over this piece, reworking the original as well as numerous preliminary drawings and oil sketches.

Mother and Child on a Couch James Abbott McNeill Whistler, c. 1870s, watercolor, London: Victoria & Albert Museum. Whistler wished his art to appear to be effortless. The hidden reality was very different.

James Abbott McNeill
Whistler

● 1834–1903 ◼ AMERICAN

🎨 England; France   🎨 oils; engravings
🏛 London: Tate Collection. Glasgow: Hunterian Museum   📈 $2.6m in 2000, *Harmony in Gray, Chelsea in Ice* (oils)

A small, egocentric, quarrelsome, witty, and dandy artist who was born in the US, and later lived in Europe (France and England). Leading figure of the Aesthetic movement, he developed a new style of painting and role for the artist. Was a contemporary of Oscar Wilde.

Look for painting as an aesthetic object and experience—the subject matter taking second place to the visual pleasure of color and form. Note the subtle harmonies of soft color, carefully placed shapes, and suppression of detail. He chose simple subjects, expressive of mood. His portraits say little about the sitter's personality. Why was he so tentative? Was he never at ease with painting? Arguably his best works are his prints, in which he never lacked self-confidence.

The thin paint surface belies the fact that he worked and reworked his pictures, wiping away his efforts until he had reached his notion of perfection (which must have been agonizing for his portrait sitters). Some works are still in their original frames, designed by Whistler to harmonize with the painting. Look for his famous "butterfly" signature, which he used after 1870. Much influenced by Japanese art, Velasquez, and Manet (he had to be up to date and in the forefront of fashion), he became interested in Oriental art and decoration in general. Played a major role in introducing modern ideas to British art.

KEY WORKS *The White Girl*, 1862 (London: Tate Collection); *Nocturne: Blue and Gold*, 1872–77 (London: Tate Collection); *Arrangement in Gray and Black: Portrait of the Painter's Mother*, 1871 (Paris: Musée d'Orsay); *Nocturne in Black and Gold: The Falling Rocket* (see page 323); *Upright Venice*, 1879–80 (Private Collection)

> **"If the man who paints [only what] he sees before him were an artist, the king of artists would be the photographer."**
>
> JAMES ABBOTT McNEILL WHISTLER

SYMBOLISM AND AESTHETICISM

From the mid-19th century, a literary cult developed in France that explored the mystical, the spiritual, and the morbid. It found an outlet in the visual arts in Symbolism, "the ambiguous world of the indeterminate," in the words of the painter Odilon Redon. Across the Channel in England, it was echoed by Aestheticism.

SYMBOLISM

Prompted by the poet Théophile Gautier, who had argued for the rejection of conventional morality and the primacy of "pure sensation," a series of poets and painters in France increasingly elaborated a world in which imagination was allowed free rein. For Gustave Moreau, as to some extent for the more Classically minded Puvis de Chavannes, it was a means of infusing Academic figure painting with an allusive and richly imaginative new pictorial language. Odilon Redon, whose later painting was based directly on his dreams, went further still. Semi-human figures inhabit fantastic landscapes made more mysterious by brushwork that eventually approached the abstract.

The Cyclops Odilon Redon, c. 1914 (oil on canvas), Otterlo, Netherlands: Kröller-Müller Museum. Redon's highly personal vision later made him a hero of the Surrealists.

ART FOR ART'S SAKE

The idea that art could be an end in itself with no higher purpose—whether moral, spiritual, or political—than the pursuit of pure "artistic sensation" reached a peak toward the end of the 19th century. In England, it was exemplified by the Aesthetic movement. Oscar Wilde was its best-known literary exponent, the American-born Whistler its chief (and most notorious) champion in the visual arts, going so far as a court appearance to defend the integrity of the movement. This was "a crusade on behalf of beauty," a "poetic passion," which utterly rejected utilitarianism in favor of the exquisite.

JAPANESE ART

The impact of Japanese prints on the transformation of the visual arts in Europe in the second half of the 19th century was crucial. Their use of everyday subjects, unusual viewpoints, tilted perspectives, bold, flat colors, and strong outlines amounted to a pictorial language entirely different to anything then known in the West.

Japanese Ghost Katsushika Hokusai, 1830s, woodblock, London: Victoria & Albert Museum. From series of One Hundred Stories, this features a man turned into a snake on his death, a theme that resonated with the Symbolists' obsession with spiritual transformation.

WHAT TO LOOK FOR

That color and form, irrespective of their subject matter, could be expressive in themselves had been commonplace since the days of Delacroix. But Whistler went much further. His nominal subject matter is dissolved until it becomes nothing but a complex interplay of color and form infinitely delicately rendered. The result is a beguiling, haunting surface pattern.

Nocturne in Black and Gold: The Falling Rocket James Abbott McNeill Whistler, c. 1875, 23¾ x 18½ in (60 x 47 cm), oil on panel, Detroit Institute of Arts.

The painting captures the drama and beauty of the fleeting instant in which a rocket explodes, scattering a shower of sparks into the night

Whistler was deeply influenced by Japanese prints, in particular their non-naturalistic handling of space and concentration on expressive surface patterns

Like the Impressionists, Whistler continually sought ways to represent immediacy and the infinitely changeable nature of light

Rapid brushwork, however painstakingly arrived at, conveys a sense of an instant captured, of the transient made permanent

TECHNIQUES

Rather than build up thick layers of paint, Whistler would wipe away his mistakes to leave only a thin film of transparent paint. The loose, light brushwork and subtle color harmonies were influenced by Velasquez.

Whistler's unusual signature has similarities with the collector's seals found on Chinese art. He was an enthusiastic and early collector of Oriental blue and white porcelain.

Gustave **Moreau**

◔ 1826–98   ⚑ FRENCH

🏛 France   ◉ oils; watercolors; drawings
🏛 Paris: Musée Gustave Moreau   ⚡ $2.5m
in 1989, *Le poète et la sirène* (oils)

An intense, talented, prolific, workaholic, and successful artist, determined to revive the tradition of history painting (actually in terminal decline) and to be a rival of the greatest old masters.

He was noted for erudite, imaginative, literary, and mythological subjects. His idiosyncratic style is halfway between the strange, fantasy world of Bosch and the surreal dream world of Max Ernst. His work is sometimes dark and mysterious, sometimes bright and shimmering, but always sinister, oozing romantic decadence and symbolism. Used deeply worked surfaces and textures with inventive impasto, glazes, and colors that unlocked his imagination.

He produced a huge quantity of sketches and watercolors; these preceded his finished oil paintings, either as experiments or to work out their final design and details. His late watercolors (and some unfinished oils) are as free and sketchy as modern abstraction. He was active at the same period as the Impressionists, who were everything he was not. A gifted teacher, he influenced many who seem impossibly far removed from his style (such as Matisse). Moreau was much influenced by a tour of Italy (1857–59).

KEY WORKS *Diomedes Devoured by Horses*, 1851 (Los Angeles: J. Paul Getty Museum); *Orpheus*, 1865 (Paris: Musée d'Orsay); *Salome*, 1876 (Paris: Musée Gustave Moreau); *Hesiod and the Muse*, 1891 (Paris: Musée d'Orsay)

Pierre **Puvis de Chavannes**

◔ 1824–98   ⚑ FRENCH

🏛 France   ◉ oils   🏛 Paris: Hôtel de Ville
(murals); Sorbonne University; Panthéon;
Musée d'Orsay. Boston: Public Library (murals)
⚡ $850,000 in 1998, *L'enfance de Sainte Geneviève* (oils)

Puvis de Chavannes was internationally sought after in his day as the leading painter of large-scale murals to decorate public buildings. Worked on canvas, then affixed to walls. His smaller works were also admired by avant-garde painters such as Seurat, Gauguin, and Munch.

His statuesque figures in landscapes are the direct descendants of the great Classical tradition. He had a very recognizable dry technique, using a chalky white coloring with a stiff style that made his work look like a fresco. His was a valiant but ultimately unsuccessful attempt to make the Classical and Academic tradition relevant to the modern world. Tried to touch big emotions such as hope and despair, but missed the target; his work now looks at best decorative, at worst, lifeless.

His archaic, flat style searches for a "modern" simplification of form and color, and a timeless monumentality for the figure, detached from literary connections; it was only in the next generation (Matisse) that this would be fully unlocked. To do his work full justice, it needs to be seen in situ in the elaborate Beaux-Arts Renaissance-revival buildings that he decorated (and which were themselves to be overtaken by the simplified architecture of Modernism).

KEY WORKS *The Beheading of St. John the Baptist*, c. 1869 (London: National Gallery); *The Prodigal Son*, c. 1879 (Washington, DC: National Gallery of Art); *Young Girls by the Edge of the Sea*, 1879 (Paris: Musée d'Orsay); *The Poor Fisherman*, 1881 (Paris: Musée d'Orsay); *Woman on the Beach*, 1887 (St. Petersburg: Hermitage Museum)

Odilon **Redon**

◔ 1840–1916   ⚑ FRENCH

🏛 France   ◉ oils; pastels; prints; drawings
🏛 Washington, DC: National Gallery of Art
⚡ $3.4m in 2004, *Vase au guerrier japonais*
(works on paper)

Redon became one of the principal *fin de siècle* Symbolist artists, and was a Surrealist before his time.

His *oeuvre* divides in two: pre- and post-1894. His early small-scale, black-and-white drawings and prints had neurotic, introspective subject matter (he had a classic Freudian, unhappy childhood). After 1894 he overcame his neuroses and his art blossomed into radiant color and joyful subject matter. His inspiration came from the inner mind, not the outer eye. Today, he is better known for his later work.

His poetic, contemplative works have no specific meaning. His fascinating early subject matter anticipated Surrealism—floating heads, curious creatures, strange juxtapositions, all drawn from the depths of the imagination (and from Symbolist writers such as Poe and Baudelaire). Observe his very fine drawing and print techniques, with beautiful tonal treatments. Later, he developed an exquisite pastel technique and the ability to produce saturated, unreal colors of astonishing richness and intensity.

KEY WORKS *The Trees*, 1890s (Houston: Museum of Fine Arts); *Ophelia Among the Flowers*, c. 1905–08 (London: National Gallery); *The Shell*, 1912 (Paris: Musée d'Orsay); *Anemones and Lilacs in a Blue Vase*, 1914 (Paris: Petit Palais)

Maurice **Denis**

◔ 1870–1943   ◪ FRENCH

▣ France; Switzerland   ▨ oils; fresco   ▥ St. Petersburg: Heritage Museum   ⚡ $467,087 in 2000, *Les communiantes, la promenade au jardin* (oils)

He was a leading Symbolist who led reaction against Impressionism. Driven by theory. Founder member of Nabis.

No realistic representation, insignificant subject matter; small-scale easel painting is king. The result is paintings with deliberately flat, decorative, stylized or Art Nouveau appearance; strange colors; trivial, everyday subjects. As effective (more so?) with his stage and costume design and book illustrations. A committed Catholic who applied his art to the service of church decoration.

KEY WORKS *The Two Sisters*, 1891 (Amsterdam: Van Gogh Museum); *Gaulish Goddess of Herds and Flocks*, 1906 (Munich: Neue Pinakothek); *Orpheus and Eurydice*, 1910 (Minnesota: Minneapolis Institute of Arts)

Arnold **Böcklin**

◔ 1827–1901   ◪ GERMAN

▣ Switzerland; Germany; Italy   ▨ oils   ▥ Basel (Switzerland): Kunstmuseum   ⚡ $168,300 in 1993, *Kentaurenkampf* (oils)

Leading German Symbolist painter. Swiss-born, Düsseldorf-trained but most influenced by Italian art (especially

Raphael). Meticulous craftsman of Classical, mythological figures in intense moody landscapes that are intended to trigger dreamlike reveries. Very much the languid *fin de siècle* fashion, but now seems cloying and artificial.

KEY WORKS *Pan in the Reeds*, 1857 (Munich: Neue Pinakothek); *Self-Portrait with Death as a Fiddler*, c. 1871–74 (Berlin: Staatliche Museum); *The Isle of the Dead*, 1883 (Berlin: Staatliche Museum)

Aubrey **Beardsley**

◔ 1872–98   ◪ BRITISH

▣ England   ▨ drawings; prints   ⚡ $135,000 in 2004, Design for the front cover of *The Savoy, No. 4* (works on paper)

A self-taught, tubercular, workaholic, master of the sinuous, sensual, erotic (sometimes pornographic), black-and-white drawing and print. Brilliant but controversial. Art Nouveau illustrator. Highly original and gifted, capturing the essence of *fin de siècle* decadence. Had a boring private life—his eroticism was all in his mind. Died of tuberculosis at the age of only 25.

KEY WORKS *Salome*, 1892 (New Jersey: Princeton University Library); *How King Arthur Saw the Questing Beast*, 1893 (London: Victoria & Albert Museum); *A Nightpiece*, 1894 (Cambridge: Fitzwilliam Museum)

Thomas Wilmer **Dewing**

◔ 1851–1938   ◪ AMERICAN

▣ US   ▨ oils   ▥ Washington, DC: Sackler and Freer Galleries   ⚡ $3.1 million in 2002, *Song* (oils)

A painter of accomplished works depicting elegant, stately, distant women in tastefully furnished interiors or wandering in lush, dreamy landscapes. They are often large in scale and were turned into Japanese-style screens. Also produced studies for the above, pastels and silverpoints. Good example of Aestheticism—a pot-pourri of Pre-Raphaelites, Whistler, and Japan. Note the frames.

KEY WORKS *The Letter*, 1895–1900 (New York: Metropolitan Museum of Art); *Lady with a Lute*, 1886 (Washington, DC: National Gallery of Art); *The Gossip*, c. 1907 (Minnesota: Minneapolis Institute of Arts)

Walter Richard **Sickert**

● 1860–1942 ▶ BRITISH

🏛 England; France; Italy 🖌 oils; prints
🏛 London: Tate Collection 💲 $286,000
in 1993, *Brighton Pierrots* (oils)

The leading British painter of the
Impressionist and Post-Impressionist
period, Sickert had personal links with
French artists such as Degas. Style
perhaps best described as a French idiom
spoken with a very strong English accent.

He chose down-to-earth subjects—street
scenes, cheap interiors, music halls, and
prostitutes, and painted them in an earthy
manner, without glamor, with a disregard
for fashion, in a palette of muddy colors,
and thick, heavily worked paint. He was
fond of and used the sense of intimacy and
unobtrusive observation that is one of the
qualities of photography. The imagery
for many late works was taken directly
from newspaper photographs—a mistake,
as it destroyed any sense of intimacy.

High-quality craftsman—his pictures
are very carefully composed, sometimes
with striking or unusual viewpoints, behind
which lay much work and preliminary
drawing. Note the careful and diligent
application of paint in his work; his
unusual color combinations and
interesting light effects. In his late work,
look for the lines of the underlying grid
he used for squaring up (enlarging) the
photographs. Also made good etchings.

KEY WORKS *Interior of St. Mark's, Venice*, 1896
(London: Tate Collection); *La Hollandaise*,
1906 (London: Tate Collection); *Jack the Ripper's
Bedroom*, c. 1906 (Manchester: City Art Gallery)

John Singer **Sargent**

● 1856–1925 ▶ AMERICAN

🏛 France; England; US 🖌 oils; drawings
🏛 Washington, DC: National Gallery of Art
💲 $21m in 2004, *Group with Parasols* (oils)

Sargent was the last seriously successful
portrait painter in the grand manner.
Born in Florence, he lived mostly in

The Daughters of Edward Darley Boit *John Singer
Sargent, 1882, 87 x 87 in (221 x 221 cm), oil on canvas,
Boston: Museum of Fine Arts.* The painting was
enthusiastically reviewed by Henry James in 1883.

Europe. He was very talented, successful, and rich. He captured the spirit of the golden age that perished in World War I.

In the 1880s and 1890s, he succeeded with large-scale portraits of the *nouveaux riches* of the UK, US, and France, showing them at their glittering best, in flattering and relaxed poses. After 1900, he painted the English aristocracy but made them more formal and aloof. Grew bored with faces and spoiled clientele: look for his preferred small-scale plein-air landscape sketches, intimate glimpses of family and friends, and rapid charcoal sketches. Also produced uninspired, time-consuming murals for public buildings in Boston (1890–1921).

He had a brilliant oil technique—his assured fluid paint and bold compositions match the confident faces and expensive well-cut clothes of his sitters. His real interest was in light (he was friendly with the Impressionists, especially Monet) and precise matching of tones. Was trained in Paris to use "au premier coup" technique—one exact brushstroke and no reworking. His watercolor technique was less assured. Influenced by Velasquez. His work successfully bridges the divide between the old masters and Impressionism.

KEY WORKS *Madame X (Madame Pierre Gautreau)*, 1883–84 (New York: Metropolitan Museum of Art); *Mrs. Adrian Iselin*, 1888 (Washington, DC: National Gallery of Art); *The Bridge of Sighs*, c. 1905 (New York: Brooklyn Museum of Art)

Joaquin **Sorolla y Bastida**
◔ 1863–1923 ♙ SPANISH

♙ Spain; US 🖌 oils; prints 🏛 New York: Hispanic Society of America (murals)
📈 $5.61m in 2003, *Bathing Time* (oils)

Born and raised in Valencia, he was an accomplished, prolific, and internationally acclaimed painter with an easy, fluent style. Successfully bridged the divide between old masters and Moderns (like Sargent and Zorn). Sorolla y Bastida was a painter of beach scenes, landscapes, society portraits, and genre scenes; he had an enviable facility with light effects. Shows a nice balance between (social) realism and idealism. Painted directly onto canvas—fast.

KEY WORKS *The Relic*, c. 1893 (Bilbao: Museo de Bellas Artes); *Wounded Foot*, 1909 (Los Angeles: J. Paul Getty Museum); *Court of Dances*, 1910 (Los Angeles: J. Paul Getty Museum)

Girls from Dalarna Having a Bath *Anders Zorn, 1908, 33⅓ x 20⅝ in (86 x 53 cm), oil on canvas, Stockholm: Nationalmuseum. Zorn did much to preserve the folk traditions of the Dalarna region, where he was born.*

Anders **Zorn**
◔ 1860–1920 ♙ SWEDISH

♙ Sweden; Europe; US 🖌 watercolors; oils; prints 🏛 New York: Metropolitan Museum of Art
📈 $2,608,000 in 1990, *Les Baigneuses* (oils)

Zorn was a prolific, talented, and very successful painter with a popular line in worldly-looking, fleshy nudes in plein-air settings. He also painted elegant portraits of the rich and famous. He had a virtuoso, free paint technique, which cleverly—like Manet—suggests 1) equality with the old masters (Titian) and the modern (the Impressionists); and 2) (false) spontaneity. Made brilliant watercolors, etchings, and the odd sculpture.

KEY WORKS *Mrs. Walter Rathbone Bacon*, 1897 (New York: Metropolitan Museum of Art); *Hugo Reisinger*, 1907 (Washington, DC: National Gallery of Art); *Mrs. John Crosby Brown*, c. 1900 (New York: Metropolitan Museum of Art)

POST-IMPRESSIONISM　　　late 19th/early 20th century

However liberating Impressionism was, its concentration on surface appearance and the moment inevitably limited its emotional range. From about 1880, a number of painters sought to fuse the new visual freedom generated by Impressionism with greater emphasis on form and content. The four giants of the Post-Impressionist era were Cézanne, Gauguin, Seurat and Van Gogh.

SUBJECTS AND STYLE

Modern life provides the dominant subject matter. Seurat pioneered a new monumentality, producing large-scale groups of figures painted using precise dots of paint, a technique known as divisionism. Cézanne achieved a similar sense of grave serenity by very different means, painstakingly reworking his paintings to reveal the

Landscape at Pont Aven
Paul Gauguin, 1888, oil on canvas, Private Collection. Gauguin developed his non-naturalistic style during a stay in Pont Aven, Brittany.

world's underlying reality. Gauguin and Van Gogh both sought ways to express troubled, often dreamlike emotions. Gauguin used flat color and distorted perspective, Van Gogh harsh colors, and strong outlines.

WHAT TO LOOK FOR

The sheer variety of styles covered by the term Post-Impressionism highlights a crucial feature of the period: that the absolute standards governing Western art established in the Renaissance no longer applied. This belief, which has remained unchallenged ever since, was the first claim that art was what the artist asserted it to be. Furthermore, "truth" in art did not have to mean naturalism, the attempt to show the world "as it actually is." This inevitably led to a wide diversity of styles, with the result that the term "Post-Impressionism" can really only be applied to the period rather than a particular style. Where Cézanne's work was intensely contemplative and minutely observed, Van Gogh's was tortured and highly expressive.

KEY EVENTS

1886	Van Gogh joins brother in Paris. Cézanne moves to Provence. Term "Neo-Impressionism" coined
1888	Van Gogh moves to Arles; after bouts of madness, shoots himself in 1890
1889	Norwegian Edvard Munch in Paris; *The Scream* (1893) combines northern brooding with Symbolist imagery
1891	Gauguin goes to Tahiti; returns to Paris 1893, then back to Pacific 1895
1895	Cézanne's first major show

Van Gogh's Bedroom at Arles *Vincent van Gogh, 1889, oil on canvas, Art Institute of Chicago.* This is the third version of the painting that Van Gogh produced. It was painted for his mother while recovering from a mental breakdown.

Paul **Gauguin**

● 1848–1903 📮 FRENCH

📄 France; Tahiti 🎨 oils; sculpture; prints
🏛 Washington, DC: National Gallery of Art.
St. Petersburg: Hermitage Museum. Paris: Musée
d'Orsay 💰 $35m in 2004, *Maternité II* (oils)

Gaugin was a successful stockbroker who, at the age of 35, abandoned his career and family to become an artist. Yearned for the simple life and died, unknown, from syphilis, in the South Seas. Had a decisive influence on the new generation (including Matisse and Picasso).

His best work is from his visits to Pont Aven, in Brittany (especially in 1888) and from Tahiti in the 1890s. Powerful subjects expressed with a strong sense of design: bold, flattened, simplified forms; intense, saturated colors. Constant search for a personal and spiritual fulfilment, which remained unsatisfied. Highly attracted to Tahitian feminine beauty, and many works are as full of sexual as well as spiritual yearning. Also produced interesting woodcarvings, pottery, and sculpture.

Although an acute observer of nature, he believed that the source of inspiration had to be internal, not external (which sparked a major quarrel with Van Gogh). Hence, look for symbolic, not natural, colors;

Nevermore *Paul Gauguin, 1897, 23⅝ x 45⅔ in (60.5 x 116 cm), oil on canvas, London: Courtauld Institute of Art.* Gauguin had a poetic ability to evoke moods that were haunting, ambiguous, and suffused with melancholy.

complex, sometimes biblical, symbolism. Plenty of scope for detective work on his visual sources, among them: South American art, Egyptian art, medieval art, Cambodian sculpture, Japanese prints, and Manet.

KEY WORKS *Landscape*, 1873 (Cambridge: Fitzwilliam Museum); *The Vision After the Sermon*, 1888 (Edinburgh: National Gallery of Scotland); *Sunflowers*, 1901 (St. Petersburg: Hermitage Museum); *Primitive Tales*, 1902 (Essen: Museum Folkwang); *Riders on the Beach*, 1902 (Essen: Museum Folkwang)

The Meal *Paul Gauguin, 1891, 28¾ x 36¼ in (73 x 92 cm), oil on canvas, Paris: Musée d'Orsay.* Rich coloring and distorted perspective combine to produce a work that is part still life, part enigmatic portrait of three Tahitian children.

Vincent **van Gogh**

● 1853–90   ⚑ DUTCH

⚑ Netherlands; England; France

🖌 oils; drawings; engravings

🏛 Amsterdam: Van Gogh Museum. Otterlo (Netherlands): Kröller-Müller Museum   🔨 $75m in 1990, *Portrait of Dr. Gachet* (oils)

Self-Portrait *1889, 25⅝ x 21½ in (65 x 54.5 cm), oil on canvas, Paris: Musée d'Orsay.* Following his violent breakdown in Arles in May 1889, Van Gogh produced this painting in the asylum at St. Rémy four months later.

He was a happy child who became grim, impoverished, melancholic, difficult to love, and suicidal—but he painted works that are now among the world's best known, best loved, and most expensive. He took up painting at the age of 27 and wanted his art to be a consolation for the stresses and strains of modern life. His subjects are wholly autobiographical, tracing every moment and emotion in his life. While the popular image of Van Gogh is of the tormented genius, he was also an educated, cultured man, who, despite the rapid pace of his output, put deep thought and planning into his art.

LIFE AND WORKS

Van Gogh came late to his artistic vocation, after years of unfulfilling careers, failed love affairs, poverty, and spiritual crises. Dismissed from his post as lay preacher for his too literal interpretation of Christ's command to give away worldly goods to the poor, he found a new mission in art. His early subjects were Dutch peasants and workers, whose honest struggle he sought to portray. This moralistic tone disappeared from his later art, which, under the influence of Impressionism and Japanese woodcuts encountered on his move to Paris, developed into an expressive, swirling style. An unsuccessful attempt to found an artists' cooperative at Arles with Gauguin led to a breakdown (he cut off part of his left ear during a quarrel), and he briefly entered an asylum in 1889. Although an enormously productive period, his depression finally overcame him, and he died at his own hand, virtually unknown to the art world, leaving 800 paintings and 850 drawings, completing 200 paintings in last 15 months alone. His obsessive letters to his devoted brother, Theo, which often explain work in detail, formed the source material for the quickly emergent cult that continues to grow around him.

Sunflowers 1888, 36½ x 28¾ in (92.1 x 73 cm), oil on canvas, London: National Gallery. One of a series of 12 sunflower paintings by Van Gogh, the majority of which were done during his stay in Arles.

STYLE

Van Gogh had an instinctive, self-taught, hurried style that is instantly recognizable. He used paint straight from the tube, applied as thick as furrows; strange perspectives; firm outlines, like a child's drawing; thrilling use of color, which takes on a life of its own. He distorted form and color in order to express inner feelings, moving away from the reproduction of literal visual appearances toward a symbolic and expressive synthesis. His swirling brushwork bristles with energy and emotional power.

He was able to endow inanimate objects with human personality (as did his favorite author, Charles Dickens), so that his yellow chair becomes a symbol or image of Van Gogh himself. He had a passionate belief in the importance of first-hand observation, which can be electrifying; but he also used color symbolism, with yellow being especially significant in his works. He ranks with Cézanne and Gauguin as the greatest of the Post-Impressionist artists.

KEY WORKS *The Artist's Father*, 1866 (Cambridge: Fitzwilliam Museum); *Abduction*, c. 1867 (Washington, DC: National Gallery of Art); *French Street Scene with Access to a Vantage Point*, 1887 (Amsterdam: Van Gogh Museum); *Portrait of Armand Roulin*, 1888 (Essen: Museum Folkwang); *Young Peasant Girl in a Straw Hat Sitting in Front of a Wheatfield*, 1890 (Private Collection)

Starry Night 1889, 29 x 36 in (73 x 92 cm), oil on canvas, New York: Museum of Modern Art. At the time he was planning Starry Night, Van Gogh was reading a collection of poems by the American writer Walt Whitman, one of which uses similar imagery.

Portrait of Doctor Paul Gachet, the Man with the Pipe 1890, 7 x 6 in (18 x 14 cm), etching, Paris: Bibliothèque Nationale.

Emile **Bernard**

● 1868–1941   🏳 FRENCH

🏛 France   🎨 oils   🏛 Madrid: Museo Thyssen-Bornemisza   💲 $450,000 in 1998, *Madeleine au Bois D'Amour* (oils)

A close friend of Gauguin, Van Gogh, and Cézanne, Bernard painted his own competent versions of Gauguin's style (clear outline; solid, flat color). Good, but not as good as he thought (although he did influence the Nabis). Most important now for his writings—especially interviews with Cézanne—and as the editor of Van Gogh's letters. In the 1920s, he gave up painting and retired to Venice to write.

KEY WORKS *Buckwheat Harvest*, 1888 (New York: Josefowitz Collection); *Study of Breton Women*, c. 1888–90 (Quimper, France: Musée des Beaux-Arts); *Breton Women on a Wall*, 1892 (New York: Josefowitz Collection)

Paul **Sérusier**

● 1863–1927   🏳 FRENCH

🏛 France   🎨 oils   🏛 Boston: Museum of Fine Arts   💲 $550,000 in 2003, *Deux lavandières au bord de la cascade* (oils)

His stiff, decorative style (firm outline, bright, flat colors, simplification) is largely indebted to Gauguin, with lesser

The Talisman Paul Sérusier, 1888, 160¼ x 84⅔ in (270 x 215 cm), oil on panel, Paris: Musée d'Orsay. Sérusier's landscape was named *The Talisman* because it was so influential in the development of Symbolism.

borrowings from Egyptian and medieval art. Sérusier's favored subject was Breton women at work. A disciple of Gauguin, who spread his ideas and was a founder member of Nabis. Well-heeled and popular with fellow artists, but was too hung up on theory—needed to loosen up his art.

KEY WORKS *Farmhouse at Le Pouldu*, 1890 (Washington, DC: National Gallery of Art); *Solitude*, 1891 (Rennes: Musée des Beaux-Arts); *Breton Landscape*, 1895 (Boston: Museum of Fine Arts)

Félix **Vallotton**

● 1865–1925   🏳 SWISS

🏛 France   🎨 oils; woodcuts; sculpture   🏛 St. Petersburg: Hermitage Museum   💲 $1,473,577 in 2000, *On the Beach* (oils)

There was a short period when he was at the forefront of new ideas (1890–1901), painting scenes of everyday life in original, simplified form (he disliked straight lines, preferred curves, round tabletops, etc.). Was influenced by Japanese prints and French Symbolists. Produced good, often satirical, prints; otherwise forgettable, traditional, realistic works.

KEY WORKS *Seated Female Nude*, 1897 (Musée de Grenoble); *Interior*, 1903–04 (St. Petersburg: Hermitage Museum); *Woman in a Black Hat*, 1908 (St. Petersburg: Hermitage Museum)

Henri **Rousseau**

● 1844–1910   🏳 FRENCH

🏛 France   🎨 oils; woodcuts; sculpture   🏛 Paris: Musée d'Orsay   💲 $4,023,000 in 1993, *Portrait of Joseph Brummer* (oils)

He was a minor customs official who took up painting on retirement to supplement his pension. He was lionized by the young avant-garde (Picasso et al) because of the childlike vitality of his work.

His work has an unconscious (genuine) naïvety. He painted like a child, but on a bigger scale. He had all the qualities of a child, including the "art is my favorite subject" enthusiasm; wobbly perspective; smiley faces; big signature; obsession with arbitrary detail (every leaf in a tree, or every blade of grass), and a desire to please. He usually worked around a simple idea with a central single object.

He did what most children grow out of, or are taught not to do; he is a reminder that we may flourish best and achieve unexpected recognition if we are what we are and do not constantly strive to be what we are not.

KEY WORKS *Self-Portrait of Rousseau, from L'Ile Saint-Louis*, 1890 (Prague: National Gallery); *Artillerymen*, 1893–95 (New York: Guggenheim Museum); *Child with a Puppet*, c. 1903 (Winterthur, Switzerland: Kunsthalle); *Jaguar Attacking a Horse*, 1909 (Houston: Museum of Fine Arts)

The Rugby Players Henri Rousseau, 1908, 39⅝ x 31⅝ in (100.5 x 80.3 cm), oil on canvas, New York: Guggenheim Museum. In 1908, Picasso organized a banquet with other avant-garde painters in Rousseau's honor.

their uncertain, shadowy world; you sense that he was part of that world, not just an observer.

The economy of the brushstrokes and the simplicity of the materials are as direct and basic as his subjects. He used paint thinned with turpentine that allowed fine, rapid marks, and unprimed cardboard, which he did not try to disguise—exploiting its rawness and color and the way it absorbs diluted oil paint.

KEY WORKS *Woman Doing her Hair*, 1891 (Paris: Musée d'Orsay); *Quadrille at the Moulin Rouge*, 1892 (Washington, DC: National Gallery of Art); *At the Moulin Rouge*, 1892–95 (Art Institute of Chicago); *Rue des Moulins*, 1894 (Washington, DC: National Gallery of Art)

Henri de **Toulouse-Lautrec**

🌐 1864–1901   🏳 FRENCH

🏛 Paris   🖌 oils; prints   🏛 Paris: Musée d'Orsay. Albi: Musée Toulouse-Lautrec

📈 $13.2m in 1990, *Danseuse assise aux bas roses* (works on paper)

Toulouse Lautrec was the epitome of the bohemian artist: the crippled aristocrat who haunted the Parisian cafés and brothels, and commemorated their inhabitants in art of supreme quality.

There is an extraordinary immediacy and tension in his work, resulting from his mastery of his subject matter and technique. The prostitutes and drunks, although sometimes close to caricature, are shown without sentiment or criticism—he loved them and understood them. The brilliant, wiry draftsmanship and thin, nervous paint seem to reflect

Le Divan Japonais Henri de Toulouse-Lautrec, 1892, 30 x 23½ in (76.2 x 59.7 cm), lithograph, Paris: Bibliothèque Nationale. Passionate about lithography, Toulouse-Lautrec created many lithographic posters advertising Montmartre nightlife.

Paul **Cézanne**

◉ 1839–1906 ◪ FRENCH

🏛 Paris; Aix-en-Provence 🎨 oils; watercolors; drawings 🏛 Philadelphia: Barnes Foundation. Paris: Musée d'Orsay 📈 $55m in 1999, *Rideau, cruchon et compotier* (oils)

Cézanne is considered the Mother and Father of modern art. A solitary, pioneering, difficult workaholic. He thought that his life and work were failures.

LIFE AND WORKS

Cézanne's ambitious businessman father from Aix-en-Provence terrified his son, who was saved by his determined artistic sensibility. His father eventually allowed him to go to Paris to study art, giving him a small allowance, and later a fortune. Cézanne never had to sell his work to live—a rare privilege. In 1870, he married Hortense Fiquet and they had one son, Paul.

Cézanne's early efforts were as inept as his social behavior, and he was rejected as "incompetent" by the École des Beaux Arts. His subsequent lifelong struggle to find a coherent way of painting resulted miraculously in work that became a key influence on Modern Art. His first one-man show in 1895 caused huge

Self-Portrait *Paul Cézanne, c. 1873–76, 25⅛ x 20⅞ in (64 x 53 cm), oil on canvas, Paris Musée d'Orsay. Hailed by Picasso as "My one and only master ... father of us all."*

excitement for young artists such as Matisse and Picasso.

His last years were marked by loneliness and poor health. Already suffering with diabetes, he died from pneumonia after being soaked in a downpour while painting outdoors.

STYLE

At the heart of Cézanne's painting was a determination to continue the highly disciplined French Classical tradition epitomized by Poussin, but to do so outdoors and "from nature." In all his works, he combines a remarkable faithfulness to what he observes with a deep awareness of his emotional response. His palette is usually restricted to earthy greens, reds, and blues, and there may be an instinctive underlying gridlike structure, as if to hold the composition together and define the different areas.

Cézanne did not originate new subjects: rather his originality was in his way of seeing and painting. For example, his landscapes often took him weeks or months to complete. The difficulty was that the detail was always changing as the light changed—and even as he moved position. In other words, there never came a moment when he deemed any work to be finished—one of the reasons for his sense of failure, and why he rarely signed his work.

WHAT TO LOOK FOR

His works have multilayered significance: central to Cézanne are the same (traditional) subjects painted over and over again in a constant attempt to record accurately what he sees, to express what he feels, and to produce

Still Life with Basket *Paul Cézanne, 1888–90, 25¾ x 31½ in (65 x 81 cm), oil on canvas, Paris: Musée d'Orsay. Cézanne worked so slowly that the fruit often rotted and he had to substitute plaster replicas.*

Montagne Sainte-Victoire with Trees and a House *Paul Cézanne, 31 x 39 in, (78 x 99 cm), oil on canvas, Moscow: Museum of Modern Art of the West.* Mt. St. Victoire is a well-known landmark near Aix-en-Provence, revisited frequently by Cézanne.

an aesthetically satisfying picture. Not easy, as these goals are constantly changing and are often in conflict; he achieves it in the works of 1885–1901.

The Large Bathers *Paul Cézanne, c. 1900–05, 81¾ x 98 in (208 x 249 cm), oil on canvas, Philadelphia: Museum of Art.* The artist never painted from naked models; instead he assembled his nude compositions from photographs.

Cézanne's paintings have an extraordinary power, as though you were seeing through his own eyes.

Examine the marks that he makes— small, precise, beautiful, each in place for a reason. He only makes marks when he has seen and felt something. He also weaves the marks together to produce a harmony of color and design. Every picture surface trembles with the thrill and anxiety of his intense seeing, feeling, and making.

KEY WORKS *The Artist's Father*, 1866 (Cambridge: Fitzwilliam Museum); *Abduction*, c. 1867 (Washington, DC: National Gallery of Art); *Still Life with Apples and Oranges*, c. 1895–1900 (Paris: Musée d'Orsay); *Le château noir*, 1900–04 (Washington, DC: National Gallery of Art)

Pierre **Bonnard**

● 1867–1947   ⚑ FRENCH

🏛 France   🎨 oils; drawings   💰 $6,232,000 in 2003, *Matinée au Cannet* (oils)

He was one of the great masters of color. If Matisse is the king of color, Bonnard is the queen. Though less intellectual than Matisse, he shared his view that art should be a celebration of life and a source of visual joy.

Painted the places, rooms, and people that he knew most intimately, notably his neurotic, bath-obsessed wife, Marthe. Early work is progressive, later work is deeply personal and stands outside the mainstream. Lovely, free drawings that are masterpieces of observation. The paintings were done in his studio from memory and from black and white notes and sketches—all that glowing color came out of his head.

Stand well back and see how he creates thrilling spaces (rich, textured foregrounds and hazy distances). Walk forward and see how glorious color harmonies take over (blues, violets, greens, with glowing pinks and oranges). When really close, let the detail of flickering brushwork and subtle color weavings fill your eye. His work becomes brighter with age (unusual). **KEY WORKS** *The Letter*, c. 1906 (Washington, DC: National Gallery of Art); *Table Set in a Garden*, c. 1908 (Washington, DC: National Gallery of Art); *Bathing Woman, Seen from the Back*, c. 1919 (London: Tate Collection)

The Almond Tree in Blossom *Pierre Bonnard, 1947, 21⅔ x 14¾ in (55 x 37.5 cm), oil on canvas, Paris: Musée National d'Art Moderne. Bonnard's last painting, which he was still perfecting while on his deathbed.*

Edouard **Vuillard**

● 1868–1940   ⚑ FRENCH

🏛 France   🎨 oils; prints   💰 $7m in 1989, *La table de toilette* (oils)

Vuillard was a shy, highly talented painter and printmaker who was in the forefront of new artistic ideas up to 1900, after which he retreated into his own comfortable, intimate world.

He is best known for his glimpses of middle-class life—mostly cluttered domestic interiors. Had a nervous style, with busy surfaces that flicker with light or allow the image to build up like a mosaic. Was fascinated by repeating patterns, such as woven material or wallpaper. Rich, earthy palette. Warm sense of color.

Pioneered simple design, strong color, and energetic brushwork. An enthusiastic photographer—his works show this, having a snapshotlike quality. **KEY WORKS** *Landscape: Window Overlooking the Woods*, 1899 (Art Institute of Chicago); *Vase of Flowers on a Mantelpiece*, c. 1900 (Washington, DC: National Gallery of Art) *Portrait of Théodore Duret*, 1912 (Washington, DC: National Gallery of Art)

Mother and Child *Edouard Vuillard, 1900, 20¼ x 19¾ in (51.4 x 50.2 cm), oil on board, Private Collection. Vuillard never married, but remained deeply devoted to his widowed mother, who was a dressmaker.*

Sir William **Nicholson**

1872–1949 BRITISH

England oils; prints $246,750 in 2001, Le début de la rue Montagne Sainte-Geneviève (oils)

Nicholson was a highly accomplished painter of landscapes, portraits, and still lifes, with an easy, fluid, intimate style and a wonderful eye for observation, composition, color, and light—and an ability to edit out the superfluous. Successful, and knighted for his achievements. Also made poster and theater designs, and woodblock prints. Ben Nicholson's father.

KEY WORKS *Beerbohm,* 1905 (London: National Portrait Gallery); *The Lowestoft Bowl,* 1911 (London: Tate Collection)

Ferdinand **Hodler**

1858–1918 SWISS

Geneva oils Bern: Kunstmuseum $2,705,727 in 1998, *Lake Silvaplaner* (oils)

A talented painter of monumental figure paintings, portraits, and landscapes.

He painted modern narratives and allegories with a confident drawing style and strong outlines. Powerful, intensified color; his hatched brushstrokes and broken color give optical vibrancy. Untroubled by self-doubt, but sometimes falls into the trap of the pompously overserious statement. Liked silhouetted figures or mountains against a sky.

KEY WORKS *Tired of Life,* 1892 (Munich: Neue Pinakothek); *Silence of the Evening,* c. 1904 (Winterthur, Switzerland: Kunstmuseum)

Lovis **Corinth**

1858–1925 GERMAN

Germany; Paris oils; watercolors; prints Berlin: Staatliche Museum $1,310,400 in 2004, *Walchensee, Morning Fog* (oils)

His work is rarely seen outside Germany. Major figure who tried to reinvent the tradition of the old masters in a modern idiom. Ambitious, gifted, Prussian.

In his traditional style he painted established subjects (portraits, still lifes, mythologies), using an earth palette and influenced by old masters, especially Rembrandt and Hals. In his modern style he painted frank, direct interpretations. Free and expressive paint-handling—he used painting as a personal and emotional release. After a stroke in 1911, his work became increasingly loose, reflecting his physical handicap, awareness of death, isolation (he disliked Modernism), and melancholy at the defeat of the German Empire in 1918.

Impressively versatile, he produced stunning, small, late watercolors and prints, which were easier to handle after his stroke and show thrilling emotional and technical invention. His plein-air landscapes (especially those around his house at Walchensee, Bavaria) hover between Impressionism and Expressionism and were a great commercial success in Berlin. Compositions in late works often lean curiously to the left. He painted a series of self-portraits every year on his birthday (after 1887).

KEY WORKS *Nude Girl,* 1886 (Minnesota: Minneapolis Institute of Arts); *Centaurs Embracing,* 1911 (London: Courtauld Institute of Art); *Samson Blinded,* 1912 (Berlin: Staatliche Museum); *Magdalen with Pearls in her Hair,* 1919 (London: Tate Collection); *Self-Portrait with Straw Hat,* 1923 (Basel, Switzerland: Kunstmuseum)

Carl **Milles**

1875–1955 SWEDISH

Sweden; Europe; US sculpture Lidingö (Sweden): Millesgården $540,567 in 1989, *The Small Water-Nymph* (bronze)

Greatest Swedish sculptor, and one of the most famous sculptors since Rodin (who was a big early influence). Best known for his large-scale fountains, which show his strong grasp of architecture. Widely traveled in Europe; later taught in the US, where he did most of his best work.

Combined eclectic influences from his travels into highly individual style. Fused classical and Nordic cultures to create vigorous, unusual groupings. His figures are full of vitality, while his fountains are conceived as an architectural whole: figures must be viewed against the background of sky and water.

KEY WORKS *Folke Filbyter (Le cavalier de la légende),* 1920s (Lidingö, Sweden: Millesgården); *Fountain,* 1936–40 (St. Louis, Missouri: Market Street); *Orpheus Fountain,* 1930s (Michigan: Cranbrook Art Museum); *Pegasus and Bellerophon,* 1940s (Iowa: Des Moines Art Center)

SECESSION AND ART NOUVEAU late 19th/early 20th century

In the 1890s, several groups of painters in Vienna, Munich, and Berlin sought to break away from the official academies and promote new ideas and styles. They labeled their new groupings *Sezession*, and their avant-garde exhibitions created considerable outrage and scandal. In the end, these groups were splintered by internal politics, leading to further breakaway groupings.

VIENNA SECESSION

Founded by Gustav Klimt, who aimed to put Vienna on the international stage artistically by pursuing new avant-garde ideas, with links to other progressive artists all over Europe. In particular, Klimt wanted to create a union between the fine arts of painting and sculpture and architecture, and the applied arts of design and decoration.

Façade of Secession Building, Vienna
The new home for art, designed and built in just six months in 1898, was a rejection of the traditional architectural styles of the Austro-Hungarian empire.

ART NOUVEAU

French for "new art;" also known as *Jugendstil* or *Sezessionstil* in Austria and Germany and *Stile Liberty* in Italy. Art Nouveau describes a highly decorative style, most often seen in architecture and the applied arts, which was at the forefront of fashion in the 1890s. It aimed to reject historical influences and create one encapsulating style for all the arts. The French-speaking version is organic and free-flowing; the German/Scottish version is geometric.

KEY EVENTS

1892	Rejection of Munch's early work by Berlin Artists' Association. German artists start Munich Secession
1897	Klimt breaks away from the main Austrian academy and patron, Künstlerhaus, and establishes hugely successful exhibition (57,000 visitors) and magazine *Ver Sacrum*
1899	Leading German Impressionist Max Liebermann starts Berlin Secession movement
1900	First of Hector Germain Guimard's Art Nouveau designs for Paris Metro

Sarah Bernhardt *Alphonse Mucha, 1896, color lithograph, Prague: Mucha Trust.* Mucha was a Czech painter and designer who settled in Paris. His work was important in the development of French Art Nouveau.

Gustav **Klimt**

● 1862–1918   ⚑ AUSTRIAN

🏛 Austria   🎨 oils; mixed media; drawings
🏛 Vienna: Österreichische Galerie   💰 $26m
in 2003, *Landhaus am Attersee* (oils)

Klimt was the leading Viennese painter
who broke away from convention to
found the Viennese Secession movement
and develop a highly original, sensitive
style. Some of his most impressive
projects were interior decoration.

The intense, introverted subject matter
reflects Klimt's own personality (he was
an oversexed workaholic), and *fin de siècle*
Vienna (neurotic, idle, adulterous, gossipy,
deeply conservative, but also packed with
original talent and fresh ideas from Freud,
Richard Strauss, Mahler, and so on). It
also expresses his wish to explore modern
sensibility and break free from old, stifling
taboos and restrictions, and his wish to

The Kiss Gustav Klimt, 1907–08, 71 x 71 in (180 x 180 cm),
oil on canvas, Vienna: Österreichische Galerie. The couple
are surrounded by a cloud of gold, intended as a symbolic
expression of the power of love.

demolish the snobby distinction between
the fine artist and the craftsman.

Klimt's brilliant, inventive technique
reflects his training (at the School for
Decorative Arts, where he learned
craft techniques), and his fascination
with Egyptian art (flat and decorative)
and Byzantine art (gold and mosaic).
Notice the sensitive hands, hidden faces,
private symbolism—he worked through
suggestion rather than description
in order to touch the inner feeling
rather than the outward show.

KEY WORKS *Judith*, 1901 (Vienna: Österreichische
Galerie); *Hope II*, 1907–08 (New York:
Museum of Modern Art); *Baby (Cradle)*,
1917–18 (Washington, DC: National
Gallery of Art)

MODERNISM
c. 1900–1970

Young artists and writers in Western Europe welcomed the dawn of the 20th century with excitement and great expectation. They hoped and believed it would usher in a new era fueled by technological advances and democratic ideals that would result in economic and social improvements for the great majority of humankind.

Artists, architects, and ensgineers were to be at the heart of creating this brave new modern world that was to look different from anything seen before. In many ways their dreams were realized. The plethora of new styles and technical innovations that followed in rapid succession radically changed art and the environment, and testified to a freedom of thought and expression that was at times bewildering in its range and diversity.

REACTION

What the idealists failed to predict, however, was the effectiveness of those forces that would seek to destroy, and very nearly extinguish, these new freedoms. They could not foresee the fierceness of the political confrontations or the terrifying destruction of human life and material heritage that would ensue.

THE WORLD WARS

The most terifying manifestations of the political struggle were the two world wars (1914–18 and 1939–45). By 1919, after more than four years of debilitating warfare on the Western Front, Britain and France, the victors of World War I and the world's leading colonial powers, could still assert their dominant position in the world, despite the growing realities of American financial and political muscle. Germany, by contrast, was prostrate, politically and economically in turmoil, Austria-Hungary was destroyed as a single entity, and Russia launched on a communist experiment that would bring misery and death to millions. After 1929, the Western economies, including that of the mighty US,

Young Lady and Her Suite Alexander Calder, 1970, painted steel, height 33 ft (10 m), Detroit, Michigan. One of the dreams of the first generation of Modern artists and architects was the creation of an ideal city.

Frieze showing heroic Soviet workers, Moscow
Soviet art, like Nazi art, was monumental and deeply conservative. Both regimes ruthlessly crushed any form of individual expression.

suffered catastrophic depression. Germany and the Soviet Union, meanwhile, set about establishing totalitarian regimes that were irreconcilably opposed in their political ideologies, but had many features in common.

Soon after Hitler began World War II in 1939, France was forced into ignominious surrender, and Britain into Churchillian defiance. In the end it was the unlikely alliance between American manufacturing might and Soviet manpower that secured a victory over Nazi Germany.

After 1945, Europe had to acknowledge the reality of American dominance within the Western world. Neither Britain nor France had been able to contain the growth of prewar fascism in Europe, or offer a creditable alternative to communism.

REVIVAL
The efforts of France and Britain after the war to hold on to their empires were clearly doomed. Europe entered a period of austerity and introspection. From the late 1940s it was the threat of conflict between the US and the Soviet Union that defined international relations. Further, after 1949, a new factor was added to the balance of world power: the threat of nuclear war and humankind's complete self-destruction.

By 1970 the picture was very different. Whereas Germany in 1945 was a country reduced to rubble and occupied by its former enemies, its Western entity now boasted the largest economy in Europe. Over the

---

TIMELINE: 14TH—15TH CENTURY

1900 Freud's *The Interpretation of Dreams* published, Vienna

1914–18 First World War

1919 Versailles peace settlement shrinks Germany and dissolves Austria-Hungary

1936 Stalinist purges in USSR; Spanish Civil War begins (to 1939)

1933 Hitler elected German chancellor

1900　**1910**　**1920**　**1930**

1907 Picasso's *Les Demoiselles d'Avignon*

1917 Russian Revolution

1929 Wall Street Crash precipitates global slump

same period, almost every European country enjoyed an unprecedented period of economic growth. The roots of this lay in the even more spectacular buoyancy of the US economy in the 1950s and 60s. American financial aid to Western Europe, the Marshall Plan, launched in 1947, kick-started Europe's war-ravaged economies, and thereafter America's dynamism and its tempting vision of a consumer society, drove developments around the world. Even the economies of Soviet-dominated Eastern Europe grew. The European Economic Community which started idealistically in 1957, slipped into strategies for securing comfortable prosperity rather than achieving any great ideal.

INTERLINKING
Against this turbulent background, artistic innovation was, in fact, greatest in those places that had experienced foreign occupation, or where freedom of expression

was most under threat or was a new discovery. At the end of the 19th century this meant France, and Paris became the capital of the avant-garde, a role it retained until 1939. Germany, Russia, and the Netherlands, and to a lesser degree Italy and Spain, made major contributions, but in Britain and the US, where freedom of speech and conscience were taken for granted, Modern Art was of less interest. After 1945, as the US became the standard bearer for the Western democracies, the center of gravity shifted to New York City, but perhaps what is most striking is the degree to which Modern Art and its early development in Europe and the US is interlinked with the fight for democratic freedom.

Chrysler Building, New York
This Art Deco skyscraper, a landmark of 20th-century architecture, was conceived in prosperity but opened during the Great Depression.

Soviet postcard from World War II
Hitler suffers in the Russian winter as he runs from a hail of shells. All countries in the war used art to project their propaganda messages.

СКВЕРНЫЙ РУССКИЙ КЛИМАТ.   Рис. Бор. Ефимова и Н. Долгору..

1939 German invasion of Poland sparks World War II

1941 German invasion of Soviet Union

1947 New York takes over from Paris as the capital of the artistic avant garde

1956 Anti-Soviet uprising in Hungary suppressed

1962 Andy Warhol's *Twenty-five Colored Marilyns*, New York

1969 US succeeds in landing men on the Moon

1940   **1950**   **1960**   **1970**

1938 Hitler annexes Austria and border regions of Czechoslovakia

1945 German surrender ends war in Europe; atomic bomb dropped on Hiroshima; Japanese surrender

1955 Warsaw Pact established

1957 Treaty of Rome: EEC created

1962 Cuban missile crisis

1967 Year of "Flower Power" and growing protests against war in Vietnam

Henri **Matisse**

◔ 1869–1954   🏳 FRENCH

🏠 Paris; Vence (South of France)   🎨 oils;
sculpture; collage; drawings   🏛 Paris: Musée
d'Art Moderne. Pennsylvania: Barnes Foundation
💰 $17m in 2000, *La robe persane* (oils)

The King of Color—he celebrated the
joy of living through color. Major hero
of the Modern Movement and one of
its founders. Professorial and social, but
not convivial, and a bit of a loner.

LIFE AND WORKS

Matisse first studied law in Paris and
worked as a legal clerk before taking
up art studies at the influential Académie
Julian and under Moreau at the Ecole
des Beaux-Arts, where he met several
of the future Fauves. In fact, he came
to art late and almost by chance, when,
aged 21, he was given a box of paints
while recovering from an appendicitis
operation. In the late 1890s, he
experimented with Divisionism and
absorbed a deep knowledge of color
theory. In 1899, he turned to Cézanne.
Although penniless, he bought from art
dealer, Vollard, a small Cézanne *Bathers*
which he kept all his life and used as
inspiration at low or critical moments

Self-Portrait Henri Matisse, 1918, 25¼ x 21¼ in
(65 x 54 cm), oil on canvas, Nice: Musée Matisse. A rare
full painting of the master at work. Matisse usually hides
small images of himself in intimate portraits of others.

of his career. Coming from the gray
cold light of northern Europe, the
discovery of the brightness and warmth
of Mediterranean light, which he first
experienced in Collioure, on the French-
Spanish border in the summer of 1904,

Large Reclining Nude Henri Matisse, 1935, 26 x 36½ in
*(66 x 92.7 cm), oil on canvas, Maryland: Baltimore Museum
of Art.* He reworked this picture 22 times, altering the
background and model's proportions until he was happy.

"I cannot copy nature in a servile way. I must interpret nature and submit it to the spirit of the picture."

HENRI MATISSE

was a revelation. From 1905–07, as the foremost Fauve painter, he was champion of the young avante-garde, and opened a school for young artists. His *Notes of a Painter* (published 1908) is one of the most important statements of the principles of modern art. At this period he also visited Morocco and came under the influence of Islamic and Persian art, both of which emphasize pattern and bold but subtle color. In the 1920s, Matisse settled semi-permanently in Nice, and his art continued to flourish with ever-increasing richness, and fascination with light and color, even when a bedridden invalid, with very few false turnings. In many ways, his later years are among his most fertile and inventive, as he experimented with paper cutouts and collages, the illustrations for *Jazz* and *La Cirque*, plus the stained glass windows and vestments for the Chapel of the Rosary at Vence, near Nice.

SUBJECTS AND STYLE

Look for his life-enhancing, joyous combination of subject matter (notably the open window, still life, and female nude), and his glorious color which takes on a life of its own and is free to do its own thing, without necessarily imitating nature. Explored color independently from subject matter and turned it into something you want to touch and feel. As a result, he loved exploring the exotic, especially oriental fabrics and ceramics with their strong decorative feel and heightened colors. This is brilliantly explored through his superb *Odalisque* nudes of 1920–25. His late gouaches on paper cutouts enabled him to carve into color. Also a brilliant and innovative printmaker (1952 being the year of his printed blue nudes, now still gracing the walls of many students as posters) and sculptor, sculpture often being an explorative extension of his painting.

WHAT TO LOOK FOR

His work explores the full range of what color can do, by crowding, juxtaposing, intensifying, relaxing, purifying, heating,

cooling. Look for white spaces around bright colors, allowing them to "breathe" and reach their full visual potential. The open brushwork is deliberate, to give movement and life to the color and to register Matisse's own presence and activity. Matisse said he "dreamt of an art of balance and purity and serenity, devoid of troubling or depressing subject matter … a mental soother … like a good

Luxe, calme, et volupté (Luxury, Serenity, and Pleasure) *Henri Matisse, 1904, 38¾ x 46½ in (98 x 118 cm), oil on canvas, Paris: Musée d'Orsay. His hallmark piece when first exhibited, reminiscent of Cézanne's* Bathers.

armchair." It was this apparent lack of aggression or need for controversy that puzzled Picasso. If in their earlier years they had competed for leadership of the avant-garde, in later life they kept a respectful distance, each aware of the other's innovations, even influenced by them, yet never in competition. To the end, Matisse's principal concern was always with color, and the way it could be used to create form, emotion, and sensation. In his own words, "I am unable to distinguish between the feeling I have for life and my way of expressing it."

KEY WORKS *The Joy of Living*, 1905–06 (Pennsylvania: Barnes Foundation); *Statuette and Vases on an Oriental Carpet*, 1908 (Moscow: Pushkin Museum); *The Black I–IV*, 1909– c. 1929 (London: Tate Collection); *Reclining Nude, Back*, 1927 (Private Collection); *The Snail*, 1953 (London: Tate Collection)

LES FAUVES

The name was given to the movement at the 1905 Salon d'Automne exhibition held in Paris. Art critic of the review *Gil Blas*, Louis Vauxcelles, insultingly labeled the brightly colored style of the paintings as the work of wild beasts (*fauves*). But the group, loosely formed around liaisons between the artists about the turn of the century, loved the term.

Matisse and Derain studied together in 1898 and Vlaminck, a friend of Derain, was introduced two years later. They were heavily influenced by Van Gogh and Cézanne, as well as the Pointillism of Seurat. Color harmony is a central theme, although the dotted style eventually gave way, in the main, to wide choppy brushstrokes of stunning pure color, freely applied in flat patterns. It embodied Derain's ideal of "color for color's sake." Now an object could generate its own brightness. The chief group members were Matisse, Dufy, Derain, Vlaminck, and Braque. One of the principal places of inspiration was Collioure in the South of France. By 1907, most of the artists had moved on to explore new personal ideals.

Charing Cross Bridge *André Derain, 1906, 32 x 39½ in (81.2 x 100.3 cm), oil on canvas, Washington, DC: National Gallery of Art.* Derain was influenced by Monet's paintings of the Thames River.

Maurice de **Vlaminck**
1876–1958   FRENCH

France   oils; drawings   St. Petersburg: Hermitage Museum $10,721,805 in 1990, *Les pêcheurs à Nanterre* (oils)

He was both a volatile and boastful character who made a brief splash as one of the avant-garde Fauve artists in France c. 1905–06. As a youth, he earned an income from his winnings as a racing cyclist, and from performing as an orchestral violinist. Painting was very much a secondary vocation at this time. He also wrote novels and memoirs.

His early landscapes are full of color, thickly and freely painted, and with strong simplified designs. They express the mood of adventure and experimentation that captured the imagination of progressive young French artists at the time. His later landscapes degenerated into a boring formula; superficially they look modern, but they are not.

Separate the subject matter (which is actually not very innovative) from the way it is painted (which is), and maybe question the reason for this balance between the old and new. He used a not very subtle palette of four colors—red, blue, yellow, and green—but wove them together to create a strong visual "fizz."

KEY WORKS *The Blue House*, 1906 (Minnesota: Minneapolis Institute of Arts); *Tugboat on the Seine, Chatou*, 1906 (Washington, DC: National Gallery of Art); *View of the Seine*, c. 1906 (St. Petersburg: Hermitage Museum); *Still Life*, c. 1910 (Paris: Musée d'Orsay); *The River*, c. 1910 (Washington, DC: National Gallery of Art)

Tugboat at Chatou *Maurice de Vlaminck, 1906, 19 x 25 in (50 x 65 cm), oil on canvas, Private Collection.* Vlaminck and André Derain were named the "Chatou Couple" after the Paris suburb where they painted together.

Albert **Marquet**

⬤ 1875–1947   🇫🇷 FRENCH

🏛 France   🎨 oils; watercolors; drawings
🏛 Paris: Musée National d'Art Moderne
📈 $1,309,549 in 1989, *Le carnaval à Fécamp* (oils)

Marquet was a disciple of Matisse, who developed an appealing and poetic style: strong, simple design; clear, harmonious color; the elimination of unnecessary detail (Matisse compared him favorably with the Japanese artist Hokusai). He produced small-scale works in oil and watercolor. The scenes of Paris, around the Seine, and French ports are the most effective and popular.
KEY WORKS *André Rouveyre*, 1904 (Paris: Musée d'Orsay); *Le Pont-Neuf*, 1906 (Washington, DC: National Gallery of Art); *Winter on the Seine*, c. 1910 (Oslo: National Gallery)

André **Derain**

⬤ 1880–1954   🇫🇷 FRENCH

🏛 Paris; London   🎨 oils; sculpture; drawings
🏛 St. Petersburg: Hermitage Museum   📈 $8.79m in 1989, *Bateaux dans le port, Collioure* (oils)

He is best remembered as Matisse's main partner in creating Fauvist paintings in the South of France, in the early 20th

The Seine at Paris Albert Marquet, c. 1907, 25¾ x 31⅞ in (65 x 81 cm), oil on canvas, Private Collection. Fauvist Marquet is well known for his panoramic views of the Seine and various French ports, featuring docks, cranes, tugs, and ships at anchor.

century. He was one of the first artists to take an interest in African sculpture.

Derain's early works were extremely influential in the development of the use of color in Modern art. Stayed (mostly) with traditional landscape themes, with an important series of views of London (Thames River) painted in 1906. Then he unwisely abandoned color and concentrated on form. His later work is mediocre and currently overrated.

Early work is notable for attractive paint handling, open brushwork, and strong, confident compositions. He makes subtle use of color, exploiting color harmonies as well as color contrasts, and placing half-tones and full tones together. Intensifies local colors, but never gets away from them (unlike Matisse). Thus skies are always blue, leaves green (Matisse skies can be yellow, green … anything).
KEY WORKS *Portrait of Matisse*, 1905 (London: Tate Collection); *Charing Cross Bridge* (see opposite); *The Pool of London*, 1906 (London: Tate Collection); *Southern France*, 1927 (Private Collection)

Les Demoiselles d'Avignon

Pablo Picasso 1907

This celebrated painting is now hailed as one of the most momentous paintings in the history of art. Yet, the often forgotten reality is that for 30 years, it was known only to a handful of Picasso's friends and was hardly ever seen in public until purchased by MoMA in New York in 1938.

The painting explores, although never fully resolves, a plethora of new ideas. Its significance is that through it, Picasso decisively broke with his own past, with all the traditions of Western art, established himself as the undisputed leader of the avant-garde, and immediately launched into a period of astonishing and profoundly influential creativity. He had been planning a large figure piece, and had experimented with a brothel scene, from which this work evolved. The title (not chosen by Picasso, and he disliked it), refers to a notorious brothel in Barcelona.

In 1907, Picasso was working in Montmartre, Paris, in a cramped and cluttered space with two dark rooms in an artistic colony known as the Bateau Lavoir, which was a building like a rabbit warren. This large canvas would have filled one entire wall of his studio.

Picasso would later turn this type of still-life imagery into small brightly painted sculptures

Picasso believed that art and the human figure could have a redemptive or "exorcizing" power. Here the target is prostitution and sexual disease

This is the first indication from Picasso of an interest in still life. It would become a regular feature in his early Cubist paintings and throughout his life. It is also a theme that links him to Cézanne and Spanish art. Picasso always wanted to be seen as a reinventor of tradition rather than an iconoclast.

Les Demoiselles d'Avignon

Medium oil on canvas
Dimensions 96 x 92 in (244 x 233 cm)
Location New York: Museum of Modern Art

TECHNIQUES

After seeing Cézanne's work in
the autumn of 1906, Picasso began
to experiment spatially with flat,
splintered planes and patterns of
light and dark rather than rounded
volumes to create a sense of, rather
than an illusion of, space and form.

The faces of these
figures were repainted
after Picasso had a
"revelation" about
African sculpture at the
Ethnographic Museum
in Paris in 1907

Early Iberian sculpture influenced the
faces of the figures. In March 1907, Picasso
acquired two such pieces that had been
stolen from the Musée du Louvre

This figure begins to explore what
would become a hallmark of Cubism:
the combination of different viewpoints
and profiles in a single figure

CUBISM   1907–1918

Cubism was the most significant art and design innovation of the 20th century, similar in effect and consequence to the invention of the internal combustion engine, manned flight, and wireless communications—all of them developed at about the same time. The principles of Cubism were worked out in 1907–1914.

PICASSO AND BRAQUE

The movement's inventors were Picasso and Braque. Their early Cubist works were all small scale, with conventional subjects such as still life, landscape, and the human figure. The great innovation was use of fragmented and chopped-up forms, creating an effect like a puzzle that has been put together with the pieces wrongly joined. The works of 1910–11 are given the

label "Analytical Cubism," and used monochromatic paint on canvas. In the works after 1912, they stuck on the contents of wastepaper baskets in addition—this development is known as "Synthetic Cubism."

Woman with a Guitar (Ma Jolie)
Pablo Picasso, 1911, 39⅓ x 25¾ in (100 x 65 cm), oil on canvas, New York: Museum of Modern Art. The woman in the title is Picasso's mistress Eva Gouel (also known as Marcelle Humbert).

PRINCIPLES

Cubism rewrote the rules and expectations as to how paintings and sculpture could be made. Paintings were no longer like a window, but a forum where almost anything might happen.

Sculpture was to be open and transparent rather than a solid object. Any sort of material, however humble or everyday, could be used to make art. In the eyes of the Cubists, art was to be about cumulative experience rather than mere observation.

KEY EVENTS

1907	Picasso's *Les Desmoiselles d'Avignon* (see pages 348–349) introduces the principle of collapsing form and figure distortion
1909	Braque and Picasso work closely as a team to create first "Analytical Cubist" works
1911	Picasso's *The Guitar* first sculpture made by constructing parts rather than reducing
1913	Birth of collage and *papier collés* as "Synthetic Cubism" evolves
1918	Cubism's effects influence Italian and Russian Futurist/Orphic movements

Portrait of Pablo Picasso *Juan Gris, 1912, 36¾ x 29¼ in (93 x 74 cm), oil on canvas, Art Institute of Chicago. Gris wanted to acknowledge Picasso as the father of the historic new artistic era.*

Georges **Braque**

● 1882–1963 ◪ FRENCH

🇵 Paris ◪ oils; mixed media
⚡ $8.64m in 1986, *Femme
lisant* (oils)

Braque was one of the most
innovative and majestic
painters of the 20th century.
He built on the example
of Cézanne and the 18th
century to lift decorative
painting (especially still
life) to new heights.

   He was one of the key
early leaders of the avant-
garde. Produced important
Fauve paintings, and then
invented Cubism with
Picasso. Later work concentrates on still
life, the human figure, and studio interiors.
Be totally at ease to enjoy the way he
develops the language of Cubism, and
his instinct for color, texture, and paint.
This is work that delights the eye, in the
way romantic music delights the ear, and
touches the heart rather than the intellect.

   Cubist innovations included the use
of letters, *papiers collés*, sand mixed with
paint, and trompe-l'oeil wood graining.
Braque used rich, earthy colors and
images built up layer by layer. His works
show a wonderful sense of controlled
freedom as he moves images and details
around to create lyrical harmonies of
color, line, and shape (he loved music and
you can sense it going through his head
as he paints). Late work famous for the
bird image as a simple symbol of human
spiritual aspiration.

KEY WORKS *Landscape near Antwerp*, 1906
(New York: Guggenheim Museum); *Café-Bar*,
1919 (Basel, Switzerland: Kunstmuseum);
Le Guéridon, 1921–22 (New York: Metropolitan
Museum of Art); *Still Life: Le Jour*, 1929
(Washington, DC: National Gallery of Art)

*Studio V Georges Braque, 1949, 57 x 68¾ in (145 x 175 cm),
oil on canvas, Private Collection.* The artist rarely left the
intimate world of his studio for subject matter, transforming
everyday objects, such as guitars, tabletops, and fruit bowls
into masterpieces of color and form.

Juan **Gris**

● 1887–1927 ◪ SPANISH

🇵 Paris ◪ oils; sculpture; collage
🏛 London: Tate Collection ⚡ $7.7m
in 2002, *Pot de géranium* (oils)

He was third in the hierarchy of the
inventors of Cubism (after Picasso and
Braque), concentrating mainly on still life.

Gris moved to Paris from Spain in 1906,
and in his formative years he drew witty
pieces for various publications. It wasn't
until 1910 that he turned to painting as
a serious vocation.

   He had a masterly reinterpretation of
the traditional still life. Stand back and
see how his meticulously crafted, stylish,
highly decorative pictures look like
expensive jewelry; they are often (and
very effectively) shown in elaborate
frames like mounts for brooches. Stand
close to them and play the Cubist game
of piecing together the final image from
the fragmented images and clues.

   He often used a dark palette to great
effect, especially blacks and blues. His
works have complex geometric designs
and grids, with the images slipping in and
out of the different planes. Playful use of
lettering and speckled patterns. His
brilliant and inventive *papier collés* get
better as they get older, browner, and
more antique. Somehow reminiscent of
French 18th-century marquetry furniture
and its fine craftsmanship?

KEY WORKS *Violin and Playing Cards*, 1913
(New York: Metropolitan Museum of Art);
Bottle of Rum and Newspaper, 1914 (New York:
Guggenheim Museum); *Fantômas*, 1915
(Washington, DC: National Gallery of Art);
Still Life, 1917 (Minnesota: Minneapolis
Institute of Arts)

believed art should touch and transform all corners of everyday life. Portrayed hands as pieces of machinery. His early Cubist work was pioneering.

KEY WORKS *The Smokers*, 1911–12 (New York: Guggenheim Museum); *The Wedding*, 1912 (Paris: Musée National d'Art Moderne); *The Mechanic*, 1920 (Ottawa: National Gallery of Canada); *The Two Sisters*, 1935 (Berlin: Staatliche Museum)

Julio **González**

● 1876–1942 🏴 SPANISH

🏴 Spain; France 🎨 sculpture; drawings; oils 🏛 Amsterdam: Stedelijk Museum. Paris: Musée National d'Art Moderne 📈 $3.1m in 2002, *Homme gothique* (sculpture)

He was one of the first artists to use iron as a sculptural medium. Taught by his goldsmith/sculptor father how to use metals, but spent his early years mainly as a painter.

After meeting Picasso in Barcelona, González moved to Paris where he was reacquainted with his fellow countryman and they struck up a lifelong friendship. Making jewelry and metalwork occupied González up until the 1920s, but at the age of 50, he made a total commitment to sculpture, concentrating specifically on welded metal as a material. Look for semi-abstract works on a grand scale, incorporating Picasso's brutal humor.

KEY WORKS *Woman with Hair in a Bun*, 1929–34 (Art Institute of Chicago); *Head Called "The Rabbit,"* 1930 (Madrid: Reina Sofia National Museum); *Daphné*, 1937 (Madrid: Reina Sofia National Museum)

Fernand **Léger**

● 1881–1955 🏴 FRENCH

🏴 France; US 🎨 oils 🏛 Philadelphia: Museum of Art. New York: Guggenheim Museum. London: Tate Collection 📈 $20m in 2003, *La femme en rouge et vert* (oils)

Léger was one of the giants of the Modern Movement and an ardent believer in the moral and social function of art and architecture. Refreshingly cheerful and extrovert.

His ambition was to create a new democratic art for and about ordinary people. He achieved it through strong, straightforward imagery, style, and technique: the modern, blue-collar worker and his family at work and play, plus the machine-made objects of their world. Shows muscular happiness and spiritual joy in an ideal world where work and play become one (if it can be so for children, why can it not be so for adults?).

He was simple but not simplistic. He had a modern, moral message, which was romantic and idealistic but also challenging (a fresh restatement of "man the measure of all things"). He produced simple images and designs that contain sophisticated spatial and color relationships. Also made beautiful and strong drawings, stage sets, tapestries, murals, films, books, and posters—he

Jacques **Lipchitz**

● 1891–1973 🏴 FRENCH

🏴 France; US 🎨 sculpture 🏛 New York: Museum of Modern Art 📈 $1.4m in 1989, *Figure* (sculpture)

A talented sculptor of Lithuanian origin, Lipchitz settled in Paris in 1909 and emigrated to the US in 1941. He was an early, sensitive, and personal interpreter of Cubism in traditional materials (plaster, stone, terracotta, and bronze) in the 1920s. This led to a more figurative, arabesque style; then to a flirtation with Surrealism and, finally, complex Symbolism. He was always original, if sober and monumental.

KEY WORKS *Man with a Guitar*, 1916 (New York: Museum of Modern Art); *Seated Figure*, 1917 (Ottawa: National Gallery of Canada); *Mother and Child*, 1949 (Alabama: Birmingham Museum of Art)

Frank **Kupka**

◔ 1871–1957 ⚑ FRENCH/CZECH

🏛 France 🖌 oils; drawings 🏛 Prague: National Gallery 💰 $1,029,657 in 1990, *Contrastes gothiques* (oils)

Kupka was a natural anarchist who settled in Paris at the age of 24 and stayed forever. He was one of the first to create a true abstract art, characterized by solid, geometric blocks of color. He had the potential to develop as a great pioneer of abstraction, but lacked an underlying philosophical drive and the single-minded dedication to fulfil it—he was distracted by too many ideas.

KEY WORKS *Planes by Colors, Large Nude*, 1909–10 (New York: Guggenheim Museum);

Vertical and Diagonal Planes, c. 1913–14 (New York: Metropolitan Museum of Art); *The Colored One*, c. 1919–20 (New York: Guggenheim Museum)

Raoul **Dufy**

◔ 1877–1953 ⚑ FRENCH

🏛 France 🖌 oils; watercolors; drawings 🏛 Paris: Musée d'Art Moderne de la Ville de Paris 💰 $2.8m in 2004, *Fête à Sainte-Adresse* (oils)

He was a talented painter who in the early days might have made the big time with Braque and Matisse—but who lacked their grit. Best known for accomplished, colorful, decorative works, much admired by fashionable *beau monde* of 1920s and 30s. Free, linear drawing; clear, floating colors; easy subjects such as horse racing and yachting. Prints and tapestry designs.

KEY WORKS *Portrait of Suzanne Dufy, the Artist's Sister*, 1904 (St. Petersburg: Hermitage Museum); *The Baou de Saint-Jeannet*, 1923 (London: Tate Collection)

The Regatta at Cowes *Raoul Dufy, 1934, 32¼ x 39 in (82 x 100 cm), watercolor on paper, Private Collection.* Dufy was not interested in art theories or questioning the meaning of life. His vivacious art, which included book and stage design, was much praised in the 1930s–1950s.

Maurice **Utrillo**
- 1883–1955   FRENCH
- Paris   oils   London: Christie's Images $1,296,612 in 1990, *Le café de la Tourelle à Montmartre* (oils)

He was a popular painter known for not very challenging, crustily painted views of Montmartre, characterized by sharp perspectives and deserted streets. His best work was c. 1908–16. Later work is less gloomy and contains small figures. Had a personal history of mental instability.
KEY WORKS *Saint-Denis Canal*, 1906–08 (Tokyo: Bridgestone Museum of Art); *Marizy-Sainte-Geneviève*, c. 1910 (Washington, DC: National Gallery of Art)

Georges **Rouault**
- 1871–1958   FRENCH
- France   oils; drawings   St. Petersburg: Hermitage Museum $1.6m in 1990, *Fille de cirque* (oils)

Rouault was an important French painter with a highly individual style. An unhappy loner who deliberately stood outside the mainstream of Modern art.

He chose losers and the exploited as his subjects, expressing through them his bleak view of life and the activities and rituals used by human beings as they prey on each other in a struggle for survival. He was one of the very few committed Christian artists of the 20th century.

His dark palette reflected his gloomy subjects. Uses faces to convey expression. The black outlines and his choice of colors give a deliberate appearance of stained glass to his paintings—there is an iconlike quality in his figures.
KEY WORKS *Les Filles*, 1904 (St. Petersburg: Hermitage Museum); *Nude with Raised Arm*, 1906 (St. Petersburg: Hermitage Museum); *Christ in the Outskirts*, 1920 (Tokyo: Bridgestone Museum of Art)

Kees van **Dongen**
- 1877–1968   FRENCH
- Paris   oils   Moscow: Pushkin Museum $5.3m in 2004, *Femme fatale* (oils)

He was Dutch-born but considered an honorary Frenchman (settled in Paris 1897). Best remembered for the work he produced from 1905 to 1913: they are genuinely original, boldly painted works, in saturated, vibrant colors, which made him one of the leading Fauve painters and placed him almost on a par with Matisse. His later work is lively, but repetitive and unimaginative.
KEY WORKS *The Red Dancer*, 1907 (St. Petersburg: Hermitage Museum); *Woman in a Black Hat*, 1908 (St. Petersburg: Hermitage Museum)

Robert **Delaunay**
- 1885–1941   FRENCH
- France; Spain; Portugal   oils   New York: Guggenheim Museum $4.7m in 1991, *Premier disque* (oils)

Delaunay was one of the pioneers of modern art. Sought new types of subject matter and made an early breakthrough to abstract painting. Much supported by Russian-born wife, Sonia, who produced equally talented art in a similar style, and was also a theater and textiles designer.

His early work takes modern themes such as cities, the Eiffel Tower, manned flight, and soccer. Delaunay used color in a free and highly inventive way, most famously in his discs, which are abstract, lyrical, full of light and pleasure, and intended to celebrate the emotional and joyful impact of pure color.
KEY WORKS *Red Eiffel Tower*, 1911 (New York: Guggenheim Museum); *Simultaneous Open Windows*, 1912 (London: Tate Collection); *Homage to Blériot*, 1914 (Basel, Switzerland: Kunstmuseum)

Marc **Chagall**
- 1887–1985   RUSSIAN/FRENCH
- France; Russia   oils   Nice: Musée Marc Chagall $13.5m in 1990, *Anniversaire* (oils)

He was a Russian-born Hasidic Jew whose inspiration was his early cultural roots.

His unique and personal marriage of subjects, themes, and quirky, personal style perpetuate an enduring air of childlike innocence and wonder. He was very prolific—paintings, prints, ceramics, stained glass, murals—which inevitably leads to uneven quality. Best paintings generally early and pre-1950; worst work is sugary, sentimental, and slight (but has never lost its popularity). Chagall concentrated on major stained-glass projects after 1950. Do the odd floating heads and bodies and his combination of simultaneous events in one picture reflect his own strange, peripatetic life and consequent cultural eclecticism?

KEY WORKS *The Fiddler*, 1912–13 (Washington, DC: National Gallery of Art); *Paris through the Window*, 1913 (New York: Guggenheim Museum); *The Rooster*, 1929 (Madrid: Museo Thyssen-Bornemisza); *War, 1917*, 1964–66 (Zurich: Kunsthaus)

The Juggler *Marc Chagall, 1943, 52 x 39⅓ in (132 x 100 cm), oil on canvas, Private Collection.* Chagall settled in France in 1914. His art combines Russian folk art, Cubist fragmentation, and Expressionist color.

Bird in Space

Constantin Brancusi 1923

A wonderful simplification of form
and deeply sacred approach to
his work made Brancusi highly
influential in the development
not only of 20th-century sculpture
but of abstract art generally.

Often seen as the pinnacle of Brancusi's
work, this gleaming, highly polished
bronze stands five feet tall, simply but
gracefully capturing the gentle elegance
of a bird in flight. Some see it as a bird
lifting into the air, others as a gigantic
golden feather denoting the whole motion
of flight. Its Minimalist poise and
haunting presence creates a meditative
stillness. Brancusi, a Romanian who
settled in Paris, always sought to achieve
a mystic symbolism in his work, fascinated
by universal symbols of life and fertility.
He made 28 versions of this piece.

**Nothing symmetrical or
geometrical** means this
graceful turning bronze
captures an innate sense
of flightlike motion

**The light beautifully
catches** the yellow bronze
as the sculpture starts to
widen out and commence
its gentle turn

> "Simplicity is not
> an end in art but
> we arrive at
> simplicity in spite
> of ourselves."
>
> CONSTANTIN BRANCUSI

Bird in Space

Medium bronze
Height 56¾ in (144 cm)
Location New York: Metropolitan
Museum of Art

The stone base is a
wonderful contrast in
texture and color to the
lightness of the metal

Constantin **Brancusi**

● 1876–1957   ⚑ ROMANIAN/FRENCH

🏛 Paris   🔨 sculpture   🏛 Paris: Musée National
d'Art Moderne (with a recreation of his studio)
📈 $16.5m in 2002, *Danaïde* (sculpture)

Brancusi was a seminal figure in 20th-
century art, with a profound influence
on sculpture and design. Born into a
Romanian peasant family, settled in Paris
in 1904. Student of Rodin. Remained
indifferent to honor and fame.

His work shows tireless refinement
and search for purity. Constant reworking
of selected themes—children, human
heads, birds, modular columns. Interested
in abstract ideals such as the purity
of primordial (simple) forms, but was
never an abstract artist—a reference to
a recognizable nature is always present.

Emphasis on the inherent qualities
of materials. Touches something very
basic in the human psyche. As soothing
as the sound of the waves of the sea.

Endless pleasure can be derived from
the contemplation of pure line, simplicity
of form (such as an egg shape), light
reflecting off surfaces, materials unadorned
and unadulterated. Notice the bases that
are an integral part of the whole work.
His studio became a work of art in its
own right because of the way he grouped
his work in it to bring out comparisons
and reflections of light.

KEY WORKS *The Kiss*, 1909 (Paris: Montparnasse
Cemetery); *Princess X*, 1916 (Paris: Musée
National d'Art Moderne); *Mademoiselle Pogani*,
1920 (Paris: Musée National d'Art Moderne);
Maquettes for the Endless Column, 1937 (Paris:
Musée National d'Art Moderne)

From 1900 to 1950 Paris was the center of artistic innovation and attracted artists, collectors, dealers, and connoisseurs from all over the world. All the major innovations from Cubism to Surrealism originated in Parisian studios, and could be first seen there in avant-garde exhibitions. This diversity of styles, artists, and activity has been labeled loosely as "Ecole de Paris" (School of Paris).

Chaïm Soutine

◉ 1894–1943   ⚑ FRENCH

🏛 France   🎨 oils   🏛 Pennsylvania: Barnes Foundation   💰 $8,460,001 in 2005, *Le pâtissier de Cagnes* (oils)

He was a Lithuanian-born Jew who worked in Paris. Undisciplined, tragic, and depressive. Unknown in his own lifetime although was recognized and supported by a few dedicated collectors.

Look for portraits, landscapes, and flayed carcasses. He had a wide emotional range—from angelic choirboys to dead meat. At a distance, the paintings look controlled and neat, but close up, the churning distortions and paint handling become dominant.

He had acute color sense and produced lovely harmonies of color. His work shows uncontrolled distortion, but this is not arbitrary. Cracked painting surfaces show the speed with which he worked, painting over layers not yet dry. Many influences, such as Cézanne and El Greco.

KEY WORKS *Self-Portrait*, 1916 (St. Petersburg: Hermitage Museum); *Landscape at Ceret*, c. 1920 (London: Tate Collection); *Side of Beef*, 1925 (Buffalo: Albright-Knox Art Gallery)

Amedeo Modigliani

◉ 1884–1920   ⚑ ITALIAN

🏛 France   🎨 oils; sculpture   🏛 Milan: Mattioli Collection   💰 $28m in 2004, *Jeanne Hébuterne devant une porte* (oils)

He was a neurotic, spoiled, tubercular, drug-addicted, woman-beating, poverty-stricken but talented pioneer who achieved a genuine and satisfactory synthesis between the priorities of the old masters and those of modern art.

Modigliani created very recognizable portraits and splashy nudes, both highly stylized, simplified, painterly, poetic, decorative, and moody. Notice the inclined heads with long faces on long necks; elongated noses; almond-shaped eyes with a glazed and far-away stare, which show the influence of his original, gifted, carved stone sculptures and his study of African and Oceanic art. Good sculptures. Sensitive drawings.

He had many influences: African art; Art Nouveau; Matisse-like simplification; Cézanne- and Cubist-like fragmentation of space around the figures; Picasso-like intensity and confident, fluent line. Would he have gone on to greater things or was he burned out? His early death probably saved his reputation.

KEY WORKS *Head*, c. 1911–12 (London: Tate Collection); *Paul Guillaume*, 1916 (Milan: Galleria d'Arte Moderna); *Chaïm Soutine*, 1917 (Washington, DC: National Gallery of Art); *Nude on a Blue Cushion*, 1917 (Washington, DC: National Gallery of Art)

Jeanne Hébuterne in a Yellow Sweater *Amedeo Modigliani, 1918–19, 39½ x 25¾ in (100 x 65 cm), oil on canvas, New York: Guggenheim Museum.* She was the artist's common-law wife and frequent subject.

EXPRESSIONISM AND ABSTRACTION

Expressionism and Abstraction were key early trends in the development of Modern Art, and their influence continues in full force to the present day with many different individual styles. Early practitioners wanted art to become more like music, conveying emotion and meaning by suggestion, heightened sensation, and free association, rather than by description of forms and appearances.

EXPRESSIONISM

Any style that conveys heightened sensibility through distortion of e.g. color, drawing, space, scale, form, and/or intense subject matter, or a combination of these. Expressionism was a particularly strong tendency in German art as a way of facing up to the spiritual and social crises that arose at the time of World War I.

Storm Tide in Hamburg Oskar Kokoschka, 1962, 35¾ x 46½ in (90 x 118 cm), oil on canvas, Hamburg: Kunsthalle. Painted in the year of his Tate Gallery retrospective.

ABSTRACTION

A true example of abstract art has intellectual or emotional meaning (or both), but does not represent or imitate any visible object or figure. Good abstract art is not easy to get to grips with, but it will reward the effort involved. You may need to see a large number of works together as well (for example, in an exhibition devoted to the artist) in order for you to begin to see fully and understand what the artist is trying to put over. One piece in a mixed show is often—frankly—meaningless, because all that you can hope to notice are the eye-catching or superficial qualities of the work.

KEY EVENTS

1910	Kandinsky paints his first abstracts
1911	Kandinsky writes the abstract artists' chief treatise *On the Spiritual in Art* and establishes Blaue Reiter group
1914	Outbreak of World War I. Several artists are killed in action, including Franz Marc and August Macke
1919	Weimar Republic takes control in Germany. Period of cultural and artistic diversity. Egon Schiele dies in influenza pandemic
1934	Expressionism condemned as "degenerate art" by Nazi party

Faultier Franz Marc, 1912, 5⅔ x 8⅔ in (14.3 x 21.4 cm), woodcut, Hamburg: Kunsthalle. In 1911, Marc embarked on a series of paintings of animals; these have since become the cornerstone of his reputation.

early 20th century

WHAT TO LOOK FOR

Starting out as a figurative painter, Wassily Kandinsky was among the first to create a truly abstract art in which color and form take on an expressive life of their own. Painted at the height of his creative powers, this work encapsulates his theories about the emotional properties of shape, line, and color. It was painted after he settled in Germany for the second time in 1922. He left his academic posts in Russia, disillusioned with the outcome of the Revolution.

Red was described as giving "the impression of a strong drum beat," whereas green was "the attenuated sounds of a violin"

For Kandinsky, horizontal lines were "cold and flat," verticals "warm, strong, and yellow," right angles "cold, controlled, and red"

Black Frame *Wassily Kandinsky, 1922, oil on canvas, Paris: Musée National d'Art Moderne.* Painted just after Kandinsky began teaching at the Bauhaus.

The artist contrasts curved lines, which are "mature," with angular lines, which are "youthful"

A painting such as this should not be analyzed intellectually but allowed to reach those parts of the brain that connect with music

According to Kandinsky's theories, yellow possesses a capacity to "attain heights unbearable to the eye and the spirit"

Kandinsky was interested in the connections between art and music. He could literally "hear" colors, a quality that is known as synaesthesia.

TECHNIQUES

Works such as this were planned and executed with the utmost care and precision by Kandinsky. Colors, angles, and the places where lines touched and planes overlapped had to be absolutely exact.

Egon **Schiele**

◗ 1890–1918   🇩🇪 GERMAN

📕 Vienna   🎨 oils; watercolors; drawings
🏛 Washington, DC: National Gallery of Art
💹 $18,871,000 in 2003, *Krumau Landscape, Town and River* (oils)

An intense, tragic, short-lived genius whose art expressed his own self-destructive personality and the claustrophobic introspection of Sigmund Freud's Vienna. He died, together with his pregnant young wife, in the great flu epidemic.

His art concentrates on sexually intense subjects, including portraits, self-portraits, and (at end of his life) religious works. Look for isolated, single figures, often shown in silhouette; couples or groups of figures in highly charged relationships; bodies in contorted positions; gaunt faces lost in inner thoughts; cityscapes in Art Nouveau style. A precocious, gifted draftsman, he also made many drawings and watercolors. His paintings have a tense, nervous, probing outline, rapidly filled with color, which gives them a strong sense of immediacy and urgency.

Self-Portrait Nude *Egon Schiele, 1910, 43 x 14½ in (110 x 35.5 cm), oil on canvas, Vienna: Graphische Sammlung Albertina.* Schiele often isolates his figures against a plain background—like specimens on a dissecting table.

His work can still extract a genuine gasp, if not the shock or horror of 100 years ago. It attracted fierce opposition from conservative society, and Schiele was arrested and imprisoned on the charge of depraving children. He was, however, recognized and successful in advanced circles. He saw the human figure or spirit as animal rather than moral. Insisted on absolute freedom for creative individuality and self-determination.

KEY WORKS *Mourning Woman*, 1912 (New York: Museum of Modern Art); *Houses on the River (The Old Town)*, 1914 (Madrid: Museo Thyssen-Bornemisza); *Embrace*, 1917 (Vienna: Österreichische Galerie)

Edvard **Munch**

◗ 1863–1944   🇳🇴 NORWEGIAN

📕 Oslo; Paris; Berlin   🎨 oils; prints; woodcuts
🏛 Oslo: Munch Museum; National Gallery
💹 $6,627,000 in 2002, *Haus in Aasgaardstrand* (oils)

The best-known Norwegian and Scandinavian painter, and a forerunner of Expressionism. His early life was tortured by sickness, death, insanity, rejection, unhappy love affairs, and guilt—a textbook case for Freud.

Observe the way he worked through his neuroses in his paintings. The best, most intense, works are before his nervous breakdown in 1908. They are full of recognizable (almost clichéd) images of isolation, rejection, sexuality, and death, but he had a rare ability to portray such intimate emotions in a universal way, so that we can recognize and even come to terms with our own inner fears, as well as being able to touch his. He made anxiety beautiful.

The sketchy, unfinished style, using scrubby paint (with scratch marks from the handle of the brush), alongside simple and balanced compositions reveals much of his inner uncertainty and search for peace and stability. Look for intense color combinations, strange flesh colors, an obsessive interest in eyes and eye sockets, phallic symbols. His woodcuts, which exploit the grain of the wood, are some of the most accomplished things he did.

KEY WORKS *The Sick Child*, 1885–86 (Oslo: National Gallery); *Starry Night*, 1893 (Los Angeles: J. Paul Getty Museum); *Madonna*, 1893–94 (Oslo: Munch Museum)

The Scream

Edvard Munch c. 1893

Munch's *The Scream*—one of the world's most recognizable paintings—was part of his *The Frieze of Life*, "a poem about life, love, and death." The project occupied him for much of his life: an attempt to find pictorial means to represent inner turmoil and angst.

The Scream

Media oil, tempera, and pastel on cardboard
Dimensions 35 x 29 in (91 x 73 cm)
Location Oslo: National Gallery

Much like Van Gogh, by whom he was deeply influenced, Munch devised a startling visual language to give expression to the neuroses that dogged his life: despair, rejection, and loneliness. The obvious primal quality of *The Scream*—Munch in fact painted two versions—conveys this profound sense of alienation and nightmare with shocking directness.

Lurid reds, greens, and yellows fill the sky, their unnaturalness a striking metaphor for the central figure's despair

The composition is simple: the strong, unsettling diagonal of the bridge and rail contrasting with the opposing diagonal of the water. The horizon is relatively high and strongly emphasized. The principal figure is placed firmly in the center of the picture

TECHNIQUES

Paint is applied with a seemingly violent action—often with the brush handle— creating a potent sense of restlessness and distortion. The apparent haste with which the picture was painted is deceptive; it was planned and executed meticulously.

A near formless landscape suggests a world dissolving into chaos. Like the vivid sky, these patterns prefigure fully abstract painting

Staring, hollow eyes on a skull-like face are a recurring feature of Munch's deeply disturbed figures

Emil **Nolde**

○ 1867–1956   ▣ GERMAN

🏛 Munich; Paris; Germany; Asia
🎨 oils; watercolors; prints; engravings
🏛 Seebüll, Germany: Stiftung Ada und Emil Nolde
📈 $2.9m in 2002, *Blumengarten* (oils)

A pioneering Expressionist and member
of Die Brücke, Nolde's art hides a unique
radical-regressive complexity. He
was very interested in non-European
"primitive" art, but believed in racial
purity and the concept of a master race.

This was Expressionism done with flair.
He shares Expressionism's strengths
(spontaneity, passion, visual challenge)
and weaknesses (too strident, soon runs
out of steam). Creator of landscapes,
seascapes (his best work), and figure
painting. Uses bright, clashing colors
and thick paint, resulting in simplification
and a conscious crudeness. Had an instinct
for color; most apparent when his work
is seen from a distance.

His early work was on the cutting
edge of the avant-garde, but he never
developed; he was painting the same work
in 1940 as in 1910 (but only Beckmann
was able to sustain his original levels of
Expressionist creativity and freshness after
the age of 40). Great watercolorist. Was a
fully paid-up Nazi and never understood

> ### DIE BRÜCKE   1905–13
>
> Important avant-garde group of German
> Expressionists based in Dresden, founded by
> Kirchner, Schmidt-Rottluff, Heckel, and Fritz
> Bleyl. They expressed radical political and
> social views through modern, urban subject
> matter or landscapes and figures. Later
> associated artists included Nolde, Pechstein,
> and Van Dongen. They were influenced by
> the latest Parisian ideas and primitive non-
> European art. Look for bright colors, bold
> outlines, and deliberately unsophisticated
> techniques (most of the group were without
> proper training). Influential in the revival
> of the woodcut as an expressive medium.

why they rejected his art—perhaps he
was (sadly) a curious case of arrested
development, artistically and politically?
KEY WORKS *Young Black Horses*, 1916 (Dortmund:
Museum am Ostwall); *Orchids*, 1925 (Private
Collection); *The Artist and his Wife*, c. 1932
(Detroit Institute of Arts)

Otto **Müller**

○ 1874–1930   ▣ GERMAN

🏛 Germany   🎨 prints; oils   🏛 Berlin:
Brücke Museum   📈 $1.62m in 1997,
Zigeunerinnen am Lagerfeuer (oils)

Müller was an important but short-lived
contributor to the German avant-garde,
1906–14 (Die Brücke). Powerful images
of nudes in landscape. "Primitive," rough
texture, bold outline and color, deriving
from Matisse and the Cubists. Painted
gypsy subjects after 1920.
KEY WORKS *Two Bathers*, c. 1920 (Washington,
DC: National Gallery of Art); *Adam and Eve*,
1920–22 (San Francisco: Fine Arts Museums)

Ernst Ludwig **Kirchner**

○ 1880–1938   ▣ GERMAN

🏛 Dresden; Berlin; Frauenkirch (Switzerland)
🎨 prints; oils; sculpture   🏛 Davos (Switzerland):
Kirchner Museum. Berlin: Brücke Museum
📈 $4,704,000 in 2003, *Akte in der Sonne,
Moritzburg* (oils)

A key member of Die Brücke, Kirchner
was sensitive, prone to mental and
physical breakdown (terrible war
experiences). Expressed the schizophrenic
mood of his times in a highly charged,

The Dancers *Emil Nolde, 1920, oil on canvas, Stuttgart:
Staatsgalerie.* Nolde had been much influenced by a visit
to New Guinea in 1913, saying "Everything which is
primeval and elementary captures my imagination."

> ## "Everyone who renders directly and honestly whatever drives him to create is one of us."
>
> ERNST LUDWIG KIRCHNER, DIE BRÜCKE MANIFESTO

tense, Expressionist style. Had a sketchy, wiry technique, making use of heightened, intensified color. Committed suicide.
KEY WORKS *Artillerymen*, 1915 (New York: Guggenheim Museum); *Self-Portrait as a Soldier*, 1915 (Ohio: Allen Memorial Art Museum)

Max **Pechstein**
◉ 1881–1955 ⚑ GERMAN

🏛 Dresden; Berlin; Palau Islands (South-East Asia) 🎨 prints; oils; engravings 🏛 Berlin: Brücke Museum
💰 $1,261,600 in 1997, *Seated Girl* (oils)

A leading member of Die Brücke, Pechstein was a painter and engraver who also designed decorative projects and stained glass. Was called "the Giotto of our time." Characteristic flat style, using pure, unmixed colors and lyrical subjects of figures, nudes, and animals in landscape. Influenced by Matisse and Oceanic art. Commercially successful, he alienated his fellow avant-garde artists.
KEY WORKS *Nelly*, 1910 (San Francisco: Museum of Modern Art); *Seated Nude*, 1910 (Berlin: Staatliche Museum)

Erich **Heckel**
◉ 1883–1970 ⚑ GERMAN

🏛 Dresden; Berlin; Flanders; Lake Constance 🎨 prints; engravings 🏛 Berlin: Brücke Museum 💰 $1,584,000 in 2000, *Dangast, Village Landscape* (oils)

Heckel was a leading German Expressionist (member of Die Brücke). Untrained. Painted powerful, pessimistic images of nudes, portraits, sickness, and anguish with a corresponding fierce and angular style, using strident colors. His landscapes are more decorative.
KEY WORKS *Two Bathers*, c. 1920 (Washington, DC: National Gallery of Art); *Adam and Eve*, 1920–22 (San Francisco: Fine Arts Museums)

Berlin Street Scene *Ernst Ludwig Kirchner, 1913, 47½ x 37½ in (121 x 95 cm), oil on canvas, Berlin: Brücke Museum.* Kirchner moved to Berlin in 1911 and became fascinated by the edginess of street life.

Karl **Schmidt-Rottluff**
◉ 1884–1976 ⚑ GERMAN

🏛 Dresden; Berlin 🎨 oils; prints; woodcuts; sculptures 🏛 London: Victoria & Albert Museum. Leicester: Leicestershire Museum 💰 $3.6m in 2001, *Die Lesende* (oils)

A leading German Expressionist and member of Die Brücke, noted for his instinctive, forceful, angular, monumental style, which uses consciously harsh color and aggressive simplification. His later style (after 1945) is softer and more fluid, but still involves intense color. Made powerful woodcuts and lithographs. Reviled by the Nazis.
KEY WORKS *Gap in the Dyke*, 1910 (Berlin: Brucke Museum); *Red Tower in the Park*, 1910 (Frankfurt: Städel Museum)

Accent in Pink *Wassily Kandinsky, 1926, 39¼ x 31½ in (100 x 80 cm), oil on canvas, Paris: Musée National d'Art Moderne. Painted in the same year that the Bauhaus published his major treatise Point and Line to Plane.*

Gallery of Art); *Black Frame*, 1922 (Paris: Musée National d'Art Moderne); *Several Circles*, 1926 (New York: Guggenheim Museum)

Wassily **Kandinsky**
● 1866–1944   ⬤ RUSSIAN

🏛 Munich; Russia; Weimar (Germany); Paris   ⬤ oils; prints   🏛 New York: Guggenheim Museum. Munich: Städtische Galerie   📈 $19m in 1990, *Fugue* (oils)

One of the pioneers of the Modern Movement and reputedly the painter of the first abstract picture. Lived in Germany 1896–1914 and 1923–33, and taught at the Bauhaus in the 1920s.

He worked slowly from increasingly simplified figurative work through to sketchy abstracts and then hard-edge abstract. Had a complex, multifaceted personality. For example, he cultivated an intellectual rather than instinctive approach to art, backed up by much theoretical writing, but at the same time he had a strong physical sensitivity to color, which he could hear as well as see (a phenomenon called synesthesia).

Stand close to the paintings, let them fill your field of vision, then try to relax the eye and the mind so the color and shapes reach that part of the brain that responds to music—don't analyze them, but float into them and let yourself go. If you have never looked at a picture this way before, it can often be a strange, exhilarating, spiritual experience, but it will need time and patience.

KEY WORKS *St. George I*, 1911 (St. Petersburg: Hermitage Museum); *Improvisation 31 (Sea Battle)*, 1913 (Washington, DC: National

Gabriele **Münter**
● 1877–1962   ⬤ GERMAN

🏛 Düsseldorf; Munich   ⬤ oils   🏛 Munich: Lenbachhause   📈 $600,000 in 2000, *Kind mit Puppe* (oils)

Strongly influenced by Fauvism, Münter was a leader of Der Blaue Reiter Group and Kandinsky's partner and mistress from 1903 until 1914. During this time she painted bold, expressive, original, and colorful still lifes and landscapes. She broke for good from Kandinsky in 1917 and ceased to paint.

KEY WORKS *Interior*, 1908 (New York: Museum of Modern Art); *View From her Brother's House in Bonn*, 1908 (Madrid: Museo Thyssen-Bornemisza); *Future (Woman in Stockholm)*, 1917 (Ohio: Cleveland Museum of Art)

Franz **Marc**

● 1880–1916 🏳 GERMAN

🏛 Munich; Paris   🎨 oils   🏛 New York:
Guggenheim Museum   📊 $7.59m in 1999, *Der
Wasserfall: Fraeun unter einem Wasserfall* (oils)

The son of a Munich painter, Marc was
a key member of the Der Blaue Reiter
group. Author of richly sourced, very
personal art, which explores a vision
of a unified world in which animals
and the rest of nature exist in perfect
harmony. Combined progressive French
Cubist structure; Matisse-like expressive
color; Kandinsky's spiritualism, and old-
fashioned, German Romantic notions
of nature. By 1914 he had become more
abstract. Was killed in action at Verdun.
KEY WORKS *The Tiger*, 1912 (Munich: Städtische
Galerie); *Animals*, 1913 (Moscow: Pushkin
Museum); *The Mandrill*, 1913 (Munich:
Staatsgalerie Moderner Kunst)

Little Blue Horse Franz Marc, 1912, 22¾ x 28¾ in
(58 x 73 cm), oil on canvas, Saarbrüken (Germany):
Saarland Museum. Marc thought that animals had an
inherent innocence that gave them access to greater
truths than humans, and that their fate paralleled the
apocalyptic future to be visited on mankind.

DER BLAUE REITER   1911–14

An important, loosely grouped association
of avant-garde German Expressionists,
based in Munich. Kandinsky and Marc
were the key members, but the group
included Klee, Macke, and Münter. Their
name, meaning "The Blue Rider," came
from the Kandinsky painting used on the
cover of their Almanac. They wanted to
put spiritual values
into art and
used abstraction,
simplification,
and the power of
color as a means
of doing this.

The Almanac of 1912
included articles and
illustrations by Der
Blaue Reiter artists
and the composer
Arnold Schoenberg,
and even a play
by Kandinsky.

> "A work of art is a
> parable, it is man's
> thought, an autonomous
> idea of an artist."
>
> AUGUST MACKE

August **Macke**

● 1887–1914 🏳 GERMAN

🏛 Berlin; Paris; Munich: Tunisia   🎨 oils;
watercolors   🏛 Bonn: Kunstmuseum
📊 $3,744,000 in 2000, *Market in Tunis* (oils)

A leading German Expressionist of
Der Blaue Reiter group and the most
French in outlook and expression—a
joyful, rather than anguished, agenda
(Rhinelanders are more cheerful?). Made
lyrical use of clear, vibrant color and
figurative subject matter. A possibly great
talent, but he died, aged 27, in the first
German offensive in World War I.
KEY WORKS *Garden on Lake Thun*, 1913 (Bonn:
Städtisches Kunstmuseum); *Woman in a Green
Jacket*, 1913 (Cologne: Museum Ludwig);
Lady in a Park, 1914 (New York: Museum of
Modern Art); *Promenade* (*with Half-Length of
Girl in White*), 1914 (Stuttgart: Staatsgalerie)

James **Ensor**

- 1860–1949   **🇧🇪** BELGIAN
- **🇧🇪** Ostend; Brussels   **▪** oils; engravings
- **🏛** Ostend: Museum of Fine Arts
- **⚡** $705,600 in 2004, *Bons Juges* (oils)

Christ's Triumphant Entry into Brussels James Ensor, 1888, 101¾ x 169⅔ in (258 x 431 cm), oil on canvas, Los Angeles: J. Paul Getty Museum. An early masterpiece motivated more by a belief in the future triumph of Socialism than in Christian religion.

A talented loner remembered for his eccentric, brightly colored, nervously painted, and macaber imagery (skulls, skeletons, self-portraits, suffering Christ), much of it deriving from childhood memories of objects in his parents' souvenir shop. Best work between 1885 and 1891 (he tends to repeat himself after that). Belated recognition. High-quality drawings and engravings.

KEY WORKS *Still Life with Ray*, 1892 (Bruges: Musées Royaux des Beaux-Arts); *Still Life with Sea Shells*, 1923 (Boston: Museum of Fine Arts)

Käthe **Kollwitz**

- 1867–1945   **🇩🇪** GERMAN
- **🇩🇪** Berlin; Flanders; Russia   **▪** prints; sculpture; woodcuts; watercolors; engravings   **🏛** Berlin: Käthe-Kollwitz-Museum   **⚡** $149,063 in 2003, *Self-Portrait* (watercolors)

From a family of strong moral and social convictions, Kollwitz became one of the great printmakers (especially of black-and-white woodcuts). Also a sculptor. She placed emphasis on strength: of emotion, of the human body (she saw it as monumental), and gave importance to expressive hands and faces. Chose personal themes—mother and child, son's death (World War I), self-portraits. She was politically committed, a social reformer (but never revolutionary), and much honored (except by the Nazis).

KEY WORKS *Weavers' Revolt Series*, 1895–98 (Berlin: Käthe-Kollwitz-Museum); *Peasants' War Series*, 1902–08 (Berlin: Käthe-Kollwitz-Museum); *The Widow I, the Mothers, and the Volunteers*, 1922–24 (New York: Museum of Modern Art)

DIE ÜBERLEBENDEN   KRIEG DEM KRIEGE!

The Survivors; War against War; Antiwar Day September 21, 1924 Käthe Kollwitz, 1924, print, Florida: Holocaust Museum. The poster was published by the International Federation of Trade Unions, Amsterdam.

Oskar **Kokoschka**
● 1886–1980   ♙ GERMAN

🏛 Vienna; Dresden; Prague; London; Switzerland
🎨 oils; prints; watercolors   🏛 London: Courtauld
Institute of Art   📈 $2.7m in 1989,
Dresden, Neustadt I (oils)

From the same generation as Sigmund
Freud, also from Vienna, he was best
known for his powerful Expressionist
portraits and self-portraits, very freely
painted and rich in color. Also painted
landscapes and townscapes. Responded
best to strong, famous faces and views.
A deep-thinking, deep-feeling humanist.
KEY WORKS *Bride of the Wind*, 1914 (Basel,
Switzerland: Kunstmuseum); *Jerusalem*,
1929–30 (Detroit Institute of Arts)

Francis **Picabia**
● 1879–1953   ♙ FRENCH

🏛 Paris; US; Barcelona; Côte d'Azur   🎨 oils;
mixed media   🏛 New York: Museum of Modern
Art   📈 $4.15m in 1990, *Petite Udnie* (oils)

He was a quixotic, anarchic character,
best remembered for his involvement
with Dada. He flirted with Cubism,
Expressionism, and Surrealism. His most
effective work was in his "machine style"
phase (1913–1920s), when he used the
inspiration of technical drawings to
produce telling images that comment
ironically on man's relationship with
machines (often with erotic overtones).
KEY WORKS *I See Again in Memory My Dear
Udnie*, 1914 (New York: Museum of
Modern Art); *Very Rare Picture on Earth*,
1915 (New York: Guggenheim Museum)

Marcel **Duchamp**
● 1887–1968   ♙ FRENCH

🏛 Paris; New York   🎨 oils; sculpture; mixed
media   🏛 Philadelphia: Museum of Art
📈 $1.6m in 2002, *Bicycle Wheel* (sculpture)

The father of Conceptual art, Duchamp
was applauded as one of the great gurus
and heroes of the Modern Movement,
but his work is possibly one of its
greatest bores (it is possible to achieve
both at the same time).

The ragbag of his few works are
now icons of the Modern Movement
(notably the urinal; see below). None
are very interesting to look at per se,
but Duchamp was the first to propose
that the interest and stimulus of a work
of art can lie solely in its concept or
intellectual content—it doesn't matter
what it looks like, as long as you can
pick up the message.

To speak ill of Duchamp is to invite
the wrath and derision of the entire
modern art establishment. However,
although he was significant in his day, in
all honesty his work is quite limited and
now looks distinctly tired. Not quite a
case of the Emperor's clothes, but time
to say that the suit is now threadbare and
old-fashioned. A brilliant, charming but
arrogant, intellectual thug who continues
to mesmerize and intimidate the art
world from beyond the grave.
KEY WORKS *Nude Descending Staircase, No. 2*,
1912 (Philadelphia: Museum of Art); *The
Bride*, 1912 (Philadelphia: Museum of Art);
Fountain (replica), 1917 (London: Tate
Collection); *In Advance of the Broken Arm*, 1945
(New Haven: Yale University Art Gallery)

DADA   1915–22

The first of the modern antiart movements, with
strands in Europe and New York. Its prominent
figures (Arp, Duchamp, Ernst, Man Ray, and
Picabia) deliberately used the absurd, banal,
offensive, and tatty to shock and to challenge
all existing ideas about art, life, and society.
The name (French for "hobbyhorse") was
probably chosen by randomly inserting a
penknife into a dictionary.

Fountain (Urinal) (replica, original lost), Marcel
Duchamp, 1917 (remade 1964), height 24 in (61 cm),
porcelain, London: Tate Collection. Made for a US
exhibition; the artist had decamped to the US in 1915.

Kurt **Schwitters**

◉ 1887–1948 ᴘᴊ GERMAN

🏛 Hanover; Norway; UK 🎨 collage; mixed
media; oils; sculpture 🏛 Hanover: Sprengel
Museum 💲 $327,800 in 1993, *Merzbild mit
Kerze* (sculpture)

He was a pioneering, poetic, romantic
loner who used the fragments no one

YMCA Flag, Thank You, Ambleside *Kurt Schwitters,
1947, mixed media, Kendal, Cumbria (UK): Abbot Hall Art
Gallery. The title refers to the English Lake District, where
the artist settled in 1945.*

bothered with to make sense of a world
that he found politically, culturally, and
socially mad—Germany from 1914
to 1945. Schwitters ran a successful,
pioneering advertising agency from
1924 to 1930. Died in England as a
refugee. Was influential, especially in
the 1960s and 1970s.

His small-scale "Merzbilder" collages
were created in great number and with
extraordinary care, both in composition,
content, and arrangement. He used
material that he, literally, picked up in
the streets of his native Hanover. His
work of 1922–30 is more consciously
constructed (and influenced by Russian
Constructivism and Dutch De Stijl).
Produced a few high-quality, traditional
paintings and sculptures as a deliberate
contrast to his avant-garde activities.

His early roots were in Dada, but he
was never political, polemical, or satirical.

His work is always personal or
autobiographical—the artist as sacrificial
victim or spiritual leader. His major
(manic) project was "Merzbau"—a whole
building filled with personal *objets trouvés*—
a collage gone mad. (It was destroyed by
Allied bombs in 1943; a successor near
Oslo was destroyed by fire in 1951.)
Poignant attempt to create a new beauty
on the ruins of German culture.

KEY WORKS *Merzbild 5B (Picture-Red-Heart-
Church)*, 1919 (New York: Guggenheim
Museum); *Merz 163, with Woman Sweating*,
1920 (New York: Guggenheim Museum);
Merz Picture 32A (The Cherry Picture), 1921
(New York: Museum of Modern Art);
Flight, 1946 (Kendal, Cumbria, UK:
Abbot Hall Art Gallery)

Jean (Hans) **Arp**

◉ 1886–1966 ᴘᴊ FRENCH

🏛 France; Germany; Switzerland
🎨 collage; sculpture; oils 💲 $2,671,233
in 2003, *Femme* (sculpture)

A poet, painter, and sculptor as well
as an experimenter, best remembered
for wood reliefs, cardboard cutouts,
torn paper collages, and (after 1931)
stone sculptures. His early work is
modest in scale and appearance. Arp
liked simplicity, biomorphic shapes, and
chance. Took natural forms and sought

Head *Jean (Hans) Arp, 1929, 26⅜ x 22¼ in (67 x 56.5 cm),
relief, Private Collection. Arp regarded his simplified
shapes as emblems of natural growth and forms, using
light-hearted inspiration from plants, animals, and man.*

to perfect their shape and inner spirit. Founder of Dada and Surrealism.

KEY WORKS *Collage with Squares Arranged According to the Laws of Chance*, 1916–17 (New York: Museum of Modern Art); *Birds in an Aquarium*, c. 1920 (New York: Museum of Modern Art)

John **Heartfield** (Helmut Herzfelde)

● 1891–1968 ▨ GERMAN

▨ Berlin; London   ▣ photomontage   ▣ New York: George Eastman House   ▨ $7,920 in 2000, *Family, Sunday Walk* (watercolors)

An artist and journalist, founder of Dada in Berlin in 1910, Heartfield is perhaps best known for developing political photo-montage in Berlin in the 1920s and 1930s. Took refuge in England from 1938 to 1950. Settled in East Germany from 1950.

He had an intense social and political commitment (left wing, anti-Nazi), and anglicized his name as a protest against German nationalism. Original manipulator of media imagery and lettering, producing biting and memorable satire, highly expressive of its age.

Notice the economy of means: Heartfield knew exactly what he wanted to say and went for the jugular with one simple, unforgettable image—less is more.

KEY WORKS *Adolf the Superman: Swallows Gold and Spouts Junk*, 1920 (Berlin: Akademie der Künste); *Five Fingers has the Hand*, 1928 (New York: Smithsonian Cooper-Hewitt National Design Museum)

Max **Ernst**

● 1891–1976 ▨ GERMAN

▨ Bonn; Cologne; Paris; New York   ▣ prints; collage; sculpture; oils   ▣ Bruhl, Germany: Max Ernst Museum   ▨ $2.2m in 2002, *Le roi jouant avec la reine* (sculpture)

One of the leading Surrealists, Ernst lived in France after 1921 (and in the US from 1941 to 1953). After serving in World War I, he became with Jean Arp, his lifelong friend, the leader of the Dada movement in Cologne.

His witty and inventive experimentation unites subject and technique to great effect. Pioneer of the Surrealist desire to explore the subconscious and create a sense of disturbing out-of-this-world reality. His experimental techniques were a means of activating or liberating his own imagination and, by extension, ours. Don't be tempted into an overly serious, analytical, or historical approach to his work. Relax, and enter into the imaginative play he sets up.

Look for his own childhood memories, such as forests and little bird "Loplop." Enjoy his unusual techniques: witty play with collaged images (one of the first to use them); frottage (rubbed patterns); and

The Entire City *Max Ernst, 1935, 23¾ x 31¾ in (60 x 81 cm), oil on canvas, Zürich: Kunsthaus.* The artist created a whole series of works portraying cityscapes using different media, including oils and frottage.

décalcomania (liquid paint patterns), where accident is used to liberate images in the subconscious. Early strange, figurative images that seem to be painted dreams. Although his work is always imaginative, his later work is more abstract and lyrical, and loses bite. Better when small scale.

KEY WORKS *Massacre of the Innocents*, 1921 (Private Collection); *The Elephant Celebes*, 1921 (London: Tate Collection); *The Fall of an Angel*, 1922 (Private Collection); *Forest and Dove*, 1927 (London: Tate Collection); *La toilette de la mariée*, 1940 (Venice: Peggy Guggenheim Gallery)

Alexei von **Jawlensky**

◔ 1864–1941   ⚑ RUSSIAN

🄿 Germany; Paris; Switzerland   ⬛ oils; drawings   🏛 California: Norton Simon Museum. London: Christie's Images   ⤢ $7.4m in 2003, *Schokko—Schokko mit Tellerhut* (oils)

Jawlensky was one of the minor masters of Modernism, much influenced by Kandinsky and Matisse. He created sensitive, mystical, small-scale works, with simplified forms, pure colors, and bold blue outlines. Note his birth date—earlier than you might think—he was the same age as Matisse and Kandinsky.

KEY WORKS *Landscape with a Red Roof*, c. 1911 (St. Petersburg: Hermitage Museum); *Portrait of Alexander Sacharoff*, 1913 (Wiesbaden: Städtisches Museum); *Head: Red Light*, 1926 (San Francisco: Museum of Modern Art)

***Head of a Woman** Alexei von Jawlensky, 1911, 20½ x 19¾ in (52 x 50 cm), oil on cardboard laid on plywood, Edinburgh: National Gallery of Modern Art. The artist gave up a military career for art at age 35.*

Mikhail **Larionov**

◔ 1881–1964   ⚑ RUSSIAN

🄿 Russia; Switzerland; Paris   ⬛ watercolors; oils; drawings   🏛 Musée d'Art Moderne de la Ville de Paris   ⤢ $420,000 in 2004, *Reclining Nude* (oils)

He is best remembered as the founder of Rayonism (one of the briefly flourishing sub-Cubist movements before 1914), which showed objects broken up by prisms of light. Otherwise his work is not memorable. His later years were blighted by ill health and poverty.

KEY WORKS *Soldier on a Horse*, c. 1911 (London: Tate Collection); *Rayonist Composition*, c. 1912–13 (New York: Museum of Modern Art)

Natalia **Goncharova**

◔ 1881–1962   ⚑ RUSSIAN

🄿 Moscow; Paris   ⬛ oils; watercolors; drawings; prints   🏛 New York: Guggenheim Museum   ⤢ $664,200 in 2003, *Bathing Boys, Simultaneous Perception* (oils)

Goncharova was the leading member of the Russian avant-garde; well born and connected (links to Pushkin family tree). Well traveled in Europe and had an openly radical lifestyle. Settled in Paris (together with Larionov, her lifelong companion and collaborator) in 1915. She was versed in early Cubism, Fauvism, and Futurism. Used a progressive, visual language with a consciously strong, Russian peasant, religious-icon accent. Bold, strong, earthy, masculine colors.

KEY WORKS *The Laundry*, 1912 (London: Tate Collection); *Rayonism, Blue-Green Forest, 1913*, dated 1911 (New York: Museum of Modern Art); *Lady with a Hat*, 1913 (Paris: Musée National d'Art Moderne)

> **"Imagination is more important than knowledge, because imagination is infinite."**
>
> ALBERT EINSTEIN

Alexandra **Exter**

◔ 1882–1949   ⚑ RUSSIAN

🄿 Russia; Paris   ⬛ prints; sculpture; drawings   ⤢ $1.78m in 1989, *Composition* (works on paper)

She was a leading member of the Russian avant-garde. From Kiev, but well traveled. Effective emissary between the avant-garde movements in Russia and the West. Left Russia in 1924. Sophisticated work with strong French-Italian appearance and sensibility. Designs for book illustrations, theater, film, ceramics, textiles.

KEY WORKS *Construction*, 1922–23 (New York: Museum of Modern Art); *American Policeman*, 1926 (Washington, DC: Hirshhorn Museum)

Suprematist Compostion No. 56 *Kasimir Malevich, 1911, 31 x 28 in (80 x 71 cm), oil on canvas, St. Petersburg: State Museum of Russia.* Malevich wanted to represent the nonobjective supremacy of pure feeling through the suggestion of geometric forms floating in pure white space.

Kasimir **Malevich**

● 1878–1935 ⶮ RUSSIAN

Ⱪ Russia; Berlin   ✍ oils; collage
🏛 Amsterdam: Stedelijk Museum. New York: Museum of Modern Art   ⚡ $15.5m in 2000, *Suprematist Composition* (oils)

He is regarded as the most important Russian avant-garde painter of the Modern Movement.

From 1913 to the late 1920s he developed a new type of abstract art and the aesthetic and social philosophy of Suprematism. This new art reflects the search for a new utopia in which all the old, familiar values were to be replaced by new social organizations and new beliefs. The new Soviet world was to have been designed by and for engineers, both social and mechanical.

Don't try and read the simple abstract forms in a literal or material way. See them as shapes floating in space, independent of gravity, ready to regroup or twist and turn, or plunge into infinity. If you can do this, you can experience the excitement and optimistic uncertainty of this revolutionary period, bravely facing an unknown future.

KEY WORKS *The Knife Grinder,* 1912 (New Haven: Yale University Art Gallery); *Suprematist Composition,* 1915 (Amsterdam: Stedelijk Museum); *Dynamic Suprematism,* 1916 (Cologne: Museum Ludwig); *Black Square,* c. 1929 (St. Petersburg: State Russian Museum)

Naum **Gabo**

◔ 1890–1977   🅿 RUSSIAN

🅿 Russia; Oslo; Berlin; UK; US   ♟ sculpture
🏛 University of Cambridge: Kettle's Yard
💰 $458,200 in 1999, *Vertical Construction No. 1* (sculpture)

Also known as Naum Neemia Pevsner. A peripatetic, self-taught pioneer of Russian Constructivism. He lived in Russia, Germany, Paris, London, and the US. Worked closely with elder brother, Antoine Pevsner. His 3-D work emphasizes modern materials (such as Plexiglas), space, light, and kinetic movement. Expresses sophisticated aesthetic values plus social ideals—a vision of a transcendental order.

KEY WORKS *Head No. 2*, 1916 (London: Tate Collection); *Construction in Space with a Crystalline Centre*, 1938–40 (Museum of London)

Linear Construction in Space No. 1 *Naum Gabo, 1944–45, height 11¾ in (30 cm), plastic and nylon thread, University of Cambridge: Kettle's Yard.* Gabo created form through the description of space rather than mass.

Birth of the Universe *Antoine Pevsner, 1933, 29½ x 41⅓ in (75 x 105 cm), oil on canvas, Paris: Musée National d'Art Moderne.* Pevsner's later work was characterized by spiraling three-dimensional forms.

Antoine **Pevsner**

◔ 1886–1962   🅿 RUSSIAN/FRENCH

🅿 Russia; Paris; Oslo   ♟ oils; mixed media; sculpture   🏛 Paris: Musée National d'Art Moderne   💰 $240,000 in 2001, *Developable Surface* (sculpture)

He was the leading exponent of Russian avant-garde, nonobjective art. Creator of 2-D and 3-D pieces. Fascinated by modern technology and engineering, he made conscious use of modern materials such as Perspex, glass, and iron. Note his mastery of the dynamics of spherical surfaces, the way he loves to use projections in space and expresses the poetry of technology, especially flight. He left Russia (together with his brother Nuam Gabo) in 1921 and settled in Paris in 1923. Died a much-respected figure.

KEY WORKS *Construction in Space*, 1929 (Basel, Switzerland: Kunstmuseum); *Anchored Cross*, 1933 (New York: Guggenheim Museum); *Meeting of Planets*, 1961 (Musee d'Art Moderne de la Ville de Paris)

CONSTRUCTIVISM   1917–21

Important Russian avant-garde movement. Vladimir Tatlin, later joined by Rodchenko and brothers Antoine Pevsner and Naum Gabo, developed "constructed," architectural art to reflect the modern world. They were concerned with abstraction, space, new materials, 3-D form, and social reform. Soviet disapproval meant the group fragmented across Europe, influencing the fields of architecture and decoration, and the Bauhaus and De Stijl movements.

Model of the *Monument to the Third International* Tatlin's unrealized visionary project was for a steel-and-glass monument to the Revolution, larger than the Eiffel Tower, standing in Petrograd, pointing at the North Star—linking the world and the universe.

El **Lissitsky**

1890–1941   RUSSIAN

Russia; Germany; Switzerland   prints; sculpture; mixed media $550,000 in 1990, *Proun No. 95* (works on paper)

A pioneering Modernist architect and artist, he was a creator of Constructivist abstractions, which develop the links between art, design, and architecture, and art as a material and spiritual experience.
KEY WORKS *Untitled*, c. 1919–20 (New York: Guggenheim Museum); *Proun*, c. 1923 (New York: Guggenheim Museum)

Vladimir **Tatlin**

1885–1953   RUSSIAN

Russia; Paris   mixed media; sculpture; oils   Moscow: Tretyakov Gallery $28,980 in 1987, *Project for Construction* (drawing)

He was the heroic, legendary founder of Russian Constructivism. Lived in Paris in 1913 and was much influenced by Picasso

The Sailor (Self-Portrait) *Vladimir Tatlin, 1911–12, 28¼ x 28¼ in (71.5 x 71.5 cm), tempera on canvas, St. Petersburg: State Russian Museum.*

and Futurism. Famous for his relief constructions, especially corner reliefs, and his never-built tower (*Monument to the Third International*). Made stage and industrial designs in the 1920s. Believed in art at the service of Revolution. Deadly rival of Malevich. Died in oblivion.
KEY WORKS *The Fishmonger*, 1911 (Moscow: Tretyakov Gallery); *Mother and Child*, c. 1912–13 (Private Collection)

Aleksandr **Rodchenko**

1891–1956   RUSSIAN

Russia   photography; oils; prints; sculpture   Moscow: Tretyakov Gallery $504,000 in 1988, *Line* (oils)

An active Bolshevik with strong ideals, he believed that art must be in the service of the Revolution to create an ordered, technological society. Always demanded active participation from viewers. He was rejected by Stalin.
KEY WORKS *Line and Compass Drawing*, 1915 (New York: Museum of Modern Art); *Composition*, 1916 (Private Collection); *Black on Black*, 1918 (New York: Metropolitan Museum of Art)

Giacomo **Balla**

● 1871–1958 Ⓟ ITALIAN

Ⓟ Rome Ⓞ oils; sculpture; mixed media Ⓜ Rome: Galleria Nazionale d'Arte Moderna ⓩ $4.4m in 1990, *La scala degli addii—salutando* (oils)

He was a leading Italian Futurist who had a brief, important, innovative, key period from 1912 to 1916. Interested in sensations: speed, flight, movement, and light, which he represented by using fragmentation and color—progressing from Divisionism via Cubism to clean-cut Abstraction. Declined after 1916 into decorative figuration. Also produced theater design and poems.

KEY WORKS *Girl Running on a Balcony,* 1912 (Milan: Civica Galleria d'Arte Moderna); *Mercury Passing in Front of the Sun,* 1914 (Private Collection)

Dynamism of a Dog on a Lead *Giacomo Balla, 1912, 38¾ x 43¼ in (89 x 109 cm), oil on canvas, New York: Albright-Knox Art Gallery.* Balla recreated speed in this painting by superimposing several images in layers.

French Cubist interlocking planes and fragmentation, then adding color as a means of representing his ambitious subjects.

His work is always on a small scale and not always successful—his ambitions often outran his technical abilities and the means at his disposal. Ditto for his sculptures, of which only four remain. He is to later artists what Bleriot's flying machine is to jet aircraft.

KEY WORKS *Street Noises Invade the House,* 1911 (Hanover: Niedersächsische Landesmuseum); *Dynamism of a Cyclist,* 1913 (Milan: Collection Gianni Mattioli); *Dynamism of a Man's Head,* 1914 (Milan: Civico Museo d'Arte Contemporanea); *The Charge of the Lancers,* 1915 (Milan: Ricardo Jucker Collection)

Umberto **Boccioni**

● 1882–1916 Ⓟ ITALIAN

Ⓟ Italy Ⓞ oils; sculpture Ⓜ Milan: Collection of Riccardo and Magda Jucker; Civica Galleria d'Arte Moderna ⓩ $1.38m in 1988, *Romanza di una cucitrice* (oils)

Boccioni was a leading Futurist painter and sculptor who embraced the verve of modern life and enjoyed conflict. Joined a World War I bicycle brigade, but died falling from a horse, at the age of 34.

His work was pioneering in subject and style. He was interested in highly charged modern subjects, such as dynamic, collective experience (crowds and riots); movement and speed; memories and states of mind shown as continuous time; emotions and experiences beyond the incidental trivia of time and place. Innovative in adopting

Unique Forms of Continuity in Space *Umberto Boccioni, 1913, height 43 in (111 cm), bronze, New York: Museum of Modern Art.* The sculpture was first exhibited in plaster form in Paris in 1913, and later cast in bronze.

Carlo **Carrà**

● 1881–1966 ▥ ITALIAN

▥ Italy ▥ oils ▥ New York: Museum
of Modern Art ▥ $739,000 in 1990,
Autunno, ritratto di Emilio Colombo (oils)

He was a prominent Futurist painter and
later a leading figure in the Metaphysical
movement. Early works combined
Futurism's dynamism with a Cubist feel
for structure. Under Chirico's influence he
turned to Metaphysical painting, but later
rejected the avant-garde and advocated
a return to a more naturalistic type of
art. Influential critic and writer on art.
KEY WORKS *Horsemen of the Apocalypse*, 1908
(Art Institute of Chicago); *The Funeral of
the Anarchist Galli*, 1911 (New York: Museum
of Modern Art)

Gino **Severini**

● 1883–1966 ▥ ITALIAN

▥ Italy; Paris ▥ oils; gouache; drawings
▥ Rome: Galleria Nazionale d'Arte Moderna
▥ $3.3m in 1990, *Sea = Dancer* (oils)

Severini was one of the creators of
Futurism. Painter, stage designer, writer,
and intellectual. Long-lived and adaptable.
  His early work was dull, until he
discovered Impressionism (in Paris, 1906).
His most significant works are his Futurist
paintings, 1911–16, which have dynamic
subjects, such as trains, buses, city streets,
dancers, and war machinery—all of them
animated by Cubist fragmentation and
strong colors. After 1916 his paintings
become less dynamic and more formally
pure, with precise adherence to geometric

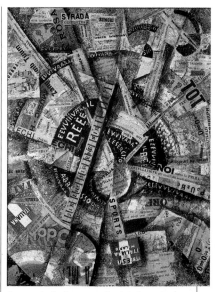

Interventionist Demonstration *Carlo Carrà, 1914,
15¼ x 11½ in (38.5 x 30 cm), collage, Venice: Peggy
Guggenheim Collection. The spiraling collage was inspired
by a plane dropping leaflets onto the Piazza del Duomo.*

> ## "Art is nothing but
> ## humanized science."
>
> GINO SEVERINI

rules. In the 1920s he made mural
decorations (especially mosaics in
churches); and in the 1930s grand
Fascist monuments.
  His work is of uneven quality—the
Futurist paintings can be very good, or else
very formulaic and trite. His later work
is hardly known outside Italy. Like other
bright lights of the early avant-garde (such
as Derain), he had only a brief period of
real significance. Does a lasting reputation
require longevity and large output more
than talent? Fascist Italy (unlike its
equivalent in Germany or Russia)
produced some very fine architecture and
public art. Why? And does evil political
patronage irrevocably taint the art?
KEY WORKS *Dynamic Rhythm of a Head in a Bus*,
1912 (Washington, DC: Hirshhorn Museum);
Red Cross Train Passing a Village, 1915 (New
York: Guggenheim Museum); *Suburban
Train Arriving in Paris*, 1915 (London: Tate
Collection); *Still Life with Fish*, 1958 (San
Francisco: Fine Arts Museums)

FUTURISM   1909–15

Originating in Italy (although it had
adherents in Russia), Futurism was one
of the most important early avant-garde
art movements, and the only one not
to center around Paris. Its main figures
included Bocconi, Balla, Carrà, Severini,
Wyndham Lewis, and Joseph Stella.
It was widely influential, with goals set
out in a series of manifestoes urging a
break with the past. Futurism noisily
promoted a worship of machinery,
speed, modernity, and revolutionary
change, using the latest avant-garde
styles such as Cubism.

VORTICISM

An avant-garde British art movement, short-lived but significant as the first organized movement toward abstraction in English art. Vorticism took Cubist and Futurist ideas, aiming to shake up the stuffy British art world and society generally. Its lynchpin was Percy Wyndham Lewis, editor of *Blast*, the Vorticist review. Another prominent figure was Christopher Richard Wynne Nevinson, a difficult personality who had a brief flowering as a leading member of the English avant-garde, producing his best work as an official war artist in World War I. The movement foundered after its sole exhibition in 1915, but left a legacy on the development of British modernism.

Front cover of the *Blast* War Number, featuring a Wyndham Lewis woodcut. The issue included articles by Ezra Pound (who coined the movement's name) and T. S. Eliot.

(Percy) Wyndham **Lewis**

◖ 1882–1957   🇵 BRITISH

🏛 Paris; UK   🎨 oils; drawings; mixed media
🏛 London: Victoria & Albert Museum
📈 $73,350 in 1993, *Timon of Athens—The Thebaid* (watercolors)

Lewis was a painter, writer, and journalist. An angry young man who, with his fellow Vorticists, brought Modern art to Britain. Later became a right-wing misfit and admirer of Fascism.

His work is always angular and awkward, rather like the artist himself. His powerful and original early work was among the first abstract art in Europe.

He was also the author of very strong drawings and paintings of World War I battlefields (he was an official war artist). Interesting later portraits.

Note his skilled, spikey draftsmanship and his personal and inventive use of Cubist and Futurist styles and ideas. Inventive, creative use of faceted space and figures. Interesting exploration of the concept of the man-cum-machine. Was happier with words than images.

KEY WORKS *Praxitella*, c. 1921 (Leeds: City Art Gallery); *Self-Portrait*, 1921 (Manchester: City Art Gallery); *The Mud Clinic*, 1937 (New Brunswick, Canada: Beaverbrook Art Gallery)

A Battery Shelled
(Percy) Wyndham Lewis, 1919, 72 x 125 in (182.8 x 317.8 cm), oil on canvas, London: Imperial War Museum. Lewis was one of several young professional artists employed by the government to record their experience of the battlefront.

Edward **Wadsworth**

◔ 1889–1949   🏳 BRITISH

🏴 UK   🎨 oils   🏛 tempera   💹 $274,500
in 1992, *The Cattewater, Plymouth Sound* (oils)

He was a successful member of the
avant-garde who ran through the voguish
styles of his time: geometric and Cubist
pre-1914; representational in the 1920s; a
figurative Surrealist in the 1930s; abstract
in the 1940s. He produced rather good
work, in a derivative way. His skill at Cubist
fragmentation led him to design and
paint ship camouflage in World War I.
KEY WORKS *Abstract Composition*, 1915 (London:
Tate Collection); *Satellitium*, 1932 (Nottingham:
Castle Museum); *The Perspective of Idleness*,
1940 (Bolton, UK: Museums, Art Gallery,
and Aquarium)

David **Bomberg**

◔ 1890–1957   🏳 BRITISH

🏴 London; Palestine; Spain   🎨 oils;
drawings; prints   🏛 London: Victoria
& Albert Museum   💹 $240,700 in 1998,
San Miguel, Toledo, Afternoon (oils)

Bomberg was the son of Polish Jewish
immigrants. Briefly on the cutting edge
of the avant-garde (c. 1914) when he
pioneered Cubism and Vorticism in
Britain. Then changed style, producing
gloomy, minor Expressionist paintings.
KEY WORKS *In the Hold*, 1913–14 (London:
Tate Collection); *The Mud Bath*, 1914
(London: Tate Collection)

William **Roberts**

◔ 1895–1980   🏳 BRITISH

🏴 France; Italy; UK   🎨 oils; drawings;
watercolors   🏛 London: Bonhams
💹 $124,500 in 1990, *Birth of Venus* (oils)

Individual Modernist who developed an
interesting and curiously homey version
of the working man/urban life/machine-
age imagery and style pioneered by Léger.
His early experience as an advertising-
poster designer is (too?) evident, and his
weakness is that he established a formula
that became overrepetitive. Member of
pioneering Vorticists, c. 1914.
KEY WORKS *The Return of Ulysses*, 1913
(London: Tate Collection); *People at Play*,
c. 1920 (London: Christie's Images)

Sir Jacob **Epstein**

◔ 1880–1958   🏳 AMERICAN/BRITISH

🏴 France; UK   🎨 sculpture; oils; drawings
🏛 London: Tate Collection. Leeds: City Art Gallery
💹 $102,920 in 1998, *Tin Hat* (sculpture)

He was an audacious and original sculptor,
frequently attacked by conservative critics
for indecency. Studied in Paris 1902–05,
where he developed a lasting interest in
ancient and primitive sculpture, which
inspired much of his later work. Settled in
England in 1905, and carried out a series
of controversial commissions, labeled as
indecent by his critics. Was influenced by
Picasso, Modigliani, and Brancusi in Paris
while working on Oscar Wilde's tomb,
and associated with Wyndham Lewis and
the Vorticists in London. In later years he
concentrated on bronze portrait busts of
luminaries, which were widely admired.
KEY WORKS *The Rock Drill*, 1913–14 (London:
Tate Collection); *Rima*, 1922 (London: Hyde
Park); *The Tomb of Oscar Wilde*, 1912 (Paris:
Père Lachaise Cemetery)

St. Michael Vanquishing the Devil *Jacob Epstein,
1958, height 236¼ in (600 cm), bronze, Coventry Cathedral
(UK).* Epstein created a number of large-scale biblical
subjects, hoping to encourage a "new hope for the future."

"A great man of action into whose hands the fairies had placed a paintbrush instead of a sword."

(PERCY) WYNDHAM LEWIS ON AUGUSTUS JOHN

Augustus **John**

◉ 1878–1961 ▣ BRITISH

▣ UK ◪ oils; drawings; chalks ▥ London: National Portrait Gallery ↗ $180,400 in 2003, *Dorelia in a Red Dress* (oils)

He was truly gifted and one of the best draftsmen of any period. His romantic bohemian temperament made him an increasing misfit—should have lived in first half of 19th century, not the 20th. His wonderful early pieces show his great originality and talent; after 1918 it went to seed and he ended up doing competent, unexceptional work—although always recognizably John.

His best works were his early drawings and the sensitive, simplified, intensely

colored landscapes—a personal interpretation of Post-Impressionism. He painted society portraits with style and panache. Unjustly underrated—deserves reinstatement.

KEY WORKS *William Butler Yeats*, 1907 (Manchester: City Art Gallery); *The Smiling Woman*, c. 1908 (London: Tate Collection)

Gwen **John**

◉ 1876–1939 ▣ BRITISH

▣ UK; Paris; Meudon (France) ◪ oils
▥ Cardiff (UK): National Museum of Wales. London: Tate Collection ↗ $265,650 in 1990, *The Seated Woman* (oils)

She was the sister of Augustus John and mistress of Rodin. Author of tight, overintense (neurotic?), minutely worked, rather monochromatic portraits and interiors. Had a sensitive talent, although limited in range and currently overrated compared with her brother.

KEY WORKS *Girl Holding a Rose*, c. 1910–20 (New Haven: Yale Center for British Art); *Interior (Rue Terre Neuve)*, c. 1920s (Manchester: City Art Gallery)

Robert Polhill **Bevan**

◉ 1865–1925 ▣ BRITISH

▣ UK; France ◪ oils; drawings
▥ London: Agnew & Sons ↗ $173,850 in 1992, *Horse Dealers at the Barbican* (oils)

Bevan was an interesting, underrated painter who studied in Paris in the 1890s and met Gauguin at Pont-Aven, in Brittany. Painted traditional subjects, with successful, if limited, individual Modernist style—stiff, angular, simplified, with luminous colors. Rather better than the contemporaneous Bloomsbury set (Bell, Fry, and Grant).

KEY WORKS *Hawkridge*, 1900 (Private Collection); *The Cab Horse*, c. 1910 (London: Tate Collection); *Parade at Aldridge's*, 1914 (Boston: Museum of Fine Arts)

Dorelia in a Landscape *Augustus John, c. 1916, 24⅔ x 16 in (62 x 41 cm), oil on canvas, Private Collection.* Gypsy life fascinated John. Dorelia (Dorothy McNeil) was his mistress, and after his wife's death, his lifelong companion.

THE BLOOMSBURY GROUP   1920s–1930s

A loosely knit group of writers, artists, poets, and designers, taking their name from the London district where they were based. An intellectual elite in rebellion against Victorian restrictions, priding themselves on their sexual freedom but frequently accused of snobbery. On the artistic side, they practiced and promoted modern French art. Vanessa Bell, Duncan Grant, and Roger Fry were the artistic leading lights: their output was variable, but their confidence unshakeable.

A Group of "Bloomsberries" in Vanessa's Bell's Sussex backyard. Grant is third from right; Fry kneels with arm around bust.

Sir Alfred **Munnings**

◉ 1878–1959   ⚑ BRITISH

🏴 UK   🎨 oils; drawings   🏛 Dedham (England): Sir Alfred Munnings Art Museum; Castle House
💰 $7m in 2004, *The Red Prince Mare* (oils)

The brilliant and successful Munnings was an artist who believed (like his clientele) that anything "modern" was a horrible mistake. Though blind in one eye, he had acute vision. Socially he saw only what he wanted to see. He was president of the Royal Academy.

He is remembered primarily for his hunting and racing portraits of humans and horses. He had rare flashes of inspiration, but too often his work lapses into a stock formula: half-way horizon, human upper torsos and heads plus horses' heads and ears silhouetted against a sky piled high with clouds. Though fascinating as social documents, such paintings are his least interesting artistically. He always painted a good "picture," just as some writers always write a good "story."

At his best when he was at his most informal and inventive—in his pictures of horse fairs, local races, landscapes, or gypsies. Within them (and tucked away in portraits), note his genius for capturing a specific light effect, the play of light on landscape or horses' flanks, movement, unexpected viewpoints, and spontaneous slices of life. Munnings never doubted his own talent or the values that he celebrated (and it shows).

KEY WORKS *My Wife, My Horse and Myself,* c. 1910 (Dedham, England: Castle House); *Shrimp on a White Welsh Pony,* 1911 (Dedham, England: Castle House); *The Friesian Bull,* 1920 (Wirral, UK: Lady Lever Art Gallery)

Mark **Gertler**

◉ 1891–1939   ⚑ BRITISH

🏴 UK; Southern France   🎨 oils   🏛 Leeds: City Art Gallery   💰 $90,750 in 1997, *Boxers* (oils)

He was a talented artist from a poor, Jewish immigrant family. Came to inhabit the fringes of the snobbish Bloomsbury set. Shared their interest in modern French art and painted better than they did. Figure studies (back views of nudes) and still lifes. Good design and paint handling. Committed suicide.

KEY WORKS *Head of the Artist's Mother,* 1910 (London: Victoria & Albert Museum); *Merry-Go-Round,* 1916 (London: Tate Collection)

ASHCAN SCHOOL c. 1891–1919

A progressive group of American painters and illustrators, comprising Sloan, Bellows, Glackens, Luks, and Henri. They believed that art should portray the everyday, sometimes harsh, realities of life—especially New York City life—and rejected officially sanctioned art (which they said was "fenced in with tasseled ropes and weighed down with bronze plates"). They generally painted gritty, poor, urban scenes in a spontaneous, unpolished style.

Robert **Henri**

🌐 1865–1929 🏴 AMERICAN

🏛 Philadelphia; Paris; New York 🎨 oils; drawings
🏛 Washington, DC: National Gallery of Art
💲 $420,000 in 2003, *Berna Escudero* (oils)

Henri was a charismatic, hard-drinking, rebellious, and anarchic man, but a great teacher and believer in young people. He chose down-to-earth, urban subjects (note his portraits of "my people"—Irish peasants, Chinese coolies, American Indians) and had a direct, "real" style using dark tonal contrast, limited color, and liquid brushstrokes.

Leader of the Ashcan School, in 1908 he founded The Eight, who put together

The Little Dancer Robert Henri, c. 1916–18, 40½ x 32½ in (102.8 x 82.5 cm), oil on canvas, Ohio: Butler Institute of American Art. Henri produced a number of paintings of dancers—some of unknowns like the model for this portrait, others of stars such as Isadora Duncan.

the first art exhibition independently curated by artists in the US.

Henri links Eakins (he studied at Pennsylvania Academy) and Manet (he was in Paris from 1888 to 1890)—and his students: George Bellows, Stuart Davies, Edward Hopper, Rockwell Kent, Man Ray, and Trotsky (yes, Trotsky).
KEY WORKS *Antonio Banos*, 1908 (Houston: Museum of Fine Arts); *The Irish Girl*, c. 1910 (Arizona: State University Art Museum); *Himself* (self-portrait), 1913 (Art Institute of Chicago)

George **Luks**

🌐 1867–1933 🏴 AMERICAN

🏛 Europe; Philadelphia; New York 🎨 oils; watercolors; drawings 🏛 Washington, DC: Hirshhorn Museum 💲 $600,000 in 1990, *Knitters, High Bridge Park* (oils)

Luks was a vaudeville comedian. He was also pugnacious, a braggart, and hard-drinking (he is said to have died from injuries in a brawl). Painted Ashcan School scenes of New York lower-class life, but ignored the reality of poverty and overcrowding, favoring the romance of teeming humanity, male supremacy, and adventure. Note his bravura brushwork. Painted notable watercolors of his native Pennsylvania mining country.
KEY WORKS *The Café Francis*, c. 1906 (Ohio: Butler Institute of American Art); *The Bersaglieri*, 1918 (Washington, DC: National Gallery of Art)

William James **Glackens**

🌐 1870–1938 🏴 AMERICAN

🏛 Philadelphia; New York; France
🎨 drawings; oils 🏛 Fort Lauderdale: Museum of Art 💲 $1.55m in 1998, *Vacation Home* (oils)

Philadelphia-born, he studied in Paris and was a protégé of Robert Henri. Initially a newspaper illustrator. Produced attractive and competent images of everyday New York life (interiors and exteriors), overtly derived from Manet and the Ashcan School. His work is popular imagery or illustration aspiring to the level of art.
KEY WORKS *May Day, Central Park*, c. 1905 (San Francisco: Museum of Modern Art); *Italo-American Celebration, Washington Square*, c. 1912 (Boston: Museum of Fine Arts)

McSorley's Bar *John Sloan, 1912, 26 x 32 in (66 x 81.2 cm), oil on canvas, Detroit Institute of Arts.* Sloan was a regular drinker at this working-class, men-only Irish tavern, and some of his sketches still decorate the walls.

Square, 1909 (Ohio: Butler Institute of American Art); *Austrian-Irish Girl*, c. 1920 (Washington, DC: Hirshhorn Museum)

John **Sloan**

● 1871–1951   ◪ AMERICAN

🏛 Philadelphia; New York; Santa Fe
🎨 drawings; oils   🏛 Washington, DC: National Gallery of Art   💲 $2.7m in 2003, *Easter Eve* (oils)

He was a member of the Ashcan School. Started as an illustrator/cartoonist with Socialist sympathies but was opposed to the idea of art as propaganda. Produced New York scenes of the working classes, but modified harsh reality with an ideal of honest, cozy, vaguely erotic, urban happiness. Caught fleeting moments well. After 1914, worked in Santa Fe. Lost the plot after 1928. Superb etchings.
KEY WORKS *Wake of the Ferry*, 1907 (Washington, DC: Phillips College); *Recruiting in Union*

George Wesley **Bellows**

● 1882–1925   ◪ AMERICAN

🏛 New York   🎨 oils; prints; drawings
🏛 Washington, DC: National Gallery of Art
💲 $25m in 1999, *Polo Crowd* (oils)

Bellows was a leading member of the Ashcan School. His best period was pre-1913, when he tackled tough, gritty subjects, such as construction sites (Penn Station), slum dwellers, boxing matches—depictions of raw energy. Later work too self-conscious and affected by theories of symmetry and the Golden Section.
KEY WORKS *Cliff Dwellers*, 1913 (Los Angeles: County Museum of Art); *Mrs. T in Cream Silk, No. 2*, 1920 (Minneapolis Institute of Arts)

A Stag at Sharkey's *George Wesley Bellows, painted 1909, 18½ x 23¾ in (47 x 60.4 cm), lithograph by George Miller (1917), Houston: Museum of Fine Arts.* Bellows's evocation of an illegal boxing match was acclaimed at the time as a landmark of realism.

Marsden **Hartley**

● 1877–1943 ⚑ AMERICAN

📓 US; Europe 🎨 oils; prints; drawings
🏛 San Francisco: Fine Arts Museum.
Washington, DC: National Gallery of Art
📈 $2.5m in 2002, *Painting No. 6* (oils)

The greatest American artist of the
first half of the 20th century: original,
mystical, homosexual.

His early Impressionist work was
followed by paintings influenced by
the German Expressionists, whom he
knew (met Kandinsky and Jawlensky
in Berlin and Munich, c. 1913).
Experimented with abstraction. His
"Portrait of a German Officer" series
(which commemorates his male lover) is
the major monument of early American
Modernism. Later produced several
important series of paintings in Provence
(France), New Mexico, and Maine. Used

Abstraction *Marsden Hartley, c. 1914, 24¼ x 20 in
(61.5 x 50.8 cm), oil on paperboard mounted on panel,
Houston: Museum of Fine Arts.* Typical of Hartley's work
of the period, this painting shows the influence of
Delaunay and Kandinsky in its interest in geometric
arrangements of bands and circles, and color relationships.

vigorous brushstrokes and jarring color
contrasts, such as rust and acid green.

KEY WORKS *The Aero*, 1914 (Washington, DC:
National Gallery of Art); *Mount Katahdin,
Maine*, 1942 (Washington, DC: National
Gallery of Art)

Max **Weber**

● 1881–1961 ⚑ RUSSIAN/AMERICAN

📓 New York; Europe 🎨 woodcuts; oils;
chalks 🏛 Washington, DC: National Gallery
of Art. Boston: Museum of Fine Arts
📈 $1.5m in 2002, *New York* (oils)

Russian-born, he was a gifted artist.
Studied with Matisse (in Paris 1905–08)
and produced important Cubist paintings.
One of the first Americans to use modern
idiom. Later, Expressionist work (à la
Soutine), with Jewish subjects based on
Russian memories. Moved easily between
established styles—produced pleasing
results but compromised originality.

KEY WORKS *Interior of the Fourth Dimension*, 1913
(Washington, DC: National Gallery of Art);
Rush Hour, New York, 1915 (Washington, DC:
National Gallery of Art)

Patrick Henry **Bruce**

● 1881–1937　▣ AMERICAN

▣ New York; Paris　🎨 oils; drawings
🏛 Washington, DC: Hirshhorn Museum
📈 $1.1m in 2000, *Still Life* (oils)

Bruce was a member of an old Virginia family. Early American Modernist. Visited Paris in 1904, was influenced by Matisse, Steins, and Delaunay. Good, semiabstract still lifes with spare, geometric shapes, primary colors, hot pinks, and thick paint like cake icing. Unrecognized. Work did not sell. Gave up painting, destroyed work, and sold antiques; later committed suicide.
KEY WORKS *Painting*, 1922–23 (New York: Whitney Museum of American Art); *Still Life: Transverse Beams*, 1928–32 (Washington, DC: Hirshhorn Museum)

Stanton **Macdonald-Wright**

● 1890–1973　▣ AMERICAN

▣ US; Paris; London　🎨 oils　🏛 Washington, DC: Smithsonian American Art Museum
📈 $440,000 in 1990, *Conception Synchromy* (oils)

He was an avant-garde American painter. Studied in Los Angeles and went to live in Paris in 1913. Developed Synchronism—abstract, kaleidoscopic symphony of swirling, fragmented rainbow colors—derived from French artists such as Delaunay. Lost the plot on return to US.
KEY WORKS *Dragon Trail*, 1930 (Washington, DC: Hirshhorn Museum); *Mural for the Santa Monica Library*, 1934–35 (Washington, DC: Smithsonian American Art Museum)

Arthur Garfield **Dove**

● 1880–1946　▣ AMERICAN

▣ US; Europe　🎨 drawings; oils; mixed media
🏛 Washington, DC: National Gallery of Art
📈 $1.1m in 2003, *Snowstorm* (oils)

A shy, reclusive farmer *manqué*, avid sailor. First American artist to paint an abstract picture (1907–09). Produced small-scale lyrical work, derived from a love of land and seascape, full of natural shapes, rhythms, and essences of nature; also witty collages and assemblages. Unappreciated in his lifetime.
KEY WORKS *Foghorns*, 1929 (Colorado Springs: Fine Arts Center); *Sand Barge*, 1930 (Washington, DC: Phillips College); *Reflections*, 1935 (Indianapolis: Museum of Art)

Burgoyne **Diller**

● 1906–65　▣ AMERICAN

▣ US　🎨 oils; sculpture　🏛 Washington, DC: Hirshhorn Museum　📈 $95,000 in 1995, *First Theme* 1959–60 (oils)

He is one of the most important American abstract artists. Produced 3-D abstract painted reliefs and geometric paintings. Simple shapes, primary colors on white or black, and understated brushwork. Much influenced by Mondrian and the Dutch De Stijl movement (see page 389), both in appearance and his aspiration for social and spiritual reformation.
KEY WORKS *Untitled (Three Men with Hats in City Street)*, 1932 (Ohio: Cleveland Museum of Art); *Second Theme*, 1949 (New York: Metropolitan Museum of Art)

Stuart **Davis**

● 1894–1964　▣ AMERICAN

▣ New York; Paris　🎨 oils　🏛 Washington, DC: Hirshhorn Museum　📈 $2.2m in 1997, *Odol* (oils)

Davis was a leading American Cubist. Initially trained in advertising (it shows to his advantage), and studied with Robert Henri (see page 380). From 1924, developed striking and individual abstract paintings and collages, notable for bright colors and jazzy rhythms. Borrowed motifs from popular culture; considered a progenitor of Pop Art. Fascinated by urban scenes and advertising posters.
KEY WORKS *House and Street*, 1931 (New York: Whitney Museum of American Art); *The Mellow Pad*, 1945–51 (Private Collection)

> **"I don't want people to copy Matisse or Picasso, although it is entirely proper to admit their influence. I don't make paintings like theirs. I make paintings like mine."**
>
> STUART DAVIS

Max **Beckmann**

1884–1950   GERMAN

Frankfurt; Amsterdam; US   oils;
woodcuts; drawings   Minnesota:
Minneapolis Institute of Art $20.5m
in 2001, *Self-Portrait with Horn*

One of the great painters of the 20th century. Generally overlooked because never one of the Modernist "gang," and difficult, even now, for officialdom to pigeonhole. To sustain such Expressionist intensity and quality is a rare (unique?) achievement.

Produced beautiful, expressive, somber paintings; rich colors, strong drawing. Many portraits, self-portraits, and allegories full of symbolism. Beckmann's works are very much of their time, but do not belong to any "school" or "ism." Their underlying theme is the human condition and concern for the triumph of the human spirit.

Beckmann's use of black (one of the most difficult pigments) is stunning and worthy of Manet; his understanding of the human condition is worthy of Rembrandt. His work charts a central vein of the spiritual anguish of 20th-century Europe. Born into the gifted, optimistic generation of the 1880s, he experienced the horrors of World War I and the collapse of civilized values in Germany in the 1920s and 1930s. In 1937, classed as a "degenerate"

Self-Portrait in Olive and Brown *Max Beckmann, 1945, 23¾ x 19¾ in (60.3 x 49.8 cm), oil on canvas, Detroit Institute of Arts.* Painted while he was writing his autobiography, *A Little Yes and a Big No.*

by the Nazis, he chose voluntary self-exile to Amsterdam. In 1947, he emigrated to the US, where he taught and painted.

KEY WORKS *The Dream*, 1921 (Missouri: St. Louis Art Museum); *Departure*, 1932–33 (New York: Museum of Modern Art); *Journey on the Fish*, 1934 (Stuttgart: Staatsgalerie); *Carnival*, 1942–43 (University of Iowa Museum of Art)

THE NAZIS AND DEGENERATE ART   1930s

Nazi ideologues believed that any art that did not conform to a bourgeois ideal of well-crafted, figurative images portraying ideal heroism or comfortable day-to-day living was the product of degenerate human beings and perverted minds. The German term, *entartete Kunst*, was coined by Hitler and the party's chief theoretical spokesperson, Alfred Rosenberg. "Degenerate" modern artists could not exhibit or work, and many confiscated works were burned. A Nazi-backed touring exhibition of modern and abstract art (with works by Beckmann, Dix, Grosz, Kandinsky, Mondrian, and Picasso) opened in 1937 to show how foul Degenerate art was. The plan backfired and introduced modern art to huge crowds.

Adolf Hitler and Hermann Goering, probably at the 1937 exhibition. Before he rose to power, Hitler supported himself through painting and continued to paint throughout his life.

Otto **Dix**

◔ 1891–1969   ⏚ GERMAN

⬚ Germany   🎨 prints; drawings; mixed media
🏛 San Francisco: Fine Arts Museum. New York:
Museum of Modern Art   💰 $5,445,000 in 1999,
Portrait of the Lawyer Dr. Fritz Glaser (oils)

Dix was a mocking, bitter observer
and recorder of German society during
World War I and the 1920s and 1930s as
its moral and social values collapsed. Anti-
Nazi. Ugliness fascinated him—reflected
in a powerful distortion of realistic
observation with intense line, detail,
and acid color; expressed in portraits
of friends and powerful engravings.
He was recognized only after 1955.
KEY WORKS *Card-Playing War Cripples*, 1920
(Private Collection); *The Artist's Parents*,
1921 (Basel, Switzerland: Kunstmuseum)

George **Grosz**

◔ 1893–1959   ⏚ GERMAN

⬚ Berlin; New York   🎨 prints; drawings; oils
🏛 San Francisco: Fine Arts Museum. New York:
Museum of Modern Art   💰 $2,041,000
in 1996, *Wildwest* (oils)

Best remembered as the biting and
original chronicler of the sad and
corrosive period of Germany history
between 1918 and the rise of Hitler.
   His small-scale works (especially
prints and drawings) are of a
consciously artless, angular,
modern style (in the sense of
uncomfortable, provocative, and
anarchic). They chronicle the
uncomfortable truth behind the
respectable bourgeois façade. He
was fascinated by street life yet,
for all his apparent criticism of
it, he seems to end up loving
the ugly corruptness he records.
   Note the repetition of certain stock
types and faces; poisonous colors
and artless style to create a feeling
of instability and menace. He was
an early user of photomontage. His
terrifying personal World War I
experiences made him a pessimist,
misanthrope, and political activist
(Communist). His style softened
c. 1924 after marriage and fatherhood.
He emigrated to the US in 1933 and
reverted to being a graphic artist.

KEY WORKS *Suicide*, 1916 (London: Tate
Collection); *Grey Day*, 1921 (Berlin:
Nationalgalerie); *Pillars of Society*, 1926
(Berlin: Staatliche Museum)

Christian **Schad**

◔ 1894–1982   ⏚ GERMAN

⬚ Munich; Berlin; Zurich   🎨 oils; prints; collage
🏛 London: Tate Collection   💰 $492,200 in 1998,
Bildnis einer Unbekannten (oils)

He was a painter who also made collages
and prints (woodcuts), and took photos in
the manner of Man Ray (see page 394).
Best known for his Neue Sachlichkeit
work—a cool, uncompromising, critical
depiction of the German bourgeois
society of the 1920s, including cold, steely
portraits. The exaggerated, emphasized
detail serves to highlight its emptiness.
The alienating spaces show how things
and people become disconnected.
KEY WORKS *Agosta, the Pigeon-Chested Man,
and Rasha, the Black Dove*, 1929 (London:
Tate Collection); *Operation*, 1929 (Munich:
Städtische Galerie)

Self-Portrait with Model *Christian Schad, 1927,
30 x 24¼ in (76 x 62 cm), oil on canvas, Private Collection.
Neue Sachlichkeit ("New Objectivity") describes a
tendency for German art, after 1925, to turn away from
Expressionism. Schad abandoned painting in the Nazi era.*

At Coffee *László Moholy-Nagy, c. 1926, 11¼ x 8¼ in (28.3 x 20.6 cm), vintage gelatin silver photograph, Houston: Museum of Fine Arts.* Moholy-Nagy tried to expand the scope of photography through experimental techniques and innovative compositions. An inspirational teacher, his influence on art and design training has been profound.

KEY WORKS *Photogram*, 1923 (Los Angeles: J. Paul Getty Museum); *A II*, 1924 (New York: Guggenheim Museum); *Dual Form with Chromium Rods*, 1946 (New York: Guggenheim Museum)

Lyonel **Feininger**
● 1871–1956   AMERICAN/GERMAN

 Berlin; New York   woodcuts; drawings; watercolors   San Francisco: Fine Arts Museum $4.03m in 2004, *Newspaper Readers II* (oils)

Son of a concert violinist, Feininger was New York-born and -based, but spent most of his life in Germany (1887–1937). Quiet, personal style, akin to a broken glass pane in which buildings and seascape are the central subject. He blended Cubist fragmentation of form (he studied in Paris) and the misty light and dreaminess of Romanticism (his German heritage). A founder of Bauhaus, remaining there until it was closed in 1933. Talented printmaker (etchings). He influenced set designs for early films such as Max Reinhardt's *Cabinet of Doctor Caligari*.
KEY WORKS *The Bicycle Race*, 1912 (Washington, DC: National Gallery of Art); *Sailing Boats*, 1929 (Detroit Institute of Arts); *Market Church at Evening*, 1930 (Munich: Alte Pinakothek)

László **Moholy-Nagy**
● 1895–1946   HUNGARIAN/GERMAN

 Europe; Chicago   collage; photomontage; drawings; prints   Los Angeles: J. Paul Getty Museum $981,500 in 2000, *A XI* (oils)

He was a lawyer-turned-artist and theoretical writer. Geometric Abstract artist and leading member of, and teacher at, the Bauhaus. Provided the basis for the New Photographer's movement. Sought to create order and clarity using design, abstraction, architecture, typography, constructions, and photography. He settled in Chicago in 1937.

THE BAUHAUS   1919–33

The most famous modern art school, on which so many others have been modeled, highly influential in the fields of architecture and design. Its teachers included Albers, Feininger, Klee, Kandinsky, Moholy-Nagy, and Schlemmer. It opened in Germany in 1919 and was closed by the Nazis in 1933—the New Bauhaus was set up in Chicago by Moholy-Nagy in 1937. The Bauhaus tried to teach the virtues of simple, clean design; abstraction; mass production; the moral and economic benefits of a well-designed environment; democracy and worker participation.

Poster by Joost Schmidt for Bauhaus Exhibition in Weimar, July–September 1923. Bauhaus artists recognized early on the importance of graphic design as a medium to express a corporate identity and image for the school.

Paul **Klee**

● 1879–1940   🏳 GERMAN

🏳 Germany; Bern (Switzerland)   🖌 mixed media; drawings   🏛 Bern: Paul Klee Center
📈 $4,788,000 in 1989, *Auftrieb und Weg, Segelflug* (oils)

The Golden Fish Paul Klee, 1925–26, 19¾ x 27¼ in (50 x 69 cm), oil and watercolor on paper and board, Hamburg: Kunsthalle. In 1925 Klee joined the staff of the Bauhaus, published his *Pedagogical Sketchbook*, and displayed his work at a Surrealist exhibition in Paris.

Klee was a prolific author of drawings, watercolors, and etchings. Dedicated teacher (Bauhaus), and a talented poet and musician. Had a fey, spiritual character and was one of the most original pioneers of the Modern Movement.

Creator of the chamber music of modern art—finely wrought, small-scale works in many media, which are reminiscent in some ways of medieval manuscript illumination (perhaps he drew on this tradition?). Note his quirky, personal imagery and the delicate, unpretentious abstracts. His work is always very sensual, visually and mentally, and delightfully and poetically odd. Had an exquisite color sense and produced neat, precisely worked surfaces.

Don't try to understand or intellectualize Klee—just enjoy his work and follow him wherever he chooses to take your eye and imagination (one of his well-known writings is called "Taking a line for a walk"). Above all, let him take you back to the realm of childhood imagery, imagination, and humor. You will return to adulthood immensely refreshed, enriched, and stimulated.

KEY WORKS *Ancient Sound*, 1925 (Basel, Switzerland: Kunstmuseum); *Ad Parnassum*, 1932 (Hamburg: Kunsthalle); *Diana in the Autumn Wind*, 1934 (Bern, Switzerland: Kunstmuseum); *Death and Fire*, 1940 (Bern, Switzerland: Kunstmuseum)

> "The more horrifying this world becomes ... the more art becomes abstract; while a world at peace produces realistic art."
>
> PAUL KLEE

Josef **Albers**

● 1888–1976   ⚑ GERMAN/AMERICAN

▥ Weimar; US   ✎ prints; woodcuts; oils
🏛 Essen: Albers Museum, Bottrop Collection.
New Haven: Yale University Art Gallery
⚡ $600,000 in 1996, *Despite Mist, Study
for "Homage to the Square"* (oils)

One of the great artist-educators of the
Modern Movement. Pillar of the Bauhaus
1923–1933. Emigrated to US in 1933.

His highly original work combines
investigations into perception with
a simple beauty. Best known for his
"Homage to the Square" series (1949–70),
in which he experiments with nests of
squares that explore values of light and
degrees of temperature in contrasting
colors and hues. He uses the square
because it is the most static of geometric
forms, able to accentuate the color

relationship, and is without movement. He
was also an accomplished photographer
and designer in stained glass.

"Homage to the Square" sounds boring,
but is visually fascinating because Albers
understood that you can never predict
scientifically what color is going to
do, and how it constantly catches you
unaware and delights you. "Homage
to the Square" is the ultimate proof
of this, but you need to get involved
and experiment (by half closing your
eyes, for instance) to really enjoy
and appreciate what is going on.
KEY WORKS *Glass, Color, and Light*, 1921
(New York: Metropolitan Museum of
Art); Study for *Homage to the Square Mild
Scent*, 1965 (Hamburg: Kunsthalle)

Oskar **Schlemmer**

● 1888–1943   ⚑ GERMAN

▥ Weimar; Breslau; Berlin   ✎ oils; prints;
sculpture   🏛 San Francisco: Fine Arts Museum.
Basel (Switzerland): Kunstmuseum   ⚡ $3.08m
in 1998, *Grosse Sitzendengruppe I* (oils)

A leading member of the Bauhaus. Painter
and sculptor. Most effective and at ease
designing mural decorations for ballet
and theater. He preferred simplification,
the interplay of shape and form, and
reflective inner states of mind, rather
than expression and dramatic impact.
Liked quiet exploration and experiment.
KEY WORKS *Head in Profile, with Black Contour*,
1920–21 (San Francisco: Fine Arts Museums);
Group of Fourteen Figures in Imaginary Architecture,
1930 (Cologne: Wallraf-Richartz-Museum);
Bauhaus Stairway, 1934 (New York: Museum
of Modern Art)

DE STIJL   1917–31

De Stijl (from the Dutch for "the style,"
was the name of a group of Dutch artists,
and the journal they published—the
1920s' most influential avant-garde art
magazine. Members and contributors
included Piet Mondrian, Theo van
Doesburg, and the architect and designer
Gerrit Rietveld. The collective advocated
a geometrical type of abstract art,
simplification, social and spiritual form,
seeking laws of harmony that would be
equally applicable to life and art.

Red Blue Chair *designed by
Gerrit Rietveld, 1918.* The hard
surfaces and strong colors are
a rejection of familiarity and
sentimentality in favor of
dynamic rationality.

Piet **Mondrian**

● 1872–1944   ⚑ DUTCH

▥ Netherlands; Paris; London; New York
✎ oils; mixed media   🏛 New York:
Museum of Modern Art   ⚡ $18.75m
in 2004, *New York, Boogie Woogie* (oils)

One of the pioneers of pure abstract art.
Austere, reclusive character who hated the
green untidiness of nature. Theoretically
and intellectually influential in his lifetime.
Had no commercial success.

The most familiar works are the abstracts
of the 1920s and 1930s. They have simple

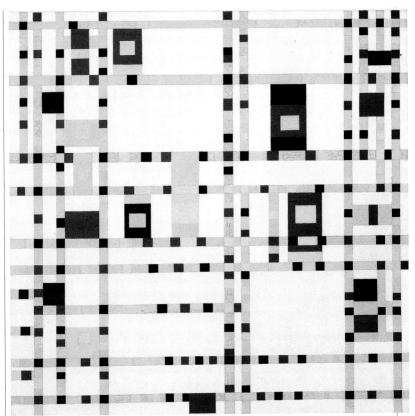

Broadway Boogie Woogie Piet Mondrian,
1942–43, 50 x 50 in (127 x 127 cm), oil on canvas,
New York: Museum of Modern Art. © 2005
Mondrian/Holtzman Trust, c/o HCR International,
Warrenton, Virginia, US

elements: black, white, and primary colors only, horizontal and vertical lines. His goal was to find and express a universal spiritual perfection, but his imagery has become a commonplace of 20th-century commercial design. Look out, also, for his late, jazzily colorful work, completed in New York. His slow and painstaking progress through Symbolism and Cubism to abstraction repays patient study.

You have to see Mondrian's work in the flesh to understand it. Reproductions make his abstracts look bland, mechanical, and easy, with immaculate, anonymous surfaces. In fact, you can (and are supposed to see) the brush marks, the alterations, the hesitations—the struggle to achieve that harmonious balance and purity that he desperately wanted, but found so hard to attain. Note also the deliberate small scale and intimacy of most of his work.

KEY WORKS *The Gray Tree*, 1912 (The Hague: Gemeentemuseum); *Pier and Ocean*, 1915 (Otterlo, Netherlands: Kröller-Müller Museum); *Tableau No. IV with Red, Blue, Yellow, and Black*, 1924–25 (Washington, DC: National Gallery of Art); *Composition in Red and Blue*, 1939–41 (Private Collection)

> **"Abstract art ... is opposed to a natural representation of things ... it is not opposed to nature ... It is opposed to the raw, primitive animal nature of man, but it is at one with human nature."**
>
> PIET MONDRIAN

SURREALISM

Surrealism was the most influential avant-garde movement of the interwar years. Its chief goal, asserted by its founder and leader, André Breton, was to meld the unconscious with the conscious to create a new "super reality"—a *surréalisme*. Cubism, Dada, and Freud were its starting points. Its enduring influence can be found notably in present-day advertising and avant-garde humor.

STYLE

Still from the 1929 Surrealist film *Un Chien Andalou* by Salvador Dalí and Luis Buñuel. Film was an ideal medium for Surrealism. Buñuel, working closely with Dalí, created a disconcerting and deliberately unfathomable masterpiece.

Perhaps not surprisingly for a movement whose origins were largely literary and which actively championed anarchy, Surrealism in the visual arts almost immediately developed a bewildering variety of styles. It could be highly finished, aiming at a kind of heightened realism (Dalí, for example), or, at the other end of the spectrum, entirely abstract (Miró, for example). In whatever style it was executed, it generally aimed to surprise, often to shock, frequently to disturb, and always to create a dreamlike atmosphere, sometimes highly specific, at other times vague and suggestive.

SUBJECTS

The personal nature of the subconscious necessarily resists categorization; Surrealist subject matter literally knew no limits. Ernst experimented with a visual equivalent of stream of consciousness writing: *frottage*—rubbings taken from worn surfaces to create chance patterns. Magritte's deadpan paintings exploit enigmatic juxtapositions, often sexual. Arp, painter and sculptor, favored simple, vaguely biomorphic shapes, seemingly randomly assembled, in bold, flat colors.

KEY EVENTS

1919	André Breton and Philippe Soupault write *Les Champs Magnétiques*
1924	First *Surrealist Manifesto* issued, largely written by Breton, in Paris
1930	Breton formally allies Surrealism with the Proletarian Revolution
1936	London International Surrealist Exhibition held
1937	Leon Trotsky and Breton write *Manifesto for an Independent Revolutionary Art*
1939	Outbreak of World War II sees exodus of Surrealist artists to New York

Object *Meret Oppenheim, 1936, diameter 9½ in (23.7 cm) height 23¾ in (7.3 cm), fur, china, and metal, New York: Museum of Modern Art.* Oppenheim's fur-covered cup, saucer, and spoon encapsulate Surrealism's determination to subvert the everyday world.

WHAT TO LOOK FOR

Ernst was the most complete Surrealist artist in the sense that he experimented with all techniques: figuration, abstraction, and collage. In this archetypal, pioneering work he explores methods of creating imagery that were to become a commonplace of Surrealist painting. In particular, he synthesizes his study and understanding of Freud's ideas, notably about the juxtaposition of polarities such as the rational/irrational, constructive/destructive, dead/alive, with his own experiences and desires. Oedipus means "swollen foot"; in Greek mythology he was the hero who unwittingly killed his father, married his own mother, and gouged out his eyes on realizing what he had done. Freud's "Oedipus Complex" is an inability to break infantile dependence on parents, and so become fully mature.

Oedipus Rex *Max Ernst, 1922, 36⅔ x 40 in (93 x 102 cm), oil on canvas, Private Collection.* Ernst knew he had to escape the dominance of his father, who was an academic painter and devout Catholic.

In Freudian analysis, the balloon and the birds represent a longing for escape and freedom

The hand that cracks the nut is a metaphor for sexual intercourse. The spike and the arrow stand for pain, and the distorted scale suggests the struggle in gender relationships

Ernst was obsessed by birds, death, and gender ever since his pet cockatoo died on the day his sister was born. The birds have human, upside-down eyes

TECHNIQUES

Paint is applied in a precise but anonymous manner. Imagery has been copied from magazines and prints. Ernst was a self-taught painter and a pioneer of collage.

The psychosexual interpretation is that the nut represents the female (the crack suggesting the vulva)

The mechanical device that pierces the finger is one that was used to punch holes in the webbed feet of chicken so as to mark their age. It suggests pain, penetration, and intercourse.

Salvador **Dalí**

● 1904–89 ⚑ SPANISH

🏠 Spain; Paris; New York 🎨 mixed media; oils; sculpture 🏛 Figueras (Spain): Salvador Dalí Museum. St. Petersburg (Florida): Salvador Dalí Museum 💲 $3.77m in 2000, *Ma femme nue regardant son propre corps devenir marches* (oils)

Soft Construction with Boiled Beans: Premonition of Civil War Salvador Dalí, 1936, 43⅓ x 32⅓ in (110 x 83 cm), oil on canvas, Philadelphia: Museum of Art. The second half of the painting's title was added on the outbreak of the Spanish Civil War.

Dalí was a flamboyant self-publicist, and one of the most popular painters of the 20th century. Made a brief but major contribution to Surrealism.

He was an artist of astonishing technical precocity and virtuosity. He mastered almost any style (see early work), finally choosing one based on the detailed, "realistic," 17th-century Dutch masters—instantly popular and recognizable as "very skillful" (the optical illusions are breathtaking). Ultimately just a flashy showman with a big ego and a long moustache—like a singer who churns out popular arias in a spectacular way, but devoid of any real expression, meaning, or freshness.

There is one exception to the above. Look for the works of 1928–33, which are great and profound. Briefly, as a true pioneer of the Surrealist movement, Dalí created works to explore his "paranoia-critical method." Using Freudian ideas about dreams and madness, he produced obsessional images in which detailed reality is suddenly transformed into different, intricate, and disturbing images. Technically and imaginatively brilliant. He ought to have persisted with it.

KEY WORKS *Seated Girl Seen from the Rear*, 1925 (Madrid: Museo Nacional Centro de Arte Reina Sofia); *The Persistence of Memory*, 1931 (New York: Metropolitan Museum of Art); *Surrealist Composition with Invisible Figures*, c. 1936 (Private Collection); *Christ of St. John of the Cross*, 1951 (Kelvingrove, Glasgow: Art Gallery and Museum)

Joan **Miró**

◔ 1893–1983   ▣ SPANISH

▣ Barcelona; Paris; Mallorca   ◑ mixed media;
ceramics; sculpture; prints   ▣ Barcelona:
Foundation Joan Miró. Mallorca: Pilar and Joan
Miró Foundation and Museum   ▨ $11.5m
in 2001, *Portrait of Mme. K* (works on paper)

He was a leading Surrealist painter and
sculptor: experimental, unconventional,
influential. Searched for a new visual
language, purged of stale meanings
and appealing to the senses.

Miró is best known for his abstract and
semiabstract works—highly structured,
poetic, dreamy; simple forms floating on
fields of color. Let them suggest anything
(especially something biological, sexual,
primitive). Enjoy the naughty thoughts,
silliness, color, beauty, light, warmth.

Uses a limited number of forms, but
repeats and makes rhymes of them. He
draws on an (unconscious) memory bank
of natural and landscape forms, which
suggest generative power in nature.
He experimented with "magic realism"
before breaking into a new style, c. 1924.
KEY WORKS *Le port*, 1945 (Private Collection);
The Red Sun Gnaws at the Spider, 1948 (Private
Collection); *Woman and Bird in the Moonlight*,
1949 (London: Tate Collection)

Harlequin's Carnival Joan Miró, 1924, 26 x 36¾ in
(66 x 93 cm), oil on canvas, Buffalo: Albright-Knox
Gallery. Miró claimed that his imagery was sometimes
the result of hallucinations caused by extreme hunger.

André **Masson**

◔ 1896–1987   ▣ FRENCH

▣ France; Spain; US   ◑ mixed media;
drawings; engravings; sculpture   ▣ New York:
Museum of Modern Art   ▨ $883,945 in 1989,
La femme paralytique (oils)

An artist whose reputation and influence
is better known than his work. Deeply
affected by World War I injuries. Leading
Surrealist who explored the irrational and
subconscious in intense, finely wrought
paintings and drawings. Disliked order;
liked experimentation and spontaneous
action. Lived in the US after 1940—had
a big impact on Abstract Expressionists.
KEY WORKS *Pedestal Table in the Studio*, 1922
(London: Tate Collection); *Card Trick*, 1923
(New York: Museum of Modern Art)

Yves **Tanguy**

◔ 1900–55   ▣ FRENCH

▣ Paris; New York; Connecticut   ◑ oils
▣ New York: Museum of Modern Art
▨ $6.77m in 2005, *Derniers Jours* (oils)

A self-taught Surrealist who, from c. 1927,
evolved (but never developed further) a
style of imaginary landscapes (or seabeds?)
full of weird and curiously compelling half-
vegetable, half-animal forms.
KEY WORKS *The Look of Amber*, 1929 (Washington,
DC: National Gallery of Art); *Promontory Palace*,
1931 (New York: Guggenheim Museum)

Man Ray

1890–1976 AMERICAN

New York; Paris; Hollywood
photography; prints; mixed media
Los Angeles: J. Paul Getty Museum
$1.5m in 2003, *Impossibilité Dancer-Danger* (oils)

The creator of memorable avant-garde Surrealist images, usually through photography. He was inventive (imaginatively and technically), witty, and anarchic. Cultivated a carefree persona with maxim that the least possible effort would give the greatest possible result. Painted documentary portraits of the Dada and Surrealist heroes.

KEY WORKS *Silhouette*, 1916 (New York: Guggenheim Museum); *Duchamp with Mill*, 1917 (Los Angeles: J. Paul Getty Museum)

> "A certain amount of contempt for the material employed to express an idea is indispensable to the purest realization of this idea."
>
> MAN RAY

The Aged Emak Bakia Man Ray, 1970, after the original of 1924, height 18¼ in (46 cm), silver, Private Collection. The sculpture is named after an earlier Man Ray Surrealist film of 1927, Emak Bakia, which means "leave me alone" in Basque.

Meret Oppenheim

1913–85 GERMAN

Berlin; Paris sculpture; mixed media
Boston: Museum of Fine Arts $74,592 in 2002, *Tout Toujours* (oils)

She will always be remembered for her Surrealist fur teacup *Object* (see page 390). Oppenheim produced engaging, delicate, whimsical work on many themes and in many media and styles—individually slight but collectively expressing her refusal to be categorized and pinned down. Had a free spirit and disliked prescribed roles, especially for women. Witches and snakes are recurring images.

KEY WORKS *Object (Le déjeuner en fourrure)*, 1931 (Houston: Museum of Fine Arts); *Sitzende Figur mit verschränkten Fingern*, 1933 (Bern, Switzerland: Kunstmuseum); *Red Head, Blue Body*, 1936 (New York: Museum of Modern Art)

Sir Roland Penrose

1900–84 BRITISH

London mixed media; collage; sculpture London: Tate Collection
$26,884 in 2003, *Union Nocturne* (oils)

He was a rich and eccentric painter, writer, dilettante, connoisseur, and collector—another shining example of the uniquely British "gifted amateur." A friend of Picasso and Ernst, he was a champion of Surrealism. Made and painted good (if derivative) Surrealist works.

KEY WORKS *Night and Day*, 1937 (Private Collection); *The Last Voyage of Captain Cook*, 1936–67 (London: Tate Collection)

Paul Delvaux

1897–1994 BELGIAN

Belgium oils Bruges: Palais des Beaux-Arts. St. Idesbald (Belgium): Paul Delvaux Foundation and Museum
$4,698,000 in 1999, *Le miroir* (oils)

He was a loner who created a limited and repetitive *oeuvre* of finely detailed, vaguely erotic, and symbolic, nighttime, dreamland images based on themes of naked women, semideserted railroad stations or landscapes, and classic buildings. Admired by, but not allied with, true Surrealists. Influenced by Magritte and De Chirico exhibition of 1926.

KEY WORKS *A Siren in Full Moonlight*, 1940 (New Haven: Yale Center for British Art); *The Red City*, 1941 (Private Collection)

René **Magritte**

◐ 1898–1967 ⋈ BELGIAN

🏛 Brussels; Paris 🎨 oils; gouache; prints
🏛 New York: Museum of Modern Art. Minnesota: Minneapolis Institute of Art 💰 $11.5m in 2003, *Empire des lumières* (oils)

Magritte was a leading Surrealist painter who made a virtue of his bowler-hatted, cheap-suited provincialism. Famous for use of everyday objects plus deadpan style, creating mildly disturbing images suggesting the dislocated world of dreams.

He painted small(ish) oil paintings. Used deliberately banal technique, without aesthetic virtue—imagery is everything. Transformed the familiar into the unfamiliar by weird juxtapositions, changes of scale and texture, and contradiction of expectation. The titles of his works (sometimes chosen by friends) are designed deliberately to confuse and obscure. His best work dates from the 1920s and 1930s. Change of style after 1943. Worked as a freelance advertising artist from 1924 to 1967.

Used classic Freudian symbols and references—death and decay (coffins, night); sex (naked women, pubic parts); phallic symbols (guns, sausages, candles). Themes of claustrophobia (closed rooms, confined spaces = sexual repression?); yearning for liberty (blue sky, fresh landscapes). Witnessed his mother's suicide aged 13. Married. His work risked becoming a tired formula (his very late work is), but is saved by an active imagination and a sense of the absurd.
KEY WORKS *The Menaced Assassin*, 1926 (New York: Museum of Modern Art); *Reproduction Prohibited*, 1937 (Rotterdam: Museum

The Human Condition *René Magritte, 1933, 39⅖ x 32 in (100 x 81 cm), oil on canvas, Washington, DC: National Gallery of Art.* The term "magic realism" was coined to describe the conceptual tensions between the possible and the impossible in Magritte's work.

Boymans-van Beuningen); *The Song of Love*, 1948 (Private Collection); *Golconde*, 1953 (Houston: Menil Collection)

Matta

◐ 1911–2002 ⋈ CHILEAN

🏛 Paris; Rome; New York 🎨 oils; prints; drawings
🏛 San Francisco: Museum of Modern Art
💰 $1.5m in 1995, *Disasters of Mysticism* (oils)

Roberto Sebastián Echaurren, revolutionary spirit who was born in Santiago but settled in France in 1933 and became an early Surrealist. Like many other artists, left for the US when World War II broke out but resettled in Paris in 1954. Author of strange, dreamlike paintings with complex spaces and totemlike figures. Had a poetic agenda: searching for links between the cosmos, the eroticism of the human body, and the human psychic space. Intended his work to exalt freedom and aid mankind's struggle against oppression.
KEY WORKS *Psychological Morphology*, 1939 (Toronto: Art Gallery of Ontario); *La Rosa*, 1943 (Ohio: Cleveland Museum of Art)

Pablo **Picasso**

● 1881–1973 ⚑ SPANISH

🏛 Barcelona; Paris; Rome; South of France
🎨 oils; sculpture 🏛 Paris: Musée National
Picasso. Barcelona: Museu Picasso 💲 $93m
in 2004, *Garçon à la Pipe* (oils)

Picasso stands as the undisputed master
and chief innovator of the Modern
Movement. You have to go
back to Michelangelo to
find anyone of equal genius
or stature. He was convivial
and energetic, and led a
turbulent, intense, and
often unhappy personal
life (his many love affairs
are legendary). His output
of work was vast; he
was equally inventive
as painter, sculptor,
printmaker, ceramicist,
and theater designer.

LIFE AND WORKS

Born into an artistic family
in Barcelona, his prodigious
talent showed itself at an
early age. He visited Paris for the first
time at the age of 19, and he divided
his early years between France and Spain,
developing his "Blue Period," with its
themes of death and deprivation. In 1904
he settled permanently in France, first
evolving the "Rose Period," with images
of the circus and harlequins; by 1907 he
was the champion of the avant-garde and
the pioneer of Cubism (see page 350).

Self-Portrait *1901, 40 x 23¾ in
(81 x 60 cm), oil on canvas, Paris:
Musée National Picasso.* The
starving artist aged 20, painted
in Paris during his "Blue Period."

Although deeply committed to Spain, its
art, and its people, Picasso effectively lived
in voluntary exile, based in Paris, where he
became the focus for the emerging School
of Paris (see page 357), and latterly in the
south of France. Passionately opposed
to Franco's political regime, which he
attacked in his art, he vowed never to
set foot in his land of birth while Franco
lived. The dictator outlived
him by 32 months.

PAINTINGS

His paintings display a
bewildering range of technical
and stylistic originality:
he was the master of
Classicism, Symbolism, and
Expressionism; the inventor
of Cubism, and anticipator of
Surrealism. However, pure
abstraction never interested
him. Central to his art is a
wide-ranging post-Freudian
response to the human figure
and the human condition—
with frequent intimate
references to sex and death,
sometimes blissful, sometimes anguished.
All his work was highly egocentric in
some way, but he had the rare ability to
turn self-comment into universal truths.

> **"Art is a lie that makes
> us realize the truth."**
>
> PABLO PICASSO

Out of many themes, two invite
immediate exploration: the almost daily
autobiography from ambitious, half-starved
young hopeful to husband and womanizer
to sexually frustrated old man; and the
ease with which he switched styles,
images, and techniques, always conscious
of which was the most appropriate for his
subject matter and mood.

SCULPTURE

There is a tendency to judge Picasso by
his paintings, whereas his true forte was
for work in 3-D. These became more
numerous and interesting as he grew
older (the quality of his paintings declines
after 1939). Here, too, he was the master
of traditional techniques and a dazzling

Minotaur Caressing a Sleeping Girl *1933,
13¼ x 17½ in (33.6 x 43.9 cm), drypoint engraving, Private
Collection.* The bull is a metaphor for Picasso himself:
frustratingly caught up in a marriage he wished to dissolve
while committed to a secret, young, pregnant lover.

Weeping Woman *1937, 21⅔ x 18 in (55 x 46 cm), oil on canvas, Melbourne: National Gallery of Victoria.* Showing typical Cubist distortion, the model for this depiction of female grief is said to be Picasso's then mistress, Dora Maar. The picture was used as a study for *Guernica* (1937), painted in response to the bombing of the Spanish city by the Germans in 1937.

innovator through welding, constructions, and ceramics. In fact, many two-dimensional works are simply ideas that itch to be realized in 3-D.

KEY WORKS *Child with a Dove*, 1901 (London: National Gallery); *Family of Saltimbanques*, 1905 (Washington, DC: National Gallery of Art); *Girl on a Ball*, 1905 (Moscow: Pushkin Museum); *The Lovers*, 1923 (Washington, DC: National Gallery of Art); *Guernica*, 1937 (Madrid: Museo Nacional Centro Arte Reina Sofia)

A Bull *c. 1950, ceramic plate, London: Bonhams.* After World War II, Picasso moved to Antibes with Françoise Gillot and began his carefree, inventive work in ceramics, which have the attributes of paintings and sculpture.

Paul **Nash**
● 1889–1946 🏴 BRITISH

🇬🇧 Kent; Sussex; Dorset (all UK) 🎨 oils; mixed media; photography 🏛 London: Tate Collection
💰 $146,400 in 2004, *Autumn Landscape* (oils)

One of the best British artists before 1950, he successfully blended an English pastoral vision with an awareness of European modern art. The voice of "I am English first and foremost, of Europe but not in Europe."

His small-scale works in oil, pastel, or watercolor show a deeply personal firsthand response to landscape, coastline, Sun, and Moon, and to objects in nature. He was careful in every sense and very English, of a certain type: self-contained, serious, gentle, parochial, romantic, polite, self-assured, independent, but not too progressive. Lean, spare, well-focused imagery and style. Earthy English palette.

He worked as a war artist in both world wars. Focused on trench landscape and its destruction in World War I; flight and aircraft in World War II. His capacity for juxtaposing the unexpected and transposing one object into another by association links him with the Surrealists. Note how he abstracts from nature and organizes his perceptions, feelings, and paintings to capture the essential feel of a place—the so-called "genius loci."

KEY WORKS *Mineral Objects*, 1935 (New Haven: Yale Center for British Art); *Circle of Monoliths*, 1937–38 (Leeds: City Art Gallery); *Monster Field*, 1939 (South Africa: Durban Art Gallery); *Totes Meer (Dead Sea)*, 1940–41 (London: Tate Collection)

Sir Stanley **Spencer**
● 1891–1959 🏴 BRITISH

🇬🇧 Berkshire 🎨 oils; drawing 🏛 Cookham (UK): Stanley Spencer Gallery. London: Tate Collection; Imperial War Museum 💰 $1,992,000 in 1990, *Crucifixion* (oils)

A difficult, argumentative but inspired personality with a unique and personal vision and great talent. Preached, practiced, and illustrated sexual liberation at a time when such things were "not done."

His work shows English eccentricity at its best and most convincing. Disregarded prevailing conventions (social and moral,

Travoys Arriving with the Wounded at a Dressing Station, Smol, Macedonia *Sir Stanley Spencer, 1916, 72 x 86 in (83 x 218.5 cm), oil on canvas, London: Imperial War Museum.* Spencer served in the army as a medical orderly and infantryman.

as well as artistic), and had an utterly personal agenda and unshakeable belief in his own vision and ability. Focus of his life and major work was around his home village of Cookham, which he saw as an earthly paradise. It also provided the setting for his profound belief in the return of Christ for and among ordinary people.

Observe his humanity, humor, and acerbic wit. He had a dry, careful, deliberately outdated technique inspired by early Italians, Pre-Raphaelites, and Dutch and Flemish painters. Was a masterly and inspired draftsman. His best works are his religious and World War I subjects. Potboiler landscapes earned him money. Like all true visionary eccentrics, he managed to be separate from his own time and era, yet totally of it.

KEY WORKS *The Centurion's Servant*, 1914 (London: Tate Collection); *The Resurrection: Cookham*, 1924–26 (London: Tate Collection); *Self-Portrait with Patricia Preece*, 1936 (Cambridge: Fitzwilliam Museum); *A Village in Heaven*, 1937 (Manchester: City Art Gallery)

Ivon **Hitchens**
● 1893–1979 🏴 BRITISH

🇬🇧 London; Sussex 🎨 oils; drawings
🏛 London: Tate Collection 💰 $255,000 in 2003, *Boy at Breakfast* (oils)

He was a sensitive painter who made a slow, patient progress from figuration to abstraction. His main theme was landscape, often in long horizontal format, in which color and form are increasingly abstracted to simple elements. Among the first in England to sustain a development of post-Cubist painting. Also painted still lifes and nudes.

KEY WORKS *Balcony at Cambridge*, 1929 (London: Tate Collection); *Winter Stage*, 1936 (London: Tate Collection)

Henry **Moore**

● 1898–1986 🅿 BRITISH

🅵 Leeds; London; Hertfordshire   🗿 sculpture; drawings   🏛 Washington, DC: National Gallery of Art   💹 $7.5m in 2004, *Three-piece Reclining Figure: Draped* (sculpture)

Moore was a tough, gritty, ambitious Yorkshireman, one of the best-known British modern masters. His work is a popular choice for international sculptural monuments but it looks best when in a landscape setting rather than in a gallery.

His romantic response to nature and the human figure is often expressed as a synthesis of the two, so that his forms can be read simultaneously as organic nature (rocks, cliffs, trees), and as human figures. He consciously rejected Renaissance notions of ideal beauty, but was much influenced by Mexican, Egyptian, and English medieval sculpture. Direct carving

and truth to materials were an imperative of his early work; this was gradually replaced by a desire for monumentality.

Walk around his sculptures to investigate the constantly changing relationships between the different parts. Moore was fascinated by the reclining nude, and mother-and-child images. He investigated ideas in his drawings and was a superb sculptural draftsman. Flirted with Surrealism in the 1930s; important war drawings in 1940s. Declined when he used assistants for late public monuments.

KEY WORKS *Mother and Child*, 1936–37 (Leeds: City Art Gallery); *UNESCO Reclining Figure*, 1957 (Paris: UNESCO Headquarters); *Mirror Knife Edge*, 1977 (Washington, DC: National Gallery of Art)

> "… a work must first have a pent-up energy, an intense life of its own, independent of the object it may represent."
>
> HENRY MOORE

Reclining Figure (LH 175) Henry Moore, 1936, height 25¼ in (64 cm), elmwood, West Yorkshire: Wakefield Art Gallery. Moore was a founder of the English Surrealist Group in 1936.

Dame Barbara **Hepworth**
◔ 1903–75   ◳ BRITISH

◳ England; Italy; St. Ives   ◨ sculpture
▥ St Ives: Barbara Hepworth Museum and
Sculpture Garden   ⚡ $1m in 2004, *The Family
of Man: Figure I, Ancestor I* (sculpture)

Hepworth was a leading member of
the first generation of British modern
masters. She expressed in sculpture,
for the first time, the tradition of
English Romantic landscape. She
was much honored and revered both
in her lifetime and subsequently.

Look for a deeply emotional response
to, and identification with, nature and
landscape. Her inspiration came from
light, seasons, natural materials, mysteries
of nature. She searched for (and found)
fundamental essences and elements. These
were distilled and abstracted, for instance,
into simplified forms and pure color like
Matisse (she had contact with the French
avant-garde in 1932), although Hepworth's
starting point was nature, not the human
figure. Made some geometric carvings in
the 1930s; also beautiful drawings.

> ## "In the contemplation
> ## of nature we are
> ## perpetually renewed."
> ### DAME BARBARA HEPWORTH

Involute 1 *Dame Barbara Hepworth, 1946, height 18 in
(45.7cm), white stone, Private Collection.* Pierced abstract
form became a distinctive feature, allowing Hepworth to
explore the physical essence and inherent poetry of her
materials. Her first such piece dates from 1931–32.

ST. IVES GROUP   1940s–1960s

St. Ives in Cornwall became a creative
colony for British artists after the arrival
in 1939 of sculptor Barbara Hepworth
and her then husband Ben Nicholson,
who had discovered retired fisherman
painter Alfred Wallis on an earlier visit
to the town. Wallis's naïve paintings
later inspired many of the group, which
included artists Terry Frost, Patrick
Heron, and sculptor Henry Moore.

Tate St. Ives, Cornwall, England Opened in 1993,
the gallery overlooks Porthmeor Beach and exhibits
modern and contemporary art.

She had a lifelong belief in truth to
materials—taking stone, wood, bronze
(after 1950) and making apparent the
unique quality of each individual piece,
adapting the final form to its own
peculiarities. Initiated and developed
pierced form to explore materials and
evoke nature's mystery and organic
growth. Used strings to express emotional
response and tension. Greek titles, after
visit to Greece (1953), indicate respect
for Classical tradition.

KEY WORKS *Doves*, 1928 (Manchester: City
Art Gallery); *Two Forms*, 1933 (London:
Tate Collection); *Sculpture with Colour
(Oval Form) Pale Blue and Red*, 1943
(Private Collection); *Minoan Head*, 1972
(Cambridge: Fitzwilliam Museum)

Ben **Nicholson**
◔ 1894–1982   ◳ BRITISH

◳ England; Paris; Switzerland   ◨ oils;
sculpture   ▥ London: Tate Collection
⚡ $1,936,000 in 1990, *La Boutique Fantastique* (oils)

Doyen of the St. Ives School, Nicholson
was a pioneer of abstract art in Britain,
and one of the UK's first modern artists.
Son of Sir William Nicholson; he married
Barbara Hepworth in 1934.

September 1963 *Ben Nicholson, 1963, oil and collage on fibrocement, Private Collection.* In the 1930s, Nicholson explored abstraction through carved relief sculptures. In the 1950s, he returned to the theme, making constructions out of boards that he cut, assembled, and painted.

He chose traditional subject matter (landscapes and still lifes) for his paintings, reliefs, and drawings. Moved easily between a pared-down figuration and pure abstraction, making interesting use of materials and scratched textures. The lean, athletic look and sense of calculation rather than spontaneity was central to his competitive persona, which enjoyed playing games (ball and psychological). His work shows debt to modern European art—Cubism, Mondrian, and Braque.

Notice the way in which he imposed English virtues of politeness or understatement on the unruly appearance of the European avant-garde, making it as well-tailored as a Savile Row suit and as well-mannered as a game of gentlemen's cricket (both express deep passions as well as reserve). Does the fact that his work looks equally at home in modern or traditional, country or urban, British or European settings suggest that it is bland—or does it mean it is the essence of international savoir faire?

KEY WORKS *St. Ives Bay: Sea with Boats*, 1931 (Manchester: City Art Gallery); *White Relief*, 1935 (London: Tate Collection); *February 1956 (menhir)*, 1956 (New York: Guggenheim Museum)

John **Piper**
◉ 1903–92 ◪ BRITISH

▣ London ◨ oils; prints ▥ London: Tate Collection ◲ $131,200 in 2003, *Rocky Valley, North Wales* (oils)

A serious, well-regarded painter and printmaker notable for a very personal, stylized, romantic imagery of landscape and architecture. Was also a book illustrator and stage designer. Once the epitome of acceptable modernity, his work now looks dated, but will come back into fashion one day.

KEY WORKS *Beach with Starfish*, 1933–34 (London: Tate Collection); *Autumn at Stourhead*, 1939 (Manchester: City Art Gallery)

Graham **Sutherland**
◉ 1903–80 ◪ BRITISH

▣ England; France ◨ engravings; oils ▥ San Francisco: Fine Arts Museums ◲ $247,050 in 2004, *Toad* (oils)

His work is a fascinating example of English tradition and modern idiom cohabiting. Sutherland's landscapes reveal a fascination with organic forms and metamorphosis. His portraits (his best work?) show a fascination for facial forms that contain the inner personality (like a fossil in a rock). Underrated.

KEY WORKS *Somerset Maugham*, 1949 (London: Tate Collection); *Christ in Glory*, 1962 (Coventry Cathedral)

The March of Humanity in Latin America David Alfaro Siqueiros, 1964, area 50,000 sq. ft (4,645 sq. meters), mural painting, Mexico City: Polyforum Siqueiros. Siqueiros considered this his greatest achievement and the union of all his discoveries.

David Alfaro **Siqueiros**

◔ 1896–1974 ⚑ MEXICAN

🏢 Mexico; Europe 🎨 oils; acrylics 🏛 Mexico City (murals for public buildings) 💰 $330,000 in 1989, *Niña Madre* (works on paper)

A prolific painter and writer who was deeply involved in progressive, political causes in Mexico in the 1920s and 1930s. He is revered as Mexico's greatest painter.

Produced solemn (gloomy?) works with strong political commitment—art in the service of the people's revolution. Look for monumental, sculptural peasants and faces; direct, earthy subjects. Was technically accomplished and quietly experimental (he made very early use of industrial paints and drip techniques), and was unshakeably consistent in his style and belief.

His crowning achievements are the vast in-situ murals in Mexico, which are revolutionary manifestos in their own right and exploit daring, cinema-inspired angles and perspectives.
KEY WORKS *Seated Nude*, 1931 (San Francisco: Fine Arts Museums); *Zapata*, 1931 (New York: Metropolitan Museum of Art)

Diego **Rivera**

◔ 1886–1957 ⚑ MEXICAN

🏢 Mexico; Paris; Italy; US 🎨 oils; fresco 🏛 Mexico City (fresco decorations in public buildings). Detroit Institute of Arts 💰 $2.8m in 1995, *Baile en Tehuantepec* (oils)

Rivera was a giant—physically (6 ft, 300 lbs); in terms of his charismatic personality (political revolutionary and turbulent love life); and in the quantity and scale of his work—representing

social realism at its most convincing. A Marxist, loved and financed by US mega-capitalists.

The large-scale murals he created in the 1920s and 1930s were designed for public spaces and express a utopian view of society—they are political statements of art in the service of society. His vision was a union between Mexico's Indian history and a machine-age future in which past, present, and future, nature, science, humanity, male and female, and all races and cultures coexist in harmony. He revived the art of monumental, true fresco, physically and conceptually.

The way he turns his vision into vast, crowded images is truly miraculous. He synthesized first-hand knowledge of pre-Columbian art, Modernism (Cubist space), realism, and early Renaissance frescoes (monumental, simplified forms of Giotto, Masaccio, Piero) into brilliantly organized and controlled decorative pageants, with a storyteller's instinct for memorable detail. Also produced seductive, smaller-scale easel paintings and sketches: portraits, figures, narrative scenes, and still lifes.
KEY WORKS *Still Life*, 1913 (St. Petersburg: Hermitage Museum); *Table on a Café Terrace*, 1915 (New York: Metropolitan Museum of Art); *The Aztec World*, 1929 (Mexico City: Palacio Nacional)

José Clemente **Orozco**

◔ 1883–1949 ⚑ MEXICAN

🏢 Mexico; US 🎨 oils; watercolors 🏛 Guadalajara: Orozco Workshop-Museum. Mexico City: Carrillo Gil Museum 💰 $883,200 in 2004, *Cellar* (oils)

Orozco was one of the three great Mexican muralists (with Diego Rivera and David Alfaro Siqueiros). His public-building murals, in a cold and austere style, are based on his experiences of the Mexican Revolution and Civil War, showing the struggles and sacrifices of the people and the pain of needless suffering.

KEY WORKS Fresco series, 1926 (Mexico City: Casa de los Azulejos); *The Coming and the Return of Quetzalcoatl*, 1932–34 (New Hampshire: Dartmouth College)

Frida **Kahlo**

● 1907–54 ⓟ MEXICAN

ⓟ Mexico 🎨 oils 🏛 Coyoacan (Mexico): Museo Frida Kahlo 📈 $2.9m in 1995, *Autorretrato con chango y loro* (oils)

Kahlo was one of the best-known Mexican painters, who created powerful, figurative images that synthesized her

sufferings, both physical (she was crippled in a car accident aged 15) and emotional (stormy marriage to Diego Rivera), with an exploration of themes of Mexican politics and identity. Is her art merely parochial, or does it touch deeper levels of emotion?

KEY WORKS *Self-Portrait with Monkey*, 1938 (Buffalo: Albright-Knox Art Gallery); *The Two Fridas*, 1939 (Mexico City: Museo de Arte Moderno); *Self-Portrait with Cropped Hair*, 1940 (New York: Museum of Modern Art)

Suicide of Dorothy Hale Frida Kahlo, 1939, 23½ x 19½ in (59.7 x 49.5 cm), oil on masonite with painted frame, Arizona: Phoenix Art Museum. Dorothy Hale was a beautiful socialite who, after losing her husband and her financial security, threw herself to her death from the window of her New York apartment.

Giorgio de **Chirico**

● 1888–1978   ▶ ITALIAN

▣ Greece; Italy; Paris; US
▣ oils; sculpture   ▣ New York:
Museum of Modern Art   ▨ $6.4m
in 2004, *The Great Metaphysician* (oils)

De Chirico was the originator
of metaphysical painting.
Melancholic curmudgeon with
a brief period of true greatness,
around 1910–20. Haunting
paintings of deserted Italianate
squares with exaggerated
perspectives, irrational
shadows, trains, clocks, over-
sized objects, and a sense of
latent menace and ungraspable
meaning. Much influenced by
Nietzsche. Late work is weak.

KEY WORKS *The Uncertainty of
the Poet*, 1913 (London: Tate
Collection); *The Painter's Family*,
1926 (London: Tate Collection)

The Mystery and Melancholy of a Street Giorgio
de Chirico, 1914, 34⅔ x 28⅓ in (88 x 72 cm), oil on canvas,
Private Collection. De Chirico's poetic suggestions of the
unpredictable were an inspiration for the Surrealists.

Giorgio **Morandi**

● 1890–1964   ▶ ITALIAN

▣ Bologna   ▣ oils; engravings
▣ San Francisco: Fine Arts Museums
▨ $1.35m in 1990, *Natura Morta* (oils)

He was reclusive, isolated, and gifted,
best known for his post-1920 still lifes of
simple objects (such as bottles) of great
delicacy and seductive, poetic simplicity.
Small scale, low key; almost monochrome,
almost abstract, to be enjoyed in silence.
Good pre-1920 metaphysical paintings.
Beautiful etchings.

KEY WORKS *Still Life*, 1948 (Parma:
Fondazione Magnani-Rocca); *Still Life*,
1957 (Hamburg: Kunsthalle)

Balthus

● 1908–2001   ▶ FRENCH

▣ France; Italy; Switzerland   ▣ oils
▣ New York: Museum of Modern Art
▨ $3.4m in 2004, *Golden Afternoon* (oils)

His full name was Balthasar Klossowski de
Rola Balthus. Self-taught and precocious,
with Polish antecedents; well-connected
intellectually (Bonnard and Rilke were
family friends). Reclusive. Consciously
worked against the modern grain—

ideologically opposed to abstract art,
determined to establish the importance
of craftsmanship.

He painted landscapes and portraits. His
work probes the area between innocence
and perversity, reality and dream. Slow,
careful workmanship. Affirmation of
time-honored virtues such as precise
draftsmanship, oil paint, observation
from life, conscious creation of beauty,
muted tones, delicate color, light, and
the primacy of human figure.

KEY WORKS *The Living Room*, 1941–43 (Minnesota:
Minneapolis Institute of Arts); *Sleeping Girl*,
1943 (London: Tate Collection); *Japanese Girl
with Red Table*, 1967–76 (Private Collection)

Hans **Hofmann**

● 1880–1966   ▶ GERMAN/AMERICAN

▣ Paris; Munich; US   ▣ oils; drawings
▣ Washington, DC: National Gallery of Art
▨ $980,000 in 2003, *In Upper Regions* (oils)

A pioneering, but only moderately
successful, abstract painter (his style was
never fully resolved—principally large

squares modified by thick pigment and bright color). Hugely gifted and influential as a teacher. Was the key figure in bringing news of the European giants (like Picasso) to the younger generation of soon-to-be American Abstract Expressionists.

KEY WORKS *Autumn Gold*, 1957 (Washington, DC: National Gallery of Art); *City Horizon*, 1959 (San Francisco: Museum of Modern Art)

Elie **Nadelman**

◉ 1882–1946   ▶ POLISH/AMERICAN

🅿 Paris; London; US   🄲 sculpture
🏛 Washington, DC: Smithsonian American Art Museum   ⓩ $2.6m in 1987, *Tango* (sculpture)

A gifted Polish sculptor of great charm, Nadelman moved to Paris in 1904. His Parisian style was eclectic in the Classical Greek tradition. He

> "Imitation of objective reality is not creation... it is a purely intellectual performance, scientific and sterile..."
>
> HANS HOFMANN

moved to London around 1914 before emigrating to New York at the onset of World War I. There he counted cosmetics queen Helena Rubinstein among his patrons; she commissioned Nadelman to create a set of marble heads for her beauty salons. In 1919, he married an heiress and became a pioneer collector of folk art. He himself created charming folk art—inspired wood sculptures (with a hint of the Hellenistic). After a decade of living the high life, he lost everything financially in the economic depression that followed the Wall Street Crash of 1929.

His sculptures often have the silhouettes of figures in Seurat's paintings. His work is an interesting and successful synthesis of ancient and modern, the common denominator being a search for purity in form and materials.

KEY WORKS *Classical Head with Headdress*, 1908–09 (Wisconsin: Milwaukee Art Museum); *Standing Female Nude*, c. 1909 (Washington, DC: Hirshhorn Museum); *Man in the Open Air*, 1915 (New York: Museum of Modern Art); *The Dancer*, 1920–22 (New York: Jewish Museum of Art)

Tango Elie Nadelman, c. 1918–24, height approx. 34⅓ in (88 cm), cherry wood and gesso, Houston: Museum of Fine Arts. Impressed by American popular culture, the artist also borrowed from folk art to make observations of high society.

Louise **Nevelson**

● 1899–1988 🏳 GERMAN/AMERICAN

🏛 US; Munich 🎨 sculpture; mixed media; oils 🏛 San Francisco: Fine Arts Museums 💰 $230,000 in 1989, *Dawn's Wedding Chapel I* (sculpture)

Born Louise Berliawsky in Kiev (family emigrated to the US in 1905), Nevelson was brought up with wood (the family business was timber) and was always dedicated to being a sculptor (to the point of abandoning her husband and child). She only discovered her signature style in the 1950s—open-sided boxes made into reliefs, each box containing an assortment of forms created from wood scraps, painted in monochrome, usually black.

Her sculpture is most impressive when on a large scale. It is distinguished work that carries in it the sort of accumulated experience and mysterious gravitas that comes with old age. It must be absorbed slowly just like the company or wisdom of the ancients. This is a welcome reminder that no one is ever too old to be creative: Nevelson's best work was done in her 70s and 80s.

KEY WORKS *White Vertical Water*, 1932 (New York: Guggenheim Museum); *Sky Cathedral*, 1958 (Buffalo: Albright-Knox Art Gallery)

Mirror Image 1 *Louise Nevelson, 1969, height 210¼ in (534 cm), painted wood, Houston: Museum of Fine Arts.* Nevelson took the boxes that she had previously used as pedestals for her work and turned them into art, filling them with carved wooden forms. This inspiration led her to create wall-sized assemblages.

Joseph **Cornell**

● 1903–c. 1972 🏳 AMERICAN

🏛 US 🎨 sculpture; mixed media; oils 🏛 Washington, DC: Smithsonian American Art Museum 💰 $2.3m in 2005, *Untitled (Medici Princess)* (mixed media)

The creator of strange, small-scale, imaginative boxes. Though often pigeon-holed as Surrealist, they are poetic reveries rather than Freudian dream worlds. Lived lonely, reclusive life in Flushing, New York, with his mother and crippled brother. Scoured junk shops for bits and pieces, which he filed away meticulously.

Many of the reveries are about travel that he never undertook (maps and images of Paris, for instance) or film stars he never met. Often tinkered for years with images and contents of individual boxes. The glass fronts of the boxes symbolically separate the real world from the dream. No sexual imagery—he disapproved of Surrealism's dark, "unhealthy" aspects.

KEY WORKS *Tilly Losch*, 1935 (Private Collection); *Untitled (The Hotel Eden)*, 1945 (Ottawa: National Gallery of Canada)

Grant **Wood**

● 1892–1942 🏳 AMERICAN

🏛 Iowa 🎨 oils; tempera 🏛 Art Institute of Chicago 💰 $1.25m in 1985, *Arbor Day* (oils)

He was a painter of fantastical, childlike landscapes. Also portraits, murals, and stained glass. His quirky work reflects

Steam Turbine Charles Sheeler, 1939, 22 x 18 in (56 x 45.7 cm), oil on canvas, Ohio: Butler Institute of American Art. The fifth in the series of six "Power" paintings commissioned by *Fortune* magazine.

calculated, precise, and free of human presence as any mass-produced objects. Worked for Henry Ford and shared his belief that factories are temples of worship. Replaced the sublimity of wild nature with the sublimity of the urban landscape. In 1959, he suffered a stroke and had to give up painting and photography.

KEY WORKS *Fugue*, 1940 (Boston: Museum of Fine Arts); *Aerial Gyrations*, 1953 (San Francisco: Museum of Modern Art); *Stacks in Celebration*, 1954 (New York: Berry-Hill Galleries)

old-fashioned virtues: sobriety, strict parents, and sexual morality. He had a painstaking, stiff, old-fashioned style, often working in tempera. Iowa-raised, Wood was the (closet gay) altar boy of American regionalism.

American Gothic is as famous in American art as the *Mona Lisa* is in Italian art, and just as enigmatic. Does it parody the chaste and sober virtues it proclaims or is it admiring them? His work never reveals the answer, and he never confessed to anyone.

KEY WORKS *American Gothic*, 1930 (Art Institute of Chicago); *The Midnight Ride of Paul Revere*, 1931 (New York: Metropolitan Museum of Art); *Daughters of the Revolution*, 1932 (Ohio: Cincinnati Art Museum)

Charles **Sheeler**

● 1883–1965   🏴 AMERICAN

🏴 US; Europe   🎨 oils; photography
🏛 Washington, DC: National Gallery of Art
💰 $1.7m in 1983, *Landscape* (oils)

Sheeler was a dour, romantic painter and photographer who turned the industrial landscape into works of art as carefully

Charles **Demuth**

● 1883–1935   🏴 AMERICAN

🏴 US; Europe   🎨 oils; watercolors   🏛 New York: Memorial Art Gallery, University of Rochester
💰 $750,000 in 1992, *Welcome to our City* (oils)

The leading Precisionist of the 1920s and 1930s, who produced small-scale views of industrial architecture (factories, water towers, and silos), carefully painted with a front-on view and emphasis on simplified geometry. Note his subtle colors and acute observation of light and shade, and the total absence of human presence.

KEY WORKS *My Egypt*, 1927 (New York: Whitney Museum of American Art); *I Saw the Figure Five in Gold*, 1928 (New York: Metropolitan Museum of Art)

"Paintings must be looked at and looked at and looked at... No writing, no talking, no singing, no dancing will explain them."

CHARLES DEMUTH

Edward **Hopper**

● 1882–1967   🏴 AMERICAN

📖 US; Europe   🎨 oils; engravings; watercolors
🏛 New York: Whitney Museum of American Art
💹 $12.5m in 2005, *Chair Car* (oils)

He was a taciturn, monosyllabic, New York inhabitant with a small-town puritan upbringing, who became a successful and quintessential American painter.

His imagery is the American urban landscape and its inhabitants; and also Cape Cod. Marvelous observation and recording of light (perhaps most notably harsh, electric light). Spare, lean, tough technique (like many of his subjects). Strong color sense and ability to create tense, confined spaces. Influenced by photography and the movies (avid moviegoer), and Impressionism (visited Paris in 1906–07 and 1909–10).

How is he able to make the commonplace and banal so uneasy, significant, and memorable? Is it his magic way with light? His ability to simplify and generalize—to express a universal mood, not just an anecdotal story? His subtle space distortions that create a sense that something is wrong or about to happen? Similar talents are shown by the great black-and-white movie producers (like Hitchcock)—many of his pictures could be stills from a movie.

KEY WORKS *Early Sunday Morning*, 1930 (New York: Whitney Museum of American Art); *Cape Cod Evening*, 1939 (Washington, DC: National Gallery of Art); *Nighthawks*, 1942 (Art Institute of Chicago)

Grandma **Moses**

● 1860–1961   🏴 AMERICAN

📖 US   🎨 oils   🏛 Vermont: Bennington Museum
💹 $180,000 in 1993, *Country Fair* (oils)

Née Anna Mary Robertson. A self-taught farmer's wife from Virginia in Vermont who, in the 1930s, aged 70+, became a celebrity. Her paintings are in a naïve style with nostalgic images of idyllic rural life, full of women and children. She copied details from popular prints; her work was in turn endlessly reproduced as greeting cards, wallpaper, and fabrics.

KEY WORKS *My Hills of Home*, 1941 (New York: University of Rochester); *Black Horses*, 1942 (Private Collection); *Making Apple Butter*, 1958 (Art Institute of Chicago)

Chop Suey Edward Hopper, 1929, 31¼ x 38 in (81 x 96.5 cm), oil on canvas, Collection of Mr. and Mrs. Barney A. Ebsworth. Even when successful, Hopper preferred cheap restaurants, secondhand cars, and old clothes.

Down on the Farm in Winter *Grandma Moses, 1945, 19½ x 23⅜ in (49.5 x 60 cm), oil on masonite, Tokyo: Fuji Museum.* Grandma Moses spent most of her life on a farm; first as hired help and then as the wife of a farmer. Many of her paintings depict her memories of that time.

Georgia **O'Keefe**

● 1872–1986   **[PI]** AMERICAN

[PI] US   **[]** oils   **[fm]** Washington, DC: National Gallery of Art   **[$]** $3.3m in 1997, *From the Plains* (oils)

An influential but one-off artist, outside the mainstream of modern art. Her work will be remembered and valued far longer than many other 20th-century names that are currently in fashion or overpraised.

Her intense and exotic imagery lay in that intriguing area between figuration and abstraction. She made very powerful images of nature and architecture, which have a strong period feel of the 1920s, 1930s, and 1940s. Her ability to simplify and intensify color, movement, and pattern has something in common with the best of the classic Disney cartoons, notably *Fantasia*, with which her work was contemporary (Walt Disney: 1901–66).

Many of her paintings have the shifting and fantastic qualities seen in cloud patterns in the sky. Look for plants and flowers (often in close-up), mountains, animal bones. Notice how she transformed all of them into something that has a strong unreal, even surreal, poetic life: mountains become flesh; plants become organisms like sea anemones; skulls live and see. Unusual and intense color combinations; bold and simple patterns.

KEY WORKS *Black Iris*, 1926 (New York: Metropolitan Museum of Art); *Ranchos Church*, 1929 (Washington, DC: Phillips College); *Jack-in-the-Pulpit No. IV*, 1930 (Washington,

DC: National Gallery of Art); *Red Hills with White Shell*, 1938 (Houston: Museum of Fine Arts); *White Iris No.7*, 1957 (Madrid: Museo Thyssen-Bornemisza)

Thomas Hart **Benton**

● 1889–1975   **[PI]** AMERICAN

[PI] Paris; US   **[]** oils   **[fm]** Missouri: Jefferson City, for murals in Capitol Building   **[$]** $1.4m in 1989, *Homeward Bound* (oils)

Considered the High Priest of American Regionalism, Benton came from a national, political family and was a cantankerous, homophobic, anti-Modern and energetic self-publicist. Determined painter of subjects that proclaim the authentic virtues of the Midwest, non-urban American life— bulging, restless figures in heaving swirling spaces. Was a keen user of vulgar colors. Very popular, and his works influenced Jackson Pollock.

KEY WORKS *Martha's Vineyard*, c. 1925 (Washington, DC: Corcoran Gallery of Art); *Cattle Loading, West Texas*, 1930 (Andover, Massachusetts: Addison Gallery of American Art); *Roasting Ears*, 1930 (New York: Metropolitan Museum of Art)

Jacob **Lawrence**

● 1917–2000   **[PI]** AMERICAN

[PI] US   **[]** oils   **[fm]** Washington, DC: National Gallery of Art   **[$]** $290,000 in 2003, *Ten Fugitives* (oils)

Lawrence's was the first voice of an authentic art by and for African– Americans. Born in Atlanta, resided in Harlem. Researched and understood the Great Migration and Ku Klux Klan persecution. He is most famous for the "Migration" series—60 small powerful paintings in a spare, lean, modern style with intense colors, which are strengthened by their understatement and the lack of any expression of hatred.

KEY WORKS *John Brown Forming an Organization among the Colored People of Adirondack Woods to Resist the Capture of Any Fugitive Slaves*, 1941 (Detroit Institute of Arts); *The Wedding*, 1948 (Art Institute of Chicago); *Street to Mbari*, 1964 (Washington, DC: National Gallery of Art)

Mark **Tobey**

◉ 1890–1976   ⚑ AMERICAN

🏛 US; England; Far East; Switzerland
🎨 oils   🏛 San Francisco: Fine Arts
Museums   💰 $130,000 in 1999, *Untitled* (oils)

Tobey was a sensitive artist who developed
a very personal abstract style, serene
and luminous, out of small calligraphic
marks and gestures. This did not happen
until the mid-1940s when he was aged
50+ (he was a contemporary of Picasso,
rather than Pollock). Was influenced
by spiritual faith (a convert to Bahai),
Far East calligraphy, Amerindian art,
and Japanese woodcuts.

KEY WORKS *Fragments in Time and Space*, 1956
(Washington, DC: Hirshhorn Museum);
Advance of History, 1964 (New York:
Guggenheim Museum); *Composition*, 1967
(San Francisco: Fine Arts Museums)

David **Smith**

◉ 1906–65   ⚑ AMERICAN

🏛 US   🎨 sculpture   🏛 Washington,
DC: National Gallery of Art   💰 $3.7m in
1994, *Cubi V* (sculpture)

Smith created beautiful, inventive, poetic
works made from iron, steel, and found
objects, which he welded, manipulated,
and coaxed into constructions of great
originality. His quiet modesty, honest
beliefs, and deep feeling touched his work
with a profound sense of the presence
of fundamental and universal forces,
and of human worth. One of the most
influential and original modern sculptors
of his generation.

KEY WORKS *Hudson River Landscape*, 1951 (New
York: Whitney Museum of American Art);
Books and Apple, 1957 (Harvard University:
Fogg Art Museum); *Cubi XXVII*, 1965
(New York: Guggenheim Museum)

> "Painting is a state of
> being ... Painting is self-
> discovery. Every good painter
> paints what he is ... When
> I am in my painting I'm not
> aware what I'm doing."
>
> JACKSON POLLOCK

Jackson **Pollock**

◉ 1912–56   ⚑ AMERICAN

🏛 US   🎨 oils; enamels; mixed media
🏛 New York: Museum of Modern Art. Venice:
Peggy Guggenheim Collection   💰 $10.5m
in 1989, *Number 8, 1950* (watercolors)

This pioneering abstract painter of
the New York School, nicknamed
"Jack the Dripper," was a tortured
alcoholic, who swung between sensitivity
and machismo, elation and despair.

His work is at its best when on a large
scale, such as 12 x 24 ft (3.6 x 7.2 m), as
it is only then that the passionate, heroic,

Number 6 *Jackson Pollock, 1948, 22⅓ x 30¾ in
(57 x 78 cm), oil on paper laid down on canvas,
Private Collection. Pollock first showed his drip paintings
in 1948 at the Betty Parsons Gallery, New York.*

monumental nature of his achievement becomes apparent. (A child of five cannot conceive or create on this scale.) He put the canvas on the floor and stood in the middle with a large can of household paint—he consciously wanted to be "in" the painting and to become physically part of it.

Look for the rhythms and flow in the threads of paint (they may be instinctive, but not arbitrary or careless). How many separate layers of paint can you see? It is just about possible to reconstruct his movements, and so be "in" the painting at second hand. But why no footprints?

KEY WORKS *The Blue Poles: Number 11, 1952* (Canberra: National Gallery of Australia); *Lavender Mist: Number 1, 1950,* (Washington, DC: National Gallery of Art); *The Deep, 1953* (Paris: Musée National d'Art Moderne)

The Moon-Woman Cuts the Circle *Jackson Pollock, 1943, 43 x 41 in (109.5 x 104 cm), oil on canvas, Paris: Musée National d'Art Moderne.* Inspired by a North American Indian myth about the moon and the feminine.

ABSTRACT EXPRESSIONISM

Abstract Expressionism grew out of the human tragedies of the Great Depression and World War II, reaching maturity in the early years of the Cold War. Faced with the real possibility of the denial of freedom of expression and the extinction of the human race, artists felt compelled to act, and create art that would take up these issues.

STYLE

It grew out of Surrealism but was never a coherent movement and had no program. Styles were wholly personal. It was also entirely American, and New York replaced Paris as the capital of artistic creativity. Among its leaders, Pollock dripped and flung paint onto his giant canvases, torn between the desire to allow chance to determine how it fell and to control the final result. Rothko's immense areas of subtly modulated color had precise, meditative ends in mind.

Ballantine *Franz Kline, 1948–60, Los Angeles: County Museum of Art, oil on canvas.* Kline's early work was black and white; later he used color. The spontaneity is illusory: each "gesture" was painted slowly and deliberately.

SUBJECTS

Sometimes energized forms (such as Jackson Pollock's) were intended to be a near-documentary account of the artist's struggle to create in his or her direct encounter with the canvas. Other artists aimed to express the deepest and most universal of emotions and anxieties in distorted figurative images, or fields of pure, deliberately modulated or contrasting color. Yet as with music, ultimately all Abstract Expressionist works can only be felt intuitively rather than understood.

KEY EVENTS

1943	Rothko, Still, and Gottlieb assert the basic goals of their art in a letter to *The New York Times*
1946	*New Yorker* art critic Robert Coates coins the term "Abstract Expressionism"
1947	Pollock develops new style of Surrealist-influenced "automatic" painting, dripping paint onto huge canvases laid on the ground
1956	Pollock killed in car crash
1970	Rothko, suffering from deep depression, commits suicide in his studio

Man on the Dunes *Willem de Kooning, 1971, oils, Private Collection.* Part of the artist's passionate outpourings during the 1970s when his painting became an extreme frenzy of bold colors and paint layering, then smeared by newspapers.

late 1940s – 1950s

WHAT TO LOOK FOR

Heroic imperatives dominate Abstract Expressionism. It is alternately bold and assertive, contemplative and questioning. Its impact derives in large measure from scale, large canvases—"portable murals"—that overwhelm and dazzle, seeming to draw the spectator into what can feel like a parallel universe. Texture is important, too, whether Pollock's rivulets and rivers of paint, Still's thick, almost relieflike blocks of color, or Rothko's layers of thinly applied color. However, Rothko spoke for them all when he said "… if you are moved only by the color relationships, you miss the point … I'm interested only in exploring basic human emotions."

The Black and the White *Mark Rothko, 1956, 93¾ x 53½ in (238 x 136 cm), oil on canvas, Harvard: Fogg Art Museum.* Abstract Expressionist works were displayed unframed so that they would be perceived as a "presence" rather than a tangible object.

Within a limited range, Rothko's colors have an exceptional richness, a seemingly infinite series of subtle gradations

TECHNIQUES

In a typical motif, Rothko paints two hazy, soft-edged blocks of color, the upper stacked weightlessly over the lower, with both appearing to hover over a delicate red base. The effect of the work is deliberately sublime, inducing a kind of quasi-religious feeling.

Black in Rothko's hands achieves a gentle luminosity: the sense of an "infinite void" is palpable

Mark **Rothko**

● 1903–70 ⏀ AMERICAN

⏀ US ⏀ oils ⏀ London: Tate Collection.
Houston: St. Thomas University. New York:
Museum of Modern Art ⏀ $14.6m in 2003,
White and Black on White (oils)

A melancholic Russian émigré who settled
in the US at the age of 10, Rothko
became a leading member of the New
York School and pioneer of Color Field
abstract painting. Committed suicide.

His deceptively simple abstract paintings
have deliberately plain, soft-edged shapes
and luminous, glowing colors. His work is
at its best seen on a large scale, completely
filling a space such as the Rothko room at
Tate Modern or the chapel at St. Thomas
University. Look for his early work to see
how slowly and carefully he reached this
final, very personal, expression.

Treat the works with the respect and
care with which they were created and
give them time to reach you. Move
around them so as to get to know them;
stand close to the works, relax, wait, so
that the color completely fills your field
of vision and seeps through your eyes
into your mood and feelings. Rothko
said his paintings were about "tragedy,
ecstasy, and doom"—about fundamental
(and romantic) emotions and passions.

KEY WORKS *Multiform*, 1948 (Canberra: National
Gallery of Australia); *Untitled (Violet, Black,
Orange, Yellow on White and Red)*, 1949 (New
York: Guggenheim Museum); *Green and Maroon*,
1953 (Washington, DC: Phillips College)

Willem de **Kooning**

● 1904–97 ⏀ DUTCH/AMERICAN

⏀ US ⏀ oils; sculpture ⏀ Washington,
DC: National Gallery of Art ⏀ $18.8m in
1989, *Interchange* (oils)

A Rotterdam-born painter and decorator
who went to New York in 1926, and
became one of the most consistent and
longest-lived Abstract Expressionists.

He produced his best work between
1950 and 1963. One of the few artists
to achieve a genuine synthesis between
figuration and abstraction—the image
(most famously, the woman) and the
abstract expressive gesture coexist and
interact as equal partners. After 1963, he
lost control and direction, turning out

work with arbitrary gestures, flabby
colors, and splodgy decoration. His
last paintings were, sadly, feeble (he
had Alzheimer's disease).

Wonderful color sense, using thrilling
and unusual color juxtapositions, and
complex textures and interweaving of
paint, which are a pleasure to look at. He
creates a truly exciting balance and tension
between uncontrolled freedom and
conscious control; between aggression and
beauty; between abstraction and figuration
(as skilled, daring, and breathtaking as a
high-wire act). In the complexity of paint
and imagery lurk subtle layers of meaning.
Who can or will explain the tortured female?

KEY WORKS *Woman and Bicycle*, 1952–53 (New
York: Whitney Museum of American Art);
Marilyn Monroe, 1954 (Private Collection);
Door to the River, 1960 (New York: Whitney
Museum of American Art)

Barnett **Newman**

● 1905–70 ⏀ AMERICAN

⏀ US ⏀ oils; sculptures ⏀ $3.5m
in 2002, *White Fire 1* (oils)

Newman, a leading Abstract Expressionist,
developed a personal style of large-scale
Color Field painting that attempted to
touch emotions and aspirations beyond
the power of words to express.

Look for everything or nothing. If you
see the intense color fields with the simple
vertical stripes as nothing more than that,

Vir Heroicus Sublimis Barnett Newman, 1950–51, 95⅜ x 213¼ in (242.2 x 513.6 cm), oil on canvas, New York: Museum of Modern Art. Originally an art critic, Newman was an articulate advocate for the Abstract Expressionists.

you will not see much. But if you see, for example, the red background drawing aside to reveal an expanding opening into an infinite blue space (the blue stripe), or the yellow stripe as a flash of cosmic light, then you will see everything.
KEY WORKS *Moment*, 1946 (London: Tate Collection); *Dionysius*, 1949 (Washington, DC: National Gallery of Art)

Franz **Kline**
◗ 1910–62   🇺 AMERICAN

🄿 US   🎨 oils   🏛 Washington, DC: National Gallery of Art   💰 $5.7m in 2005, *Crow Dancer* (oils)

Kline was a leading Abstract Expressionist who grew up in the industrial coal-mining region of Pennsylvania. Studied in Boston and London. Lived a lonely life in New York and died young.

At first, his big black-and-white abstract paintings from the 1950s and 1960s look like enlarged Chinese calligraphy. They are typical for their time: gestural, personal, spontaneous, moody, full of existential angst. But further acquaintance shows that this is the opposite of what they are.

Kline was not spontaneous. He worked out the compositions and placing of the brush marks very carefully. Painted well-balanced, serene pictures with astonishing

cerebral and sensual harmony. Visitors to a Kline exhibition become noticably deeply engaged with the works and each other.
KEY WORKS *Ballantine*, 1948–60 (Los Angeles: County Museum of Art); *Chief*, 1950 (New York: Museum of Modern Art)

Robert **Motherwell**
◗ 1915–91   🇺 AMERICAN

🄿 US   🎨 oils; collage   🏛 San Francisco: Fine Arts Museums   💰 $2.6m in 2004, *Elegy to the Spanish Republic No.71* (oils)

Motherwell was an urbane, erudite, fluent, influential painter, writer, and philosopher who was a leading Abstract Expressionist. He married Helen Frankenthaler.

His abstract paintings, drawings, and collages are always elegant. His work ranges from small-scale, intimate collages to grand, large-scale paintings. Enjoys paint, accident, the unexpected, calculated simplicity. Restrained use of color.

His major achievement, the "Spanish Elegies" series of paintings (more than 150 canvases done over his lifetime), form a deeply emotional response to the Spanish Civil War and Motherwell's realization that civilization can regress. The collages he built around wine labels, cigarette wrappers, and music are a diary of association, not an autobiography.
KEY WORKS *Personage (Autoportrait)*, 1943 (New York: Guggenheim Museum); *Black on White*, 1961 (Houston: Museum of Fine Arts)

Adolph **Gottlieb**

● 1903–74   ⚑ AMERICAN

🏛 US   🎨 oils   🏛 Washington, DC: National
Gallery of Art   ⚡ $850,000 in 2003, *Blast II* (oils)

Gottlieb was a well-known Abstract
Expressionist, but too schematic to be
one of the great artists. He had two
styles: 1941–51—pictographs, loose
compartments filled with schematic and
symbolic shapes (he was into Freud and
Surrealism); 1950s onward—imaginary
semi-abstract landscapes, typically with
a simple, round, celestial body floating
above loosely painted earthly chaos.
KEY WORKS *Romanesque Façade*, 1949
(Champaign, Illinois: Krannert Art
Museum); *Ascent*, 1958 (New York:
Adolph and Esther Gottlieb Foundation)

Clyfford **Still**

● 1904–80   ⚑ AMERICAN

🏛 US   🎨 oils   🏛 New York: Guggenheim
Museum   ⚡ $2.8m in 2004, *1960-F* (oils)

One of the leading Abstract Expressionist
painters, Still was intense, serious, painterly,
heroic, romantic, and difficult to live with.
A sensitive intellect in a rugged exterior,
he was brought up in the big open spaces
of Alberta, Canada, and Washington.

His early figurative work explored the
relationship between humans and
landscape. His later large-scale (for
their time) abstract paintings are heavily
worked, having rough surfaces with thick
paint. Used intense colors and simple
"imagery" consisting of "flames" or
"flashes" of color on a field of single
color, with a vertical format for paintings
and "images." His works manifest a
deliberate cragginess, intransigence,
and awkwardness that reflect both the
character of the artist and the agenda
shared by his fellow Abstract Expressionists.

You have to spend time with the paintings
and be prepared to meet the artist halfway.
He saw art as a moral power in an age of
conformity; life as a force pitted against
nature—especially earth and sky. Thus
the vertical "necessity of life" arises from
the horizontal. He continued the 19th-
century tradition of Romantic landscape.
KEY WORKS *Jamais*, 1944 (New York:
Guggenheim Museum); *1953*, (London:
Tate Collection)

Sam **Francis**

● 1923–94   ⚑ AMERICAN

🏛 US; France; Japan   🎨 acrylics; watercolors;
prints; sculpture   🏛 Washington, DC: National
Gallery of Art   ⚡ $3.1m in 1999, *Towards
Disappearance I* (oils)

Francis took up art as therapy while
recovering from spinal injuries as a World
War II fighter pilot. Large-scale abstracts
in which splattered and dribbled pure
translucent color floats with weightless
ease over a white background, conjuring
up a magical, open, light-filled space.
KEY WORKS *Red and Pink*, 1951 (San Francisco:
Museum of Modern Art); *Around the Blues*,
1956–57 (London: Tate Collection)

In Lovely Blueness *Sam Francis, 1955–57, 118 x 275¼
in (300 x 700 cm), acrylic on canvas, Paris: Musée National
d'Art Moderne.* Francis was inspired by memories of light
patterns on his hospital ceiling and the Pacific sky.

Untitled Arshile Gorky, 1946, 21 x 29 in (53.3 x 73.6 cm), mixed media, Private Collection. During the 1940s, Gorky spent part of each year in Virginia, where his wife's family had a farm, making drawings while in the countryside and then exploring multiple versions of the shapes and colors he had observed.

Arshile **Gorky**

● 1904–48   ⚑ ARMENIAN/AMERICAN

🏛 US   🎨 oils   🏛 Washington, DC: National Gallery of Art   💰 $3.6m in 1995, *Scent of Apricots on the Fields* (oils)

Gorky emigrated from Turkey to the US in 1920. Original lyrical, gentle, and poetic abstract painterly style, deriving inspiration from landscape and nature. Natural colors, biomorphic forms (influence of Miró and Surrealism). Tragic, early death (like many fellow Abstract Expressionists); committed suicide after cancer, car accident, and disastrous studio fire.

KEY WORKS *The Artist and his Mother*, 1926–29 (New York: Whitney Museum of American Art); *Hugging/Good Hope Road II*, 1945 (Madrid: Museo Thyssen-Bornemisza)

Richard **Diebenkorn**

● 1922–93   ⚑ AMERICAN

🏛 US   🎨 oils   🏛 Washington, DC: National Gallery of Art   💰 $3.2m in 2001, *Ocean Park No.67* (oils)

Considered an American West Coast Matisse (whom he was much taken with), Diebenkorn was talented, influential, very visual, but lacked the master's range and tough-minded certainty.

His early abstracts (abstraction from nature) of 1948–56 were reactions to specific places (color, topography, light).

Vigorous figurative work from 1956, with bold, simple designs, glowing color, and juicy paint. Returned to abstraction with the Ocean Park series (from 1966); these works are large scale, translucent, investigative, and statuesque. It is important to see pieces by natural light—hard, artificial light kills subtleties. Don't rush: let the eye bask and play.

His most confident work is figurative. His abstracts are always oddly tentative—justified as sensitive, responsive, and so on, but somehow he could never reach that final distillation of sensation that so distinguishes Matisse. His early abstract work can be repetitive and unstructured, and can kill color (perhaps the reason he moved on to figuration?). Stunning response to light (as good as Hopper's). Lovely small-scale work (cigar-box lids 1976–79) and late work (still small, as a heart disease prevented him from working large scale).

KEY WORKS *Seated Nude, Black Background*, 1966 (Private Collection); *Seated Figure with Hat*, 1967 (Washington, DC: National Gallery of Art); *Still Life: Cigarette Butts and Glasses*, 1967 (Washington, DC: National Gallery of Art); *Ocean Park No.64*, 1973 (Pittsburgh: Carnegie Museum of Art)

Jean **Tinguely**

◔ 1925–91   ⚑ SWISS

🏛 Switzerland   ✪ sculpture; mixed media
🏛 Basel (Switzerland): Museum Jean Tinguely
📈 $265,600 in 1997, *Untitled, Welded Sculpture Fountain* (sculpture, 1968)

The creator of bizarre, unpredictable, clanking machines, made from junk, which move and whizz, sometimes to the point of self-destruction. His work is highly original and very humorous. Thought that change is the only constant in life. Delighted in expressing an anarchic freedom (against neat, orderly Switzerland?). Married Niki de Saint-Phalle and worked with her on his most famous work, *Beaubourg Fountain*.

KEY WORKS *The Sorceress*, 1961 (Washington, DC: Hirshhorn Museum); *Débricollage*, 1970 (London: Tate Collection); *Beaubourg Fountain*, 1980 (Paris: Centre Pompidou)

CoBrA   1948–51

First founded in Paris by Belgian poet and essayist Christian Dotrement, the group were mainly inspired by their Marxist beliefs. Including Karel Appel, Asger Jorn, and Pierre Alechinsky, their art was experimental and sympathetic to Expressionism and Surrealism but showed its greatest affinity to folk art and children's art, and to works of Paul Klee and Joan Miró. CoBrA's name was adopted from the names of the three capital cities of the countries of its principal members: Co from Copenhagen, Br from Brussels, and A from Amsterdam.

Asger **Jorn**

◔ 1914–73   ⚑ DANISH

🏛 Denmark; Paris   ✪ oils; drawings
🏛 San Francisco: Fine Arts Museums   📈 $1.9m in 2002, *In the Beginning was the Image* (oils)

A founder member of CoBrA. Boldly and freely painted, intensely colored, gestural works, sometimes abstract, sometimes with figurative imagery. At the forefront of European art until the mid-1960s, when Pop art became the fashion.

KEY WORKS *My Spanish Castle*, 1953 (Boston: Museum of Fine Arts); *The Three Sages*, 1955 (Bruges: Musées Royaux des Beaux-Arts)

Karel **Appel**

◔ 1921–   ⚑ DUTCH

🏛 Denmark; France; US   ✪ oils; sculptures; drawings; prints; ceramics   🏛 San Francisco: Fine Arts Museums   📈 $680,000 in 2002, *Women, Children, Animals* (oils)

An important postwar artist and founder member of CoBrA, he is recognizable for thickly painted, brightly colored Expressionist paintings that attempt to capture the spontaneity of children's painting, but also benefit from adult sophistication/organization and aesthetic sensibility, along with an ability to create on a large scale. Appel has also produced scenery for a ballet.

KEY WORKS *Burned Face*, 1961 (Private Collection); *Hip Hip Hooray*, 1949 (London: Tate Collection)

Turning of Friendship of America and France *Jean Tinguely, 1961, 80½ in (204 cm), mixed media, Private Collection.* The artist had shown in New York in 1960.

Pierre **Alechinsky**

● 1927–   🇫🇷 FRENCH

🏠 Belgium; Paris; Far East   🎨 oils; acrylics;
prints   🏛 San Francisco: Fine Arts Museums
💰 $440,100 in 1990, *Epave* (oils)

A painter and printmaker who creates
decorative, joyful, abstract paintings,
notable for their spontaneity, lightness
of touch, and glowing translucent
color. Often uses formula of a central
panel surrounded by complementary
border of small calligraphic images.
Pleasure-giving work that is mercifully
free from introspection or pretension
to profound meaning.
KEY WORKS *Hors de Jeu*, 1962 (Rome:
L'Archimede – Galleria d'Arte);
To Day Red Hot, Too Hot, 1964 (San
Francisco: De Young Museum)

Octave *Pierre Alechinsky, 1983, print, Private Collection.*
A one-time member of the CoBrA group, Alechinsky
settled in Paris in 1951 where he developed an interest
in Japanese calligraphy and visited the Far East.

Nicolas de **Staël**

● 1914–55   🇫🇷 FRENCH

🏠 Belgium; Europe; France   🎨 oils   🏛 London:
Tate Collection   💰 $1.9m in 1990, *Syracuse* (oils)

An orphaned Russian aristocrat émigré
who took French citizenship in 1948,
de Stael started with admiration for
old masters, not Modernism. Evolved
a successful style that bridged the divide
between figuration and abstraction, using
thick, tactile paint, rich colors, and simple
forms (suggestive of landscape or still life).
Committed suicide (because overwrought
or overworked?). His work is neglected.
KEY WORKS *Composition*, 1950 (London:
Tate Collection); *Le Parc des Sceaux*, 1952
(Washington, DC: Phillips College);
Mediterranean Landscape, 1953 (Madrid:
Museo Thyssen-Bornemisza)

Jean **Dubuffet**

● 1901–85   🇫🇷 FRENCH

🏠 France   🎨 oils; sculpture; prints
🏛 Périgny-sur-Yerres (Paris): Dubuffet Foundation
💰 $4.3m in 2002, *Paris Montparnasse* (oils)

A painter, sculptor, printmaker, collector,
and writer who was also the son of a
wine merchant. Turned full-time artist
in 1945 after an early life of the wine
trade, military service, divorce, and
dilettantism. Developed a challenging
and consciously anti-aesthetic, anti-art

establishment style—but ended up as
the art establishment's favorite example
of radical chic.

His art went through a succession of
cycles. In each case, he had a thought-
out agenda and different experiments
with materials, which he then promoted
via exhibitions: 1942–50 portraits and
graffiti; early 1950s obese nudes in
smeary oil paint; late 1950s "Earth"
themes and sand-gravel textures;
1960s black outlined "jigsaw" style
and polystyrene sculpture. He sought
intensity, not beauty. Promoted Art
Brut and tapped into the unschooled
creativity of children and psychotics.

Dubuffet raised naïvety to the highest
level of sophistication and knew exactly
what he was doing—one of the few
occasions where this "game" works.
The trouble with most *faux naïf* work
is that you have no idea (unless told)
whether the work is to be admired
because it is by an untrained and
innocent eye, or by an overeducated
sophisticate trying to amaze us by
how "simple" he or she can be.
KEY WORKS *Spinning Round*, 1961 (London: Tate
Collection); *The Triumpher*, 1973 (Périgny-sur-
Yerres, Paris: Dubuffet Foundation)

Composition *Alfred Otto Wolfgang Schulze Wols, c. 1950, 9¾ x 6¼ in (24.8 x 15.9 cm), gouache on paper, Private Collection.* From his Tachist phase, a method involving "taches" or stains of color splashed on canvas.

Together they are strangely beautiful and moving to look at and be with.

KEY WORKS *Painting*, 1944–45 (New York: Museum of Modern Art); *Bateau*, 1951 (Boston: Museum of Fine Arts)

Pierre **Soulages**

◐ 1919– ⦿ FRENCH

🇵 France; US; Japan 🎨 oils; prints
🏛 Paris: Musee National d'Art Moderne
💰 $387,200 in 1990, *Peinture 41-58* (oils)

He produced large-scale, heavily textured, gestural, painterly abstracts in which black is predominant. Intended to be more visual than emotional in impact—he considers black to be the means of making light and color visible and alive.

KEY WORKS 23 *May 1953* (London: Tate Collection); 6 *August 1956* (Canberra: National Gallery of Australia)

César (César Baldaccini)

◐ 1921–1998 ⦿ FRENCH

🇵 France 🎨 sculpture; mixed media 🏛 New York: Museum of Modern Art 💰 $513,655 in 1999, *L'homme de la liberté* (sculpture)

César is celebrated for constructions and compressions in metal, often with unusual material, such as car parts. Very visual, human, witty, active work. Liked animal skeletons, bones, structure, surfaces like bats' wings. His work in paper and plastic lacks strength and tension (as if the material bored him?) and can be kitsch. Disturbing self-portraits.

KEY WORKS *Italian Flags*, 1960s (Private Collection); *Thumb*, 1965 (Martigny, Switzerland: Fondation Pierre Gianadda)

Alfred Otto Wolfgang Schulze **Wols**

◐ 1913–51 ⦿ GERMAN/FRENCH

🇵 Germany; France 🎨 oils; watercolors; drawings 💰 $932,800 in 1990, *Untitled* (oils)

Wols was a lost soul, typical of many dispossessed, destitute, and unhappy people who were victims of political and social upheavals in central Europe during this era. Found solace in artistic activity and drink. Born in Germany, lived in France.

He made small-scale works in oils and watercolors. The oils are often composed of compulsive pouring, smearing, spraying, and scratching. The watercolors frequently have an obsessive concern with detail. What distinguishes Wols from many lesser jotters and scribblers is the quantity, consistency, and integrity of his work. Unrecognized in his lifetime, he persisted with, and pioneered, a new style of expressive abstraction.

He was remarkable for his attention to detail. Every mark is there for a reason. (This is real integrity.) Try to see a group of works together: the end result, individually and collectively, is a remarkable record of someone using art to rise above hardships that killed many others—literally or spiritually.

Yves **Klein**

◐ 1928–62 ⦿ FRENCH

🇵 France; Japan 🎨 mixed media; sculpture 🏛 Hamburg: Kunsthalle 💰 $6.1m in 2000, *Re I* (works on paper)

Untrained (except at judo), uneducated, megalomaniac dreamer, who had a brief, high-profile and influential presence.

His paintings, objects, and records of "happenings" (notably those saturated with his trademark YKB "Yves Klein Blue") give a unique, intense glow. The rhetoric he and his supporters used is huge: blue is the infinite immateriality of the heavens; blue fills the space between object and viewer with spiritual energy; blue leads to Zenlike transcendental experience, and so on. With a leap of imagination similar to his own, this is possible. Klein was also infamous for his scandalous behavior throughout his short-lived career.

Is the attraction of his objects the aesthetic and spiritual experience they seek to convey? Or is it that they were and remain as instantly recognizable and as chic as the Gucci loafer or Chanel No. 5—all of them proclaiming the possessor to be a (self-elected) member of the international club of connoisseurship and savoir-faire? Is this the first example of art as a high-class fashion accessory? And, if so, is it any the worse for that?

KEY WORKS *IKB 79*, 1959 (London: Tate Collection); *Untitled Blue Monochrome (IKB 82)*, 1959 (New York: Guggenheim Museum); *Requiem Blue*, 1960 (Houston: Menil Collection)

Armand Fernandez **Arman**

● 1928–98 ◾ FRENCH

France; US   ◾ sculpture; conceptual art
Hamburg: Kunsthalle   ◾ $330,000 in 1989, *Subida al cielo* (sculpture)

Arman was a stimulating and witty manipulator of objects. His work was more visual than conceptual. Avid collector since childhood; father a furniture and knickknack dealer; grandmother an obsessive accumulator of junk.

His work is transformed through accumulations, combustions, cut-ups. Obsessive interest in manufactured objects (such as keys, car parts, machines, dolls, or paint tubes). Their repetitive accumulation, and luxurious and bizarre presentation out of context (for instance, Perspex boxes, resin beds, and wall mounts), endow them with a kind of poetry. Cut-up musical instruments or charred furniture simultaneously shock and cause reappraisal of the true function of objects.

KEY WORKS *Accumulation of Sliced Teapots*, 1964 (Minneapolis: Walker Art Center); *Diana (Noli me tangere)*, 1986 (Toronto: Miriam Shiell Gallery); *Self-Portrait-Robot*, 1992 (Florence: Galleria degli Uffizi)

Office Fetish Armand Fernandez Arman, 1984, 30 x 30 in (76.2 x 76.2 cm), rotary telephones and metal poles, Detroit Institute of Arts. Together with Yves Klein and Jean Tinguely, Arman was a member of the Nouveaux Réalistes, who rejected painting and used real materials.

Henri **Michaux**

● 1899–1984 ▶ BELGIAN

▣ Belgium; France; Africa; Asia
▣ watercolors; prints ▣ Paris: Musée National d'Art Moderne
▣ $65,910 in 1990, *Composition* (works on paper)

He was the author of highly original, experimental, introverted paintings. Michaux sought to use art as an escape from the material world. Worked very rapidly, without preconceptions; he used wash and diluted inks for his watercolors, as they do not allow for revision and second thoughts. After 1956 he sometimes worked under the influence of the hallucinogenic drug mescalin.

KEY WORKS *Meidosems*, 1948 (Boston: Museum of Fine Arts); *La bataille des éperons d'or*, 1960 (Bruges: Musées Royaux des Beaux Arts)

The Andes Cordillera Henri Michaux, 1958, 15¾ x 11¾ in (40 x 30 cm), gouache on paper, Private Collection. Even before he used drugs, Michaux regarded painting as an art of psychic improvisation.

Marcel **Broodthaers**

● 1924–1976 ▶ BELGIAN

▣ Belgium; Germany; UK ▣ sculpture; photography; installations; video ▣ $687,600 in 1992, *Armoire blanche et table blanche* (sculpture)

Broodthaers was an unsuccessful poet turned untrained artist (in 1964) who created bizarre objects and installations or exhibitions of objects and real works of art. His goal? To investigate issues such as the meaning of art; the definition of art; art institutions and power structures; the art market and aesthetics—and in doing so to challenge received opinion. Subtle, humorous, influential, successful.

KEY WORKS *Armoire charbonnée (Armoire à charbon)*, 1966 (Bruges: Musées Royaux des Beaux Arts); *Le drapeau noir. Tirage illimité*, 1968 (Bruges: Musées Royaux des Beaux Arts)

Henri van Herwegen **Panamarenko**

● 1940– ▶ BELGIAN

▣ Belgium ▣ sculpture; installations
▣ $120,000 in 1998, *Flugobjekt—Rakete* (sculpture)

He is an eccentric visionary who designs weird Leonardo-like machines. They do not work in reality but they do wonders for the imagination. The theme is liberating humanity from physical constraints by suggesting ways to jump farther, to fly, to defy gravity, to reinvent time and space, and so on. Beautiful machines.

KEY WORKS *Feltra*, 1966 (Ghent: Stedelijk Museum voor Actuele Kunst); *Airplane*, 1967 (Wolfsburg: Kunstmuseum); *The Aeromodeler*, 1969–71 (New York: Dia:Chelsea)

> **"One must never forbid oneself anything. One must also be able to go back, one must always be able to change ..."**
>
> HANS HARTUNG

Hans **Hartung**

● 1904–89 ▶ GERMAN

▣ Germany; France ▣ oils; acrylics; prints
▣ Paris: Musée National d'Art Moderne
▣ $1,424,497 in 1990, *T 47-10* (oils)

Hartung is recognized as having been one of the first painters of gestural abstraction.

His style is spontaneous, neat, wiry, free, with pencil lines crawling over the paper and brushstrokes that have some of the characteristics of Chinese calligraphy but are never uncontrolled or arbitrary. His strong sense of (complex) composition and color identifies him as European rather than American. His aim was to create images expressing his innermost being. His paintings are not always as spontaneous as they look: they may be enlarged versions of small, free sketches, in which he replicates the gestures or accidental marks (but does that make the end result any less valid?).

KEY WORKS *T-1954-20*, 1954 (Canberra: National Gallery of Australia); *Lines and Curves*, 1956 (San Francisco: Fine Arts Museums)

Fritz **Hundertwasser**

◕ 1928–2000 🏳 AUSTRIAN

🏳 Austria 🎨 oils; mixed media
🏛 Vienna: KunstHausWien 💰 $441,600 in 2004, *La tour de Babel perfore le soleil—un spiraloid—Tower of Babel* (oils)

Born Friedrich Stowasser. Produced small, detailed, richly colored, ornamental and jewel-like abstract works, often with a spiral motif, which is organic and labyrinthine in character (a deliberate metaphor for the self-regenerative processes of life). Used mixed media, gold and silver, wrapping paper, and jute. Refreshingly romantic and lyrical.

KEY WORKS *460 Hommage au Tachisme*, 1961 (Vienna: KunstHausWien); *224 The Big Way*, 1955 (Vienna: Österreichische Galerie)

686 Good Morning City *Friedensreich Hundertwasser, 1970, 33½ x 21¾ in (85 x 55.5 cm), silkscreen, Private Collection.* In 1972 the artist designed posters for the Munich Olympics. He subsequently worked on town planning projects in many parts of the world.

FLUXUS   1962–1970s

Originating in Germany, literally meaning "flow," the Fluxus movement advocated a shift from aesthetics to ethics in artistic values. It held a similar attitude to that of Dadaism, promoting artistic exploration and sociopolitical activism. Ignoring art theories, members often created mixed-media works from any found materials and developed the performance art movement, called "Aktions" or "Happenings." Fluxus artists shifted the importance from what an artist creates to the artist's actions, opinions, and emotions.

Literature Sausage *Dieter Roth, 1967, 25 in (63 cm), mixed media, Hamburg: Kunsthalle.* The work consists of Hegel's 20-volume *oeuvre*, ground up and stuffed into sausage skins.

Günther **Uecker**

◕ 1930– 🏳 GERMAN

🏳 Germany 🎨 sculpture 🏛 Venice: Peggy Guggenheim Collection 💰 $97,415 in 2004, *Large Field* (works on paper)

His typical work (after 1955) consists of nails hammered into a board that are arranged in patterns that are reminiscent of electromagnetic fields. Monotony and repetition are deliberate and integral to his work. He is motivated by Zen and visions of purity and silence; it is his personal belief that he should establish harmony between people and nature.

KEY WORKS *Tactile Rotating Structure*, 1961 (Venice: Peggy Guggenheim Collection); *TV 1963*, 1963 (Venice: Peggy Guggenheim Collection)

Renato **Guttuso**

● 1912–87 **ITALIAN**

Italy ● oils; watercolors
St. Petersburg: Hermitage Museum
$174,195 in 2004, *Spaghetti Eater* (oils)

Guttuso was much praised in the 1950s when considered by many (left-wing) critics to be on the cutting edge of the avant-garde; his social realist works were seen as an antidote to American gestural abstraction, thus he does capture something specific about postwar European art and politics. Founder member of the anti-Fascist association Corrente. His originality declined rapidly after the late 1950s when he became too derivative (too many borrowings from Picasso and Goya).
KEY WORKS *Crucifixion*, 1941 (Rome: Galleria Nazionale d'Arte Moderna); *Sulfur Miners*, 1949 (London: Tate Collection)

Death of a Hero *Renato Guttuso, 1953, 34⅔ x 40½ in (88 x 103 cm), oil on canvas, London: Estorick Collection. The artist was staunchly anti-Fascist and a resistance fighter. After the war he became a Communist politician.*

Alberto **Burri**

● 1915–95 **ITALIAN**

US; Italy ● collage Rome: Galleria Nazionale d'Arte Moderna $2.62m in 1989, *Umbria Vera*, 1952 (works on paper)

He was a doctor-turned-artist who had some success in the 1950s with original work (for the time), using sacking and other nonarty materials, to produce serious looking collages. (Some connection with doctors bandaging patients—he liked to recreate blood with splashes of red paint—and using splints? Commentary on the state of postwar Europe?)

KEY WORKS *Abstraction with Brown Burlap (Sack)*, 1953 (Turin: Galleria Civica d'Arte Moderna e Contemporanea); *Composition*, 1953 (New York: Guggenheim Museum)

Lucio **Fontana**

● 1899–1968 **ARGENTINIAN/ITALIAN**

Italy ● oils; sculpture; ceramics; installations
Rome: Galleria Nazionale d'Arte Moderna
$1,862,500 in 2002, *Concetto spaziale, Il Cielo di Venezia* (oils)

Fontana was an unknown who in middle age became a significant figure in postwar European art, finding a successful if limited "formula" that was in tune with the mood of the times.

He is most famous for monochrome canvases with single or multiple precision cuts, and for canvases and supports that have been pierced or lacerated. Can be very good indeed—but can be oh, so dull! Better when several works are seen together—a single work can look merely superficial or silly.

The cuttings and piercings had a meaning in the 1960s, as part of a (then new, but now worn out) exploration of the meaning of existence and the role of art. Perhaps they are now best seen as engaging period pieces with an innocent 1950s or 1960s view of the creative act and gesture as a bid for freedom (and he was over 50 when he started them). His earlier ceramic work searched for a freedom of expression, but he needed a different medium to find full utterance.
KEY WORKS *Spatial Concept*, 1958 (London: Tate Collection); *Spatial Concept: Expectations*, 1959 (New York: Guggenheim Museum); *Nature*, 1959–60 (London: Tate Collection)

Mario **Merz**

● 1925–2003 **ITALIAN**

Italy ● installations; sculpture; conceptual art
Berlin: Nationalgalerie $1,323,000 in 2005, *Igloo object cache-toi* (sculpture)

He was a leading member of Arte Povera who in the 1960s and 1970s created works that addressed geographical and environmental issues—notably metal-

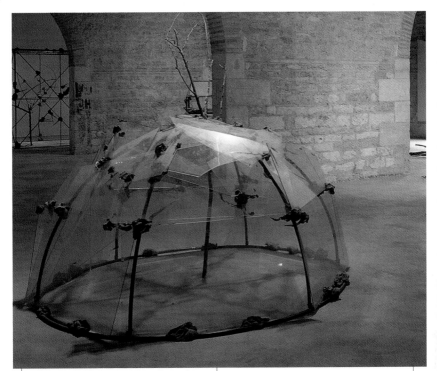

What's to be Done? Mario Merz, 1969, shown here in an exhibition in 1991, mixed media, Bordeaux: CAPC Musée d'Art Contemporain. One of Merz's "igloos," part of a larger installation involving painting and sculpture.

framed "igloos" covered with clay, wax branches, broken glass, etc. Produced transient, temporary work to reveal art as a process of change (like nature itself) and the artist as nomad. There are references to Fibonacci numbers (an infinite sequence of numbers in which each number equals the sum of the previous two).

KEY WORKS *Crocodile in the Night*, 1979 (Toronto: Art Gallery of Ontario); *Igloo*, 1983 (London: Courtauld Institute of Art); *Unreal City, Nineteen Hundred Eighty-Nine*, 1989 (New York: Guggenheim Museum)

Michelangelo **Pistoletto**

● 1933– ⚑ ITALIAN

🏛 Italy   🎨 conceptual art; sculpture; performance; video   💰 $184,690 in 2004, *Woman Walking* (oils)

Pistoletto is a conceptual artist best known for work using mirrors arranged so that the spectator keeps on seeing

him/herself. This is often achieved by means of polished steel sheets on which life-size photographed images of people are overlaid, thereby creating a relationship between image and spectator. Effective, puzzling, and amusing, but not as profound as claimed.

KEY WORKS *Architecture of the Mirror*, 1990 (Turin: Castello di Rivoli Museum of Contemporary Art); *In the First Place*, 1997 (Turin: Castello di Rivoli Museum of Contemporary Art)

ARTE POVERA   1970–

An Italian term meaning "Poor Art" or "Impoverished Art." It was coined by the Italian art critic Germano Celant to describe a type of work first seen in Turin in 1970, which is now commonplace in contemporary art. The art objects are made from natural or cheap and tacky materials and carry a strong political agenda, with the proposal that the elevation of humble materials as art corresponds with the wish for the elevation of poor social classes. It also hopes to defy any possibility of being commercially exploited.

Jannis **Kounellis**

● 1936– GREEK/ITALIAN

Italy sculpture Hamburg: Kunsthalle
$1,058,940 in 1990, *Senza titolo* (oils)

Kounellis is a leading member of Arte Povera who creates strange objects and constructions out of materials such as blankets, mattresses, sacks, and blood, and likes to show evidence or traces of flames and smoke. His intention is to draw attention to, and make one think about, the dark side of 20th-century experience, especially social deprivation and spiritual starvation.

KEY WORKS *Carboniera*, 1967 (London: Courtauld Institute of Art); *Untitled*, 1987 (New York: Guggenheim Museum)

Piero **Manzoni**

● 1933–63 ITALIAN

Italy conceptual art; sculpture; mixed media Hamburg: Kunsthalle $840,000 in 1998, *Achrome* (sculpture)

He was a cherubic-looking aristocrat who was a short-lived (cirrhosis of liver), experimental artist in the forefront of releasing art from traditional ideas, processes, and forms.

He created objects and ideas that are now the commonplace of mainstream, official art, but were genuinely cutting-edge in the late 1950s and 1960s: strange white objects with no specific meaning, made by dipping material in kaolin or plaster; devices or strategies to preserve the evanescent (like the artist's breath) and challenge the idea of art as a tradable commodity; incorporating public and environment into a work of art. His work was provocative, but he was blessed with delicacy and humor.

KEY WORKS *Artist's Breath*, 1960 (London: Tate Collection); *Declaration of Authenticity No. 025*, 1961 (Boston: Museum of Fine Arts)

Luciano **Fabro**

● 1936– ITALIAN

Italy sculpture $223,300 in 2002, *Italia d'Oro* (sculpture)

Fabro is currently working on elegant, refined, carved sculptures using traditional materials, such as marble. He takes delight in visual and physical properties of material. Interested in craftsmanship and aesthetics—a contemporary interpretation of a tradition that goes back to Classical Greece. His work needs sunlight to bring it to life.

Enjoy his work for what it is. Let it play freely on your imagination through your own eyes. Close your ears to the wordy jargon of those catalogers and curators who spend more time looking at keyboards and playing with words than looking at works of art. These works have all the gloriously refined qualities of haute couture: they are an open invitation for the eye and imagination to have a truly fulfilling private feast.

KEY WORKS *Italio d'Oro (Golden Italy)*, 1971 (Los Angeles: Museum of Contemporary Arts); *Iconografia*, 1975 (Private Collection); *Road Map of Italy*, 1979 (Turin: Castello di Rivoli Museum of Contemporary Art)

Alighiero **Boetti**

🌐 1940-94   🏳 ITALIAN

🇮🇹 Italy   ▨ sculpture; conceptual art; mixed media   💰 $431,200 in 2002, *Tempo in tempo col tempo* (works on paper)

Boetti was a leading member of Arte Povera. Specialized in colored-wood creations. He created bits and pieces (such as assemblages, embroideries, drawings) that scratch away at attempting to make sense of a "fragmented but all embracing world" (so what's new?). Naïve systems, which the viewer is supposed to decode. Fashionable, not trivial, but ultimately insignificant. Untrained (it shows).

He is a useful reminder that the ideas, appearance, and agenda of the young,

"cutting-edge" art of the 1990s have been in play for a good 30 years.

KEY WORKS *The Thousand Longest Rivers in the World*, 1977-85 (New York: Museum of Modern Art); *Aerei*, 1984 (New York: Gagosian Gallery); *Map*, 1993-94 (Private Collection)

Mimmo **Paladino**

🌐 1948-   🏳 ITALIAN

🇮🇹 Italy   ▨ oils; prints; sculpture

🏛 New York: Metropolitan Museum of Art

💰 $225,000 in 1990, *Pozzo di eroi* (sculpture)

Creator of consciously individual, showy, expressively painted, colorful, large-scale figurative work made up of dislocated parts of animals, death masks, and bodies. Has a personal, mythical, and mystical agenda, which is probably (and deliberately?) impenetrable. A leading member of the Italian Transavanguardia movement, which included Sandro Chia and Francesco Clemente.

KEY WORKS *Canto Guerriero*, 1981 (Indiana: Ball State Museum of Art); *Untitled*, 1985 (New York: Metropolitan Museum of Art); *Sette*, 1991 (Buffalo: Albright-Knox Art Gallery)

Bringing the World into the World Alighiero Boetti, 1973–79, 53¼ x 70 in and 53¼ x 80 in (135 x 178 cm and 132 x 201 cm); ballpoint pen on paper mounted on linen, Private Collection. The alphabet is part of the art work.

Antoni **Tàpies**

● 1923–   SPANISH

Spain   mixed media; oils; prints
Barcelona: Fundació Antoni Tàpies
$753,608 in 1990, *Bois et marron
troué* (mixed media)

He is a talented self-taught artist whose
best work dates from the 1950s and early
1960s, when he used coarse materials to
produce somber heavily textured canvases
expressing the uncertain, stressful mood
of Cold War Europe. His later work is
less convincing because it is less in tune
with the times. Much highly praised,
so-called avant-garde art of the 1970s
and 1980s is anticipated by Tàpies.
KEY WORKS *Great Oval or Painting*, c. 1955
(Bilbao: Fine Arts Museum); *Le Chapeau
Renverse*, 1967 (Paris: Musée National
d'Art Moderne)

Juan **Muñoz**

● 1953–2001   SPANISH

Spain; UK; US   sculpture;
installations $125,000 in 1997,
From One to Five, Two (sculpture)

Born in Madrid, he studied in London
and New York. Creator of large-scale
installations that fill a whole gallery—such
as marquetry floors with extreme false
perspective, constructions with architectural
elements (such as iron balconies) that
have distorted scale, and groups of
figure sculptures in unexplained silent
relationships. He creates feelings of
disequilibrium, danger, and absurdity.
    If the new museums of modern and
contemporary art are no longer places

for individual, spiritual, and aesthetic
refreshment, nor for genuinely eye-
opening artistic and political challenge,
but are effectively adult adventure
playgrounds driven by management
targets for admissions, budgets, shop
sales, fund raising, and commercial
sponsorship (and why not?—everyone
and everything must move with the
times), then these (and other similar
works) are good-quality content for them.
KEY WORKS *Last Conversation Piece*, 1984–85
(Washington, DC: Hirshhorn Museum);
Dwarf with a Box, 1988 (London: Tate
Collection); *Double Bind*, 2001
(London: Tate Collection)

Eduardo **Chillida**

● 1924–2002   SPANISH

Spain   sculpture   Bilbao:
Guggenheim Museum $644,000
in 2001, *Besaka* (sculpture)

He was a Basque artist,
notable for abstract
constructions, mainly in
forged or welded iron, that
combine several Spanish
influences: modern, such
as Picasso, and traditional,
such as old farm implements.
These sculptures are

Berlin Eduardo Chillida, 2000,
iron sculpture, Berlin-Tiergarten:
Bundeskanzleramt. The installation
of Chillida's sculpture in the Court of
Honor of the Berlin Federal Chancellery
coincided with the opening of his own
dedicated museum, the Museo Chillida-
Leku, in his hometown of Hernani.

> ## "The conditions you need to be a good goalkeeper are exactly the same conditions you need to be a good sculptor! You must have a very good connection, in both professions, with time and space."
>
> ### EDUARDO CHILLIDA

sometimes monumental, but always graceful—often without a base, so they touch the ground with a dancer's lightness. Many have interlocking and embracing themes.

KEY WORKS *Tximista (Lightning)*, 1957 (Washington, DC: Hirshhorn Museum); *Modulation of Space*, 1963 (London: Tate Collection); *Silent Music II*, 1983 (New York: Metropolitan Museum of Art)

Jaume **Plensa**

● 1955– ﾉﾘ SPANISH

🇪🇸 Spain   🔵 conceptual art; installations; sculpture   💰 $27,209 in 1990, *Lau II* (mixed media)

The Spaniard Jaume Plensa is a good example of the new academic modern orthodoxy that is heavily promoted by the official art establishment.

He works with large-scale industrially made objects made to look significant, portentous, and profound, by being displayed in isolation or attached to big white walls in large official spaces. He "uses" steel, glass, and neon light, but the artist is only the designer: the physical creation is done anonymously, presumably in a factory.

If you remove the words that embellish the pieces ("Rembrandt," "womb," "desire," "Giotto," "a fool sees not the same tree a wise man sees"), what do they amount to? Profundity or banality? Is this art with deep meaning, or a clever exercise in marketing and packaging? Is this a good example of the way art establishments are mesmerized by big, slick machines?

KEY WORKS *Knock Knock*, 1999 (Kirishima, Japan: Kirishima Open-Air Museum); *Crown Fountain*, 2004 (Chicago: Millennium Park)

Laurence Stephen **Lowry**

● 1887–1976   ⊯ BRITISH

📟 NW England   🎨 oils   🏛 Salford: Lowry Centre
💹 $2.8m in 1999, *Going to the Match* (oils)

Lowry was a quirky painter who became critically and commercially successful with his instantly recognizable scenes of the bleak north of England—industrial landscapes inhabited by busy "stick" people. His "spontaneous naïvety" appeals to critics and intellectuals, his everyday directness to popular taste. At his best he is very good indeed, at all levels.

KEY WORKS *An Organ Grinder*, 1934 (Manchester: City Art Gallery); *The Fever Van*, 1935 (Liverpool: Walker Art Gallery)

Victor **Pasmore**

● 1908–98   ⊯ BRITISH

📟 England   🎨 oils; sculpture   🏛 Southampton: City Art Gallery   💹 $330,000 in 1997, *The Studio of Ingres* (oils)

He was an interesting pioneer of British abstraction. Started off as a spare-time painter (1927–37), then became a full-time figurative painter who went abstract in 1948 (which was a difficult decision for him). His line and form was very sensitive (oversensitive and contrived?). His spare, cool, calculated, consciously artificial works now look dated.

KEY WORKS *Parisian Café*, 1936–37 (Manchester: City Art Gallery); *Chiswick Reach*, 1943 (Ottawa: National Gallery of Canada)

Sir Terry **Frost**

● 1915–2003   ⊯ BRITISH

📟 Cornwall, England   🎨 oils
🏛 London: Tate Collection
💹 $70,300 in 2004, *Yellow Quay* (oils)

Frost was a leading St. Ives Group painter. Produced sensitive early works with gentle, fundamental shapes and colors abstracted from nature, often invoking sensations of movement, flight, or waves. His later work is more purely abstract. Took inspiration from the natural world. Wanted to convey the ecstatic and poetic experiences he found in nature.

You could go around a Sir Terry Frost exhibition looking for modern art influences and color theories (they are there to be found and that is all some people do), but what a waste of an opportunity that would be. If you go around looking for sunlight, water, leaves, and woods, and your memory or evocation of them and their interaction with you, your sight, or your emotions, you will be as uplifted as if you had spent your ideal day in the country.

KEY WORKS *Brown and Yellow*, c. 1951–52 (London: Tate Collection); *Green, Black, and White Movement*, 1951 (London: Tate Collection); *Blue Moon*, 1952 (London: Tate Collection)

Sir Sidney **Nolan**

● 1917–92   ⊯ AUSTRALIAN

📟 Australia; UK   🎨 oils   🏛 Lanyon (Australia): Nolan Gallery. London: Tate Collection
💹 $719,048 in 2000, *Death of Constable Scanlon* (oils)

Widely traveled and acclaimed, Nolan was one of the few contemporary artists to have established a place for narrative, mythological painting, notably the "Ned Kelly" (romantic Australian outlaw) series. His distinctive style combines abstraction and figuration, and conveys a strong sense of the heat and emptiness of the vast Australian landscape. Was an exponent of expressive brushwork and color.

KEY WORKS *The Trial*, 1947 (Canberra: National Gallery of Australia); *Kelly in Spring*, 1956 (London: Hayward Gallery)

Patrick **Heron**

● 1920–99   ⚑ BRITISH

🏛 England   🎨 oils; prints   🏛 London: Tate Gallery   💹 $364,000 in 2001, *Lux Eterna* (oils)

He is greatly revered and respected as one of the pioneers of large-scale, postwar abstract art in the UK. Had a difficult, combative personality. His last years were marked by illness and personal tragedy.

Was the creator of a prolific and impressive body of work that is intensely visual, colorful, and inspired by personal emotion and things seen. One of the few artists who sought to bridge the gap between European aesthetic sensibility and American direct rawness.

If possible, see his work in daylight—preferably sunlight—so the individual colors and color contrasts and interactions reach their full potential of Mediterranean intensity.

His most powerful work dates from the late 1960s and early 1970s—big works with intense, simple, hard-edge color forms that generate intense color sensations and pulsating spaces. Stand close to them for the full power to develop in your eye. His earlier work shows the inspiration of landscape, seascape, and the light of Cornwall. His later works are looser in style. Nevertheless, everything he created was done with very great, but not always obvious, technical exactitude.

KEY WORKS *Boats at Night*, 1947 (London: Tate Collection); *Vertical: January 1956* (London: Tate Collection); *Red and Yellow Image*, 1958 (London: Tate Collection)

Alan **Davie**

● 1920–   ⚑ BRITISH

🏛 UK; Europe   🎨 oils; prints   🏛 London: Tate Collection   💹 $85,000 in 1989, *Oh to be a Serpent that I May Love you Longer* (oils)

Davie is an unusual but well-regarded painter, working today in a totally individual manner. Talented athlete and jazz musician. Prolific. Magic. His work is all about trying to express the inexpressible and how to reach the primal and mystical forces of humankind (the kind of experience that the hippy generation sought). If you cannot accept the possibility of magic, or are unwilling to travel with him, his work will remain meaningless and appear no more than a design for a cover to a handbook on Indian mysticism.

He needs a large scale to express fully the magnitude of his endeavors. Early work is thickly painted in an Abstract Expressionist style. Since the 1960s he has worked in a figurative style, full of signs and symbols that are highly reminiscent of Indian art and decoration.

KEY WORKS *Thoughts for a Giant Bird*, 1940s (London: Bonhams); *Entrance to Paradise*, 1949 (London: Tate Collection); *Peggy's Guessing Box*, 1950 (Venice: Peggy Guggenheim Gallery)

Red and Blue *Sir Terry Frost, 1959, 50 x 30 in (127 x 76 cm), oil on canvas, Leicester: New Walk Museum.* Frost began to paint after being taken prisoner during the German invasion of Crete in 1941.

Leon **Kossoff**

● 1926 – ⚑ BRITISH

🏠 England 🎨 oils 💲 $460,800 in 2001, *Children's Swimming Pool, 12 o'clock Saturday Morning, September* (oils)

Kossoff is a somewhat shadowy and neglected figure, influenced by his Jewish cultural heritage. The human figure is always central to his work, which is of high quality, very thickly and crudely painted, in a strongly Expressionist style. He is inclined to gloominess, although his swimming-pool series are full of life.

KEY WORKS *Portrait of Father*, 1978 (Edinburgh: National Gallery of Modern Art); *Two Seated Figures No. 2*, 1980 (London: Tate Collection)

Frank **Auerbach**

● 1931 – ⚑ BRITISH

🏠 UK 🎨 oils 🏛 New York: Auerbach Collection 💲 $600,000 in 1990, *Mornington Crescent with the Statue of Sickert's Father-in-law* (oils)

Auerbach is German-born, but British by adoption. Chiefly produces small-scale paintings in which the paint can be as thick a bread crust, the result of constant revisions piled on one another. Images mostly of central, urban London, but also nudes. His work is an almost defiant declaration that although the art of painting may be considered by some to be out of fashion, it will certainly never die.

KEY WORKS *The Sitting Room*, 1964 (London: Tate Collection); *J. Y. M. 1*, 1981 (Southampton: City Art Gallery)

R. B. **Kitaj**

● 1932 – ⚑ AMERICAN/BRITISH

🏠 US; England 🎨 oils; pastels 🏛 London: Marlborough Fine Art. Edinburgh: National Gallery of Modern Art 💲 $341,000 in 1994, *Value, Price, and Profit* (oils)

He was born in the US, but settled in the UK in the 1960s. Maintains and advances a definition of art that is central to European painting in the "grand manner"—life drawing, literary subjects, exposition of human, intellectual, and moral issues. Sees himself as a martyr crucified by ignorant British critics (with some justification).

He has a very personal style. Makes large-scale, "exhibition" pieces, with many personal and biographical references, sometimes hidden. There are cross-references to literature and philosophy, sometimes to specific passages. He is concerned with the Jewish diaspora. Fine draftsman and instinctive colorist. Independent of eye and mind, and (to his credit) difficult to pigeonhole. His refusal to compromise can seem arrogant—is this why he was recently savaged by art critics in Britain (but not in the US)?

KEY WORKS *The Murder of Rosa Luxembourg*, 1960 (London: Tate Collection); *The Ohio Gang*, 1964 (New York: Museum of Modern Art); *The Hispanist (Nissa Torrents)*, 1977–78 (Bilbao: Fine Arts Museum)

Value, Price, and Profit, or Production of Waste
R. B. Kitaj, 1963, 60 x 60 in (152.4 x 152.4 cm), oil on canvas, Private Collection. Kitaj's self-image is that of a pilgrim existing in a cold, ugly, and exploitative world whose saving grace is the warmth generated by human creativity and intellect.

Francis **Bacon**

● 1909–92 ⴲ BRITISH

🖾 UK; Germany; Paris 🎨 oils; watercolors;
drawings 🏛 Art Institute of Chicago 💲 $7.8m
in 2001, *Studies of the Human Body* (oils)

He was one of the most significant
figurative painters of the postwar period.
Largely self-taught. A loner, personally
and artistically. His long-term significance
has yet to be assessed and will depend on
whether he is followed, or if he proves to
be a dead end.

> ## "The feeling of desperation and unhappiness are more useful to an artist than the feeling of contentment, because desperation and unhappiness stretch your whole sensibility."

FRANCIS BACON

Pope I—Study after Pope Innocent X by Velasquez
*Francis Bacon, 1951, 78 x 54 in (197.8 x 137.4 cm), oil on
canvas, Aberdeen: Art Gallery and Museums.* An existential
protest against authoritarian political power.

Bacon shows genuine originality in his
imagery, and the way he constructs it
and handles paint. His central (only?)
image is of an isolated figure, usually
male, often naked, under stress, in bare,
brightly lit, or colored space. Said
by Bacon (and others) to indicate the
condition of postwar Europe and modern
human isolation. His work is beautifully
crafted, with controlled drawing and
line, and tense, emotional color. There
is creative interplay between what he
intends and what happens accidentally.

Three Studies for Portraits (including Self-Portrait)
*Francis Bacon, 1969, 14 x 12 in (35.5 x 30.5 cm) each, oil
on canvas, Private Collection.* Bacon would only paint
protraits of friends, and worked from photographs.

Like many contemporary artists, he has
suffered from unhelpful excess of praise,
but in truth, he has only one image and
one emotion, which he repeats with
variation. Late developer—nothing of
sustained significance until his late 30s,
then 20 years or so of very powerful
work; after about 1971 (aged 61 and
following the death of his lover George
Dyer) he declined into repetitive formula.

KEY WORKS *Three Studies for Figures at the Base of
a Crucifixion*, 1944 (London: Tate Collection);
Study after Velasquez I, 1950 (New York: Tony
Shafrazi Gallery); *Three Figures in a Room*, 1965
(Paris: Musée National d'Art Moderne); *Study
for Head of Lucien Freud*, 1967 (Private Collection)

Roger **Hilton**

◔ 1911–75 ⚑ BRITISH

🏴 UK; France 🎨 oils; gouache 🏛 London:
Tate Collection 💰 $49,000 in 1990, *Untitled* (oils)

A producer of gutsy paintings, sometimes
abstract, sometimes with rudimentary
female or abstract forms. He delighted in
color, paint, female form, causing offence,
and maintaining a rough humor in the
face of considerable personal problems.
KEY WORKS *January 1957* (London:
Tate Collection); *Oi Yoi Yoi*, 1963
(London: Tate Collection)

Lucian **Freud**

◔ 1922– ⚑ BRITISH

🏴 UK 🎨 oils 🏛 London: Tate Collection
💰 $6,993,000 in 2005, *Red-haired Man on Chair* (oils)

He is the senior living British painter.
German-born grandson of Sigmund
Freud, the founder of psychoanalysis.
Became a British subject in 1939.
  His main subject is the human figure,
often naked, posed artificially as models
in a studio. Sometimes paints views from
windows, but anything other than the
human figure he considers "frivolous."
All his models are known to him personally,
so there is an intimate sense of deep
knowledge (love even?), not detachment.
His work reveals extraordinary powers
of concentration (which is not the same
as intensity). Powerful portraits.
  Look how carefully the eyes are painted
and how much of the inner person they
reveal, even when closed. How well he
knows all those blemishes, bulges, lumps,
private parts of the flesh that we study
and examine intimately in our own
bodies, but rarely see or care to look at
in others. He knows every corner of his
studio and the space that the models
occupy. He knows exactly what he can
do with his paint—and what he can't.
KEY WORKS *In the Silo Tower*, 1940–41 (Private
Collection); *Girl with Roses*, 1947–48 (London:
British Council); *Naked Man on a Bed*, 1987
(London: Saatchi Collection); *Naked Woman*,
1988 (Missouri: St. Louis Art Museum)

The Painter's Mother *Lucian Freud, 1982–84,
41½ x 50¼ in (105.5 x 127.5 cm), oil on canvas, Private
Collection.* Freud once remarked, "I paint people not
because of what they are like, not exactly in spite of
what they are like, but how they happen to be."

Sir Anthony **Caro**

◔ 1924– ⚑ BRITISH

🏴 UK; US 🎨 sculpture 🏛 London: Tate
Collection 💰 $96,850 in 2002, *Strand* (oils)

Caro is usually proclaimed (how correctly?)
as *the* leading contemporary British
sculptor. Studied engineering at Cambridge
(which shows) and worked with Henry
Moore (which doesn't show).
  He is a creator of sculpture constructed
out of heavy metal, which is usually
welded together, recycling the elements
of the engineering and construction
industries (plates, beams, propellers).
Emphasis on structure, space, horizontals,
verticals, and constructions hugging the
ground or tabletop like well-organized

scrap. Displays truth to (industrial) materials? His early work (1960s) is brightly painted; later work undecorated other than with carefully controlled rust.

Under the modern outer garment is a deeply traditional soul. Solid, honest, plain speaking, down-to-earth (literally), no-frills work that emphasizes the basic values (space, construction, materials) but can be didactic and schoolmasterish, suggesting the deep-seated, sometimes stubborn, values of middle England (and none the worse for that). It isn't art full of fantasy or poetic imagination.

KEY WORKS *Sculpture 3*, 1961 (Venice: Peggy Guggenheim Gallery); *Early One Morning*, 1962 (London: Tate Collection); *Yellow Swing*, 1965 (London: Tate Collection)

Michael **Andrews**

● 1928–95 ◪ BRITISH

◪ UK; Australia ◪ acrylics; oils ◪ London: Tate Collection ◪ $75,680 in 2003, *Untitled* (oils)

Andrews produced sensitive work that reflected his inner personality. Large-scale paintings of places and people he knew well and felt deeply about. He possessed a delicate, unassertive technique (mainly working with spray-painted acrylic). A shy, reclusive personality. Painstakingly slow worker (hence few works), totally absorbed by his subjects and activity. English sensibility to light and nature.

KEY WORKS *The Colony Room*, 1962 (London: Tate Collection); *The Deer Park*, 1962 (London: Tate Collection)

Bridget **Riley**

● 1931– ⚑ BRITISH

🏛 England; France   🎨 oils; watercolors; prints
🏛 Birmingham (UK): Museums and Art Gallery
💰 $700,000 in 2004, *Serif* (works on paper)

An eminent major abstract painter, Riley
has a strong international reputation and
a lifelong dedication to the exploration of
both the visual and emotional properties
of color. Widely traveled.

She creates intensely visual, abstract
paintings whose appearance and form
(large scale, stripes, blocks of color) do
not result from any theory or formula
but are a means of using color and form
to create sensations of light and space.

The colors interact at their edges
and generate the illusion of other
colors or jumps of color. Some colors
jump forward, others back. Dark (often
black) stripes create a rhythmic pulse
across the surface. There is emotional
as well as visual involvement.
KEY WORKS *Winter Palace*, 1981 (Leeds:
Museums and Art Gallery); *Fall*, 1963
(London: Tate Collection); *Orphan Elegy I*,
1978 (London: British Council)

Victor **Vasarely**

● 1908–97 ⚑ HUNGARIAN/FRENCH

🏛 France   🎨 oils; prints   🏛 Aix-en-Provence:
Fondation Vasarely. Pécs (Hungary): Victor Vasarely
Museum   💰 $195,600 in 1990, *Cintra* (oils)

Vasarely was one of the key figures
in the creation of Op Art in the 1950s.
Hungarian-born, but was awarded French
citizenship in 1959. He produced hard-
edge abstract paintings designed to give
powerful optical effects and illusions
that can often be explored and activated
by moving around the paintings. His
work was satisfying, but limited.
KEY WORKS *Neves II*, 1949–58 (London:
Tate Collection); *Quasar*, 1966 (San
Francisco: Fine Arts Museums)

Morris **Louis**

● 1912–62 ⚑ AMERICAN

🏛 US   🎨 oils; acrylics   💰 $1.5m
in 2002, *Untitled* (oils)

Louis created large-scale lyrical works.
The subject matter is color, which is
trickled and floated onto bare canvas

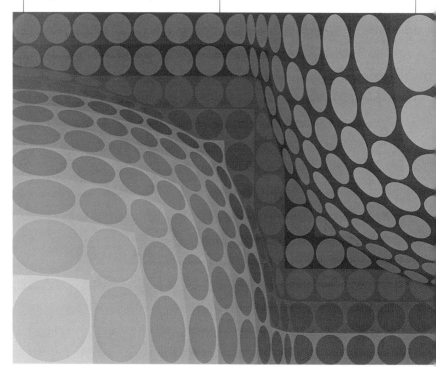

in such an inventive way that, if you suspend disbelief, the pigment can seem to be rivers, waterfalls, liquid mists of fresh pure color (if you can enjoy a landscape, why not this?). Easy-going but satisfying.

KEY WORKS *Tet*, 1958 (New York: Whitney Museum of American Art); *Gamma Epsilon*, 1960 (Private Collection)

Robert **Rauschenberg**

● 1925– ⚑ AMERICAN

📖 US 🎨 mixed media; prints 🏛 Detroit Institute of Arts. New York: Museum of Modern Art. Hamburg: Kunsthalle 💰 $6.6m in 1991, *Rebus* (works on paper)

He is a major pioneering postwar artist. Prolific, creative, and influential. Very New York. Deeply committed to international cooperation for social change and human rights.

Produces a very consistent, personal, and visual work. Explores how to make materials (screen printing, paint, found objects, papers, fabrics, or metals) and images (from contemporary media images, words, abandoned urban detritus) work together. The whole constitutes a chronicle of his own activities and of his culture and times. Like Canaletto, he produces works that mirror a particular society, reflecting, distorting, or glamorizing it, and are sought after by its members as souvenirs.

Has a passionate involvement, with an underlying innocence (not naïvety)— takes evident delight in collecting material and putting it together, without self-consciousness or rules. His best work is beautiful to look at, technically intriguing, layered, memorable, and puzzling. Since the 1980s his work has declined; impersonal and overblown.

Bi-Vega Victor Vasarely, 1974, 45 x 31 in (114 x 79 cm), screenprint, London: Hayward Gallery. Vasarely regarded the artist as a workman who produces prototypes for reproduction by others.

Bellini Robert Rauschenberg, 1986, 56½ x 35 in (143.5 x 88.9 cm), intaglio printed in color on woven paper, Detroit Institute of Arts. A late work by Rauschenberg, which combines high and low art imagery.

KEY WORKS *Bed*, 1955 (New York: Leo Castelli Gallery); *Odalisk*, 1955–58 (Cologne: Museum Ludwig); *Soviet/American Array II*, 1988 (Detroit Institute of Arts)

Larry **Rivers**

● 1923–2002 ⚑ AMERICAN

📖 US 🎨 oils; sculpture; mixed media; collage 🏛 New York: Museum of Modern Art 💰 $425,000 in 1990, *Africa I* (oils)

He was a multifaceted bohemian: painter, poet, and jazz musician from a Russian-Jewish émigré family. An influential guru. Created versatile and many-sided works, which are difficult to summarize—they can switch, within the same work, between figuration and abstraction, sharp detail and lush brushstrokes. One of the parents of Pop Art, he was also one of the first to use mass-media imagery. Also reworked famous hackneyed paintings.

KEY WORKS *Washington, Crossing the Delaware*, 1953 (New York: Museum of Modern Art); *Camels*, c. 1962 (Cambridge: Fitzwilliam Museum); *French Money*, 1962 (Private Collection)

Alexander **Calder**

● 1898–1976 🏴 AMERICAN

🏴 US; France 🎨 sculpture; gouache
🏛 New York: Whitney Museum (the
video of him playing with his circus
is its best-loved exhibit) 💰 $5.2m
in 2003, *Untitled* (sculpture)

The man who gave the world
the mobile, thus making it
a better and happier place.
Child of a sculptor father
and painter mother. Trained
as an engineer and industrial
draftsman, and cartoonist.

Enjoy the movement and *joie
de vivre* in his mobiles (from mid-
1930s)—those famous, delicately
balanced constructions of wire and
disks painted in primary colors or
black. Tiny or large scale, they are
marvels of endless variety. Stabiles are
steel constructions firmly planted on
the ground and immobile but their
swooping shapes suggest movement. Early
work includes wire figures and a circus
of tiny figures, which he could animate.

Let the child in you come alive and
forget worldly cares. Animate the mobiles
into life (a breath of wind is usually
enough); walk around and through
the large stabiles to explore their life.
Deceptive simplicity and soothing
unpredictability are among the life-
enhancing qualities of Calder's works.
If you must speak art jargon, talk about
drawing in space, negative space,
spatial relationships, form, and color.
Wonderful, energy-filled gouaches.

KEY WORKS *Lobster Trap and Fish Tail*, 1939
(New York: Museum of Modern Art); *The
Spider*, 1940 (Private Collection); *Vertical
Constellation with Bomb*, 1943 (Washington,
DC: National Gallery of Art)

Blue Feather *Alexander Calder, c. 1948, 42 x 55 x 18 in
(106.6 x 139.7 x 45.7 cm), painted sheet metal and wire,
Private Collection.* This piece combines Calder's two
inventions: "stabile" (the static base) and "mobile" parts.

His very simple, large canvases are
saturated with pure color. Let the eye
and the mind relax fully and absorb the
colors, shapes, and the razor-sharp edges.
Enjoy them for what they are and let
them play on the imagination, stretch the
eye and stretch the mind's eye. Look at
the meticulously painted surfaces (he
always uses oil paint for richness of color).

His works are sometimes to be enjoyed
as objects seeming to float on the wall;
sometimes to be seen as spaces through
the wall giving onto fields of blue (sky or
sea?), or red (earth or fire?). He mixes his
own colors, and what he creates is a final
distillation of something once seen in the
world (especially architecture). It uplifts
the eye and the spirit—as refreshing as
chilled champagne. The canvases must
be in pristine condition (damage and
dirt ruin the purity and experience).

KEY WORKS *Rebound*, 1959 (London: Anthony
d'Offay Gallery); *Red Curve*, 1960s (Private
Collection); *Blue, Green, Yellow, Orange, Red*,
1966 (New York: Guggenheim Museum)

Ellsworth **Kelly**

● 1923– 🏴 AMERICAN

🏴 US 🎨 oils; prints; drawings
🏛 London: Christie's Images 💰 $2.6m
in 2004, *Chatham XIII—Yellow Red* (oils)

He is one of the contemporary masters,
who has continued Matisse's exploration
of color. Traditional values of painting—
technical perfection, visual pleasure,
spiritual uplift—are still alive and well.

Philip **Pearlstein**

● 1924– 🏴 AMERICAN

🏴 US 🎨 oils; prints; drawings 💰 $52,500
in 1990, *Two Nudes on a Mexican Blanket* (oils)

Pearlstein is a leading figurative painter
with a raw, objective style depicting
the human body as it appears, with
the minimum of interpretation.

Notice the artificiality within the reality: highly finished surfaces (rather than imitation of perceived textures), hidden or cut-off faces, odd viewpoints. The artificiality forces the question "why?"— which in turn demands an answer or interpretation. Pearlstein lays claim to having given dignity back to the figure by rescuing it from both Expressionist and Cubist distortion, and from pornographic exploitation. His early, pre-1960s, work is Abstract Expressionist.

KEY WORKS *Nude Torso*, 1963 (New York: National Academy of Design); *Male and Female Nudes with Red and Purple Drape*, 1968 (Washington, DC: Hirshhorn Museum); *Model in Green Kimono*, 1974 (San Francisco: Fine Arts Museums)

Andrew **Wyeth**

● 1917– ⚑ AMERICAN

▣ US ✦ tempera; watercolors
▥ New York: Museum of Modern Art
⚡ $1.55m in 1997, *Christina Olson* (oils)

Wyeth is the son of famous book illustrator. First achieved fame with the watercolors he painted in Maine in the late 1930s. Has a brilliant realist technique, is popular and much collected, but is unjustly derided by many contemporary critics.

His subjects are carefully chosen and have deep personal meaning. At first sight they look ordinary, but part of Wyeth's magic is his ability to make the commonplace hauntingly memorable. He is unconcerned by fashion or being up to date. His large-scale paintings are done in tempera (not oil), which is painstakingly slow to work with and enables him to exploit his love of detail and focus on the quality of draftsmanship rather than painterliness.

Observe the way he heightens realism by using strong design and unusual, artificial compositions; note also the way he contrasts fine detail with large areas of abstraction. His watercolors and dry-brush paintings are painted in a frenzy (they are often tossed onto the ground, which is why they may have smudges, tears, or attached pieces of vegetation).

KEY WORKS *Winter*, 1946 (North Carolina Museum of Art); *Christina's World*, 1948 (New York: Museum of Modern Art); *Snow Flurries*, 1953 (Washington, DC: National Gallery of Art)

Claes **Oldenburg**

● 1929– ⚑ AMERICAN

▣ US ✦ sculpture; mixed media ▥ New York: Museum of Modern Art. London: Tate Collection
⚡ $1.3m in 2004, *Sewing Machine* (sculpture)

Oldenburg was born in Europe, but brought up in the US (his father was appointed Swedish Consul in Chicago, 1936). He is one of Pop Art's most original and inventive talents.

His highly original creations work on several levels by constantly reversing normal expectations. He starts with commonplace consumer-society objects (such as a hamburger or a typewriter) and metamorphoses them into something strange and comical by altering their scale, texture, or context. Also asks questions about what constitutes a painting, sculpture, work of art, or a consumer object.

He enjoys experimenting with paradox and contradiction. He mocks the self-absorbed seriousness of consumer society but is always teasing and humorous, never threatening. Has always been a compulsive drawer, even as a child, forever imagining transpositions that carry witty and significance resonances—such as a woman's lipstick, which becomes a rocket with a warhead and doubles as a sculptural monument in a public place.

KEY WORKS *Two Cheeseburgers with Everything (Dual Hamburgers)*, 1962 (New York: Museum of Modern Art); *Lipsticks in Piccadilly Circus, London*, 1966 (London: Tate Collection)

Jim **Dine**

● 1935– ⚑ AMERICAN

▣ US; UK ✦ oils; acrylics; mixed media; prints; installations ▥ New York: Guggenheim Museum ⚡ $600,000 in 1996, *Hearts* (oils, acrylic on 57 canvases)

He is one of the pioneers of Pop Art. His work has a strong biographical element in which tools (childhood memories of grand-father's hardware store), paint, palettes (artist's studio), and domestic objects, are prominent. Full of wit and simple poetry, released by sensitive juxtaposition of objects, color, and stenciled labels.

KEY WORKS *Bedspring*, 1960 (New York: Guggenheim Museum); *Pearls*, 1961 (New York: Guggenheim Museum)

POP ART

Pop Art emerged independently in New York and London in the mid-1950s, and remained the dominant avant-garde movement until the late 1960s. In America, its initial motivation was a reaction against the self-absorption of Abstract Expressionism and a determination that art should re-engage with the real world. In the US, Pop Art celebrated the new consumer society; in Britain, there was always an undertow of nostalgia.

SUBJECTS AND STYLE

The commonplace and the ordinary dominate: famously, Coca-Cola bottles, hamburgers, comic strips, household products, images from newspapers, advertisements—in short, almost anything produced by Western consumer society. In part, this was because Pop Art held that it was the duty of art to take the modern world as its subject. By extension, in an age of mass production, styles aimed at anonymity.

Just What is it that Makes Today's Homes so Different, so Appealing? Richard Hamilton, 1956, 10¼ x 9¾ in (26 x 24.8 cm), collage, Tübingen: Kunsthalle. Witty, mocking, challenging: Pop Art is born.

WHAT TO LOOK FOR

As with pop music, look for a world of youthful energy, more excited by mass advertising than the obscurities of high and abstract art. Pop Art was designed to be consciously different, irreverent, easy to look at and remember. Fun and economic freedom, however banal and cheap, were considered more interesting than contemplating life's deepest mysteries.

Campbell's Soup Can Andy Warhol, 1962, 35¾ x 24 in (90.8 x 60.9 cm), screen print, New York: Leo Castelli Gallery. Bold, simple, unadorned: in short, Pop Art epitomized, the everyday made epic.

KEY EVENTS

1952	Independent Group (IG) formed in London: actively seeks to celebrate "pulp imagery"
1955	Robert Rauschenberg's *The Bed*, key proto-Pop Art work
1958	English critic Lawrence Alloway coins term "Pop Art;" Jasper Johns has first one-man show in New York
1962	Pop Art announces itself with its first major exhibition, held at the Sidney Janis Gallery in New York. Lichtenstein, Warhol, Oldenburg, and other artists are present

Wayne **Thiebaud**

● 1920– ⚑ AMERICAN

🏵 US 🎨 oils 🏛 New York: Memorial Art Gallery, University of Rochester

📈 $2.8m in 2002, *Freeways* (oils)

A painter of portraits, landscapes, and still lifes, which are lavishly executed in thick, buttery paint and clear, bright colors. Takes a loving but unromantic interest in the anonymous faces and products seen in the supermarket, cafeteria, or deli. His simplified style comes from his early experience as an advertising artist and cartoonist. Paints clear light, and thick blue shadows you feel you can touch.

KEY WORKS *Display Cakes*, 1963 (San Francisco: Museum of Modern Art); *Freeway Curve*, 1979 (San Francisco: Museum of Modern Art)

Roy **Lichtenstein**

● 1923–97 ⚑ AMERICAN

🏵 US 🎨 acrylics; oils; sculpture

🏛 San Francisco: Fine Arts Museums

📈 $6.5m in 2002, *Happy Tears* (oils)

He was a leading American Pop artist with an instantly recognizable style, which at first sight seems to be just large-scale blow-ups of comic-book images.

Had a great ability to contradict expectations with wit and elegance—nothing is what it seems. He transformed the comic-book images (traditionally dismissed as mere trash) into elegant large-scale paintings, which are in the tradition of a serious art gallery experience. He achieves this by the sophistication of his technique and the probing nature of his subject matter. (Caravaggio and Manet did something similar in their days.)

Note how he turns the mechanized impersonality of the comic-book image into something very personal. He organizes, redefines, and exaggerates his images with the skill and knowledge of an old master. Has a meticulous technique: highly controlled use of black outline; use of Ben Day dot; intense color. Deep interest in life, love, and death (traditional high-art subjects) and in modern American society. He parodies other artists and (like Manet) plays with art history.

Anxious Girl *Roy Lichtenstein, 1964, oil on canvas, Private Collection*. Lichtenstein first showed in New York in 1962 with the brilliant Leo Castelli whose gallery first promoted Pop Art in the US.

KEY WORKS *Drowning Girl*, 1963 (New York: Museum of Modern Art); *Whaam!*, 1963 (London: Tate Collection); *As I Opened Fire*, 1964 (Amsterdam: Stedelijk Museum); *M-Maybe (A Girl's Picture)*, 1965 (Cologne: Museum Ludwig)

Edward **Ruscha**

● 1937– ⚑ AMERICAN

🏵 US 🎨 oils; acrylics; prints 🏛 Washington, DC: National Gallery of Art 📈 $3.2m in 2002, *Talk About Space* (oils)

An Oklahoma boy who went LA hip in 1956, Ruscha's early work is Pop—icily perfect images of gasoline stations and billboards, plus booklets of photos of similar subjects. His recent work plays with images and words; for instance, a painting of water may have that word spelled out in a trompe-l'oeil spill of water. Uses unconventional media such as fruit juice instead of watercolor.

KEY WORKS *Lisp*, 1968 (Washington, DC: National Gallery of Art); *Accordion Fold W/ Vaseline Stains*, 1973 (New York: UBS Art Collection)

Alex **Katz**

● 1927– ⋈ AMERICAN

▣ US ◆ oils; drawings
🏛 San Francisco: Fine Arts Museums.
Waterville, Maine: Colby College
Museum of Art ⚡ $600,000 in
2001, *Blue Umbrella No.2* (oils)

Katz is a veteran, very visual,
American figurative painter who
reruns traditional themes and
techniques in a contemporary
American idiom.

He replays, with genuine
inventiveness, themes and ideas
beloved of the French Impressionists
and Post-Impressionists (Manet, Monet,
Seurat especially): airy landscapes,
the middle class at play, fascination
with recording the effects of light.
Direct wet-in-wet oil technique; color
harmonies and dissonances; open
brushwork that jumps into a focused
image at a distance. Look for the self-
absorbed faces, gestures, and intriguing
psychology that you find in Manet's work.

He is to French art what Californian
Cabernet Sauvignon wine is to French
Bordeaux—not necessarily better or
worse, but noticeably different: on a
bigger scale, more direct, less complex.
Enjoy his works for what they are:
a refreshing, eye-filling pleasure with
a distinguished and recognizable
pedigree. Try to view the paintings by
daylight, and also notice the sketches
done from life, which he works up into
large scale in the studio.

KEY WORKS *Ada and Alex*, 1980 (Waterville,
Maine: Colby College Museum of Art);
Rudy, 1980 (Waterville, Maine: Colby College
Museum of Art); *Tracy on the Raft at 7:30*, 1982
(Waterville, Maine: Colby College Museum of
Art); *Varick*, 1988 (London: Saatchi Collection)

Dusk *Alex Katz, 1986, 54 x 72 in (137.2 x 183 cm), oil on canvas, Private Collection.* The artist's flat style and lean technique connects with his early experiences as a designer of stage sets and costume.

Jasper **Johns**

● 1930– ⋈ AMERICAN

▣ US ◆ oils; encaustic paints; sculpture; prints
🏛 Washington, DC: National Gallery of Art
⚡ $15.5m in 1988, *False Start* (oils)

Johns was a key figure in postwar American
art and a founding father of Pop Art. Very
influential, very much admired. Is (and
will be) to American 20th-century art
what Poussin is to 17th-century French art.

His art is cerebral, philosophical, closed,
and self-referential. He loves polarities—
works that are simultaneously cerebral
and sensual, light-hearted and serious,
simple and complex, beautiful and banal,
realistic and illusionistic.

The classic Johns are his early American
flag paintings. They caused excitement
because no one could work out (and still
can't?) whether they were paintings or
objects, abstract works of art or literal
reproductions of the flag, banal or deeply
emotional—he enjoys riddles about
definitions. He can work on a small scale
(the ale cans), or a large scale
(through canvases with objects
attached). Used encaustic (wax)
technique for his early work.

KEY WORKS *Target with Plaster Casts*,
1955 (New York: Leo Castelli
Gallery); *White Flag*, 1955 (New
York: Leo Castelli Gallery); *0 through
9*, 1961 (London: Tate Collection)

Three Flags *Jasper Johns, 1958, 30¾ x
45 in (784 x 115.6 cm), encaustic on canvas,
New York: Whitney Museum of American Art.*
A teasing play on reality and illusion.

Ale Cans

Jasper Johns c. 1964

Jasper Johns's *Ale Cans*—cast in bronze and painstakingly painted—is key not just in the evolution of Pop Art but of modern art as a whole. It plays a brilliantly sophisticated game with notions about the perception of, and expectations from, a work of art.

Ale Cans	
Medium painted bronze	
Dimensions 5½ x 8 x 4¾ in (14 x 20.3 x 12 cm)	
Location Private Collection	

Johns was hugely influenced by the most radical (and intellectual) of the Dada artists, Marcel Duchamp. Duchamp likened art to playing a game of chess, but Johns goes further and deeper than Duchamp, and has a genuine wit. His *Ale Cans*—this is the second version he made—is a work of craftsmanship, yet it poses puzzles that are teasingly unanswerable. Is it just a worthless, throwaway object as its subject suggests? Is it a painting? Or a sculpture? Does it matter? The result is both playful and challenging, a product of the artist's engagement with contemporary artistic debates. Many have tried to follow in Johns's footsteps, but it is a difficult game and few succeed.

> ## "Sometimes I see it and then paint it. Other times I paint it and then see it."
>
> JASPER JOHNS

The use of bronze and the solid base raise expectations that it is traditional sculpture

The use of two cans side by side (rather than a single one) is artistic and sculptural, yet the subject matter is a trivial, disposable object from everyday life

The large oval labels are exceptionally carefully painted, raising the question, "Is it a painting rather than a sculpture?"

Andy **Warhol**

⬤ 1928 – 87 🏳 AMERICAN

🏛 US   🎨 oils; acrylics; prints; sculpture; video
🏛 Pittsburgh: Andy Warhol Museum   💲 $15.75m
in 1998, *Orange Marilyn* (works on paper)

A neurotic surrounded by drug addicts, Warhol was a key figure: his work represents one of art's turning points, changing the role of the artist and his or her way of seeing and doing things, as did Leonardo in the 16th century and Courbet in the 19th century. A great voyeur.

Look for instantly recognizable, talented work. His images were drawn from the world of Hollywood, films, TV, glamor, mass media, and advertising (Marilyn Monroe, Chairman Mao, Coca-Cola bottles, Campbell's soups). He deliberately recalled and exploited the values of the world by using its visual language: bright colors, silkscreen technique, repetition, commercial simplification, and compelling (sometimes shocking) images. Was also a (mediocre) fashion designer and filmmaker.

He set up a new role model for the artist (much aspired to by today's young stars): no longer the solitary genius expressing intense personal emotion (as Picasso and Pollock did), but the artist as businessman—the equal of Hollywood movie stars and directors and Madison Avenue advertising executives. Son of Czech immigrants, he acted out an American dream cycle—pursued a driving need to be famous and rich, like his subjects, and ended up destroying himself.

KEY WORKS *Campbell's Soup Can* (see page 440); *Green Disaster Ten Times*, 1963 (Frankfurt: Museum für Moderne Kunst); *Suicide*, 1963 (New York: Leo Castelli Gallery); *Jacqueline Kennedy No.3*, 1965 (London: Hayward Gallery)

> **"I wanted to be an art businessman or a business artist. Being good in business is the most fascinating kind of art."**
>
> ANDY WARHOL

Twenty Marilyns *Andy Warhol, 1962, 77½ x 45⅜ in (197 x 116 cm), silk screen, Private Collection.* At about the time he produced this famous work, Warhol directed his assistant friends and hangers-on into an organization that he called The Factory.

Philip **Guston**

◔ 1913–80   ℙ AMERICAN

🄿 Mexico; US; Europe   🄰 oils
🏛 Canberra: National Gallery of Australia
💲 $6.5m in 2005, *The Street* (oils)

He was a well-regarded and influential
artist whose work has had several distinct
and different phases.

His early work is figurative. In about
1950 he became an Abstract Expressionist,
producing shimmering, nervously painted,
high-minded abstract paintings. Around
1970 he returned to figuration, with crude,
but perversely poetic, cartoonlike imagery
that conjures up a bizarre world of
everyday junk remnants.

It is difficult to explain Guston's
changes of direction other than as
autobiographical. He was probably
working out the consequences of a
traumatic childhood (father's suicide,
brother's death, memories of Ku
Klux Klan). His crudity perhaps
reflects an element of self-loathing?

KEY WORKS *The Native's Return*, 1957
(London: Phillips Collection); *The
Painter's Table*, 1973 (Washington, DC:
National Gallery of Art)

James **Rosenquist**

◔ 1933–   ℙ AMERICAN

🄿 US   🄰 oils; prints   🏛 Ottawa:
National Gallery of Canada   💲 $1.1m
in 2005, *Be Beautiful* (oils)

One of the leading Pop artists, he
was initially trained, and became very
successful, as a New York billboard

Legend *Philip Guston, 1977, 65¼ x 78¾ in (175 x 200 cm),
oil on canvas, Houston: Museum of Fine Arts.* Guston
said of his works around this time: "You see, I look at
my paintings, speculate about them, they baffle me, too.
That's all I'm painting for."

painter and designer. Creates large-scale
works that are chronicles of an era (1960s).
Pieces together immaculately painted
layers of commonplace imagery, which
jump in scale and, because of their
seeming disconnections, are resistant
to (but demanding of) interpretation.

KEY WORKS *Study for Marilyn*, 1962 (London:
Mayor Gallery); *President Elect*, 1961–64
(Paris: Centre Pompidou)

Robert (John Clark) **Indiana**

◔ 1928–   ℙ AMERICAN

🄿 US   🄰 oils; prints   🏛 San Francisco:
Fine Arts Museums   💲 $550,000 in 2002,
American Sweetheart (oils)

He is remembered for the brief period
when he created imagery of simple words
and numbers painted on a large scale in
blazing color. Work is flat, razor-edged,
and heraldic; has effective, eye-bombarding
optical impact. Often uses a single, monosyllabic command—EAT; LOVE; DIE.
Influenced by billboard signs. Very
Pop Art, very 1960s; now very dated.

KEY WORKS *The American Dream 1*, 1961 (New
York: Museum of Modern Art); *LOVE*, 1967
(New York: Museum of Modern Art); *American
Dream*, 1971 (Boston: Museum of Fine Arts)

F-111 *(detail) James Rosenquist, 1964–65, 10 x 86 ft
(3.48 x 26.21 m), oil on canvas and aluminum, New York:
Museum of Modern Art.* A detail from a vast composition,
which was a protest against the Vietnam War and
American defense spending.

Richard **Hamilton**

◐ 1922–   ▣ BRITISH

▣ UK   ◪ oils; prints; photomontage
▥ London: Tate Collection   ▨ $182,000
in 2004, *Fashion-Plate* (works on paper)

The former intellectual guru of British
Pop Art who still holds court, Hamilton
has an austere, rather self-conscious style,
which can come across as aloof and
patronizing. Seems to have a need to
address his work to the high priests of the
art world rather than the public at large
(an odd attitude for one who claimed to
be a true "pop," that is popular, artist).
KEY WORKS *Chromatic Spiral*, 1950
(London: Tate Collection); *Just what
is it that Makes Today's Homes so Different,
so Appealing?* (see page 440)

Sir Eduardo **Paolozzi**

◐ 1924–2005   ▣ BRITISH

▣ UK; Europe; US   ◪ sculpture; prints; collage
▥ London: Tate Collection. San Francisco:
Museum of Fine Arts   ▨ $90,200 in 2003,
Portrait of the Artist (sculpture)

Born in Edinburgh, Paolozzi was the son
of an Italian immigrant family who had
settled in Scotland. Passionate, consistent,
generous. A founder of Pop Art and one
of the great (though underrated) artists of
the second half of the 20th century.

His sculptures, constructions, and prints
(lithographs) are kaleidoscopes of images
and ideas. At their heart is a dialog about
the human condition in the modern
world. The fragmentation and unexpected
juxtapositions of images are never arbitrary
but part of a clearly thought-out strategy,
commenting on questions such as: How
do we fit into our fragmentary modern
world? How do we use our powers over
life and death? Can technology be poetic?

This is the art of a quick-firing, endlessly
demanding imagination, which got more
alert with age. To connect with it, be
willing to be as freely imaginative yourself,
ready to see and revise all your familiar
certainties. Look for the clues: the life and
loves of Hollywood idols that equal those
of Greek gods (we still need mythology);
references to other fertile minds (for
example, Burl Ives, who combined folk,
band, and classical music); and to places
of imagination (such as museums).

KEY WORKS *I was a Rich Man's Plaything*,
1947 (London: Tate Collection); *Bird*,
1949 (London: Tate Collection); *Real
Gold*, 1949 (London: Tate Collection);
Mosaics, 1983–85 (London Underground:
Tottenham Court Road Station)

Sir Peter **Blake**

◐ 1932–   ▣ BRITISH

▣ UK   ◪ oils; prints; mixed media
▥ London: Tate Collection   ▨ $115,500
in 2000, *Little Lady Luck* (oils/collage)

Blake was one of the founders of British
Pop Art in the 1960s. Finely crafted work
that is rather fey and increasingly has
more to do with a nostalgic and often
witty longing for a world that was the
stuff of schoolboy dreams—comics,
badges, pop and film stars, girls and
wrestlers, corner stores—rather than
anything modern. A Peter Pan figure.
KEY WORKS *Self-Portrait with Badges*, 1961
(London: Tate Collection); LP cover for
Sgt. Pepper's Lonely Hearts Club Band, 1967
(London: Victoria & Albert Museum)

Patrick **Caulfield**

◐ 1936–   ▣ BRITISH

▣ UK   ◪ oils; prints   ▥ London: Tate Collection
▨ $301,950 in 2004, *Window at Night* (oils)

A pioneering Pop artist whose work
was very recognizable, with a 1960s
style using mass media images and spare,
simple shapes. His colors are bright and
flat with a strong, black outline. Somehow
he has got stuck and has never moved on.
KEY WORKS *Black and White Flower Piece*, 1963
(London: Tate Collection); *Still Life with
Dagger*, 1963 (London: Tate Collection)

Allen **Jones**

◐ 1937–   ▣ BRITISH

▣ UK   ◪ oils; prints; sculpture   ▥ London:
National Portrait Gallery   ▨ $100,040 in 2003,
General and his Girl (oils)

One of the founders of Pop Art, Jones
uses simple, figurative imagery, often with
erotic charge (likes fetish symbolism—high
heels, body-clinging garments, and so on),
combined with bright, bold, "modern"
abstract color. A product of the swinging

London of the 1960s and not ashamed to continue the theme.

KEY WORKS *Wet Seal*, 1966 (London: Tate Collection); *What do you Mean, what do I Mean?*, 1968 (Private Collection).

David **Hockney**

🌑 1937 –   🏳 BRITISH

🏳 UK; US   🎨 acrylics; oils; prints; photography
🏛 London: Tate Collection   💰 $2.6m in 2002, *Portrait of Nick Wilder* (oils)

A genuinely gifted artist with an acute eye and fertile imagination. Once the bad boy of British art, now a respected elder statesman. Sadly, he seems to have decided not to extend his talents (like Degas) and has settled to live the good life on undemanding potboilers (like Millais).

A truly great draftsman—focused, precise, observant, free, who has a brilliant ability to extract only the essentials. Timely reminder of the pleasure and novelties of seeing and recording perception with feeling, still important for art even after 500 years. Has stunning technique with pencil, pen, and crayon and an immaculate sense of color. Can make the commonplace memorable and moving. Chooses autobiographical subjects.

At his best as a draftsman (drawing, prints, and paintings). Brilliant observer and re-creator of light, space, and character in portraits, but not as convincing (though never uninteresting) when he tries to work solely from the imagination or to be a painterly painter (from the 1980s onward). Inspired designer of sets for theater, opera, ballet. Is experimenting with Cubism and photography.

KEY WORKS *Peter C*, 1961 (Manchester: City Art Gallery); *We Two Boys Together Clinging*, 1961 (London: Arts Council Collection); *California Bank*, 1964 (London: Mayor Gallery); *A Bigger Splash*, 1967 (London: Tate Collection)

Sunbather *David Hockney, 1966, 72 x 72 in (183 x 183 cm), acrylic on canvas, Cologne: Ludwig Museum. 1966 was the era of the Beatles, Rolling Stones, and the Beach Boys. Homosexuality was legalized in the UK in July 1967.*

CONTEMPORARY ART
1970 –

With the art and politics of the present and recent past it is impossible not to be subjective. It is probably wiser to identify what is in fashion than try to write instant history or make predictions. Fashion and technology have always been important factors in determining the priorities of contemporary art and politics.

Every age has its obsessions. An artist of limited talent who plays up to these will receive a measure of critical acclaim and exposure that a talented artist whose interests lie elsewhere will not be granted. But fashion shifts and it might be fair to propose that a list of today's fashionable obsessions (what is "in " and "out") is a complete reverse of the list of 50 years ago. For example: today's most exhibited art often means large-scale works, shock, and gritty realism with an emphasis on headline-grabbing social issues or neurotic revelations about an artist's private life. Artworks that play with concepts and words are put before the public more frequently than those concerned with looking and seeing. Celebrity status, self-aggrandizement

The Spectrum of Brick Lane *David Batchelor, 2003, mixed media.* Post-Modernism often uses technology combined with installations and plays to an audience for whom presentation is a greater priority than content.

and satisfying the demands of rich collectors are "in"; modesty, self-doubt, the quiet contemplation of the dignity, or absurdity of humanity, or a wish to create a better world for humankind is "out." An interest in beauty, clarity, and spiritual values is "out" (as is Picasso), whereas material values, obfuscation, and Marcel Duchamp are "in." Detachment and irony are widely praised as virtues whereas genuine passion and belief are out of fashion. Lip service is paid to personal manual skill but sloppiness can be applauded as spontaneity, and subcontracting all aspects of physical creation to anonymous hands or computers accepted without question.

ART AND TECHNOLOGY
The place of new technologies in contemporary art is ambiguous. Sometimes it seems we might be in the presence of a break out as

Germans celebrating the fall of the Berlin Wall
Built in 1960 as a key element in the Iron Curtain
dividing East and West, the popular uprisings of
1989 caused the wall to fall.

seems that ancient traditions of
creativity such as that of Chinese art,
are being lost in the rush to emulate
fashionable Western modernism.

POLITICS

Similar observations might be
ventured about politics. In the 1970s
and 1980s the Western democracies
had a roller-coaster ride, sometimes
staring into the abyss of economic
turmoil, at other times adopting the
mantra "greed is good." In Europe
the postwar consensus of a welfare
state has been opposed by those
wanting a more individualistic

the presence of a break out as
significant as that of the early
Renaissance with the PC playing
a world-changing role akin to
Gutenberg's moveable type (see page
75). But it may be that we are merely
continuing a revolution that was
started 100 years ago, and that what
is sometimes lauded as profound
innovation is more similar to the
artistically mannered and short-
lived extravagances that
followed the High Renaissance
(see page 108). What is more
certain is that contemporary art
is currently ubiquitous as a
recreational and consumer
activity not seen since the craze
for Academic art in the later
half of the 19th century. It also

The Pompidou Center (Beaubourg), Paris
Completed in 1978, the gallery's popularity and
visitor numbers took the authorities by surprise.

TIMELINE: 1970—

1974 President Nixon forced to resign after Watergate scandal	**1976** Death of Chairman Mao	**1980** Iran–Iraq War (to 1988)	**1988** Gorbachev initiates reforms (*perestroika* and *glasnost*) in Soviet Union
1970		**1980**	
1973 US withdraws from Vietnam; Yom Kippur War in Middle East	**1975** Khmer Rouge impose Marxist rule of terror in Cambodia (to 1979)	**1979** Islamic Revolution in Iran; Soviet invasion of Afghanistan	**1987** Palestinian protests (intifada) begin

THE RISE OF THE COMPUTER

The first true computers, using punch cards for memory, were built in Britain to crack enemy codes during World War II. The world's first electronic computer was built in the 1940s. But it was not until 1962 that computers began to reach their real potential, with the introduction of the microchip allowing the creation of much smaller machines. In 1971 the first mass-produced computers became available, with Microsoft supplying software from 1975. Sales of home computers soared during the 1980s with total of 1.7 billion sold by 2004. In 1993 the arrival of the Internet, a worldwide network linked by telephone lines, gave users access to almost limitless information.

approach. Currently in high fashion is the idea that market forces should drive everything, and that technology will somehow supply a way out of moral dilemmas. In this postmodern world beliefs in political causes or moral principles appears to have given way to a detached and ironic relativism. The shared bonds that tied the Western Alliance together since 1945, not least the idea that there were identifiable common enemies, has begun to unravel. It is also tempting to suggest that the ideal of creating a better democratic world, which was fought for in blood, has degenerated into attitudes of self-satisfaction and self-indulgence in which everyone is encouraged to act and consume what he or she wishes,

with many individual "rights" but few communal obligations. Confusingly, the US, which was the champion of freedom and sacrificed much to defeat totalitarianism, is now the world's greatest corporate and military power. Europe similarly having fought authoritarian bureaucracies and one-party systems seems tempted to turn her collective self into a labyrinthine bureaucracy in the name of harmonization.

THE FUTURE

Western art reflects many of today's headline issues: among them, political correctness, green issues and global warming, gender matters, health, and the wish to deny the inevitability of aging and death. However, whatever one's subjective view of art or current events, it is the everyday interaction of both that has always made art so fascinating. To quote the 19th-century critic and historian John Ruskin, "A nation's art is its only biography."

Satellite tracking station in New Mexico
For those who control them, satellites offer endless opportunities for communication and military targeting.

| 1989–91 Collapse of Soviet communism in Eastern Europe, followed by collapse of USSR (1991) | 1998 India and Pakistan test nuclear weapons | 1999 NATO bombing campaign to halt Serbian persecution of Albanians in Kosovo | 2003 Second Gulf War: US invades Iraq, overthrows Saddam Hussein |

1990   **2000**

| 1990 Iraqi invasion of Kuwait: first Gulf War | 1993 Oslo Accords: limited Palestinian self-rule | 2001 US "War against Terrorism" declared after al-Qaeda terror attacks; US overthrows Taliban regime in Afghanistan | 2005 French and Dutch electorates reject proposed EU constitution |

Louise **Bourgeois**

◗ 1911– ◪ FRENCH/AMERICAN

◪ France; US   ◪ sculpture; oils; engravings
◫ Washington, DC: National Gallery of Art
◪ $1.3m in 2002, *Blind Man's Buff* (sculpture)

A current heroine of feminists,
Bourgeois was unknown until she was
in her 60s. Daughter of an emotionally
dysfunctional family, she works out the
consequent trauma through her art.

Her work is eclectic and uses many
materials—sculpture, constructions,
installations; images of bodily experiences
such as pregnancy, birth, breastfeeding;
images of the house. She plays on notions
of desire, attraction, repulsion, and
male-female relationships. References
to mother's activities of sewing and
tapestry. She's not trying to illustrate
anything but to recreate the way she
feels: anxiety, loneliness, defenselessness,
vulnerability, aggression, sex, and death.

Her womanizing father installed a
young mistress in the family home who
was hated by her mother; Louise was
caught in the middle. Like many from
Van Gogh onward, she has turned to
artistic activity to relieve her pain
and find a role. Is she among
those who have the ability to
communicate to someone
with completely different
experiences? Or is she
among those whose
very insistence and
(neurotic) predictability
eventually kills the
emotion or message?
KEY WORKS *Dagger Child*,
1947–49 (New York:
Guggenheim Museum);
Winged Figure, 1948
(Washington, DC: National
Gallery of Art); *Mortise*,
1950 (Washington, DC:
National Gallery of
Art); *Eyes*, 1982 (New
York: Metropolitan
Museum of Art)

Quarantania Louise
Bourgeois, 1947–53, cast
1984, 78¾ x 30 x 29¼ in
(200 x 68.5 x 74.2 cm) bronze,
Houston: Museum of Fine
Arts. An early work suggestive
of crowds and phalluses.

Agnes **Martin**

◗ 1912–2004 ◪ AMERICAN/CANADIAN

◪ US   ◪ acrylics; oils   ◫ New York:
Guggenheim Museum   ◪ $2.3m in
2003, *Leaves* (oils)

Martin was a much-admired
painter of gentle, lyrical
abstracts, which reflect her
search for spiritual purity
and her rejection of
material encumbrances
and cares. Lived a simple
life in New Mexico.

Her largish, square-
shaped canvases of pure,
pale colors and simple design are
intended to reflect the qualities she values.
They are beautiful, with a haunting
luminosity, and should be experienced
as much as looked at. Let your mind go
free, as when contemplating the ocean.

Notice the soothing delicacy with which
they are made: paint gently stroked on,
precise pencil marks creating something
close to those organic traces, webs, and
honeycomb structures found in nature;
subtle color gradations like sunlight on
early-morning mist or snow; horizontal
lines suggestive of landscape spaces.
KEY WORKS *White Flower*, 1960 (New York:
Guggenheim Museum); *Leaf in the Wind*,
1963 (Pasadena: Norton Simon Museum)

Tony **Smith**

◗ 1912–80 ◪ AMERICAN

◪ US   ◪ sculpture; oils   ◫ Washington,
DC: National Gallery of Art   ◪ $150,000 in
1989, *Throne* (sculpture)

Smith was an architect (until 1950s),
and a sculptor (from 1960s), and
painter. He created simple, satisfying,
engineered structures (he designed
and created the models, others built
the end products). They are of varying
size and scale but always with human
proportions—romantic rather than
minimal. Sleek black surfaces add
a stylish, sophisticated presence.
Space is as important as form.
KEY WORKS *Moondog*, model 1964,
fabricated 1998–99 (Washington,
DC: National Gallery of Art);
Wandering Rocks, 1967 (Washington,
DC: National Gallery of Art)

Joseph **Beuys**

● 1921–86 ⚑ GERMAN

⚑ Germany 🎨 sculpture; performance art
🏛 Darmstadt (Germany): Hessisches
Landesmuseum 💰 $413,100 in
1994, *Stapelkopf Siegel* (mixed media)

A star of the 1980s, highly regarded by
intellectuals and lionized by ambitious
curators and dealers, Beuys was a serious,
gentle, mystic and charismatic figure who
sought to comment on his own times, and
was also (paradoxically) a victim of them.

To establish a connection with these
works, you have to establish a rapport with
the whole Beuys phenomenon—the man,
his appearance, his lifestyle, his biography,
and his beliefs. Thus the lumps of fat,
fur, or felt that you find in the museum
showcases are like fragments of a total
work; or, they are like the traces that
a wild animal makes to establish its
presence or the extent of its territory.

Only by accepting the Beuys
phenomenon can you begin to "see" the
energy of the world references, harmony
with nature, the dilemmas of modern
Germany, Beuys's early childhood
experiences, and so on. If you don't want
to or can't cross this threshold, don't worry
—it may all be self-deception anyway. The
phenomenon is an unexpected alliance of

Earth Telephone Joseph Beuys, 1968, 8 x 18½ x
30 in (220 x 47 x 76 cm), telephone, earth, and grass,
connecting cable on wooden board, Hamburg: Kunsthalle.
Beuys saw himself as part witchdoctor, part magician.

the artist's ego with museum or commercial
interests, looking for instant history.
KEY WORKS *How to Explain Pictures to a Dead Hare*,
1965 (performance); *Felt Suit*, 1970 (London:
Tate Collection); *Four Blackboards*, 1972
(London: Tate Collection); *Encounter with Beuys*,
1974–84 (New York: Guggenheim Museum)

Jules **Olitski**

● 1922– ⚑ AMERICAN

⚑ US 🎨 acrylics; sculpture 🏛 Canberra:
National Gallery of Australia 💰 $320,000 in
1990, *Strip Heresy* (oils)

Born in Russia, Olitski trained in old-
master painting techniques. Creator of
large-scale decorative abstract paintings.
Uses a stain and spray-gun technique,
which creates a field of atmospheric color
that seems to dissolve the picture surface.
There is often a band of rich pigment
along one edge or at a corner. Sensual,
slightly precious, self-conscious work.
KEY WORKS *Ino Delight*, 1962 (Saskatchewan,
Canada: Mackenzie Art Gallery); *Prince
Patutsky's Command*, 1966 (Canberra:
National Gallery of Australia)

> "In places like universities, where everyone
> talks too rationally, it is necessary for a kind of
> enchanter to appear … I am calling for a better
> kind of form of thought, of feeling, of willpower."
>
> JOSEPH BEUYS

Kenneth **Noland**

● 1924– **P** AMERICAN

P US 🖌 acrylics; sculpture
🏛 Houston: Museum of Fine Arts
📈 $1.85m in 1989, *Empyrean* (oils)

Noland creates simple, direct works in which the impact is purely visual, coming solely from color on the canvas—there is no "meaning," drawn line, or spatial depth. He plays with color variations and simple, dynamic shapes (such as a bull's eye or a chevron) and their relationship to the shape or edge of canvas. He also plays with irregular-shaped canvases. Very American, very good.

KEY WORKS *Song*, 1958 (New York: Whitney Museum of American Art); *Half*, 1959 (Boston: Museum of Fine Arts); *Hade*, 1973 (Private Collection)

George **Segal**

● 1924–2000 **P** AMERICAN

P US 🖌 sculpture 🏛 Ottawa: National Gallery of Canada 📈 $600,000 in 2001, *Chance Meeting* (sculpture)

A creator of environments that are like banal settings with real objects from everyday life, but in which the people are replaced by white plaster figures. Segal makes casts from real live people, wrapping them in plaster-soaked gauze bandages like a mummy. Powerful and sensitive evocation of the lonely anonymity of everyday life. His work is highly distinctive and original.

KEY WORKS *Cinema*, 1963 (Buffalo: Albright-Knox Art Gallery); *The Gas Station*, 1963 (Ottawa: National Gallery of Canada)

Duane **Hanson**

● 1925–96 **P** AMERICAN

P US 🖌 sculpture 🏛 Florida: Norton Museum of Art 📈 $280,000 in 2001, *Security Guard* (sculpture)

The maker of hyperrealistic sculptures (since 1967). A modern reworking of the "everyday life" realism much loved by Victorian middle classes. His early work was strongly political.

He created unnervingly lifelike, life-size sculptures of people who are almost indistinguishable from the

> "I am interested in the everyday types of things that people do, the common denominator, those things that are down to earth."
>
> DUANE HANSON

Homeless Person Duane Hanson, 1991, height 66¼ in (168 cm), mixed media, Hamburg: Kunsthalle. Hanson is often quoted: "… men lead lives of quiet desperation …"

gallery-goers who look at them. His subjects are tourists, shoppers, construction workers, children—middle America at work and play. He took molds from live models, which were then cast in polyester resin or bronze and painted; he then added real accessories, such as shoes and clothes. His stated aim was to ennoble the commonplace and ordinary by turning it and its inhabitants into art.

Slow worker—a single figure could take a year to complete. Note the realism of flesh textures, such as bruises, varicose veins, hair on forearms or legs. His figures are often in movement but always self-absorbed and introspective (even when in a group); sometimes they are asleep. The impact comes in part from his astonishing technical skill, in part from his contemporaneity. How powerful will these works be when they eventually look like historical figures, not part of the here and now?

KEY WORKS *Tourist*, 1970 (Edinburgh: National Gallery of Modern Art); *Salesman*, 1992 (Missouri: Kemper Museum of Contemporary Art)

Untitled John Chamberlain, c. 1960s, sheet metal, Rome: Galleria Nazionale d'Arte Moderna. Chamberlain taught at the famous Black Mountain College, near Asheville in North Carolina, which established a model for an ideal liberal education.

KEY WORKS *Essex*, 1960 (New York: Museum of Modern Art); *Dolores Jane*, 1962 (New York: Guggenheim Museum); *Koko-Nor II*, 1967 (London: Tate Collection)

John **Chamberlain**

◉ 1927– ◪ AMERICAN

◪ US ◪ sculpture ◪ Texas: Chinati Foundation ◪ $500,000 in 2003, *Murmurous Moto, Maestro* (sculpture)

Influenced by David Smith in his early work, Chamberlain was famous for sculptures (freestanding and wall reliefs) made from welded-together car parts. They are not arbitrarily made, but carefully planned and painted for aesthetic effect (look for the inclusion of chrome parts). Many of his compositions are designed to be hung on walls, rather than stood on the ground. Don't look for a social comment on car-obsessed consumer society—his later work uses non-car materials such as aluminum foil, polyurethane foam, and paper bags.

Donald (Don) **Judd**

◉ 1928–94 ◪ AMERICAN

◪ US ◪ sculptures; installations; oils ◪ Texas: Chinati Foundation ◪ $4.2m in 2002, *Untitled* (sculpture)

Judd created sculptures by giving instructions for the industrial production of modular (often large) box-shaped objects in polished metal and Plexiglas, which are often stacked and cantilevered. They are simple, minimal, with proportions and spaces based on mathematical progressions, and all of a piece in shape, color, and surface. The works are detached and cool, with no human presence or reference.

KEY WORKS *Untitled*, 1969 (New York: Guggenheim Museum); *Untitled*, 1970 (New York: Guggenheim Museum); *Untitled (Six Boxes)*, 1974 (Canberra: National Gallery of Australia)

49 Three-Part Variations of the Three Different Kinds of Cubes *Sol Lewitt, 1967–71, 49 units, each 24 x 8 x 8 in (60 x 20 x 20 cm), enamel on steel, Hamburg: Kunsthalle.* LeWitt was a leading exponent of Minimalism, a reaction against Abstract Expressionism and Pop.

A Wall Divided Vertically into Fifteen Equal Parts, Each with a Different Line Direction and Color, and All Combinations, 1970 (London: Tate Collection); *Steel Structure (formerly Untitled),* 1975–76 (San Francisco: Museum of Modern Art); *Wavy Brushstrokes,* 1996 (Washington, DC: National Gallery of Art)

Sol **Lewitt**

● 1928– ◪ AMERICAN

▣ US   ◪ sculpture; conceptual art; prints
🏛 Washington, DC: National Gallery of Art
⯈ $320,000 in 2004, *Untitled* (sculpture)

A pioneering Minimalist, now one of the "Grand Old Men." At first sight, Lewitt's structures and wall drawings look as if they are merely mechanical applications of established mathematical systems, but they are not.

He creates a type of pure beauty that comes out of an order that is logical but not rigid or predictable. He starts with a system, ratio, or formula, which can be quite arbitrarily chosen, and employs assistants to make the modular structure or wall drawing that follows from it. His works can be on a large or small scale, but the bigger and more complex the better; they are completely self-referential and self-contained.

You can take the works intellectually and try to unravel the system, or you can take them visually for what they are and enjoy their unexpected, peaceful beauty and the way in which they generate light as well as space, thus creating a sense of emotional openness and purity. His wall drawings are created for each new location and then whitewashed out. His early work was in monochrome or white; he gradually introduced color and his recent work is richly colorful (and less pure and less effective as a result?).
KEY WORKS *Floor Structure Black,* 1965 (Washington, DC: National Gallery of Art);

Cy **Twombly**

● 1928– ◪ AMERICAN

▣ US; Rome   ◪ oils; drawings
🏛 Washington, DC: National Gallery of Art
⯈ $5.1m in 2002, *Untitled* (oils)

Twombly is much admired for his highly personal abstract style consisting of apparently random scribbles and marks, sometimes incorporating bits of text and diagram. If you require order, clarity, structure, and specific meaning, you will hate it; if you like improvisation, hints, whispers, and teases, you will love it.
KEY WORKS *Vengeance of Achilles,* 1962 (Zurich: Kunsthaus); *Quattro Stagioni* (a painting in four parts), 1993–94 (London: Tate Collection)

Untitled *Cy Twombly, 1970, mixed media on paper, Private Collection.* Twombly settled in Rome in 1957 and some see his calligraphic style as akin to the marks found on ancient walls.

Untitled (Felt Tangle)
*Robert Morris, 1967,
74⅞ x 157½ x 86¾ in
(190 x 400 x 220 cm), felt
and metal eyes,
Hamburg:
Kunsthalle.* Morris
started making his felt
constructions in 1967 after
moving to a studio in
Colorado, which used to be
an old felt factory, and
where remnants were still
lying around.

Robert **Ryman**

● 1930– 🏳 AMERICAN

🏳 US 🎨 oils; mixed media
🏛 Schaffhausen, Switzerland: Hallen für
Neue Kunst 📈 $2.1m in 1989, *Summit* (oils)

A self-taught abstract painter from
Nashville, Tennessee, Ryman has a limited
but highly visual theme. Musical enthusiast
(Charlie Parker and Thelonius Monk).
His works should be seen by daylight.

His paintings are about what paintings
are made from, what paint can do, and
what they look like (and why not?).
So don't look for subjects, concepts, and
spirituality. Look instead at the way he
uses oil paint (thick, thin, shiny, flat); his
use of textured canvases, paper, metal
surfaces, and so on; and how he attaches
these works to the wall. It sounds banal,
but actually they are beautiful to look
at if you don't expect too much. Is it
a dead end or a new beginning?

He wants his work to be shown by
daylight so that the textured surfaces will
look different and interesting as the light
changes (white attracts light). Look at
his different choices of brush marks and
surface and the way they change in the
same work; also at what he does with
canvas (stretched or unstretched, for
instance). Look also at the edges and the
way he incorporates his signature. The
choice of frame, or lack of one, is also his.
KEY WORKS *Classico IV,* 1968 (New York:
Guggenheim Museum); *Surface Veil,* 1970–71
(San Francisco: Museum of Modern Art);
Monitor, 1978 (Amsterdam: Stedelijk Museum)

Robert **Morris**

● 1931– 🏳 AMERICAN

🏳 US 🎨 sculpture; conceptual art; land art;
performance art 🏛 New York: Guggenheim
Museum 📈 $57,500 in 1990, *Untitled* (sculpture)

Morris produces large-scale simple
forms, either geometric and hard-edge, or
curvilinear and soft-edge (such as mounds
of hanging felt). He creates the blueprint,
others make the pieces. He wants you to
focus on an analysis of an activity of your
perception and/or the decisionmaking
process by which he arrives at final form
—the classic agenda for Minimal art, of
which he was a pioneer.
KEY WORKS *Untitled (Corner Piece),* 1964 (New
York: Guggenheim Museum); *House of
Vetti I,* 1983 (Hamburg: Deichtorhallen)

Fernando **Botero**

● 1932– 🏳 COLOMBIAN

🏳 Colombia; US 🎨 oils; prints 📈 $1.4m
in 1992, *La Casa de las Gemelas Arias* (oils)

Botero is a creator of immediately
recognizable paintings and sculptures
that are wholly out of the mainstream
of "serious" contemporary art. Tubby,
cheerful, over-inflated (literally and
metaphorically) figures, meticulously
painted in bright colors, through which
he ridicules the pomposities of life, art,
and officialdom. A breath of fresh air.
KEY WORKS *Our Lady Fatima,* 1963 (Bogota:
Museo de Arte Moderno); *Dancing in Colombia,*
1980 (New York: Metropolitan Museum of Art)

Richard **Estes**

● 1932– ◪ AMERICAN

◪ US ◪ oils; prints ◫ San Francisco: Fine Arts Museums ◪ $420,000 in 2000, *Gourmet Treats* (oils)

The king of Photorealism, Estes uses many of the same techniques as Canaletto, but not place-specific. His views could be of any modern city.

His fine, detailed paintings of the modern urban streetscape look at first sight as though they are merely enlarged photographs—but they are not. Estes paints from photographs to create a highly complex, composite view that heightens reality in a way impossible in a single photograph, but it gives the illusion of freezing a split second, as does a photo.

Produces carefully organized compositions that divide the scene into distinct areas—for example, he might create a diptych. Uses a multipoint perspective or viewpoint and reflecting windows to show what is happening outside the picture frame, behind the back of the viewer. Note the absence of human figures and activity. Rich, intense color harmonies. Within his self-imposed limitations, he creates haunting, moody images that have beauty and detachment.

KEY WORKS *Parking Lot*, undated (New York: National Academy of Design); *Nedicts*, 1970 (Madrid: Museo Thyssen-Bornemisza); *Diner*, 1971 (Washington, DC: Hirshhorn Museum)

Nam June **Paik**

● 1932– ◪ KOREAN

◪ Japan; Germany; US ◪ sculpture; installations; performance art ◫ Washington, DC: Smithsonian American Art Museum ◪ $120,004 in 2002, *Vol de Nuit* (sculpture)

Once a young "bad boy" with an instinct for public scandal; now he has "grand old man" status. His first interest was music (John Cage). From the 1960s, he has wanted to turn TV from a medium for passive mass audiences into an individual and dynamic medium, like painting. He uses the TV screen like collage and creates large-scale installations with banks of screens. Pioneering and impressive.

KEY WORKS *Global Groove*, 1973 (Pittsburgh: Carnegie Museum of Art); *Video Flag*, 1985–96 (Washington, DC: Hirshhorn Museum)

Gerhard **Richter**

● 1932– ◪ GERMAN

◪ Germany ◪ oils; prints ◫ San Francisco: Museum of Modern Art ◪ $4.9m in 2001, *Drei Kerzen* (oil)

A refugee from Communist East Germany (1961), Richter trained as an orthodox Communist trompe-l'oeil social realist, then had to assimilate Western

S. with Child *Gerhard Richter, c. 1995, oil on canvas, Hamburg: Kunsthalle.* One of a series of eight paintings Richter made of his wife with their newborn child, showing his characteristic blurred Photorealistic technique. The compositions revisit the religious motif of the Madonna and Child.

Modernism. He is often pigeonholed with cutting-edgers now in their 30s and 40s, but is in fact old enough to be their father.

He produces three different types of work: schematic, Minimalist abstracts; splashy, messy abstracts; finely painted, soft-focus photographic imagery (most typical). What is not in doubt is his technical ability and high critical esteem. What is less clear is his meaning (he seems to deny any). Supporters says the deadpan blurriness shows his "dialectical tension" and virtuous ambivalence. Detractors ask how is it that such "important" work can be so boring?

KEY WORKS *Passage*, 1968 (New York: Guggenheim Museum); *Korn*, 1982 (New York: Guggenheim Museum); *St. John*, 1988 (London: Tate Collection); *Abstract Painting (726)*, 1990 (London: Tate Collection)

George **Deem**

● 1932– 🏳 AMERICAN

🇺 US 🖌 oils 🏛 New York: Allan Stone Gallery 💰 $3,750 in 1998, *School of Winslow Homer* (oils)

Deem is a New York-based painter famous for his "School of" paintings. Takes elements from well-known works by famous artists, such as Vermeer, and arranges them in a schoolroom setting—which is itself borrowed from a painting by Winslow Homer. Witty, perceptive, inventive. Uses subtle brushwork, which reproduces the techniques of the old masters. Makes you look and think twice.

KEY WORKS *Visitation*, 1978 (Private Collection); *Vermeer's Chair*, 1994 (New York: Nancy Hoffman Gallery)

Dan **Flavin**

● 1933–96 🏳 AMERICAN

🇺 US 🖌 installations 🏛 New York: Guggenheim Museum 💰 $650,000 in 2004, *Untitled* (sculpture)

He was noted for constructions using fluorescent tubes and neons, usually arranged across a corner of a darkened empty room. Claimed to be playing with space of the room; illuminating dull corners (of life?) and expressing mystical notions about light. Early nostalgic references to Russian Constructivists.

KEY WORKS *The Nominal Three (to William of Ockham)*, 1963 (New York: Guggenheim

Museum); *Greens Crossing Greens (to Piet Mondrian, Who Lacked Green)*, 1966 (New York: Guggenheim Museum)

Carl **André**

● 1935– 🏳 AMERICAN

🇺 US 🖌 sculpture 🏛 New York: Guggenheim Museum 💰 $800,000 in 2004, *Steel-Magnesium Plant* (sculpture)

One of the first exponents of Minimal art, Andre's work reflects his boyhood in a Massachusetts shipyard town and his early job on the Pennsylvania railroad—surrounded by metal plates, girders, railway lines, industry, quarries.

Notorious for the *Pile of Bricks*, which hit the headlines in the 1970s (the Tate Gallery and André were ridiculed in the popular press). His most successful work is typically of industrially made components (such as bricks or metal plates), which are arranged in mathematical order; also chunky, rough-cut wood constructions made from pre-cut units. In the 1970s, genuinely challenged the gallery-goer to question what is and what is supposed to be art. In 1985, he was charged with the murder of his wife (who fell from a window), but was later acquitted.

KEY WORKS *Equivalent VIII*, 1966 (London: Tate Collection); *Venus Forge*, 1980 (London: Tate Collection); *Bandolin*, 2003 (New York: Paula Cooper Gallery); *Carbon Quarry*, 2004 (Düsseldorf: Konrad Fischer Galerie)

Tomb of the Golden Engenderers
Carl André, c. 1976, 36 x 108 x 36 in (91.4 x 274.3 x 91.4 cm), western red cedar wood, Private Collection. André was a leading Minimalist, also writing in the tradition of concrete poetry.

Christo & Jeanne-Claude

● BOTH 1935– ♙ AMERICAN

🏛 Europe; US; Asia; Australia ⬛ sculpture; environmental art ⚡ $320,000 in 1999, *Yellow Store Front* (sculpture)

Christo and Jeanne-Claude—a husband and wife partnership based in New York—travel the world to create highly original, memorable projects.

They wrap objects. They started in 1958 with small items and moved on to very large ones in 1961, e.g. wrapping the Pont Neuf in Paris and the Reichstag in Berlin, in fabric and ropes, which both suggest and conceal the thing wrapped. Also creators of landscape projects such as a 24-mile (40-km)-long curtain (literally) running across open

Wrapped Trees *Christo and Jeanne-Claude, 1997–98, Fondation Beyeler and Berower Park, Basel, Switzerland.* For this installation, 178 trees were wrapped in 592,000 sq ft (55,000 sq m) of woven polyester fabric and ropes.

countryside. The big projects are deliberately temporary, so one only has a limited opportunity of seeing them.

Their underlying purpose isn't social but aesthetic—the transformation of the well-known into the unfamiliar or disquieting while at the same time touching and involving everyone in the creative process.
KEYWORKS *Wrapped Coast*, 1968–69 (New South Wales, Australia: Little Bay); *Surrounded Islands*, 1983 (Florida: Biscayne Bay)

Eva **Hesse**

● 1936–70 ♙ GERMAN/AMERICAN

🏛 US; Germany ⬛ sculpture; conceptual art; oils 🏛 London: Mayor Gallery ⚡ $2m in 1997, *Unfinished, Untitled, or Not Yet* (sculpture)

A short-lived, deeply sensitive (and perhaps troubled) young woman of fragile health (she died of cancer), who has

temporarily become a cult figure. She and her work epitomize one type of high art of the 1960s.

She had deadly serious intention and personal expression but at times was totally impenetrable. Creator of a wide range of work: abstract paintings, sculpture and Minimalist, conceptual constructions—perhaps the sign of a lost soul searching for her own reality. Her work addressed her own anxieties: Nazi persecution; being a refugee in New York; her parents' divorce; her mother's suicide; being a professional woman in a male world; her own painful divorce; her determination to be an outsider.

She was committed to the handmade, but the concept was more important than the details. Her work makes constant allusion to female sexual anatomy. Employed repetitive binding with strings and ropes. Hated decoration, hence the materials she used and the way they are used—works are repellent to sight and touch.
KEY WORKS *Tomorrow's Apples (5 in White)*, 1965 (London: Tate Collection); *Hang Up*, 1966 (Art Institute of Chicago); *Vertiginous Detour*, 1966 (Washington, DC: Hirshhorn Museum)

Frank **Stella**

● 1936– ♙ AMERICAN

🏛 US ⬛ oils; acrylics; mixed media
🏛 San Francisco: Fine Arts Museums
⚡ $4.6m in 1989, *Tomlinson Court Park* (oils)

One of today's leading abstract painters, Stella is prolific and very varied—but a constant theme is investigating what paintings are and what they can or should look like.

His early work reduced painting to all but its most pure, minimal, and indispensable properties: simple, flat, shaped, monochrome. He then introduced pure, bright, hard-edge color with increasing complexity. After the early 1970s, he started to investigate how impure a painting can be and yet still remain a painting, by making constructions that are rich, interlocking clusters of shape and color. Uses varied materials.

Likes to work on a large scale. He steals ideas and techniques from sculpture and architecture, but always creates "pictures"—his creations have a back to the wall and are viewed from the front.

KEY WORKS *Six Mile Bottom*, 1960 (London: Tate Collection); *Agbatana II*, 1968 (St Étienne: Musée de l'Art et de l'Industrie); *Harran II*, 1967 (New York: Guggenheim Museum)

Georg **Baselitz**

◯ 1938– 🏴 GERMAN

🏴 Germany   🎨 oils; sculpture; mixed media
🏛 Canberra: National Gallery of Australia
💰 $1m in 2001, *Der Hirte* (oils)

The creator of big, lively, colorful, energetically painted, not very original paintings (neither in technique nor subject), in which bodies are often portrayed upside down. Acclaimed in official art circles. Also makes large-scale, crudely hewn sculptures out of wood.

Baselitz claims (perhaps honestly?) that his works have no particular meaning, although this does not deter the art establishment from endowing them with deep significance and cheerfully paying enormous prices for them. Notice direction of the paint

Picture-Eleven Georg Baselitz, 1992, 113¾ x 181½ in (289 x 461 cm), oil on canvas, Hamburg: Kunsthalle. Baselitz was one of a number of artists born and trained in East Germany who escaped to the West.

drips—at least they prove the figures were painted upside down and that he hasn't just up-ended his canvases.

KEY WORKS *Studio Corner*, 1973 (Hamburg: Kunsthalle); *Three-legged Nude*, 1977 (Hamburg: Kunsthalle)

Brice **Marden**

◯ 1938– 🏴 AMERICAN

🏴 US   🎨 oils   🏛 San Francisco: Museum of Modern Art   💰 $2.2m in 2003, *10 Dialog 2* (oils)

Marden is a leading American Abstract painter who is not easy to pigeonhole and who has not got stuck in a rut like many of his contemporaries.

His earlier works are either single spreads of voluptuous color or combinations of rectangular forms (panels) playing on the rectangular nature of his canvas. Uses velvety, textured paint (also beeswax and encaustic) for these. Titles of his pieces often refer to art history.

His recent works take a new direction. At first sight they look just like other examples of over-praised, messily painted abstracts. But linger and let them be what they are: the lines become like the rhythmic, moving patterns on the surface of clear deep water; the colors have the hues of autumn leaves. Reminisce about landscape.

KEY WORKS *Blonde*, 1970 (Boston: Museum of Fine Arts); *Green (Earth)*, 1983–84 (New York: Mary Boone Gallery); *Corpus*, 1991–93 (New York: Matthew Marks Gallery)

Robert **Smithson**

● 1938–73　▣ AMERICAN

▣ US　◧ land art; conceptual art; sculpture
🖹 $240,000 in 1998, *Double Nonsite, California and Nevada* (sculpture)

Smithson was a pioneer land artist, who was tragically killed in his 30s. He had a pessimistic view of the world: he foresaw it ending in a new ice age, not a golden age, reduced to self-destructive banality by the anonymity of urban developments and indifference to the environment. He reacted against this by offering his workings on the land (and the documentation of the process) as works of art.
KEY WORKS *Yucatan Mirror Displacements (1–9)*, 1969 (New York: Guggenheim Museum); *Spiral Jetty*, 1970 (situated at Great Salt Lake, Utah)

Judy **Chicago**

● 1939–　▣ AMERICAN

▣ US　◧ installations; conceptual art
🏛 San Francisco: Museum of Modern Art
🖹 $2,400 in 1989, *And then there was Light* (works on paper)

She is best known for the collaborative venture *Dinner Party* (1973–79), a room-size installation of a triangular table, and elaborate named place settings for 39 key historic and mythological females. Her activities are a celebration of sisterhood, but they are more popular with the public than with feminists.
KEY WORKS *Dinner Party*, 1973–79 (New York: Brooklyn Museum of Art); *The Rejection Quartet*, 1974 (San Francisco: Museum of Modern Art)

Broken Circle Robert Smithson, 1971, diameter 140 ft (42.7 m), green water, white and yellow sand flats, Emmen (Holland). Smithson was interested in historic man-made environments such as burial grounds and pyramids.

A. R. **Penck**

● 1939–　▣ GERMAN

▣ Germany　◧ oils; prints; woodcuts
🏛 Hamburg: Kunsthalle　🖹 $220,000 in 1989, *O A TE MI 2* (works on paper)

Born Ralf Winckler in East Germany (his earliest memory is of the fire bombing of his home town of Dresden in 1945). Creates highly individual works that have a consciously primitive and crude appearance. His hallmarks are his stylized, spindly, silhouetted figures; archaic symbols; fragmented writing. Has a personal political agenda, which is not always easy to fathom.
KEY WORKS *View of the World, Psychotronic-Strategic-Art*, 1966–71 (Frankfurt: Städel Museum); *Standart-Bild*, 1971 (Basel, Switzerland: Kunstmuseum)

Richard **Serra**

● 1939–　▣ AMERICAN

▣ US　◧ sculpture　🏛 London: Tate Collection. Washington, DC: National Gallery of Art
🖹 $390,000 in 1999, *Sign Board* (sculpture)

The foremost American creator of sculpture for public spaces. Produces huge works, which have a commanding presence and are held together only by gravity.

Look for giant, minimal, monumental slabs of metal, often exhibited in open urban spaces. They are unmissable and unavoidable—and often seem to be unstable, as though the pieces could fall over. Take pleasure in his interest in massive weight and the way he likes to play with the sense and appearance of it: propped, balanced, rotated, moving, about to move, added to, subtracted from, towering, ground-hugging. Loves playing with the force and direction of weight.

He is also interested in the psychology of weight, in two ways: 1) observing the impact that his massive, apparently unstable or dangerous objects have on the viewers' own space and on their bodily and mental reactions to them; 2) as a metaphor for social realities, such as the weight of government control or personal tragedy. Legal actions have been taken to have some of his works removed.

KEY WORKS *Strike: To Roberta and Rudy*, 1969–71 (New York: Guggenheim Museum); *Five Plates, Two Poles*, 1971 (Washington, DC: National Gallery of Art); *Balance*, 1972 (Washington, DC: Hirshhorn Museum)

Chuck **Close**

● 1940 – ◪ AMERICAN

◪ US ◪ oils; acrylics; prints ◪ San Francisco: Museum of Modern Art
◪ $4.3m in 2005, *John* (acrylics)

Close produces huge portraits of himself and his friends, always from the neck up. Works from photographs, which are squared up and the final images created tiny square by tiny square, according to a complex, time-consuming, and mechanical procedure. Uses color after 1971. The end result is a compelling one.

KEY WORKS *Frank*, 1969 (Minnesota: Minneapolis Institute of Arts); *Big Self-Portrait*, 1977–79

Self-Portrait Chuck Close, 2000, 58¾ x 47¼ in (149.5 x 120.5 cm), screen print, New York: Museum of Modern Art. Close was paralyzed in 1988 but continues to work with brushes strapped to his wrists.

(Minnesota: Minneapolis Institute of Arts); *Georgia*, 1984 (Youngstown, Ohio: Butler Institute of American Art)

Jan **Dibbets**

● 1941 – ◪ DUTCH

◪ Netherlands ◪ photography; installations
◪ $60,000 in 1995, *Octagon II* (collage)

Photographer (black-and-white and color) and installation maker.

His photographs are to be admired for their rigorous and meticulous qualities—formal and dry—and their limited experiments with perspective and space. Also produces installations that are strong sociological or political observations and critiques of capitalism.

His photo experiments are said to be part of a traditional Dutch interest in perspective and order that goes back to Saenredam via Mondrian. Maybe, but Dibbets does not have their feel for the poetry of space and light.

KEY WORKS *Spoleto Floor*, 1981 (Turin: Castello di Rivoli Museum of Contemporary Art); *Four Windows*, 1991 (Tilburg, Netherlands: De Pont Foundation for Contemporary Art)

Bruce **Nauman**

● 1941–   ▣ AMERICAN

▣ US   ⚡ installations; performance art; sculpture; conceptual art; video   🏛 London: Tate Collection   📈 $9m in 2001, *Henry Moore Bound to Fail, Back View* (sculpture)

Regarded as one of the gurus of the official art world, Nauman aims to examine, document, and involve the viewer in experiences of pointless activity, humiliation, stress, and frustration.

He works in many media—video, performance, conventional sculpture, neon … you name it. Claims to be communicating his observations of human nature and examining our perceptions of it, but focuses on activities that are pointless, repetitive, and deliberately inept. Fair enough, but does it result in anything of significance, or merely the trivial and banal? If the answer is "that's the point," then isn't it just an exercise in perversity?

To answer the above, trust your own judgment; ignore museum labels and their over-anxious insistence on significance (translation: we have committed significant money and professional credibility to this; if it isn't deemed to be significant and profound, we will look like complete idiots). Better still, as this is overtly public art, to study the reactions of gallery goers. Are they engaged and interested? Dismissive and disinterested? They will tell you if his strategies amount to meaningful art.

KEY WORKS *Shelf Sinking into the Wall with Copper-Painted Plaster Casts of the Spaces Underneath*, 1966 (London: Tate Collection); *The True Artist Helps the World by Revealing Mystic Truths (Window or Wall Sign)*, 1967 (Canberra: National Gallery of Australia)

Sigmar **Polke**

● 1941–   ▣ GERMAN

▣ Germany   ⚡ photography; oils; mixed media   🏛 San Francisco: Museum of Modern Art   📈 $1.5m in 2005, *Bavarian* (oils)

His family migrated from East to West Germany in 1953. Produces large-scale work, which often appears to be a chaotic appropriation of images from consumer society, painted onto unorthodox grounds (such as woollen blankets or furs). Claims to be attacking cliché-ridden banalities of current society and aspires to make contact with a higher spiritual level of consciousness.

Flight—Black, Red, and Gold Sigmar Polke, 1997, 118¼ x 157½ in (300 x 400 cm), mixed media, polyester fabric, Private Collection, Hamburg: Kunsthalle. Polke's most recent works reflect an interest in exploring the relationship of abstract and figurative art.

Gilbert and George

● 1943– AND 1942– British

🏴 London 🎭 performance art; photomontage; video; mixed media 🏛 London: Tate Collection 💰 $420,000 in 2004, *Seed* (photographs)

Gilbert Proesch and George Passmore. Highly successful, narcissistic couple who regularly appear in their own work as two cheap-suited "nerds." They have a big international following. Started as real-life "living sculptures."

Their large "photopieces" (produced since 1974) are made by an unknown process and are technically very impressive. Subject matter comes out of inner-city decay and is often deliberately "in-yer-face" and offensive

Street *Gilbert and George, c. 1983, 47⅓ x 39⅓ in (121 x 100 cm), mixed media, Private Collection.* Gilbert and George were among the first artists to move to the East End of London, attracted by its affordability and roughness. The area is now a fashionable art Mecca, acting as a shop window for dealers and collectors.

to all sides: to liberals (racist overtones, admiration for Thatcherism, swastikas, crude little England nationalism) as much as to old-school conservatives (overt homosexuality with young boys, turds, ridicule of religion and the monarchy).

Their work unquestionably reflects something significant about British society and its art world (1970s to the 1990s), but what? Are they criticizing the physical, moral, social, and educational decay of society (the period when Britain became "a nation state equivalent of Woolworths")? Are they praising it? Exploiting it? Or pandering to chattering-class voyeurism? Their work may rapidly begin to look very dated. Are they Hogarth's successors? Do they have a true message, or is their inability to set an agenda a comment in itself on present-day British society?

KEY WORKS *A Portrait of the Artists as Young Men*, 1970 (London: Tate Collection); *Balls: the Evening Before the Morning After—Drinking Sculpture*, 1972 (London: Tate Collection);

Blinky **Palermo**

● 1943–77 German

🏴 Germany 🗿 sculpture; oils; mixed media 🏛 Frankfurt: Städel Museum. New York: Dia:Beacon 💰 $600,000 in 2002, *Stoffbild* (fabric painting)

Real name Peter Heisterkamp, he was a short-lived refugee from Communist East Germany to Düsseldorf (1954). Was a disciple of Beuys. Had a charismatic personality and adopted the pseudonym (Palermo) of a notorious boxer and Mafioso. Made objects, fabric works, and abstract paintings. His utopian dream was to use art as a means of modern salvation. Perhaps another case where ambition ran too far ahead of the achievement.

KEY WORKS *Staircase*, 1970 (London: Tate Collection); *Untitled (Fabric Painting)*, 1970 (Frankfurt: Städel Museum); *To the People of New York City (1976–77)*, (New York: Dia:Beacon)

James **Turrell**

● 1943– American

🏴 US 🗿 installations; land art 🏛 Houston: Museum of Fine Arts 💰 $100,000 in 2000, *Raetho* (sculpture)

Turrell produces gallery installations and land-art creations that are light-filled spaces. Wants to capture the physical reality (rather than the illuminating quality) of light (natural and artificial). You, the viewer, are to move about and become so involved and absorbed that you experience a different level of consciousness (spiritual or cosmic).

KEY WORKS *Lunette*, 1974 (New York: Guggenheim Museum); *Night Passage*, 1987 (New York: Guggenheim Museum)

Christian **Boltanski**

- 1944– FRENCH

France ⚡ sculpture; installations; photography
Hamburg: Kunsthalle 📈 $175,258 in 1990, *Les saynètes comiques: le baiser caché* (works on paper)

The Frenchman produces disturbing installations that are gloomy, dimly lit, labyrinthine, and claustrophobic. He collects items such as photographs, old clothes, and personal relics to address his central themes of lost childhood, death, anonymity, and the Holocaust. He attempts to create a visual requiem for all innocent victims. Familiar war subject matter, to which he brings a new twist.

KEY WORKS *The Reserve of Dead Swiss*, 1990 (London: Tate Collection); *Gymnasium Chases*, 1991 (San Francisco: De Young Museum)

Rebecca **Horn**

- 1944– GERMAN

Germany; UK; US ⚡ installations;
video London: Tate Collection
📈 $49,680 in 2004, *Libelle* (sculpture)

Horn is the creator of highly original installations incorporating machines that move, click, whirr, flick paint, or flap wings, and are generally surprising or unpredictable. Her work is compulsive viewing, entertaining and unnerving, and has the ability to set off odd and possibly alarming or subversive trains of thought (which is what she is after). Machines need perfecting (too many breakdowns).

KEY WORKS *The Hydra-Forest Performing Oscar Wilde*, 1988 (San Francisco: Museum of Modern Art); *Concert for Anarchy*, 1990 (London: Tate Collection)

Monuments: The Children of Dijon Christian Boltanski, 1986, 275¾ x 157½ in (700 x 400 cm), installation, Hamburg: Kunsthalle. Displaying photographs of anonymous French children, Boltanski has described his work as a monument to the glory of childhood.

Jorg **Immendorff**

- 1945– GERMAN

Germany ⚡ oils; sculpture Hamburg: Kunsthalle 📈 $193,993 in 1990, *Tor I, Design* (resin on canvas)

He produces heavily painted Expressionist work that is essentially traditional and derivative (of 1920s German Expressionism and Beckmann). Addresses political issues such as the divided Germany or the environment. Typical imagery of his work is a café interior with an anonymous crowd, and symbolism of watchtowers, uniforms, barbed wire, and eagles.

KEY WORKS *The Rake's Progress*, 1992 (New Jersey: World House Gallery); *Untitled*, 1993 (New York: Philip Isles Collection)

World of Work Jorg Immendorff, 1984, 111¾ x 130 in (284 x 330 cm), oil on canvas, Hamburg: Kunsthalle. Never shy of publicity, Immendorff opened a bar in Hamburg's red light district in 1984.

Sean **Scully**

● 1945– IRISH/AMERICAN

 UK; US   oils; pastels   London: Tate
Collection. San Francisco: Museum of Modern Art
 $310,000 in 1990, *Untitled* (oils)

He is noted for his high-minded abstract
art (he believes in pure painting as high
art). The favored form is large, simple,
horizontal and vertical stripes, and the
technique emphasizes the qualities of
paint through earthy gray colors and
the subtle interplay of two and three
dimensions. His works are sometimes
made from separate panels. An "art
for art's sake" of great refinement.
KEY WORKS *Paul*, 1984 (London: Tate
Collection); *Pale Fire*, 1988 (Texas:
Modern Art Museum of Fort Worth)

Anselm **Kiefer**

● 1945– GERMAN

 Germany   oils; acrylics; mixed media;
sculpture; photography   London: Tate
Collection $1.05m in 2001, *Athanor* (oils)

Kiefer creates very large-scale, gloomy,
superficially simple images, thickly
painted, often with applied or collaged
material. The intention is to draw your
imagination in via perspectives, textures,
and layers, to confront difficult
conceptual issues, such as Nazi horrors
and guilt for the Jewish Holocaust. A
sort of modern history painting. Uses
art as a means of expunging the past.
Look for the Hans Makart of our times.
KEY WORKS *Parsifal I*, 1973 (London: Tate
Collection); *Margarethe*, 1981 (New York:
Marion Goodman Gallery)

Susan **Rothenberg**

● 1945– AMERICAN

 US   oils; acrylics; prints; drawings
 San Francisco: Museum of Modern Art.
London: Tate Collection $460,000 in
1991, *Cabin Fever* (oils)

A former dancer who came to prominence
as a painter in the mid-1970s, now much
displayed. Her large-scale works usually
contain a human or animal form, emerging
from a hazy background, on the point
of mutating into something else. Weird,
vaguely disturbing, and symptomatic of
the American love of anxious self-analysis.
KEY WORKS *Bone Man*, 1986 (New York:
Museum of Modern Art); *Vertical Spin*,
1986–87 (London: Tate Collection)

Red Banner Susan Rothenberg, 1979, 90 x 123¾ in
(228.6 x 314.6 cm), acrylic on canvas, Houston: Museum
of Fine Arts. During this decade, Rothenberg explored
themes based on horses, regarding the activity and
investigation as akin to painting a self-portrait.

Richard **Long**

● 1945–   卫 BRITISH

卫 UK   🎨 land art; conceptual art; sculpture; photography   🏛 London: Tate Collection   📈 $190,000 in 1989, *Whitechapel Slate Circle* (sculpture)

Long is a leading British land artist who achieved much early success. He was a winner of awards and attained international recognition in his 30s, but from the age of 50+ has gone rather quiet.

He is an artist with very serious intentions. He works with the land, assembling bits of it (rocks, sticks, mud) in aesthetic configurations (typically, large-scale stone arrangements in a circle or line, or walls "painted" with the mud). His earlier work is in photographic form, recording marks made by him on and in the landscape he walked over.

Is he, as some claim, a development of the Constable-Wordsworth tradition (man's harmony with nature) or is he the opposite? Does he perhaps represent the modern city dweller's incomprehension of, and puzzlement at, nature—seeking to cover it in urban developments, transform it into municipal parks (however sensitively done), and bring it back to the city art gallery in chunks and buckets?

KEY WORKS *A Square of Ground*, 1966 (London: Tate Collection); *A Line Made by Walking*, 1967 (London: Tate Collection); *Red Slate Circle*, 1980 (New York: Guggenheim Museum); *Wessex Flint Line*, 1987 (Southampton: City Art Gallery)

Jeff **Wall**

● 1946–   卫 CANADIAN

卫 Canada   📷 photography; conceptual art   🏛 Hamburg: Kunsthalle   📈 $250,000 in 2000, *The Well* (photographs)

Wall produces immaculate cibachrome photographs presented in steel frames and illuminated from behind by fluorescent tubes. The expectation created by their detailed photographic realism is that they are "from life." In fact, they are carefully selected and posed artificial tableaux, maybe using actors. A neat play on what is reality and what is art.

KEY WORKS *A Sudden Gust of Wind (After Hokusai)*, 1993 (London: Tate Collection); *Citizen*, 1996 (Basel, Switzerland: Kunstmuseum)

Anthony **Gormley**

● 1950–   卫 BRITISH

卫 UK; India; Sri Lanka   🗿 sculpture; installations   🏛 London: Tate Collection   📈 $145,600 in 2004, *Quantum Cloud XIV* (sculpture)

He is an artist of increasing stature who has never been afraid to go against the grain of fashion.

His characteristically (but not exclusively) life-size human figures have no specific features and are made of metal, visibly

Angel of the North Anthony Gormley, 1997–98, height 65 ft (20 m), steel sculpture, Gateshead (UK). The work has a poetic significance as a memorial to the area's now defunct coal mining industry.

soldered together in static poses. They are casts of the artist's own body. He is wrapped in plastic wrap, then cloth, then coated with wet plaster, which dries. He is then cut out of the resulting mold, which is reassembled, and lead or other metal is pressed into the void, or beaten to take his form, and the pieces are welded together.

Gormley studied Buddhism in India, and there can be little doubt that he is an artist trying to say something (in which he may or may not succeed) rather than to play to a market. His 65-ft (20-m)-high *Angel of the North* dominates the main highway toward Tyneside, England.

KEY WORKS *Bed*, 1980–81 (London: Tate Collection); *Three Ways: Mould, Hole, and Passage*, 1981 (London: Tate Collection); *Untitled (Man Falling)*, 1985 (Private Collection); *Maquette for Leeds Brick Man*, 1986 (Leeds: City Art Gallery)

Julian **Schnabel**

● 1951 –   ◫ AMERICAN

◫ US   ◮ oils; mixed media; prints
🏛 Michigan: Detroit Institute of Arts
💲 $325,000 in 1999, *Portrait of a Girl* (oils)

He is a much-hyped charismatic figure, considered very "bankable" in the "greed is good" boom of the 1980s. His energetic, thickly painted figurative work has striking additions, such as broken crockery and black or red velvet. Claims to deal with weighty subjects, in the tradition of great art (Van Gogh, for instance). Fashionable, but forgettable in the long term.

KEY WORKS *Jacqueline*, 1987 (Salzburg: Rupertinum Gallery of Modern Art); *Self-Portrait in Andy's Shadow*, 1987 (Santa Monica: Broad Art Foundation)

Bill **Viola**

● 1951 –   ◫ AMERICAN

◫ US   ◮ video; installations; photography
🏛 Berlin: Guggenheim Museum   💲 $59,600 in 2002, *Incrementation* (sculpture)

Viola is one of a very small minority that uses video to genuinely creative effect. He tackles age-old subjects such as birth, death, and human relationships with experience and understanding, and builds up imagery in ways analogous to the processes of a painting. Also uses the technology to involve the viewer in creating the final image. Moving, perhaps even profound, work.

One of the reasons why he is so successful and convincing is that he does not use the video medium and technology as an end or phenomenon in itself. He has something he wishes to say about the human condition and uses video technology to express it. Like all the best artists, he is totally in control of his chosen medium and can take it to the edge of its limitations.

KEY WORKS *The Sleep of Reason*, 1988 (Pittsburgh: Carnegie Museum of Art); *Nantes Triptych*, 1992 (London: Tate Collection); *The Crossing*, 1996 (New York: Guggenheim Museum)

Francesco **Clemente**

● 1952 –   ◫ ITALIAN/AMERICAN

◫ Italy; US   ◮ tempera; watercolors; oils
🏛 Bilbao: Guggenheim Museum   💲 $310,000 in 1994, *The Celtic Bestiary* (works on paper)

He was born in Naples, lives in New York. One of the most respected members of the current art establishment. Prolific, multifaceted, multinational—multi-everything. The epitome of official contemporary artistic acceptability.

Clemente creates both large-scale works and smaller ones. Explores dual themes that are the meat of political correctness, such as the relationship between the past and present, the human and animal, Europe and America, man and woman, East and West. Uses a wide variety of impeccable source material (Italian Renaissance, Indian art). Technically very sound and intellectually complex, with much symbolism to unravel.

With such correct, self-assured, firmly controlled agendas, technique, and subject matter, it is difficult to find fault. But why are the faces, eyes, and imagery in general so sad and lonely? Any art that takes itself so deadly seriously risks becoming passionless. Why the obsession with genitalia? Seems like joyless self-obsession: subjects are often sexual but not erotic. And it is the sort of art that public institutions want.

KEY WORKS *Tondo*, 1981 (New York: Museum of Modern Art); *Fire*, 1982 (Zurich: Thomas Ammann Fine Art); *Head*, 1984 (London: Victoria & Albert Museum)

Mona **Hatoum**

◔ 1952– 🏳 LEBANESE

🏳 UK; US; Canada; France   🎦 video; installations; performance art; sculpture   🏛 London: Tate Collection   💱 $130,000 in 2000, *Silence* (sculpture)

She is an involuntary refugee working in London. Creates installations and videos whose subjects are about exile, loneliness, and authoritarian politics, which she interweaves and interlinks with an examination of the undemocratic boundaries of traditional art practices.
KEY WORKS *Measures of Distance*, 1988 (London: Tate Collection); *Socle du Monde*, 1992–93 (Toronto: Art Gallery of Ontario)

David **Salle**

◔ 1952– 🏳 AMERICAN

🏳 US   🎨 oils; acrylics; prints   🏛 London: Tate Collection   💱 $500,000 in 1989, *Tennyson* (sculpture)

Salle creates large-scale figurative paintings, which are a ragbag of familiar, not very taxing, images culled from art history, adverts, design, porn, and so on. Facile and technically feeble when examined closely at first hand, they fortunately for him look quite convincing as small-scale reproductions in books or catalogs.

If you find this—or any other—artist's work awful or incomprehensible, but don't want to to say so or alienate yourself at private views, say "He (or She) has a style that is distinctly his own" (which is always true); "he neutralizes and subverts narrative and artistic conventions" (no one will dare disagree); "he appropriates art and images and simultaneously critiques them in his work" (people will be impressed, especially if they have no idea what you actually mean).
KEY WORKS *Sextant in Dogtown*, 1987 (New York: Whitney Museum of American Art); *Walking the Dog*, 1992 (London: Tate Collection)

Sophie **Calle**

◔ 1953– 🏳 FRENCH

🏳 France   🎦 photography   💱 $20,000 in 2004, *In Romance in Granada* (photographs)

Calle makes gallery displays with photographs and texts. Acts as a recorder and chronicler of society—spying on strangers, photographing them, recording what they say, involving them in her own deliberate role play. Fascinated by the interplay of public and private, fiction and reality, exhibitionism and secrecy.
KEY WORKS *The Birthday Ceremony*, 1981 (Chicago: Donald Young Gallery); *The Bronx*, 1991 (Boston: Barbara Krakow Gallery)

Nan **Goldin**

◔ 1953– 🏳 AMERICAN

🏳 US   🎦 photography   🏛 London: Tate Collection   💱 $250,000 in 2002, *Thanksgiving* (photographs)

She takes large-scale photographs, often in series, that create a visual diary of her social circle, travels, and emotional crises. She is especially concerned with so-called taboo (gay, lesbian, or transvestite) relationships and public awareness of their intimacies. Honest, often moving, and beautifully crafted.
KEY WORKS *Nan One Month after Being Battered*, 1984 (London: Tate Collection); *Siobhan in my Bathtub, Berlin*, 1992 (Winterthur, Switzerland: Fotomuseum)

Martin **Kippenberger**

◔ 1953–97 🏳 GERMAN

🏳 Germany   🎨 oils; installations; performance art; prints   🏛 San Francisco: Museum of Modern Art   💱 $650,000 in 1999, *Untitled* (oils)

Created drawings, paintings, installations, and performances. Provocative, cynical, and anti-authority, he attempted to raise the trivial and "subcultural" to the status of high art (a mainstream activity of artists since 1900). His last work, *MetroNet*, is of an imaginary, underground railway world.
KEY WORKS *Das Ende des Alphabets (ZYX)*, 1990 (Ghent: Stedelijk Museum voor Actuele Kunst); *The Raft of the Medusa*, 1996 (San Francisco: Museum of Modern Art)

Anish **Kapoor**

◔ 1954– 🏳 BRITISH/INDIAN

🏳 UK; India   🎨 sculpture   🏛 London: Tate Collection   💱 $368,000 in 2004, *Untitled* (sculpture)

Born in Bombay, India, he settled in the UK. Creates 3-D objects in which color, space, and the interplay between the visible and invisible predominate—high-quality toys for adults, in the best sense.

His strange-looking objects are made from materials such as steel, fiberglass, or stone. They have highly polished or intensely pigmented surfaces, often on a large scale. Be prepared to suspend disbelief—stop seeing them as manmade objects and allow them to act freely on your perception and imagination. Go on, play with them.

If you let go and allow your mind and eye to follow their own course—rather as you may have been able to do as a child, looking at the sky and clouds—there is a lot there. Enjoy thrilling and strange spaces to sink into, colorful "magic kingdoms" to explore, the familiar made strange. Lots of simple, unthreatening, genuinely "out of this world" experiences. A fresh, inspiring affirmation of art's role in celebrating and creating some *joie de vivre*.

KEY WORKS *As if to Celebrate, I Discovered a Mountain Blooming with Red Flowers*, 1981 (London: Tate Collection); *Untitled*, 1983 (London: Tate Collection); *Void Stone*, 1990 (Leeds: City Art Gallery)

Marsyas Anish Kapoor, 2002, 508½ x 114¾ ft (155 x 35 m), steel and PVC, London: Tate Modern. This giant sculpture was covered by a dark red fleshy-textured PVC membrane—hence the reference to Marsyas, the Greek satyr who was flayed alive.

Cindy **Sherman**

● 1954–   🏴 AMERICAN

🏴 US   📷 photography   🏛 New York: Metropolitan Museum of Art   💰 $300,000 in 2001, *Untitled Film Still No.48* (photographs)

Sherman is a leading New York artist beloved by art critics who swoon over the powerful manner in which she deconstructs and comments on women's role in a male-dominated consumer society.

She produces very large-scale photographs, often in high-key color. Works in series. She acts the parts, makes the sets, and takes the photographs herself. There is no other (and no male) involvement. In the early series, she depicted herself as media stereotypes and as ordinary girls and women. From 1985, she has produced series of grotesque images—teddy bears, dolls, or toys in a stew of vomit or slime; dehumanized medical dummies; also parodies of old-master portraits.

She seems to have less of a specific agenda than most commentators wish on her. She claims to have discovered this style of work almost by accident. Her grotesque images are said to be a commentary on consumerism's excessive binges and purges. Try identifying with the stereotypes that Sherman portrays—career girl, runaway teenager, Ingres portrait, and so on.

KEY WORKS *Untitled A-D,* 1975 (London: Tate Collection); *Untitled Film Stills* (series), 1977–80 (New York: Museum of Modern Art); *Nr. 261,* 1992 (Hamburg: Kunsthalle)

Kiki **Smith**

● 1954–   🏴 AMERICAN

🏴 US   🗿 sculpture; screenprints; body art   🏛 New York: Museum of Modern Art   💰 $210,000 in 1997, *Pee Body* (sculpture)

The daughter of sculptor Tony Smith, Kiki Smith trained briefly as a medical technician. She is obsessed with bodily fluids and parts, such as blood and saliva. She either displays these in jars or makes paper cutouts that suggest skin, and wax figures that seem to drip secretions. The underlying agenda for this need to play with the repellent is not clear.

KEY WORKS *Ribs,* 1987 (New York: Guggenheim Museum); *Untitled (Train),* 1994 (Santa Barbara, California: Museum of Art)

Thomas **Schuette**

● 1954–   🏴 GERMAN

🏴 Germany   🗿 sculpture; mixed media; drawings   🏛 Ghent: Stedelijk Museum voor Actuele Kunst   💰 $210,000 in 1998, *Grosse Geister* (sculpture)

Schuette is an artist who uses techniques and ideas from several disciplines. Makes sculptures, which range from small doll-like models to large pieces, drawings, and architectural models in wood similar to doll's houses. The human figure, scale, and presence are always apparent. His work encourages an open-ended, imaginative, nonaggressive questioning of the human condition and experience.

KEY WORKS *Weinende Frau,* 1989 (Ghent: Stedelijk Museum voor Actuele Kunst); *Belgian Blues,* 1990 (Ghent: Stedelijk Museum voor Actuele Kunst)

Robert **Gober**

● 1954–   🏴 AMERICAN

🏴 US   🗿 sculpture; installations; oils; mixed media   🏛 San Francisco: Museum of Modern Art   💰 $800,000 in 2005, *Untitled Leg* (sculpture)

A maker of objects and installations, Gober is well regarded and much exhibited on the international circuit.

He explores various fashionable ideas, such as subversion of conventions and social norms (the happy family as oppressive rather than beneficial), gay politics, green and conservation issues. Some of his objects look like found objects but are in fact made by Gober; others are everyday objects that overtly don't work (like an unconnected sink).

Does the work at times risk becoming too humorless, oblique, obscure, and overly didactic? Does he sometimes seem to say: "Today, class, we are going to consider issues of normality and abnormality in contemporary society and strategies of how we might debate those issues by creating objects that will subvert our normal expectations?" Which interests him more: his strategies or the human issues? Aren't some of his chosen social issues very parochial?

KEY WORKS *The Subconscious Sink,* 1985 (Minneapolis, Minnesota: Walker Art Center); *Prison Window,* 1992 (San Francisco: Museum of Modern Art); *Rat Bait,* 1992 (San Francisco: Museum of Modern Art)

Jeff **Koons**

● 1955– 🏳 AMERICAN

🏳 US 🎨 sculpture; conceptual art; oils; photography 🏛 New York: Guggenheim Museum 💰 $5.1m in 2001, *Michael Jackson and Bubbles* (sculpture)

He's good-looking, clever, witty, articulate, popular, good at self-publicity, successful. A former salesman and Wall Street commodity broker; now one of the darlings of the contemporary art world. Married La Cicciolina (famous Italian porn star and politician).

He glorifies and deifies the banal consumer object as a work of art. For instance, he presented pristine vacuum cleaners in the airtight, fluorescent-lit museum cases usually reserved for precious objects; he cast an inflatable toy rabbit as a polished sculpture like a Brancusi; he presented a kitsch Michael Jackson model like a Meissen figurine;

Popples *Jeff Koons, 1988, 29½ x 23¾ x 15¾ in (75 x 60 x 40 cm), porcelain, Hamburg: Kunsthalle.* This porcelain sculpture recreates in detail a stuffed toy that was marketed by a cartoon show. Part of the artist's "Banality" series, it failed to sell at Sotheby's in New York in 2003.

and filmed himself and his wife making love in a sanitized, Disneylike setting. He has an obsession with newness.

His work displays layers of clever, deliberate symbolism: the pristine vacuum cleaner = phallic (male) + sucking (female) + cleaning (purity or goodness) + brand new (virginity and immortality). He comments on consumer society's relentless promotion of success and the luxury lifestyle—and also how art functions, since commodities can be turned into high art, and art into commodities.

KEY WORKS *Lifeboat*, 1985 (Hamburg: Kunsthalle); *Three Balls Total Equilibrium Tank*, 1985 (London: Tate Collection); *Pink Panther*, 1988 (New York: Sonnabend Gallery); *Blue Poles*, 2000 (New York: Guggenheim Museum)

Andreas **Gursky**

● 1955– 🏳 GERMAN

🏳 Germany 🎨 photography 🏛 London: Tate Collection 💰 $550,000 in 2005, *May Day IV* (photographs)

Gursky is a commercially and critically successful capturer of the high-tech, fast-paced, modern world. Produces large-scale, highly colored photographs capturing various aspects of late capitalist society. The scope of his images has expanded in size and subject matter (looking outside his native Germany to an increasingly global stimulus) since the late 1980s. Particularly interested in the exchange mechanisms of capitalist societies, he produces highly formalized photos of North American and East Asian stock exchanges, where the crowds are color-coordinated in an almost Abstract Expressionist way.

Gursky can be seen as a modern descendant of history painting, cataloguing our cultural mythologies. But don't expect documentary: his interest lies in the collective and anonymous, not the individual and personal.

KEY WORKS *Schiphol*, 1994 (New York: Metropolitan Museum of Art); *Singapore Stock Exchange*, 1997 (New York: Guggenheim Museum); *Parliament*, 1998 (London: Tate Collection); *99 Cent*, 1999 (New York: Metropolitan Museum of Art)

Andy **Goldsworthy**

● 1956– ⚑ BRITISH

🏴 UK � sculpture; mixed media; photography 🏛 London: Courtauld Institute of Art 💰 $13,300 in 2001, *Snow Cone, Grise Fjord, Ellesmere Island* (photographs)

He works mostly in the open air with, and in response to, natural materials and particular places. Creates art with leaves, ice, trees, or stones.

His deeply sensitive response to nature, places, and seasons is in the English Romantic landscape tradition (like Constable or Palmer) but he offers new forms and interpretations. He weaves together the materials he uses in ways that rival nature's own ingenuity and beauty. Most works are made for, or left, out of doors where, as he intends, they eventually melt, fall over, or disintegrate.

Makes photographic records of these outdoor works, which he presents in book form as beautiful images and objects in themselves. Also produces work for gallery spaces and urban settings, though these tend to be less successful.

KEY WORKS *Conch Shell Leafwork*, 1988 (Leeds: City Art Gallery); *Red Pool, Scaur River, Dumfriesshire*, 1994–95 (Virginia: Sweet Briar College Art Gallery)

Felix **Gonzalez-Torres**

● 1957–96 ⚑ CUBAN/AMERICAN

🏴 US 🔑 conceptual art; installations; mixed media 🏛 San Francisco: Museum of Modern Art 💰 $1.5m in 2000, *Untitled, Blood* (sculpture)

He was the acme of political correctness: Cuban, gay, urban; had sad untimely death (AIDS). His work is conceptual, featuring piles of candies or paper, photographs, light

Arch at Goodwood Andy Goldsworthy, 2002, sandstone, Goodwood: Cass Sculpture Foundation. The quarried slabs of sandstone forming the arch weigh over 100 tons. The old flint wall it straddles was built by French prisoners during the Napoleonic Wars.

bulbs, and so on. Said to explore issues of illness, death, love, loss—life's sadness and transience—with a poetic aura.

Maybe his works don't achieve their stated ends unless accompanied by curatorial handouts, catalogs, or didactic writings—in which case, who is creating the art work: the artist or the curator? Well and sincerely intentioned, but in the end may amount to very little.

KEY WORKS *Untitled (Death by Gun)*, started 1990 (ongoing) (New York: Museum of Modern Art); *Untitled (Portrait of Ross in L. A.)*, 1991 (Art Institute of Chicago); *Untitled (Public Opinion)*, 1991 (New York: Guggenheim Museum)

Keith **Haring**
● 1958–90   ▣ AMERICAN

▣ US   🎨 drawings; oils; mixed media; sculpture
🏛 San Francisco: Museum of Modern Art
📈 $550,000 in 2004, *Untitled—People* (oils)

Haring was formally trained and first made his mark as a graffiti artist in the New York subway. In later life, he was principally interested in marketing his easily recognizable images (simplistic pin men depicted with thick black outlines, participating in various inconsequential activities) via T-shirts, pins, and so on. The epitome of art and the artist as a brand image. Died from AIDS in 1990.

KEY WORKS *Subway Drawing*, 1980–81 (New York: Hyde Collection Art Museum); *Self-Portrait*, 1989 (Florence: Galleria degli Uffizi)

Francis **Alÿs**
● 1959–   ▣ BELGIAN

▣ Mexico City   🎨 conceptual art; oils; performance art; mixed media   📈 $160,000 in 2003, *Untitled* (oils)

He is a painter, and conceptual and performance artist. Active principally in Mexico City, where he sets up elaborate projects that are said to catalog the (banal or surreal?) urban experience. Some involve other people, such as advertisement painters. On one occasion he dragged through the city a small magnetic dog that attracted metal debris.

KEY WORKS *The Last Clown*, 1995–2000 (London: Lisson Gallery); *61 out of 60*, 1999 (London: Lisson Gallery)

Jean-Michel **Basquiat**
● 1960–88   ▣ AMERICAN

▣ US   🎨 acrylics; mixed media; collage
📈 $5m in 2002, *Profit I* (oils)

A young, black, middle-class New Yorker, who died of a drug overdose aged 28. Frenzied and prolific self-taught artist whose work powerfully reflects the obsessions and conflicts of his city and his decade.

His large-scale work has the appearance, content, and crudity of graffiti on buildings (he began his career by secretly and illegally painting on public buildings). Their sheer energy, size, number, and consistency indicate an intelligence seeking release or crying for help. Shocking, controversial, ugly, drug-crazed they may be—boring and dismissable they are not.

Words, images, and collaged materials reflect the street life in which he grew up and lived, notably: racism, money (the art market took him up and his works sold for high prices), exploitation, Third World cultures, comics, TV and films, rap music, break-dancing, junk food, black heroes, urban ghettos, and sex.

KEY WORKS *Untitled (Skull)*, 1981 (Santa Monica: Broad Art Foundation); *Saint*, 1982 (Zurich: Galerie Bruno Bischofberger)

Jake and Dinos **Chapman**
● 1962– AND 1966–   ▣ BRITISH

▣ UK   🎨 conceptual art; sculpture; mixed media   🏛 London: Tate Collection   📈 $83,520 in 2001, *Cyber-iconic Man* (sculpture)

The brothers create life-size resin and fiberglass figures, usually of pubertal or pre-pubertal children. In part rendered with startling realism, in part distorted by grotesque, obscene, and impossible sexual organs; also mutilated anatomies, which recreate realistically the imagery of Goya's *Disasters of War*.

The brothers admit that their purpose is totally cynical—to create an aesthetic of indifference, insensitivity, with no cultural value. Shock has always been a legitimate artistic weapon, but shock for its own sake alone is worthless.

KEY WORKS *Hell*, 1999–2000 (London: Tate Collection); *Insult to Injury*, 2003 (London: Tate Collection)

Tracey **Emin**

● 1963– ▣ BRITISH

▣ UK ⚡ installations; conceptual art; sculpture;
video 🏛 London: Saatchi Collection; Tate Collection
💰 $252,000 in 2000, *My Bed* (installation)

She of the now notorious unmade bed.
Candidate for (but not winner of) Turner
Prize, Tate Gallery 1999. All her work is
a public and manic working out (exorcism)
of her traumatically unhappy youth and
adulthood (rape at 13; endless promiscuity;
transient relationships; abortion). Is it art
or should it be considered a cry for help?
Where does she go from here?

Can a cry for help, alone, make art?
Van Gogh cried for help, but used art as
a means of attempting self-reconstruction,
and he had a vision of a better world he
wished to create for himself and others.
Without this sort of reaching out, there
is always a danger of simply lapsing into
self-indulgence and self-pity—which may
be necessary personally, but it isn't art.

KEY WORKS *CV Cunt Vernacular*, 1997 (London:
Tate Collection); *Just Love Me*, 1998 (Bergen,
Norway: Kunstmuseum); *Hate and Power Can Be
a Terrible Thing*, 2004 (London: Tate Collection)

Rachel **Whiteread**

● 1963– ▣ BRITISH

▣ UK ⚡ sculpture; drawings; prints
🏛 London: Tate Collection 💰 $420,000
in 2004, *Untitled—16 Spaces* (sculpture)

Once one of the most fashionable
of the 30-something British artists
who gained international attention.
She is much featured in the media.

Whiteread creates single-minded work
of very serious, austere appearance. She
makes physical casts in concrete, resin,
rubber, and so on, of everyday objects
and spaces (yes, spaces), such as the inside
of a bath, spaces under chairs, and, most
famously, the inside of complete rooms
of a Victorian house (the house was then
demolished by the local authority). The
rationale behind her compositions is that
she makes concrete the ordinary, banal
spaces we inhabit and on which we leave
the imprint of our existence.

So far has had one good and worthwhile
idea, which has caught attention and
which she has explored in a dedicated
and conscientious manner. But do the

actual objects she
creates have lasting
merit? Will what she
creates turn out to
be profound or just
parochial? Where
on earth does she go
next? Is she a seven-
day wonder, or at
the beginning of a
long and memorable
career? Such
unanswerable
questions are the
stuff and fun of
an involvement
with high-profile
contemporary art.

KEY WORKS *Untitled
(Freestanding Bed)*, 1991
(Southampton: City Art Gallery);
Untitled (Air Bed II), 1992 (London:
Tate Collection); *Untitled (Floor/Ceiling)*,
1993 (London: Tate Collection)

Damien **Hirst**

● 1965– ▣ BRITISH

▣ UK ⚡ conceptual art; installations; sculpture;
mixed media; video 🏛 London: Saatchi Collection;
White Cube Gallery 💰 $1,969,000 in 2004,
Fragile Truth (sculpture)

Now middle-aged, once the biggest
young name in the UK. Famous for
cows preserved in formaldehyde,
but he makes "art" with almost
anything—cigarette butts, paint,
video… Able entrepreneur, who knows
his market. As an artist and personality,
he will probably auto-destruct eventually.

Hirst claims that his art is a serious
discussion of death and decay. Has
undoubtedly an uncanny ability to
comment on current social obsessions—
his recent works touched that sensitive
nerve of fears over the health industry,
genetic engineering, getting old and
infirm, etc. Equally, he and his work have
the fascination of a freak show at a circus.
Is he saying something long-lasting, or
is his art as significant as an executive
toy? The comparisons with great artists
such as Picasso are silly. And when he's
finished delivering the goods and wowing
the media, will Hirst's work amount to
more than fashion statements?

Away From the Flock (second version) Damien Hirst, 1994, 37¾ x 58⅔ x 20 in (96 x 149 x 51 cm), steel, glass, formaldehyde solution, and lamb, London: White Cube Gallery. A replica replacing the vandalized original.

KEY WORKS *Forms Without Life*, 1991 (London: Tate Collection); *In and Out of Love*, 1991 (London: Saatchi Gallery); *Prodigal Son*, 1994 (London: White Cube Gallery)

Matthew **Barney**

● 1967– ▮▯ AMERICAN

▮▯ US ▮ conceptual art; installations; video; multimedia ▮ New York: Guggenheim Museum
▮ $350,000 in 1999, *Cremaster 4* (sculpture)

He is a former medical student, well known for creating events of interlinked film performances, installations, videos, and art books with a common narrative or theme. Attracted by the repellent—strange, nightmarish forms made from horrible synthetic materials, slime made from Vaseline, mutants padded with cushions, bizarrely made-up models, etc.

The underlying message is unclear: is he trying to make a meaningful comment on, or critique of, Western consumer society? Or, even if he is, is he merely pandering to that society's inherent voyeurism and narcissism—its love of looking at itself even (especially?) when it is particularly distorted, repellent, or violent?

KEY WORKS *Metabolism of the Hubris Pill*, 1992 (Ghent: Stedelijk Museum voor Actuele Kunst); *The Cremaster Cycle*, 1994–2002 (New York: Guggenheim Museum); *Transexualis and Repressia*, 1996 (San Francisco: Museum of Modern Art)

Mariko **Mori**

● 1967– ▮▯ JAPANESE/AMERICAN

▮▯ Japan; UK; US ▮ video; photography ▮ Chicago: Museum of Contemporary Art
▮ $140,000 in 2002, *Red Light* (photographs)

She is the creator of strange, technically immaculate cibachrome or video images, which project a fantasy world that is a cocktail of futuristic science fiction, retro, Barbie dolls, kitsch, fashion, realism, and West and East. Her own extravagantly dressed image is central. She claims to be projecting an image of Utopia and the necessity of believing in utopias and optimism.

Can Utopia be so anodyne? This is not the vision of Utopia that sets out to reform the key moral, social, political, and environmental issues. It is the dream world of the global mega-shopper whose ambition is the latest "must have" brand. It is effective, but as yet narcissistic.

KEY WORKS *Birth of a Star*, 1995 (Chicago: Museum of Contemporary Art); *Empty Dream*, 1995 (Chicago: Museum of Contemporary Art)

Chris **Ofili**

● 1968– ▮▯ BRITISH

▮▯ UK; Zimbabwe ▮ mixed media; collage ▮ London: Tate Collection ▮ $210,000 in 2001, *X plus Y equals O* (oils)

Ofili produces largish-scale technically complex works—layers of paint, resin, glitter, and collage. Famously uses elephant dung in the painted surface, or under the picture as a support (the result of a trip to his cultural homeland, Zimbabwe, in 1992). Addresses issues of black identity and experience via cultural references to the Bible, jazz, and porn. Has potential, but as yet undeveloped.

KEY WORKS *Monkey Magic*, 1995 (Los Angeles: Museum of Contemporary Art); *No Woman No Cry*, 1998 (London: Tate Collection)

Glossary

ABSTRACT ART (*See* p. 358) Art that does not represent objects or people from the observable world. *See* Delaunay (p. 354); Kandinsky (p. 364); Kupka (p. 353); Malevich (p. 371); Miró (p. 393); Mondrian (p. 389); Pollock (p. 410); Rothko (p. 414); Stella (p. 462)

ABSTRACT EXPRESSIONISM (*See* pp. 412–413) The avant-garde art of the New York School, which flourished after World War II: big, challenging, personal, emotional, painterly, and influential. *See* Gorky (p. 417); Kline (p. 415); De Kooning (p. 414); Newman (p. 414); Pollock (p. 410); Rothko (p. 414); Still (p. 416)

ABSTRACTION (*See* pp. 358–359) The word used when talking about an artist whose work distills natural forms or appearances into simpler forms, but who stops short of creating abstract art. *See* Hepworth (p. 400); Matisse (pp. 344–345); Nicholson (p. 400); Wols (p. 420)

ABSTRACTION LYRIQUE The type of European painting of the 1940s and 1950s in which a loose and painterly abstraction was used to express subconscious fantasy. *See* Burri (p. 424); Michaux (p. 422); Tàpies (p. 428); Wols (p. 420)

ACADEMIC STYLE The highly polished, finely detailed style that was promoted by the conservative 19th-century academies. Most of it was worthy but boring. A lot of it was appallingly bad. Ingres was its supreme and brilliant master. *See* Bouguereau (p. 285); Cabanel (p. 285); Ingres (p. 264); Leighton (p. 287); Puvis de Chavannes (p. 324)

ACADEMICISM The clever but laborious reworking of established models. Exists in every age.

ACADEMIES (*See* p. 284) The official institutions set up in many European countries to organize and promote exhibitions, art education, and aesthetic rules and standards. *See also* Museum of modern art; Royal Academy

ACRYLIC Modern synthetic emulsion paint that combines some of the characteristics found in traditional oil paint (such as thick impasto) with some of those found in watercolors (such as transparent washes). Hockney has been particularly successful with acrylics (*See* p. 447)

ACTION PAINTING Painting produced by the emphatic physical activity of the artist: for instance, throwing paint or dripping it onto a canvas. Needs to be done on a large scale for maximum impact. Messiness and accidents are among its considered virtues. *See* Michaux (p. 422); Pollock (p. 410)

AERIAL PERSPECTIVE The illusion of receding space created by the use of warm colors (such as reds and oranges) in the foreground and cool colors (such as blues) in the distance. Pinturicchio was one of the first to combine linear, or geometric, perspective with aerial perspective. Leonardo was the first to study aerial perspective scientifically. *See* Cuyp (p. 209); Lorrain, Claude (p. 182); Pinturicchio (p. 97); Turner (p. 281)

AESTHETICISM, AESTHETIC MOVEMENT *See* Art for art's sake

AESTHETICS According to the *Oxford English Dictionary*: "The philosophy or theory of taste, or of the perception of the beautiful in nature."

AFTER ... "After Rembrandt" (or whomever) means a copy by someone other than Rembrandt of an actual work by Rembrandt, made at any date.

AIRBRUSH A tool that uses compressed air to spray paint. Can produce exceedingly fine gradations of color, or a fine line. *See* Andrews (p. 435)

ALLA PRIMA Painting onto a surface directly without any underpainting or preliminary working out of the design. *See* Titian (p. 143)

ALLEGORY A work of art where symbols or symbolic messages are used to convey the "meaning" of the work. Thus it alludes to more than is apparent at first sight. The hidden meanings, symbols, and cross-references may not always be easy to follow, and may be deliberately obscure in the manner of a brain-teasing puzzle. Allegory and realism were combined with notable success by the Dutch 17th-century masters, and by 19th-century realists such as Winslow Homer. (*See* p. 294)

ALTARPIECE The picture or sculpture made to go behind or on an altar and so enhance its part in the act of Christian worship. Many are now seen removed from this context, in the setting of the secular art gallery. Altarpieces are often designed to be seen from a kneeling position, so the perspective and design is worked out accordingly (to look at them properly you need to kneel before them, even in an art gallery).

ALTO RILIEVO *See* Relief

AMBIGUITY Something that can be understood or seen in more than one way is ambiguous. When carefully and knowingly used by an artist, it is a quality that has great value. The word is much used currently in descriptions or explanations of contemporary art, where occasionally it has a genuine meaning or expresses a genuine virtue. However, it often seems to be a coded signal that the writer finds the message from the artist so obscure, meaningless, or confused that it is virtually incomprehensible.

ANALYTICAL CUBISM (*See* p. 350) The works of Picasso and Braque of c. 1901–11 in which they fragmented form but still used conventional painting techniques. *See* Braque (p. 351); Picasso (pp. 396–397)

ANAMORPHIC A perspective trick. An object depicted in anamorphic perspective looks distorted and unrecognizable when seen from the front. This is because the viewpoint for it is placed exaggeratedly to one side, and only by looking at it from this point will the distortions correct themselves to produce a recognizable image. The best-known example of anamorphic perspective is the skull in the foreground of Holbein's *The Ambassadors*.

ANTIQUE, ANTIQUITY Terms used to describe the art of Ancient Greece and Rome

APOTHEOSIS Elevation to divine status. Senior Christian figures and monarchs who require flattery are usually the prime candidates for images of apotheosis.

APPLIED ART Works of art that are deemed to be useful and ornamental, rather than intellectual or spiritual—such as furniture, ceramics, wallpaper, tapestries, and metalwork

APPROPRIATION ART Objects, images, or texts removed from their normal context and placed unchanged in a new one, thereby gaining (it is said) a new, highly charged significance. Often presented as a new, "cutting-edge" idea, it could also be said to be old hat—something artists have been doing since time immemorial—the caves of Lascaux being the first examples of appropriation art. *See* Polke (p. 464)

AQUATINT A method of printmaking that produces soft, often grainy, gradations in tone. *See* Goya (pp. 262–263)

ARA Associate of the Royal Academy, London. There are 30 at any one time. *See also* RA; Royal Academy

ARCHAISM Imitating early, often primitive, styles

ARMORY SHOW The exhibition held in 1913 that introduced Modern art to the United States. So called because it was held in a famous army building in New York.

ARRICCIO The smooth layer of plaster onto which the design of a fresco is made

ARS LONGA VITA BREVIS One of those semi-learned Latin phrases, more used historically than now, which is often said to mean "Art is long-lasting, but life is short." Actually it means "Life is short and art takes a long time to create."

ART BRUT Crude pictures and graffiti on walls made by untrained amateurs and psychotics. *See* Dubuffet (p. 419)

ART DECO The popular and fashionable decorative style of the 1920s and 1930s. Cinema designers loved it—Radio City Music Hall, New York, for instance.

ART FOR ART'S SAKE (*See* p. 322) The idea that art is not concerned with storytelling, morality, religion, spiritual or intellectual enlightenment, and suchlike, but only with its own aesthetic properties of color, form, and so on. *See* Chase (p. 316); Dewing (p. 325); Whistler (p. 321)

ART HISTORY An academic discipline that originated in the 19th century to discuss and analyze works of art in a historical context, and which now includes other fields such as feminism, political and socioeconomic theories, and psychology. Can be profoundly revealing and illuminating, but can also kill a work of art stone dead when it fails to acknowledge that true art—that which engages the imaginative experience of mankind—transcends mere history and academic theorizing.

ART INFORMEL A type of European abstract painting of the 1940s and 1950s, which paralleled Abstract Expressionism in the United States. Had some general visual similarities but lacked the scale, focus, and drive of American art. *See* Dubuffet (p. 419); Michaux (p. 422); Wols (p. 420)

ART NOUVEAU (*See* p. 338) The highly decorative style (called *Jugendstil* in Germany, *Liberty* or *Floreale* in Italy, and *Modern* or *style moderne* in Russia) that was at the forefront of fashion in the 1890s. *See* Beardsley (p. 325); Denis (p. 325); Ensor (p. 366); Klimt (p. 339); Modigliani (p. 357); Schiele (p. 360)

ARTE POVERA (*See* p. 425) Describes the work of the group of Italian avant-garde 1960s artists with a strong political agenda who made *arte povera* (poor art) objects created from cheap and tacky materials. Kounellis, who was one of the leading proponents of *arte povera*, had a particular liking for sacking, blood, and marks made by flames and smoke. *See* Boetti (p. 427); Kounellis (p. 426); Merz (p. 424)

ARTIST'S PROOF Limited-edition prints, exclusively for the artist's own use or sale. They are marked A/P and are not numbered.

ARTS COUNCIL OF GREAT BRITAIN Founded in 1945 to promote art. Government-funded but not government-controlled. Currently going through a difficult period (being pressured by the government) but fighting back.

ASHCAN SCHOOL (*See* p. 380) Important group of late-19th-century American painters and illustrators who believed that art should portray the day-to-day harsh realities of life and that artists should be seen to get their hands (and clothes) dirty. *See* Bellows (p. 381); Glackens (p. 380); Henri (p. 380); Luks (p. 380); Sloan (p. 381)

ASSEMBLAGE A 3-D picture made from different everyday materials

ATELIER French word for "studio"

ATELIER LIBRE A studio where you pay a fee for organized group sessions to paint from a model, but where there is no tuition. Important feature of the Parisian avant-garde in the late 19th century.

ATTRIBUTE Symbol associated with a figure that enables it, for example, to be identified as a particular saint or god; thus Juno always has a peacock, St. Catherine the wheel on which she was nearly martyred, and so on.

ATTRIBUTED TO … "Attributed to Rembrandt" (or whomever) means that a work is probably by that artist, but there is still some doubt about how much of it was done by the master.

ATTRIBUTION An informed opinion as to the authorship of a work of art when there is no definite proof. *See also:* Attributed to …; By …; Follower of …; Manner of …; Studio of …

AUREOLE Circle of light surrounding the head or body of a holy figure

AUTOGRAPH A work of art believed to be entirely by a particular artist

AUTOMATISM High-class doodling directed by the unconscious mind. Much in vogue with the Surrealists. *See* Ernst (p. 369); Miró (p. 393)

AVANT-GARDE Art that is so innovative as to be ahead of the mainstream art of its time and rejected as unacceptable by the official system and institutions. Most work that is currently called avant-garde by the official museum and gallery system is not—simply because once officialdom adopts it and blesses it, it becomes part of the mainstream. The heroic period of the modern avant-garde was 1880–1960.

"BAD PAINTING" Name for a small group of artists with no fixed agenda who created messily painted figurative images as a reaction against Minimal art and Conceptual art in the 1970s. They were well named! *See* Salle (p. 470); Schnabel (p. 469)

BALDACCHINO Italian word for "canopy." A fringed canopy in cloth or a structure in metal or stone that is fixed like a roof over an altar, a throne, or a holy object.

BAMBOCCIATA Small old-master painting (usually 17th century) of humble, peasant subject matter and street life. Named after a minor Dutch artist called Pieter van Laer (c. 1592–1642), who worked in Rome and was nicknamed Bamboccio ("rag doll") because he was small and deformed.

BARBIZON SCHOOL (*See* p. 305) Group of progressive, mid-19th-century French landscape painters who worked in and around the village called Barbizon in the forest of Fontainebleau, near Paris. *See* Corot (p. 304); Rousseau, Théodore (p. 304)

BAROQUE (*See* pp. 178–179) The dominant style of the 17th century. Look for: illusion, movement in space, drama, love of rich color and materials; heaviness, seriousness, pomposity. *See* Bernini (pp. 173–175); Champaigne (p. 182); Cortona (p. 177); Rembrandt (pp. 200–201); Rubens (p. 191); Snyders (p. 190); Thornhill (p. 217)

BAS RELIEF *See* Relief

BAUHAUS (*See* p. 386) Famous modern art school, opened in Germany in 1919 and closed by the Nazis in 1933. Highly influential in the fields of architecture and design. *See* Albers (p. 388); Feininger (p. 386); Kandinsky (p. 364); Klee (p. 387); Moholy-Nagy (p. 386); Schlemmer (p. 388)

BEAUX ARTS The fine arts

BELLE PEINTURE Beautiful paint handling in the sense of a rather self-indulgent love of luscious paint, elegant brushstrokes, and a lively paint surface—perhaps at the expense of any other quality such as subject matter and observation.

BEN DAY Cheap, simple printing process invented in 1879 by Benjamin Day, a New York newspaper engraver. Uses patterns of dots that differ in density to create a halftone image. Employed extensively in newspapers and magazines, and suitable for both black-and-white and color. With a magnifying glass, the dot patterns are clearly visible. *See* Lichtenstein (p. 441)

BIEDERMEIER The predominant style in Austria and Germany in the first half of the 19th century. Plain, bourgeois, modest, conservative, well made.

BINDER Material (such as oil) that holds particles of pigment together and so makes paint

BIOMORPHIC FORMS Softly contoured organic (rather than geometric) forms used in abstract art. *See* Arp (p. 368); Gorky (p. 417); Miró (p. 393)

BISTER Brown pigment made from charred wood, used as ink or chalk. *See* Rembrandt (pp. 200–201)

BITUMEN Rich, brown, tarry pigment. Looks wonderful when fresh but it is disastrous because it never dries and soon turns into a black, bubbly mess. *See* Géricault (p. 269); Reynolds (p. 239); Ryder (p. 295)

BLAUE REITER, DER (THE BLUE RIDER) (*See* p. 365) Important avant-garde group of German Expressionists, based in Munich c. 1911. Wanted to put spiritual values into art and used abstraction, simplification, and the power of color as a means of doing this. *See* Kandinsky (p. 364); Klee (p. 387); Macke (p. 365); Marc (p. 365); Münter (p. 364)

BLEED 1) What happens when one layer or area of color seeps into another and changes it. 2) In printing, a picture or text that runs off the edge of the paper is said to bleed.

BLOOM Blue or white "film" that develops on badly stored oil paintings

BLOOMSBURY GROUP (*See* p. 379) The name of a group of English writers, artists, poets, and designers, who practiced and promoted modern French art in the 1920s and 1930s. *See* Lewis, (Percy) Wyndham (p. 376)

BLOT DRAWING Using deliberate or accidental stains or blots on a piece of paper to get the imagination going. *See* Cozens, Alexander (p. 244); Leonardo (pp. 132–133)

BODY ART Art that takes the body as its subject or object (or both). Refers to such use in performance art, contemporary sculpture, or video.

BODY COLOR Watercolor mixed with opaque white

BOLOGNESE SCHOOL (*See* p. 166) Important 17th-century Italian school of artists based in and around Bologna, who successfully combined Classicism and theatricality. *See* Carracci (p. 167); Domenichino (p. 168); Guercino (p. 172); Reni (p. 166)

BOOK OF HOURS A prayer book used by laymen for private devotions. The hours refer to the times of day when prayers are said.

BOTTEGA The area of an old master's studio used by his apprentices

BRÜCKE, DIE (THE BRIDGE) (*See* p. 362) Important avant-garde group of German Expressionists based in Dresden, 1905–13, with radical political and social views expressed through modern, urban, subject matter or landscapes and figures. *See* Kirchner (p. 362); Heckel (p. 363); Nolde (p. 362); Pechstein (p. 363); Schmidt-Rottluff (p. 363)

BRUSH Instrument for applying paint that has been in use since the early Stone Age

BRUSHWORK A painter's individual handling of paint texture, especially oils. Can be very distinctive—thin, thick, flat, juicy, rough, and so on—and a major element in an artist's style. Or can be virtually anonymous, even mechanical and boring. *See* Ingres—anonymous (p. 264); Rembrandt—interesting (pp. 200–201)

BUCRANIUM (PL. BUCRANIA) Decorative motif featuring the horned head or skull of an ox

BUON FRESCO True fresco—the real thing, painting into wet plaster. *See also* Fresco; Mezzo fresco

BURIN The main tool used in engraving. You push it like a chisel and it plows out a line on the metal or wooden surface.

BURR When you engrave a line with a burin, like a plow, it leaves a ridge of dug-out material (burr) on either side of the furrow. If this is retained, the printed line has an extra rich, soft quality, though the burr soon wears away.

BY … One of the shortest but most important words in the commercial and academic art world. The description "by Rembrandt" (or any other master) means that there is definite proof (or, at least, substantial evidence) that the artist painted it. *See also* Attribution

BYZANTINE ART The artistic tradition that flourished in Byzantium (Constantinople), the capital of the Eastern Roman Empire from c. 330 CE to the mid-15th century. Notable for stylized depictions of Christianity and Imperial Rome in mosaics, frescoes, and relief sculpture.

CADMIUM The metal cadmium was discovered in the early 19th century and from then on new cadmium pigments (yellow, orange, and red) were produced. Popular because it was cheap and durable.

CALLIGRAPHY The art of fine handwriting

CAMDEN TOWN GROUP Small, progressive group of English painters who lived and worked in Camden Town, London, 1911–14. They were influenced by the Post-Impressionists.

CAMERA LUCIDA Latin for "light chamber." A machine for drawing and copying that uses a prism and gives the illusion of seeing a real object as if it were on a piece of paper.

CAMERA OBSCURA Latin for "dark chamber." A boxlike device that projects an image through a small hole or lens onto a sheet of paper or other material so that its outline can be traced. Same principle as a simple photographic camera. *See* Canaletto (p. 235); Vermeer (p. 213)

CANVAS The material on which most largish pictures are painted. Inexpensive, flexible, durable, shapable. In common use by 1500. Linen is the traditional material; cotton duck has been used widely since 1945.

CAPRICCIO A fantasy townscape combining both real and imaginary buildings. Used to good advantage by decorative 18th-century artists such as Panini. *See* Canaletto (p. 235); Guardi (p. 236); Van der Heyden (p. 210); Panini (p. 234)

CARAVAGGISTI Followers of Caravaggio (*See* pp. 170–171), from all over Europe, who were influenced by his subjects, realism, and dramatic lighting. *See* Gentileschi (p. 169); Zurbarán (p. 185)

CARICATURE An exaggerated, ludicrous, or satirical portrait. *See* Carracci (p. 167); Daumier (p. 307); Hogarth (p. 238)

CARMINE A red pigment that is ostensibly good for flesh tones, but has the fatal disadvantage of rapidly losing its color, which is why some of Reynolds's sitters look like white-faced ghosts (*See* p. 239)

CAROLINGIAN ART Produced in Europe in the 8th and 9th centuries during the reign of Charlemagne (800–14) and his successors

CARTOON A full-size drawing that is used as the design for a painting or tapestry. *See* Leonardo (pp. 132–133); Michelangelo (p. 136); Raphael (p. 131)

CASEIN Strong adhesive made from curd (milk)

CASSONE Elaborately decorated Italian Renaissance marriage chest, sometimes with lid(s) and sides painted by leading artists

CATALOGUE RAISONNÉ A complete, annotated, and scholarly catalog of all known and attributed works by an artist

CHALK Soft, fine, grained rock used for drawing. The white variety is processed from calcium carbonate, the black from carbonaceous shale, and the red (sanguine) from hematite (iron ore).

CHARCOAL Charred twigs or sticks used for drawing

CHIAROSCURO Pronounced contrast between brightness and darkness. From the Italian *chiaro* (bright), *oscuro* (dark). *See* Bol (p. 202); Caravaggio (pp. 170–171); La Tour (p. 184); Rembrandt (pp. 200–201); Ribera (p. 185); Zurbarán (p. 185)

CHINESE WHITE White pigment with the same chemical components as zinc white but less transparent

CHINOISERIE Works of art reflecting a fanciful idea of China. Especially in vogue in Europe from the late-17th to the mid-18th centuries.

CIBACHROME A color print made from a slide. Usually large scale and with high definition and clarity. *See* Wall (p. 468)

CINQUECENTO Italian for "16th century" (1500–99)

CIRCLE OF ... "Circle of Rembrandt" (or whomever) means a work done in the artist's time and showing his influence

CIRE PERDUE *See* Lost wax

CLAIR-OBSCUR French term for *chiaroscuro*. *See* Chiaroscuro

CLASSIC Much used and abused word. Sometimes it means logical, symmetrical, well established, archetypal; sometimes it means the moment of highest achievement by an artist or of a general style. Not an alternative word for Classical.

CLASSICAL Belonging to, or deriving from, Ancient Greece and Rome

CLAUDE GLASS A small, portable, dark, convex mirror. Hold it up to a real landscape and you get a miniaturized, subtle, colored version of it that looks a bit like a painting by Claude. *See* Lorrain, Claude (p. 182)

CLEANING *See* Restoration

CLICHÉ VERRE (OR GLASS PRINT) A cross between photography, printmaking, and etching. You draw the design on a glass plate and print it onto light-sensitive paper. *See* Corot (p. 304); Millet (p. 305); Rousseau, Théodore (p. 304)

CLOISONISM From the French *cloison*, meaning "partition." A style of painting in which areas of pure color are surrounded by narrow bands of black or gray. Looks like *cloisonné* enamel decoration of metals. Although Gauguin took the credit for inventing the style, and most fully realized its possibilities, it was Emile Bernard who first showed it to Gauguin. *See* Bernard (p. 332); Gauguin (p. 329)

CoBrA (*See* p. 418) A group of post-World War II European avant-garde artists known for colorful, expressive, abstract work. So called because of the initial letters of their native cities: Copenhagen, Brussels, Amsterdam. *See* Alechinsky (p. 419); Appel (p. 418); Jorn (p. 418)

COGNOSCENTI From the Italian *conoscere*, "to know." Those who have inside knowledge.

COLL. From the collection of the person or organization named

COLLAGE Photographs, bits of newspaper, magazines, wallpaper, and so on, pasted down, and sometimes painted around and over. An art form much used by the Cubists. *See* Braque (p. 351); Picasso (pp. 396–397); Rodchenko (p. 373); Schwitters (p. 368)

COLOR-FIELD PAINTING A type of Abstract Expressionism painting whose principal feature is a large expanse of color with no obvious point of focus or attention. *See also* Abstract Expressionism. *See* Newman (p. 414); Rothko (p. 414)

COLOR WHEEL A circular diagram showing the relationships between primary, secondary, tertiary, and complementary colors. An indispensable tool for anyone working with color.

COMMERCIAL ART Art commissioned exclusively for commercial purposes, such as advertising or packaging

COMPLEMENTARY COLORS Each primary color—red, yellow, blue—has its own, exclusive, complementary color—green, purple, orange. These are made by mixing the other two primaries. When the corresponding pair of primary and complementary colors are placed side by side, they cause an optical vibration in the eye and activate each other.

COMPOSITION The arrangement of the shapes and areas of a picture, considered as surface pattern only

COMPUTER ART Works of art made with the aid of a computer. *See* Paik (p. 458)

CONCEPTUAL ART Works of art where the only thing that matters is the idea or concept. No value or merit is awarded in materials or to physical or technical skill. The problem for many people is that the ideas and concepts offered often seem utterly banal, and the works appear to have no visual or aesthetic interest. Came into fashion in the late 1960s; still very much the thing for many official art establishments and museum curators. *See* Beuys (p. 453); Duchamp (p. 367); Gonzalez-Torres (p. 474); Hesse (p. 460)

CONNOISSEURSHIP Knowledge, understanding, and appreciation of works of art, with emphasis on visual and aesthetic qualities.

CONSERVATION Creating the environment in which a work of art is properly taken care of, without undue interference, and without the need to restore and repair. Not to be confused with restoration.

CONSTRUCTIVISM (*See* p. 372) Very important avant-garde movement (1917–21) concerned with abstraction, space, new materials, 3-D form, and social reform. *See* Gabo (p. 372); Pevsner (p. 372); Tatlin (p. 373)

CONTÉ A French brand of chalk or crayon, named after Nicolas-Jacques Conté (1755–1805), the scientist who invented it. Seurat used black conté crayon on rough, grainy paper to create exquisite small-scale drawings, which show simplified forms and subtle gradations of tone.

CONTEMPORARY ART Usually taken to mean works of art produced since 1960

CONTEXT ART Art that criticizes the commercial activities and institutions of the art world with a view to investigating or revealing its political machinations and manipulations.

CONTRAPPOSTO From the Italian *contrapporre*, meaning "to oppose." A pose in which the body below the hips is twisted in the opposite direction from the body above the hips.

CONTRE-JOUR "Against the light"—looking at things that are strongly lit from behind, and so almost silhouetted. Bingham's *Fur Traders* is a masterpiece of *contre-jour*, reflection, and bathed light.

CONVERSATION PIECE A group portrait set in a room or a garden showing polite conversation or a related activity such as a tea party. *See* Devis (p. 239); Hogarth (p. 238); Zoffany (p. 241)

COPY An imitation of an original. May be honest, may be a forgery. *See also* Forgery

C-PRINT Color print made from a color negative

COULISSE A compositional device (*en coulisse* is French for "in the wings") in which rocks, trees, and so on are placed at the sides of a painting to lead the eye into the center.

CRAQUELURE The network of cracks that can develop on the surface of old oil paintings

CRAYONS Chalks mixed with oil or wax

CROSS HATCHING Criss-crossing parallel lines, which can be varied to create tone

CUBISM (*See* p. 350) The most significant art and design innovation of the 20th century, Cubism overturned conventional systems of perspective and ways of perceiving form. *See* Braque (p. 351); Gris (p. 351); Léger (p. 352); Picasso (pp. 396–397)

CURATOR Someone who organizes an exhibition, sets the agenda for it, and chooses the participating artists

DADA (*See* p. 367) The first of the modern anti-art movements. Deliberately used the absurd, banal, offensive, and tatty to shock and to challenge all existing ideas about art, life, and society. Originated in New York in 1915, and in Zurich in 1916. *See* Arp (p. 368); Duchamp (p. 367); Ernst (p. 369); Man Ray (p. 394); Picabia (p. 367)

DANUBE SCHOOL The group of painters from middle Europe who developed landscape painting in the early 16th century. *See* Altdorfer (p. 158); Cranach (p. 125)

DEACCESSION A work of art that has been cataloged as part of a collection needs a formal act of deaccession to undo the formality of officially cataloging it. Whether or not museums should have the power to deaccession is a subject of hot debate.

DECALCOMANIA Technique in which paint is splashed onto paper with a big brush and covered while still wet with another sheet of paper before the two are rubbed together. The result is a pattern that looks like a weird, fantastic forest or jungle. Used by the Surrealists as a means of harnessing accidents to create spontaneous, unpreconceived subjects and forms. *See* Ernst (p. 369)

DECONSTRUCTION The currently fashionable idea that the true meaning of a work of art is found, not by examining what an artist professed to mean or tried to say, but by analyzing the way he or she expressed it

DECORATIVE ARTS *See* Applied art

DEGENERATE ART ("ENTARTETE KUNST") (*See* p. 384) The Nazi term for any art they believed to be the product of degenerate human beings and perverted minds and which did not conform to a bourgeois ideal of well-crafted, figurative images portraying heroism or comfortable day-to-day living, .

DE GUSTIBUS NON EST DISPUTANDUM Latin maxim meaning "There is no accounting for taste"

DEL., DELIN. Found on prints after an artist's name. Means the artist drew the design, but that the print may have been made by someone else.

DEVICE An emblem or motto that an artist or printmaker uses instead of a signature. *See* Whistler—butterfly device (p. 321)

DIDACTIC Consciously teaching or instructing

DIFFICULTY All major works of art are difficult in that they require time and effort, and test the perception, intellect, and emotions of both creator and viewer. However, it does not follow, as some commentators seem to think, that because something is difficult to unravel or understand it is therefore a major work of art.

DIGITAL ART Art that uses computers and the Internet. *See* Paik (p. 458)

DILETTANTE Today a disparaging word to describe someone with a superficial and unserious interest in the arts. But in the 18th century it was used as a word of praise, denoting a deep and profound interest and pleasure not just in the visual arts but in the whole richness of human possibility.

DIORAMA A peepshow with artistic pretensions. Can be the size of a small box or a large building.

DIPTYCH A picture made in two parts. An altarpiece that is a diptych usually has the two parts hinged together.

DISEGNO Italian term covering both drawing and design. Skill in *disegno* was very highly valued in the Renaissance. *See* Michelangelo (p. 136); Raphael (p. 134)

DISTEMPER Powdered colors mixed with size; impermanent. Used by scene painters in the theater. Old paintings in distemper have a very dark and dusty appearance.

DISTRESSED One way of saying "in poor condition"

DIVISIONISM (*See* p. 320) A way of painting in which color effects are obtained optically rather than by mixing colors on the palette. Seurat was the originator of Divisionism but died young, so Signac became its chief promulgator. *See* Pissarro (p. 314); Seurat (p. 320); Signac (p. 320)

DONOR Someone who commissions a work of art and gives it to an institution (such as a church). In the Renaissance, the image of the donor was often included in the picture.

DRAGGING Paint pulled across a surface in an uneven way so that the underneath layer of paint shows through

DRAPERY MAN (DRAPERY PAINTER) A studio assistant who painted the unimportant bits of drapery

DRAFTSMAN Someone who draws, but you have to do it very well to deserve the name

DRY BRUSH A technique whereby a watercolor brush is squeezed almost dry, to produce a fine, opaque line. See Dürer (pp. 126–127); Wyeth (p. 439)

DRY POINT A type of print technique. A metal plate is scratched with a sharp point, producing a burr. Often used to add extra touches to etching and engraving. See also Burr. See Rembrandt (pp. 200–201)

DUCK A type of canvas, usually made of cotton

EARTH ART See Land art

EARTH COLORS Pigments such as ocher and umber made from earth

EASEL PICTURE A picture of a size to fit on and be painted at an easel in a studio—so in practice a bit taller than 6 ft (2 m)

ECLECTIC Borrowing freely from a wide variety of sources. See Carracci (p. 167)

ÉCORCHÉ French for "flayed." A drawing or model that shows a human or animal body without its skin.

EDITION All the impressions made from a single printing plate and issued at the same time

EIGHT, THE Important group of eight avant-garde American artists (Arthur Davies, William Glackens, Robert Henri, Ernest Lawson, George Luks, Maurice Prendergast, Everett Shinn, and John Sloan) formed in 1907 for a New York exhibition and which gained notoriety. Some were part of the Ashcan School; some were colorfully modern. See also Ashcan School. See Glackens (p. 380); Henri (p. 380); Luks (p. 380); Sloan (p. 381)

ELEVATION View of a building from one vantage point

EMBLEM 1) An object symbolizing or suggesting another object. 2) A picture, possibly with a motto or set of verses, that spells out a message of moral instruction. Very popular in 17th-century Holland.

EMPATHY Transferring your feelings and personality onto a person or a work of art

EMPIRE STYLE Grand imperial decorative style that started in Paris and spread throughout Europe. The style of choice in Napoleon's era, it consisted of hyped-up Neo-Classicism with the addition of other motifs, often Egyptian. Sometimes called Regency in England.

EMULSION A medium containing materials that will not mix naturally—such as oil and water—but that are made to do so by adding an emulsifying agent. Egg yolk is such an agent; tempera is an emulsion. See also Tempera

ENCAUSTIC Pigments mixed with molten wax and fused to a surface. Much used by the ancient Greeks. Has had a recent revival. See Johns (p. 442); Marden (p. 461)

ENGRAVING Print technique. A sharp V-shaped tool is pushed across a metal plate producing precise, clear-cut lines. Widely used since the early Renaissance. Dürer's incomparable engraving technique strongly influenced young Aubrey Beardsley, who loved the dramatic and erotic qualities of bold black-and-white illustrations. See Beardsley (p. 325); Dürer (pp. 126–127)

ENLIGHTENMENT (THE) In the mid-18th century, upholders of The Enlightenment believed that human reason could (and would) solve most problems and create heaven on earth. Also known as the Age of Reason (pp. 218–221)

ENTARTETE KUNST See Degenerate art

ENVIRONMENT ART Creating an environment (such as a room, but can be outside) so that the presence of the visitor in it becomes an integral part of the experience or event. Early works tended to bombard onlookers with light, sound, smell, and touch, so they had to react. Developed in the 1960s. See also Installation

ESQUISSE French word for "sketch"

ETCHING Print technique widely used since the 17th century. The line is first drawn by hand, then acid is used to make the line eat into the metal plate. It produces a delicate, free-flowing line with a soft outline. Picasso's The Vollard Suite is arguably the greatest achievement in all 20th-century etching. See Picasso (pp. 396–397); Rembrandt (p. 200); Whistler (p. 321)

EUSTON ROAD SCHOOL English group founded in the 1930s who promoted realism à la Cézanne. See Pasmore (p. 430)

EX-VOTO Latin: "from a vow." A work of art made as an offering to a god, usually to ask a favor or as a thank you for a prayer answered.

EXC., EXCUDIT Latin for "he executed it." Found on prints, identifying the engraver or publisher.

EXISTENTIALISM The fashionable philosophy among the Western intellectual elite in the immediate postwar period. Says, in essence, that individuals are only responsible to themselves and therefore they are free, even obliged, to express themselves as personally and individually as possible. Very influential with avant-garde artists and writers of the time. See Pollock (pp. 410–411)

EXPRESSIONISM (See pp. 358–359) Style conveying heightened sensibility through distortion of color, drawing, space, scale, form, or intense subject matter, or a combination of these. One of the principal strands of 20th-century German art. See also Blaue Reiter, Der; Brücke, Die

EYE LEVEL Everything we see is at, above, or below eye level. When looking at a figurative picture, this needs to be worked out in order to read the objects and space relationships correctly.

FACSIMILE An exact copy

FACTURE *See* Handling

FAKE A work of art deliberately made or altered so as to appear to be better, older, or other than what it, in fact, is. *See* p. 25. *See also* Forgery

FANCY PICTURE English 18th-century pictures of a single figure, or a group of figures, in an open-air setting doing nothing very much other than looking sweet, appealing, and picturesque. *See* Gainsborough (p. 240)

FAUVES, LES (*See* p. 346) French avant-garde movement, which originated in 1905. One of the key early movements in Modern art. Decorative and expressive works full of bright color and flat patterns, loosely painted. *Fauve* is the French word for "wild beast." *See* Braque (p. 351); Derain (p. 347); Dufy (p. 353); Matisse (pp. 344–345); Vlaminck (p. 346)

FEC., FECIT., F. Latin for "he/she made it." Sometimes accompanies an artist's signature, as a sort of double declaration of authenticity.

FÊTE CHAMPÊTRE French for "outdoor feast." A group of elegant ladies and gents having a relaxed and happy time in a landscape setting and evidently absorbed with each other, love, and music. Much in vogue in 18th-century France. Also sometimes referred to as *fête galante*. *See* Lancret (p. 224); Pater (p. 224); Watteau (pp. 222–223)

FIGURATIVE ART Art that represents recognizable nature and objects. The opposite of abstract art.

FIGURE The human form

FIN DE SIÈCLE Refers to the jaded, decadent attitudes in vogue at the end of the 19th century

FINE ARTS Painting, sculpture, and architecture

FINISH A work of art that is executed in meticulous detail is called "highly finished." *See* Ingres (p. 264)

FIXATIVE A transparent spray that fixes chalks, charcoal, and pastel to paper, and stops them from smudging and rubbing

FL., FLOREAT Latin for "he/she flourished." If the actual birth and death dates of an artist are not known, it is customary to give the dates when he or she was known to be working (i.e. flourished). Same as "active."

FLUXUS (*See* p. 423) International group of artists set up in Germany in 1962. Promoted "happenings" with spectator participation. Opposed to anything that smacked of tradition or professionalism. *See* Beuys (p. 453)

FOLLOWER OF ... Somebody working in the style of a particular artist, but not necessarily a pupil or assistant. *See also* Attribution; Manner of ...

FORESHORTENING A perspective trick. An extreme example is a painting that gives the illusion of an arm pointing directly at the spectator; in fact only the hand is shown, the arm being hidden behind the hand. *See* Caravaggio (pp. 170–171); Lanfranco (p. 168); Mantegna (p. 107); Masaccio (p. 88); Sebastiano del Piombo (p. 135); Uccello (p. 92)

FORGERY Something made in fraudulent imitation of another thing already existing. *See also* Fake

FORM The shape, size, movement, texture, color, and tone of an object

FOUND OBJECT *See* Objet trouvé

FRENCH REVOLUTION 1789—a key date. The most important political event of the 18th century and a watershed for the arts, as for so much else in European history.

FRESCO Italian for "fresh." Painting on the wet plaster of a wall so that when it dries, the painting is the plaster. This has to be done rapidly and with absolute certainty, as there is no possibility for corrections other than hacking off the plaster and starting again. Michelangelo's ceiling in the Sistine Chapel is fresco painting at its most magnificent. *See also* Buon fresco; Mezzo fresco

FROTTAGE From the French *frotter*, "to rub." Making an impression of a textured surface by placing a piece of thin material over it and rubbing it with something like a wax crayon. Used by the Surrealists to stimulate ideas and painting. *See* Ernst (p. 369)

FUTURISM (*See* p. 375) One of the most important early avant-garde art movements. Originated in Italy between 1909–15 and was widely influential. Noisily promoted a worship of machinery, speed, modernity, and revolutionary change, using the latest avant-garde styles such as Cubism. *See* Balla (p. 374); Boccioni (p. 374); Lewis, (Percy) Wyndham (p. 376); Severini (p. 375)

GAMBOGE A rich golden-yellow pigment

GENDER SURFING Mixing up sexual roles in order to entertain and amuse

GENRE A particular category of subject matter—such as portrait, landscape, marine, or history painting

GENRE PAINTING A type of picture that purports to show a reassuring glimpse of everyday life. Usually small scale and intimate. Invented in 17th-century Holland and much in vogue in other prosperous bourgeois circles, such as 18th-century France, Biedermeier Germany, and 19th-century Britain. The French artist James Tissot was deservedly successful in 1870s Victorian London. *See* Chardin (p. 224); Greuze (p. 224); Hooch (p. 211); Maes (p. 208); Terborch (p. 210); Tissot (p. 302); Vermeer (p. 213); Wilkie (p. 280)

GEORGIAN A vague term much loved by real estate agents and antique dealers meaning anything British, of the 18th and early 19th centuries, and therefore desirable—all British monarchs between 1714 and 1830 were called George, from George I to George IV.

GESAMTKUNSTWERK Untranslateable German word meaning "total work of art." The idea is the creation of a totality in which architects, painters, sculptors, writers, musicians, poets, and so on, all make an equal contribution so that the whole is greater than the sum of the individual parts. Wagner was enthused by the idea—but with himself as the creative controlling genius.

GESSO A white absorbent ground for painting in tempera or oil. Made from chalk or gypsum mixed with glue.

GESTALT A one-word way of saying that the mind tries to turn chaos into order. It organizes what it perceives and senses, and tends to make the final result greater than the sum of the individual parts.

GESTURE PAINTING See Action painting

GILDING Covering a surface with gold leaf

GLASS PRINT See Cliché verre

GLAZING 1) Old-master technique of covering a layer of already-dried oil paint with a transparent layer of a different color. One of the reasons for the rich, resonant, and subtle color effects in old masters. A very strong, durable technique. 2) Putting glass, in a frame, over a picture to protect it.

GOLDEN SECTION A mathematical proportion thought to be very beautiful. Take a line AB and divide it by C so that the ratio AC : CB = AB : AC. In practice it works out at approximately 8 : 13. Widely used. See Poussin (pp. 180–181)

GOTHIC The principal European style in the arts (and especially architecture) before the Renaissance, from the 12th to 15th centuries. Characterized by the soaring vertical and pointed arch. The underlying message is spiritual uplift and devotion.

GOTHIC REVIVAL The reawakened interest in medieval art in the 18th and 19th centuries. Called by the French *style troubadour*.

GOUACHE Opaque watercolor. Ideal for Jacob Lawrence who wanted to work on a small scale with spare, lean, and intense colors. See Calder (p. 438); Lawrence (p. 409); Lewis, John Frederick (p. 288); Matisse (pp. 344–345); Watteau (pp. 222–223)

GRAFFITO Strictly speaking, "graffito" (or "sgraffito") describes any design scratched through a layer of paint or other material, to reveal a different ground underneath. The plural "graffiti" now describes unauthorized designs or words that are painted, sprayed, scratched, or scribbled onto walls or other publicly visible surfaces, sometimes by political activists, sometimes by vandals, and sometimes by those with highly sophisticated artistic and graphic skills. See Basquiat (p. 475); Dubuffet (p. 420)

GRAND MANNER An ambitious type of painting that promotes the idea of heroic characters and events, and resonates with implications of history, authority, and greatness. History painting and portraiture are the usual subjects. Showy, eloquent, and rhetorical; at its best convinces by overwhelming, at its worst looks insincere, artificial, and ludicrous.

Reynolds fervently believed in the merits of grand manner painting. He succeeded with it in his portraits, but failed spectacularly when it came to history painting. See Copley (p. 256); Kitaj (p. 432); Reynolds (p. 239); Sargent (p. 326); Stuart (p. 257)

GRAND TOUR (See p. 234) Once-in-a-lifetime tour around Europe to see the major sights and works of art, and to experience life—very much the done thing in the 18th and 19th centuries.

GRAPHIC ART Art primarily dependent on the use of line, not color, such as drawing, illustration, engraving, and printmaking

GRISAILLE A painting made with different grays and no colors

GROTESQUE Decorative design incorporating fanciful human, animal, and plant features. The inspiration was the designs found in excavated crypts of grottoes (hence the name) in Rome in the early 16th century, notably the Golden House of Nero. In the 18th century the word came to mean something ridiculous and unnatural. See Raphael (p. 134)

GROUND 1) The final, prepared surface of a support, which will be painted on. 2) Also the name of the substance used for such preparation. The purpose of the ground is to create a smooth surface with a sympathetic texture for the artist to paint on, and which also isolates the paint from the support. A ground can be of any color. The old masters traditionally used a middle tone so that they could paint brighter than the ground for highlights, and darker for shadows. Since Impressionism, grounds are usually white to make colors as bright as possible. See also Primer; Sinking in; Support

GUILD Medieval organization that trained and protected its members. Painters often belonged to the Guild of St. Luke (he was the patron saint of painters). The High Renaissance masters despised them, and the academies took over their role. See also Academies

GUM ARABIC Binder used for watercolors—the gum comes from certain varieties of acacia tree

HALFTONE Any tone or shade that lies between the extremes of light and dark

HALO Circle endowed with divine light surrounding the head of a holy person

HANDLING The way a medium—such as paint, clay, or charcoal—is used and manipulated. All artists have their own individual way of handling their material, which is as personal as handwriting.

HAPPENING "Artistic" event, supposedly spontaneous, similar to a theatrical performance and presented as a work of art. Typical 1960s phenomenon. See also Fluxus; Beuys (p. 453); Dine (p. 439); Klein (p. 422); Oldenburg (p. 439); Rauschenberg (p. 437)

HARDBOARD See Masonite

HARD-EDGE PAINTING Abstract painting using solid areas of color with clear, sharp outlines. See Kelly

(p. 438); Morris, Robert (p. 457); Noland (p. 454); Riley (p. 436)

HATCHING Parallel lines put side by side in differing densities, used in drawing to create tone and shadow

HELLENISTIC Greek and Greek-influenced art of the 4th century to the 1st century BCE (sometimes identified as the period from the death of Alexander the Great in 323 BCE to the defeat of Antony and Cleopatra at Actium in 31 BCE).

HERM Figure with a bearded head on a column tapering from top to bottom, sometimes with a big phallus. Named after the Greek god Hermes.

HIERATIC From the Greek for "priestly." 1) Stylized conventional portrayal of a religious figure. 2) Cursive form of hieroglyphic script used by the priests in ancient Egypt.

HIGH ART Every age proposes certain subjects or styles (or both) as its own appropriate and acceptable high art—art that is very seriously intentioned and aims to express a profound intellectual and spiritual meaning. In the 18th century, this was history painting; in the 19th century, landscape painting; in the early 20th century, abstract art; in the late 20th century, Conceptual art. Whether or not the aim is achieved is another matter—sometimes the individual results never rise above banality. *See also* Conceptual art; Grand manner

HIGH RELIEF *See* Relief

HISTORICISM An obsessive interest in the past, often adopted by those unable to face the present, let alone the future

HISTORY Our relationship with the past is constantly changing. It is only recently that we have characterized the past as a series of separate epochs, removed from the present, each with its own unique values. Thus we now go to great lengths to preserve the past as a relic and call it a national heritage. Nowadays, we worship old art, antiques, and memorabilia, and officially approve of "modern" types and styles of art that look consciously different from the art of the past. In earlier times, there was perceived to be a continuum between past and present, which made history, mythology, and antiquity part of the here and now.

HISTORY PAINTING Subjects of classical mythology, history, and biblical themes. Until the end of the 19th century, any seriously ambitious painter had to succeed as a history painter or settle as an also-ran. *See also* Grand manner; High art. *See* David (p. 252); Moreau (p. 324); Poussin (pp. 180–181); Reynolds (p. 239); West (p. 256)

HOLOGRAM, HOLOGRAPH A 3-D image produced by a complex process of light from a laser striking a special photographic image. Clever, but is it any more impressive than using paint to create the illusion of space or movement on a static flat surface?

HORIZON LINE The horizontal line across a picture that is at the artist's eye level

HUDSON RIVER SCHOOL (*See* p. 290) Loosely organized group of American painters who established a new tradition for landscape painting in the United States. *See* Bierstadt (p. 292); Church (p. 290); Cole (p. 290); Moran (p. 292)

HUE Commonly described as color. Normal vision can differentiate between approximately 10 million different hues.

ICON 1) A sacred image—especially the images of Christ, the Virgin, and the saints produced for the Greek and Russian Orthodox churches. 2) A highly influential and widely admired cultural image.

ICONOCLASM The destruction of images—either literally or metaphorically

ICONOGRAPHY The language of images or language created by images—especially symbols, allegory, and so on

ICONOLOGY The study or interpretation of iconography

IDEAL That physical, intellectual, or emotional perfection that humans can never achieve. It can only be imagined or aspired to, but art can represent it. *See* Raphael (p. 134)

ILLUMINATED MANUSCRIPT A handwritten text decorated with paintings and ornaments

ILLUMINATION (*See* p. 77) The embellishment of a written text with gold, silver, or color

ILLUSIONISM Deceiving the eye into believing that what is painted is real

IMITATOR OF ... *See also* Manner of ...

IMP. Latin for "he has printed it." Appears on prints, along with the name of the printer or publisher.

IMPASTO Oil paint thickly applied (think of toothpaste). *See* Auerbach (p. 432); Rembrandt (pp. 200–201); Van Gogh (pp. 330–331)

IMPRESSION A print made by pressing a plate or block onto a piece of paper

IMPRESSIONISM (*See* pp. 312–313) The famous progressive movement that started the dethronement of Academic art. The Impressionists went back to nature with the intention of painting only what the eye could see and created small-scale works of contemporary scenes, landscapes freely and directly painted en plein air (outdoors), portrait, and still lifes. *See* Caillebotte (p. 311); Cezanne (pp. 334–335); Degas (p. 315); Manet (p. 307); Monet (p. 310); Morisot (p. 314); Pissarro (p. 314); Renoir (p. 311); Sisley (p. 314)

IMPRIMATURA A type of colored primer applied over a white background

INCUNABULA Books printed before 1500, generally illustrated with woodcuts

INDIGO A dark blue vegetable dye or color made from a tropical plant of the pea family

INDIAN INK Black ink made with carbon particles. So-called because it was originally imported from India.

INSTALLATION A work of art that integrates the exhibition space into its content. Currently the most pervasive form of official or museum art—probably for administrative and economic reasons as contemporary art usually have vast spaces to fill. It is much more economical and labor-saving for them to fill each space with one huge installation (particularly if you can persuade artists to set it up themselves) than to employ an army of people to hang, arrange (and keep a security check on) dozens of small-scale objects. *See* Barney (p. 477); Bourgeois (p. 452); Chicago (p. 462); Gober (p. 472); Hirst (p. 476); Muñoz (p. 429); Whiteread (p. 476)

INTAGLIO A design that is cut into a surface such as metal, jewel, or stone

INTENSITY The strength or brightness of a color

INTERNATIONAL GOTHIC A style of painting in favor in the late 14th and early 15th centuries. Colorful, very decorative, and rather artificial, with lots of realistic detail in costumes, animals, and landscapes. It often depicts court life. *See* p.74; Gentile da Fabriano (p. 83); Limbourg brothers (p. 77); Pisanello (p. 84); Sassetta (p. 83)

INTIMISME Small-scale, Impressionist-style pictures showing domestic interior scenes. *See* Bonnard (p. 336); Vuillard (p. 336)

IN., INV., INVENIT Latin for "he created, designed, invented it." Found on prints, along with the name of the artist who made the original design.

IRONY To convey a meaning by expressing the opposite. It is a term much used currently when commenting on contemporary art. As with "ambiguity," it is often a way of masking the fact that the commentator may have no idea about what the artist is trying to say. *See also* Ambiguity

"ISM" Shorthand way of referring to a succession of artistic movements from the late 19th century onward —Impressionism, Fauvism, Cubism, Surrealism, Expressionism, and so on.

ISOMETRIC DRAWING Technical drawing that keeps the scale of height, width, and depth constant, and does not use perspective

ITALIANATE Strictly speaking, a work of art that recalls the Italian Renaissance, but sometimes used to describe a work with an Italian character, especially a golden light. The Dutch artist Jan Both (*See* p. 212) studied in Rome and introduced the arcadian Italianate landscape to Holland.

JACOBEAN Works of art produced in England during the reign of James 1 (1603–25), and works in that style

JAPONISM (*See* p. 322) The influence of Japanese art on Western art. *See* Cassatt (p. 316); Dewing (p. 325); Gauguin (p. 329); Tobey (p. 410); Vallotton (p. 332); Whistler (p. 321)

JOURNEYMAN From the French *journée* (day). Someone employed to work by the day— perhaps a skilled worker who has completed his apprenticeship but is not yet a master craftsman

JUGENDSTIL *See* Art Nouveau

KAOLIN Fine white clay used for making porcelain

KEY A painting is in a high key if the colors are predominantly bright and light, and in a low key if dark and somber. Like major and minor keys in music.

KINETIC ART Works of art with moving parts. *See* Calder (p. 438); Gabo (p. 372)

KITCHEN SINK SCHOOL Group of British artists active in the 1950s, whose subjects were slummy interiors

KITSCH Mass-produced, decorative, popular, cheap knick-knacks, which are widely bought and condescendingly dismissed by the well educated as in bad taste, sentimental, rubbish. Art that has such characteristics or is deliberately "vulgar" or "trashy."

LACQUER Varnish made from natural resins. Tends to go yellow with age. Modern synthetic equivalents are also commonly referred to as lacquer.

LAND ART Fashioning land into a work of art. Cannot be exhibited in a museum or gallery, but photographs of Land art projects are shown. Developed in the late 1960s. *See* Long (p. 468); Smithson (p. 462); Turrell (p. 465)

LANDSCAPE A painting in which natural scenery is the principal subject and the motivating idea. Began to come into its own in the 17th century, and by the end of the 19th century replaced history painting as the main aim of any ambitious young artist. *See also* Barbizon School

LAYERS OF MEANING *See* Ambiguity

LAY FIGURE A jointed wooden model of the human figure, often life-size, which could be dressed up and used in the studio in place of a live model. Like the mannequins seen in store displays.

LAYING IN *See* Underpainting

LAYOUT Drawing or design that shows what the final appearance of a decorative scheme, ad, book cover, or newspaper page will look like.

LEAN Oil paints with a low oil content. They look spare and lack bulk, just like a lean person.

LIBERTY Italian name for Art Nouveau, so named after Liberty's store in London. *See also* Art Nouveau

LIFE CLASS A group of artists drawing or painting from a live model

LIMITED EDITION An edition of a specific number of prints, each one numbered and marked. Thus 7/50 means the 7th print out of a limited number of 50. Nowadays, sometimes used as a promotional hype or catchphrase to trap the unwary—

do you seriously believe an edition of several hundreds or even thousands is "limited?"

LIMNER Out-of-date word for an artist. Usually describes a portrait painter, and probably a painter of miniatures.

LINEAR Describes a work of art in which outlines predominate

LINEAR PERSPECTIVE *See* Perspective

LINOCUT A relief print made from a piece of linoleum. Linoleum floor covering is nice to use because it is strong but soft, and carves well and more easily than a block of wood. *See* Picasso (pp. 396–397)

LITHOGRAPHY This complicated printmaking process produces an image that looks as if it has been made with a soft or greasy crayon. Came into its own in the early 19th century. *See* Daumier (p. 307); Géricault (p. 269); Schmidt-Rottluff (p. 363)

LOCAL COLOR The actual color of an object. Local color is changed and modified by light and shade, distance, the color of nearby objects, and so on —so what you see may be rather different from the actual local color.

LOST WAX (CIRE PERDUE) A complicated method of casting sculpture. To oversimplify: make your model out of wax; encase it in a heat-resistant layer of plaster or clay; drill a hole in the plaster; heat it all up until you know the wax is melted; pour it out and fill the resulting space with bronze; let it cool; crack open the mold and there is your sculpture.

LOW RELIEF *See* Relief

LUMINISTS A group of mid-19th-century American landscape and marine painters notable for a polished realism in which all signs of brushstrokes were eliminated, and fine gradations of tone were used to produce luminous effects. The result is often one of eerie, breathless, clear stillness. Impending storms also feature. *See* Heade (p. 291); Lane (p. 291)

LUNETTE A semicircular painting, such as a half moon. Usually a decorative element over a window or door.

MAGENTA A brilliant red-purple. Named after the textile town in northern Italy.

MAHLSTICK A thick cane with a soft padded head (a bit like a drumstick). Used by painters to support an arm or wrist. The head can rest on the painting without damaging it.

MANDORLA An almond-shaped outline around the body of a holy person endowed with divine light, usually Christ

MANGA Popular Japanese comics and cartoons

MANIKIN A small lay figure. *See* Lay figure

MANNER OF … "Manner of Rembrandt" (or whoever) means that the work is in Rembrandt's style but done at a later date, by someone else. *See also* Attribution; By …; Follower of …; Studio of …

MANNERISM (*See* p. 146) The predominant style c. 1520–1600: elongated figures, artificial poses, complicated or obscure subject matter, vivid color, unreal textures, deliberate lack of harmony and proportion Seen at its best in Italy and France. *See* Bronzino (p. 148); Pontormo (p. 148)\

MAQUETTE A small clay or wax model to show what a finished full-size sculpture will look like

MARBLING A decorative effect that swirls colored paints around so that it has the same sort of quality as the patterns found in colored marble

MARINE PAINTING A seascape with a narrative action, such as a naval battle

MAROUFLAGE From the French *moroufle*, "strong glue." To pin a painted canvas to a wall or panel.

MASKING To protect one area of a work of art from what is being done to another area or to the work as a whole. Masking can be done by using protective tape or a varnish that can later be removed.

MASONITE Compressed fiberboard—a cheap alternative to canvas or panels. Called hardboard in the UK.

MASTER OF … A title given to an artist of unidentified personality, but one whose hand has been detected because a group of works are all in the same style. He is usually named after his best known work, his patron, or the region where he worked— e.g. the Master of the St. Bartholomew Altarpiece. *See* Campin (Master of Flemalle) (p. 111)

MASTERPIECE A work of art of outstanding quality. Originally it was the work that an artist had to submit to his guild to prove his ability so that he could become a master. *See also* Guild

MASTIC Gum or resin

MATTE (OR MATT) Not shiny or glossy

MEDIUM 1) (pl. media) The material worked with and manipulated to make a work of art—such as oil paint, watercolor, charcoal, or clay. 2) (pl. mediums) A liquid that can be added to paints to make them act differently (for instance, to thin them or make them dry more quickly).

MEMENTO MORI A reminder of death

METALPOINT A means of drawing using a fine needle of pure metal to make a mark on specially prepared paper. *See also* Silverpoint

METAMORPHOSIS The change of something into something else, often the transformation of a human being or god into an animal or vegetation. Ovid's great book *Metamorphoses*, in which he narrates with compelling verbal imagery stories of the Classical deities who often changed their form in order to achieve their desires, is one of the main sources of mythological imagery in art. Metamorphosis appeals to artists since the visual transformation of the known and familiar into something recognizable but beyond reality is one of art's great possibilities

METAPHOR Using a subject or object in a work of art to bring to mind one that is not actually represented

METAPHYSICAL ART Italian avant-garde art movement of the 1920s that depicted a seemingly real world, but where all the spaces, relationships, and situations are outside everyday human experience. *See* Chirico (p. 404); Morandi (p. 404)

MEZZO FRESCO Fresco painting, but onto dry plaster so that the paint is only partially absorbed. *See also* Buon fresco; Fresco

MEZZOTINT A type of print. It was used mostly in the 18th century in England for portraits and is recognizable by very rich blacks and good halftones. *See* Gainsborough (p. 240); Reynolds (p. 235)

MINIATURE A very small picture, usually a portrait, very finely painted, usually on ivory, vellum, or artboard. The term comes from the Latin "minium"—the red lead that produced the red ink used in medieval illuminated manuscripts to emphasize initial letters—it has nothing to do with the Latin *minutus*, "tiny."*See* Copley (p. 256); Hilliard (p. 161); Holbein (p. 160); Oliver (p. 161)

MINIMAL ART A type of art that first became fashionable in the 1960s, designed for gallery and museum exhibition. Usually three-dimensional, large scale, and geometric, with the slick, anonymous, precision qualities of manufactured or machinemade objects and little obvious visual significance or personal craftsmanship. The artistic significance lies in the ideas embodied but … *See also* Conceptual art. *See* André (p. 459); Flavin (p. 459); Judd (p. 257); Lewitt (p. 456); Morris, Robert (p. 457)

MISERICORD A hinged seat found in church choir stalls. Look for glorious carvings underneath.

MISERICORDIA Latin word for "mercy"

MIXED MEDIA Describes a work of art made with a variety of materials and techniques

MOBILE A hanging sculpture with shapes or solids hung from wires or strings so that they move freely. If you see them, don't be afraid to blow on them so that they move and come to life (but do not touch them). *See* Calder (p. 438)

MODELLO A small version of a large picture done to impress a patron and show what the commission will be like

MODERN ART The great flowering of Modern art occurred between 1880 and 1960, and it embraces all the avant-garde works produced at that time. It starts with Manet and the Impressionists and continues until the New York School. Three characteristics are worth mentioning: 1) A claim to break with the past—all other previous art movements emphasized their inheritance from the art of the past. 2) A defiance of all existing art institutions and the creation of works of art that were "homeless," in the sense that they belonged in no existing institution. 3) A plethora of styles and ideas. Modern artists were at their most active in those places where freedom of speech and thought was most at risk, or under threat (pp.340–343)

MONOCHROME *See* Grisaille

MONOLITH A sculpture carved or cast as a single piece

MONOTYPE A single print made by painting onto glass or metal and then transferring the image onto a piece of paper pressed over it

MONTAGE Use of cut-up, readymade photographic and printed images (such as magazine advertisements) arranged and stuck down to make a work of art. *See* Grosz (p. 385); Heartfield (p. 369)

MORBIDEZZA Italian word for "softness," used to mean soft-focus effects

MORDANT From the French verb *mordre*, "to bite." An acid that eats away at a metal plate, for example.

MOSAIC A design or picture made of small bits of stone or colored glass, or other materials. Widely used by the Greeks and Romans, and a favorite of Byzantine art.

MOTIF A recurring or dominant theme, pattern, or subject

MOUNT Works on paper are usually mounted on a piece of board and have a border between them and the frame. Good mounting and framing can bring a picture alive. In general, make the bottom border about 20 percent deeper than the others.

MULTIFACETED *See* Ambiguity

MULTIPLE Catch-all term for editioned works of art that do not belong to traditional categories such as prints, cast sculptures, or tapestries

MURAL A painting on a wall or ceiling

MUSEUM OF MODERN ART The dominant art institution of the second half of the 20th century. The first museum of modern art was MoMA, which opened in New York in 1929. They now exist all over the world and are as important and influential for contemporary art (and increasingly as dictatorial and stultifying) as the academies were in the 19th century.

NABIS Group of progressive artists working in France c. 1892–99. Believed in art for art's sake, decoration, simplification, emotion, and poetry. The name means "prophets" in Hebrew. Paul Sérusier was one of the group's founders and was much indebted to Gauguin and Bernard. *See* Bonnard (p. 336); Denis (p. 325); Sérusier (p. 332); Vallotton (p. 332); Vuillard (p. 336)

NAÏVE ART Art that looks as if it is done by someone who has had no professional training—with childish subject matter, bright local colors, strange perspective, and unsophisticated enthusiasm. Can be genuine, but can be a consciously adopted pose—and it is not always easy to tell which is which. One is genuine and heartfelt, the other is artificial play-acting. Douanier Rousseau, a retired customs official, was one of the genuine. *See* Grandma Moses (p. 408); Rousseau (Le Douanier) (p. 332) (both genuine)

NARCISSISM Triumphant bourgeois capitalism invariably produces an art that is obsessed with its own way of life, image, and material prosperity (true for 15th-century Netherlands, 17th-century Holland, Second Empire France, and Victorian England; at no time more true than today). Extravagant contemporary claims are also made for the quality and significance of the art (capitalist success is very dependent on convincing marketing).

NARRATIVE ART Art that tells a story. Hogarth's narrative pictures, which he called "modern moral subjects," depicting the follies of human behavior, show how a good story never fails to appeal.

NATIONAL ACADEMY OF DESIGN Founded in New York in 1825, to be the American equivalent of the Royal Academy in London

NATURALISM The representation of nature with the least possible formal distortion or subjective interpretation

NATURE MORTE French for "still life"

NAVICELLA A representation of the story of Christ walking on the water

NAZARENES (*See* p. 273) Group of progressive young Germans who formed a group in 1809 to revive the spirit and techniques of early Christian and Renaissance art

NEGATIVE SPACE The space between objects. In a painting or sculpture, it can have as much significance or shape as the objects represented and can be manipulated and colored. Of great importance to artists, but often unnoticed or ignored by those looking at works of art (if you have difficulty seeing negative spaces, try turning the work upside down and then looking at them). *See* Whiteread (p. 476)

NEOCLASSICISM The predominant fashionable style from about 1770 to 1830, emphasizing the spirit and appearance of Classical Greece and Rome. Tends to be severe, authoritative, didactic, well made, and architectural (prefers straight lines). Succeeds best in architecture, furniture, and sculpture; seen at its finest in England (the Adam style) and France (Louis XVI style). *See* p. 258–261; Canova (p. 254); David (p. 252); Hamilton (p. 241); Houdon (p. 252); Mengs (p. 249); Vien (p. 252)

NEOEXPRESSIONISM A type of large-scale painting, fashionable in the 1970s, made in an aggressively raw and Expressionist manner with surfaces heavily laden with paint and sometimes including objects, like smashed earthenware. Lays claims to portentous or doom-laden subject matter. *See* Baselitz (p. 461); Clemente (p. 469); Kiefer (p. 467); Schnabel (p. 469)

NEO-IMPRESSIONISM Impressionist subject matter painted through the strict application of the scientific color theories of Divisionism. *See also* Divisionism. *See* Seurat (p. 320); Signac (p. 320)

NEOPLASTICISM The philosophy of De Stijl. *See* Stijl, De

NEO-ROMANTICISM British painting of the 1930s, 1940s, and 1950s that gave a modern interpretation to the romantic and visionary landscape tradition that stemmed from Blake and Palmer. *See* Sutherland (p. 401); Piper (p. 401)

NEUE SACHLICHKEIT German, meaning "New Objectivity." A stern, precise, and detailed style often socially critical in content, fashionable in Germany in the 1920s. *See* Dix (p. 385); Grosz (p. 385); Schad (p. 385)

NEW ENGLISH ART CLUB Founded in Britain in 1886 as a progressive anti-academic group committed to spontaneity and plein-air painting. *See* Sargent (p. 326); Sickert (p. 326)

NEW OBJECTIVITY *See* Neue Sachlichkeit

NEW REALISM Term applied to a diverse group of European artists working in the 1960s who used disposable everyday materials to create unusual-looking works with obscure but vaguely symbolic or mystical meanings. *See* Arman (p. 421); Christo & Jeanne-Claude (p. 460); Klein (p. 421)

NEW YORK SCHOOL *See* Abstract Expressionism

NONOBJECTIVE ART *See* Abstract art

NORWICH SCHOOL (*See* p. 276) Important group of landscape and seascape painters based in Norfolk, England c. 1805–25. Inspired by the flat Norfolk landscape, with big skies, and by the Dutch masters. They were brilliant water colorists. "Old Crome" was the School's principal founder.

NUDE, NUDITY The unclothed human body. As man is God's highest creation, painting and sculpting the nude has traditionally been the highest aspiration for art. Nudity implies dignity; nakedness implies shame.

OBJET D'ART Small decorative objects such as snuff boxes, scent bottles, and figurines

OBJET TROUVÉ An object found by chance (such as a piece of wood or even a bicycle wheel), which an artist uses or displays for its aesthetic merit. *See* Duchamp (p. 367); Nash (p. 398); Schwitters (p. 368)

OCHER A pigment made from clay. Ranges from pale yellow to reddish brown depending on the clay. The stuff you buy in tubes is a kind of dirty yellow.

ODALISQUE From the Turkish word *odalik* (*oda* = chamber; *lik* = function). An Asian female slave, usually half-naked and reclining. Ingres and Matisse both favored the subject. Ingres's celebrated *Grande Odalisque* annoyed the public and the critics because they thought the anatomy was wrong. *See* Ingres (p. 264); Matisse (pp. 344–345)

OEUVRE An artist's entire output

OIL The principal oil used in painting is linseed oil, which is made from flax seeds. It is slow-drying (can take days or weeks) and can go yellow with age. Poppy oil is also widely used.

OIL PAINT, OILS Oil painting, in the sense known today, developed in the 15th century and became the dominant type of painting in the 16th and 17th centuries. Among the advantages of oil paints are their flexibility, versatility, portability, strength, and rich appearance, and the fact that they are most pleasurable to work with. Oil paints are made by mixing powdered pigments with oil.

OLD MASTER Strictly speaking describes any artist from the early Renaissance to roughly the mid-19th century. Popularly speaking describes any such artist whose reputation has stood the test of time, although reassessments and rediscoveries do occur. For example Vermeer was rediscovered at the end of the 19th century. Georges de La Tour is currently being reassessed.

OLEOGRAPH A special type of print made on a textured surface that deliberately imitates the look of an oil painting

OMEGA WORKSHOPS An avant-garde British enterprise (c. 1913–15) that produced modern furniture, pots, screens, and so on. A brave attempt, but the products were often rather shoddy. *See* Lewis, (Percy) Wyndham (p. 376)

OMP 1) Old master picture. 2) Ordinary member of the public.

OP ART (ABBREV. OF OPTICAL ART) A type of abstract art that was at the forefront in the 1960s. Typified by hard-edge paintings, often in black and white, which bombard the eyes and cause them to "see" colors or shapes that are not actually there. Can be disorientating and exhausting to look at. Suited to psychedelic experiences and bright lifestyles of the 1960s. *See* Vasarely (p. 436)

OPTICAL MIXTURE *See* Divisionism

ORGANIC What is usually meant is that everything in a work of art hangs together, with nothing extraneous or irritatingly out of place

ORIGINAL PRINT A print where the artist originates the image to be printed—not a reproduction of an already existing painting

ORPHISM An early Parisian-based abstract art movement in which loosely painted areas of rainbow colors were the dominant theme. *See* Delaunay (p. 354); Kupka (p. 353)

ORPIMENT Brilliant lemon-yellow pigment. Poisonous.

ORTHOGONAL A line that works as perspective, apparently leading the eye from the surface of the picture toward its vanishing point

OVERPAINTING Layers of paint applied over the initial layers once they have dried, so that the layers don't mix

PAINT Paint consists of coloring matter dispersed in a binder. There are many types of coloring matter and binders, which produce anything from watercolors to oil paints.

PAINTERLY A picture painted in a painterly manner is one in which the artist has deliberately used the physical properties of paint. Thus, for oils, it might be intensity or subtlety of color, thick impasto, and juicy swirls; for watercolor, it might be transparency and washes. *See also* Handling

PALETTE 1) The flat surface on which artists lay out and mix their paints. Traditionally, it is oval in shape with a hole for the thumb. 2) The term also refers to the range of colors that an artist uses. Most artists establish a preferred and limited range, which they get to know well and which is very recognizable: for example, Monet used rainbow colors, Rembrandt used earth colors.

PALETTE KNIFE A knife with a blunt, flexible blade used for mixing paint and for scraping paint off, or spreading it on, a canvas

PALLADIAN Gutsy Classical style influenced by, or imitating the architecture of, the Venetian Andrea Palladio (1508–80). Much in fashion in Britain in the first half of the 18th century.

PANEL A firm support (such as wood, board, or metal) on which a picture is painted. Canvas, even when tightly stretched, is not firm.

PANORAMA A scene or landscape painted on a cylindrical surface. The viewer stands in the middle with a 360-degree view and hopes to have the illusion of a real open-air view.

PANTOGRAPH A simple tool for enlarging or reducing drawings in size by tracing their outline. It looks like four rulers hinged together.

PAPER First made in China 100 CE and in the West in the 13th century. Paper is made from cellulose fibers, beaten to a pulp, and spread out in a thin film and dried. The best paper is still made from linen rag. Cheap paper is made from wood pulp and soon discolors and goes brown (like newspaper).

PAPIER COLLÉ French for "pasted paper." Pieces of paper prepared by the artist—not newspaper cuttings or similar, as used in collage—stuck down and incorporated into a painting. *See also* Collage. *See* Braque (p. 351); Gris (p. 351); Matisse (pp. 344–345)

PAPIER MÂCHÉ French, lit. "chewed paper." Shredded paper mixed with a flour-and-water paste to form a pulp that can be shaped into 3-D objects. These are lightweight but firm when the mixture dries.

PARADIGM Example or pattern

PARCHMENT The skin of an animal prepared as a material for writing or painting. Parchment is usually sheep or goat; vellum is cow.

PARQUET Thin wooden strips attached to the back of a warped wooden panel to straighten and strengthen it. Not used now, as current wisdom is that it does more harm than good.

PASSAGE A small but distinctive part of a work of art

PASTEBOARD A stiff support made by pasting layers of paper together

PASTEL Powdered pigment mixed with gum or resin. It is applied directly on paper and then often smudged and softened with the fingers, producing soft, chalky tones. Fragile and easily damaged. *See* Carriera (p. 229); Degas (p. 315)

PASTICHE A work of art created in the manner of a specific artist, not a copy of a known work

PASTORAL A scene portraying the life of shepherds and country people in an idealized way. The general atmosphere is usually sunny, fertile, peaceful, innocent, and carefree. The French painter Claude Lorrain originated the pastoral landscape in the mid-17th century.

PATINA The mellow tone and slightly worn look that surfaces acquire with age, especially metal and wood. Usually considered to be attractive.

PATRON Somebody who commissions works of art from living artists—and so often influences the content or appearance of the work.

PEDESTAL The base on which a statue is placed

PENDANT A painting designed to make a pair with, or companion to, another

PENSIERO Italian for "thought." A preliminary drawing or sketch.

PENTIMENTO Italian for "repentance." A mark or alteration made during the creation of a painting that is subsequently painted over but that can be seen or detected, maybe as a ridge in the paint, maybe because the top surface becomes transparent with age, or perhaps through infrared photography or X-rays.

PERCEPTUAL ART Any art that places importance on engaging the eye by the visual appearance and visual interest of a work. Conceptual art is more concerned with ideas than with engaging the eye.

PERFORMANCE ART The 1970s follow-on to 1960s "happenings;" same sort of thing but more structured, theatrical, and sometimes even scripted. There is still a lot of it around. *See* Beuys (p. 453); Hatoum (p. 470); Klein (p. 422); Morris, Robert (p. 457); Nauman (p. 464)

PERSPECTIVE The basic rules of linear or geometric perspective were established in the Renaissance and are: a fixed, single viewpoint with lines that meet at a vanishing point, so creating the illusion of 3-D space on a flat surface. *See* Angelico (p. 89); Bellotto (p. 236); Canaletto (p. 235); Christus (p. 115); Estes (p. 458); Piero della Francesca (p. 100); Uccello (p. 92)

PHALANX Influential group of Munich artists, led by Kandinsky in 1901, who were opposed to the old-fashioned Academy and all conservative views, and who organized exhibitions and ran a Modern art school. *See* Kirchner (p. 362); Kandinsky (p. 364); Münter (p. 364)

PHILISTINE Somebody with a complete lack of interest in art or culture of any sort

PHOTOGRAPHY The invention of photography had a profound impact on artists, and at once raised a host of practical and aesthetic issues: for example, hack portrait painters were put out of business. Progressive artists such as Degas openly welcomed photography's influence and uses; others used it and pretended they had not. Some tried to rival its meticulous accuracy; others sought to record sensations beyond the reach of photography (Impressionists). Whether photography was "proper art" was hotly debated (and still is by some)—Ingres said it could never be. The earliest surviving photograph was taken in France in 1827. Daguerre established it as a serious medium in 1837. *See* Degas (p. 315); Ingres (p. 264)

PHOTOGRAVURE A commercial printing process invented in the 19th century

PHOTOMONTAGE A technique of cutting up photographs, newspaper pieces, or advertisements and combining them with drawings and lettering to produce striking, provocative, or illogical images. The German artist John Heartfield produced powerful work commenting on the turmoil and ideological struggles in Germany and Eastern Europe between the two World Wars. *See* Ernst (p. 369); Grosz (p. 385); Heartfield (p. 369)

PHOTOREALISM Paintings that look like large, color photographs but are in fact meticulously executed paintings. They often take shiny, reflecting surfaces as their motif. Became a popular style in the 1970s. *See* Estes (p. 458)

PICTOGRAPH, PICTOGRAM A pictorial symbol representing an object or idea. Road signs are a good example; so are hieroglyphs.

PICTURE PLANE When a picture acts as a window onto a real or imaginary world, the picture plane is the equivalent of the sheet of glass that divides the spectator's world from the world of the picture

PICTURESQUE Today it means little more than attractive or charming. In the 18th century, it embraced serious ideas about what was beautiful in nature, usually involving irregularity, informality, and a bit of wildness. These notions had considerable influence on 18th-century English landscape design.

PIGMENT The coloring matter in paint. It does not dissolve in the liquid that carries it, such as oil or water. Coloring matter that does dissolve is called a stain or dye.

P., PINX., PINXIT Latin for "he/she has painted it." Found on prints to show who painted the original picture that has been copied in the print.

PLAQUETTE A small cast metal relief, or replica, of a small work of art, usually in bronze or lead, which is applied as decoration to another object such as a piece of furniture or stone vase. Can be made in multiple copies. The sculptural equivalent of a print.

PLASTIC ARTS Strictly speaking, only those arts that involve molding and modeling (such as sculpture made from clay). In practice, it often refers to all the visual arts.

PLASTICITY 1) Any material that is pliable, stretchable, and durable, so that it can be modeled and molded, has plasticity. 2) A drawing is said to have plasticity if it gives a convincing illusion of a 3-D form.

PLATE MARK In printmaking, the indentation left on a sheet of paper by the pressure of a metal plate or wooden block carrying the print design

PLEIN AIR (*See* p. 305) A painting begun and completed in the open air, or one that conveys the qualities and sensations of open-air painting. Boudin's plein-air spontaneity was genuine and greatly influenced the young Monet. *See* Boudin (p. 304); Constable (p. 277); Corinth (p. 337); Corot (p. 304); Landseer (p. 288); Monet (p. 310); Rousseau, Théodore (p. 304); Sargent (p. 326); Zorn (p. 327)

POCHADE A small oil sketch made outdoors in one sitting. *See* Bonington (p. 268); Constable (p. 277); Corot (p. 304)

POINTILLISM Divisionism as practiced by Seurat, Signac, and Camille Pissarro. *See also* Divisionism

POINTING MACHINE A machine perfected in the 19th century that enabled the dimensions of a small 3-D model (sometimes made by the sculptor) to be mechanically transferred to a larger block of stone so that an exact but bigger version could be carved, either by the sculptor or by someone else. *See* Rodin (p. 318)

POLYCHROME Many colored. Used especially in reference to painted sculpture.

POLYMER PAINTS Similar to acrylics

POLYPTYCH An altarpiece made of more than three panels that are hinged together

POP ART (*See* p. 440) Predominant movement of the 1950s and 1960s, especially in the US and UK. Played around with the popular fetishes of the consumer society (such as advertisements, comics, and well-known brand images like Coca-Cola). Often used quick and inexpensive commercial art techniques. The US version used exclusively contemporary imagery; the UK version carries a heavy dose of nostalgia and whimsy. *See* Blake, Sir Peter (p. 446); Caulfield (p. 446); Indiana (p. 445); Johns (p. 442); Jones (p. 446); Lichtenstein (p. 441); Rosenquist (p. 445); Warhol (p. 444)

POPPY OIL An oil extracted from poppy seeds. Similar to linseed oil, but thicker, and even slower to dry. *See also* Oil

PORTFOLIO A case, usually big and flat, for carrying works of art on paper

PORTRAIT A likeness of a person or an animal. What is like, and what is not, is of course where the arguments begin.

POSTER PAINT Inexpensive, brightly colored gouache. *See* Gouache

POST-HUMAN The buzz phrase to describe subjects that focus on media or consumer obsessions and new technology (such as computers, genetic engineering), and their influence on the human body.

POST-IMPRESSIONISM (*See* p. 328) Catchy phrase that doesn't mean very much, except that it includes all the more or less progressive artists from about 1885 to 1905. Can be used as widely or as narrowly as you please. The four principal Post-Impressionists, who did indeed start with Impressionism and then sought to develop a more formal or symbolic style, are Cézanne (pp. 334–335); Gauguin (p. 329); Seurat (p. 320); and Van Gogh (pp. 330–331)

POST-MODERNISM The triumph of style over substance. Art and architecture (but literally anything or anyone in fashion, politics, music, literature—you name it) of the 1980s and 1990s and now, with nothing much to say of real substance or meaning (although it might be claimed otherwise), presented in a very cool, self-conscious, stylish (and overdesigned?) manner. Not art for art's sake, but style for style's sake. "Branding" and designer clothes are very post-modern, as are many dot.com companies and many Internet websites.

POST-PAINTERLY ABSTRACTION Cult term for American large-scale, colorful, simple-design abstract painting in the 1960s, either hard-edge, or loose, or lyrical. *See* Kelly (p. 438); Louis (p. 437); Noland (p. 454); Olitski (p. 453); Stella (p. 460)

POTBOILER A work of art produced merely to earn the necessities of life—or in the case of the already successful, just to make money

POUNCING Pricking small holes in the drawn outlines of a cartoon. You can then transfer the design to another surface by sprinkling the cartoon with fine soot so that it falls through the holes and leaves a mark.

PRECISIONISTS Group of American artists prominent in the 1920s and 1930s whose theme was modern industry and urban landscapes, portrayed in an idealized and romantic way with acute observation and a smooth, precise technique. *See* Demuth (p. 407); Sheeler (p. 407)

PREDELLA In an altarpiece, the strip of small-size paintings set in the frame at the bottom of the main painting. They are usually narrative scenes related to the subject of the main painting.

PRE-RAPHAELITES (*See* p. 297) Small and influential group of young British artists who came together in 1848 and aimed to challenge conventional views by championing the artists who came before Raphael. *See* Hunt (p. 298); Millais (p. 298); Rossetti (p. 296); Ruskin (p. 296)

PRIMARY COLORS Red, yellow, and blue. In theory, all other colors can be made from them—but colored pigments and colored lights can and do behave differently.

PRIMER A primer is applied to a support to isolate the support from the ground and the final paint surface. Without a primer, raw canvas or raw wood would simply absorb the paint and/or react chemically with it, thereby making the artist's task impossible or even destroying the work—unless, of course, the artist wants the effect of the paint being absorbed by (therefore staining) raw canvas or wood. *See also* Ground; Sinking in; Support

PRIMITIVE ART Old-fashioned and politically incorrect way of describing the early or traditional art of societies, such as African tribes and the Inuits. In fact, most of it is highly sophisticated, if properly understood. *See also* Naïve art

PRINT The image made by pressing an inked or painted surface onto a piece of paper

PROBLEMATIC Useful word and concept currently much used by critics and commentators, especially in the United States. Can mean there is a genuine problem that is worth discussing. More often it is a polite and coded way of saying "meaningless." If you find a work of art or someone's point of view incomprehensible or futile, don't admit defeat or tell the truth. Look serious and describe it as "problematic."

PROFIL PERDU French, lit. "lost profile." A head that is turned away so that the back of the head, along with the outline of the cheek and chin, can be seen—the rest of the profile being lost from view.

PROOF A trial print. It allows the artist and the printmaker to see what is happening. They can then make adjustments before arriving at the final version from which the print run will be made.

PROVENANCE The pedigree of a work of art—a list of who owned it and when

PURE COLOR Color used straight from the tube without mixing

PURISM Fashionable Parisian art movement of the 1920s. Used Cubist ideas to produce figurative art (lots of still lifes) that was supposedly pure in design, form, and color. Most of it was rather boring and forgettable.

PVA Polyvinyl acetate: manmade resin used as a paint medium and in varnishes and adhesives

QUADRATURA A painting on a ceiling or wall that gives the illusion of extending the real space of a room. Often includes illusionistic details or extensions of the architecture, such as columns.

QUADRA RIPORTATO Italian, lit. "carried picture." A picture painted on a ceiling to look as if it were an easel painting hung overhead.

QUATTROCENTO Italian for "15th century" (1400–99)

RA Full member of the Royal Academy, London. There are 40 at any one time; they have to give the Royal Academy a work that they have produced. *See also* Royal Academy

RAYONISM Avant-garde Russian movement c. 1913, which came near to abstraction, whose subject was light and rays of light. *See* Goncharova (p. 370); Larionov (p. 370)

READY-MADE A mass produced object taken by an artist and turned into his/her own "creation" by the addition of a signature or some other small alteration. The most famous ready-made is Duchamp's urinal, which he called *Fountain* (*See* p. 367) and exhibited as a work of art in 1917. *See also* Objet trouvé

REALISM (*See* pp. 300–301) 1) Every generation seems to define realism in its own way. For example, Renaissance artists thought their art was real because they opened a "window on the world," showing 3-D space and human emotion with an accuracy and intensity not seen before. On the other hand, some modern abstract painters thought they were more real by showing the reality that a picture is just paint on a flat surface. At the moment, some contemporary artists regard themselves as realists because they confront current social, green, or gender issues … and so on. 2) Realism with a capital "R" was the progressive movement in art and literature in the mid-19th century (especially in France) that was concerned with social realities and showing fact rather than ideals and aesthetics. The early novels of Zola are a good example. *See* Courbet (p. 306)

RECESSION The illusion of depth in a picture. *See also* Aerial perspective; Perspective

RED CHALK *See* Sanguine

REFORMATION Sixteenth-century religious movement that sought to modify Roman Catholic doctrine and practice. It led directly to the establishment of the Protestant churches.

REGENCY *See* Empire style

REGIONALISM American movement of the 1930s that was the first expression of a consciously independent American art. Its vision was of a real American art, springing from American soil and seeking to interpret American life. *See* Benton (p. 409); Wood (p. 406)

RELIEF From the Italian *rilevare*, "to raise." Sculpture carved from a flat or curved surface so that part of the image projects. If the image projects slightly, it is known as bas relief (low relief). If it projects more boldly, it is known as alto rilievo (high relief).

RELIEF PRINT A print made from a block or plate in which the area not to be printed is cut away, leaving the part to be inked standing in relief. *See also* Wood engraving; Woodcut

RELINING The process by which a damaged canvas is stuck down on a new one

REMARQUE PROOF A trial print on which an artist has written or drawn instructions as notes for what to do next. *See also* Proof

RENAISSANCE (*See* pp. 86–87; pp. 108–109; pp. 138–139). French, lit. "rebirth." The flowering of new ideas in Italian art between 1300 and 1550, which has influenced the subsequent development of all Western art. The three key ideas that developed during the Renaissance with increasing sophistication were: 1) The work of art as a window on the world— the illusion of looking at space, light, the human figure, or landscape. 2) Man as the measure of all things—human scale, proportion, emotion, ideals, or spirituality as the central theme and yardstick for art. 3) Reverence for Christianity, the Bible, and Classical antiquity—the interpretation of the Christian message by illustrating the Old and New Testaments, and the adaptation and use of Classical (Greek and Roman) ideas, literature, and images.

REPLICA In art-collecting terminology, a copy of a picture or sculpture made by the artist himself

REPOUSSOIR From the French *repousser*, "to push back." A figure or object in a painting that directs the eye to the main point of interest. Same as *coulisse*. *See* Coulisse

REPRESENTATIONAL ART Art that depicts recognizable objects and figures, although they may not necessarily be true to life

REPRODUCTION A copy of a picture or print made by mechanical means, such as photography

REREDOS The decorated screen behind an altar. It is usually sculpted, sometimes painted, and can take the form of a tapestry or hanging or decorative metalwork.

RESIN The main ingredient of varnish. Natural resins come from trees and plants.

RESIST Something applied to a surface to prevent the penetration of liquids. Usually a varnish, or a similar coating, or masking tape.

RESTORATION Repairing a work of art that has become damaged through accident, decay, or neglect. The ethics of restoration are as complicated as medical ethics. How much transplanting, patching-up, and cleaning can occur before the object dies aesthetically or becomes unrecognizable? Best motto: if in doubt, leave well alone, because once it is dead or ruined, there is nothing you can do. A terrifying number of paintings have been ruined by over-cleaning in the last 50 years, and as yet no one has properly faced up to the fact. The *Mona Lisa* had eyebrows—until an unwise early restorer accidentally removed them.

RETABLE An altarpiece of one or more fixed (not hinged) framed panels

RETARDANT A medium that slows down the rate at which paint dries

RETARDATAIRE From the French *retard*, "delay." Not up to date.

RETINAL PAINTING Another name for Op art. *See* Op art

RETOUCHING Repainting very small areas of a picture that have become damaged

RETRO An object made with current-day materials or technology. Its external appearance is stylized to make it appear as an authentic product of another era (especially the 1930s or 1940s); for instance, a transistor radio in a case that makes it look to be a 1930s wireless.

RETROSPECTIVE An exhibition that shows a comprehensive selection of an artist's works covering his or her whole life, or a particular period. Can make or break the artist's reputation or spirit: works that are incomprehensible or neglected when seen in isolation can blossom when seen in their full context; works that looked wonderful on their own can suddenly seem boringly repetitive when shown together. Picasso would not allow retrospectives, arguing that the only thing that mattered was what he was doing now.

ROCAILLE A decorative motif using shells and rocks, or shell-like swirls and curls

ROCOCO (*See* pp. 226–227) The predominant style of the first half of the 18th century. Look for curves, pretty colors, playfulness, youth, elegance, fine craftsmanship, extravagance, carefree attitudes, and references to real and fanciful nature (flowers, leaves, rocks, birds, monkeys, or dragons). *See* Boucher (p. 224); Gainsborough (p. 240); Guardi; (p. 236) Tiepolo (p. 230); Watteau (pp. 222–223)

ROMANESQUE The main style of Christian Europe in the 11th and 12th centuries, seen mostly in architecture and recognizable by thick walls, small windows, and rounded arches. Look also for wall paintings, tapestries (such as the Bayeux tapestry), stained glass, and illuminated manuscripts.

ROMANISTS A group of Flemish painters who went to Italy in the early 16th century and were influenced by the contemporary Italian art they saw there. *See* Gossaert (p. 116)

ROMANTICISM (*See* pp. 266–267) The movement in art, music, and literature in the late-18th and early 19th centuries that produced some of the greatest and best-loved works of art of all time. The Romantics believed in new experiences, individuality, innovation, risk-taking, heroism, freedom of imagination, love, and living life to the full. *See* Constable (p. 277); Delacroix (p. 268); Friedrich (p. 272); Géricault (p. 269); Turner (p. 281)

ROYAL ACADEMY Prestigious organization founded in London in 1768 to promote high standards in art, to run an art school, and to exhibit work by artists, both living and dead. Very successful in promoting British art in the 18th and 19th centuries. Privately funded, and therefore never an instrument of state control. In the 20th century, it gained (rightly) a reputation for stuffiness and for being anti-modern, but it is now becoming more up to date. *See* Reynolds (p. 239)

SACRA CONVERSAZIONE The Madonna and Child surrounded by saints. They are all in a single space and aware of each other though not necessarily communicating with each other. Much exploited in Venetian Renaissance art. *See* Mantegna (p. 107); Bellini (103); Angelico (p. 89); Filippo Lippi (p. 88)

SALON The French official annual public art exhibition, controlled by the Académie. Immensely influential, especially in the 19th century, when it was the bastion of conservative attitudes. *See also* Academies; Impressionism

SALON D'AUTOMNE Annual autumn exhibition of contemporary art in Paris. Much used by early pioneers of Modern art as a means of showing their work. *See* Bonnard (p. 336); Marquet (p. 347); Matisse (pp. 344–345); Rouault (p. 354)

SALON DES INDÉPÉNDANTS Annual spring show of contemporary art in Paris. It is open to all newcomers, with no selection by a jury. Much used by early pioneers of Modern art as a means of getting their work seen by the public. *See* Matisse (pp. 344–345); Redon (p. 324); Seurat (p. 320); Signac (p. 320)

SALON DES REFUSÉS The exhibition held in Paris in 1863 that showed work by artists who had been turned down by the official Salon. One of the key events in late-l9th-century art. *See* Cézanne (pp. 334–335); Courbet (p. 306); Fantin-Latour (p. 302); Manet (p. 307); Pissarro (p. 314); Whistler (p. 321)

SANGUINE Red chalk. Used finely it can produce exquisite small drawings. Michelangelo achieved a mastery of the medium, which was not seen again until the early 18th century, in France. *See* Michelangelo (p. 136); Rubens (p. 191); Watteau (pp. 222–223)

SARCOPHAGUS Stone coffin (Roman, Egyptian, etc.), often decorated with relief sculpture

SATURATION The degree of intensity of a color

SCHEMA A very basic diagrammatic drawing, such as an egg shape to indicate a head

SCHOOL Group of artists whose work shows some similarities. A useful, but often very imprecise, term.

SCHOOL OF BOLOGNA (*See* p. 166). Term encompassing 16th-century artists working in Bologna, fusing Venetian and Florentine influences into a distinctive Bolognese style. *See* Carracci (p. 167); Domenichino (p. 168); Guercino (p. 172); Reni (p. 166)

SCHOOL OF FONTAINEBLEAU (*See* p. 153) Group of 16th-century Italian, French, and Flemish painters who decorated the Palace of Fontainebleau for Henri IV. *See* Abbate (p. 154)

SCHOOL OF PARIS (*See* p. 357) A useful term embracing the various artists, schools, and movements who pioneered new ideas in Paris in the first half of the 20th century

SCOTTISH COLORISTS Four progressive Scottish painters—Cadell, Fergusson, Hunter, and Peploe—who were active before 1914, producing high-quality work in bright colors with simplified stylization that was much influenced by French Fauvism. Peploe spent several years in Paris, and was among the first to put modern French ideas into practice in Britain.

SCULP. , SCULPSIT, SC., SCULPEBAT Latin for "he cut it" or "he carved it." Found on prints to indicate the name of the person who made the plate or block. Sometimes found on sculpture to indicate an original carving, not a cast.

SCULPTURE Three-dimensional work of art made by carving, modeling, or constructing. Like a picture, it has no useful function in itself.

SCUMBLE A thin layer of oil paint dragged over a bottom layer of paint in such a way that the scumble breaks up, allowing the bottom layer to show through

SEASCAPE A picture that takes the sea as its subject. If the subject is ships, it is called a marine painting.

SECESSION (*See* p. 338) Groups of progressive German and Austrian artists who challenged the ideas and authority of the academies in the 1890s. In Vienna, Gustav Klimt, a leading member of the Secession, explored the themes of love and sexuality that obsessed both the conservatives and the radical modernizers.

SECONDARY COLORS The colors produced by mixing primary colors: blue + yellow = green; yellow + red = orange; blue + red = purple

SECULAR Belonging to the everyday world, not to the spiritual or religious world

SEICENTO Italian for "17th century" (1600–99)

SEMANTICS The study of the meaning of words

SEMIOTICS The study and interpretation of signs and the way they signal an underlying state of affairs, attitudes, observations, ideas, and actions. A simple example is the way we all understand and react to the convention that a red traffic light means stop and a green one go.

SEPIA Brown pigment used for ink and watercolor. It comes from an octopus or cuttlefish and fades easily.

SERIGRAPHY General term for the art of silkscreen printing. *See* Silkscreen printing

SETTECENTO Italian for "18th century" (1700–99)

SFUMATO Soft outlines and a smooth, smoky transition between areas of color. *See* Leonardo (pp. 132–133)

SGRAFFITO *See* Graffiti

SICCATIVE 1) Adjective; means that it will dry—linseed oil is siccative, olive oil is not. 2) Noun; means a drying agent—something added to oil to speed up the rate at which it dries.

SIGNIFICANT FORM The idea that beauty in a work of art lies solely in color, composition, and line. It was influential in early 20th-century English art and helped to develop abstract art.

SILHOUETTE Black paper cutout of the profile of a face, invented by a French Minister of finance called M. de Silhouette in the 18th century

SILKSCREEN PRINTING (OR SERIGRAPHY) A printmaking method in which ink or paint is squeezed through a fine mesh screen, usually made of silk, on which the design has been made. Invented c. 1900 and used widely by modern artists, especially those with an eye for bold designs and bright colors. *See* Warhol (p. 444)

SILVERPOINT A method of drawing using an

instrument with a fine silver tip, which makes a fine gray line on specially prepared paper. *See* Dürer (pp. 126–127); Leonardo (pp. 132–133)

SIMILE In art, more or less the same as metaphor and allegory. *See* Allegory

SIMULACRUM An illusionary image that is so effective that it supplants reality.

SIMULTANEOUS CONTRAST The effect whereby if you project a white light onto a screen already illuminated with a light in one of the primary colors, the white light will appear in that color's complementary color. For instance, if you project a white light onto a screen already illuminated with a blue light, the white light will appear orange.

SINKING IN This happens when oil is absorbed from paints into the ground—the canvas, for instance. It leaves the paint looking dry and dull.

SINOPIA (PL. SINOPIE) The underdrawing for a fresco; it is usually made in red ocher

SIZE Gelatine or animal skin glue—when melted and made into a solution it can be painted onto a surface to make it waterproof and suitable for painting on. *See also* Distemper

SKETCH A rapidly executed work in any medium. Used by artists to sort out general ideas for a painting (or sculpture), or to note the essential features of it. *See* Constable (p. 277)

SOCIAL REALISM Describes works of art showing every day life—often its harsher aspects. In the 19th-century, social realist pictures showed the laboring classes, prostitutes, sickness, death, or adultery painted in photographic detail. Today, they are conceptual works addressing such issues as AIDS, gender, race, feminism, sexuality, anxiety, and loneliness. In the 1850s and 1860s, Ford Madox Brown addressed the issues of forced emigration from the UK, inspired by the departure for Australia of his sculptor friend, Thomas Woolner. *See also* YBAs

SOCIALIST REALISM The official art of the Communist dictatorship of the Soviet Union, mostly heroic portrayals of the Party faithful and ardent workers. Copied in other hard-line communist countries, such as Mao's China and Castro's Cuba.

SOFT-GROUND ETCHING A type of etching producing an effect that looks like a pencil or chalk drawing. Complex technique and rare. *See* Etching

SOFT SCULPTURE Sculpture made from soft materials such as cloth, fur, or felt

SOPRA PORTE From the Italian, lit. "over the doors." Paintings made to go in the space above doorways—often landscapes or still lifes.

SOTTO IN SU Latin for "from below upward"— an illusionistic effect so that when you look up at figures painted on a ceiling, they appear to float in space. *See* Correggio (p. 150); Mantegna (p. 107); Tiepolo (p. 230); Veronese (p. 142)

SOVIET REALISM *See* Socialist Realism

SPATTER Paint flicked off the end of a brush

SPREZZATURA From the Italian, meaning "nonchalance," "ease." The ability to do things with speed and ease.

SQUARING UP A reliable way of transferring a drawing accurately onto a larger surface. You draw a grid of squares over the drawing and an equivalent grid with the same number of squares over the larger surface. Copy the contents of each square of the drawing into the equivalent square on the larger—and, presto, it works. *See* Robinson (p. 317); Sickert (p. 326)

SQUEEGEE A rubber blade or roller used for pressing the ink through a silkscreen to make prints. *See also* Silkscreen

ST. IVES GROUP (*See* p. 400) Group of British artists working in St. Ives, in Cornwall, England, in the 1940s, 1950s, and 1960s. See Frost (p. 430); Hepworth (p. 400); Heron (p. 431); Moore (p. 399); Nicholson (p. 400)

STAFFAGE People or animals in a landscape that are incidental to the general theme or view but add scale or a bit of human interest, act as repoussoir, or help the perspective. *See also* Repoussoir

STATE When working on a print, artists will often take an impression to see what is happening and help them decide what to do next. Each such impression is called a "state" and may carry a number. Dedicated print collectors love them because they are rare and show how the artist arrived at the final state, which is the one that is printed in quantity.

STEEL ENGRAVING An engraved or etched copper plate that has been faced with steel by electroplating to make it harder and therefore able to produce more impressions. Some of the softness and subtlety of the image is lost in the process.

STIJL, DE (*See* p. 389) Dutch for "the style." The most influential avant-garde art magazine in the 1920s, founded and promoted by a group of Dutch artists (it is also the name of their movement). Advocated a geometrical type of abstract art, simplification, social and spiritual form. *See* Mondrian (p. 389)

STILL LIFE A depiction of inanimate objects such as fruit, flowers, plates, bottles, or dead birds or animals. Seventeenth-century Holland liked lavish still lifes (and Jan Davidsz de Heem excelled at them). Simple ones were favored in the Enlightenment. The pioneers of Modern art used them to break new ground in ways of seeing. The only Perceptual art subject that can be prearranged and (almost) totally controlled by the artist. *See* Cézanne (pp. 334–335); Chardin (p. 224); de Heem (p. 199)

STIPPLE ENGRAVING Ingenious marriage of engraving and etching techniques, which produces a print that looks like a chalk drawing. Much used in the 18th century for portraits.

STIPPLING Small dots or strokes applied in differing densities to create areas of tone or of light and shade

STREET ART Works of art in public places, such as murals on buildings, graffiti, sidewalk art, and "happenings." *See also* Happening

STRETCHER The wooden frame over which canvas is stretched to make a surface for painting. Never forget to look at the backs of paintings—sometimes they are more interesting than the front, and the labels attached to stretchers can tell a history in themselves.

STRUCTURALISM Buzzword for the study of the meaning of signs. Used to be called "iconology."

STUDIO OF ... Describes a work made by the assistants in a master's studio. Looks as though it has been created by the master, but it has not and usually appears a bit mechanical, tired, or overfamiliar. *See also* Attribution; By ...; Follower of ...; Manner of ...; Studio of ...

STUDY A preliminary drawing or painting made before going on to the final version, but worked out in considerable detail

STURM, DER German for "the storm." Name of a magazine and art gallery in Berlin, which was a major influence in promoting German and foreign modern art in Germany between 1912 and 1932.

STYLE A distinctive way of doing things, which can be analyzed and its unique combination of characteristics identified. To be one of the memorable greats, you need a style that is new, instantly recognizable, technically accomplished, easy to describe in words, and easy for the public and other professionals to mimic.

STYLE OF ... In the same style as a particular artist, but not by that person. *See also* Attribution; By ...; Follower of ...; Manner of ...; Studio of ...

SUBJECT, SUBJECT MATTER The theme(s) of a work of art. An artist may be seeking to show ideas or issues that are wider or deeper than the actual objects and figures represented.

SUBLIME A feeling of grandeur or awe induced by a work of art or nature—an aesthetic concept much discussed in the 18th century, reaching its fullest expression in the late-18th and early 19th centuries. Someone standing on a mountain top and gazing into a ravine that has a powerful waterfall, while storm clouds gather overhead, is a typical example, and one much used in art. Turner lusted after sublime experiences in both life and art. *See* Friedrich (p. 272); Martin, John (p. 280); Turner (p. 281)

SUCCESSIVE CONTRAST Take a brightly colored sheet of paper in a primary color (red, for example). Stare at it for a minute, then look at a white wall. You will "see" a ghostlike image of the sheet of paper in its complementary color (green in this case). This automatic creation in the mind's eye of the complementary color is called successive contrast.

SUPERREALISM *See* Photorealism

SUPPORT A painting needs a support, which may be canvas, a wood panel, a copper sheet, paper, etc. The artist needs to prepare the support by painting on to it a primer, and then a ground, to create a suitable smooth surface on which the picture can be painted. *See also* Ground; Primer

SUPREMATISM Russian avant-garde movement, pre-World War I, that strove to create a new spiritual awareness by developing an abstract art based on simplified geometric form, simple color, and floating spatial relationships, unlike anything found in the material world. *See* Lissitsky (p. 373); Malevich (p. 371)

SURREALISM (*See* pp. 390–391) The leading avant-garde movement of the 1930s. It sought to reach a new "super reality" by defying logic and accessing the unconscious (it was strongly influenced by Freud's theories). Used almost every artistic style from abstraction to realism. Magritte turned reality on its head by confounding normal experiences, but in a way that was more poetic than shocking. *See* Arp (p. 368); Dali (p. 392); Delvaux (p. 394); Ernst; (p. 369) Magritte (p. 395); Man Ray (p. 394); Masson (p. 393); Matta (p. 395); Miró (p. 393); Tanguy (p. 393)

SYMBOLISM (*See* pp. 322–323) Started as a progressive movement in 19th-century French poetry (Rimbaud, Baudelaire, Mallarmé, Verlaine), which influenced a number of painters interested in the mystical and spiritual. Look for strange, enigmatic, and allegorical subjects designed to play on the emotions and come close to the power of dreams. *See* Ensor (p. 366); Moreau (p. 324); Puvis de Chavannes (p. 324); Redon (p. 324)

SYNAESTHESIA The rare ability to experience color sensations as a physical (as opposed to an imaginative) experience when other senses such as taste and hearing are stimulated. *See* Kandinsky (p. 364)

SYNCHRONISM American version of Orphism. *See* Macdonald-Wright (p. 383)

SYNTHESIS Bringing two or more separate things or ideas together to create another, different one

SYNTHETISM *See* Cloisonism

SYNTHETIC CUBISM (*See* p. 350) The works done by Picasso, Braque, and Gris c. 1912–15, featuring fragments of newspapers, tickets, and so on, incorporated into paintings.

TABLEAU VIVANT French, lit. "living painting." A depiction of a scene by silent and motionless costumed participants. Many old-master paintings can be turned into *tableaux vivants.*

TACHISME From the French *tâche* for "patch" or "spot." Group of postwar French painters, contemporary with the Abstract Expressionists, who produced freely painted abstract pictures. Interesting, but not major. *See* Soulages (p. 420)

TEMPERA Emulsion made of powder pigments bound together with egg yolk and thinned with water. Very quick-drying, tough, and permanent. Has to be applied in short strokes, so covering a large area is painstakingly slow. The favored medium in early-Renaissance Italy until replaced by oil paint. Still used occasionally. *See* Clemente (p. 469); Ghirlandaio (p. 95); Michelangelo (p. 136); Piero della Francesca (p. 100); Wyeth (p. 439)

TENEBRISM A style of painting with bright lights and dark shadows as practiced by Caravaggio and his Spanish and Neopolitan followers. Same sort of thing as *chiaroscuro*. Spanish-born José Ribera, who settled in Naples, used dramatic lighting to emphasize his deliberate realism. *See also* Chiaroscuro *See* Caravaggio (pp. 170–171); Ribera (p. 185); Zurbarán (p. 185)

TERM *See* Herm

TERRIBILITÀ Italian for "awe." A sense of awe and foreboding about the human condition—in particular its essentially tragic nature, its unpredictability, the inevitability of pain and suffering, and the certainty of God's final judgment. *See* Michelangelo (p. 136)

TERTIARY COLORS The result of mixing a primary and a secondary color (such as red and green) or two secondary colors (such as green and orange). The latter, in particular, results in muddy colors—browns, grays, and blacks.

TESSERAE (SING. TESSERA) The small pieces of material used to make a mosaic

THUMBNAIL SKETCH A small, rapidly executed sketch that captures all the essential features of the subject

TINT The variation in a color made by mixing it with another

TITANIUM WHITE White pigment with the purest whiteness and best opacity. Perfected in the 1920s and now the largest selling pigment.

TONDO Italian, meaning "round." A circular painting or relief sculpture.

TONE The lightness or darkness of a color. Also described by referring to the lightness, value, intensity, or brilliance of a color.

TOOTH The degree of roughness of a painting support (such as paper or canvas)

TOPOGRAPHY The detailed depiction of an actual place. R. p. Bonington excelled at it, and produced luminous and detailed watercolors and oils of picturesque places such as Verona. *See* Bonington (p. 268)

TRANSAVANGUARDIA Italian movement of the late 1970s that sought to re-establish so-called traditional artistic priorities, such as expressive painting, color figuration, and individuality. More a reaction against the anonymity of Minimalism than a coherent agenda for something. *See* Clemente (p. 469); Paladino (p. 427)

TRECENTO Italian for "14th century" (1300–99)

TROMPE L'OEIL French, lit. "deceives the eye." A *trompe l'oeil* painting is designed to trick viewers into thinking that what they see is the real thing.

TURPENTINE Strong-smelling, quick-drying, thin liquid made from pine resin, used for diluting oil paints

UKIYO-E Popular Japanese paintings and woodblock prints made in the 17th, 18th, and 19th centuries. Decorative and brightly colored with strong designs, they portray courtesans, landscapes, animals and birds, narrative scenes, etc. Ukiyo-e means "floating world," but for some reason no Western writer seems able to explain convincingly the idea it enshrines. Hiroshige, one of the masters of Ukiyo-e, is noted for his poetic reverence for nature, and his deftness in expressing the effects of mist, rain, and snow.

UMBER A dark brown earth pigment. Raw umber is dark yellow-brown; burned umber is dark reddish-brown.

UMBRIAN SCHOOL Italian artists who worked in and around Perugia in the 15th and 16th centuries. *See* Piero della Francesca (p. 100); Raphael (p. 134); Signorelli (p. 95)

UNDERPAINTING Complete detailed design for a picture made in a dull monochrome then painted over to make the finished work

UT PICTURA POESIS Latin saying expressing the idea that paintings can fulfil the function of written texts, especially poetic and lyrical ones

UTRECHT SCHOOL A group of 17th-century Dutch artists who visited Rome and were strongly influenced by the works of Caravaggio. The leading member of the Utrecht School was Gerrit van Honthorst, who is especially known for his striking use of artificial light. *See* Honthorst (p. 204); Terbrugghen (p. 199)

VALUE, COLOR VALUE The lightness or darkness of a color: low value is dark; high value is bright

VANISHING POINT *See* Perspective

VANITAS A still life containing symbolic references (such as skulls or extinguished candles) to death and the transitory nature of life

VARIANT A copy that is slightly different from the original

VARNISH A hard-drying transparent protective substance, which is painted onto the surface of a painting to protect that surface and give the colors a unity of texture and appearance. Varnish is suitable for paintings on a panel or canvas, but it tends to make the pictures go darker with age.

VARNISHING DAY *See* Vernissage

VEDUTA Italian from *vedere*, "to view." A more-or-less accurate view of a town or city. The 18th-century artists who painted them were called *vedutisti*. *See* Bellotto (p. 236); Canaletto (p. 235); Piranesi (p. 249)

VEHICLE The liquid that binds pigments together to make paint; oil, for instance

VELLUM Fine parchment made from the skin of a calf. (Same derivation as "veal.")

VERDIGRIS 1) A poisonous, green or greenish-blue pigment made from copper; it is fugitive and eventually goes dark brown. First used by the ancient Greeks

(it comes from *vert de Grèce*, green from Greece).
2) The greenish or bluish patina that forms on copper, brass, and bronze.

VERMILION Bright-red pigment made from mercury and sulfur. First made by the ancient Greeks.

VERNISSAGE French word for "varnishing day." This was the day before an exhibition opened, when artists added the finishing touches or final varnish to their work, which was already hanging on the wall. Today, *vernissage* is simply a chic name for private viewing.

VIDEO ART A work of art made to be viewed on one or more television screens installed in a gallery. Claims to investigate and use the artistic possibilities of the medium—the unique color, brightness, and movement that television has. It usually has no narrative or documentary content and so is utterly different from what you see on television at home. *See* Hatoum (p. 470); Hirst (p. 476); Paik (p. 458); Viola (p. 469)

VIGNETTE Either a small, usually figurative, design, such as a portrait or a still life, without a border and shading off at the edges, or a scene describing a brief, often domestic, narrative incident. Originally it meant a design of vine leaves and tendrils.

VINGT, LES Influential avant-garde Belgian group of the 1880s, who showed their own work alongside most of the progressive French artists from Manet onwards. *See* Ensor (p. 366)

VIRIDIAN A bright-green chrome-based pigment, non-poisonous, introduced in the early 19th century

VORTICISM (*See* p. 376) Avant-garde British art movement, 1913–15. Took up Cubist and Futurist ideas and aimed to shake up the stuffy British art world and society generally. *See* Bomberg (p. 377); Lewis, (Percy) Wyndham (p. 376); Roberts (p. 377)

WASH Very watery watercolor or ink flooded on to paper from a brush to cover a large area. Ruskin used watercolor wash with great effect to capture the texture of architectural brick- and stonework as well as light and atmosphere.

WATERCOLOR Any type of painting medium soluble in water is, technically, watercolor. What is usually meant, however, are those works on paper with thin washes of transparent watercolor paint that the English find so appealing. The technique is fiendishly difficult. Notice how the greatest masters have the ability to combine luminous atmospheric effects and minute detail in the same work; for some reason no other medium can do this so successfully. Thomas Girtin was a genuine innovator, and potentially one of the greatest watercolor masters, but he died of tuberculosis at the age of 27. *See* Cézanne (pp. 334–335); Girtin (p. 244); Turner (p. 281)

WET INTO WET Painting wet paint into wet paint. In oils, this produces a very luscious, juicy result. *See* Manet (p. 307); Ribera (p. 185); Sargent (p. 326); Velasquez (p. 187)

WHITE LEAD The most important pigment in the history of Western painting. The only white pigment available until the 19th century, made from lead strips. It absorbs X-rays and so allows X-ray photography to reveal what goes on under the visible surface of a painting.

WHITE SPIRIT A turpentine substitute

WOOD ENGRAVING A printmaking process that uses a block of very hard fine-grained wood, such as box. Look for small-scale works in black and white, which have minute and fine detail.

WOODBLOCK PRINT Usually refers to Japanese woodcuts

WOODCUT One of the most basic printing techniques, whereby the design to be printed is cut into a block of wood. Most 15th- and 16th-century prints, especially for book illustration, use the technique. It was replaced by metal engraving and then revived at the end of the 19th century. No one has ever surpassed the mastery of Dürer. *See* Cranach (p. 125); Dürer (pp. 126–127); Gauguin (p. 329); Holbein (p. 160); Kollwitz (p. 366); Munch (p. 360); Schad (p. 385); Schmidt-Rottluff (p. 363)

WORKSHOP OF … *See* Studio of …

W. P. A. Stands for Works Progress Administration, an American government scheme to give employment to artists during the 1930s Depression. Involved all the arts and sponsored 100,000 paintings, 2,500 murals, and 2 million posters.

X-RAY A standard conservation and restoration technique. Because underpainting is often done with paints mixed with white lead, X-ray photographs will show what went on under the surface of a surface (since X-rays don't pass through lead). *See also* White lead

XYLOGRAPHY Rarely used word for woodcut or wood engraving

YBAs Young British Artists. Band of so-called "cutting-edge" artists who captured an international following in the 1990s, when they were mostly aged around 30. Many trained at Goldsmiths College, London. Work is mostly Conceptual. Themes tend to be current social issues. Very efficient at "making art," but curiously passionless. *See also* Social realism. *See* Hirst (p. 476); Ofili (p. 477); Whiteread (p. 476)

YELLOWING Oil paintings can darken or yellow with age. Yellowing is caused by old linseed oil or by dirt or by smoke (nicotine leaves a yellow deposit), or a combination of these.

ZIGGURAT Ancient Mesopotamian pyramid-shaped tower with a square base

ZINC WHITE An alternative pigment to white lead. It is not poisonous and is the least opaque of all white pigments.

Index

Page numbers in **bold** refer to main entries.

A

Abbate, Niccolò dell' **154**
Abstract Expressionism 405, **412–13**, 414–17, 431, 440, 445
Abstraction 353, 356, **358–9**, 374, 383, 389, 393, 400, 410, 436, 457, 467
  Color Field 414
  Geometric 386, 388
  Synchronism 383
  see also Abstract Expressionism; CoBrA
Academic Art **258–61**
Academies 22–3, **284**
  Britain 238, 239, 241, 284, 298, 379
  France 284, 306, 312
acrylics **35**
Adam, Robert 242, 250
  Kedleston Hall, Derbyshire 250
Aegean World, Early **52–3**
Aertsen, Pieter **156**
  The Adoration of the Shepherds 156
Aestheticism 321, **322–3**, 325
African sculpture 347, 349, 357
Agasse, Jacques-Laurent **247**
  Miss Casenove on a Gray Hunter 247
Age of Reason 219, 224, 246
Albers, Josef 386, **388**
  Homage to the Square 388
Alechinsky, Pierre 418, **419**
  Octave 419
Algardi, Alessandro **169**
Allan, David **246**
Alma-Tadema, Sir Lawrence **288**
  The Tepidarium 288
Altdorfer, Albrecht **158**
  Beheading of St. Catherine 158
Alÿs, Francis **475**
André, Carl **459**
  Tomb of the Golden Engenderers 459
Andrews, Michael **435**
Angelico, Fra **89**
  The Beheading of St. Cosmas and St. Damian 89
  Santa Trinità Altarpiece 22
Antonello da Messina **104**
Appel, Karel **418**
Arcimboldo, Giuseppe **159**
  Water 159
Arellano, Juan de **186**

Still Life of Flowers in a Basket 186
Arman, Armand Fernandez **421**
  Office Fetish 421
Arp, Jean (Hans) 367, **368–9**, 390
  Head 368
Art Brut 419
Art Nouveau 325, **338**, 357
Arte Povera **425**, 426, 427
artist,
  masterpiece, definition 26–7
  role of 18–20
  through history 16–17
Ashcan School **380**, 381
Auerbach, Frank **432**
Avercamp, Hendrick **208**
  Winter Scene with Skaters near a Castle 209

B

Baldung Grien, Hans **125**
Balla, Giacomo **374**, 375
  Dynamism of a Dog on a Lead 374
Balthus **404**
Bandinelli, Baccio 20
  Cosimo de' Medici 20
Barbizon School 304, **305**
Barney, Matthew **477**
Barocci, Federico **151**
  The Circumcision of Christ 151
Baroque Era 39, 146, 151, **162–5**, 173, 174–5, 177, **178–9**, 185–9, 190–3
  architecture 164–5
Barry, James **241**
Bartolommeo, Fra Baccio della Porta **135**
Baselitz, Georg **461**
  Picture-Eleven 461
Bassano, Jacopo **151**
Batchelor, David 448–9
  The Spectrum of Brick Lane 448–9
Batoni, Pompeo Girolamo **237**
Baudelaire, Charles 270
Bauhaus 364, 372, **386**, 387, 388
Beardsley, Aubrey **325**
Beckmann, Max 362, **384**
  Self-Portrait in Olive and Brown 384
Bell, Vanessa 379
Bellini, Gentile **102**
  Procession in St. Mark's Square 102–3
Bellini, Giovanni 102, **103**, 143
  Agony in the Garden 103
Bellini, Jacopo **102**
  The Madonna of Humility adored by Leonello d'Este 102
Bellotto, Bernardo **236–7**
  View of Warsaw from

the Royal Castle 236
Bellows, George Wesley 380, **381**
  A Stag at Sharkey's 37, 381
Benton, Thomas Hart **409**
Berenson, Bernard 24, 142
Bernard, Emile **332**
Bernini, Gianlorenzo 169, **173–5**, 178
  Apollo and Daphne 173
  Cornaro Chapel **174–5**
  Fontana del Moro 178
  Fountain of the Four Rivers 162
Berruguete, Pedro **118**
Beuys, Joseph 41, 43, **453**
  Earth Telephone 453
Bevan, Robert Polhill **378**
Bible 130, 297, 302
  Title Page, the Great Bible, 1539 130
Bierstadt, Albert **292**
Bingham, George Caleb **292**
Blake, Sir Peter **446**
Blake, William **248**, 280
  The Ancient of Days 248
Blaue Reiter, Der 364, **365**
Bloomsbury Group 378, **379**
Boccioni, Umberto **374**, 375
  Unique Forms of Continuity in Space 374
Böcklin, Arnold 325
Boetti, Alighiero **427**
  Bringing the World into the World 426–7
Bol, Ferdinand **202**
  Portrait of a Husband and Wife 202
Bologna, School of **166**
Boltanski, Christian 41, **466**
  Monuments: The Children of Dijon 466
Bomberg, David **377**
Bonington, Richard Parkes **268–9**
  The Undercliff 268–9
Bonnard, Pierre **336**
  The Almond Tree in Blossom 336
Bordone, Paris **151**
Bosch, Hieronymus **121**, 324
  The Garden of Earthly Delights: Hell 120
  Triptych of the Temptation of St. Anthony 120–1
Botero, Fernando **457**
Both, Jan **212**
Botticelli, Alessandro 26, 88, 96, **98–9**, 299
  The Adoration of the Magi 96
  Birth of Venus 26, 44–5
  La Primavera **98–9**
Boucher, François **224–5**, 226, 227
  Bacchus and Erigone 227
Bouguereau, William-Adolphe **285**

The Birth of Venus 285
Bourdichon, Jean **119**
  Anne of Brittany with St. Anne, St. Ursula, and St. Helen 119
  Grandes Heures 119
Bourgeois, Louise **452**
  Quarantania 452
Bouts, Dieric **114**
  Hell 114
Bramante 138
Brancusi, Constantin 39, **356**
  Bird in Space **356**
Braque, Georges 35, 346, 350, **351**, 401
  Studio V 351
Brett, John **298**
Breton, André 390
  Les Champs Magnétiques 390
  Manifesto for an Independent Revolutionary Art 390
  Surrealist Manifesto 390
Britain
  Academic Art 259, 260, 261, 286–9
  contemporary 465, 468, 470–1, 474, 475–6, 477
  modern masters 398–401, 430, 431–6, 446–7
  painting, 18th century 219–21, 238–48
  Romanticism 259, 260, 261, 266, 276–82
  see also Bloomsbury Group; English Landscape Tradition; Pre-Raphaelites; St. Ives Group; Vorticism
bronze sculpture **38**
Bronzino, Agnolo 146, **148–9**
  An Allegory with Venus and Cupid 148
Broodthaers, Marcel **422**
Brown, Ford Madox **296**
  Work 296
Browning, Robert 297
Bruce, Patrick Henry **383**
Brücke, Die **362**, 363
Brueghel, Jan **195**
Bruegel, Pieter (the elder) **157**, 195
  Hunters in the Snow—February 157
  Tower of Babel (detail) 157
  The Triumph of Death 74
Brueghel, Pieter (the younger) **195**
  A Village Festival in Honor of St. Hubert and St. Anthony 195
Brunelleschi, Filippo 75
  Dome of Florence Cathedral 75
Burgundian School 85
Burne-Jones, Sir Edward Coley 297, **298–9**
  St. George and the Dragon 299
Burri, Alberto **424**
Byron 268
Byzantine Art **64–5**, 78,

79, 155
Christ Pantocrator 64–5
Emperor Justinian I and his Retinue 65
Madonna and Child 64

C

Cabanel, Alexandre **285**
Cleopatra Testing Poisons on Those Condemned to Death 285
Caillebotte, Gustave **311**
Calder, Alexander 40, 340–1, **438**
Blue Feather 438
studio 40
Young Lady and her Scribe 340–1
Calle, Sophie **470**
Callot, Jacques 164
The Hanging 164
Campin, Robert **111**
Canaletto, Giovanni Antonio **235**, 236, 237
The Basin of San Marco on Ascension Day 234–5
Canova, Antonio **254**, 255
Cupid and Psyche 254
Paulina Bonaparte Borghese as Venus 250, 254
Caravaggio 168, 169, **170–1**, 172, 177, 185, 199
Judith and Holofernes 170
The Sick Bacchus 171
The Supper at Emmaus 170–1, 178
Caro, Sir Anthony **434–5**
Carpaccio, Vittore **141**
Dream of St. Ursula 141
Carrà, Carlo **375**
Interventionist Demonstration 375
Carracci, Annibale **167**, 178, **179**
Farnese Palace, Rome 167, 179
Fishing 167
The Holy Women at Christ's Tomb 167
Venus and Anchises **179**
Carriera, Rosalba Giovanna **229**
Caterina Sagredo Barbarigo as "Bernice" 229
Cassatt, Mary 30, **316**
Castiglione, Baldassare 129
The Book of the Courtier 129, 138
Catena, Vincenzo **142**
Caulfield, Patrick **446**
cave painting 48–9
The Great Hall, Lascaux 48–9
Cellini, Benvenuto **149**
Saltcellar 149
Celtic Art **66–7**
Book of Kells 67
Cennini, Cennino 30
César (César Baldaccini) **420**
Cézanne, Paul 26, 180, 184, 331, 332, **334–5**, 344, 346, 349, 351, 357

The Large Bathers 335, 344
Montagne Sainte-Victoire with Trees and a House 333–4
Self-Portrait 334
Still Life with Basket 334
Chagall, Marc **354–5**
The Juggler 355
chalks **30**
Chamberlain, John **455**
Untitled 455
Champaigne, Phillippe de **183**
Chapman, Jake and Dinos **475**
charcoal **30**
Chardin, Jean **224**
Still Life 224
Charles I 165, 194, 198
Charles II 216, 217
Charles V Holy Roman Emperor, 129, 130
Chase, William Merritt **316–17**
Portrait of a Lady in Black 316
Chia, Sandro 427
chiaroscuro 184, 203
Chillida, Eduardo **428–9**
Berlin 428–9
Chirico, Giorgio de 375, 394, **404**
The Mystery and Melancholy of a Street 404
Christo & Jeanne-Claude 43, **460**
The Gates 2–3
Surrounded Islands 43
Wrapped Trees 460
Christus, Petrus **115**
Church, Frederick Edwin **290–1**
Cotopaxi 291
Church, conflict, 16th century 129–31
conflict, 17th century 162
Counter-Reformation 164
Patronage 17, 20, 129
Cimabue (Cenni di Peppi) **78**, 80
Madonna and Child Enthroned with Eight Angels and Four Prophets (or Maestà) 78
Classical Antiquity 17, 18, 86, 105, 139, 170, 180, 239, 325, 400
Classical Greece 32, 33, 38, 39, **54–5**
Altar of Zeus 57
The Battle of Issus 56
Boy from Antikythera 55
Centaur Triumphing over a Lapith 54
Derveni krater 57
Dying Gaul 56
Kouros 39, 53
Laocoön **58–9**
Red-figure vase 54
see also Aegean World, Early; Hellenistic Art
Classical Rome 32, 33,

38, **60–1**
Ara Pacis (Imperial) 60
Equestrian statue of Emperor Marcus Aurelius (Imperial) 60, 61
Nile in Flood (Imperial) 60–1
see also Late Roman and Early Christian Art
Claude Lorrain 154, **182–3**, 212, 243
Landscape with the Marriage of Isaac and Rebekah 182–3
Clemente, Francesco 427, **469**
Clodion, Claude Michel *Arc de Triomphe* 250
Close, Chuck **463**
Self-Portrait 463
Clouet, François **154**
Charles IX 154
Coates, Robert 412
CoBrA **418**, 419
Coello, Claudio **186**
Cole, Thomas **290**
Scene from "The Last of the Mohicans" 290
Coleridge, Samuel 266
collage **35**
collectors 20–2
Columbus, Christopher 75
computers 42, 451
Conceptual Art 367, 460
connoisseurs 24
Constable, John 31, 245, **277**, 278–9, 304, 314, 468
Dedham Church 266
Flatford Old Mill Cottage on the Stour 277
The Hay Wain **278–9**
Stour Valley 266
Constructivism 40, 368, **372**, 373
Contemporary Art 29, **448–79**
The Pompidou Center, Paris 450–1
Copernicus 131
Copley, John Singleton **256–7**
Corinth, Lovis **337**
Cornell, Joseph **406**
Cornelius, Peter von **273**
Faust 273
Corot, Jean-Baptiste-Camille **304**
Woman with a Pearl 304
Correggio, Antonio **150–1**, 154, 249
Cortona, Pietro da **177**
Cosimo I de' Medici 20, 91, 146, 147, 149
Cosway, Richard **242**
Cotman, John Sell 276
The Marl Pit 276
Courbet, Gustave 18, 300, **301**, **306**, 307
Caricature of Gustave Courbet 19
The Painter's Studio 300, **301**
Stonebreakers 300
Cox, David 276, **277**
Cozens, Alexander **244**

Cozens, Robert **244**
London from Greenwich Hill 243
Cranach, Lucas (the elder) **125**
The Nymph of the Fountain 125
Credi, Lorenzo di **96–7**
criticism **24**, 25
Crivelli, Carlo **105**
The Annunciation with St. Emidius 105
Crome, John 276
View of Mousehold Heath, near Norwich 276
Cubism 35, **350**, 351, 352, 357, 362, 365, 370, 374, 375, 382, 383, 386, 389, 390, 396
Cuyp, Aelbert **209**
A Herdsman with Five Cows by a River 209

D

Dada 41, 43, **367**, 368, 369, 390, 394, 443
Dadd, Richard **289**
Daddi, Bernardo **76**
Polyptych with the Crucifixion and Saints 76
Dahl, Michael **217**
Dali, Salvador 390, **392**
Soft Construction with Boiled Beans: Premonition of Civil War 392
Daniels, Harvey
Tree 35
Dante 78, 268
Divine Comedy 101, 319
Daumier, Honoré **307**
The Third-Class Carriage 307
David, Gerrit **117**
God the Father Blessing 117
David, Jacques-Louis 247, 250, **251**, **252–3**, 267
Napoleon Crossing the Alps on 20th May 1800 253
The Oath of the Horatii **251**
Davie, Alan **431**
Davis, Stuart **383**
dealers 20, **21**
Deem, George **459**
Degas, Edgar 30, 312, **315**, 316, 326
Blue Dancers 30
Little Dancer 312
The Star, or Dancer on Stage 315
Woman Drying Herself 315
Delacroix, Eugene 223, **268**, 269, **270–1**, 323
Liberty Leading the People **270–1**
Scenes from the Massacre of Chios 268
Delaunay, Robert **354**
Delaunay, Sonia 354
Delft School 194
Delvaux, Paul **394**
Demuth, Charles **407**
Denis, Maurice **325**
Derain, André 346, **347**

Devis, Arthur **239**
Dibbets, Jan 463
Dickens, Charles 331
Diebenkorn, Richard **417**
"Ocean Park"
series 417
Diller, Burgoyne **383**
Dine, Jim **439**
Divisionism 314, **320**,
344, 374
Dix 384, **385**
Dobson, William **216**
Doesburg, Theo van 389
Domenichino **168**
The Last Sacrament of
St. Jerome 168
Donatello 88, **90–1**,
101, 318
David **90**
Dongen, Kees van **354**
Dossi, Dosso **141**
Dotrement, Christian 418
Dou, Gerrit **202**
The Village Grocer 202
Dove, Arthur
Garfield **383**
drawing **30–1**
Dubuffet, Jean **419**
Duc de Berry, Jean 77
Duccio di Buoninsegna
78–9, 82, 84
Duchamp, Marcel 41,
367, 443
Fountain (Urinal) 41, 367
Hat Rack 41
Dufy, Raoul 346, **353**
The Regatta at Cowes 353
Dughet, Gaspard **183**
Durand-Ruel, Paul 21
Dürer, Albrecht 36,
115, 116, 124, **126–7**,
148, 273
Altarpiece of the Rose
Garlands 126–7
Melancolia 127
Self-Portrait at the Age
of Twenty-eight 126
A Young Hare 126
Dutch art
see Netherlands

E

Eakins, Thomas
295, 380
Earl, Ralph **257**
Early art 29, **47–71**
see also Aegean World;
Byzantine; Celtic;
Saxon & Viking;
Classical Greece;
Classical Rome; Gothic;
Early; Egypt, Ancient ;
Medieval; Romanesque;
egg tempera **32**
Egypt, Ancient 32, 38,
39, **50–1**
Bird-scarab pectoral from
Tutankamun's tomb 50
Book of the Dead 50–1
Mask from mummy-case
of Tutankhamun 47
Palette of Narmer 50
Relief from tomb of
Ramose 51
El Greco 146, **155**, 357
The Burial of Count

Orgaz, from a Legend of
1323 155
The Resurrection 155
Eliasson, Olanus 41
The Forked Forest Path 41
Elsheimer, Adam **158**
Emin, Tracey **476**
encaustic **32**
beeswax 32
English Landscape
Tradition **243**, 304
engraving **36**
copperplate 36
The Engraver 36
tools 36
Enlightenment, The 219,
221, 262, 266
Ensor, James **366**
Christ's Triumphant
Entry into Brussels 366
Epstein, Sir Jacob **377**
St. Michael Vanquishing
the Devil 377
Ernst, Max 35, 324, 367,
369, 390, **391**
The Entire City 369
Oedipus Rex **391**
Estes, Richard **458**
Eworth, Hans **161**
Queen Mary I 161
exploration 75, 130, 131
Expressionism **358–9**,
360–7, 382, 396, 418,
432, 466
Exter, Alexandra **370**

F

Fabritius, Carel **203**
Fabro, Luciano **426–7**
Falconet, Etienne **226**
Education de l'Amour 226
Fantin-Latour, Henri **302**
Fauves, Les **346**, 351,
354, 364, 370
Feininger, Lyonel **386**
fête galante 222, 223
Fildes, Sir Luke **288**
Doctor 288
Fiorentino, Rosso
146, **153**
Flavin, Dan **459**
Flemish painting 33,
114–15, 116, 149, 156,
157, 158, 190–5
Flinck, Govaert **202**
Florence **74–5**, 78, 80,
83, 88–100, 105, 132,
135–7, 148
Fluxus **423**
Fontainebleau **153**,
154, 305
Fontana, Lucio **424**
Fouquet, Jean **118–19**
Fragonard, Jean-Honoré
226, **228–9**
The Swing 226, 228
France
Academic Art 258–61,
284, 285, 306, 312
classical landscape
180–2
contemporary 452,
466, 470
Impressionism 277, 302
304, 310–14
industrialization, 261

Neoclassicism
218–221, 251, 252–3
Realism 300–1,
304, 306
Renaissance 118–19
Revolution 18, 221,
223, 227, 228, 253, 266
Rococo 218–221,
222–9
Romanticism 258–61,
266, 267, 268,
269–70, 304
Thirty Years' War, effect
of 164
see also Art Nouveau;
Barbizon School;
Cubism; Divisionism;
Les Fauves; Post-
Impressionism; School
of Paris; Symbolism
Francis I 130, 131
Château de Chambord,
Loire Valley 131
Francis, Sam **416**
In Lovely Blueness 416
Frederigo da Montefeltro,
Urbino, Duke of 106
fresco **33**
Freud, Lucian **434**
The Painter's Mother
434–5
Freud, Sigmund 339,
360, 367, 390, 391,
392, 395, 396
Friedrich, Caspar, David
266, **272**, 273
Monk by the Sea 266
The Stages of Life 272
Winter Landscape 272
Frith, William Powell **287**
Derby Day 286
Frost, Terry 400, **430**
Red and Blue 430–1
Fruosino, Bartolomeo di,
illuminated "P" 77
Fry, Roger 379
Fuseli, Henry **248**
The Nightmare 248
Futurism 350, 370, 373,
374, **375**

G

Gabo, Naum **372**
Linear Construction in
Space No. 1 372
Gaddi, Taddeo **78**
Gainsborough, Thomas
186, **240**
Mr. and Mrs. Andrews 240
The Painter's Daughters
Chasing a Butterfly 240
Galileo Galilei 165
Gallego, Fernando **118**
Pietà with Two Donors 118
galleries 22–4
Grand Gallery of the
Louvre 22
Guggenheim Museum,
Bilbao 24
Hermitage, St.
Petersburg 11
Gauguin, Paul 324, 328,
329, 331, 332
Landscape at Pont
Aven 328
The Meal 329

Nevermore 329
Gentile da Fabriano **83**
The Presentation in the
Temple (from the Altarpiece
of the Adoration of the
Magi) 83
Gentileschi, Artemisia **172**
Judith and her
Maidservant 172
Gentileschi, Orazio
169, 172
Rest on the Flight into
Egypt 169
George I 217
George II 216
George IV (Prince
Regent) 280
Géricault, Théodore
267, **269**
Portrait of a Woman
Addicted to Gambling 269
The Raft of the Medusa
267, 269
Germany,
contemporary 453,
458, 460, 461, 462,
464, 465, 466, 467,
470, 472, 473
Expressionism 121,
358, 360, 362–3,
364–5, 382, 384, 466
printing 36, 75
Romanticism 259,
260–1, 272–3, 274, 365
Thirty Years' War
163–4
Gertler, Mark **379**
Ghiberti, Lorenzo 84,
86, **88**
The Sacrifice of Isaac 86
Ghirlandaio, David 95
Ghirlandaio, Domenico
95
The Visitation 95
Giambologna **149**
The Rape of the
Sabines 149
Gibbons, Grinling **217**
Woodcarving of a
Cravat 217
Gilbert and George **465**
Street 465
Giordano, Luca **177**
The Crucifixion of
St. Peter 177
Giorgione **140**, 141,
143, 151, 223
The Sleeping Venus 140
The Tempest 140
The Three Philosophers 140
Giotto di Bondone 76,
78–9, **80–1**, 82, 88
Campanile of the
Duomo, Florence 80
Cappella degli Scrovegni,
frescoes, Padua 81
The Ecstasy of St.
Francis 81
Giovanni di Paolo **84**
Girardon, François **184**
Girodet-Trioson,
Anne-Louis **264**
Girtin, Thomas **244**
The White House,
Chelsea 243
Glackens, William
James **380**

Gober, Robert **472**
Goes, Hugo van der
108, **116**
 *The Adoration of
 the Shepherds* 116
 Portinari Altarpiece
 108, 116
Goethe, Johann Wolfgang
von 221, 273
Goldin, Nan **470**
Goldsworthy, Andy
43, **474**
 Arch at Goodwood 474
Goncharova, Natalia **370**
Gonzaga family 106, 147
González, Julio **352**
Gonzalez-Torres, Felix
474–5
Gorky, Arshile **417**
 Untitled 1946 417
Gormley, Anthony **468–9**
 Angel of the North 468
Gossaert, Jan **116**
Gothic style 73–5, **74**,
76, 79, 89, 121
 carvings, Chartres
 (Early) 71
 Early **70–1**
 International 74, 83,
 84, 86
 Roettgen Pietà 74
 Romantic 272, 273
 Rose window,
 Chartres, 70
Gottlieb, Adolph 412, **416**
gouache **34**
Goya, Francisco
262–3, 308
 Los Caprichos 36, 262
 The Clothed Maja 262–3
 *Here Neither, Plate 36, The
 Disasters of War* 262, 263
 *Of What Ill Will He
 Die?* 36
 The Third of May 266
Gozzoli, Benozzo 86,
92–3
 *The Procession of the
 Magi* 86, 93
 *The Triumph of
 St. Aquinas* 92
Grand Tour **234**,
235, 237
Grant, Duncan 379
Greece *see* Aegean World,
Early; Classical Greece
Greuze, Jean-Baptiste **225**
 Le Geste Napolitain 225
Gros, Antoine-Jean **264**
 *Napoleon in the Plague
 House at Jaffa* 264
 *Portrait of Madame
 Bruyère* 264
Grosz, George 384, **385**
Grünewald, Mathis
121, **122–3**
 Crucifixion (from *The
 Isenheim Altarpiece*)
 122–3
 *The Isenheim
 Altarpiece* 121
 *The Resurrection
 of Christ* 121
Guardi, Francesco **236**
 Landscape with Ruins 236
Guercino **172**
Guimard, Hector

Germain 338
Gursky, Andreas **473**
Guston, Philip **445**
 Legend 445
Gutenberg, Johannes 75
Guttuso, Renato **424**
 Death of a Hero 424

H

Hals, Frans 196, **198**, 337
 The Laughing Cavalier 198
Hamilton, Gavin **241**
Hamilton, Richard
440, **446**
 *Just what is it that Makes
 Today's Homes so Different,
 so Appealing?* 440
Hanson, Duane **454**–5
 Homeless Person, 454
Haring, Keith **475**
Hartley, Marsden **382**
 Abstraction 382
Hartung, Hans **422–3**
Hassam, Childe **316**
Hatoum, Mona **470**
Heade, Martin
 Johnson **291**
Heartfield, John **369**
Heckel, Erich **363**
Heem, Jan Davidsz
de **199**
 *Still Life of Fruit
 and Flowers* 199
Heemskerck, Maerten
van **156**
 Family Group 156
Hellenistic Art **56–9**
 Altar of Zeus 57
 The Battle of Issus 56
 Derveni krater 57
 Dying Gaul 56
Henri, Robert **380**, 383
 The Little Dancer 380
Henry VIII 129
Hepworth, Dame
 Barbara 39, **400**
 Involute 1 400
Heron, Patrick 400
Hesse, Eva 40, **460**
Hey, Jean **119**
Hicks, Edward **275**
 Peaceable Kingdom 275
Hilliard, Nicholas **161**
 *Portrait of Robert Devereux,
 Earl of Essex* 161
Hilton, Roger **434**
Hirst, Damien **476–7**
 Away from the Flock 477
history, art 24–5
Hitchcock, Alfred 408
Hitchens, Ivon **398**
Hobbema, Meyndert **210**
Hockney, David **447**
 Sunbather 447
Hodler, Ferdinand **337**
Hofmann, Hans **404–5**
Hogarth, William
231, **238**
 *Marriage à la Mode: VI,
 The Lady's Death* 238
 The Rake's Progress 238
 Self-Portrait 238
Hokusai, Katsushika
322, 347
 Japanese Ghost 322
Holbein, Hans (the

younger) **160**
 *Lady with a Squirrel
 and a Starling* 160
 *Portrait of a Youth in a
 Broad-brimmed Hat* 160
Holland *see* Netherlands
 painting, 17th century
20, 157, 196–215,
244, 302, 392
 Realism **196–7**
Homer, Winslow **294**
 Eight Bells 294
Honthorst 172
Hooch, Pieter de **211**
Hopper, Edward **408**
 Chop Suey 408
Horn, Rebecca 41, **466**
Houdon, Jean-Antoine
252
 *François-Marie Arouet
 Voltaire* 252
Hudson River School **290**
Hugo, Victor 270
Humanism 86, 91
Hundertwasser, Fritz **423**
 686 Good Morning City
 37, 423
Hunt, Holman, William
276, 297, **298**
 *Isabella and the Pot
 of Basil* 297

I

illumination 32, 76,
77, 82, 84
Immendorff, Jorg **466**
 World of Work 466
Impressionism 21,
312–13, 325, 326,
327, 328, 375
Indiana, Robert
 (John Clark) **445**
Industrialization
220, 260–1
 James Watt, rotary
 steam engine 220
Ingres, Jean-Auguste-
Dominique 31, 258–9,
264–5, 287
 The Turkish Bath 258–9
 The Valpinçon Bather 265
Innocent X, Pope 169
Installations **41**
Italy
 Baroque 151, 162,
 164–5, 166–79
 Neoclassicism
 250, 254
 Renaissance **74–5**,
 86–7, 106, 128–31,
 138–9
 Rococo 229–33
 see also Classical Rome;
 Futurism

J

James II 165
Japanese art 36, 321,
322, 325, 329, 331
Jawlensky, Alexei **370**
 Head of a Woman 370
John, Augustus **378**
 *Dorelia in a
 Landscape* 378
John, Gwen **378**

Johns, Jasper 32,
440, **442–3**
 Ale Cans **443**
 Three Flags 442
Jones, Allen **446–7**
Joos van Cleve **117**
Jordaens, Jacob **190**
Jorn, Asger **418**
Judd, Donald (Don) **455**
Julius II, Pope 138, 139

K

Kahlo, Frida **403**
 *Suicide of Dorothy
 Hale* 403
Kandinsky, Wassily 358,
359, **364**, 365, 370,
384, 386
 Accent in Pink 364
 Black Frame **359**
Kapoor, Anish **470–1**
 Marsyas 471
Katz, Alex **442**
 Dusk 442
Kauffmann, Angelica **242**
Kelly, Ellsworth **438**
Kiefer, Anselm **467**
Kippenberger,
 Martin **470**
Kirchner, Ernst Ludwig
362–3
 Berlin Street Scene 363
Kitaj, R. B. 30, **432**
 *Value, Price, and Profit, or
 Production of Waste* 432
Klee, Paul 34, 386,
387, 418
 The Golden Fish 387
Klimt, Gustav 338, **339**
 The Kiss 339
Klein, Yves 43, **420–1**
Kline, Franz 412, **415**
 Ballantine 412
Kneller, Sir Godfrey
216, 217
Købke, Christen, **289**
 *River Bank at
 Emilliekilde* 289
Kokoschka, Oskar
358, **367**
 *Storm Tide in
 Hamburg* 358
Kollwitz, Käthe **366**
 *The Survivors; War
 against War* 366
Koninck, Philips **207**
 Panoramic Landscape 207
Kooning, Willem de
412, **414**
 Man on the Dunes 412
Koons, Jeff **473**
 Popples 473
Kossoff, Leon **432**
Kounellis, Jannis **426**
Kupka, Frank **353**

L

La Tour, Georges de
170, **184**, 229
 St. Joseph the Carpenter 184
Lancret, Nicolas **224**, 231
land art **43**
Landseer, Sir Edwin **288**
Lane, Fitz Hugh **291**
Lanfranco, Giovanni

151, **168**
Christ and the Woman
of Samaria 168–9
Larsson, Carl **303**
Lastman, Pieter **198**, 200
The Expulsion of
Hagar 199
Late Roman and Early
Christian Art
Holy Women at the
Tomb of Christ 62
Mummy-case portrait
from Fayum 62
Lawrence, Jacob **409**
"Migration" series 409
Lawrence, Sir Thomas
286–7
Portrait of Arthur Wellesley,
1st Duke of Wellington 287
Le Nain Brothers **184**
LeBrun 284
Léger, Fernand **352**
Two Women holding a
Pot of Flowers 352
Leighton, Lord
Frederic **287**
Garden of the
Hesperides 287
Lely, Sir Peter **216**
Anne Hyde, Duchess
of York 216
Leonardo da Vinci 30, 96,
115, **132–3**, 135, 138
The Last Supper
132–3, 138
Mona Lisa 13, 17,
133, 138
Two Horsemen 132
The Virgin on the
Rocks 133
Leutze, Emmanuel
Gottlieb **274–5**
Washington Crossing the
Delaware River, 25th
December 1776 274–5
Lewis, John Frederick **289**
Indoor Gossip, Cairo 289
Lewis, (Percy) Wyndham
375, **376**, 377
A Battery Shelled 376
Blast Front cover of
War Number 376
Lewitt, Sol **456**
49 Three-Part Variations
of the Three Different
Kinds of Cubes 456
Lichtenstein, Roy 440, **441**
Anxious Girl 441
Liebermann, Max
302, 338
A Country Brasserie,
Brannenburg, Bavaria 302
Limbourg brothers **77**
Les Belles Heures 77
Death, One of the Four
Riders of the Apocalypse 77
Les Très Riches Heures 77
Linnell, John 276, **280**
Lipchitz, Jacques **352–3**
Lippi, Filippino **95**
Lippi, Fra Filippo
88–9, 95
Lissitsky, El **373**
Lithography **37**
Lochner, Stephan **85**
The Last Judgment 84–5
Lombardo family

105, 106
Monument to Doge
Pietro Mocenigo 105
Long, Richard **468**
Longhi, Pietro **231**
Exhibition of a Rhinoceros
at Venice 231
Lorenzetti brothers **79**
Allegory of Good
Government: Effects of
Good Government in
the City 78–9
Lorenzo il Magnifico 90
Lorenzo Monaco **82**
Madonna Enthroned
between Adoring Angels 82
Lorrain, Claude see
Claude Lorrain
Lotto, Lorenzo **142**
Louis XIII 180, 183
Louis XIV 163, 164,
165, 178, 184, 220,
226, 284
Louis XV 224, 255
Louis XVI 266
Loutherbourg, Jacques
Philippe de **245**
Battle Between Richard I
Lionheart and Saladin in
Palestine 245
Lowry, Laurence
Stephen **430**
Luks, George **380**
Luther, Martin 126, 130
95 Theses 130

M

Macdonald-Wright,
Stanton **383**
Macke, August 358, **365**
Maes, Nicolaes **203**
An Eavesdropper with
a Woman Scolding 203
Magritte, René 390,
394, **395**
The Human Condition 395
Mahler 339
Makart, Hans **286**
Malevich, Kasimir **371**
Suprematist Composition
No. 56 371
Malory,
Morte d'Arthur 297
Man Ray 42, 367,
385, **394**
The Aged Emak Bakia 394
Rayograph 42
Manet, Edouard 198,
300, **307**, **308–9**, 314,
317, 321, 329, 380, 442
The Bar at the Folies-
Bergère 306–7
Le Déjeuner sur l'Herbe
300, 308
Olympia **308–9**
Manfredi, Bartolommeo
172
Mannerism **131**,
146, 148, 150, 153,
154, 158
Mantegna, Andrea
73,106, 114, 151
Camera degli Sposi 73
Manzoni, Piero **426**
Marc, Franz 358, **365**

Faultier 358
Little Blue Horse 364–5
Marden, Brice **461**
Marlow, William **245**
The Pont de Gard,
Nîmes 245
Marquet, Albert **347**
The Seine at Paris 347
Martin, Agnes **452**
Martin, John **280**
Masaccio (Tommaso
Giovanni di Mone)
84, **88**
The Trinity 88
Masolino da Panicale **84**
masterpiece, definition
26–7
Masson, André **393**
Massys, Quentin **115**
The Money Lender and
his Wife 115
materials 29–43
Matisse, Henri 324, 329,
336, **344–5**, 346, 347,
354, 362, 365, 370,
400, 438
La Cirque 345
Jazz 345
Luxe, calme, et volupté
(Luxury, Serenity, and
Pleasure) 345
Large Reclining Nude 344
Notes of a Painter 345
Odalisque 345
Self-Portrait 344
Matta **395**
Matteo di Giovanni **101**
Madonna and Child with
Sts. Catherine and
Christopher 101
media and materials
28–43
Medici 75, 90, 91, 116,
132, 146, 147, 149
Medieval Art 17, 19, 39,
68–9
Book cover 69
Cross of Gero 68–9
Otto II, Holy Roman
Emperor 69
St. Mark from Carolingian
Gospel Book 68
Memling, Hans 114
Portrait of a Man 114
Mengs, Anton Raphael
249
Merz, Mario **424–5**
What's to be Done? 425
Messerschmidt, Franz
Xaver **249**
Metaphysical movement
375
Metsu, Gabriel **212**
Mexico, modern painting
35, 402–3
Michel, Louis 229
Michelangelo 20, 26, 30,
33, 39, 88, 91, 94, 95,
126, 129, 135, **136–7**,
138, 139, 146, 147, 148,
149, 155, 167, 248,
269, 287, 299, 318
The Creation of Adam 33
David 26, 138
The Delphic Sibyl 128–9

Holy Family with St.
John (Doni Tondo) 136
The Last Judgment 136
Pietà 137
Study of a Man
Shouting 31
Millais, Jean-François
300, **305**
The Angelus 305
The Gleaners 300
Millais, Sir John Everett
297, **298**
The Rescue 297
Miller, George 37
lithograph of A Stag
at Sharkey's 37
Milles, Carl **337**
Milton, John 248
Minimalist art 456, 460
Minoan art 52–3
Bull-leaping fresco 52–3
Miró, Joan 390, 393,
417, 418
exhibition poster 11
Harlequin's Carnival 393
Modernism 21, 40–3, 80,
134, 337, **340–3**, 344,
352, 261, 364, 370,
371, 376, 377, 387, 388
see also Abstraction;
Constructivism; Cubism;
Dada; Expressionism;
Futurism; Op Art; Pop
Art, Surrealism
Modigliani, Amedeo
357, 377
Jeanne Hébuterne in
a Yellow Jumper 357
Moholy-Nagy, László **386**
At Coffee 386
Mondrian, Piet 384,
389, 401
Broadway Boogie
Woogie 389
Monet, Claude 304,
310, 312, 317, 327
Impression Sunrise 312
The Japanese Bridge at
Giverny 310
Waterlily Pond 310
Moore, Henry 39,
399, 400
Reclining Figure 399
Moran, Thomas **292**
The Grand Canyon of
the Yellowstone 292
Morandi, Giorgio **404**
Moreau, Gustave
322, **324**
Mori, Mariko **477**
Morisot, Berthe **314**
Morland, George 277
Moroni, Giovanni
Battista **149**
Morris, Robert **457**
Untitled (Felt Tangle) 457
Morris, William 297, 298
Moses, Grandma **408**
Down on the Farm in
Winter 409
Motherwell, Robert **415**
"Spanish Elegies" 415
Mount, William
Sidney **295**
Mozart 240, 246
Mucha, Alphonse 338
Sarah Bernhardt 338

Müller, Otto **362**
Munch, Edvard 324, 328, 338, **360–1**
The Scream 328, **361**
Muñoz, Juan **428**
Munnings, Sir Alfred **379**
Münter, Gabriele **364**
Murillo, Bartolomé 185, **186**
Muybridge 260
photograph of a jumping horse 260
Mycenaean culture 52, 53
Mytens, Daniel **198**

N

Nabis 325, 332
Nadelman, Elie **405**
Tango 405
Napoleon 221, 250, 253, 259, 260, 266
Napoleonic Era 259–60
Nash, Paul **398**
Nauman, Bruce **464**
Nazarenes **273**
Nazis **384**
Neoclassicism **218–21**, 223, 241, 249, **250–1**, 252–5, 273
Netherlands 77, 110–14, 116, 117, 119, 120, 163
Neumann, Balthasar 232
Nevelson, Louise **406**
Mirror Image 1 406
Nevinson, Christopher Richard Wynne 376
New Photographer's movement 386
Newman, Barnett 412, **414–15**
Vir Heroicus Sublimis 414–15
Newton, Isaac 165
Nicholson, Ben 337, **400–1**
September 1963 401
Nicholson, Sir William **337**
Nolan, Sir Sidney **430–1**
Noland, Kenneth **454**
Nolde, Emil 34, **362**
The Dancers 362
Norwich School **276**

O

Ofili, Chris **477**
oil painting 28–9, **33**
O'Keefe, Georgia **409**
Oldenburg, Claes 40, **439**, 440
Giant Hamburger 40
Olitski, Jules **453**
Oliver, Isaac **161**
Op Art 436
Oppenheim, Meret 390, **394**
Object 390, 394
Orozco, José Clemente 35, **402–3**
Overbeck, Friedrich 273

P

Pacher, Michael **124**
The St. Wolfgang

Altarpiece 124
Paik, Nam June **458**
painting, materials, and techniques **32–5**
Paladino, Mimmo **427**
Palma Giovane 141
Palma Vecchio, Jacopo **140–1**
Lady with a Lute 141
Palermo, Blinky **465**
Palmer, Samuel **280**
Panamarenko, Henri van Herwegen **422**
Panini, Giovanni Paolo **234**
Ruins with Figures 234
Paolozzi, Sir Eduardo **446**
Parker, Cornelia 16
Cold Dark Matter: An Exploded View 16
Parmigianino, Girolamo 146, **150**, 154, 155
The Madonna of the Long Neck 150
Self-Portrait in a Convex Mirror 146
Pasmore, Victor **430**
Pastels **30**
Patenier, Joachim **116–17**
St. Jerome in a Rocky Landscape 108
Pater, Jean-Baptiste **224**
Pearlstein, Philip **438–9**
Pechstein, Max **363**
Pellegrini, Giovanni Antonio **230**
pen and ink **31**
pencil **31**
Penck, A. R. **462**
Penrose, Sir Roland **394**
Performance art **43**
Permoserin, Balthasar 252
Perugino, Pietro 97, 273
St. Sebastian 97
Pevsner, Antoine **372**
Birth of the Universe 372
Photography **42**, **260**, 386, 458
Photorealism 458
Picabia, Francis **367**
Picasso, Pablo 30, 35, 136, 329, 332, 345, **348–9**, 351, 352, 357, 373, 377, 384, **396–7**, 405
A Bull 397
Les Demoiselles d'Avignon **348–9**, 351
The Guitar 351
Minotaur 35
Minotaur Caressing a Sleeping Girl 396
Self-Portrait 396
Weeping Woman 397
Woman with a Guitar 351
Piero della Francesca **87**, **100**, 106
The Flagellation of Christ 87
Palace at Urbino 106
Resurrection of Christ 100
Piero di Cosimo **93**
Pinturicchio, Bernardino di Betto **97**
Pope Pius II Canonizes St. Catherine of Siena 97
Piper, John **401**

Piranesi, Giovanni **249**
Carceri d'Invenzione (Prisons) Plate IV 249
Pisanello (Antonio Pisano) **84**
Portrait of Ginevra d'Este 84
Pisano, Nicola and Giovanni **76**
Fontana Maggiore, Perugia 76
Pissarro, Camille 312, **314**
Pistoletto, Michelangelo **425**
Pittoni, Giovanni Battista **230**
The Delivery of the Keys to St. Peter 230
Plein air painting 304, **305**, 312
Plensa, Jaume **429**
Pointillism 320, 346
see also Divisionism
Polke, Sigmar **464–5**
Flight—Black, Red, and Gold 464
Pollaiuolo brothers **94**
Battle of the Ten Naked Men 94
Pollock, Jackson 409, **410–11**, 412, 413
The Moon-Woman Cuts the Circle 411
Number 6 410
Pontormo, Jacopo 146, **148**
Cosimo de' Medici (Il Vecchio) 146
Deposition 146
Pop Art 383, 418, **440**, 441–6
Post-Impressionism 223, 326, **328**, 331, 378
Potter, Paulus **208**
The Young Bull 208
Poussin, Nicolas 154, 167, 169, **180–1**, 182, 183, 334
Arcadian Shepherds 180–1
Portrait of the Artist 180
The Rape of the Sabines 181
Pre-Raphaelites 273, 296, **297**, 298–9, 325, 398
Preti, Mattia **177**
Primaticcio, Francesco 153
Primitive art *see* Early art
Printmaking **36–7**
Provost, Jan **115**
Pucelle, Jehan **79**
Puvis de Chavannes, Pierre 322, **324**

R

Raeburn, Sir Henry **242**
Portrait of Sir Walter Scott 242
Ramsay, Allan **239**
Raphael 26, 94, **134**, 135, 138, 139, 146, 147, 150, 166, 167, 168, 180, 186, 241, 249, 264, 273, 297, 325
Madonna of the Pinks 27

Pope Leo X with Cardinals Giulio de' Medici and Luigi de' Rossi 134
The School of Athens 138–9
The Sistine Madonna 134
Rauschenberg, Robert **437**
The Bed 440
Bellini 437
Sleep for Yvonne Rainer 34
Rayonism 42, 370
Realism **300–1**, 304, 306
Redon, Odilon 30, 322, **324–5**
The Cyclops 322
Rembrandt 31, 170, 196, 198, **200–1**, 202, 203, 207, 239, 307, 337
Jacob Blessing the Children of Joseph 200–1
Lion Resting 31
Self-Portrait at the Age of 63 201
Studies of Old Men's Heads and Three Women with Children (detail) 200
The Three Crosses 201
Remington, Frederic **293**
The Blanket Signal 293
Renaissance 33, 79, 89, 90, 264, 312, 328
Early Renaissance 20, 26, **73–5**, 83, 84, **86–7**, 88, 91, 92, 95, 100, 103, 135, 299
High Renaissance 17, 19, 39, **128–31**, 132, 135, **138–9**, 143, 146
France 118–19
see also Italy; Florence; Rome; Siena; Venice
Northern Renaissance **108–9**
Reni, Guido **166**
Atalanta and Hippomenes 166
Renoir, Pierre-Auguste 228, **311**, 312, **313**
Bather Arranging her Hair 311
Boating Party 313
reproductions 29
Reynolds, Sir Joshua 186, 238, **239**, 240, 242
Master Thomas Lister (The Brown Boy) 239
Ribera, José **185**
The Club Foot 185
Ricci, Marco **229**
Ships in a Gale 229
Ricci, Sebastiano **229**
Richter, Gerhard **458**
S. with Child 458
Riemenschneider, Tilman **121**, 124
Rietveld, Gerrit 389
Red Blue Chair 389
Riley, Bridget **436**
Rivera, Diego **402**
Rivers, Larry **437**
Robbia, Andrea della 91
Robbia, Luca della **91**
Cantoria 91
Robert, Hubert 22
Grand Gallery of the Louvre 22
Roberts, William **377**

Robinson, Theodore **317**
  At the Piano 317
Rococo 186, **218–21**,
  226–7, 222–33, 250, 252
Rodchenko, Aleksandr
  373
Rodin, Auguste 38,
  318–19, 337, 356, 378
  *The Burghers of
  Calais* 318
  The Gates of Hell
  318, 319
  The Kiss 38, **319**
  The Thinker 38
Romanesque Art
  39, **70–1**
  Nave of Pisa
  Cathedral 70
Romano, Giulio **147**
  Madonna and Child 147
Romanticism 18, 248,
  249, **258–61**, **266–7**,
  297, 304, 386, 416
  see also Britain;
  France; Germany;
  United States
Rome 138, 139,146,
  162, 164
  see also Renaissance;
  Baroque
Rome, Classical *see*
  Classical Rome
Rosa, Salvator **176**
  Self-Portrait 176
Rose, Joseph 250
Rosselli, Cosimo **94**
Rossetti, Dante
  Gabriel **296**, 297
Rosenquist, James **445**
  F-111 445
Roth, Dieter **423**
  Literature Sausage 423
Rothenberg, Susan **467**
  Red Banner 467
Rothko, Mark 412,
  413, **414**
  *The Black and the
  White* 413
Rouault, Georges **354**
Roubiliac, Louis-François
  252
Rousseau, Henri **332–3**
  The Rugby Players 333
Rousseau, Théodore
  304, 305
Rowlandson, Thomas **247**
  A French Coffee House 247
Rubens, Sir Peter Paul
  20, 156, 167, 178,
  186, 190, **191–3**,
  195, 239, 269
  *Battle of the Amazons
  and Greeks* 191
  *Hélène Fourment in a
  Fur Wrap* 191
  Marie de' Medici
  series 222
  Samson and Delilah **192–3**
Runge, Philipp Otto **273**
  Die Farbenkugel 273
  Self-Portrait 273
Ruscha, Edward **441**
Ruskin, John **296**,
  298, 299
Russell, Charles M. **293**
Russia 32, 41, 359, 364,
  368, 370–3

Entombment of Christ 32
Frieze showing heroic
  Soviet workers,
  Moscow 342
Soviet Postcard from
  World War II 343
Ryder, Albert
  Pinkham **295**
  Jonah and the Whale 285
  Roadside Meeting 295
  *Siegfried and the
  Rhinemaidens* 295
Ryman, Robert **457**

S

Saenredam, Pieter
  Jansz **205**
Salle, David **470**
Sargent, John
  Singer **326–7**
  *The Daughters of
  Edward Darley Boit* 326
Sarto, Andrea del **135**,153
  *Lamentation over the
  Dead Christ* 135
Sassetta, Stefano di
  Giovanni **83**
Savery, Roelandt **190**
Saxon Art **66**
Schad, Christian **385**
  *Self-Portrait with
  Model* 385
Schiele, Egon **360**
  Self-Portrait Nude 360
science, 17th century **165**
  Isaac Newton's
  telescope 165
  Visit of Louis XIV to
  the Académie Royale
  des Sciences in 1667
Schlemmer, Oskar
  386, **388**
  Unterhaltung I 388
Schmidt, Joos 386
  Poster for Bauhaus
  Exhibition 386
Schmidt-Rottluff, Karl **363**
Schnabel, Julian **469**
Schongauer, Martin **125**
School of Paris **357**
Schuette, Thomas **472**
Schwitters, Kurt 35, **368**
  *YMCA Flag, Thank
  You, Ambleside* 368
screen prints **37**
  silkscreen printing 37
Scully, Sean **467**
sculpture
  materials, and
  techniques **38–40**, 41
Sebastiano del
  Piombo **135**
Secession **338**
Segal, George **454**
Senefelder, Aloys 37
Serra, Richard **462–3**
Sérusier, Paul **332**
  The Talisman 332
Seurat, Georges
  320, 324, 328
  *A Sunday Afternoon
  on the Island of La
  Grande Jatte* 320
Severini, Gino 375
Shakespeare, William
  170, 248, 297

Sheeler, Charles **407**
  Steam Turbine 407
Sherman, Cindy **472**
Sickert, Walter
  Richard **326**
Siena 76, 78, 82, 101
Signac, Paul **320**
Signorelli, Luca **94–5**
Simone Martini **82**
Siqueiros, David Alfaro
  35, **402**
  *The March of Humanity
  in Latin America* 402
Sisley, Alfred 312, **314**
  The Bridge at Moret 314
Sistine Chapel 128, 138,
  139, 167
Sloan, John **381**
  McSorley's Bar 381
Sluter, Claus **85**
  The Moses Well 85
Smith, David 40, **410**
  Four Units Unequal 40
Smith, Kiki **472**
Smith, Tony **452**
Smithson, Robert 43, **462**
  Broken Circle 462
Snyders, Frans **190**
  *Pantry Scene with a
  Page* 190
Sorolla y Bastida,
  Joaquín **327**
Soulages, Pierre **420**
Soutine, Chaïm **357**
Spain
  Baroque 129, 131,
  178, 185–9
Spencer, Sir Stanley **398**
  *Travoys Arriving with
  the Wounded at a
  Dressing Station, Smol,
  Macedonia* 398
Spranger, Bartholomeus
  158
St. Ives Group **400**, 430
  Tate St. Ives,
  Cornwall 400
St. Peter's, Rome
  138, 139, 178
Staël, Nicolas de **419**
Steen, Jan **211**
  The Christening Feast 211
Steenwyck, Harmen 197
  *The Vanities of
  Human Life* **197**
Stella, Frank **461–2**
Stella, Joseph 375
De Stijl 368, 372, **389**
Still, Clyfford 412,
  413, **416**
stone sculpture **39**
stone-age sculpture 47
  Venus of Willendorf
  39, 47, 48
Stoss, Veit **124**
Strauss, Richard 339
Stuart, Gilbert **257**
Stubbs, George **246**
  Anatomy of the Horse 246
  *A Horse Frightened by
  a Lion* 246
Sueur Brothers, Le 220
  *Cry of Liberty and
  the Departure for the
  Frontier* 220
Suh, Do-Ho 41
  Some/One 41

Surrealism 43, 324–5,
  353, 369, 377, **390–1**,
  392–5, 398, 404, 406,
  412, 417, 418
Sutherland, Graham **401**
Symbolism **322–3**,
  324–5, 325, 332,
  353, 389, 396
Synchronism 383

T

Tanguy, Yves **393**
Tàpies, Antoni **428**
  Composition, LXIV 428
Tatlin, Vladimir 372, **373**
  *Monument to the Third
  International* 373
  *The Sailor
  (Self-Portrait)* 373
Teniers, David **195**
  Boors Carousing 195
Tennyson 297
Terborch, Gerard **210**
  *The Flea-Catcher (Boy
  with His Dog)* 196
Terbrugghen, Hendrick
  172, **199**
Thiebaud, Wayne **441**
Thornhill, Sir James **217**
Thorvaldsen, Bertel **255**
  *Jason with the
  Golden Fleece* 255
Tiepolo, Giambattista
  226, **230–1**, **232–3**
  *Abraham and the
  Three Angels* 231
  *Apollo Bringing the
  Bride* **232–3**
Tiepolo, Giandomenico
  231
Tinguely, Jean **418**
  Beaubourg Fountain 418
  *Turning of Friendship of
  America and France* 418
Tintoretto 146, **152**
  *St. George and the
  Dragon* 152
  Susanna Bathing 152
Tischbein, Johann
  Heinrich Wilhelm 221
  *Goethe in the
  Campagna* 221
Tissot, James **302–3**
  Portrait of Mlle. L. L. 303
Titian 135, 138, 141,
  143–5, 151, 155,
  167, 186, 249, 287,
  299, 308
  Bacchus and Ariadne
  144–5
  *The Emperor Charles
  V on Horseback in
  Mühlberg* 138
  Venus and Adonis 143
Tobey, Mark **410**
Toulouse-Lautrec,
  Henri de **333**
  Le Divan, Japonais 333
Trumbull, John **274**
  *Portrait of Alexander
  Hamilton* 274
Tuby, Jean-Baptiste 21
  Fountain of Apollo 21
Tunick, Spencer 43
  Nude Installation 43
Turner, J. M. W. 31, 34,

244, 245, 266, 276, **281–3**, 292
Couvent du Bonhomme, Chamonix 266
Crichton Castle (Mountainous Landscape with a Rainbow) 281
The Fighting Téméraire **282–3**
Rain, Steam, and Speed—The Great Western Railway 281
Sunset over a Ruined Castle 34
Turrell, James **465**
Twombly, Cy **456**

U

Uccello, Paolo **92**
The Hunt in the Forest 92
Uecker, Günther **423**
Ugolino di Nerio **82**
United States
  American School, rise of 256, **257**
  Contemporary 452–7, 458, 459–3, 464, 467, 469, 470, 472–3, 474–5, 477
  Declaration of Independence 221
  Early Modernists 380–3
  expansion 261
  Impressionism 316–17
  Modernists 37, 404–17, 436–45
  Romanticism 274, 275, 290–5
Utrecht School 196, 199, 200, 204
Utrillo, Maurice **354**

V

Valdés Leal, Juan de **186**
Valetin, Moïse 172, **182**
Vallotton, Félix **332**
van de Velde, Esaias **204**
van de Velde, Willem (the elder) **204**
van de Velde, Willem (the younger) **205**
Sea Battle of the Anglo-Dutch Wars 205
van der Heyden, Jan **210**
van der Neer, Aert **207**
van Dyck, Sir Anthony 186, **194–5**
King Charles I of England 194
van Eyck 33, 108, **109–11**, 115, 117, 126
Ghent Altarpiece 108
A Man in a Turban 110
The Marriage of Arnolfini 33, 109
van Gogh, Vincent 32, 328, 329, **330–1**, 332, 346, 476
Portrait of Doctor Paul Gachet, the Man with the Pipe 331
Self-Portrait 330
Starry Night 330

Sunflowers 331
Van Gogh's Bedroom at Arles 328
van Goyen, Jan **205**
River Landscape with Ferries Docked Before a Tower 205
van Honthorst, Gerrit **204**
Supper with the Minstrel and his Lute 204
van Huysum, Jan **212**
van Loo, Carle **229**
van Ostade, Adriaen **206**
The Piper 206–7
van Ruisdael, Jacob **208–9**
van Ruysdael, Salomon 196, **206–7**, 209
River Landscape with Peasants Ferrying 196
Varley, John **276**
Vasarely, Victor **436**
Bi-Vega 437
Vasari, Giorgio 147
The Annunciation 147
Lives of the Artists 147
Vauxcelles, Louis 346
Gil Blas 346
Vecchietta **101**
Pope Pius II, Crowned by Two Cardinals 101
Velasquez 170, 185, 186, **187–9**, 321, 327
Christ on the Cross 187
Les Meninas **188–9**
Waterseller of Seville 187
Veneziano, Domenico **91**
Venice 33, 103–6, 135, 138, 140–4, 151–2, 230, 286
Vermeer 211, **213–15**
The Artist's Studio **214–5**
Christ in the House of Martha and Mary 25
Girl with a Pearl Earing 213
View of Delft 213
Vernet, Antoine-Charles Horace 260
Napoleon Giving Orders before Austerlitz 260
Vernet, Claude-Joseph **255**
The Storm 255
Veronese, Paolo **142**
Marriage at Cana 142
Verrocchio, Andrea del **93**, 96, 132
Equestrian Monument to Bartolomeo Colleoni 93
Versailles 163, 164, 232
  Chapelle Royale 164
Victoria, Queen 25
video art **42**
Vien, Comte Joseph-Marie **252**
Vienna Secession 338, 339
Facade of Secession Building, Vienna 338
Vigée-Lebrun, Elisabeth **255**
Portrait of a Young Woman 255
Viking Art **66**
Viola, Bill 42 **469**
The Crossing 42

Vivarini family **104–5**
Madonna and Child with Sts. Peter, Jerome, and Mary Magdalene with a Bishop 104
Vlaminck, Maurice de **346**
Tugboat at Chatou 346
Vollard, Ambroise 21 344
  portrait of Vollard 21
Vorticism **376**, 377
Vos, Marten de **156**
Vuillard, Edouard **336**
Mother and Child 336

W

Wadsworth, Edward **377**
Wall, Jeff **468**
Wallis, Alfred 400
Ward, James **277**
Gordale Scar 277
Warhol, Andy 12, 18, 37, 440, **444**
Campbell's Soup Can 440
Twenty Marilyns 12, 444
watercolor **34**
Watteau, Jean-Antoine **222–3**, 224
L'Enseigne de Gersaint 222
Head of a Negro 223
A Journey to Cythera 222–3, 226
Pierrot: Gilles 222
Watts, George Frederick **299**
Weber, Max **382**
Weenix, Jan **212**
Still Life 212
Weir, Julian Alden **317**
West, Benjamin **256**
The Death of General Wolfe 256–7
Weston, Edward 42
Weyden, Rogier van der 108, **111–13**, 114, 115, 117, 124, 126
The Deposition **112–13**
Portrait of a Young Woman in a Pinned Hat 108
Whistler, James Abbott McNeill **321**, 322, **323**, 325
Mother and Child on a Couch 321
Nocturne in Black and Gold: The Falling Rocket 323
Whiteread, Rachel **476**
Wilde, Oscar 321, 322, 377
Wilkie, Sir David **280**
The Chelsea Pensioners Reading the Waterloo Dispatch 280
William III 217
Wilson, Richard **244**
Snowdon 244
Winckelmann, Johann 250
Thoughts on the Imitation of Greek Works of Art 250
Winterhalter, Franz Xavier **286**
Wols, Alfred Otto **420**
Composition 420
Wood, Grant **406–7**
American Gothic 407

woodcarving **39**
woodcuts **36**
Woodington, W. F. 282
Wordsworth, William 266, 468
Wouvermans, Philips **208**
Wren, Sir Christopher 217
Wright, John Michael **216**
Wright, Joseph **246**
Wyeth, Andrew **439**

Z

Zimmermann, Johann Baptiste
The Last Judgment 226
Zoffany, Johann **241**
The Drummond Family 241
Zola, Emile 300
Zorn, Anders **327**
Girls from Dalarna 327
Having a Bath 327
Zuccarelli, Francesco **237**
An Italianate River Landscape 237
Zuccaro, Taddeo 158
Zurbarán, Francisco de **185**

PICTURE CREDITS

The publisher would like to thank the following for their kind permission to reproduce their photographs.

a = above; bg = background; b = below; c = center; l = left; r = right; rh = running header; t = top

AKG = akg-images; AL = Alamy Images; ART = The Art Archive; BAL = www.bridgeman.co.uk; Co = Corbis

1 Corbis/Alinari Archives; **2-3** Photo: Wolfgang Volz © Christo 2005; **4** Getty Images/Photo: Gjon Mili/Time Life Pictures/© Succession Picasso/DACS 2005; **5** Alamy Images/Robert Harding Picture Library Ltd; **6-7** Corbis/William Manning; **9** BAL/Bargello (br); Stapleton collection (cl); **9** Rex Features/Roger-Viollet (t); **10-11** Corbis/D. Hudson (b); **11** Christie's Images Ltd/© Succession Miro, DACS, 2005 (t); **12** BAL Private Collection/© The Andy Warhol Foundation for the Visual Arts, Inc/ARS, NY and DACS, London 2005; **13** Empics Ltd/Gorassini Giancarlo/ABACA; **14-15** Alamy Images/Angus Oborn; **16** © Tate, London 2005/Courtesy Frith Street Gallery; **18** BAL/Musee de la Ville de Paris, Musee du Petit-Palais, France (t); **18-19** Rex Features/Richard Young (b); **19** BAL/Private Collection (t); **20** BAL/Bargello (t); **20-21** Corbis/Dave G. Houser (b); **21** Rex Features/Roger-Viollet (tr); **22** BAL/Museo di San Marco dell'Angelico, Florence (t); **22-23** BAL/Giraudon/Louvre, Paris (b); 23 Alamy Images © David R. Frazier Photolibrary, Inc. (br); **24** Alamy Images/Donald Nausbaum (t); **24** Getty Images/Photo: David Lees/Time Life Pictures (b); **25** BAL/National Galleries of Scotland (t); **25** Reuters/De Kunsthal Gallery, Rotterdam (t); **26** BAL/Accademia, Florence; **27** National Gallery, London; **28** Corbis/Royalty Free; **30** BAL/Gabinetto dei Disegni e Stampe, Uffizi, Florence (tra), (trb); Pushkin Museum, Moscow, Russia (bcl), (bcr); **31** BAL/Peter Willi/Louvre, Paris (cl); Private Collection; 31 DK Images/Musee Marmottan; Stephen Oliver (b). **32** Alamy Images/Visual Arts Library (London) (bc); **32** BAL/Louvre, Paris (cr); (tr); **33** BAL/National Gallery, London (bcr), (bl). **33** DK Images/Steve Gorton (bc), (br); **33** Photo Scala, Florence/Vatican Museums and Galleries, Vatican City (tr); **34** Photonica/John Wilkes (bcr); **34** © Tate, London 2005 (tr); **35** BAL/Daniels, Harvey/Private Collection, (tl); Private Collection/© Robert Rauschenberg/VAGA, New York/DACS, London 2005 (b); **35** Art Archive/Museum of Modern Art, New York/© Succession Picasso/DACS 2005 (br); **36** BAL/Private Collection (tl); On Loan to Hamburg Kunsthalle, Hamburg (b); **36** Christie's Images Ltd (c); **36** Corbis/Austrian Archives (tr). **36** DK Images/Artichoke prints (br); **37** BAL/ Private collection/© Hundertwasser Archives, Vienna (br); **37** Corbis/John Garrett (bl); Wolfgang Kaehler (tr); **37** Mary Evans Picture Library (t); **37** Rex Features/Peter Brooker (cr); **38** Corbis (b); © Ted Soqui (c), (tl); **39** Corbis/Elio Ciol (tl); **39** Getty Images/John Millar (cr); **40** BAL/Private collection/© ARS, NY and DACS, London 2005 (bl); Private Collection/© Estate of David Smith/VAGA, New York/DACS, London 2005 (cr); **40** Getty Images/Greg Pease (t); **41** Alamy Images/Roger Bamber © Olafur Eliasson (t); **41** BAL/Private collection/© Succession Marcel Duchamp/ ADAGP, Paris and DACS, London 2005 (b); **42** BAL/© Man Ray Trust/ADAGP, Paris and DACS, London 2005 (tr); **42** Photo: Kira Perov/© Bill Viola; **42** Zefa Visual Media UK Ltd/A. Green (tl); **43** Photo: Wolfgang Volz, © Christo 1983 (b); **43** Magnum Photos/Alec Soth (cl); **43** Rex Features/Erik Pendzich (t); **44-45** BAL/Giraudon/Galleria degli Uffizi, Florence; **45-46** Corbis/Gian Berto Vanni (t); **46** Corbis/Sandro Vannini; **48** BAL/Naturhistorisches Museum, Vienna, Austria (b); **48** Getty Images/National Geographic/Sissie Brimberg (t); **49** BAL/Iraq Museum, Baghdad, Iraq, Giraudon; **50** BAL/Egyptian National Museum, Cairo, Egypt (bl), (t); **51** BAL (t); **52** BAL (b); Giraudon (t); **53** BAL/Giraudon (bl); Peter Willi (br); **54** BAL/British Museum, London (b); Giraudon/Louvre, Paris (tr); **54** Corbis/Charles O'Rear (cl); **55** akg-images/Nimatallah; **56** Alamy Images/Adam Eastland (b); **56** BAL/ Alinari /Museo Archeologico Nazionale, Naples (t); **57** Corbis/Gianni Dagli Orti (br); **57** Corbis/Royalty Free (t); **58-59** akg-images/Nimatallah; **60** BAL/Lauros/Giraudon (tr); **61** Corbis/Sandro Vannini (b); **61** Art Archive: Museo Capitolino Rome/Dagli Orti (t); **62** BAL/Giraudon/Louvre, Paris (t); **63** BAL/Castello Sforzesco, Milan; **64** Art Archive/Dagli Orti (A)/Cathedral of St Just Trieste (t); Art Archive/Dagli Orti (A) (b); **65** BAL/San Vitale, Ravenna (b); **66** BAL/British Museum, London/Boltin Picture Library (t); **66** Corbis/Werner Forman (bl); **67** BAL/MS 58 fol.34r Chi-rho (initials of Christ's name) Gospel of St. Matthew, chap. 1 v. 18, Irish (vellum)/Board of Trinity College, Dublin, Ireland; **69** akg-images/Erich Lessing (t); **69** Art Archive/Dagli Orti (A)/Archaeological Museum Cividale Friuli(bl); Dagli Orti/Bibliothèque Municipale Abbeville; Dagli Orti/Musée Condé Chantilly (t); **70** Alamy Images/Hideo Kurihara (b); **70** BAL/Chartres Cathedral, Chartres, France (t); **71** BAL/Chartres Cathedral, Chartres, France, Peter Willi(b); **72** Corbis/Massimo Listri; **74** akg-images/Erich Lessing (b); **74** BAL/Prado, Madrid (t);

75 Alamy Images/AA World Travel Library; **76** BAL/Samuel Courtauld Trust, Courtauld Institue of Art Gallery; **77** BAL/Musee Conde, Chantilly, France (cr); Museo di San Marco dell'Angelico, Florence (bl); **78** BAL/Galleria degli Uffizi, Florence (bl); **78-79** BAL/Palazzo Pubblico, Siena; **80** Alamy Images/One World Images; **81** BAL/San Francesco, Upper Church, Assisi (br); Scrovegni (Arena) Chapel, Padua (t); **82** BAL/Fitzwilliam Museum, University of Cambridge (bc); **82-83** BAL/Louvre, Paris; **84** BAL/Louvre, Paris (bl); **85** BAL/Chartreuse de Champmol, Dijon (bc); Wallrat Richarts Museum, Cologne, Germany (t). **86** BAL/Alinari/Bargello, Florence (t); Palazzo Medici-Riccardi, Florence (b); **87** BAL/Galleria Nazionale delle Marche, Urbino; **88** BAL/Santa Maria Novella, Florence; **89** BAL/Louvre, Paris; **90** BAL/Bargello, Florence; **91** BAL/Museo dell'Opera del Duomo, Florence; **92-93** BAL/Ashmolean Museum, Oxford (t); Louvre, Paris (bc). **93** BAL/Campo Santi Giovanni e' Paolo, Venice (bc); **94** Photo Scala, Florence/Gabinetto dei Disegni e delle Stampe degli Uffizi, Florence; **95** BAL/Louvre, Paris; **96** BAL/National Gallery of Art, Washington DC, USA; **97** BAL/Hermitage, St. Petersburg, Russia (bc); Piccolomini Library, Duomo, Siena (tr); **98-99** BAL/Galleria degli Uffizi, Florence; **100** BAL/Pinacoteca, Sansepolcro; Pushkin Museum, Moscow (tc); **101** BAL/Palazzo Piccolomini, Siena (tr); **102-103** BAL/Galleria dell'Accademia, Venice; Louvre, Paris (t); **103** BAL/National Gallery, London (tr); **104** BAL/Musee de Picardie, Amiens, France; **105** BAL/National Gallery, London (br); Santi Giovanni e Paolo, Venice (tc); **106** Alamy Images/Norma Joseph (cr); **106** BAL/Walker Art Gallery, Liverpool (bc); **107** BAL/Pinacoteca di Brera, Milan; **108** BAL/Gemaldegalerie, Berlin (tr); National Gallery, London (t); **109** BAL/National Gallery, London; **110** BAL/National Gallery, London; **112-113** BAL/Prado, Madrid; **114** BAL/Galleria degli Uffizi, Florence (tr); Musee des Beaux-Arts, Lille, France (bl). **115** BAL/Louvre, Paris; **116** BAL/Galleria degli Uffizi, Florence; **117** BAL/Louvre, Paris; **118** BAL/Prado, Madrid; **119** BAL/Bibliotheque Nationale, Paris, France; **120** BAL/Musee Royaux de Beaux-Arts de Belgique, Brussels (b); Prado, Madrid (tc); **121** BAL/Musee d'Unterlinden, Calmar, France (tr); **122** BAL/Musee d'Unterlinden, Colmar, France (cl), **122-123** BAL/Musee d'Unterlinden, Colmar, France; **124** BAL/St Wolfgang, Austria; **125** BAL/Walker Art Gallery, Liverpool; **126** BAL/Alte Pinakothek, Munich, Germany (tc); Graphische Sammlung Albertina, Vienna (b); **126-127** BAL/Kunsthistoriches Museum, Vienna, Austria; **127** BAL/British Museum, London (br); **128** akg-images/Erich Lessing; **130-131** Alamy Images/naglestock.com; **130** BAL/Lambeth Palace Library, London (b); **130** Corbis/Archivo Iconografico, S.A. (t); **132** BAL/Fitzwilliam Museum, Universty of Cambridge (tr); **132-133** BAL/Santa Maria della Grazie, Milan; **133** BAL/National Gallery, London (t); **134** BAL/Galleria degli Uffizi, Florence (tr); Gemaldegalerie, Dresden, Germany (br); **135** BAL/Palazzo Pitri, Florence; **136** BAL/Galleria degli Uffizi, Florence (bc); Museums and Galleries, Vatican City (t); **137** BAL/St Peter's Vatican, Rome; **138** BAL/Louvre, Paris (br); Prado, Madrid (cra); **139** BAL/Giraudon/Vatican Museums and Galleries, Vatican City; **140** BAL/Kunsthistoriches Museum, Vienna; **141** BAL/Collection of the Duke of Northumberland (tc); Galleria dell' Accademia, Venice (br); **142** BAL/Louvre, Paris; **143** BAL/Prado, Madrid; **144-145**, Corbis/Trustees of the National Gallery, London; **146** BAL/Galleria degli Uffizi, Florence (bl); Kunsthistoriches Museum, Vienna, Austria (cra); **147** BAL/Galleria degli Uffizi, Florence (tr); Louvre, Pais, France (bc); **148** BAL/National Gallery, London; **149** BAL/Bargello, Florence; **150** BAL/Galleria degli Uffizi, Florence; **151** BAL/Louvre, Paris; **152** BAL/Kunsthistorisches Museum, Vienna, Austria (tc); National Gallery, London (bc); **153** BAL/ Giraudon/Chateau de Fontainebleau, Seine-et-Marne, France, Lauros (b); **154** BAL/Kunsthistorisches Museum, Vienna, Austria (t); **155** BAL/Prado, Madrid (tc); Toledo, S. Tome (br); **156** BAL/Gemaldegalerie, Kassel (tr); Private Collection (bl); **157** BAL/Kunsthistorisches Museum, Vienna, Austria (br), (tc); **158** BAL/Kunsthistorisches Museum, Vienna, Austria; **159** BAL/Kunsthistorisches Museum, Vienna, Austria (tl); **160** BAL/Chatsworth House, Derbyshire (br); National Gallery, London (t); **161** BAL/Beauchamp Collection (bc); Society of Antiquaries, London (cl); **162** Alamy Images/BL Images Ltd; **164** BAL/ Giraudon/Musee Bargoin, Clermont-Ferrand, France, Lauros (t); **164** Corbis/Massimo Listri (b); **165** Corbis/Bettmann (t); **165** Art Archive/Royal Society/Eileen Tweedy (t); **166** BAL/Prado, Madrid; **167** BAL/Hermitage, St Petersburg, Russia (bc); Louvre, Paris (tr); **168-169** BAL/Ashmolean Museum, University of Oxford (b); Vatican Museums and Galleries, Vatican City (tl); **169** BAL/Birmingham Museums and Art Gallery (tr); **170-171** BAL/National Gallery, London (t); Palazzo Barberini, Rome (tl); **171** BAL/Galleria Borghese, Rome (bc); **172** BAL/Palazzo Pitti, Florence; **173** BAL/ Giraudon/Galleria Borghese, Rome, Lauros; **174-175** BAL/Santa Maria della Vittoria, Rome; **176** BAL/National Gallery, London; **177** BAL/Galleria dell' Accademia, Venice; **178** BAL/Piazza Navona, Rome; **179** BAL/Palazzo Farnese, Rome (bl), (br), (c); **180-181** BAL/Louvre, Paris (b); Louvre,

Paris, Giraudon (bl); **181** BAL/Louvre, Paris (tr); **182-183** BAL/National Gallery, London; **184** BAL/Louvre, Paris; **185** BAL/Louvre, Paris; **186** BAL/Bonhams, London; **187** BAL/Apsley House, Wellington Museum, London (t); Prado, Madrid (b); **188-189** BAL/Prado, Madrid; **190** BAL/Wallace Collection, London; **191** BAL/Alte Pinakothek, Munich (b); Kunsthistorisches Museum, Vienna, Austria (t); **192-193** BAL/National Gallery, London; **194** BAL/Giraudon/Louvre, Paris, Lauros; **195** BAL/Fitzwilliam Museum, University of Cambridge; **196** BAL/Alte Pinakothek, Munich (bl); Private Collection (t); **197** National Gallery, London (bl), (br), (t) **198** BAL/Wallace Collection, London; **199** BAL/Hamburg Kunsthalle, Hamburg (t); Townley Hall Art Gallery & Museum, Burnley, Lancashire (b); **200-201** BAL/Gemaldegalerie, Kassel (b); **200** BAL/ Barber Institute of Fine Arts, University of Birmingham (t); **201** BAL/Fitzwilliam Museum, University of Cambridge (b); National Gallery, London (t); **202** BAL/Louvre, Paris (t); Giraudon/Louvre, Paris (b); **203** BAL/Harold Samuel Collection, Corporation of London (t); **204** BAL/Galleria degli Uffizi, Florence; **205** BAL/Private Collection (b); Yale Centre for British Art, Paul Mellon Collection, USA (t); **206-207** BAL/British Museum, London (t); **207** BAL/ National Gallery of Scotland, Edinburgh, Scotland (b); **208** BAL/Mauritshuis, The Hague, The Netherlands; **209** BAL/National Gallery, London (b), (t); **210-211** BAL/Wallace Collection, London; **212** BAL/Leeds Museums and Galleries (City Art Gallery); **213** BAL/Mauritshuis, The Hague (b), (t); **214-215** BAL/Kunsthistorisches Museum, Vienna; **216** BAL/ Scottish National Portrait Gallery, Edinburgh; **217** BAL/V&A Museum, London; **218** Alamy Images/Bildarchiv Monheim GmbH; **220** BAL/Musee de la Ville de Paris, Musee Carnavalet, Paris, France/Giraudon (t); **221** akg-images (tr); **222** BAL/Louvre, Paris (b); **222-223** BAL/Louvre, Paris (t); **223** BAL/British Museum, London (b); **224** BAL/ Giraudon/Louvre, Paris/Lauros **225** BAL/Worcester Art Museum, Massachusetts, USA; **226** BAL (b); Wieskirche, Wies, Germany (t); **227** BAL/Wallace Collection, London (c), (bl), (br); **228** BAL/Wallace Collection, London; **229** BAL/Indianapolis Museum of Art, USA (t); Detroit Institute of Arts (b); **230** BAL/Louvre, Paris; **231** BAL/Ca' Rezzonico, Museo di Settecento (b); Scuola Grande di San Rocco, Venice (t); **232-233** BAL/Residenz, Wurzburg; **234** BAL/Collection of the Earl of Pembroke, Wilton House, Wiltshire (tl); **234-235** BAL/National Gallery, London (b); **236** BAL/Museum Narodowe, Warsaw, Poland (b); V&A Museum, London (tr); **237** BAL/Christies Images, London (t); **238** BAL/National Gallery, London (b); Private Collection, Ken Welsh (t); **239** BAL/Hermitage, St. Petersburg, Russia (br); **240** BAL/National Gallery London (t), (b); **241** BAL/Yale Center for British Art, Paul Mellon Collection, USA (b); **242** BAL/Scottish National Portrait Gallery, Edinburgh; **243** BAL/Yale Center for British Art, Paul Mellon Collection, USA (b); Private Collection (t); **244** BAL/Private Collection; **245** BAL/Charles Young Fine Paintings, London (t); New Walk Museum, Leicester City Museum Service (b); **246** BAL/Walker Art Gallery, Liverpool, Merseyside; **247** BAL/Christie's Images (b); Fitzwilliam Museum, University of Cambridge (t); **248** BAL/Detroit Institute of Arts (t); Whitworth Art Gallery, University of Manchester (b); **249** BAL/On Loan to Hamburg Kunsthalle, Hamburg (tr); **250** BAL/Galleria Borghese, Rome (c); John Bethell (b); **251** BAL/Louvre, Paris (bc), (br), (c); **252** BAL/Bibliotheque de la Comedie Francaise, Paris; **253** BAL/ Chateau de Versailles, France; **254** BAL/Louvre, Paris; **255** BAL/Musee Calvet, Avignon, France; Museum of Fine Arts, Boston, Massachusetts, USA (b); **256-257** BAL/Private Collection, Phillips, Fine Art Auctioneers, New York, USA; **258** BAL/ Giraudon/Louvre, Paris/Lauros; **260** BAL/ Giraudon/Chateau de Versailles, France/Lauros (t); **260** Science & Society Picture Library/NMPFT (bl); **260** Science Photo Library/Eadweard Muybridge Collection/Kingston Museum (cr); **261** BAL/Guildhall Library, Corporation of London; **262-263** BAL/ Giraudon/Prado, Madrid (b); **263** BAL/Index/Private Collection (tr); **264** BAL/ Bristol City Museum and Art Gallery; **265** BAL/Louvre, Paris; **266** BAL/Fitzwilliam Museum, University of Cambridge (t); Staatliche Museen, Berlin (b); **267** BAL/Louvre, Paris (bc, (bn, (c); **268-269** BAL/Castle Museum and Art Gallery, Nottingham (t); **268** BAL/Louvre, Paris (b); **269** BAL/Louvre, Paris (t); **270-271** BAL/Louvre, Paris; **272** BAL/Museum der Bildenden Kunste, Leipzig (c); National Gallery, London (t); **273** BAL/Hamburg Kunsthalle, Hamburg; **274-275** BAL/Metropolitan Museum of Art, New York (c); **274** BAL/White House, Washington D.C. (b); **276** BAL/Norwich Castle Museum (tr); V&A Museum, London (b); **277** BAL/John Constable; **278-279** BAL/National Gallery, London; **280** BAL/Apsley House, Wellington Museum London; **281** BAL/National Gallery, London (b); Yale Centre for British Art, Paul Mellon Collection, USA (t); **282-283** BAL/National Gallery, London; **284** BAL/Giraudon/Chateau de Compiegne, Oise, France (b); Musee de la Ville de Paris, Musee du Petit-Palais, France Lauros / Giraudon (t); **285** BAL/Musee of Orsay, Paris (b); Private Collection (t); **286** BAL/Bonhams, London; **287** BAL/Apsley House, Wellington Museum, London (t); Lady Lever Art gallery, Port Sunlight, Merseyside (b); **288** BAL/Lady Lever Art Gallery, Port

Sunlight, Merseyside; **289** BAL/Louvre, Paris (t); Whitworth Art Gallery, University of Manchester (b); **290** BAL/New York Historical Society; **291** BAL/Detroit Institute of Arts, USA; **292** BAL/National Museum of American Art, Smithsonian Institute, USA; **293** BAL/Museum of fine Arts, Houston, Texas; **294** BAL/Private Collection; **295** BAL/Butler Institute of American Art; **296** BAL/Manchester Art Gallery; **297** BAL/Delaware Art Museum, Wilmington; (b); National Gallery of Victoria, Melbourne, Australia (t); **299** BAL/William Morris Gallery, Walthamstow; **300-301** BAL/Giraudon d'Orsay Paris; **302** BAL/Musee d'Orsay, Paris/© DACS 2005; **303** BAL/Musee d'Orsay, Paris; **304** BAL/Louvre, Paris; **305** BAL/Musee d'Orsay, Paris; **306-307** BAL/Courtauld Institute Gallery, Somerset House, London (t); **307** BAL/Walters Art Museum, Baltimore (br); **308-309** BAL/Musee d'Orsay, Paris; **310** BAL/Musee Marmottan, Paris (b); National Gallery, London (t); **311** BAL/National Gallery of Art, Washington DC; **312** BAL/Musee Marmottan, Paris (tl); Private Collection, Christie's Images (b); **313** BAL/Phillips Collection, Washington DC (bl), (br), (c); **314** BAL; Musee d'Orsay, Paris; **315** BAL/Musee d'Orsay, Paris (b); National Gallery, London (t); **316** BAL/Detroit Institute of Arts; **317** BAL/National Gallery of Art, Washington DC; **318** BAL/Hirshorn Museum, Washington DC; **319** BAL/Musee Rodin, Paris; **320** BAL/Art Institute of Chicago; **321** BAL/V&A Museum, London; **322** BAL/Rijksmuseum Kroller-Muller, Otterloo, Netherlands (t); V&A, London (b); **323** BAL/Detroit Institute of Arts (bl), (br), (c); **326** BAL/Museum of Fine Arts, Boston, Massachusetts; **327** BAL/Nationalmuseum, Stockholm, Sweden; **328** BAL/Art Institute of Chicago (b); Private Collection (t); **329** BAL/Courtauld Gallery, London (t); Musee d'Orsay, Paris, France (b); **330** BAL/Musee d'Orsay, Paris, France (t); Museum of Modern Art, New York (b); **331** BAL/Giraudon/ Bibliotheque Nationale, Paris (b); National Gallery, London (t); **332** BAL/Musee d'Orsay, Paris; **333** BAL/Bibliotheque Nationale, Paris, France (b); Solomon R. Guggenheim Museum, New York (t); **334** BAL/Musee d'Orsay, Paris (b); Musee d'Orsay, Paris (t); **335** BAL/Museum of Modern Art of the West, Moscow, Russia (t); Philadelphia Museum of Art, Pennsylvania (b); **336** BAL/Musee National d'Art Moderne, Paris, France/© ADAGP, Paris and DACS, London 2005 (t); Private Collection/© ADAGP, Paris and DACS, London 2005 (b); **338** BAL/© Mucha Trust (b); **339** BAL/ Osterreichische Galerie, Vienna, Austria; **340** Powerstock/ Superstock/Richard Cummins © ARS, NY and DACS, London 2005; **342** Alamy Images/Petr Svarc; **343** Alamy Images/Ambient Images Inc (t); **343** Corbis/Rykoff Collection (b); **344** Baltimore Museum Of Art/Cone Collection formed by Dr Claribel Cone and Miss Etta Cone of Baltimore, Maryland. BMA 1950.258/© Succession H. Matisse/DACS 2005 (b); **344** BAL/Musee Matisse, Le Cateau-Cambresis, France/© Succession H.Matisse/DACS 2005 (t); **345** BAL/Musee d'Orsay, Paris/© Succession H. Matisse/DACS 2005; **346** BAL/National Gallery of Art, Washington DC/© ADAGP, Paris and DACS, London 2005 (t); Private Collection/© ADAGP, Paris and DACS, London 2005 (br); **347** BAL/Private Collection/© ADAGP, Paris and DACS, London 2005; **348-349** BAL/Museum of Modern Art, New York/© Succession Picasso/DACS 2005; **350** BAL/Art Institute of Chicago (bl), Museum of Modern Art, New York/© Succession Picasso/DACS 2005 (t); **351** BAL/Giraudon/Lauros/Private Collection/© ADAGP, Paris and DACS, London 2005; **352** BAL/Christie's Images, London/© ADAGP, Paris and DACS, London 2005; **353** BAL/Private Collection/© ADAGP, Paris and DACS, London 2005; **355** BAL/Private Collection/© ADAGP, Paris and DACS, London 2005; **356** BAL/© ADAGP, Paris and DACS, London 2005; **357** BAL/Solomon R. Guggenheim Museum, New York; **358** BAL/Hamburg Kunsthalle, Hamburg (b); Hamburg Kunsthalle, Hamburg /© DACS 2005 (t); **359** BAL/Musee National d'Art Moderne, Paris, France/© ADAGP, Paris and DACS, London 2005 (c); Musee National d'Art Moderne, Paris, France/© ADAGP, Paris and DACS, London 2005 (bl), (br); **360** BAL/ Graphische Sammlung Albertina, Vienna, Austria; **361** BAL/ Nasjonalgalleriet, Oslo, Norway/© Munch Museum/Munch-Ellingsen Group, BONO, Oslo, DACS, London 2005; **362** BAL/ Staatsgalerie, Stuttgart/© Nolde-Stiftung Seebull; **363** BAL/Brucke Museum, Berlin/© Ingeborg & Dr Wolfgang Henze-Ketter, Wichtrach, Bern; **364** BAL/ Musee National d'Art Moderne, Centre Pompidou, Paris/© ADAGP, Paris and DACS, London 2005 (tl); **364-465** BAL/Saarland Museum, Saarbrucken (t); **365** BAL/ Stadtische Galerie im Lenbachhaus, Munich/© ADAGP, Paris and DACS, London 2005 (t); **366** BAL/ J. Paul Getty Museum, Los Angeles/© DACS 2005 (t); **366** Art Archive/Dagli Orti/© DACS 2005 (b); **367** Réunion Des Musées Nationaux Agence Photographique/Christian Bahier/Philippe Migeat/© Succession Marcel Duchamp/ADAGP, Paris and DACS, London 2005; **368** BAL/Abbot Hall Art Gallery, Kendal, Cumbria/© DACS 2005 (tl); Private Collection/© DACS 2005 (br); **369** BAL/Kunsthaus, Zurich, Switzerland/© ADAGP, Paris and DACS, London 2005; **370** BAL/Scottish National Gallery of Modern Art, Edinburgh/© DACS 2005; **371** BAL/State Russian Museum, St Petersburg; **372** BAL/Kettle's Yard, University of

Cambridge/The Works of Naum Gabo © Nina Williams (cl); Musee Nationale d'Art Moderne, Centre Pompidou, Paris/© ADAGP, Paris and DACS, London 2005 (tr); Private Collection (br); **373** BAL/State Russian Museum, St Peterburg, Russia/© DACS 2005; **374** BAL/Albright Knox Art Gallery, Buffalo, New York/© DACS 2005 (t); Private Collection (b); **375** BAL/Mattioli collection, Milan /© DACS 2005; **376** BAL/ Imperial War Museum, London/© Wyndham Lewis and the estate of the late Mrs G.A. Wyndham Lewis by kind permission of the Wyndham Lewis Memorial Trust (a registered charity) (b); Stapleton Collection/© Wyndham Lewis and the estate of the late Mrs G.A. Wyndham Lewis by kind permission of the Wyndham Lewis Memorial Trust (a registered charity) (tr); **377** BAL/Coventry Cathedral, Warwickshire © Estate of Jacob Epstein/Tate, London 2005; **378** BAL/Private Collection, Lefevre Fine Art Ltd, London; **379** © Tate, London: 2005; **380** BAL/Butler Institute for American Art; **381** BAL/Museum of Fine Arts, Houston Texas (b); Detroit Institute of Arts (t); **382** BAL/Museum of Fine Arts, Houston Texas; **384** BAL/Detroit Institute of Arts/© DACS 2005 (t); **384** Corbis (b); **385** BAL/© Christian Schad Stiftung Aschaffenburg/VG Bild-Kunst, Bonn and DACS, London 2005; **386** BAL/Museum of Fine Arts, Houston Texas/© DACS 2005 (t); **386** Art Archive/Dagli Orti (b); **387** BAL/Hamburg Kunsthalle, Hamburg/© DACS 2005; **389** akg-images/Erich Lessing/© DACS 2005 (b); **389** Photo Scala, Florence/© Digital image, Museum of Modern Art, New York/© 2005 Mondrian/Holtzman Trust c/o HCR International Warrenton Virginia USA (tr); **390** Kobal Collection/Bunuel-Dali (t); **390** Photo Scala, Florence/© 2005, Digital image, Museum of Modern Art, New York/© DACS 2005 (b); **391** BAL/Collection of Claude Herraint, Paris/© ADAGP, Paris and DACS, London 2005 (c), (bl), (br); **392** BAL/Philadelphia Museum of Art, Pennsylvania PA/© Salvador Dali, Gala-Salvador Dali Foundation, DACS, London 2005; **393** BAL/Albright Knox Art Gallery, Buffalo, New York/© Succession Miro, DACS 2005. **394** BAL/Private Collection/© Man Ray Trust/ADAGP, Paris and DACS, London 2005. **395** BAL/Private Collection/© ADAGP, Paris and DACS, London 2005; **396** BAL/Musee Picasso, Paris France/© Succession Picasso/DACS 2005 (t); Private Collection/© Succession Picasso/DACS 2005 (b); **397** BAL/Bonhams, London/© Succession Picasso/DACS 2005 (b); National Gallery of Victoria, Melbourne Australia/© Succession Picasso/DACS 2005 (t); **398** BAL/Imperial War Museum, London (t); **398-399** BAL/Wakefield Museums & Galleries, West Yorkshire/Reproduced by permission of the Henry Moore Foundation (b); **400** BAL/Private collection/Bowness, Hepworth Estate (b); **400** Corbis/Andy Keate; Edifice (t); **401** BAL/Private collection/© Angela Verren-Taunt 2005. All rights reserved, DACS; **402** BAL/Mexico City, Mexico/Ian Mursell/Mexicolore/© DACS 2005; **403** BAL/Phoenix Art Museum, Arizona/© 2005 Banco de Mexico Diego Rivera & Frida Kahlo Museums Trust. Av. Cinco de Mayo No.2, Col. Centro, Del. Cuauhtemoc 06059, Mexico, D.F./INBA; **404** BAL/Private Collection/© DACS 2005; **405** BAL/© Museum of Fine Arts, Houston, Texas, USA, Gift of Meredith J. and Cornelia Long; **406** BAL/© Museum of Fine Arts, Houston, Texas, USA/© ARS, NY and DACS, London 2005; **407** BAL/© Butler Institute of American Art, Youngstown, OH, USA, Museum Purchase 1950 (t); **408** BAL/Whitney Nuseum of American Art, New York; **409** BAL/Tokyo Fuji Art Museum, Tokyo, Japan/© Grandma Moses Properties Co, 1945; **410-411** BAL/Private Collection/© ARS, NY and DACS, London 2005 (b); **411** BAL/Musee Nationale d'Art Moderne, Paris/© ARS, NY and DACS, London 2005 (tr); **412** BAL/Los Angeles County Museum of Art/© ARS, NY and DACS, London 2005 (tl); Private Collection/© Willem de Kooning Revocable Trust/ARS, NY and DACS, London 2005 (br); **413** BAL/Fogg Art Museum, Harvard University Art Museums, USA/© 1998 Kate Rothko Prizel & Christopher Rothko/DACS 2005 (br), (c); **415** Photo Scala, Florence/© 2005, Digital image, Museum of Modern Art, New York/© ARS, NY and DACS, London 2005. **416** BAL/Musee National d'Art Modern, Centre Pompidou, Paris/© Estate of Sam Francis/DACS, London 2005; **417** BAL/Private Collection/© ADAGP, Paris and DACS, London 2005; **418** BAL/Private Collection/© ADAGP, Paris and DACS, London 2005; **419** BAL/Private Collection/© ADAGP, Paris and DACS, London 2005; **420** BAL/Private Collection/©

ADAGP, Paris and DACS, London 2005. **421** BAL/Detroit Institiute of Arts, USA/© ADAGP, Paris and DACS, London 2005. **422** BAL/Private Collection/© ADAGP, Paris and DACS, London 2005; **423** BAL/Hamburg Kunsthalle, Hamburg/© Estate of Dieter Roth (b); Private collection/© Hundertwasser Archives, Vienna (tr); **424** BAL/Estorick Foundation, London/© DACS 2005; **425** BAL/CAPC Musee d'Art Contemporain, France/© Estate of Mario Merz; **426-427** BAL/Private Collection/© DACS 2005; **428** BAL/Hamburg Kunsthalle, Hamburg/© Fundacio Antoni Tapies/DACS, London, 2005 (tl); **429** akg-images/L. M. Peter/© DACS 2005; **430-431** BAL/New Walk Museum, Leicester City Museum Service/© Estate of Terry Frost; **432** BAL/Private collection/© R.B.Kitaj; **433** BAL/Aberdeen Art Gallery & Museum/© Estate of Francis Bacon 2005. All rights reserved, DACS 2005 (tr); Private collection/© Estate of Francis Bacon 2005. All rights reserved, DACS (b). **434-435** BAL/Private Collection/© Lucian Freud; **436-437** BAL/Arts Council Collection, Hayward Gallery, London/© ADAGP, Paris and DACS, London 2005; **437** BAL/Detroit Institute of Arts/© Robert Rauschenberg/VAGA, New York/DACS, London 2005 (tr); **438** BAL/Private Collection/© ARS, NY and DACS, London 2005; **440** BAL/Kunsthalle, Tubingen, Germany/© Richard Hamilton 2005. All rights reserved, DACS 2005 (tr); Saatchi Collection, London/© The Andy Warhol foundation for the Visual Arts, Inc./DACS, London, 2005. Trademarks Licensed by Campbell Soup Company. All Rights Reserved (b); **441** BAL/Private collection/© Estate of Roy Lichtenstein/DACS 2005; **442** BAL/Private collection/© Alex Katz/VAGA, New York/DACS, London 2005 (t); Private collection/© Jasper Johns/VAGA, New York/DACS, London 2005 (b); **443** BAL/Private Collection/© Jasper Johns/VAGA, New York/DACS, London 2005; **444** BAL/Private collection/© The Andy Warhol Foundation for the Visual Arts, Inc./ARS, NY and DACS, London 2005; **445** BAL/Museum of Fine Arts, Houston, Texas, USA/© The Estate of Philip Guston (t); Wolverhampton Art Gallery, West Midlands/© James Rosenquist/VAGA, New York/DACS, London 2005 (b); **447** BAL/Ludwig Museum, Cologne/© David Hockney; **448** Rex Features/Ray Tang (RTR)/© David Batchelor; **450-451** Alamy Images/Ian Dagnall; **450** Corbis/Peter Turnley (tl); **451** Rex Features/Sipa Press (SIPA) (br); **452** BAL/Museum of Fine Arts, Houston, Texas, USA/© Louise Bourgeois/VAGA, New York/DACS, London 2005; **452-453** BAL/On loan to Hamburg Kunsthalle, Hamburg/© DACS 2005; **454** BAL/On loan to Hamburg Kunsthalle, Hamburg/© Estate of Duane Hanson/VAGA, New York/DACS, London 2005; **455** BAL/Galleria Nazionale d'Arte Moderna, Rome/© ARS, NY and DACS, London 2005; **456** BAL/On loan to Hamburg Kunsthalle, Hamburg/© ARS, NY and DACS, London 2005 (t); Private Collection/©Cy Twombly, Courtesy of the Gagosian Gallery (b); **457** BAL/Hamburg Kunsthalle, Hamburg/© ARS, NY and DACS, London 2005. **458** BAL/Hamburg Kunsthalle, Hamburg/Cat 827-4 © Gerhard Richter; **459** BAL/Detroit Institute of Arts,USA/© Carl Andre/VAGA, New York/DACS London 2005; **460** Photo: Wolfgang Volz, © Christo 1998; **461** BAL/On loan to Hamburg Kunsthalle, Hamburg/© Georg Baselitz; **462** Courtesy James Cohen Gallery, New York. Collection: DIA Center for the Arts, New York, Photo Gianfranco Gorgoni/© Estate of Robert Smithson/VAGA, New York/DACS, London 2005; **463** Photo Scala, Florence/© 2005, Digital image, Museum of Modern Art, New York/© Chuck Close, courtesy PaceWildenstein, New York; **464** BAL/Hamburg Kunsthalle, Hamburg/© Sigmar Polke; **465** © Gilbert & George; **466** BAL/Hamburg Kunsthalle, Hamburg/© ADAGP, Paris and DACS London 2005 (t); Hamburg Kunsthalle, Hamburg, Germany/© Jorg Immendorff (b); **467** BAL/© Museum of Fine Arts, Houston, Texas, USA, Funds from National Endowment Fund for Arts & Mrs. T.N.Law/© ARS,NY and DACS, London 2005; **468** akg-images/Richard Booth/© Antony Gormley; **471** View Pictures/Photo: Dennis Gilbert/© Anish Kapoor; **473** BAL/Hamburg Kunsthalle, Hamburg, Germany/© Jeff Koons; **474** © Andy Goldsworthy, Cass Sculpture Foundation and Michael Hue-Williams; **477-478** White Cube Gallery/Courtesy Jay Jopling/Photo: Stephen White/© Damien Hirst

AUTHOR ACKNOWLEDGEMENTS

Catalog descriptions for old master paintings sometimes contain a caveat to the effect that although the work of art is principally by the hand of the artist in question, it is possible le to detect other hands at work. So it is with this book. It came together in slightly unusual and hurried circumstances and I am very grateful to those who contributed, and whose hands are at times be detected. Nonetheless I take responsibility for what is written, and I hope that the fresh ideas outnumber the errors. In particular I would like to thank Ferdie MacDonald who was a patient and wise editor, Thomas Cussans who contributed the pages on early art and had a valuable input into many others, and Reagan Upshaw. Paintings also reveal influences and here I would like to acknowledge a few of many: Norbert Lynton, Erica Langmuir, Robert Hughes, and Umberto Morra.